Kaplan Publishing are constantly finding new v
difference to your studies and our exciting onl
offer something different to students looking f

C000160588

This book comes with free MyKaplan online re
study anytime, anywhere. **This free online resource is not sold
separately and is included in the price of the book.**

Having purchased this book, you have access to the following online study materials:

| CONTENT | ACCA (including FBT, FMA, FFA) | | FIA (excluding FBT, FMA, FFA) | |
|---|---|---|---|---|
| | Text | Kit | Text | Kit |
| Electronic version of the book | ✓ | ✓ | ✓ | ✓ |
| Check Your Understanding Test with instant answers | ✓ | | | |
| Material updates | ✓ | ✓ | ✓ | ✓ |
| Latest official ACCA exam questions* | | ✓ | | |
| Extra question assistance using the signpost icon** | | ✓ | | |
| Timed questions with an online tutor debrief using clock icon*** | | ✓ | | |
| Interim assessment including questions and answers | ✓ | | ✓ | |
| Technical answers | ✓ | ✓ | ✓ | ✓ |

* Excludes BT, MA, FA, FBT, FMA, FFA; for all other papers includes a selection of questions, as released by ACCA
** For ACCA SBL, SBR, AFM, APM, ATX, AAA only
*** Excludes BT, MA, FA, LW, FBT, FMA and FFA

## How to access your online resources

Kaplan Financial students will already have a MyKaplan account and these extra resources will be available to you online. You do not need to register again, as this process was completed when you enrolled. If you are having problems accessing online materials, please ask your course administrator.

If you are not studying with Kaplan and did not purchase your book via a Kaplan website, to unlock your extra online resources please go to www.mykaplan.co.uk/addabook (even if you have set up an account and registered books previously). You will then need to enter the ISBN number (on the title page and back cover) and the unique pass key number contained in the scratch panel below to gain access. You will also be required to enter additional information during this process to set up or confirm your account details.

If you purchased through the Kaplan Publishing website you will automatically receive an e-mail invitation to MyKaplan. Please register your details using this email to gain access to your content. If you do not receive the e-mail or book content, please contact Kaplan Publishing.

## Your Code and Information

This code can only be used once for the registration of one book online. This registration and your online content will expire when the final sittings for the examinations covered by this book have taken place. Please allow one hour from the time you submit your book details for us to process your request.

**Please scratch the film to access your unique code.**

Please be aware that this code is case-sensitive and you will need to include the dashes within the passcode, but not when entering the ISBN.

KAPLAN

PUBLISHING

# ACCA

# Strategic Professional – Options

## Advanced Audit and Assurance (INT & UK) (AAA)

## EXAM KIT

**British Library Cataloguing-in-Publication Data**

A catalogue record for this book is available from the British Library.

Published by:

Kaplan Publishing UK
Unit 2 The Business Centre
Molly Millar's Lane
Wokingham
Berkshire
RG41 2QZ

ISBN: 978-1-78740-626-1

*Acknowledgements*

These materials are reviewed by the ACCA examining team. The objective of the review is to ensure that the material properly covers the syllabus and study guide outcomes, used by the examining team in setting the exams, in the appropriate breadth and depth. The review does not ensure that every eventuality, combination or application of examinable topics is addressed by the ACCA Approved Content. Nor does the review comprise a detailed technical check of the content as the Approved Content Provider has its own quality assurance processes in place in this respect.

**IFRS**

The IFRS Foundation logo, the IASB logo, the IFRS for SMEs logo, the "Hexagon Device", "IFRS Foundation", "eIFRS", "IAS", "IASB", "IFRS for SMEs", "IFRS", "IASs", "IFRSs", "International Accounting Standards" and "International Financial Reporting Standards", "IFRIC" and "IFRS Taxonomy" are Trade Marks of the IFRS Foundation.

**IFRS**

Trade Marks

The IFRS Foundation logo, the IASB logo, the IFRS for SMEs logo, the "Hexagon Device", "IFRS Foundation", "eIFRS", "IAS", "IASB", "IFRS for SMEs", "NIIF IASs" "IFRS", "IFRSs", "International Accounting Standards", "International Financial Reporting Standards", "IFRIC", "SIC" and "IFRS Taxonomy".

Further details of the Trade Marks including details of countries where the Trade Marks are registered or applied for are available from the Foundation on request.

This product contains material that is ©Financial Reporting Council Ltd (FRC). Adapted and reproduced with the kind permission of the Financial Reporting Council. All rights reserved. For further information, please visit www.frc.org.uk or call +44 (0)20 7492 2300.

# CONTENTS

Versions of some questions in this Exam Kit may also be available on the ACCA Practice Platform on the ACCA Website. They are a very useful reference, in particular to attempt using ACCA's exam software. However, you should be aware that ACCA will decide when those questions will be amended for syllabus changes or replaced, so they may differ slightly from the versions in this Exam Kit.

This document references IFRS® Standards and IAS® Standards, which are authored by the International Accounting Standards Board (the Board), and published in the 2019 IFRS Standards Red Book.

**Key features in this edition**

In addition to providing a wide ranging bank of real past exam questions, we have also included in this edition:

- An analysis of the recent new syllabus examinations.

- Exam specific information and advice on exam technique.

- Our recommended approach to make your revision for this particular subject as effective as possible.

  This includes step by step guidance on how best to use our Kaplan material (Study Text, pocket notes and exam kit) at this stage in your studies.

- Enhanced tutorial answers packed with specific key answer tips, technical tutorial notes and exam technique tips from our experienced tutors.

- Complementary online resources including full tutor debriefs and question assistance to point you in the right direction when you get stuck.

You will find a wealth of other resources to help you with your studies on the following sites:

www.MyKaplan.co.uk

www.accaglobal.com/student

Quality and accuracy are of the utmost importance to us so if you spot an error in any of our products, please send an email to mykaplanreporting@kaplan.com with full details.

Our Quality Co-ordinator will work with our technical team to verify the error and take action to ensure it is corrected in future editions.

# INDEX TO QUESTIONS AND ANSWERS

## INTRODUCTION

The exam format of Advanced Audit and Assurance changed in September 2018. Accordingly any older ACCA questions within this kit have been adapted to reflect the new style of exam and the new guidance. Where questions have been adapted from the original version, this is indicated in the end column of the index below with the mark *(A)*. The marking schemes included are indicative schemes which have been approved by ACCA as being representative of the real exam except where indicated. One question in the kit is not adapted from a past exam question and is not exam standard but has been included to provide greater syllabus coverage.

The specimen exam is included at the end of the kit.

## KEY TO THE INDEX

### ANSWER ENHANCEMENTS

We have added the following enhancements to the answers in this exam kit:

**Key answer tips**

All answers include key answer tips to help your understanding of each question.

***Tutorial note***

All answers include more tutorial notes to explain some of the technical points in more detail.

***Top tutor tips***

For all questions, we 'walk through the answer' giving guidance on how to approach the questions with helpful 'tips from a top tutor', together with technical tutor notes.

These answers are indicated with the 'footsteps' icon in the index.

## ONLINE ENHANCEMENTS

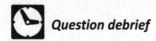

*Question debrief*

For selected questions, we recommend that they are to be completed in full exam conditions (i.e. properly timed in a closed book environment).

In addition to the examiner's technical answer, enhanced with key answer tips and tutorial notes in this exam kit, you can find an answer debrief online by a top tutor that:

- Works through the question in full

- Points out how to approach the question

- Discusses how to ensure that the easy marks are obtained as quickly as possible, and

- Emphasises how to tackle exam questions and exam technique.

These questions are indicated with the 'clock' icon in the index.

| | | | | | |
|---|---|---|---|---|---|
| 29 | Adder Group | 🔲 | 82 | 400 | Jun 15 (A) |
| 30 | Francis Group | 🔲 🕐 | 84 | 406 | Dec 14 (A) |
| 31 | Cooper | 🔲 | 85 | 414 | Jun 14 (A) |
| 32 | Poodle Group | 🔲 | 87 | 422 | Jun 13 (A) |
| 33 | Snipe | 🔲 🕐 | 88 | 427 | Jun 12 (A) |

## Other assignments

| | | | | | | |
|---|---|---|---|---|---|---|
| ✓ | 34 | Jansen & Co | 🔲 | 89 | 433 | Sept 18 |
| | 35 | Vizsla | 🔲 | 91 | 440 | M/J 18 |
| | 36 | Rope | 🔲 🕐 | 93 | 447 | S/D 16 (A) |
| | 37 | Hawk | 🔲 | 94 | 454 | Jun 12 (A) |
| ✓ | 38 | Cheetah | 🔲 | 96 | 459 | S/D 17 (A |
| | 39 | Sanzio | 🔲 | 97 | 466 | S/D 15 (A) |
| | 40 | Baltimore | 🔲 🕐 | 99 | 473 | Dec 13 (A) |
| | 41 | Jacob | 🔲 | 101 | 481 | Jun 11 (A) |
| ✓ | 42 | Moosewood Hospital | 🔲 🕐 | 102 | 487 | M/J 17 |
| | 43 | Newman & Co | 🔲 | 103 | 493 | Dec 10 (A) |
| ✓ | 44 | Beyer | 🔲 | 105 | 501 | S/D 19 |
| | 45 | Retriever | 🔲 🕐 | 106 | 509 | Jun 13 |
| | 46 | Lark & Co | 🔲 | 108 | 515 | Dec 11 (A) |
| ✓ | 47 | Squire | 🔲 🕐 | 109 | 523 | Dec 12 (A) |

## Professional and ethical considerations

| | | | | | | |
|---|---|---|---|---|---|---|
| ✓ | 48 | Thomasson & Co | 🔲 | 111 | 531 | Dec 18 |
| ✓ | 49 | Weston & Co | 🔲 🕐 | 112 | 538 | Dec 14 (A) |
| ✓ | 50 | Dragon Group | 🔲 | 113 | 546 | Jun 09 (A) |
| ✓ | 51 | Tony Group | 🔲 | 115 | 555 | Jun 15 (A) |
| ✓ | 52 | Spaniel | 🔲 | 116 | 560 | Jun 13 (A) |

## UK Syllabus only

| | | | | | | |
|---|---|---|---|---|---|---|
| ✓ | 53 | Krupt | 🔲 | 117 | 567 | S18 |
| ✓ | 54 | Kandinsky | 🔲 | 118 | 570 | S/D 15 |
| ✓ | 55 | Hunt & Co | 🔲 | 120 | 576 | Jun 12 (A) |
| ✓ | 56 | Butler (A) | 🔲 | 122 | 581 | Jun 11 (A) |

## INT Syllabus only

| | | | | | | |
|---|---|---|---|---|---|---|
| ✓ | 57 | Kandinsky | 🔲 | 124 | 587 | S/D 15 |
| ✓ | 58 | Public sector organisations | 🔲 | 127 | 594 | N/A |

# ANALYSIS OF PAST EXAMS

The table below summarises the key topics that have been tested in the new syllabus examinations to date.

| | Specimen exam Sept 19 | Sept 18 | Dec 18 | Mar 19 | June 19 | Sept 19 | Dec 19 |
|---|---|---|---|---|---|---|---|
| **Regulatory Environment** | | | | | | | |
| Regulatory framework including corporate governance | | | | | | | |
| Money laundering | | | ✓ | | | | |
| Laws and regulations | | | | ✓ | | | |
| **Professional & ethical considerations** | | | | | | | |
| Code of ethics | ✓ | ✓ | ✓ | | ✓ | ✓ | ✓ |
| Fraud and error | | | ✓ | | | | |
| Professional liability | | | | | | | |
| **Quality control & practice management** | | | | | | | |
| Quality control | ✓ | ✓ | | | | | ✓ |
| Advertising | | | | | | | |
| Tendering | | | | | | | |
| Acceptance of professional appointments | ✓ | ✓ | ✓ | ✓ | | ✓ | ✓ |
| **Planning & conducting an audit of historical financial information** | | | | | | | |
| Risk assessment: | | | | | | | |
|     Audit risk | ✓ | ✓ | | | | ✓ | ✓ |
|     Business risk | | | ✓ | | ✓ | | ✓ |
|     Risk of material misstatement | | | ✓ | ✓ | ✓ | | |
|     Group audit situation | ✓ | ✓ | | | ✓ | ✓ | |
|     Planning and materiality | | | | | | | |
|     Professional scepticism | | | | | | | |
| Audit evidence: | | | | | | | |
|     Sufficient/appropriate | | | | | | | |
|     Specific procedures | ✓ | ✓ | ✓ | ✓ | ✓ | ✓ | ✓ |
|     Analytical procedures | | | ✓ | | ✓ | | |

| | Specimen exam Sept 19 | Sept 18 | Dec 18 | Mar 19 | June 19 | Sept 19 | Dec 19 |
|---|---|---|---|---|---|---|---|
| Related parties | | | | | ✓ | | |
| Work of experts | | | | ✓ | | | |
| Work of internal audit | | | | | | | ✓ |
| Initial engagements | | | | | | | |
| Comparatives | | | | | | | |
| Joint audits | | | | | | | |
| Transnational audits | | | | | | | |
| **Completion, review and reporting** | | | | | | | |
| Evaluating misstatements and resolving outstanding issues | ✓ | ✓ | | ✓ | | ✓ | ✓ |
| Subsequent events | | | | | | | |
| Going concern | | | ✓ | | | | |
| Reporting implications | ✓ | ✓ | ✓ | ✓ | | ✓ | ✓ |
| Critical appraisal of a draft report | | | | ✓ | ✓ | | |
| Reporting in relation to other information published with FS | | | | | | | |
| Reporting to those charged with governance | | | | ✓ | ✓ | | |
| **Other assignments** | | | | | | | |
| Interim review | | | | | | | |
| Due diligence | | | | ✓ | | | ✓ |
| Prospective financial information | ✓ | ✓ | ✓ | | | | |
| Integrated reporting including social and environmental information | | | | | | | |
| Forensic audit | | | | | | ✓ | |
| Insolvency (UK only) | | ✓ | | | | | |
| Performance information (INT only) | | | | | | | |
| Levels of assurance | | | | | | | |
| Advantages and disadvantages of audit | | | | | | | |
| **Current Issues** | ✓ | | | ✓ | ✓ | | |

# EXAM TECHNIQUE

- **Skim through the whole exam**, assessing the level of difficulty of each question.

- **Divide the time** you spend on questions in proportion to the marks on offer:

  - There are 1.95 minutes available per mark in the examination.

  - Within that, try to allow time at the end of each question to review your answer and address any obvious issues.

  Whatever happens, always keep your eye on the clock and **do not over run on any part of any question!**

- **Decide the order** in which you think you will attempt each question:

  - A common approach is to tackle the question you think is the easiest and you are most comfortable with first.

  - Others may prefer to tackle the longest question first as this has the most marks attributable and you cannot afford to leave this question to last and find that you have run out of time to complete it fully.

  - It is usual, however, that students tackle their least favourite topic and/or the most difficult question last.

  - Whatever your approach, you must make sure that you leave enough time to attempt all questions fully and be very strict with yourself in timing each question.

- At the beginning of the exam take time to:

  - **Read the questions and examination requirements carefully** so that you understand them, and

  - **Plan** your answers.

- Spend the **last five minutes** of the examination:

  - Reading through your answers, and

  - Making any additions or corrections.

- If you **get completely stuck** with a question **leave it** and **return to it later**.

- Stick to the question and **tailor your answer** to what you are asked.

  - Pay particular attention to the verbs in the question.

- If you do not understand what a question is asking, **state your assumptions**.

  Even if you do not answer in precisely the way the examiner hoped, you may be given some credit, if your assumptions are reasonable.

- You should do everything you can to make things easy for the marker.

  The marker will find it easier to identify the points you have made if your **answers are well spaced out** and **clearly referenced to the requirement** being answered.

- **Written questions**:

  Marks are normally awarded for depth of explanation and discussion. For this reason, lists and bullet points should be avoided unless specifically requested. Your answer should:

  - Have a clear structure using subheadings to improve the quality and clarity of your response.

  - Be concise.

  - Address a broad range of points: it is usually better to write a little about a lot of different points than a great deal about one or two points.

- **Briefing note format**:

  Question one will ask you to present your answer in the form of briefing notes. Professional marks are awarded for this format.

  Make sure that you use the correct format – there could be easy marks to gain here.

# EXAM SPECIFIC INFORMATION

## THE EXAM

**FORMAT OF THE ADVANCED AUDIT AND ASSURANCE EXAM**

| | Number of marks |
|---|---|
| Question 1 | 50 |
| Question 2 | 25 |
| Question 3 | 25 |
| | 100 |

Total time allowed:    3 hours and 15 minutes.

From September 2019, the 'current' date in the AAA exam will be 1 July 20X5. Year-end dates will then be flexed around this depending on the nature of the question. For example, a question set at the planning stage of the audit may have a year-end of 30 June 20X5 or 31 July 20X5. A question set at the completion stage of the audit may have a year-end of 31 January 20X5 or 31 March 20X5.

Note that:

- Question 1

  This question will comprise a case study, worth 50 marks and will be set at the planning stage of the audit, for a single company, a group of companies, or potentially several audit clients.

  You will be provided with detailed information which may include extracts of financial information, strategic, operational and other relevant information for a client business, as well as extracts from audit working papers, including results of analytical procedures.

  The requirements will predominantly focus on syllabus areas A, B, C and D which cover the regulatory environment, professional and ethical considerations, quality control and practice management, and planning and conducting an audit of historical information. Other syllabus areas such as other assignments and current issues may also be included in this question.

  Four professional marks will be available and awarded based on the level of professionalism with which the answer is presented, including structure and clarity of the answer.

- Questions 2 and 3

  One question will focus exclusively on completion, review and reporting. There are a number of formats this question could adopt, including, but not limited to, assessing going concern, considering the impact of subsequent events, evaluating identified misstatements and the corresponding effect on the auditor's report. You may also be asked to critique an auditor's report or evaluate the matters to be included in a report to management or those charged with governance.

  The other question could cover any syllabus area except completion, review and reporting. Therefore the question may focus on a different aspect of the audit process such as reliance on the work of others or ethical issues arising with an audit client.

Alternatively the question may focus on non-audit engagements such as due diligence, examination of a forecast, forensic audits, etc. Current issues and developments may be examined in this question.

- All questions will be broken down into several sub-requirements that test a range of topics.

- The majority of marks are given for applying your knowledge to specific case studies. There is little scope for 'knowledge dumping'. Some questions, such as those which require detailed understanding of the auditing standards or safeguards set out in the ethical code, will award some marks for knowledge but you should restrict the amount of information you present here and should still ensure that the comments you make are relevant to the scenario presented.

- Current issues and developments within the profession are examinable. For this type of question it is likely that a technical article on the relevant topic will be issued in the weeks preceding the exam. Students are advised to check for any recent technical articles published by the ACCA Examining Team. Examiner's reports emphasise the need for students to read up on current issues and recommend that students do not solely depend on the text book for this exam.

- Discussion questions are generally disliked by students, possibly because there is no right or wrong answer. The way to approach this type of question is to provide a balanced argument. Where a statement is given that you are required to discuss, give reasons why you agree with the statement and reasons why you disagree with the statement.

**UK VARIANT SPECIFIC INFORMATION**

The following are the key differences between the UK and INT variant exams:

- Insolvency is a syllabus area which is only relevant for UK variant exams. This will not necessarily be examined every sitting. If it is examined it is likely to be one requirement that is changed from the INT variant.

- Questions on ethics and auditor's reports will require knowledge of UK guidance e.g. the FRC Ethical Standard and UK versions of the ISAs. The basic knowledge is the same for UK and INT but there are some variations in ethical safeguards and the elements of a UK auditor's report.

- Practise the UK specific questions in the Study Text and this exam kit to help prepare you for any UK specific questions.

**PASS MARK**

The pass mark for all ACCA Qualification examinations is 50%.

# DETAILED SYLLABUS

The detailed syllabus and study guide written by the ACCA can be found at:

https://www.accaglobal.com/gb/en/student/exam-support-resources/professional-exams-study-resources/p7/syllabus-study-guide.html

# KAPLAN'S RECOMMENDED REVISION APPROACH

## QUESTION PRACTICE IS THE KEY TO SUCCESS

Success in professional examinations relies upon you acquiring a firm grasp of the required knowledge at the tuition phase. In order to be able to do the questions, knowledge is essential.

However, the difference between success and failure often hinges on your exam technique on the day and making the most of the revision phase of your studies.

The **Kaplan Study Text** is the starting point, designed to provide the underpinning knowledge to tackle all questions. However, in the revision phase, pouring over text books is not the answer.

**Kaplan online progress tests** help you consolidate your knowledge and understanding and are a useful tool to check whether you can remember key topic areas.

**Kaplan pocket notes** are designed to help you quickly revise a topic area, however you then need to practice questions. There is a need to progress to full exam standard questions as soon as possible, and to tie your exam technique and technical knowledge together.

**The importance of question practice cannot be over-emphasised.**

The recommended approach below is designed by expert tutors in the field, in conjunction with their knowledge of the examiner and their recent real exams.

The approach taken for the applied skills level exams is to revise by topic area. However, with the professional stage exams, a multi topic approach is required to answer the scenario based questions.

**You need to practice as many questions as possible in the time you have left.**


## OUR AIM

Our aim is to get you to the stage where you can attempt exam standard questions confidently, to time, in a closed book environment, with no supplementary help (i.e. to simulate the real examination experience).

Practising your exam technique on real past examination questions, in timed conditions, is also vitally important for you to assess your progress and identify areas of weakness that may need more attention in the final run up to the examination.

In order to achieve this we recognise that initially you may feel the need to practice some questions with open book help and exceed the required time.

The approach below shows you which questions you should use to build up to coping with exam standard question practice, and references to the sources of information available should you need to revisit a topic area in more detail.

KAPLAN PUBLISHING

Remember that in the real examination, all you have to do is:

- Attempt all questions in the exam

- Only spend the allotted time on each question, and

- Get at least 50% of the marks allocated!

Try and practice this approach on every question you attempt from now to the real exam.

## EXAMINER COMMENTS

We have included the examiners comments to the specific new syllabus examination questions in this kit for you to see the main pitfalls that students fall into with regard to technical content.

However, too many times in the general section of the report, the examiner comments that students had failed due to:

- 'Misallocation of time'

- 'Running out of time' and

- Showing signs of 'spending too much time on an earlier question and clearly rushing the answer to a subsequent question'.

**Good exam technique is vital.**

## STRATEGIC PROFESSIONAL COMPUTER BASED EXAMINATIONS

From March 2020, all Strategic Professional exams will be assessed by computer based examination (CBE). The exam format may impact upon your approach to revision.

We advise consulting the ACCA Global website for additional CBE revision resources. On the ACCA website there is a CBE demonstration. It is **ESSENTIAL** that you attempt this before your real CBE. You will become familiar with how to move around the CBE screens and the way that questions are formatted, increasing your confidence and speed in the actual exam.

Be sure you understand how to use the **software** before you start the exam. If in doubt, ask the assessment centre staff to explain it to you.

Questions are **displayed on the screen** and answers are entered using keyboard and mouse.

For additional support with your studies please also refer to the ACCA Global website.

# THE KAPLAN AAA REVISION PLAN

## Stage 1: Assess areas of strengths and weaknesses

## Stage 2: Practice questions

Follow the order of revision of topics as recommended in the revision table plan below and attempt the questions in the order suggested.

Try to avoid referring to text books and notes and the model answer until you have completed your attempt.

Try to answer the question in the allotted time.

Review your attempt with the model answer and assess how much of the answer you achieved in the allocated exam time.

KAPLAN PUBLISHING

Fill in the self-assessment box below and decide on your best course of action.

| Comfortable with question attempt | Not comfortable with question attempts |
|---|---|

Focus on these areas by:
- Reworking test your understanding examples in Kaplan's Study Text
- Revisiting the technical content from Kaplan's pocket notes
- Working any remaining questions on that area in the exam kit
- Reattempting an exam standard question in that area, on a timed, closed book basis

Only revisit when comfortable with questions on all topic areas

Note that:

 The 'footsteps questions' give guidance on exam techniques and how you should have approached the question.

 The 'clock questions' have an online debrief where a tutor talks you through the exam technique and approach to that question and works the question in full.

## Stage 3: Final pre-exam revision

We recommend that you **attempt at least one three hour and 15 minute mock examination** containing a set of previously unseen exam standard questions.

It is important that you get a feel for the breadth of coverage of a real exam without advanced knowledge of the topic areas covered – just as you will expect to see on the real exam day.

Ideally this mock should be sat in timed, closed book, real exam conditions and could be:

- A mock examination offered by your tuition provider, and/or
- The last real examination.

# KAPLAN'S DETAILED REVISION PLAN

| Topics | | Study Text (and Pocket Note) Chapter | Questions to attempt | Tutor guidance | Date attempted | Self-assessment |
|---|---|---|---|---|---|---|
| 1 | Planning and conducting an audit including group audits. | | 1<br>2<br>3<br>4<br>5<br>6 | Evaluation of audit risk, business and risk of material misstatement is fundamental to AAA. However, rather than discussing definitions you need to be able to perform a risk assessment for specific information given in a scenario. It is imperative to understand the difference between the three types of risk in order to answer the question correctly.<br>The ability to generate audit procedures to address specific risks is essential. | | |
| 2 | Completion, review and reporting | | 15<br>16<br>17<br>18<br>19<br>20 | At the review stage of an audit you need to consider a number of issues: whether there is sufficient appropriate evidence on file; if the audit plan has been followed; whether there are any material errors in the information under review; and the impact of these issues on the reports you will have to issue.<br>One of the fundamental weaknesses identified by the examiner is a lack of understanding regarding auditor's reports. It is therefore important that you are able to assess a scenario and identify how it might impact upon your audit opinion and auditor's report.<br>You also need to be able to discuss the content and purpose of reports to those charged with governance. | | |

| 3 | Other assignments | | 34 38 42 44 47 | There are many non-audit engagements that you could be asked to plan and perform. These include:<br>• Review of interim financial information<br>• Examination of prospective financial information<br>• Due diligence<br>• Forensic audits<br>You also need to be able to discuss the ethical or professional considerations of an auditor accepting these engagements. | |
|---|---|---|---|---|---|
| 4 | Professional and ethical considerations | | 48 49 50 51 52 | You need to be able to discuss and apply the code of ethics to given scenarios. In addition you also need to consider a wide range of practice management issues, such as: quality control within the firm; legal requirements; commercial strategy; and professional liability. | |
| 5 | UK Syllabus: Auditing aspects of insolvency | | 53 54 55 56 | Students studying for the UK variant of AAA need to understand the procedures for placing a company into liquidation or administration. | |
| 6 | INT syllabus: Performance information in the public sector | | 57 58 | Students studying for the INT variant exam need to be able to comment on the relevance and measurability of performance information as well as describe procedures that can be used to audit such information. | |

Note that not all of the questions are referred to in the programme above. We have recommended an approach to build up from the basic to exam standard questions. The remaining questions are available in the kit for extra practice for those who require more question practise on some areas.

# Section 1

# PRACTICE QUESTIONS – SECTION A

## PLANNING AND CONDUCTING AN AUDIT

1    **RYDER GROUP**   *Walk in the footsteps of a top tutor*

It is 1 July 20X5. You are a manager in the audit department of Squire & Co, a firm of Chartered Certified Accountants, responsible for the audit of the Ryder Group (the Group), which has a financial year ending 30 September 20X5. The Group, a listed entity, operates in the hospitality sector, running restaurants, coffee shops and hotels.

Squire & Co audits the Group consolidated financial statements, and the individual financial statements of each Group company. All companies in the Group use IFRS® Standards as their financial reporting framework.

You are provided with the following exhibits:

1    An email which you have received from Mo Iqbal, the Group audit engagement partner.

2    Background information about the Group's current structure and business activities.

3    Notes taken at a recent meeting between Mo Iqbal and the Group finance director.

4    Selected financial projections to 30 September 20X5 and comparative financial information.

5    Notes taken by Mo Iqbal during a phone call with a representative of the audit committee.

**Required:**

**Respond to the instructions in the email from the audit engagement partner.    (46 marks)**

**Note: The split of the mark allocation is shown in the partner's email (Exhibit 1).**

**Professional marks will be awarded for the presentation and logical flow of the briefing notes and the clarity of the explanations provided.                        (4 marks)**

**(Total: 50 marks)**

**Exhibit 1 – Email from audit engagement partner**

**To: Audit manager**

**From: Mo Iqbal, Group audit engagement partner**

**Subject: Ryder Group audit planning**

**Date: 1 July 20X5**

**Hello**

You need to start planning the Ryder Group (the Group) audit, and to help with this I have provided you with some relevant information. I met with the Group finance director yesterday to discuss a number of matters including some recent business developments. I also spoke with a representative from the Group audit committee regarding several issues.

Using all the information provided, I require you to prepare briefing notes for my own use, in which you:

(a) Evaluate the significant audit risks to be considered in planning the Group audit for the financial year ending 30 September 20X5. Given the planned Group restructuring, you should evaluate audit risks relating to disclosure issues at this stage in the audit planning. **(24 marks)**

(b) Identify the additional information which should be requested from management in order to effectively audit the disposal of Primal Burgers Co, and explain why this information is required. **(4 marks)**

(c) Design the principal audit procedures to be performed in respect of:

(i) The classification of the $48 million investment in Peppers Co, and

(ii) The government grant of $20 million received in January 20X5. **(8 marks)**

(d) Using the notes from the audit committee phone call in Exhibit 5, discuss any ethical issues relevant to the Group audit, and recommend appropriate actions to be taken by our firm. **(10 marks)**

**Thank you.**


**Exhibit 2 – Background information about the Group**

The Ryder Group is one of the country's leading hospitality providers. Over the last 15 years, the Group has grown steadily and has a range of successful hospitality brands, each brand being operated by a separate, wholly owned, subsidiary of the Group.

The Group is planning some restructuring, which is discussed in the notes from the client meeting (Exhibit 3). The Group structure shown below is the Group's existing structure, before any restructuring takes place.

**Existing Group structure:**

Information about each of the Group companies is given below:

Ryder Co is the parent company of the group, a listed company, which does not trade, and holds the shares in each subsidiary company.

Mondays Coffee Co operates one of the leading coffee shop chains in the country under the 'Mondays Coffee' brand. It enjoys a strong market share and operates more than 1,200 coffee shops across the country.

Primal Burgers Co operates over 150 fast food restaurants. In recent years, revenue from Primal Burgers Co has declined, but it still provides approximately 30% of Group revenue.

Inspiral Hotels Co is a successful hotel business, with over 75 hotels across the country. The Group acquired Inspiral Hotels Co three years ago, as part of a growth strategy based on diversification.

**Exhibit 3 – Notes from client meeting**

**Group restructuring**

The Group is restructuring, as part of a strategy for continued growth in revenue and profitability. As part of this strategy, the Group is investing $48 million in a newly formed company, Peppers Co, representing 50% of the share capital of the company. The remaining 50% shareholding is owned by Smiths Co, a property development company. The contract behind this investment states that the Group and Smiths Co will work together to develop six new hotels, all based at the country's major airports. The investment in Peppers Co is likely to take place in August 20X5.

Partly to provide some of the finance needed for the restructuring, and partly because of its declining revenue, the Group is planning to dispose of Primal Burgers Co. The board approved this disposal in March 20X5. Vendor's due diligence has been carried out by Usami & Co, a firm of Chartered Certified Accountants. Usami & Co conducted an independent review of the company's financial position and future prospects and produced a report on their findings, which is made available to potential buyers. At today's date, several potential buyers have expressed an interest and the Group expects that the disposal will take place just after the financial year end.

Due to the success of the Inspiral Hotels brand, the Group plans to expand its hotel offering, and a target company for acquisition has been identified. The Group aims to acquire Valentine Co, which operates the successful Valentine Hotel chain. Negotiations are underway, and it is likely that the acquisition will go ahead in the first quarter of the next financial year. The purchase price has yet to be agreed, but is likely to be around $100 million. Due diligence performed on Valentine Co indicates that the fair value of its identifiable net assets is $85 million.

**Mondays Coffee drive-through**

The Group has previously trialled 20 drive-through coffee shops situated on busy roads, which offer customers the convenience of purchasing coffee without leaving their cars. This year the Group opened 50 new drive-through coffee shops, open 24 hours a day, seven days a week, which have proven to be extremely popular with customers. The associated capital expenditure recognised in property, plant and equipment was $43 million, which, according to the Group finance director, includes the cost of constructing the coffee shops amounting to $28 million, and the cost of acquiring three-year licences to allow 24-hour trading, at a cost of $15 million. The Group's accounting policy is to depreciate property over 20 years, and a full year's worth of depreciation will be charged in the year to 30 September 20X5 in respect of the $43 million capitalised.

According to the Group finance director, the new drive-through coffee shops are projected to account for almost all of the increase in revenue generated from the Mondays Coffee brand in the year. His comment is based on data produced from the management information system which separately records revenue generated from the drive-through coffee shops so that management can assess its performance and determine the return on the $43 million of capital expenditure.

**Government grant**

The government provides grants to organisations which commit to investing in properties to reduce carbon emissions and energy consumption. Grants are also available to organisations to promote the benefits of recycling to their customers.

In January 20X5, Ryder Co received a grant of $20 million. The only condition attached to the grant is that half of the amount must be used to upgrade existing assets to make them more environmentally friendly. None of the amount received has yet been spent, but it is planned that it will be used to finance capital expenditure across the Group's property portfolio. The other half of the grant will be used to fund an advertising campaign.

According to the Group finance director, the full $20 million is included within operating profit in the projected Group statement of profit or loss for the year (Exhibit 4).

**Exhibit 4 – Selected financial projections**

| Subsidiary | Projected to 30 September 20X5 $ million Revenue | Projected to 30 September 20X5 $ million Assets | Actual to 30 September 20X4 $ million Revenue | Actual to 30 September 20X4 $ million Assets |
|---|---|---|---|---|
| Mondays Coffee Co | 155 | 200 | 110 | 160 |
| Primal Burgers Co | 99 | 110 | 103 | 113 |
| Inspiral Hotels Co | 66 | 140 | 62 | 125 |
| **Total** | **320** | **450** | **275** | **398** |

The table above is based on management information which forms the basis of the segmental reporting disclosed in the notes to the financial statements.

Other financial information for the Group as a whole is given below:

| | Projected to 30 September 20X5 $ million | Actual to 30 September 20X4 $ million |
|---|---|---|
| Operating profit | 76 | 72 |
| Profit before tax | 20 | 18 |
| Total assets | 475 | 450 |

**Exhibit 5 – Notes from audit committee call**

The Group currently has three non-executive directors, who form the Group audit committee. Until January 20X5, there was a fourth non-executive director who was also the financial reporting expert of the Group audit committee. The Group is looking to find a replacement, but is finding it difficult to recruit for this position, and has requested that a senior partner from Squire & Co become a member of the Group audit committee while a replacement is being sought.

In addition, the Group audit committee is looking to appoint a firm of professional accountants to perform corporate finance work in relation to the planned Group restructuring. The audit committee understands that Squire & Co cannot provide this non-audit service as it would create a significant threat to auditor objectivity. However, the audit committee has asked if our firm can recommend another firm to perform the work.

Following the call, the managing partner of Squire & Co has suggested that the firm recommend Ranger Associates, an unconnected firm, to carry out the work. If Ranger Associates is appointed, Squire & Co will charge Ranger Associates a referral fee equivalent to 10% of the fee for the corporate finance engagement.

In addition, the audit committee has asked Squire & Co to work with the Group internal audit team to design internal controls over the part of the accounting system which deals with revenue, and also evaluate the operating effectiveness of the internal controls.

**2** **MARGOT**  *Walk in the footsteps of a top tutor*

You are a manager in the audit department of Snow & Co, a firm of Chartered Certified Accountants, and you are responsible for the audit of Margot Co. The company has a financial year ending 30 June 20X9, and you are about to start planning the audit.

Margot Co produces fruit-based food products using agricultural produce grown on its farms. Ben Duval, the audit engagement partner, met with the company's finance director last week to discuss business developments in the year and recent financial performance.

You are provided with the following exhibits:

1    An email you have received from Ben Duval, in respect of the audit of Margot Co.

2    Notes of a meeting which Ben held recently with the finance director of Margot Co.

3    A reference document prepared by Snow & Co containing an overview of the accounting requirements applied in the agriculture sector.

4    Extracts from the latest management accounts of Margot Co and accompanying notes, including the results of preliminary analytical procedures, which have been performed by a member of the audit team.

5    An email which the audit engagement partner received from Len Larch, a production manager working at one of the company's olive farms.

**Required:**

**Respond to the instructions in the email from the audit engagement partner.    (46 marks)**

**Note: The split of the mark allocation is shown in the partner's email (Exhibit 1).**

**Professional marks will be awarded for the presentation and logical flow of the briefing notes and the clarity of the explanations provided.                                (4 marks)**

**(Total: 50 marks)**

**Exhibit 1 – Email from Ben Duval**

To:        Audit manager

From:    Ben Duval, Audit engagement partner for Margot Co

Subject:  Audit planning for Margot Co

Hello

I have provided you with some information in the form of a number of exhibits which you should use to help you with planning the audit of Margot Co for the financial year ending 30 June 20X9.

Using the information provided, I require you to prepare briefing notes for my own use, in which you:

(a)    Evaluate the significant risks of material misstatement to be considered in planning the company's audit. You should not include risks of material misstatement relating to the valuation of the company's bearer plants or biological assets, which will be evaluated separately.                                                                                **(20 marks)**

(b)    Design the principal audit procedures to be used in the audit of:

   (i)    The impairment of the factory, and

   (ii)   The development cost capitalised in respect of the new packaging.   **(10 marks)**

(c)    Discuss the matters to be considered in planning to use an auditor's expert in the audit of the fruit, which are recognised as biological assets of the company.        **(6 marks)**

In Exhibit 5, I have provided you with an email I received from Len Larch, one of the company's production managers. In respect of this, in your briefing notes you should also:

(d)    Discuss the audit implications of the email from Len Larch, recommending any further action to be taken by our firm.                                                                **(10 marks)**

**Thank you.**


**Exhibit 2 – Notes of a meeting held on 28 February 20X9**

**Meeting attendees:**

Ben Duval, audit engagement partner, Snow & Co

Ayana Easton, finance director, Margot Co

**Business background**

Margot Co was established 30 years ago by Jim Margot, who began processing the fruit grown on his family farm to make a small range of food products including canned fruit and fruit juice. The business was relatively small until ten years ago, when the company began to expand by acquiring more farmland with different crops, and building new production facilities. This extended the range of food products which could be processed, which now includes olive oil, packaged nuts and frozen fruit. The company sells its products under the 'Fructus Gold' brand name, and the goods are sold in major supermarkets and online on the company's website.

The company is not listed, and the Margot family members are the company's majority shareholders. Jim Margot retired several years ago, his daughter, Mia Margot, is the company's chief executive officer, and other family members hold positions in senior management.

### Business developments in the year

### Online sales

In the last year, sales made through the company's website grew significantly. The finance director believes that this was in response to an advertising campaign costing $225,000, which promoted the 'Fructus Gold' brand and coincided with the launch of a new online sales portal on the company website designed to make online ordering easier. To encourage online sales, the company has regular special offers, with discounts periodically offered on a selection of product lines, and offers such as 'Buy One Get One Free' for a limited time on some products.

### Research and development

Recently, concern over the level of plastic used in packaging has encouraged food producers to investigate the use of plastic-free packaging for their products. In July 20X8, the board approved a budget of $400,000 to be spent on research and development into new packaging for its products. By 28 February 20X9, $220,000 has been spent, with this amount being paid to ProPack, a firm of packaging specialists, to design and develop a range of plastic-free bottles, bags and containers. It is anticipated that the packaging will be ready for use in two years' time at which point the company will introduce it for use across its product range. ProPack is currently testing prototypes of items which have been developed, with encouraging results.

### Loan

A loan of $375,000 was taken out during the year to support the company's research and development plans.

### Factory damage

One of the company's several factories, used to process fruit and produce fruit juice, was damaged in August 20X8 when a severe storm occurred. High winds destroyed part of the factory roof, and heavy rain led to flooding and damage to machinery and processing equipment. The factory has not operated since the storm, and the finance director has performed an impairment review on the building and plant and equipment; details of the impairment review are given in the extract from the management accounts (Exhibit 4).

### Use of an auditor's expert

The fruit growing on trees and the harvested agricultural produce are biological assets which were recognised at fair value of $3.1 million in the 20X8 audited financial statements. Due to the specialised nature of these assets, an auditor's expert will be used to provide evidence relating to their valuation. A resource document containing an overview of the accounting requirements in relation to the company's activities is provided in Exhibit 3.

**Exhibit 3 – Reference document – Extract from Snow & Co's internal technical guidance for audit staff working with clients in the agriculture sector**

**IAS® 16 *Property, Plant and Equipment* – Bearer plants**

Definition: A bearer plant is defined under IAS 16 as 'a living plant that:

–    is used in the production or supply of agricultural produce

–    is expected to bear produce for more than one period; and

–    has a remote likelihood of being sold as agricultural produce, except for incidental scrap sales.'

In line with the requirements of IAS 16, bearer plants are recorded at accumulated cost until they reach maturity and then they are depreciated over their useful life.

**IAS 41 *Agriculture* – Biological assets**

Produce growing on bearer plants, and harvested agricultural produce are biological assets and should be accounted for under IAS 41. Biological assets are measured on initial recognition and at subsequent reporting dates at fair value less estimated costs to sell, unless fair value cannot be reliably measured. A gain or loss arising on initial recognition of agricultural produce at fair value less costs to sell shall be included in the statement of profit or loss for the period in which it arises.

**IAS 2 *Inventories* – Agricultural produce**

When agricultural produce enters the production process, it should be accounted for under IAS 2.

| Fruit trees | Growing and harvested fruit | Fruit being processed |
| --- | --- | --- |
| – Bearer plants<br>– IAS 16 | – Biological assets<br>– IAS 41 | – Inventory<br>– IAS 2 |

**Exhibit 4 – Extract from management accounts and results of preliminary analytical procedures**

| | Note | As at 30 June 20X9 Projected $000 | As at 30 June 20X8 Actual $000 |
|---|---|---|---|
| **Extract from statement of financial position:** | | | |
| **Total assets** | | **12,500** | **11,900** |
| Included in total assets: | | | |
| Intangible assets | 1 | 525 | 50 |
| Property, plant and equipment | 2 | 6,150 | 6,470 |
| Total current assets | | 3,350 | 2,190 |
| Cash included in current assets | | 760 | 750 |
| Current ratio | | 2.6 | 1.4 |
| Gearing ratio | | 28% | 32% |
| **Extract from statement of profit or loss:** | | | |
| **Total revenue** | | **35,600** | **32,750** |
| Online sales included in total revenue | | 2,495 | 1,310 |
| Operating margin | | 28% | 26% |
| Return on capital employed | | 5% | 4.5% |
| **Profit before tax** | | **2,100** | **1,900** |
| **Extract from statement of changes in equity:** | | | |
| Dividend payments | | 1,200 | 1,000 |

**Notes:**

**1    Intangible assets includes the following items:**

| | 20X9 $000 | 20X8 $000 |
|---|---|---|
| Software development costs | 80 | 50 |
| Advertising costs relating to 'Fructus Gold' brand | 225 | 0 |
| Development costs in respect of new packaging | 220 | 0 |
| Total | 525 | 50 |

Software development costs of $30,000 were capitalised during the year, which relate to development of the online sales portal. The finance director suggests that both the software development costs and the advertising costs should be capitalised because the increased sales in the year are a direct result of the advertising campaign and improvements in the online sales portal.

The 'Fructus Gold' brand name is not recognised in the statement of financial position, as it is an internally generated asset. This accounting treatment has been confirmed as correct and in accordance with IAS 38 *Intangible Assets*. The notes to the 20X8 financial statements disclosed that the estimated fair value of the brand name is $18 million.

## 2 Property, plant and equipment

The carrying amount of $6.15 million includes $880,250 relating to the storm-damaged factory (referred to in Exhibit 2) and its fixtures and fittings. The factory is a cash-generating unit for the purpose of impairment testing. The finance director has provided a summary calculation, detailing the following impairment review which indicates that an impairment loss of $210,250 needs to be recognised:

|  |  | $ |
|---|---|---|
| Carrying amount at 31 August 20X8 |  | 880,250 |
| Recoverable amount |  |  |
| Higher of: Fair value less costs to sell |  | 135,000 |
| Value in use |  | 670,000 |
| Impairment loss | (880,250 – 670,000) | 210,250 |

The fair value less costs to sell has been estimated based on the sales proceeds which could be generated from selling the damaged machinery. The value in use is estimated based on the future sales which could be generated if the damage to the building is repaired and new machinery is put into the factory. The company is planning on carrying out the restoration and buying new machinery, at a total estimated cost of $450,000. This amount has been provided for within current liabilities, with a corresponding entry accounted for as a prepayment.

**Exhibit 5 – Email sent from Len Larch, employee of Margot Co, to Ben Duval, audit engagement partner**

To:     Ben Duval

From:   Len Larch

Subject: Business practices

**Hello Ben**

I obtained your contact details from your firm's website, I hope you don't mind me approaching you directly. I am emailing to voice some concerns over recent business practices at Margot Co.

In my role as production manager in one of the company's factories, I inspect samples of the fruit which comes into the factory from the company's farms, and speak to the farmers on a regular basis. Recently, several farmers told me that they have been instructed to use certain chemicals to spray the fruit trees, which should increase the fruit yield. However, some of these chemicals are prohibited for use in this country because they can be toxic to humans.

While talking to one of my friends who is a production manager from another factory, it transpired that he had also become suspicious that banned chemicals are being used in the farms. He raised the issue with one of the company directors, who allegedly gave him $10,000 and asked him not to discuss it with anyone. My friend said that I should ask for the same sum of money, but I felt uncomfortable and thought I should tell someone from outside the company about what is going on.

Please do not mention my name if you decide to investigate this further.

**Thank you, Len.**

**3    REDBACK SPORTS**  *Walk in the footsteps of a top tutor*

You are a manager in the audit department of Huntsman & Co, a firm of Chartered Certified Accountants, responsible for the audit of several companies and for evaluating the acceptance decisions in respect of potential new audit clients.

One of your audit clients is Redback Sports Co, which operates a chain of sport and leisure centres across the country. The company has a financial year ending 28 February 20X9, and you are about to start planning the audit. Stella Cross, the audit engagement partner, met with the company's finance director last week to discuss business developments in the year and recent financial performance.

In addition, Stella has been approached by Mick Emu, the managing director of Emu Gyms Co. Mick has enquired regarding whether Huntsman & Co can provide the company with an audit or limited assurance review, and Stella would like you to evaluate this request. Huntsman & Co already provides a payroll service to Emu Gyms Co and has assisted Mick with his personal tax planning in the past. Mick also has a suspicion that several employees are carrying out a fraud at the company, and he has asked whether an audit or limited assurance review would have alerted him earlier to the situation.

You are provided with the following exhibits:

1    An email you have received from Stella Cross, in respect of both Redback Sports Co and Emu Gyms Co.

2    Notes of a meeting which Stella held recently with the finance director of Redback Sports Co.

3    Extracts from the latest management accounts of Redback Sports Co.

4    Notes of a telephone conversation which Stella had yesterday with Mick Emu, managing director of Emu Gyms Co.

**Required:**

**Respond to the instructions in the email from the audit engagement partner.    (46 marks)**

**Note: The split of the mark allocation is shown in the partner's email (Exhibit 1).**

**Professional marks will be awarded for the presentation and logical flow of the briefing notes and the clarity of the explanations provided.    (4 marks)**

**(Total: 50 marks)**

**Exhibit 1 – Email from audit engagement partner**

**To:** Audit manager

**From:** Stella Cross, Audit engagement partner for Redback Sports Co

**Subject:** Audit planning for Redback Sports Co, and evaluation of accepting Emu Gyms Co as a potential audit client

Hello

I have provided you with some information in the form of a number of exhibits which you should use to help you with planning the audit of Redback Sports Co for the financial year ending 28 February 20X9.

Using the information provided in Exhibits 2 and 3, I require you to prepare briefing notes for my own use, in which you:

(a) Evaluate the business risks to be considered in planning the company's audit.

**(8 marks)**

(b) Evaluate the risks of material misstatement to be considered in developing the audit strategy and audit plan. **(18 marks)**

(c) Design the principal audit procedures to be used in the audit of the grant received from the government in September 20X8. **(6 marks)**

In Exhibit 4, I have also provided you with some information relating to Emu Gyms Co. In respect of this, in your briefing notes you should also:

(d) Evaluate the matters to be considered in deciding whether to accept an engagement to provide Emu Gyms Co with an audit or limited assurance review. **(8 marks)**

(e) In relation to the suspicion of fraud being carried out at Emu Gyms Co:

Discuss whether an audit or limited assurance review of financial statements in previous years could have uncovered the fraud. **(6 marks)**

**Thank you.**

**Exhibit 2 – Notes of a meeting held on 30 November 20X8**

**Meeting attendees:**

Stella Cross, audit engagement partner, Huntsman & Co

Aneta Bay, finance director, Redback Sports Co

**Business background**

Redback Sports Co operates 30 sport and leisure centres around the country. Each centre has a large gym and a swimming pool, and many also have tennis and badminton courts. Given the nature of the company's operations, it has to comply with health and safety regulations set by the national regulatory body, and its facilities are inspected regularly to ensure that all regulations are being followed, and for the company to retain its operating licence.

The company is not listed and therefore does not need to comply with local corporate governance regulations. However, the company's chief operating officer and chairman consider it good practice to have independent input to the board, and there are two non-executive directors. One of the non-executive directors is a leisure industry expert who was chairman of a rival company, Lyre Leisure Co, for ten years.

The second non-executive director is an academic who specialises in organisational behaviour and who has written several books on performance management in the sport and leisure industry.

The company's board has approved a plan to expand through acquiring other leisure and sport facility providers. The strategy is not likely to be implemented for another two years, when the board would like the first acquisition to take place. However, potential target companies will be identified in the next 12 to 18 months. Ultimately, the board would like to seek a flotation of the company within five years, and they consider that expanding the company would improve profits and make a stock exchange listing more feasible.

Redback Sports Co has a small internal audit department with two staff who report to the finance director, as the board does not have an audit committee.

The company offers a membership scheme whereby, for an annual subscription, members can use the facilities at any of the centres. Customers who are not members can pay to access a centre for a day under the company's 'pay as you go' plan. The membership scheme accounts for approximately 85% of the company's revenue, with the remaining revenue resulting from 'pay as you go' sales.

**Business developments in the year**

The industry is competitive and the company's strategy is to encourage customers to renew their membership and to attract new members by offering a range of new activities. According to the finance director, a successful initiative which started in March 20X8 is the 'Healthy Kids' campaign; this offers children two hours coaching per week in a range of sports including swimming and tennis. This coaching is provided free as part of their parents' membership, and it has proved to be very successful – the finance director estimates that it has led to 3,000 new members since it was launched.

In June 20X8, the company opened a new coastal sport and leisure centre which, as well as offering the usual facilities, also has a scuba diving centre and offers other water sports facilities. An investment of $12 million was also made in new gym equipment across all centres, to ensure that the company offers the most modern facilities to its customers.

An advertising campaign has been launched, to promote the company brand generally, and to make customers aware of the investments in the facilities which have been made. As part of this campaign, the company paid $1 million to a famous athlete to endorse the company for a period of two years. The athlete will appear at the opening of the new coastal sports centre and has agreed to feature in poster advertisements for the next two years.

Redback Sports Co is also involved with a government initiative to help unemployed people have access to sport facilities. The company received a grant of $2 million in September 20X8, under the terms of which it allows unemployed people three hours of free access to its facilities per month. By the end of November, 33,900 free hours of facility use have been provided under this scheme. The government intends the initiative to run for three years, to promote long-term health of participants.

A new data management system has been introduced, which integrates membership information with accounting software. This allows more efficient management of the customer database which is used extensively for marketing purposes, as well as providing more timely information on financial performance to management. Data from the previous system was transferred to the new system in July 20X8, and the two systems ran in parallel for two months while training was given to staff and the new system was monitored.

One feature of the new system is that it records and reports on the free hours of access provided to unemployed people, which the company has to report on a monthly basis to the government.

**Exhibit 3 – Extracts from management accounts of Redback Sports Co**

| | Note | Based on projected figures to 28 February 20X9 | Based on audited figures to 28 February 20X8 |
|---|---|---|---|
| Revenue | 1 | $53 million | $45 million |
| Income from government grant | 2 | $2 million | – |
| Operating margin | 3 | 15% | 10.7% |
| Profit before tax | | $6.9 million | $4.6 million |
| Capital expenditure and associated borrowings | 4 | $32 million | $20 million |
| Cash | | $1.4 million | $5.6 million |
| Total assets | | $130 million | $110 million |
| Number of sport and leisure centres | 5 | 20 | 18 |
| Number of members | 6 | 38,000 | 33,800 |
| Number of 'pay as you go' entry tickets sold | | 108,000 | 102,600 |

**Notes**

1    Revenue is forecast to increase significantly this year. This is largely due to the success of the advertising campaign featuring the celebrity athlete and the 'Healthy Kids' programme (referred to in Exhibit 2).

2    The grant received of $2 million, the details of which are explained in Exhibit 2, has been recognised in full as income for the year.

3    The company's operating expenses includes the following items:

| | 20X9 | 20X8 |
|---|---|---|
| | $000 | $000 |
| Staff costs | 15,300 | 14,300 |
| Marketing | 8,500 | 8,500 |
| Maintenance and repairs of facilities | 5,500 | 5,300 |

4    Capital expenditure was mostly financed through borrowings. On 1 March 20X8, a ten-year $30 million loan was received from the company's bank. The loan does not bear interest and is repayable at par value of $34 million. As well as the bank loan, a loan of $1 million was advanced to the company from its managing director, Bob Glider, on 1 July 20X8. The terms of this loan include 3% interest paid to Bob annually in arrears, and the capital will be repaid in seven years' time in 20Y5.

5    Two new sport and leisure centres were opened this year. As well as the coastal sport and leisure centre (referred to in Exhibit 2), a new centre was opened in an affluent urban area in the capital city.

6    The management information system shows that members visit a sport and leisure centre on average three times per week.

**Exhibit 4 – Notes of a telephone conversation between Stella Cross and Mick Emu, managing director of Emu Gyms Co**

**Notes taken by Stella Cross:**

Mick Emu phoned me this morning to discuss developments at Emu Gyms Co and to enquire whether our firm could carry out either an audit of the company's financial statements, or a limited assurance review of them. This would be the first time that the financial statements have been subject to audit or limited assurance review.

**Business background**

The company was founded by Mick in 20X5, and since that time our firm has provided a payroll service for the company's staff, which now number 35 employees working in the company's four gyms, all located in urban areas. We have also provided Mick with advice on his personal tax position and financial planning in respect of his retirement, as he wants to sell the company in a few years' time. Mick runs the company with his son, Steve, who is a qualified personal trainer, and with his daughter, Siobhan, who is the marketing director. The company employs one accountant who prepares the management and financial accounts and who deals with customer memberships.

The company has grown quite rapidly in the last year, with revenue of $8 million for the financial year to 30 September 20X8, and with total assets of approximately $5.5 million. The comparative figures for 20X7 were revenue of $6.5 million and total assets of $4.8 million.

**Loan application**

Mick thinks that it will be difficult to attract more members for his gyms in existing locations, and would like the company to expand by constructing a new gym. He has discussed a loan of $4 million with the company's bank to fund the necessary capital expenditure. The bank manager has asked for the company's financial statements for the year to 30 September 20X8 and comparative information, and has also requested a cash flow and profit forecast for the next three years in order to make a lending decision within the next two months.

Mick has asked whether a representative of the firm can attend a meeting with Mick and the company's bank manager, to support the loan application and answer questions from the bank manager, assuming that we are engaged to perform either an audit or a limited assurance review on the financial statements.

**Suspected fraud**

Mick mentioned that one of the reasons he would like an audit or limited assurance review of the financial statements is because he has noticed some unusual trends in the company's financial information. This has led him to suspect that several employees are carrying out a fraud. Each gym has a small shop selling gym wear and a café, where customers can buy light meals, drinks and snacks.

Mick has noticed that the cash receipts from sales in the shops and cafés have reduced significantly in the last year, however, there has been no reduction in purchases from suppliers. As a consequence, the gross margin for these sales as reported in the management accounts has fallen from 32% to 26%. This indicated to him that staff members could be giving away items for free to customers, or they could be taking inventories from the shops and cafés for their personal use or to sell.

The shops and cafés keep a relatively small amount of inventory which is replenished on a regular basis. Until this year, sales in the shops represented approximately 5%, and café sales represented approximately 8% of the company's revenue. The figures for this year are 3% and 6% respectively.

Mick wonders whether the potential fraud would have been uncovered earlier, had the financial statements been subject to audit or limited assurance review in previous years.

**4    EAGLE GROUP**  *Walk in the footsteps of a top tutor*

You are a manager in the audit department of Bison & Co, a firm of Chartered Certified Accountants, responsible for the audit of the Eagle Group (the Group), which has a financial year ending 31 December 20X8. Your firm is appointed to audit the parent company, Eagle Co, and all of its subsidiaries, with the exception of Lynx Co, a newly acquired subsidiary located in a foreign country which is audited by a local firm of auditors, Vulture Associates.

All companies in the Group report using IFRS® Standards as the applicable financial reporting framework and have the same financial year end.

You are provided with the following exhibits:

1    An email which you have received from Maya Crag, the audit engagement partner.

2    Background information about the Group including a request from the Group finance director in respect of a non-audit engagement.

3    Extracts from the Group financial statements projected to 31 December 20X8 and comparatives, extracted from the management accounts, and accompanying explanatory notes.

4    Management's determination of the goodwill arising on the acquisition of Lynx Co.

5    An extract from the audit strategy document prepared by Vulture Associates relating to Lynx Co.

**Required:**

**Respond to the instructions in the email from the audit engagement partner.    (46 marks)**

**Note: The split of the mark allocation is shown in the partner's email (Exhibit 1).**

**Professional marks will be awarded for the presentation and logical flow of the briefing notes and the clarity of the explanations provided.    (4 marks)**

**(Total: 50 marks)**

**Exhibit 1 – Email from audit engagement partner**

**To:**       Audit manager

**From:**     Maya Crag, Audit engagement partner

**Subject:** Audit planning for the Eagle Group

Hello

I have provided you with some information in the form of a number of exhibits which you should use in planning the audit of the Eagle Group (the Group). I held a meeting yesterday with the Group finance director and representatives from the Group audit committee, and we discussed a number of issues which will impact on the audit planning.

Using the information provided, I require you to prepare briefing notes for my use in which you:

(a)   Evaluate the audit risks to be considered in planning the Group audit. You should use analytical procedures to assist in identifying audit risks. You are not required to consider audit risks relating to disclosure, as these will be planned for later in the audit process.                                                                                                                             **(24 marks)**

(b)   Design the principal audit procedures to be used in the audit of the goodwill arising on the acquisition of Lynx Co. Management's calculation of the goodwill is shown in Exhibit 4. You do not need to consider the procedures relating to impairment testing, or to foreign currency retranslation, as these will be planned later in the audit.

                                                                                                                                           **(6 marks)**

(c)   Using the information provided in Exhibit 5, evaluate the extract of the audit strategy prepared by Vulture Associates in respect of their audit of Lynx Co and discuss any implications for the Group audit.                                                               **(10 marks)**

(d)   After considering the request in Exhibit 2 from the Group finance director in respect of our firm providing advice on the Group's integrated report, discuss the ethical and professional implications of this request, recommending any further actions which should be taken by our firm.                                                                         **(6 marks)**

Thank you.

**Exhibit 2 – Background information about the Group and request from Group finance director Group operational activities**

The Group, which is a listed entity, operates in distribution, supply chain and logistics management. Its operations are worldwide, spanning more than 200 countries. The Group's strategy is to strengthen its market share and grow revenue in a sustainable manner by expansion into emerging markets. There are over 50 subsidiaries in the Group, many of which are international. There are three main business divisions: post and parcel delivery, commercial freight and supply chain management, each of which historically has provided approximately one-third of the Group's revenue.

A fourth business division which focuses purely on providing distribution channels for the oil and coal sector was established two years ago, and in 20X8 began to grow quite rapidly. It is forecast to provide 12% of the Group's revenue this year, growing to 15% in 20X9. This division is performing particularly well in developing economies.

In recent years, revenue has grown steadily, based mainly on growth in some locations where e-commerce is rapidly developing. This year, revenue is projected to decline slightly, which the Group attributes to increased competition, as a new distribution company has taken some of the Group's market share in a number of countries. However, the Group management team is confident that this is a short-term drop in revenue, and forecasts a return to growth in 20X9.

**Innovation**

The Group has invested in automating its warehousing facilities, and while it still employs more than 250,000 staff, many manual warehouse jobs are now performed by robots. Approximately 5,000 staff were made redundant early in this financial year due to automation of their work. Other innovations include increased use of automated loading and unloading of vehicles, and improvements in the technology used to monitor and manage inventory levels.

**Integrated reporting**

The Group is proud of this innovation and is keen to highlight these technological developments in its integrated report. The Group finance director has been asked to lead a project tasked with producing the Group's first integrated report. The finance director has sent the following request to the audit engagement partner:

'We would like your firm to assist us in developing our integrated report, and to provide assurance on it, as we believe this will enhance the credibility of the information it contains. Specifically, we would like your input into the choice of key performance indicators which should be presented, how to present them, and how they should be reconciled, where relevant, to financial information from the audited financial statements.'

The publication of an integrated report is not a requirement in the jurisdiction in which the Group is headquartered, but there is a growing pressure from stakeholders for an integrated report to be produced by listed reporting entities.

If Bison & Co accepts the engagement in relation to the Group's integrated report, the work would be performed by a team separate from the audit team.

**Exhibit 3 – Extract from consolidated financial statements**

**Statement of financial position**

|  | Note | As at 31 December 20X8 Projected $ million | As at 31 December 20X7 Actual $ million |
|---|---|---|---|
| **Non-current assets** | | | |
| Goodwill | 1 | 1,100 | 970 |
| Other intangible assets | 2 | 200 | 170 |
| Property, plant and equipment | | 657 | 600 |
| Other investments | | 85 | 100 |
| | | _____ | _____ |
| Total non-current assets | | 2,042 | 1,840 |
| | | _____ | _____ |
| **Current assets** | | 1,450 | 1,420 |
| | | _____ | _____ |
| **Total assets** | | 3,492 | 3,260 |
| | | _____ | _____ |
| **Equity and liabilities** | | | |
| Equity | | | |
| Share capital | 3 | 1,250 | 1,150 |
| Retained earnings | | 840 | 780 |
| Other components of equity | | 130 | 140 |
| Non-controlling interest | | 25 | 23 |
| | | _____ | _____ |
| | | 2,245 | 2,093 |
| | | _____ | _____ |
| Non-current liabilities | 4 | 650 | 620 |
| Current liabilities | | 597 | 547 |
| | | _____ | _____ |
| **Total equity and liabilities** | | 3,492 | 3,260 |
| | | _____ | _____ |

**Statement of profit or loss**

| | Note | Year to 31 December 20X8 Projected $ million | Year to 31 December 20X7 Actual $ million |
|---|---|---|---|
| Revenue | 5 | 5,770 | 5,990 |
| Other operating income | 6 | 120 | 80 |
| Operating expenses | 7 | (5,540) | (5,800) |
| | | | |
| Operating profit | | 350 | 270 |
| Finance charges | | (28) | (30) |
| | | | |
| Profit before tax | | 322 | 240 |
| Tax expense | | (64) | (60) |
| | | | |
| **Profit for the year** | | 258 | 180 |

**Notes to the extracts from financial statements**

**Goodwill**

1 Goodwill relates to the Group's subsidiaries, and is tested for impairment on an annual basis. Management will conduct the annual impairment review in December 20X8, but it is anticipated that no impairment will need to be recognised this year due to anticipated growth in revenue which is forecast for the next two years.

In March 20X8, the Group acquired an 80% controlling shareholding in Lynx Co, a listed company located in a foreign country, for consideration of $351 million. Management's determination of the goodwill arising on this acquisition is shown in Exhibit 4.

**Other intangible assets**

2 Other intangible assets relates mostly to software and other technological development costs. During the year $35 million was spent on developing a new IT system for dealing with customer enquiries and processing customer orders. A further $20 million was spent on research and development into robots being used in warehouses, and $5 million on developing new accounting software. These costs have been capitalised as intangible assets and are all being amortised over a 15-year useful life.

**Equity and non-current liabilities**

3 A share issue in July 20X8 raised cash of $100 million, which was used to fund capital expenditure.

4 Non-current liabilities includes borrowings of $550 million (20X7 – $500 million) and provisions of $100 million (20X7 – $120 million). Changes in financing during the year have impacted on the Group's weighted average cost of capital. Information from the Group's treasury management team suggests that the weighted average cost of capital is currently 10%.

**Financial performance**

5    Revenue has decreased by 3.7% over the year, due to a new competitor in the market taking some of the Group's market share.

6    Other operating income comprises the following items:

|  | 20X8 | 20X7 |
|---|---|---|
|  | $ million | $ million |
| Reversal of provisions | 60 | 40 |
| Reversal of impairment losses on receivables and other assets | 30 | 20 |
| Foreign currency gains | 28 | 23 |
| Profit/(loss) on disposal of non-current assets | 2 | (3) |
| Total | 120 | 80 |

7    Operating expenses includes the following items:

|  | 20X8 | 20X7 |
|---|---|---|
|  | $ million | $ million |
| Staff costs | 3,650 | 3,610 |
| Cost of raw materials, consumables and supplies | 1,725 | 1,780 |
| Depreciation, amortisation and impairment | 145 | 140 |
| Other operating expenses | 20 | 270 |
| Total | 5,540 | 5,800 |

**Exhibit 4 – Determination of goodwill on the acquisition of Lynx Co**

|  | Note | $ million |
|---|---|---|
| Cash consideration – paid 1 March 20X8 |  | 80 |
| Contingent consideration | 1 | 271 |
| Total consideration |  | 351 |
| Fair value of non-controlling interest | 2 | 49 |
|  |  | 400 |
| *Less:* Fair value of identifiable net assets | 3 | (300) |
| Goodwill |  | 100 |

**Notes:**

1    The contingent consideration will be payable four years after the acquisition date and is calculated based on a payment of $525 million, only payable if Lynx Co reaches revenue and profit targets outlined in the purchase documentation. The amount included in the goodwill calculation has been discounted to present value using a discount factor based on an 18% interest rate.

2    The non-controlling interest is measured at fair value, the amount being based on Lynx Co's share price on 1 March 20X8.

3    The assets and liabilities acquired and their fair values were determined by an independent firm of Chartered Certified Accountants, Sidewinder & Co, who was engaged by the Group to perform due diligence on Lynx Co prior to the acquisition taking place. A fair value uplift of $12 million was made in relation to property, plant and equipment.

**Exhibit 5 – Extract from audit strategy – prepared by Vulture Associates in respect of the audit of Lynx Co**

The two points below are an extract from the audit strategy. Other sections of the audit strategy, including the audit risk assessment, have been reviewed by the Group audit team and are considered to be satisfactory. Lynx Co is projected to be loss making this year, and the Group audit team is confident that sufficient procedures on going concern have been planned for.

**INT & UK: Controls effectiveness**

We will place reliance on internal controls, which will reduce the amount of substantive testing which needs to be performed. This is justified on the grounds that in the previous year's audit, controls were tested and found to be highly effective. We do not plan to re-test the controls, as according to management there have been no changes in systems or the control environment during the year.

**INT: Internal audit**

Lynx Co has offered the services of its internal audit team to help perform audit procedures. We are planning to use the internal auditors to complete the audit work in respect of trade receivables, as they have performed work on this area during the year. It will be efficient for them to perform and conclude on the relevant audit procedures, including the trade receivables circularisation, and evaluation of the allowance for trade receivables, which we will instruct them to carry out.

**UK: Valuation of pension plan**

Lynx Co has a defined benefit pension plan in place for its employees. The draft financial statements recognise a non-current liability of £11 million in relation to plan assets with a value of £38 million, and plan liabilities valued at £49 million. In previous years the pension plan has been valued by an external valuer, and in 20X7 a net deficit of £3 million was recognised in non-current liabilities. However, this year the valuation has been performed by one of Vulture Associates' partners, who is a qualified actuary. The fee for providing this valuation was £35,000. It is expected that the audit fee will be £600,000 and fees for other audit-related services will be in the region of £100,000.

**5    BASSETT GROUP**  *Walk in the footsteps of a top tutor*

You are the manager responsible for The Bassett Group (the Group). The Group, a listed entity, has a financial year ending 30 April 20X8, and your firm, Whippet & Co, was appointed as Group auditor in September 20X7. Whippet & Co will audit all Group companies with the exception of Borzoi Co, a foreign subsidiary, which is audited by a local firm of auditors, Saluki Associates. The Group aims to comply fully with relevant corporate governance requirements.

You are provided with the following exhibits:

1    An email which you have received from Kerry Dunker, the audit engagement partner.

2    Background information about the Group's business activities.

3    Results of analytical procedures performed by one of the audit team.

4    Communication from the previous auditor, Grey & Co.

**Required:**

**Respond to the instructions in the email from the audit engagement partner.    (46 marks)**

**Note: The split of the mark allocation is shown in the partner's email (Exhibit 1).**

**Professional marks will be awarded for the presentation and logical flow of the briefing notes and the clarity of the explanations provided.                                  (4 marks)**

**(Total: 50 marks)**

**Exhibit 1 – Email from audit engagement partner**

**To:         Audit manager**

**From:    Kerry Dunker, audit engagement partner**

**Subject:  Bassett Group, audit planning**

Hello

I have provided you with some information in the form of a number of exhibits which you should use in planning the audit of the Bassett Group (the Group). I held a meeting yesterday with the Group finance director to discuss some aspects of the Group's business and related accounting issues. One of the audit team members has already performed limited analytical procedures based on the Group's projected financial statements and comparatives.

Using the information provided, I require you to prepare briefing notes for my use in which you:

(a)   (i)    Evaluate the audit risks to be considered in planning the audit of the Group financial statements, and                                                           **(18 marks)**

       (ii)   Identify and explain the matters which the audit team should approach with a high degree of professional scepticism.                                    **(9 marks)**

(b)     To assist the audit assistants' understanding of our audit strategy in respect of Borzoi Co:

   (i)     Explain the term 'significant component' and assess whether Borzoi Co is a significant component of the Group, and                          **(5 marks)**

   (ii)    Discuss the nature and extent of involvement which our firm should have with the audit risk assessment to be performed by Saluki Associates.          **(7 marks)**

(c)     Using the information provided in Exhibit 4, discuss the ethical and professional issues and explain the actions that Whippet & Co should have taken at the acceptance stage to avoid such issues occurring again.                          **(7 marks)**

**Thank you.**

**Exhibit 2 – Background information**

The Group is a publisher of newspapers and magazines, academic journals, and books and operates globally, with sales being made in over 100 countries. The Group has 20 subsidiaries which have been acquired over the last 30 years. All Group companies are located in the same country, with the exception of Borzoi Co, a foreign subsidiary whose operations focus on the translation of published content into a variety of different languages.

The Group's publishing activities can be categorised into three operating segments, each of which are cash generating units for the purpose of impairment reviews: newspapers and magazines, academic journals, and books.

**Software development**

During the financial year the Group has invested in software which enhances and extends the Group's range of digital publications, across all operating segments. The total investment, which is recognised as an intangible asset, was $15 million, of which $5 million relates to purchased software, and $10 million relates to internally developed software. According to management, the implementation of this software has already led to significant increases in sales of digital publications, and while this accounts for only approximately 20% of Group revenue currently, management is confident that sales of digital publications will quickly grow, and within three years is expected to overtake sales of hard copy publications across all operating segments. Using this justification, management does not consider it necessary to perform impairment reviews on any of the three operating segments this year.

**Newspapers and magazines – publication rights**

A substantial portion of the Group's newspaper and magazine publications are protected by publication rights which protect the Group's exclusive right to publish the relevant newspaper or magazine for specified periods. The Group owns more than 200 publication rights, which range in period of exclusivity from five years to 30 years. The publication rights are recognised as an intangible asset with a carrying amount of $7.9 million. The Group's accounting policy is to amortise all publication rights over an average period of 25 years.

**Books – royalty advances**

The Group commissions authors to write books for which the Group owns the copyright. When a book is commissioned, the author is paid a royalty advance, the amount of which depends on the expected sales of the book. The Group's accounting policy is to defer the cost by treating the royalty advance as a prepayment within current assets until the book is published. Once published, the cost begins to be recognised as an expense, spread over a ten-year period. The Group finance director does not have a justification for this ten-year period other than it being 'industry practice'. The total royalty advance projected to be recognised within current assets at 30 April 20X8 is $3.4 million.

**Borzoi Co**

Borzoi Co is located in Farland, a country which has recently experienced political unrest. The political situation has caused significant volatility of the local currency, the Oska. At today's date, the management accounts of Borzoi Co recognise total assets of 68 million Oska, and the exchange rate is 4 Oska:1$. In the last six months, the exchange rate has fluctuated between 10 Oska:1$ to 3 Oska:1$.

Farland requires the use of IFRS Standards and therefore Borzoi Co prepares its financial statements using IFRS Standards as its applicable financial reporting framework.

To help with the company's development of language translation operations, on 1 May 20X7, Bassett Co, the parent company of the Group, transferred a piece of translation software to Borzoi Co. The software had been purchased by the parent company for $1.5 million several years ago and prior to transfer to Borzoi Co, it was held at a carrying amount of $1 million, this being its cost less amortisation to date. Immediately prior to being transferred to Borzoi Co, the software was revalued in the parent company's financial statements to $5.4 million, this being its estimated fair value at the time of the transfer. The estimate of fair value was determined by Group management, and this amount is still outstanding for payment by Borzoi Co.

**Exhibit 3 – Results of analytical procedures**

The revenue and total assets for 20X8 (projected) and 20X7 (actual) for the Group in total and for each segment is as follows:

| Operating segment | Year to 30 April 20X8 Revenue | Year to 30 April 20X7 Revenue | % change in revenue | As at 30 April 20X8 Total assets | As at 30 April 20X7 Total assets | % change in total assets |
|---|---|---|---|---|---|---|
| | Projected $ million | Actual $ million | | Projected $ million | Actual $ million | |
| Newspapers and magazines | 64 | 67 | (4.5) | 45 | 42 | 7.1 |
| Academic journals | 47 | 46 | 2.2 | 18 | 15 | 20 |
| Books | 42 | 45 | (6.7) | 32 | 28 | 14.3 |
| Total | 153 | 158 | (3.2) | 95 | 85 | 11.8 |

**Exhibit 4 – Communication from the previous auditor, Grey & Co**

The previous Group auditor, Grey & Co, states the following in their communication to Whippet & Co:

'We have acted as Group auditor for the last four years and our audit opinion has been unmodified each year. However, we would like to bring to your attention a matter relating to the Group's corporate governance arrangements. We found that on several occasions in the last year the Group chief financial officer initially blocked our firm's access to the Group audit committee, making it difficult for us to discuss matters relating to the audit with the committee. We therefore had to rely more heavily on management information and representations than we would have liked, however, we believe that in the circumstances we obtained sufficient and appropriate audit evidence and that there was no justification for issuing a modified audit opinion. We thought that you should be aware of this difficulty.'

## 6 SUNSHINE HOTEL GROUP  *Walk in the footsteps of a top tutor*

You are a manager in the audit department of Dove & Co, responsible for the audit of the Sunshine Hotel Group (the Group), which has a financial year ending 31 December 20X7. You are about to start planning the Group audit for forthcoming year end and this is the first time that you are managing the audit.

You are provided with the following exhibits:

1   An email which you have received from John Starling, the audit engagement partner.

2   Background information about the Group's activities.

3   Notes from meeting with the finance director.

4   Extract from email from the Group finance director to John Starling, audit engagement partner.

5   Request from audit committee regarding the use of data analytics in future audits.

**Required:**

**Respond to the instructions in the email from the audit engagement partner.   (46 marks)**

**Note: The split of the mark allocation is shown in the partner's email (Exhibit 1).**

**Professional marks will be awarded for the presentation and logical flow of the briefing notes and the clarity of the explanations provided.   (4 marks)**

**(Total: 50 marks)**

**Exhibit 1 – Email from audit engagement partner**

To:       Audit manager

From:    John Starling, audit engagement partner

Subject: Audit planning, the Sunshine Hotel Group

**Hello**

I have provided you with some information in the form of a number of exhibits which you should use in planning the audit of the Sunshine Hotel Group (the Group). I held a meeting yesterday with the Group finance director and a representative from the Group audit committee, and we discussed a number of business developments during the year and plans for the future.

Using the information provided, I require you to prepare briefing notes for my use in which you:

(a)   Evaluate the business risks facing the Group.                                              **(10 marks)**

(b)   Evaluate the significant risks of material misstatement which should be considered when planning the audit.                                                                         **(18 marks)**

(c)   Using the information provided in Exhibit 4:

   (i)    Discuss the additional implications for planning the Group audit and explain any relevant actions to be taken by the firm, and

   (ii)   Design the audit procedures to be performed on the claim of $10 million, assuming that the audit team is given access to all relevant sources of audit evidence.                                                                                **(10 marks)**

(d)   In relation to the audit committee's request for information about the use of data analytics in Exhibit 5:

   (i)    Explain the term data analytics and discuss how their use can improve audit quality.

   (ii)   Explain how they could be used during the audit of the Sunshine Hotel Group and the potential limitations.                                                       **(8 marks)**

**Thank you.**

**Exhibit 2 – Background information**

The Group owns and operates a chain of 20 luxury hotels, all located in popular beachside holiday resorts. The hotels operate on an 'all-inclusive' basis, whereby guests can consume unlimited food and drink, and take part in a variety of water sports including scuba diving as part of the price of their holiday. Each hotel has at least four restaurants and a number of bars. The 'Sunshine Hotel' brand is a market leader, with significant amounts spent each year on marketing to support the brand. The hotels are luxurious and maintained to a very high standard and are marketed as exclusive adult-only luxury holiday destinations.

When customers book to stay in the hotel, they are charged a deposit equivalent to 20% of the total cost of their stay, and a further 20% is payable eight weeks before arrival. The remaining 60% is settled on departure. If a booking is cancelled prior to a week before a guest's stay commences, then a full refund is given, but no refunds are given for cancellations within the week leading up to a guest's stay.

**Exhibit 3 – Notes from meeting with finance director**

**Financial performance**

The Group has seen continued growth, with revenue for the year to 31 December 20X7 projected to be $125 million (20X6 – $110 million), and profit before tax projected to be $10 million (20X6 – $9 million).

According to the latest management accounts, the Group's total assets are currently $350 million. The 'Sunshine Hotel' brand is not recognised as an asset in the financial statements because it has been internally generated. The Group has cash of $20 million at today's date. Most of this cash is held on short-term deposit in a number of different currencies. Based on the latest management accounts, the Group's gearing ratio is 25%.

**Moulin Blanche restaurants**

In January 20X7, the Group entered into an agreement with an internationally acclaimed restaurant chain, Moulin Blanche, to open new restaurants in its five most popular hotels. The agreement cost $5 million, lasts for 10 years, and allows the Group to use the restaurant name, adopt the menus and decorate the restaurants in the style of Moulin Blanche. The cost of $5 million has been recognised within marketing expenses for the year. After a period of refurbishment, the new restaurants opened in all five hotels on 1 July 20X7.

**International expansion**

The Group is planning to expand its operations over the next three years by opening hotels in countries with increasingly popular tourist destinations.

As part of this strategy, in July 20X7 the Group purchased land in three new locations in Farland at a cost of $75 million. There are currently no specific plans for the development of these locations due to political instability in the country. In addition to the Farland acquisitions, an existing hotel complex was purchased from a competitor for $23 million. The hotel complex is located in a country where local legislation prohibits private ownership and use of beaches, so the Group's hotel guests cannot enjoy the private and exclusive use of a beach which is one of the Group's key selling points. For this reason, the Group has not yet developed the hotel complex and it is currently being used as a location for staff training.

All of these assets are recognised at cost as property, plant and equipment in the Group statement of financial position. Due to the problems with these recent acquisitions, the Group is planning to invest in alternative locations, with capital expenditure on sites in new locations of $45 million budgeted for 20X8. This will be funded entirely from an undrawn borrowing facility with the Group's bank which has a fixed interest rate of 3.5% per annum.

**Hurricanes**

Two of the Group's hotels are located in an area prone to hurricanes, and unfortunately only last week, a hurricane caused severe damage to both of these hotels. Under the Group's 'hurricane guarantee scheme', customers who were staying at the hotels at the time of the hurricane were transferred to other Group hotels, at no cost to the customer. Customers with bookings to stay at the closed hotels have been offered a refund of their deposits, or to transfer their reservation to a different Group hotel, under the terms of the scheme. The hotels are closed while the necessary repair work, which will take two months, is carried out at an estimated cost of $25 million. The repair work will be covered by the Group's insurance policy, which typically pays half of the estimated cost of repair work in advance, with the balance paid when the repair work is completed. No accounting entries have been made as yet in relation to the hurricane.

**Exhibit 4 – Extract from email from the Group finance director to John Starling, audit engagement partner**

> **John**
>
> The Group's lawyer has received a letter from Ocean Protection, a multi-national pressure group which aims to safeguard marine environments. Ocean Protection is claiming that our hotel guests are causing environmental damage to delicate coral reefs when scuba diving under the supervision of the Group's scuba diving instructors.
>
> Ocean Protection is pressing charges against the Group, and alleges that our activities are in breach of international environmental protection legislation which is ratified by all of the countries in which the Group operates. Damages of $10 million are being sought, Ocean Protection suggesting that this amount would be used to protect the coral reefs from further damage.
>
> The Group is keen to avoid any media attention, so I am hoping to negotiate a lower level of payment and an agreement from Ocean Protection that they will not make the issue public knowledge.
>
> From an accounting point of view, we do not want to recognise a liability, as the disclosures will draw attention to the matter. We will account for any necessary payment when it is made, which is likely to be next year.
>
> I understand that your audit team will need to look at this issue, but I ask that you only speak to me about it, and do not speak to any other employees. Also, I do not want you to contact Ocean Protection as this could impact on our negotiation.

**Exhibit 5 – Request from audit committee regarding the use of data analytics in future audits**

The audit committee has heard that some audit firms are now using data analytics and have asked for further information. They are keen for data analytics to be used for the audit of the Sunshine Hotel Group as soon as possible and have indicated that this will be a key deciding factor when the audit is next put out to tender. They would like Dove & Co to explain what data analytics are and how they could be used during the audit to improve efficiency and quality.

**7    LAUREL GROUP**  *Walk in the footsteps of a top tutor*

 *Question debrief*

You are a manager in Holly & Co, a firm of Chartered Certified Accountants, and you are responsible for the audit of the Laurel Group (the Group), a listed entity, with a financial year ending 31 May 20X7.

Holly & Co was appointed as Group auditor three years ago when the audit was put out for tender. Holly & Co audits all components of the Group.

You are provided with the following exhibits:

1    An email which you have received from Brigitte Sanders, the audit engagement partner.

2    A summary of relevant points from the permanent audit file.

3    Notes taken at a recent meeting between Brigitte Sanders and the Group finance director.

4    Extracts from the latest forecast financial statements with comparative figures and accompanying notes.

5    Request from the Group audit committee to perform a valuation of the shares of Oleander Co.

**Required:**

**Respond to the instructions in the email from the audit engagement partner.    (46 marks)**

**Note: The split of the mark allocation is shown in the partner's email (Exhibit 1).**

**Professional marks will be awarded for the presentation and logical flow of the briefing notes and the clarity of the explanations provided.    (4 marks)**

**(Total: 50 marks)**

**Exhibit 1 – Email from audit engagement partner**

**To:        Audit manager**

**From:    Brigitte Sanders, audit engagement partner**

**Subject:  Audit planning – the Laurel Group**

**Hello**

You need to start planning the Laurel Group audit, and to help you with this I have provided you with some relevant information. I met with the Group finance director and a representative of the audit committee yesterday to discuss recent business developments.

Using the information provided, I require you to prepare briefing notes for my use in which you:

(a)    Evaluate the risks of material misstatement to be considered in planning the Group audit. Your evaluation should utilise analytical procedures as a method for identifying relevant risks.    **(24 marks)**

(b)    Recommend any additional information which should be requested from the Group which would allow a more detailed preliminary analytical review to be performed.

**(6 marks)**

(c)    Design the principal audit procedures to be used in the audit of:

   (i)    The impairment of the Chico brand, and

   (ii)    The planned acquisition of Azalea Co.                              **(10 marks)**

(d)    Using the information provided in Exhibit 5, discuss the ethical issues raised by the request to perform the valuation of the shares of Oleander Co.              **(6 marks)**

**Thank you.**

---

 *Calculate your allowed time, allocate the time to the separate parts...............*

---

**Exhibit 2 – Points from the permanent audit file**

The Group is highly acquisitive, and there are more than 40 subsidiaries and 15 associates within the Group.

The Group produces cosmetics and beauty products which are sold under various brand names in more than 100 countries. Most of the brand names have been acquired with subsidiary companies.

Products include cosmetics, hair care products and perfumes for men and women. Research into new products is a significant activity, and the Group aims to bring new products to market on a regular basis.

**Exhibit 3 – Notes from meeting with Group finance director**

During the year the Group has incurred significant expenditure in non-current assets with $20 million being spent on the acquisition of property, plant and equipment, and $20 million investment in new product development. Half of this expenditure has been funded by a loan and half has been funded from reserves.

In December 20X6, allegations were made in the press and by customers that some ingredients used in the Chico perfume range can cause skin irritations and more serious health problems. As a result, the Chico products have been withdrawn from sale and a $30 million impairment charge has been recognised in respect of the Chico brand name. Despite this issue, Group revenues have increased by 13% and Group management is confident that no other brands are affected.

Group management is currently negotiating the acquisition of Azalea Co, a large company which develops and sells a range of fine fragrances. It is planned that the acquisition will take place in early June 20X7, and the Group is hopeful that Azalea Co's products will replace the revenue stream lost from the withdrawal of its Chico perfume range. Due diligence is taking place currently, and Group management is hopeful that this will support the consideration of $130 million offered for 100% of Azalea Co's share capital. The Group's bank has agreed to provide a loan for this amount.

**Exhibit 4 – Extract from latest forecast financial statements**

**Consolidated statement of financial position**

| | Note | 31 May 20X7 $m Projected | 31 May 20X6 $m Actual |
|---|---|---|---|
| **Non-current assets** | | | |
| Property, plant and equipment | 1 | 92 | 78 |
| Intangible asset – goodwill | 2 | 18 | 18 |
| Intangible asset – acquired brand names | 3 | 80 | 115 |
| Intangible asset – development costs | 4 | 25 | 10 |
| | | 215 | 221 |
| **Current assets** | | 143 | 107 |
| **Total assets** | | 358 | 328 |
| **Equity and liabilities** | | | |
| **Equity** | | | |
| Equity share capital | | 100 | 100 |
| Retained earnings | | 106 | 98 |
| Non-controlling interest | | 23 | 23 |
| | | 229 | 221 |
| **Non-current liabilities** | | | |
| Debenture loans | 5 | 100 | 80 |
| Deferred tax | 6 | 10 | 2 |
| **Total non-current liabilities** | | 110 | 82 |
| **Current liabilities** | | 19 | 25 |
| Total liabilities | | 129 | 107 |
| **Total equity and liabilities** | | 358 | 328 |

**Consolidated statement of profit or loss for the year to 31 May**

|  | Projected 20X7 $m | Actual 20X6 $m |
|---|---|---|
| Revenue | 220 | 195 |
| Operating expenses | (185) | (158) |
| Operating profit | 35 | 37 |
| Finance costs | (7) | (7) |
| Profit before tax | 28 | 30 |
| Tax expense | (3) | (3) |
| **Profit for the year** | 25 | 27 |

**Notes:**

1    Capital expenditure of $20 million has been recorded so far during the year. The Group's accounting policy is to recognise assets at cost less depreciation. During the year, the directors performed a review of the estimated useful lives of the company's assets. It was concluded that many were too short and as a result, asset lives were extended and the projected depreciation charge for the year is $5 million less than the comparative figure.

2    Group management has performed an impairment review at the year end and concluded that goodwill is not impaired.

3    Acquired brand names are held at cost with no amortisation being charged on the grounds that the assets have an indefinite life. An annual impairment review is conducted on all brand names. A $30 million impairment has been recognised in respect of the Chico brand name as discussed above.

4    Development costs relate to expenditure incurred to develop new beauty products. Costs incurred in the research phase are expensed until the product is determined to be technologically feasible. Costs incurred after this stage are capitalised in accordance with IAS 38 *Intangible Assets*.

5    A $20 million loan was taken out in January 20X7, the cash being used to finance a specific new product development project.

6    The deferred tax liability relates to timing differences in respect of accelerated tax depreciation (capital allowances) on the Group's property, plant and equipment. The liability has increased following changes to the estimated useful lives of assets discussed in note 1.

**Exhibit 5 – Request for additional services from the audit committee**

In addition to the planned acquisition of Azalea Co, Group management is considering purchasing the entire shareholding of Oleander Co. The Group audit committee would like Holly & Co to perform a valuation of the shares of Oleander Co to determine whether the company is a viable investment. Oleander Co is an audit client of Holly & Co.

8    ZED COMMUNICATIONS GROUP    *Walk in the footsteps of a top tutor*

The Zed Communications Group (ZCG) is an audit client of your firm, Tarantino & Co, with a financial year ending 31 December 20X6. You are the manager assigned to the forthcoming audit. ZCG is one of Tarantino & Co's largest audit clients.

You are provided with the following exhibits:

1    An email which you have received from Vincent Vega, the audit engagement partner.

2    Notes from meeting with the finance director.

3    Extracts from the latest report of the internal audit department.

4    Extracts from latest management accounts.

**Required:**

**Respond to the instructions in the email from the audit engagement partner.    (46 marks)**

**Note: The split of the mark allocation is shown in the partner's email (Exhibit 1).**

**Professional marks will be awarded for the presentation and logical flow of the briefing notes and the clarity of the explanations provided.    (4 marks)**

**(Total: 50 marks)**

**Exhibit 1 – Email from audit engagement partner**

**To:       Audit engagement manager**

**From:    Vincent Vega, audit engagement partner**

**Subject:  ZCG audit planning**

**Hello**

I have provided you with some information in the form of a number of exhibits which you should use in planning the audit of Zed Communications Group (ZCG). I held a meeting yesterday with the Group finance director regarding the forthcoming audit. We also discussed the possibility of using the Group's internal audit team to improve audit efficiency.

Using the information provided, I require you to prepare briefing notes for my use in which you:

(a)   Evaluate the audit risks relevant to planning the final audit of ZCG.    **(18 marks)**

(b)   Recommend the additional information which would be relevant in the evaluation of audit risk.    **(5 marks)**

(c)   Discuss the matters to be considered in determining the assistance which could be provided by, and the amount of reliance, if any, which can be placed on the work of ZCG's internal audit department.    **(7 marks)**

(d)   Design the principal audit procedures to be performed in the audit of:

(i)    The classification of the 50% equity shareholding in WTC as a joint venture, and

(ii)   The measurement of the intangible asset recognised in respect of the licence to operate in Farland.    **(10 marks)**

(e)   Discuss the advantages and disadvantages of a joint audit if the acquisition of the company in Neverland goes ahead.    **(6 marks)**

**Thank you.**

**Exhibit 2 – Notes from meeting with finance director**

ZCG is a listed entity, one of the largest telecommunications providers in the country and is seeking to expand internationally. ZCG also provides broadband and fixed telephone line services. One of ZCG's strategic aims is to expand internationally, either by acquiring existing telecommunications providers in other countries, or by purchasing licences to operate in foreign countries. ZCG has identified a telecommunications company located overseas in Neverland. The Group's audit committee has suggested that once the acquisition is complete, due to the distant location of the company, a joint audit could be performed with the target company's current auditors.

In March 20X6, ZCG purchased a 50% equity shareholding in Wallace Telecoms Co (WTC), a company operating in several countries where ZCG previously had no interests. The other 50% is held by Wolf Communications Co. The cost of the 50% equity shareholding was $45 million. ZCG is planning to account for its investment in WTC as a joint venture in the Group financial statements.

On 1 January 20X5, ZCG purchased a licence to operate in Farland, a rapidly expanding economy, at a cost of $65 million. The licence lasts for 10 years from the date that it was purchased. Since purchasing the licence, ZCG has established its network coverage in Farland and the network became operational on 1 July 20X6. The licence was recognised as an intangible asset at cost in the Group statement of financial position at 31 December 20X5. Since the network became operational, customer demand has been less than anticipated due to a competitor offering a special deal to its existing customers to encourage them not to change providers.

Most of ZCG's mobile phone customers sign a contract under which they pay a fixed amount each month to use ZCG's mobile network, paying extra if they exceed the agreed data usage and airtime limits. The contract also allows connection to a fixed landline and internet access using broadband connection and most contracts run for two or three years.

In order to extend its broadband services, ZCG has started to purchase network capacity from third party companies. ZCG enters a fixed-term contract to use a specified amount of the seller's network capacity, with the seller determining which of its network assets are used by ZCG in supplying network services to its customers. In the first six months of 20X6, ZCG purchased $17.8 million of network capacity from a range of suppliers, with the contract periods varying from twelve months to three years. The cost has been capitalised as an intangible asset.

**Exhibit 3 – Extracts from the latest report of the internal audit department**

ZCG has a well-established internal audit department which is tasked with a range of activities including providing assurance to management over internal controls and assisting the Group's risk management team. The internal audit department is managed by Jules Winfield, a qualified accountant with many years' experience. An extract from the executive summary of the latest internal audit report to the Group finance director is shown below:

'We are pleased to report that ZCG's internal controls are working well and there have been no significant changes to systems and controls during the year. As a result of our testing of controls we uncovered only two financial irregularities which related to:

- Failure to obtain appropriate authorisation and approval of senior management expense claims, such as travel and other reimbursements. The unsubstantiated expense claims amounted to $575,000.

- Inadequate access controls over the Group's IT systems which resulted in a payroll fraud amounting to $750,000.'

**Exhibit 4 – Extracts from latest management accounts**

|  | 8 months to 31 August 20X6 | Audited financial statements to 31 December 20X5 |
|---|---|---|
|  | $ million | $ million |
| Revenue: |  |  |
| Europe | 106 | 102 |
| Americas | 30 | 68 |
| South East Asia | 33 | 30 |
| India | 29 | 20 |
|  | —— | —— |
| Total | 198 | 220 |
|  | —— | —— |

|  | At 31 August 20X6 | At 31 December 20X5 |
|---|---|---|
|  | $ million | $ million |
| Total assets | 598 | 565 |

**9    VANCOUVER GROUP**  *Walk in the footsteps of a top tutor*

You are an audit manager in Montreal & Co, a firm of Chartered Certified Accountants, and you are responsible for the audit of the Vancouver Group (the Group). You are beginning to plan the Group audit for the financial year ending 31 July 20X6.

You are provided with the following exhibits:

1    An email which you have received from Albert Franks, the audit engagement partner.

2    Background information about the Group.

3    Projected financial information for the Group's forthcoming year-end along with comparatives and explanatory notes.

4    Notes from meeting with the audit committee representative.

**Required:**

**Respond to the instructions in the email from the audit engagement partner.    (46 marks)**

**Note: The split of the mark allocation is shown in the partner's email (Exhibit 1).**

**Professional marks will be awarded for the presentation and logical flow of the briefing notes and the clarity of the explanations provided.    (4 marks)**

**(Total: 50 marks)**

**Exhibit 1 – Email from audit engagement partner**

**To:         Audit manager**

**From:     Albert Franks, audit engagement partner**

**Subject:  The Vancouver Group – audit planning**

**Hello**

I am preparing for the audit team briefing next week at which there will be a number of recent recruits into the audit department whose first assignment will be the Vancouver Group. I have provided you with some information in the form of a number of exhibits which you should use in planning the audit of the Vancouver Group (the Group). I held a meeting yesterday with Hannah Peters, the Group finance director and a representative of the Group audit committee. We discussed some matters relevant to the Group this year and two issues raised for our attention by the committee.

Using the information provided, I require you to prepare briefing notes for my use in which you:

(a)    Explain why analytical procedures are performed as a fundamental part of our risk assessment at the planning stage of the audit.    **(4 marks)**

(b)    Evaluate the audit risks which should be considered in planning the Group audit. You should ensure that you consider all of the information provided as well as utilising analytical procedures, where relevant, to identify the audit risks.    **(24 marks)**

(c)    Design the audit procedures to be performed in respect of:

(i)    The valuation of goodwill.

(ii)    The treatment of the warehouse modernisation costs.    **(10 marks)**

(d)    Using the information provided in Exhibit 4, discuss the ethical issues relevant to Montreal & Co, and recommend any actions which should be taken by our firm.

**(8 marks)**

**Thank you.**

**Exhibit 2 – Background information about the Group**

The Group operates in the supply chain management sector, offering distribution, warehousing and container handling services.

The Group comprises a parent company, Vancouver Co, and two subsidiaries, Toronto Co and Calgary Co. Both of the subsidiaries were acquired as wholly owned subsidiaries many years ago. Montreal & Co audits all of the individual company financial statements as well as the Group consolidated financial statements.

The Group has not changed its operations significantly this year. However, it has completed a modernisation programme of its warehousing facilities at a cost of $25 million. The programme was financed with cash raised from two sources: $5 million was raised from a debenture issue, and $20 million from the sale of 5% of the share capital of Calgary Co, with the shares being purchased by an institutional investor.

**Exhibit 3 – Financial information provided by the Group finance director**

**Consolidated statement of financial position**

|  | Note | Projected 31 July 20X6 $m | Actual 31 July 20X5 $m |
|---|---|---|---|
| **Assets** | | | |
| **Non-current assets** | | | |
| Property, plant and equipment | 1 | 230 | 187 |
| Intangible assets – goodwill | | 30 | 30 |
| Deferred tax asset | 2 | 10 | 15 |
| **Total non-current assets** | | 270 | 232 |
| **Current assets** | | | |
| Inventories | | 35 | 28 |
| Trade and other receivables | | 62 | 45 |
| Cash and cash equivalents | | – | 10 |
| **Total current assets** | | 97 | 83 |
| **Total assets** | | 367 | 315 |

**Equity and liabilities**

**Equity**

| | | | |
|---|---|---|---|
| Equity share capital | | 50 | 50 |
| Retained earnings | | 126 | 103 |
| Non-controlling interest | 3 | 5 | – |
| **Total equity** | | **181** | **153** |

**Non-current liabilities**

| | | |
|---|---|---|
| Debenture | 60 | 55 |
| Provisions | 6 | 12 |
| **Total non-current liabilities** | **66** | **67** |

**Current liabilities**

| | | |
|---|---|---|
| Trade and other payables | 105 | 95 |
| Overdraft | 15 | – |
| **Total current liabilities** | **120** | **95** |
| **Total liabilities** | **186** | **162** |
| **Total equity and liabilities** | **367** | **315** |

**Consolidated statement of profit or loss for the year to 31 July**

| | Projected 20X6 $m | Actual 20X5 $m |
|---|---|---|
| Revenue | 375 | 315 |
| Operating expenses | (348) | (277) |
| **Operating profit** | **27** | **38** |
| Profit on disposal of shares in Calgary Co | 10 | – |
| Finance costs | (4) | (3) |
| **Profit before tax** | **33** | **35** |
| Tax expense | (10) | (15) |
| **Profit for the year** | **23** | **20** |

**Notes:**

1   Several old warehouses were modernised during the year. The modernisation involved the redesign of the layout of each warehouse, the installation of new computer systems, and the replacement of electrical systems.

2   The deferred tax asset is in respect of unused tax losses (tax credits) which accumulated when Toronto Co was loss making for a period of three years from 20W9 to 20X2.

3   The non-controlling interest has arisen on the disposal of shares in Calgary Co. On 1 January 20X6, a 5% equity shareholding in Calgary Co was sold, raising cash of $20 million. The profit made on the disposal is separately recognised in the Group statement of profit or loss.

**Exhibit 4 – Notes of meeting with the audit committee representative**

An investigation into the Group's tax affairs started in January 20X6. The tax authorities are investigating the possible underpayment of taxes by each of the companies in the Group, claiming that tax laws have been breached. The Group's tax planning was performed by another firm of accountants, Victoria & Co, but the Group's audit committee has asked if our firm will support the Group by looking into its tax position and liaising with the tax authorities in respect of the tax investigation on its behalf. Victoria & Co has resigned from their engagement to provide tax advice to the Group. The matter is to be resolved by a tribunal which is scheduled to take place in September 20X6.

The Group audit committee has also asked whether one of Montreal & Co's audit partners can be appointed as a non-executive director and serve on the audit committee. The audit committee lacks a financial reporting expert, and the appointment of an audit partner would bring much needed knowledge and experience.

**10   DALI**  *Walk in the footsteps of a top tutor*

You are a manager in the audit department of Mondrian & Co, a firm of Chartered Certified Accountants. This is the first year you will be responsible for the audit of Dali Co, a listed company. You are planning the audit of the financial statements for the year ending 31 December 20X5.

You are provided with the following exhibits:

1   An email which you have received from Sam Hockney, the audit engagement partner.

2   Background information on the company.

3   Notes from meeting with the finance director.

4   Request for non-audit service from the audit committee.

5   Results of preliminary analytical review performed by one of the audit team members.

**Required:**

**Respond to the instructions in the email from the audit engagement partner.** **(46 marks)**

**Note: The split of the mark allocation is shown in the partner's email (Exhibit 1).**

**Professional marks will be awarded for the presentation and logical flow of the briefing notes and the clarity of the explanations provided.** **(4 marks)**

**(Total: 50 marks)**

**Exhibit 1 – Email from audit engagement partner**

**To:** **Audit manager**

**From:** **Audit engagement partner, Sam Hockney**

**Regarding:** **Audit planning – Dali Co**

Hello

I have provided you with some information in the form of a number of exhibits which you should use in planning the audit of the Dali Co. I held a meeting yesterday with the finance director and we discussed a number of issues which will impact on the audit planning.

Using the information provided, I require you to prepare briefing notes for my use in which you:

(a) (i) Evaluate the audit risks to be considered in planning the audit of Dali Co.
**(20 marks)**

(ii) Recommend the additional information which would be relevant in the evaluation of audit risk. **(5 marks)**

(b) Design the principal audit procedures to be used in respect of:

(i) The valuation of work in progress.

(ii) The recognition and measurement of the government grant. **(10 marks)**

(c) Using the information provided in Exhibit 4, identify and discuss the relevant ethical and professional issues raised, and recommend any actions necessary. **(7 marks)**

(d) Briefly explain how the outsourcing of payroll will affect next year's audit. **(4 marks)**

**Thank you.**

**Exhibit 2 – Company background**

Dali Co was established 20 years ago and specialises in the design and manufacture of equipment and machinery used in the quarrying industry. Dali Co has become known as a leading supplier of machinery to customers operating quarries which extract stone used mainly for construction. Its customer base is located solely in its country of incorporation but most of the components used in Dali Co's manufacturing process are imported from foreign suppliers.

The machines and equipment made by Dali Co are mostly made to order in the company's three manufacturing sites. Customers approach Dali Co to design and develop a machine or piece of equipment specific to their needs. Where management considers that the design work will be significant, the customer is required to pay a 30% payment in advance, which is used to fund the design work. The remaining 70% is paid on delivery of the machine to the customer.

Typically, a machine takes three months to build, and a smaller piece of equipment takes on average six weeks. The design and manufacture of bespoke machinery involving payments in advance has increased during the year. Dali Co also manufactures a range of generic products which are offered for sale to all customers, including drills, conveyors and crushing equipment.

The projected financial statements for the 20X5 year end recognise revenue of $138 million (20X4 – $135 million), profit before tax of $9.8 million (20X4 – $9.2 million) and total assets of $90 million (20X4 – $85 million). Dali Co became listed in its home jurisdiction on 1 March 20X5, and is hoping to achieve a listing on a foreign stock exchange in June 20X6.

### Exhibit 3 – Notes from meeting with the finance director

This year has been successful from a strategic point of view in that Dali Co achieved its stock exchange listing in March 20X5, and in doing so raised a significant amount of equity finance. The company's corporate governance was reviewed as part of the flotation process, resulting in the recruitment of three new non-executive directors and a new finance director.

In March 20X5, a cash-settled share-based payment plan was introduced for senior executives, who will receive a bonus on 31 December 20X7. The amount of the bonus will be based on the increase in Dali Co's share price from that at the date of the flotation, when it was $2.90, to the share price at 31 December 20X7. On the advice of the newly appointed finance director, no accounting entries have been made in respect of the plan, but the details relating to the cash-settled share-based payment plan will be disclosed in the notes to the financial statements.

The finance director recommended that the company's manufacturing sites should be revalued. An external valuation was performed in June 20X5, resulting in a revaluation surplus of $3.5 million being recognised in equity. The finance director has informed the audit committee that no deferred tax needs to be provided in respect of the valuation because the property is part of continuing operations and there is no plan for disposal.

In July 20X5, a government grant of $10 million was received as part of a government scheme to subsidise companies which operate in deprived areas. Specifically $2 million of the grant compensates the company for wages and salaries incurred in the year to 31 December 20X5. The remaining grant relates to the continued operations in the deprived area, with a condition of the grant being that the manufacturing site in that area will remain operational until July 20Y0.

All of the company's manufacturing sites will be closed at the year-end to allow the inventory counts to take place. According to the most recent management accounts which are available, at 30 November 20X5 work in progress is valued at $12 million (20X4 – $9.5 million) and the majority of these orders will not be complete until after the year-end. In recent weeks several customers have returned equipment due to faults, and Dali Co offers a warranty to guarantee that defective items will be replaced free of charge.

### Exhibit 4 – Request for non-audit service from the audit committee

The audit committee has asked whether it would be possible for the audit team to perform a review of the company's internal control system. The new non-executive directors have raised concerns that controls are not as robust as they would expect for a listed company and are concerned about the increased risk of fraud, as well as inefficient commercial practices.

Due to the poor internal controls and the significance of the payroll cost for the company, the management team are considering outsourcing the payroll function. They have asked for a brief explanation of how this would impact next year's audit if they decide to go ahead with the suggestion.

**Exhibit 5 – Preliminary analytical review (extract) and other financial information**

|  | Based on projected figures to 31 December 20X5 | Based on audited figures to 31 December 20X4 |
| --- | --- | --- |
| Operating margin | 15% | 13% |
| Inventory holding period | 175 days | 150 days |
| Receivables collection period | 90 days | 70 days |
| Trade payables payment period | 60 days | 55 days |
| | | |
| Earnings per share | 75 cents per share | – |
| Share price | $3.50 | – |

**11    TED**    *Walk in the footsteps of a top tutor*

You are a manager in the audit department of Craggy & Co, a firm of Chartered Certified Accountants, and you have just been assigned to the audit of Ted Co, a new audit client of your firm, with a financial year ended 31 May 20X5.

You are provided with the following exhibits:

1    An email which you have received from Jack Hackett, the audit engagement partner.

2    Notes from my meeting with Len Brennan.

3    Extracts of Ted Co's draft financial statements and results of the preliminary analytical review procedures performed by one of the audit seniors.

**Required:**

**Respond to the instructions in the email from the audit engagement partner.    (46 marks)**

**Note: The split of the mark allocation is shown in the partner's email (Exhibit 1).**

**Professional marks will be awarded for the presentation and logical flow of the briefing notes and the clarity of the explanations provided.                                                   (4 marks)**

**(Total: 50 marks)**

**Exhibit 1 – Email from audit engagement partner**

**To:            Audit manager**

**From:        Jack Hackett, Audit engagement partner**

**Regarding:  Ted Co audit planning**

**Hello**

I have provided you with some information in the form of a number of exhibits which you should use in planning the audit of Ted Co. I held a meeting yesterday with the company's finance director, Len Brennan, and we discussed a number of issues which will impact on the audit planning.

Using the information provided, I require you to prepare briefing notes for my use in which you:

(a)   Discuss the matters specific to the planning of an initial audit engagement which should be considered in developing the audit strategy.                    **(6 marks)**

(b)   (i)    Evaluate the audit risks to be considered in planning the audit of Ted Co.
                                                                                     **(20 marks)**

        (ii)   Recommend the additional information which would be relevant in the evaluation of audit risk.                                                        **(5 marks)**

(c)   Design the principal audit procedures to be used in the audit of:

        (i)    The portfolio of short-term investments, and

        (ii)   The earnings per share figure.                                        **(10 marks)**

(d)   Identify and discuss the relevant ethical and professional issues raised if your firm performs the audit of both Ted Co and Ralph Co and recommend any actions necessary.                                                                        **(5 marks)**

**Thank you.**

**Exhibit 2 – Notes from meeting with Len Brennan**

Ted Co is a newly listed company which designs, develops and publishes computer games including many highly successful games which have won industry awards. The company has grown rapidly in the last few years. Ted Co was formed ten years ago by Dougal Doyle, a graduate in multimedia computing. In the last two years the company invested $100 million in creating games designed to appeal to a broad, global audience and sales are now made in over 60 countries. The software used in the computer games is developed in this country, but the manufacture of the physical product takes place overseas.

Computer games are largely sold through retail outlets, but approximately 25% of Ted Co's revenue is generated through sales made on the company's website. In some countries Ted Co's products are distributed under licences which give the licence holder the exclusive right to sell the products in that country. The cost of each licence to the distributor depends on the estimated sales in the country to which it relates, and licences last for an average of five years. The income which Ted Co receives from the sale of a licence is deferred over the period of the licence. At 31 May 20X5 the total amount of deferred income recognised in Ted Co's statement of financial position is $18 million.

As part of a five-year strategic plan, Ted Co obtained a stock market listing in December 20X4. The listing and related share issue raised a significant amount of finance, and many shares are held by institutional investors. Dougal Doyle retains a 20% equity shareholding, and a further 10% of the company's shares are held by his family members.

Despite being listed, the company does not have an internal audit department, and there is only one non-executive director on the board. These issues are explained in the company's annual report, as required by the applicable corporate governance code.

Recently, a small treasury management function was established to manage the company's foreign currency transactions, which include forward exchange currency contracts. The treasury management function also deals with short-term investments. In January 20X5, cash of $8 million was invested in a portfolio of equity shares held in listed companies, which is to be held in the short term as a speculative investment. The shares are recognised as a financial asset at cost of $8 million in the draft statement of financial position. The fair value of the shares at 31 May 20X5 is $6 million.

As a listed company, Ted Co is required to disclose its earnings per share figure. Dougal Doyle would like this to be based on an adjusted earnings figure which does not include depreciation or amortisation expenses.

The previous auditors of Ted Co, a small firm called Crilly & Co, resigned in September 20X4. The audit opinion on the financial statements for the year ended 31 May 20X4 was unmodified.

Len Brennan commented on growing competition in the computer games industry. One rapidly expanding competitor, Ralph Co, was specifically referred to. You are aware that your firm recently acquired another accountancy firm and that Ralph Co is one of their clients. It is hoped that the audit of Ralph Co will be transferred to your department to take advantage of your specialism in this industry.

**Exhibit 3 – Extract of draft financial statements and results of preliminary analytical review**

**Statement of profit or loss (extract)**

|  | Year to 31 May 20X5 Draft $000 | Year to 31 May 20X4 Actual $000 | % change |
|---|---|---|---|
| Revenue | 98,000 | 67,000 | 46.3% increase |
| Gross profit | 65,000 | 40,000 | 62.5% increase |
| Operating profit | 12,000 | 9,200 | 30.4% increase |
| Finance charge | 4,000 | 3,800 | 5.3% increase |
| Profit before tax | 8,000 | 5,400 | 48.1% increase |
| Earnings per share | 89.6 cents per share | – | |

**Note:** Earnings per share has been calculated as follows:

|  | $000 |
|---|---|
| Profit before tax | 8,000 |
| Add: Depreciation | 1,100 |
| Amortisation | 6,000 |
| Adjusted profit before tax | 15,100 |

Adjusted profit before tax 15,100,000

Number of equity shares at 31 May 20X5    16,850,000 = 89.6 cents per share

**Statement of financial position (extract)**

|  | 31 May 20X5 Draft $000 | 31 May 20X4 Actual $000 | % change |
|---|---|---|---|
| Non-current assets: | | | |
| Intangible assets – development costs | 58,000 | 35,000 | 65.7% increase |
| Total assets | 134,000 | 105,000 | 27.6% increase |

12   CONNOLLY  *Walk in the footsteps of a top tutor*

 *Question debrief*

You are an audit manager in Davies & Co, responsible for the audit of Connolly Co, a listed company operating in the pharmaceutical industry. You are planning the audit of the financial statements for the year ending 31 December 20X4.

You are provided with the following exhibits:

1   An email which you have received from Ali Stone, the audit engagement partner.

2   Background information about the company's activities.

3   Minutes of meeting between Ali Stone and the finance director, Maggie Ram.

4   Key financial information and comparative financial information.

5   Request by the audit committee for additional services.

**Required:**

**Respond to the instructions in the email from the audit engagement partner.    (46 marks)**

**Note: The split of the mark allocation is shown in the partner's email (Exhibit 1).**

**Professional marks will be awarded for the presentation and logical flow of the briefing notes and the clarity of the explanations provided.                              (4 marks)**

**(Total: 50 marks)**

**Exhibit 1 – Email from audit engagement partner**

**To:          Audit manager**

**From:       Ali Stone, Audit engagement partner**

**Subject:    Audit planning – Connolly Co**

**Hello**

You need to start planning the audit of Connolly Co, and to help with this I have provided you with some relevant information. I held a meeting yesterday with the company's finance director and we discussed a number of issues which will impact on the audit planning. I also spoke with a representative from the audit committee regarding a request for additional services Connolly Co would like our firm to provide.

Using the information provided, I require you to prepare briefing notes for my use in which you:

(a)   Evaluate the business risks faced by Connolly Co.                              **(12 marks)**

(b)   Evaluate the risks of material misstatement to be considered when planning the audit.
                                                                                    **(20 marks)**

(c)   Design the principal audit procedures to be used in the audit of the acquired 'Cold Comforts' brand name.                                                          **(7 marks)**

(d)   Using the information in Exhibit 5, discuss the ethical issues relevant to the audit firm, and recommend appropriate actions to be taken.                              **(7 marks)**

**Thank you.**

*Calculate your allowed time, allocate the time to the separate parts..............*

**Exhibit 2 – Background information**

Connolly Co is a pharmaceutical company, developing drugs to be licensed for use around the world. Products include medicines such as tablets and medical gels and creams. Some drugs are sold over the counter at pharmacy stores, while others can only be prescribed for use by a doctor. The market is very competitive, encouraging rapid product innovation. New products are continually in development and improvements are made to existing formulations. Four new drugs are in the research and development phase. Drugs have to meet very stringent regulatory requirements prior to being licensed for production and sale. Research and development involves human clinical trials, the results of which are scrutinised by the licensing authorities. It is common in the industry for patents to be acquired for new drugs and patent rights are rigorously defended, sometimes resulting in legal action against potential infringement. Once launched, products are heavily advertised to support the company's brand names. In some countries television advertising is not allowed for prescription drugs.

The success of Connolly Co relies on the retention of highly skilled scientists to develop new medicines. Most scientific personnel have worked for Connolly Co for a number of years and staff turnover has traditionally been low. However, as competition within the industry has increased, staff retention has become more difficult with people leaving to join rival companies offering larger salaries and enhanced benefits.

**Exhibit 3 – Minutes from Ali Stone's meeting with Maggie Ram**

In January 20X4, Connolly Co began to sell into a new market – that of animal health. This has been very successful, and the sales of veterinary pharmaceuticals and grooming products for livestock and pets amount to approximately 15% of total revenue for 20X4.

Another success in 20X4 was the acquisition of the 'Cold Comforts' brand from a rival company. Products to alleviate the symptoms of coughs and colds are sold under this brand. The brand cost $5 million and is being amortised over an estimated useful life of 15 years.

In May 20X4, a contract with a new overseas supplier was signed. All of the company's packaging is now supplied under this contract. Purchases are denominated in a foreign currency. Forward exchange contracts are not used.

In July 20X4, a legal claim was filed against the company by an individual who suffered severe and debilitating side effects when participating in a clinical trial. This appears to be an isolated case and no other claims have been received to date. The company's in-house legal team believe the claim will not be successful but it could take several years to settle which could cause significant reputational damage in the meantime. As a result, the company is considering offering the individual an out of court settlement. The company has asked the bank to make cash of $3 million available for this.

Connolly Co has also asked the bank for an extension of $10 million to its existing loan to support the ongoing development of new drugs.

**Exhibit 4 – Key financial information**

|  | 20X4 – Projected unaudited $000 | 20X3 – Actual audited $000 |
|---|---|---|
| Revenue | 40,000 | 38,000 |
| Operating profit | 8,100 | 9,085 |
| Operating margin | 20% | 24% |
| Earnings per share | 25c | 29c |
| Net cash flow | (1,200) | 6,000 |
| Research and development cash outflow in the year | (3,000) | (2,800) |
| Total development intangible asset recognised at the year end | 50,000 | 48,000 |
| Total assets | 200,000 | 195,000 |
| Gearing ratio (debt/equity) | 0.8 | 0.9 |

**Exhibit 5 – Request by the audit committee for additional services**

As mentioned in Exhibit 3, Connolly Co has approached its bank to extend its borrowing facilities. Davies & Co has been asked by the audit committee to provide a guarantee to the bank in respect of this loan extension.

In addition, Connolly Co's management has asked Davies & Co to provide advice on how the company's accounting and management information systems may be improved. While the systems are not considered to create any significant control deficiencies at present, management would like to develop and implement new systems over the next twelve months before they become unreliable and cause errors. Management has asked for our firm's help with this as they have little specialist in-house knowledge in this area.

## 13 GROHL  *Walk in the footsteps of a top tutor*

You are a manager in Foo & Co, responsible for the audit of Grohl Co, a company which produces circuit boards which are sold to manufacturers of electrical equipment such as computers and mobile phones. It is the first time that you have managed this audit client, taking over from the previous audit manager, Bob Halen, last month. The audit planning for the year ended 30 November 20X2 is about to commence.

You are provided with the following exhibits:

1    An email which you have received from Mia Vai, the audit engagement partner.

2    Notes from the meeting with Mo Satriani.

3    Financial information.

4    Ethical considerations affecting the audit of Grohl Co.

5    Notes from the audit senior of The Hawkins Group.

**Required:**

**Respond to the instructions in the email from the audit engagement partner.** **(46 marks)**

**Note: The split of the mark allocation is shown in the partner's email (Exhibit 1).**

**Professional marks will be awarded for the presentation and logical flow of the briefing notes and the clarity of the explanations provided.** **(4 marks)**

**(Total: 50 marks)**

**Exhibit 1 – Email from audit engagement partner**

**To:** **Audit manager**

**From:** **Mia Vai, Audit engagement partner**

**Subject: Grohl Co – audit planning**

**Hello**

I am meeting with the other audit partners tomorrow to discuss two audit clients, Grohl Co and The Hawkins Group.

I recently had a meeting with Mo Satriani, the finance director of Grohl Co and we discussed a number of issues which will impact on the audit planning. I have provided you with some information in the form of a number of exhibits which you should use when planning the audit of Grohl Co.

Using Exhibits 2 and 3, I would like you to prepare briefing notes for my use in which you:

(a) Evaluate the business risks faced by Grohl Co. **(10 marks)**

(b) Evaluate the risks of material misstatement to be considered when planning the audit. **(14 marks)**

(c) Design the audit procedures to be performed in respect of the product recall. **(6 marks)**

Using the information in Exhibit 4 I would like you to:

(d) Discuss the ethical issues raised, and recommend the relevant actions to be taken by our firm. **(8 marks)**

I have also provided you with some information relating to The Hawkins Group in Exhibit 5. The Hawkins Group has been an audit client of our firm for several years and an issue has arisen during the interim audit which is detailed in the exhibit. In respect of this, I would like you to:

(e) Discuss the implications of the information obtained by the audit senior for the planning of the audit, commenting on the auditor's responsibilities in relation to laws and regulations, and on any ethical matters arising. **(8 marks)**

**Thank you.**

**Exhibit 2 – Notes from meeting with Mo Satriani**

**Business overview**

Grohl Co's principal business activity remains the production of circuit boards. One of the key materials used in production is copper wiring, all of which is imported. As a cost cutting measure, in April 20X2 a contract with a new overseas supplier was signed, and all of the company's copper wiring is now supplied under this contract. Purchases are denominated in a foreign currency, but the company does not use forward exchange contracts in relation to its imports of copper wiring.

Grohl Co has two production facilities, one of which produces goods for the export market, and the other produces goods for the domestic market. About half of its goods are exported, but the export market is suffering due to competition from cheaper producers overseas. Most domestic sales are made under contract with approximately 20 customers.

**Recent developments**

In early November 20X2, production was halted for a week at the production facility which supplies the domestic market. A number of customers had returned goods, claiming faults in the circuit boards supplied. On inspection, it was found that the copper used in the circuit boards was corroded and therefore unsuitable for use. The corrosion is difficult to spot as it cannot be identified by eye, and relies on electrical testing. All customers were contacted immediately and, where necessary, products recalled and replaced. The corroded copper remaining in inventory has been identified and separated from the rest of the copper.

Work has recently started on a new production line which will ensure that Grohl Co meets new regulatory requirements prohibiting the use of certain chemicals, which come into force in March 20X3. In July 20X2, a loan of $30 million with an interest rate of 4% was negotiated with Grohl Co's bank, the main purpose of the loan being to fund the capital expenditure necessary for the new production line. $2.5 million of the loan represents an overdraft which was converted into long-term finance.

**Exhibit 3 – Financial information**

**Extract from draft statement of profit or loss for the year ended 30 November 20X2**

|  | 20X2 Draft | 20X1 Actual |
|---|---|---|
|  | $000 | $000 |
| **Revenue** | 12,500 | 13,800 |
| Operating costs | (12,000) | (12,800) |
| Operating profit | 500 | 1,000 |
| Finance costs | (800) | (800) |
| **Profit/(loss) before tax** | (300) | 200 |

The draft statement of financial position has not yet been prepared, but Mo states that the total assets of Grohl Co at 30 November 20X2 are $180 million, and cash at bank is $130,000. Based on draft figures, the company's current ratio is 1.1, and the quick ratio is 0.8.

**Exhibit 4 – Ethical considerations affecting the audit of Grohl Co**

Several of Grohl Co's executive directors and the financial controller left in October 20X2, to set up a company specialising in the recycling of old electronic equipment. This new company is not considered to be in competition with Grohl Co's operations. The directors left on good terms, and replacements for the directors have been recruited. One of Foo & Co's audit managers, Bob Halen, is being interviewed for the role of financial controller at Grohl Co. Bob is a good candidate for the position, as he developed good knowledge of Grohl Co's business when he was managing the audit.

At Grohl Co's most recent board meeting, the audit fee was discussed. The board members expressed concern over the size of the audit fee, given the company's loss for the year. The board members would like to know whether the audit can be performed on a contingent fee basis.

**Exhibit 5 – Notes from the audit senior of The Hawkins Group**

I have been performing the interim audit of The Hawkins Group (the Group). The Group's activities include property management and the provision of large storage facilities in warehouses owned by the Group. The projected consolidated financial statements recognise total assets of $150 million, and profit before tax of $20 million.

Customers rent individual self-contained storage areas of a warehouse, for which they are given keys allowing access by the customer at any time. The Group's employees rarely enter the customers' storage areas. It seems the Group's policy for storage contracts which generate revenue of less than $10,000, is that very little documentation is required, and the nature of the items being stored is not always known. While visiting one of the Group's warehouses during the interim audit, the door to one of the customers' storage areas was open, so I looked in and saw what appeared to be potentially hazardous chemicals, stored in large metal drums marked with warning signs. I asked the warehouse manager about the items being stored, and he became very aggressive, refusing to allow me to ask other employees about the matter, and threatening me if I alerted management to the storage of these items. I did not mention the matter to anyone else at the client.

I thought I should make you aware as it will no doubt have implications for the planning of the audit.

**14    CS GROUP**  *Walk in the footsteps of a top tutor*

You are a manager in Magpie & Co, responsible for the audit of the CS Group. You are planning the audit of the financial statements for the year ending 31 July 20X2.

You are provided with the following exhibits:

1    An email which you have received from Jo Daw, the audit engagement partner.

2    Extracts from the permanent audit file.

3    Details of the acquisition of Canary Co including calculation of the goodwill arising on acquisition.

4    Financial information of the Group.

5    Notes from meeting with Steve Eagle, finance director of the CS Group.

**Required:**

Respond to the instructions in the email from the audit engagement partner.   **(46 marks)**

Note: The split of the mark allocation is shown in the partner's email (Exhibit 1).

Professional marks will be awarded for the presentation and logical flow of the briefing notes and the clarity of the explanations provided.                                **(4 marks)**

**(Total: 50 marks)**

**Exhibit 1 – Email from audit engagement partner**

**To:**     Audit manager

**From:**   Jo Daw, Audit engagement partner

**Subject:**  CS Group audit planning

**Hello**

I have provided you with some information in the form of a number of exhibits which you should use in planning the audit of the CS Group (the Group). I held a meeting yesterday with Steve Eagle, the Group finance director and we discussed a number of issues which will impact on the audit planning. One of the issues discussed is the change in group structure due to the acquisition of Canary Co earlier this year. We need to start planning the audits of the three components of the Group, and of the consolidated financial statements.

Using the information in Exhibits 2, 3 and 4, I require you to prepare briefing notes for my use in which you:

(a)     Identify and explain the implications of the acquisition of Canary Co for the audit planning of the individual and consolidated financial statements of the CS Group.

**(8 marks)**

(b)     Evaluate the risks of material misstatement to be considered in the audit planning of the individual and consolidated financial statements of the CS Group.     **(20 marks)**

(c)     Design the principal audit procedures to be used in the audit of:

(i)     Goodwill initially recognised on the acquisition of Canary Co.

(ii)    The government grant received by Starling Co.                        **(11 marks)**

(d)     Using the information provided in Exhibit 5, discuss the ethical and professional issues raised and recommend any actions necessary.                        **(7 marks)**

**Thank you.**

**Exhibit 2 – Extracts from the permanent audit file**

Crow Co was incorporated 100 years ago. It was founded by Joseph Crow, who established a small pottery making tableware such as dishes, plates and cups. The products quickly grew popular, with one range of products becoming highly sought after when it was used at a royal wedding. The company's products have retained their popularity over the decades, and the Crow brand enjoys a strong identity and good market share.

Ten years ago, Crow Co made its first acquisition by purchasing 100% of the share capital of Starling Co. Both companies benefited from the newly formed CS Group, as Starling Co itself had a strong brand name in the pottery market. The CS Group has a history of steady profitability and stable management. Crow Co and Starling Co have a financial year ending 31 July 20X2, and your firm has audited both companies for several years.

**Exhibit 3 – Details of the acquisition of Canary Co including calculation of the goodwill arising on acquisition**

The most significant event for the CS Group this year was the acquisition of Canary Co, which took place on 1 February 20X2. Crow Co purchased all of Canary Co's equity shares for cash consideration of $125 million, and further contingent consideration of $30 million will be paid on the third anniversary of the acquisition, if the Group's revenue grows by at least 8% per annum. Crow Co engaged an external provider to perform due diligence on Canary Co, whose report indicated that the fair value of Canary Co's net assets was estimated to be $110 million at the date of acquisition. Our firm has recently been appointed as auditor of Canary Co for the year ending 30 June 20X2.

Goodwill arising on the acquisition has been calculated as follows:

|  | $ million |
|---|---|
| Fair value of consideration: |  |
| Cash consideration | 125 |
| Contingent consideration | 30 |
|  | ——— |
|  | 155 |
| Less: fair value of identifiable net assets acquired | (110) |
|  | ——— |
| Goodwill | 45 |
|  | ——— |

To help finance the acquisition, Crow Co issued loan stock at par on 31 January 20X2, raising cash of $100 million. The loan has a five-year term, and will be repaid at a premium of $20 million. 5% interest is payable annually in arrears. It is Group accounting policy to recognise financial liabilities at amortised cost.

Canary Co manufactures pottery figurines and ornaments. The company is considered a good strategic fit to the Group, as its products are luxury items like those of Crow Co and Starling Co, and its acquisition will enable the Group to diversify into a different market. Approximately 30% of its sales are made online, and it is hoped that online sales can soon be introduced for the rest of the Group's products. Canary Co has only ever operated as a single company, so this is the first year that it is part of a group of companies.

**Exhibit 4 – Financial performance and position of the Group**

The Group has performed well this year, with forecast consolidated revenue for the year to 31 July 20X2 of $135 million (20X1 – $125 million), and profit before tax of $8.5 million (20X1 – $8.4 million).

A breakdown of the Group's forecast revenue and profit is shown below:

|  | Crow Co | Starling Co | Canary Co | CS Group |
|---|---|---|---|---|
|  | $ million | $ million | $ million | $ million |
| Revenue | 69 | 50 | 16 | 135 |
| Profit before tax | 3.5 | 3 | 2 | 8.5 |

**Note:**

Canary Co's results have been included from 1 February 20X2 (date of acquisition).

Forecast information relates to 1 June - 31 July 20X2.

The forecast consolidated statement of financial position at 31 July 20X2 recognises total assets of $550 million.

**Government grant**

Starling Co received a grant of $35 million on 1 March 20X2 in relation to redevelopment of its main manufacturing site. The government is providing grants to companies for capital expenditure on environmentally friendly assets. Starling Co has spent $25 million of the amount received on solar panels which generate electricity, and intends to spend the remaining $10 million on upgrading its production and packaging lines.

**Other matters**

On 1 January 20X2, a new IT system was introduced to Crow Co and Starling Co, with the aim of improving financial reporting controls and to standardise processes across the two companies.

Starling Co's finance director left the company suddenly last week and has not yet been replaced.

**Exhibit 5 – Notes from meeting with Steve Eagle, finance director of the CS Group**

**Complaints regarding last year's audit**

Steve Eagle raised concerns about the conduct of the previous audit, stating numerous examples of when he and his staff had been interrupted when they were busy. He stated that he wanted guarantees that this year's audit will be more efficient, less intrusive and cheaper, otherwise he will seek an alternative auditor. As a result of these complaints, last year's fee has not been paid.

# Section 2

# PRACTICE QUESTIONS – SECTION B

## PLANNING AND CONDUCTING AN AUDIT OF HISTORICAL FINANCIAL INFORMATION

**15    AWDRY**  ***Walk in the footsteps of a top tutor***

(a)    The IAASB has published ISA 540 (Revised) *Auditing Accounting Estimates and Related Disclosures* (ISA-540 Revised). The revised standard states that the auditor must obtain sufficient appropriate audit evidence to evaluate whether accounting estimates and related disclosures are reasonable in the context of the applicable financial reporting framework, or are misstated. ISA-540 Revised includes enhanced requirements for risk assessment procedures and the auditor's work effort in responding to the assessed risks of material misstatement to support this evaluation.

**Required:**

**Explain why accounting estimates are considered to be a source of high audit risk and discuss the reasons for the revision of ISA-540 commenting on its requirement for an enhanced risk assessment in relation to the audit of accounting estimates.**

**(8 marks)**

(b)    You are the manager responsible for the audit of Awdry Co, a listed entity whose principal activity is the operation of a regional railway network. The audit for the year ended 28 February 20X9 is the first year your firm has audited Awdry Co. The draft financial statements recognise total assets of $58 million and profit before tax of $7.4 million. The detailed audit fieldwork has started and the audit supervisor has brought the following matters to your attention in relation to the testing of key accounting estimates:

(i)    **Cash-settled share-based payment scheme**

On 1 March 20X8, Awdry Co granted 550,000 share appreciation rights to 55 executives and senior employees of the company with each eligible member of staff receiving 10,000 of the rights. The fair value of the rights was estimated on 28 February 20X9 by an external expert using an options pricing model at $4.50 each. Awdry Co prides itself on good employee relations and the senior management team has estimated that all 55 staff will qualify for the rights when they vest three years after the granting of the rights on 1 March 20X8. The company has recognised a straight line expense in this year's draft accounts of $825,000.    **(6 marks)**

(ii)     **Regulatory penalties**

Awdry Co has been subject to a review by the national railways regulator following a complaint from a member of staff with safety concerns. The regulator identified breaches in safety regulations and issued a penalty notice on 30 September 20X8. Awdry Co has appealed against the initial penalty payable. Negotiations with the regulator are still ongoing and the amount payable has not yet been finalised. Awdry Co currently estimates that the total penalty payable as a result of the breach will be $1.3 million which it expects to repay in equal annual instalments over the next ten years with the first payment falling due on 1 March 20X9. The company's draft statement of profit or loss for the current year recognises an expense of $1.3 million and the draft statement of financial position includes a liability for the same amount.

**(6 marks)**

(iii)    **Property development**

Awdry Co owns an industrial property which it has historically used as a maintenance depot for its engines and carriages. The company has an accounting policy of revaluing its properties to fair value and at the interim audit it was noted that the depot was recorded at a carrying amount of $2.5 million in the non-current asset register. During the first week of the audit fieldwork, the audit supervisor identified a year-end journal which has uplifted the depot to a fair value of $4.9 million in this year's statement of financial position as at 28 February 20X9. Management has advised that this represents the estimated sales value of the building following Awdry Co's plan to develop the building as a residential property. The client has confirmed that the property is suitable for conversion into residential apartments at an estimated cost of $1.2 million and has negotiated secured finance for the development with their bank. The development will be subject to the payment of fees to the local council's building regulator of $173,000.               **(5 marks)**

**Required:**

(i)      **Evaluate the client's accounting treatments and the difficulties which you might encounter when auditing each of the accounting estimates described above; and**

(ii)     **Design the audit procedures which should now be performed to gather sufficient and appropriate audit evidence.**

**Note: The split of the mark allocation is shown against each of the issues above.**

**(Total: 25 marks)**

# COMPLETION, REVIEW AND REPORTING

**16 LIFESON**  *Walk in the footsteps of a top tutor*

**(a)** It is 1 July 20X5. You are a manager in the audit department of Peart & Co, a firm of Chartered Certified Accountants, responsible for the audit of Lifeson Co for the year ended 31 March 20X5. Lifeson Co is an unlisted retail company which is a new audit client of your firm this year. The company's draft financial statements recognise profit before tax of $2.15 million (20X4 – $1.95 million) and total assets of $13.8 million (20X4 – $12.7million).

The audit is nearly complete and you are reviewing the audit working papers. The audit supervisor has brought the following matters to your attention:

**(i)   Sale and leaseback transaction**

On 31 March 20X5, Lifeson Co sold a property to a leasing company, Clive Co, for its fair value at this date. The property is situated in a sought after area with a high demand for rental properties for retail purposes. Clive Co has assessed the remaining life of the property to be in excess of 50 years, and under the terms of the sales agreement, Lifeson Co will lease the property back from Clive Co for a period of ten years. Lifeson Co has treated the transaction as a sale and leaseback transaction in accordance with IFRS® 16 *Leases*, and derecognised the property in its financial statements and recorded a sale in accordance with IFRS 15 *Revenue from Contracts with Customers*.                    **(8 marks)**

**(ii)   Investment property**

Lifeson Co owns a building which it has used as a warehouse to store inventory. On 1 April 20X4 the building, which had not suffered any historic impairments, had a carrying amount based on depreciated historic cost of $323,000 and a fair value of $348,000. On this date, Lifeson Co vacated the building and moved the inventory to new larger premises. Management decided to keep the building in order to rent it out as a storage facility to local businesses and to benefit from any increases in property valuations. On 31 March 20X5, the building had not been let and it had a fair value, according to an external valuer, of $353,000. The draft financial statements for the current year recognise the building as an investment property at a carrying amount of $353,000 and include a fair value gain of $30,000 in profit before tax for the year. Since reclassification as an investment property, depreciation has not been charged in relation to the building.                    **(6 marks)**

**(iii)   Shopping mall**

Lifeson Co purchased a shopping mall on 1 April 20X3 for $9.5 million. At the date of purchase, the mall was estimated to have a remaining useful life of 20 years and a nil residual value. On 31 March 20X4 following an impairment review, the property was written down to its recoverable amount based on value in use of $8.25 million and an impairment loss of $775,000 was recognised in the statement of profit or loss for the year ended 31 March 20X4.

Lifeson Co conducted a further impairment review as at 31 March 20X5 which indicated that the property's recoverable amount, based on value in use, was now $8.85 million. As a result, Lifeson Co has recognised an impairment reversal of $1.034 million in its profit before tax for the current year. The impairment reversal of $1.034 million has been calculated as its new recoverable amount of $8.85 million less its carrying amount of $7.816 million. The audit supervisor has prepared the following working paper which summarises the accounting transactions in relation to the shopping mall:

**Summary of transactions**

| Date | | $ million | *Accounting treatment by management* |
|---|---|---|---|
| 1 April 20X3 | Cost of asset | 9.500 | |
| | Depreciation (9.5m/20 years) | (0.475) | Depreciation charge for the year to 31 March20X4 |
| | Impairment | (0.775) | Impairment loss charged to profit for the year to 31 March 20X4 |
| 31 March 20X4 | Year end carrying amount | 8.250 | |
| | Depreciation (8.25m/19 years) | (0.434) | Depreciation charge for the year to 31 March20X5 |
| | | 7.816 | Carrying amount prior to impairment review |
| | Reversal of impairment | 1.034 | Reversal of impairment credited to profit for the year to 31 March 20X5 |
| 31 March 20X5 | Year end carrying amount | 8.850 | |

**(6 marks)**

**Required:**

**Comment on the matters to be considered and explain the audit evidence you would expect to find during your review of the audit working papers in respect of the issues described above.**

**Note:** The split of the mark allocation is shown against each of the issues above.

**(b)** It is now 1 September 20X5 and the auditor's report on Lifeson Co's financial statements for the year ended 31 March 20X5 is due to be issued in the next few days.

Following discussions with management, you are satisfied that the sale and leaseback transaction has been treated correctly and that you have gathered sufficient and appropriate audit evidence to support this treatment.

However, management has indicated that they are not willing to make any further adjustments to the financial statements in relation to the investment property or shopping mall and you are now considering the form and content of the auditor's report in relation to these matters.

**Required:**

**Discuss the implications for the auditor's report on the basis that no further adjustments have been made to the financial statements in relation to the investment property or shopping mall.** **(5 marks)**

**(Total: 25 marks)**

**17    KILMISTER**  *Walk in the footsteps of a top tutor*

(a)    You are the manager responsible for the audit of Kilmister Co, a listed company specialising in the manufacture and installation of sound-proof partitions for domestic and industrial buildings. You are currently reviewing the draft auditor's report on the company's financial statements for the year ended 31 March 20X5. Extracts from the draft auditor's report are shown below:

**Independent auditor's report to the shareholders and directors of Kilmister Co**

**Basis for opinion**

We conducted our audit of Kilmister Co (the Company) in accordance with International Standards on Auditing (ISAs). Our responsibilities under those standards are further described in the auditor's responsibilities for the audit of the financial statements section of our report. We are independent of the Company in accordance with the ethical requirements which are relevant to our audit of the financial statements in the jurisdiction in which the Company operates, and we have fulfilled our other ethical responsibilities in accordance with these requirements.

We believe that the audit evidence we have obtained is sufficient and appropriate to provide a basis for our opinion.

**Opinion**

We have audited the financial statements of Kilmister Co (the Company), which comprise the statement of financial position as at 31 March 20X5, and the statement of comprehensive income, statement of changes in equity and statement of cash flows for the year then ended, and notes to the financial statements, including a summary of significant accounting policies. In our opinion, the accompanying financial statements present fairly, in all material respects, the financial position of the Company as at 31 March 20X5, and of its financial performance and its cash flows for the year then ended in accordance with IFRS® Standards.

**Material uncertainty regarding going concern**

The Company is financed by a long-term loan from its bankers which is due for redemption in August 20X5. At the date of this auditor's report, the Company is in the process of renegotiating the loan but has not yet reached a final agreement with its bankers. It is our view that the loan finance is essential to the continued survival of the Company and that at the time of reporting, therefore, the absence of a finalised agreement represents a material uncertainty regarding going concern. The financial statements have been prepared on a going concern basis but do not make any reference to the loan redemption or the ongoing negotiations with the bank. As the external auditor therefore, we are fulfilling our duty by bringing the matter to the attention of users of the financial statements.

**Other information**

The Company's principal activity is the manufacture and installation of sound-proof partitions for domestic and industrial buildings. The Company therefore engages in long-term contracts which are incomplete at the reporting date and which are material to its revenue figure. The installation process is complex and significant judgement is applied in assessing the percentage of completeness which is applied to calculate the revenue for the year. The significance of this judgement requires us to disclose the issue as other information which is relevant to the users of the financial statements.

**Required:**

**Critically appraise the extract from the draft auditor's report for the year ended 31 March 20X5.**

Note: You are NOT required to re-draft the extracts from the auditor's report.

**(10 marks)**

(b)     Your firm, Eddie & Co, has asked you to perform an independent review of the working papers of Taylor Co which is a listed entity and has been an audit client of your firm for the last ten years. The audit fieldwork is almost complete and as part of your review, you have been asked to advise the audit team on the drafting of their report to those charged with governance. Taylor Co is a discount food retailer which operates 85 stores nationally. The financial statements for the year ended 30 April 20X5 recognise revenue of $247 million (20X4 – $242 million), profit before tax of $14.6 million (20X4 – $14.1 million) and total assets of $535 million (20X4 – $321 million).

After a period of rapid expansion, 20X5 has been a year in which Taylor Co has strengthened its existing position within the market and has not acquired any additional stores or businesses. The company's draft statement of financial position for 20X5 includes a property portfolio of $315 million all of which are legally owned by the entity. In the current year, the company has chosen to adopt a policy of revaluing its property portfolio for the first time and this is reflected in the draft figures for 20X5. The audit work on property, plant and equipment included testing a sample of the revaluations. Eddie & Co requested at the planning stage that independent, external valuation reports should be made available to the audit team at the start of the final audit visit. A number of these documents were not available when requested and it took three weeks for them to be received by the audit team. The audit working papers also identify that on review of the non-current asset register, there were four properties with a total carrying amount of $11.1 million which had not yet been revalued and were still recorded at depreciated historic cost.

The audit supervisor's review of Taylor Co's board minutes identified that the company has renovated car parking facilities at 17 of its stores which has resulted in a significant increase in customer numbers and revenue at each of these locations. The total cost of the renovation work was $13.2 million and has been included in operating expenses for the current year. The audit file includes a working paper recording discussions with management which confirms that capital expenditure authorisation forms had not been completed for this expenditure.

You are aware that your firm had intended to replace the current engagement partner, Bryony Robertson, with Philip Campbell who is Eddie & Co's other specialist in food retail. Unfortunately, Mr Campbell was taken ill earlier in the year and will not now be available until next year's audit engagement. As a result, 20X5 is the eighth consecutive year in which Bryony Robertson has acted as engagement partner.

**Required:**

From the information provided above, recommend the matters which should be included in Eddie & Co's report to those charged with governance, and explain the reason for their inclusion. **(15 marks)**

**(Total: 25 marks)**

**18   DALEY**  *Walk in the footsteps of a top tutor*

Daley Co is a family owned, unlisted company which imports motor cars. The company buys cars from a variety of car manufacturers for sale to car dealerships and vehicle leasing companies within its own domestic market. Daley Co has been a client of your firm for the last three years and you are the newly appointed audit manager on the audit for the year ended 31 August 20X8. The audit for the current reporting period is nearing completion and you are reviewing the working papers of the going concern section of the audit file.

Extracts from the draft financial statements and other relevant information are given below.

**Statement of financial position**

|  | 31 August 20X8 Draft $million | 31 August 20X7 Actual $million |
|---|---|---|
| **Assets** | | |
| **Non-current assets** | | |
| Property, plant and equipment | 13.5 | 14.6 |
|  | 13.5 | 14.6 |
| **Current assets** | | |
| Inventory | 5.8 | 3.7 |
| Trade receivables | 3.7 | 2.6 |
| Cash at bank and in hand | – | 0.6 |
|  | 9.5 | 6.9 |
| Total assets | 23.0 | 21.5 |
| **Equity and liabilities** | | |
| **Equity** | | |
| Share capital | 1.0 | 1.0 |
| Retained earnings | 1.3 | 4.7 |
|  | 2.3 | 5.7 |
| **Non-current liabilities** | | |
| Long-term borrowings | 11.2 | 12.4 |
| Provisions | 3.5 | 0.5 |
|  | 14.7 | 12.9 |

**Current liabilities**

| | | |
|---|---|---|
| Trade payables | 4.2 | 2.9 |
| Bank overdraft | 1.8 | – |
| | 6.0 | 2.9 |
| **Total equity and liabilities** | 23.0 | 21.5 |

**Statement of profit or loss for the year**

| | 31 August 20X8 Draft $million | 31 August 20X7 Actual $million |
|---|---|---|
| Revenue | 11.3 | 8.8 |
| Cost of sales | (4.4) | (2.9) |
| Gross profit | 6.9 | 5.9 |
| Other operating expenses | (9.1) | (1.3) |
| Operating profit | (2.2) | 4.6 |
| Finance costs | (1.5) | (0.7) |
| Profit before taxation | (3.7) | 3.9 |
| Taxation | 0.3 | (1.3) |
| Net (loss)/profit for year | (3.4) | 2.6 |

You have also ascertained the following information during your review:

1 Daley Co has undergone a period of rapid expansion in recent years and is intending to buy new warehousing facilities in January 20X9 at a cost of $4.3 million.

2 In order to finance the new warehousing facilities, the company is in the process of negotiating new finance from its bankers. The loan application is for an amount of $5 million and is to be repaid over a period of four years.

3 The provision of $3.5 million in this year's statement of financial position relates to legal actions from five of Daley Co's largest customers. The actions relate to the claim that the company has sold cars which did not comply with domestic regulations.

4 A major new competitor has moved in to Daley Co's market in October 20X8.

5 The going concern working papers include a cash flow forecast for the 12 months ending 31 August 20X9. The cash flow forecast assumes that Daley Co's revenue will increase by 25% next year and that following the reorganisation of its credit control facility, its customers will pay on average after 60 days. The forecast also assumes that the bank will provide the new finance in January 20X9 and that the company will have a positive cash balance of $1.7 million by 31 August 20X9.

6 The financial statements have been prepared on a going concern basis and make no reference to any significant uncertainties in relation to going concern.

**Required:**

(a)    Using analytical review where appropriate, evaluate the matters which may cast doubt on Daley Co's ability to continue as a going concern.                    **(10 marks)**

(b)    Explain the audit evidence in respect of the cash flow forecast which you would expect to find in your review of the audit working papers on going concern.

**(9 marks)**

You have established through discussions with Daley Co's directors that they do not wish to disclose uncertainties over the going concern status of the company in the notes to the financial statements.

**Required:**

(c)    Explain the possible reasons why the directors may wish to exclude these disclosures and evaluate the possible implications for the auditor's report.

**(6 marks)**

**(Total: 25 marks)**

**19    CORAM & CO**   *Walk in the footsteps of a top tutor*

(a)    You are an audit manager in Coram & Co, a firm of Chartered Certified Accountants. The audit of one of your clients, Clark Co, for the year ended 31 May 20X8 is nearly complete and the auditor's report is due to be issued next week. Clark Co is an unlisted, family owned business which specialises in the service and repair of both commercial and privately owned motor vehicles. The company operates from seven geographically distinct sites, each of which is considered a separate cash generating unit for impairment review purposes. The draft financial statements recognise profit before taxation for the year of $2.3 million and total assets of $22 million.

The schedule of uncorrected misstatements included in Clark Co's audit working papers and prepared by the audit supervisor is shown below. You are due to attend a meeting with the finance director of Clark Co tomorrow, at which the uncorrected misstatements will be discussed.

| | Statement of profit or loss | | Statement of financial position | |
|---|---|---|---|---|
| | Debit | Credit | Debit | Credit |
| Schedule of uncorrected misstatements: | $ | $ | $ | $ |
| (i)   Lease of testing equipment | | | | |
|    – lease assets | | | 475,000 | |
|    – lease liabilities | | | | 475,000 |
| (ii)   Legal claim | | | | |
|    – contingent assets | | | 1,200,000 | |
|    – provision for liabilities | | | | 1,200,000 |
| (iii)   Asset impairment | | | | |
|    – assets | | | | 85,000 |
|    – expenses | 85,000 | | | |
| **Totals** | 85,000 | – | 1,675,000 | 1,760,000 |

### (i)   Lease of testing equipment

In the jurisdiction in which Clark Co operates, all motor vehicles over three years old are required to undergo an annual test of vehicle safety and roadworthiness. The annual test requires specialist testing equipment which is inspected by government officials on a regular basis. Following inspection visits in May 20X8, the government inspection report required Clark Co to replace the testing equipment at three of its sites. In order to comply with this requirement, Clark Co has agreed to lease new testing equipment from a leasing company on six-month leases. Under the terms of the leases, the company has no option to purchase the equipment. The testing equipment was made available for use by Clark Co at each of the three sites on 31 May 20X8. The client has capitalised leases with a total carrying amount of $625,000 at two of the sites but has elected to take advantage of the IFRS 16 *Leases* exemption not to capitalise short-term leases at the largest of the three sites. As a result, the present value of the lease payments of $475,000 relating to this site has not been recognised on the company's statement of financial position. **(7 marks)**

### (ii)   Legal claim

A customer of Clark Co successfully sued the company for negligence in April 20X8 after suffering a personal injury at one of its sites. The court awarded the customer $1.2 million in damages and this had not yet been paid as at 31 May 20X8. The audit working papers include a copy of a verified letter dated 25 May 20X8 from an insurance company confirming that the claim is fully covered under Clark Co's public liability insurance policy. On the basis that the company has no net liability as a result of the claim, the finance director has not recognised any amounts in the financial statements and has not made any disclosures in relation to the matter. **(5 marks)**

**(iii)** **Asset impairment**

During the year, a significant new competitor entered the market place at one of Clark Co's seven sites. As a result, the site has experienced a decline in market share and revenue. The company has therefore conducted an impairment test on the site's assets. The company's working papers for the impairment test have been audited and the following figures have been agreed by the audit team:

|  | **Site assets** |
|---|---|
|  | $ |
| Carrying amount on statement of financial position as at 31 May 20X8 | 3.6 million |
| Value in use | 2.9 million |
| Fair value | 3.9 million |
| **Related costs of selling the assets:** |  |
| – Legal costs | 126,000 |
| – Transaction taxes | 174,000 |
| – Costs of removing the assets | 85,000 |
| – Costs of reorganising the business following the asset disposals | 96,000 |

On the basis of the results of these figures, the client has calculated the recoverable amount of the assets as $3.6 million and concluded that the site has not suffered an impairment. No adjustments have therefore been made to the financial statements in this regard. **(5 marks)**

**Required:**

**Recommend and explain the matters which should be discussed with management in relation to each of the proposed adjustments, including an assessment of their individual impact on the financial statements and on the auditor's opinion if management does not make the proposed adjustments.**

Note: The split of the mark allocation is shown against each of the issues above.

**(b)** Your client portfolio as an audit manager at Coram & Co also includes Turner Co which is a listed financial institution offering loans and credit facilities to both commercial and retail customers. You have received an email from the audit supervisor who is currently supervising interim testing on systems and controls in relation to the audit for the year ending 31 October 20X8. The email gives the following details for your consideration:

One of the audit team members, Janette Stott, has provisionally agreed to take out a loan with Turner Co to finance the purchase of a domestic residence. The loan will be secured on the property and the client's business manager has promised Janette that he will ensure that she gets 'the very best deal which the bank can offer.'

The payroll manager at Turner Co has asked the audit supervisor if it would be possible for Coram & Co to provide a member of staff on secondment to work in the payroll department. The payroll manager has struggled to recruit a new supervisor for the organisation's main payroll system and wants to assign a qualified member of the audit firm's staff for an initial period of six months.

**Required:**

**Comment on the ethical and professional issues raised in respect of the audit of Turner Co and recommend any actions to be taken by the audit firm.** **(8 marks)**

**(Total: 25 marks)**

**20   BREARLEY & CO**  *Walk in the footsteps of a top tutor*

(a)   You are an audit manager in Brearley & Co, responsible for the audit of the Hughes Group (the Group). You are reviewing the audit working papers for the consolidated financial statements relating to the year ended 31 March 20X8. The Group specialises in the wholesale supply of steel plate and sheet metals. The draft consolidated financial statements recognise revenue of $7,670 million (20X7 – $7,235 million), profit before taxation of $55 million (20X7 – $80 million) and total assets of $1,560 million (20X7 – $1,275 million). Brearley & Co audits all of the individual company financial statements as well as the Group consolidated financial statements. The audit senior has brought the following matters, regarding a number of the Group's companies, to your attention:

(i)   **Dilley Co**

The Group purchased 40% of the share capital and voting rights in Dilley Co on 1 May 20X7. Dilley Co is listed on an alternative stock exchange. The Group has also acquired options to purchase the remaining 60% of the issued shares at a 10% discount on the market value of the shares at the time of exercise. The options are exercisable for 18 months from 1 May 20X8. Dilley Co's draft financial statements for the year ended 31 March 20X8 recognise revenue of $90 million and a loss before tax of $12 million. The Group's finance director has equity accounted for Dilley Co as an associate in this year's group accounts and has included a loss before tax of $4.4 million in the consolidated statement of profit or loss. **(7 marks)**

(ii)   **Willis Co**

Willis Co is a foreign subsidiary whose functional and presentational currency is the same as Hughes Co and the remainder of the Group. The subsidiary specialises in the production of stainless steel and holds a significant portfolio of forward commodity options to hedge against fluctuations in raw material prices. The local jurisdiction does not mandate the use of IFRS Standards and the audit senior has noted that Willis Co follows local GAAP, whereby derivatives are disclosed in the notes to the financial statements but are not recognised as assets or liabilities in the statement of financial position. The disclosure note includes details of the maturity and exercise terms of the options and a directors' valuation stating that they have a total fair value of $6.1 million as at 31 March 20X8. The disclosure note states that all of the derivative contracts were entered into in the last three months of the reporting period and that they required no initial net investment. **(6 marks)**

**Required:**

**Comment on the matters to be considered and explain the audit evidence you should expect to find during your review of the Group audit working papers in respect of each of the issues described above.**

**Note:** The split of the mark allocation is shown against each of the issues above.

**(b)** You are also responsible for the audit of the Blackmore Group (the Group), a listed manufacturer of high quality musical instruments, for the year ended 31 March 20X8. The draft financial statements of the Group recognise a loss before tax of $2.2 million (20X7 – loss of $1.5 million) and total assets of $14.1 million (20X7 – $18.3 million). The audit is nearing completion and the audit senior has drafted the auditor's report which contains the following extract:

**Key audit matters**

**1    Valuation of financial instruments**

The Group enters into structured forward contracts to purchase materials used in its manufacturing process. The valuation of these unquoted instruments involves guesswork and is based on internal models developed by the Group's finance director, Thomas Bolin. Mr Bolin joined the Group in January 20X8 and there is significant measurement uncertainty involved in his valuations as a result of his inexperience. As a result, the valuation of these contracts was significant to our audit.

**2    Customer liquidation**

Included in receivables shown on the consolidated statement of financial position is an amount of $287,253 from a customer which has ceased trading. On the basis that the Group has no security for this debt, we believe that the Group should make a full provision for impairment of $287,253 thereby reducing profit before taxation for the year and total assets as at 31 March 20X8 by that amount.

**Qualified opinion arising from disagreement about accounting treatment**

In our opinion, except for the effect on the financial statements of the matter described above, the financial statements have been properly prepared in all material respects in accordance with IFRS Standards.

**Emphasis of matter**

We draw attention to the loss before tax of $2.2 million for the year ended 31 March 20X8 and that the Group is in breach of loan covenants with its key finance providers. A material uncertainty therefore exists which may cast doubt on the Group's ability to continue as a going concern. Our opinion is not modified in respect of this matter.

**Required:**

**Critically appraise the extract from the auditor's report on the consolidated financial statements of the Blackmore Group for the year ended 31 March 20X8.**

**Note:** You are NOT required to re-draft the extract from the auditor's report.

(12 marks)

(Total: 25 marks)

**21 BASKING**  *Walk in the footsteps of a top tutor*

(a) Discuss the three types of misstatement identified in ISA 450 *Evaluation of Misstatements Identified During the Audit* and comment on why it is important for the auditor to consider the type of misstatement when evaluating their effect on the financial statements and determining the further actions to be taken. **(5 marks)**

(b) You are responsible for the audit of Basking Co, a large, listed package delivery company. The audit of the financial statements for the year ended 31 July 20X7 is nearly complete and you are reviewing the audit working papers. The financial statements recognise revenue of $56,360 million (20X6 – $56,245 million), profit for the year of $2,550 million (20X6 – $2,630 million) and total assets of $37,546 million (20X6 – $38,765 million).

The uncorrected misstatements identified during the audit of Basking Co are described below. The audit engagement partner is holding a meeting with the management team of Basking Co next week, at which the uncorrected misstatements will be discussed.

1    The accuracy of the depreciation charge was investigated for a sample of motor vehicles with a carrying value of $4.5 million. The investigation revealed that the accounting system had failed to correctly depreciate vehicles acquired during the year. Consequently, depreciation in the sample had been understated, and the carrying value of the vehicles overstated, by $350,000. The total value of all motor vehicles at the year end was $125 million (20X6 – $131 million).

2    In January 20X7, the board of Basking Co approved a loan to, Mrs C Angel, who is a key member of the senior management team of the company. The total amount of the loan was $75,000. Following a review of the board minutes, it was discovered that the directors agreed that the amount was clearly trivial and have, therefore, not disclosed the loan in the notes to the financial statements.

3    During the year Basking Co reduced the value of their provision for customer refunds which is recognised in the financial statements. For the past five years the value of the provision has been calculated based on 7% of one month's sales, using an average monthly sales value. Management argued that due to improved internal processing systems, such a high rate of provision was no longer necessary and reduced it to 4%. Audit procedures found that refund levels were similar to previous years and there was insufficient evidence at this early stage to confirm whether the new system was more effective or not.

**Required:**

**For each of the matters described above:**

(i)    Explain the matters which should be discussed with management in relation to each of the uncorrected misstatements, and

(ii)    Assuming that management does not adjust the misstatements identified, evaluate the effect of each on the audit opinion.

Note: The total marks will be split equally between each matter.    **(15 marks)**

**(c)**   At the start of the year Basking Co replaced its computer system with an integrated system. The new system allows for real time tracking of packages once received by Basking Co from their customer. As soon as a package is delivered to its final destination the finance system is automatically updated for the revenue and an invoice generated. The audit team have extensively tested the new system and found no deficiencies in relation to the recording of revenue.

**Required:**

**Describe the impact of the above issue, if any, on the auditor's report in accordance with ISA 701 *Communicating Key Audit Matters in the Independent Auditor's Report*.**

**(5 marks)**

**(Total: 25 marks)**

**22   MAGNOLIA GROUP**  *Walk in the footsteps of a top tutor*

You are responsible for performing Engagement Quality Control Reviews on selected audit clients of Crocus & Co, and you are currently performing a review on the audit of the Magnolia Group (the Group). The Group manufactures chemicals which are used in a range of industries, with one of the subsidiaries, Daisy Co, specialising in chemical engineering and developing products to be sold by the other Group companies. The Group's products sell in over 50 countries.

A group structure is shown below, each of the subsidiaries is wholly owned by Magnolia Co, the parent company of the Group:

Crocus & Co is engaged to provide the audit of the Group financial statements and also the audit of Hyacinth Co and Magnolia Co. Geranium Co, a new subsidiary, is audited by a local firm of auditors based near the company's head office. Daisy Co is audited by an unconnected audit firm which specialises in the audit of companies involved with chemical engineering.

The Group's financial year ended on 31 December 20X6 and the audit is in the completion stage, with the auditor's report due to be issued in three weeks' time. The Group's draft consolidated financial statements recognise profit before tax of $7.5 million and total assets of $130 million.

The notes from your review of the audit working papers are shown below, summarising the issues relevant to each subsidiary.

(a)  **Hyacinth Co – internal controls and results of controls testing**

The Group companies supply each other with various chemical products to be used in the manufacture of chemicals. Audit work performed at the interim stage at Hyacinth Co, including walk through procedures and internal control evaluations, concluded that internal controls over intra-group transactions were not effective, and this was documented in the audit file. At the final audit, tests of controls were performed to confirm this to be the case. The tests of controls confirmed that intra-group transactions are not being separately identified in the Group's accounting system and reconciliations of amounts owed between the subsidiaries are not performed.

The group audit manager has concluded on the audit working papers that 'as intra-group balances are cancelled on consolidation, this issue has no impact on the Group audit and no further work is necessary'.

As part of the audit approach it was determined that extensive testing would be performed over the internal controls for capital expenditure at Hyacinth Co as it was identified during planning that the company had made significant acquisitions of plant and equipment during the year. Following controls testing the internal controls over capital expenditure were evaluated to be effective in Hyacinth Co.

The working papers conclude that 'based on the results of controls testing at Hyacinth Co, it is reasonable to assume that controls are effective across the Group' and substantive procedures on property, plant and equipment in each Group company have been planned and performed in response to this assessment.

**(8 marks)**

(b)  **Geranium Co – new subsidiary**

This subsidiary was acquired on 30 September 20X6 and is audited by Fern & Co. The Group audit strategy contains the following statement in relation to the audit of Geranium Co: 'Geranium Co will only be consolidated for three months and the post-acquisition profit for that period to be included in the Group financial statements is $150,000. On that basis, Geranium Co is immaterial to the Group financial statements and therefore our audit procedures are based on analytical procedures only.'

Other than the analytical procedures performed, there is no documentation in respect of Geranium Co or its audit firm Fern & Co included in the Group audit working papers.

The draft statement of financial position of Geranium Co recognises total assets of $30 million. **(5 marks)**

(c)  **Daisy Co – restriction on international trade**

As well as being involved in chemical engineering and supplying chemicals for use by the other Group companies, Daisy Co specialises in producing chemicals which are used in the agricultural sector, and around half of its sales are made internationally.

Daisy Co is audited by Foxglove & Co, and the Group audit working papers contain the necessary evaluations to conclude that an appropriate level of understanding has been obtained in respect of the audit firm.

Foxglove & Co has provided your firm with a summary of key audit findings which includes the following statement: 'During the year new government environmental regulations have imposed restrictions on international trade in chemicals, with sales to many countries now prohibited.

Our audit work concludes that this does not create a significant going concern risk to Daisy Co, and we have confirmed that all inventories are measured at the lower of cost and net realisable value.'

The Group audit manager has concluded that 'I am happy that no further work is needed in this area – we can rely on the unmodified audit opinion to be issued by Foxglove & Co. This issue was not identified until it was raised by Foxglove & Co, it has not been mentioned to me by the Group board members, and it has no implications for the consolidated financial statements.'

The draft statement of financial position of Daisy Co recognises total assets of $8 million and the statement of profit or loss recognises profit before tax of $50,000.

The draft consolidated financial statements recognises goodwill in respect of Daisy Co of $3 million (20X5 – $3 million). **(7 marks)**

**Required:**

**In respect of each of the matters described above:**

(i) **Comment on the quality of the planning and performance of the Group audit discussing the quality control and other professional issues raised.**

(ii) **Recommend any further actions, including relevant audit procedures, to be taken by your firm, prior to finalising the Group auditor's report.**

**Note: the split of the mark allocation is shown next to each of the issues above.**

**(d)** Additional procedures have now been performed to assess the going concern status of Daisy Co and the group auditor has concluded that there is sufficient doubt to require disclosure of the uncertainty in the financial statements of Daisy Co. The directors of Daisy Co have stated that they do not intend to include any disclosure as they do not want to draw attention to going concern issues in case it causes further problems.

**Required:**

**Discuss the effect of this issue on the auditor's reports of Daisy Co and the Magnolia Group.** **(5 marks)**

**(Total: 25 marks)**

**23 OSIER**  *Walk in the footsteps of a top tutor*

You are the manager responsible for the audit of Osier Co, a jewellery manufacturer and retailer. The final audit for the year ended 31 March 20X7 is nearing completion and you are reviewing the audit working papers. The draft financial statements recognise total assets of $1,919 million (20X6 – $1,889 million), revenue of $1,052 million (20X6 – $997 million) and profit before tax of $107 million (20X6 – $110 million). Three issues from the audit working papers are summarised below:

**(a) (i) Cost of inventory**

Inventory costs include all purchase costs and the costs of conversion of raw materials into finished goods. Conversion costs include direct labour costs and an allocation of production overheads. Direct labour costs are calculated based on the average production time per unit of inventory, which is estimated by the production manager, multiplied by the estimated labour cost per hour, which is calculated using the forecast annual wages of production staff divided by the annual scheduled hours of production. Production overheads are all fixed and are allocated based upon the forecast annual units of production. At the year-end inventory was valued at $21 million (20X6 – $20 million). **(6 marks)**

(ii) **Impairment**

At the year end management performed an impairment review on its retail outlets, which are a cash generating unit for the purpose of conducting an impairment review. While internet sales grew rapidly during the year, sales from retail outlets declined, prompting the review. At 31 March 20X7 the carrying amount of the assets directly attributable to the retail outlets totalled $137 million, this includes both tangible assets and goodwill.

During the year management received a number of offers from parties interested in purchasing the retail outlets for an average of $125 million. They also estimated the disposal costs to be $1.5 million, based upon their experience of corporate acquisitions and disposals. Management estimated the value in use to be $128 million. This was based on the historic cash flows attributable to retail outlets inflated at a general rate of 1% per annum.

Consequently the retail outlets were impaired by $9 million to restate them to their estimated recoverable amount of $128 million. The impairment was allocated against the tangible assets of the outlets on a pro rata basis, based upon the original carrying amount of each asset in the unit. **(8 marks)**

(iii) **Warranty provision**

Each year management makes a provision for jewellery returned under warranty. The warranty is an assurance type warranty and is based on an estimate of returns levels for each product type (rings, bracelets, necklaces, watches, earrings, etc.). The warranty is calculated on an annual basis by the sales director. The breakdown for the current provision, as extracted from the notes to the financial statements, is as follows:

|  | $million |
|---|---|
| At 1 April 20X6 | 11.5 |
| Provisions charged during the year | 0.5 |
| Provisions utilised during the year | (1.9) |
| Unutilised provisions reversed | (3.1) |
| | |
| At 31 March 20X7 | 7.0 |

**(7 marks)**

**Required:**

**Comment on the matters to be considered, and explain the audit evidence you should expect to find during your file review in respect of each of the issues described above.**

**Note: The split of the mark allocation is shown against each of the issues above.**

(b) As a result of your review you have concluded that the retail outlets are overvalued due to the assumptions used in management's assessment of value in use being too optimistic. Your calculation of the value in use is $9 million lower than management's estimate. The audit engagement partner has discussed the misstatement with the management team who have refused to make the necessary adjustment to the financial statements.

**Required:**

**Discuss the effect the uncorrected misstatement will have on the audit opinion and auditor's report.** **(4 marks)**

**(Total: 25 marks)**

**24  ROCKET**  *Walk in the footsteps of a top tutor*

**(a)**  Recent developments to the auditor's report have seen the introduction of extended reports which provide more detail about the audit and the auditor's responsibilities. For listed companies the report is extended further by including a key audit matters section. In addition, the report has a new structure with the opinion being positioned towards the start of the report rather than at the end.

**Required:**

**Explain the main changes to the auditor's report and discuss the benefits of the extended auditor's report.                        (5 marks)**

**(b)**  You are a manager at Thyme & Co, a firm of Chartered Certified Accountants. You are currently involved in the completion stage of two engagements relating to different clients. Both engagements have raised issues that require your attention.

Rocket Co is a listed client operating in the engineering industry. The company manufactures machinery for use in the aircraft, defence and marine sectors. The audit for the year ended 30 April 20X7 is almost complete. The revenue and profit before tax figures recognised in the draft financial statements are $1,437 million and $139 million, respectively (20X6 – $1,489 million and $175 million respectively).

Audit procedures identified two sales transactions in the final quarter of the year that related to two different customers but where the goods were delivered to the same location. Further investigations revealed that the goods were delivered to a third party, who agreed to store them until the customers were ready to receive delivery.

The goods have yet to be delivered to the customers because they are both building new facilities and neither is sufficiently progressed to receive the new machinery. The contract terms explicitly state that Rocket Co is obliged to deliver the goods to the customers for final inspection and acceptance and the client has not agreed to any consequent amendments to these terms. The sales invoices were raised and the revenue recognised upon despatch of the goods to the storage facility. During discussions with the audit team, the finance director stated that the company had fulfilled its contractual obligations to provide the goods by a specified date. The revenue attributable to the two transactions totalled $17 million.

**Required:**

**(i)   Comment upon the matter described above and explain the further actions necessary before the auditor's report can be signed.            (7 marks)**

**(ii)  Discuss the implications for the auditor's report if no adjustments are made to the financial statements.                    (5 marks)**

**(c)**  You are reviewing the draft assurance report in relation to the examination of a forecast for Tulip Co. The forecast is included in a proposal due to be sent to Tulip Co's lenders as part of an effort to secure a new loan. Audit procedures concluded that there is no reason to believe that the forecast is unrealistic or that it has not been properly prepared. You are currently reviewing the draft assurance report, which is provided below.

> **Independent auditor's report on the forecast of Tulip Co**
>
> **To the shareholders of Tulip Co:**
>
> We have examined the forecast information of Tulip Co contained in the loan proposal in accordance with the relevant standards on assurance engagements applicable to the examination of prospective financial information. Thyme & Co is not responsible for the forecast, including the assumptions on which it is based.
>
> Based on our examination of the evidence supporting the assumptions, we believe that these assumptions provide a reasonable basis for the forecast. Further, in our opinion the forecast is properly prepared on the basis of the assumptions and is presented in accordance with IFRS.
>
> Actual results are likely to be different from the forecast since the assumptions on which the forecast is based are unlikely to be accurate.
>
> **Signed by assurance engagement partner, Thyme & Co**

**Required:**

**Critically appraise the proposed assurance report extract of Tulip Co.**

**Note: You are NOT required to re-draft the assurance report.**                    **(8 marks)**

**(Total: 25 marks)**

**25    BOSTON**  *Walk in the footsteps of a top tutor*

(a)    In 2019, the IAASB issued three exposure drafts for quality management standards to replace and revise current guidance in the area of quality control.

–    Proposed ISA 220 (Revised) *Quality Management for an Audit of Financial Statements*

–    Proposed International Standard on Quality Management (ISQM) 1 *Quality Management for Firms that Perform Audits or Reviews of Financial Statements, or Other Assurance or Related Services Engagements*

–    Proposed ISQM 2 *Engagement Quality Reviews*.

**Required:**

**Discuss the main objectives and benefits outlined in these exposure drafts on quality management.**                    **(6 marks)**

You are the manager responsible for the audit of Boston Co, a producer of chocolate and confectionery. The audit of the financial statements for the year ended 31 December 20X5 is nearly complete and you are reviewing the audit working papers. The financial statements recognise revenue of $76 million, profit before tax for the year of $6.4 million and total assets of $104 million.

The summary of uncorrected misstatements included in Boston Co's audit working papers, including notes, is shown below. The audit engagement partner is holding a meeting with the management team of Boston Co next week, at which the uncorrected misstatements will be discussed.

| | Statement of profit or loss | | Statement of financial position | |
| --- | --- | --- | --- | --- |
| | Debit | Credit | Debit | Credit |
| Summary of uncorrected misstatements: | $ | $ | $ | $ |
| (i) Impairment | 400,000 | | | 400,000 |
| (ii) Borrowing costs | | 75,000 | 75,000 | |
| (iii) Irrecoverable debt | 65,000 | | | 65,000 |
| (iv) Investment | | 43,500 | 43,500 | |
| Totals | 465,000 | 118,500 | 118,500 | 465,000 |

(i) During the year Boston Co impaired one of its factories. The carrying value of the assets attributable to the factory as a single, cash-generating unit totalled $3.6 million at the year end. The fair value less costs of disposal and the value in use were estimated to be $3 million and $3.5 million respectively and accordingly the asset was written down by $100,000 to reflect the impairment. Audit procedures revealed that management used growth rates attributable to the company as a whole to estimate value in use. Using growth rates attributable to the factory specifically, the audit team estimated the value in use to be $3.1 million.

(ii) Interest charges of $75,000 relating to a loan taken out during the year to finance the construction of a new manufacturing plant were included in finance charges recognised in profit for the year. The manufacturing plant is due for completion in November 20X6.

(iii) One of Boston Co's largest customers, Cleveland Co, is experiencing financial difficulties. At the year end Cleveland Co owed Boston Co $100,000, against which Boston Co made a 5% specific allowance. Shortly after the year end Cleveland Co paid $30,000 of the outstanding amount due but has since experienced further problems, leading to their primary lender presenting a formal request that Cleveland Co be liquidated. If successful, only secured creditors are likely to receive any reimbursement.

(iv) During the year Boston Co purchased 150,000 shares in Nebraska Co for $4.00 per share. Boston Co classified the investment as a financial asset held at fair value through profit or loss. On 31 December 20X5, the shares of Nebraska Co were trading for $4.29. At the year end the carrying value of the investment in Boston Co's financial statements was $600,000.

**Required:**

(b) Explain the matters which should be discussed with management in relation to each of the uncorrected misstatements, including an assessment of their individual impact on the financial statements; and

(c) Assuming that management does not adjust any of the misstatements, discuss the effect on the audit opinion and auditor's report.

The following mark allocation is provided as guidance for this question:

(b) 14 marks

(c) 5 marks

(Total: 25 marks)

**26    MACAU & CO**  *Walk in the footsteps of a top tutor*

You are a senior manager in Macau & Co, a firm of Chartered Certified Accountants. In your capacity as engagement quality control reviewer, you have been asked to review the audit files of Stanley Co and Kowloon Co, both of which have a financial year ended 31 December 20X5, and the audits of both companies are nearing completion.

**(a)**    Stanley Co is a frozen food processor, selling its products to wholesalers and supermarkets. From your review of the audit working papers, you have noted that the level of materiality was determined to be $1.5 million at the planning stage, and this materiality threshold has been used throughout the audit. There is no evidence on the audit file that this threshold has been reviewed during the course of the audit.

From your review of the audit planning, you know that a new packing machine with a cost of $1.6 million was acquired by Stanley Co in March 20X5, and is recognised in the draft statement of financial position at a carrying amount of $1.4 million at 31 December 20X5. The packing machine is located at the premises of Aberdeen Co, a distribution company which is used to pack and distribute a significant proportion of Stanley Co's products. The machine has not been physically verified by a member of the audit team. The audit working papers conclude that 'we have obtained the purchase invoice and order in relation to the machine, and therefore can conclude that the asset is appropriately valued and that it exists. In addition, the managing director of Aberdeen Co has confirmed in writing that the machine is located at their premises and is in working order. No further work is needed in respect of this item.'

Inventory is recognised at $2 million in the draft statement of financial position. You have reviewed the results of audit procedures performed at the inventory count, where the test counts performed by the audit team indicated that the count of some items performed by the company's staff was not correct. The working papers state that 'the inventory count was not well organised' and conclude that 'however, the discrepancies were immaterial, so no further action is required'.

The audit senior spoke to you yesterday, voicing some concerns about the performance of the audit. A summary of his comments is shown below:

'The audit manager and audit engagement partner came to review the audit working papers on the same day towards the completion of the audit fieldwork. The audit partner asked me if there had been any issues on the sections of the audit which I had worked on, and when I said there had been no problems, he signed off the working papers after a quick look through them.

When reading the company's board minutes, I found several references to the audit engagement partner, Joe Lantau. It appears that Joe recommended that the company use the services of his brother, Mick Lantau, for advice on business development, as Mick is a management consultant. Based on that recommendation, Mick has provided a consultancy service to Stanley Co since September 20X5. I mentioned this to Joe, and he told me not to record it in the audit working papers or to discuss it with anyone.'

**Required:**

**Comment on the quality of the audit performed discussing the quality control, ethical and other professional issues raised.** **(13 marks)**

**(b)** Kowloon Co works on contracts to design and manufacture large items of medical equipment such as radiotherapy and X-ray machines. The company specialises in the design, production and installation of bespoke machines under contract with individual customers, which are usually private medical companies. The draft financial statements recognise profit before tax of $950,000 and total assets of $7.5 million.

The audit senior has left the following note for your attention:

'One of Kowloon Co's major customers is the Bay Medical Centre (BMC), a private hospital. In June 20X5 a contract was entered into, under the terms of which Kowloon Co would design a new radiotherapy machine for BMC. The machine is based on a new innovation, and is being developed for the specific requirements of BMC.

It was estimated that the design and production of the machine would take 18 months with estimated installation in December 20X6. As at 31 December 20X5, Kowloon Co had invested heavily in the contract, and design costs totalling $350,000 have been recognised as work in progress in the draft statement of financial position. Deferred income of $200,000 is also recognised as a current liability, representing a payment made by BMC to finance part of the design costs. No other accounting entries have been made in respect of the contract with BMC.

As part of our subsequent events review, inspection of correspondence between Kowloon Co and BMC indicates that the contract has been cancelled by BMC as it is unable to pay for its completion. It appears that BMC lost a significant amount of funding towards the end of 20X5, impacting significantly on the financial position of the company. The manager responsible for the BMC contract confirms that BMC contacted him about the company's financial difficulties in December 20X5.

The matter has been discussed with Kowloon Co's finance director, who has stated that he is satisfied with the current accounting treatment and is not proposing to make any adjustments in light of the cancellation of the contract by BMC. The finance director has also advised that the loss of BMC as a customer will not be mentioned in the company's integrated report, as the finance director does not consider it significant enough to warrant discussion.

Kowloon Co is currently working on six contracts for customers other than BMC. Our audit evidence concludes that Kowloon Co does not face a threat to its going concern status due to the loss of BMC as a customer.'

Your review of the audit work performed on going concern supports this conclusion.

**Required:**

(i) **Comment on the matters to be considered, and recommend the actions to be taken by the auditor.** **(7 marks)**

(ii) **Explain the audit evidence you would expect to find in your review of the audit working papers.** **(5 marks)**

**(Total: 25 marks)**

## 27   DARREN      *Walk in the footsteps of a top tutor*

You are a manager in the audit department of Nidge & Co, a firm of Chartered Certified Accountants, responsible for the audit of Darren Co, a new audit client operating in the construction industry. Darren Co's financial year ended on 31 January 20X5, and the draft financial statements recognise profit before tax of $22.5 million (20X4 – $20 million) and total assets of $370 million, including cash of $3 million. The company typically works on three construction contracts at a time.

The audit is nearly complete and you are reviewing the audit working papers. The audit senior has brought the following matters to your attention:

**(a)**   Darren Co is working on a major contract relating to the construction of a bridge for Flyover Co. Work started in July 20X4, and it is estimated that the contract will be completed in September 20X5. The contract price is $20 million, and it is estimated that a profit of $5 million will be made on completion of the contract. The full amount of this profit has been included in the statement of profit or loss for the year ended 31 January 20X5. Darren Co's management believes that this accounting treatment is appropriate given that the contract was signed during the financial year, and no problems have arisen in the work carried out so far.   **(8 marks)**

**(b)**   A significant contract was completed in September 20X4 for Newbuild Co. This contract related to the construction of a 20-mile highway in a remote area. In November 20X4, several large cracks appeared in the road surface after a period of unusually heavy rain, and the road had to be shut for ten weeks while repair work was carried out. Newbuild Co paid for these repairs, but has taken legal action against Darren Co to recover the costs incurred of $40 million. Disclosure on this matter has been made in the notes to the financial statements. Audit evidence, including a written statement from Darren Co's lawyers, concludes that there is a possibility, but not a probability, of Darren Co having to settle the amount claimed.   **(6 marks)**

**(c)**   During the year Darren Co successfully tendered for a government contract to construct a military building. $7 million of expenses relating to this construction were recorded in the statement of profit or loss. The audit team was given brief summaries of the costs incurred but when asked for further corroborating evidence, management stated that they had signed a confidentiality agreement with the military and were unable to provide any further details. The construction is expected to take a further 15 months to complete.   **(5 marks)**

**(d)**   For the first time this year, the financial statements are presented as part of an integrated report. Included in the integrated report are several key performance indicators, one of which states that Darren Co's profit before tax has increased by 20% from the previous year.   **(6 marks)**

**Required:**

**Discuss the implications of the matters described above on the completion of the audit and on the auditor's report, recommending any further actions which should be taken by the auditor.**   **(Total: 25 marks)**

**28    THURMAN**  *Walk in the footsteps of a top tutor*

You are the manager responsible for the audit of Thurman Co, a manufacturing company which supplies stainless steel components to a wide range of industries. The company's financial year ended on 31 July 20X6 and you are reviewing the audit work which has been completed on a number of material balances and transactions: assets held for sale, capital expenditure and payroll expenses. A summary of the work which has been performed is given below and in each case the description of the audit work indicates the full extent of the audit procedures carried out by the audit team.

**(a)    Assets held for sale**

Due to the planned disposal of one of Thurman Co's factory sites, the property and associated assets have been classified as held for sale in the financial statements. A manual journal has been posted by the finance director to reclassify the assets as current assets and to adjust the value of the assets for impairment and reversal of depreciation charged from the date at which the assets met the criteria to be classified as held for sale. The finance director asked the audit senior to check the journal before it was posted on the basis of there being no one with the relevant knowledge to do this at Thurman Co.

The planned disposal was discussed with management. A brief note has been put into the audit working papers stating that in management's opinion the accounting treatment to classify the factory as held for sale is correct. The manual journal has been arithmetically checked by a different member of the audit team, and the amounts agreed back to the non-current asset register.                                   **(9 marks)**

**(b)    Capital expenditure**

When auditing the company's capital expenditure, the audit team selected a material transaction to test and found that key internal controls over capital expenditure were not operating effectively. Authorisation had not been obtained for an order placed for several vehicles, and appropriate segregation of duties over initiating and processing the transaction was not maintained.

The audit team noted details of the internal control deficiencies and updated the systems notes on the permanent audit file to reflect the deficiencies. The audit work completed on this order was to agree the purchase of the vehicles to purchase invoices and to the cash book and bank statement. The rest of the audit work on capital expenditure was completed in accordance with the audit programme.        **(7 marks)**

**(c)    Payroll expenses**

The payroll function is outsourced to Jackson Co, a service organisation which processes all of Thurman Co's salary expenses. The payroll expenses recognised in the financial statements have been traced back to year-end reports issued by Jackson Co. The audit team has had no direct contact with Jackson Co as the year-end reports were sent to Thurman Co's finance director who then passed them to the audit team.

Thurman Co employs a few casual workers who are paid in cash at the end of each month and are not entered into the payroll system. The audit team has agreed the cash payment made back to the petty cash records and the amounts involved are considered immaterial.                                   **(9 marks)**

**Required:**

In respect of each of the three matters described above:

(i)     Comment on the sufficiency and appropriateness of the audit evidence obtained

(ii)    Recommend further audit procedures to be performed by the audit team, and

(iii)   Explain the matters which should be included in a report in accordance with ISA 265 *Communicating Deficiencies in Internal Controls to Those Charged with Governance and Management.*

Note: The split of the mark allocation is shown against each of the matters above.

(Total: 25 marks)

**29   ADDER GROUP**  *Walk in the footsteps of a top tutor*

The Adder Group (the Group) has been an audit client of your firm for several years. You have recently been assigned to act as audit manager, replacing a manager who has fallen ill, and the audit of the Group financial statements for the year ended 31 March 20X5 is underway. The Group's activities include property management and the provision of large storage facilities in warehouses owned by the Group. The draft consolidated financial statements recognise total assets of $150 million, and profit before tax of $20 million.

(a)    The audit engagement partner, Edmund Black, has asked you to review the audit working papers in relation to two audit issues which have been highlighted by the audit senior. Information on each of these issues is given below:

(i)     In December 20X4, a leisure centre complex was sold for proceeds equivalent to its fair value of $35 million, the related assets have been derecognised from the Group statement of financial position, and a profit on disposal of $8 million is included in the Group statement of profit or loss for the year. The remaining useful life of the leisure centre complex was 21 years at the date of disposal.

The Group is leasing back the leisure centre complex to use in its ongoing operations, paying rentals annually in arrears. At the end of the 20-year lease arrangement, the Group has the option to repurchase the leisure centre complex for its market value at that time.

(ii)    In January 20X5, the Group acquired 52% of the equity shares of Baldrick Co. This company has not been consolidated into the Group as a subsidiary, and is instead accounted for as an associate. The Group finance director's reason for this accounting treatment is that Baldrick Co's operations have not yet been integrated with those of the rest of the Group. Baldrick Co's financial statements recognise total assets of $18 million and a loss for the year to 31 March 20X5 of $5 million.

**Required:**

In respect of the issues described above:

**Comment on the matters to be considered, and explain the audit evidence you should expect to find in your review of the audit working papers.**

Note: The marks will be split equally between each part.                     (16 marks)

**(b)** You are also responsible for the audit of Marr Co, with a year ended 28 February 20X5. The draft financial statements recognise profit for the year of $11 million. The materiality level used for performing the audit was $1.5 million. The audit is nearing completion, and several matters have been highlighted for your attention by the audit senior, Xi Smith. The matters have been discussed with management and will not be adjusted in the financial statements:

1      In January 20X5 a major customer went into administration. There was a balance of $2.5 million owing to Marr Co from this customer at 28 February 20X5 which is still included in trade receivables.

2      A court case began in December 20X4 involving an ex-employee who is suing Marr Co for unfair dismissal. Lawyers estimate that damages of $50,000 are probable to be paid. The financial statements include a note describing the court case and quantifying the potential damages but no adjustment has been made to include it in the statement of financial position or the statement of profit or loss.

Xi Smith has produced a draft auditor's report for your review, an extract of which is shown below:

**Extract 1**

**Basis for opinion and disclaimer of opinion**

Our audit procedures have proven conclusively that trade receivables are materially misstated. The finance director of Marr Co, Rita Gilmour, has refused to make an adjustment to write off a significant trade receivables balance. Therefore in our opinion the financial statements of Marr Co are materially misstated and we therefore express a disclaimer of opinion because we do not think they are fairly presented.

**Extract 2**

**Emphasis of Matter paragraph**

Marr Co is facing a legal claim for an amount of $50,000 from an ex-employee. In our opinion this amount should be recognised as a provision but it is not included in the statement of financial position. We draw your attention to this breach of the relevant International Financial Reporting Standard.

**Required:**

**Critically appraise the proposed auditor's report of Marr Co for the year ended 28 February 20X5.**

**Note: You are NOT required to re-draft the extracts from the auditor's report.**

(9 marks)

(Total: 25 marks)

**30    FRANCIS GROUP**  *Walk in the footsteps of a top tutor*

 *Question debrief*

**(a)**  You are a manager in the audit department of Williams & Co and you are reviewing the audit working papers in relation to the Francis Group (the Group), whose financial year ended on 31 July 20X4. Your firm audits all components of the Group, which consists of a parent company and three subsidiaries – Marks Co, Roberts Co and Teapot Co.

The Group manufactures engines which are then supplied to the car industry. The draft consolidated financial statements recognise profit for the year to 31 July 20X4 of $23 million (20X3 – $33 million) and total assets of $450 million (20X3 – $455 million).

Information in respect of three issues has been highlighted for your attention during the file review.

**(i)    Goodwill**

An 80% equity shareholding in Teapot Co was acquired on 1 August 20X3. Goodwill on the acquisition of $27 million was calculated at that date and remains recognised as an intangible asset at that value at the year end.

The goodwill calculation performed by the Group's management is shown below:

|  | $000 |
|---|---|
| Purchase consideration | 75,000 |
| Fair value of 20% non-controlling interest | 13,000 |
|  | ——— |
|  | 88,000 |
| Less: |  |
| Fair value of Teapot Co's identifiable net assets at acquisition | (61,000) |
|  | ——— |
| Goodwill | 27,000 |
|  | ——— |

In determining the fair value of identifiable net assets at acquisition, an upwards fair value adjustment of $300,000 was made to the book value of a property recognised in Teapot Co's financial statements at a carrying value of $600,000.

**(9 marks)**

**(ii)   Property complex**

In September 20X4, a natural disaster caused severe damage to the property complex housing the Group's head office and main manufacturing site. For health and safety reasons, a decision was made to demolish the property complex. The demolition took place three weeks after the damage was caused. The property had a carrying value of $16 million at 31 July 20X4.

A contingent asset of $18 million has been recognised as a current asset and as deferred income in the Group statement of financial position at 31 July 20X4, representing the amount claimed under the Group's insurance policy in respect of the disaster.

**(6 marks)**

**(iii)** **Inter-company trading**

Marks Co supplies some of the components used by Roberts Co in its manufacturing process. At the year-end, an intercompany receivable of $20 million is recognised in Marks Co's financial statements. Roberts Co's financial statements include a corresponding intercompany payables balance of $20 million and inventory supplied from Marks Co valued at $50 million.

**(5 marks)**

**Required:**

**Comment on the matters to be considered, and explain the audit evidence you should expect to find during your review of the audit working papers in respect of each of the issues described above.**

**(b)** Francis Group has recently received correspondence from their insurance company informing them that the insurance claim has been rejected as the insurance policy had expired and not been renewed at the date the disaster occurred. The going concern status is not considered to be affected as the Group has sufficient assets to acquire a new head office and continue trading. The directors have refused to remove the contingent asset.

**Required:**

**Discuss the implications of the matter described above on the auditor's report, recommending any further actions which should be taken by the auditor.** **(5 marks)**

**(Total: 25 marks)**

 *Calculate your allowed time, allocate the time to the separate parts..............*

**31** **COOPER**  *Walk in the footsteps of a top tutor*

**(a)** You are an audit manager in Rose & Co, responsible for the audit of Cooper Co. You are reviewing the audit working papers relating to the financial year ended 31 January 20X4. Cooper Co is a manufacturer of chemicals used in the agricultural industry. The draft financial statements recognise profit for the year to 31 January 20X4 of $15 million (20X3 – $20 million) and total assets of $240 million (20X3 – $230 million).

The audit senior, Max Turner, has brought several matters to your attention:

**(i)** Cooper Co's factories are recognised within property, plant and equipment at a carrying value of $60 million. Half of the factories produce a chemical which is used in farm animal feed. Recently the government has introduced a regulation stipulating that the chemical is phased out over the next three years. Sales of the chemical are still buoyant, however, and are projected to account for 45% of Cooper Co's revenue for the year ending 31 January 20X5. Cooper Co has started to research a replacement chemical which is allowed under the new regulation, and has spent $1 million on a feasibility study into the development of this chemical. **(8 marks)**

(ii)    In October 20X3, Cooper Co's finance director, Hannah Osbourne, purchased a car from the company. The carrying value of the car at the date of its disposal to Hannah was $50,000, and its market value was $75,000. Cooper Co raised an invoice for $50,000 in respect of the disposal, which is still outstanding for payment.                                                                                    **(7 marks)**

**Required:**

**Comment on the matters to be considered and explain the audit evidence you should expect to find during your review of the audit working papers in respect of each of the issues described above.**                                                               **(15 marks)**

**(b)**    You are also responsible for the audit of the Hopper Group, a listed audit client which supplies ingredients to the food and beverage industry worldwide.

The audit work for the year ended 31 January 20X4 is nearly complete, and you are reviewing the draft auditor's report which has been prepared by the audit senior. During the year the Hopper Group purchased a new subsidiary company, Seurat Sweeteners Co, which has expertise in the research and design of sugar alternatives.

The draft financial statements of the Hopper Group for the year ended 31 January 20X4 recognise profit before tax of $495 million (20X3 – $462 million) and total assets of $4,617 million (20X3 – $4,751 million). An extract from the draft auditor's report is shown below:

**Basis of modified opinion (extract)**

In their calculation of goodwill on the acquisition of the new subsidiary, the directors have failed to recognise consideration which is contingent upon meeting certain development targets. The directors believe that it is unlikely that these targets will be met by the subsidiary company and, therefore, have not recorded the contingent consideration in the cost of the acquisition. They have disclosed this contingent liability fully in the notes to the financial statements. We do not feel that the directors' treatment of the contingent consideration is correct and, therefore, do not believe that the criteria of the relevant standard have been met. If this is the case, it would be appropriate to adjust the goodwill balance in the statement of financial position.

We believe that any required adjustment may materially affect the goodwill balance in the statement of financial position. Therefore, in our opinion, the financial statements do not give a true and fair view of the financial position of the Hopper Group and of the Hopper Group's financial performance and cash flows for the year then ended in accordance with International Financial Reporting Standards.

**Emphasis of Matter Paragraph**

We draw attention to the note to the financial statements which describes the uncertainty relating to the contingent consideration described above. The note provides further information necessary to understand the potential implications of the contingency.

**Required:**

**Critically appraise the draft auditor's report of the Hopper Group for the year ended 31 January 20X4, prepared by the audit senior.**

**Note: You are NOT required to re-draft the extracts from the auditor's report.**

**(10 marks)**

**(Total: 25 marks)**

**32    POODLE GROUP**  *Walk in the footsteps of a top tutor*

You are the manager responsible for the audit of the Poodle Group (the Group) and you are completing the audit of the consolidated financial statements for the year ended 31 March 20X3. The draft consolidated financial statements recognise revenue of $18 million (20X2 – $17 million), profit before tax of $2 million (20X2 – $3 million) and total assets of $58 million (20X2 – $59 million). Your firm audits all of the components of the Group, apart from an overseas subsidiary, Toy Co, which is audited by a small local firm of accountants and auditors.

The audit senior has left a file note for your attention. You are aware that the Group's annual report and financial statements are due to be released next week, and the Group is very reluctant to make any adjustments in respect of the matters described.

**Toy Co**

The component auditors of Toy Co, the overseas subsidiary, have been instructed to provide the Group audit team with details of a court case which is ongoing. An ex-employee is suing Toy Co for unfair dismissal and has claimed $500,000 damages against the company. To comply with local legislation, Toy Co's individual financial statements are prepared using a local financial reporting framework. Under that local financial reporting framework, a provision is only recognised if a cash outflow is virtually certain to arise. The component auditors obtained verbal confirmation from Toy Co's legal advisors that the damages are probable, but not virtually certain to be paid, and no provision has been recognised in either the individual or consolidated financial statements. No other audit evidence has been obtained by the component auditors.

**Trade receivable**

On 1 June 20X3, a notice was received from administrators dealing with the winding up of Terrier Co, following its insolvency. The notice stated that the company should be in a position to pay approximately 10% of the amounts owed to its trade payables. Poodle Co, the parent company of the Group, includes a balance of $1.6 million owed by Terrier Co in its trade receivables.

**Chair's statement**

The draft chair's statement, to be included in the Group's annual report, was received yesterday. The chair comments on the performance of the Group, stating that he is pleased that revenue has increased by 20% in the year.

**Required:**

**In respect of each of the matters described:**

(a)    **Assess the implications for the completion of the Group audit, explaining any adjustments that may be necessary to the consolidated financial statements, and recommending any further procedures necessary; and**

(b)    **Describe the impact on the Group auditor's report if these adjustments are not made.**

The following mark allocation is provided as guidance for this question:

(a)    **18 marks**

(b)    **7 marks**

(Total: 25 marks)

**33   SNIPE**  *Walk in the footsteps of a top tutor*

---

 *Question debrief*

---

(a)   You are the partner responsible for performing an engagement quality control review on the audit of Snipe Co. You are currently reviewing the audit working papers and draft auditor's report on the financial statements of Snipe Co for the year ended 31 January 20X2. The draft financial statements recognise revenue of $8.5 million, profit before tax of $1 million, and total assets of $175 million.

Two issues from the audit working papers are summarised below:

**New processing area**

During the year Snipe Co's factory was extended by the self-construction of a new processing area, at a total cost of $5 million. Included in the costs capitalised are borrowing costs of $100,000, incurred during the six-month period of construction. A loan of $4 million carrying an interest rate of 5% was taken out in respect of the construction on 1 March 20X1, when construction started. The new processing area was ready for use on 1 September 20X1, and began to be used on 1 December 20X1. Its estimated useful life is 15 years.

**Assets held for sale**

Snipe Co owns a number of properties which have been classified as assets held for sale in the statement of financial position. The notes to the financial statements state that the properties are all due to be sold within one year. On classification as held for sale, in October 20X1, the properties were re-measured from carrying value of $26 million to fair value less cost to sell of $24 million, which is the amount recognised in the statement of financial position at the year end.

**Required:**

**Comment on the matters to be considered, and explain the audit evidence you should expect to find during your file review in respect of each of the issues described above.**

**Note:** The marks will be split equally between each part.                                   **(16 marks)**

(b)   Snipe Co has in place a defined benefit pension plan for its employees. An actuarial valuation on 31 January 20X2 indicated that the plan is in deficit by $10.5 million. The deficit is not recognised in the statement of financial position. An extract from the draft auditor's report is given below:

**Explanation of adverse opinion in relation to pension**

The financial statements do not include the company's pension plan. This deliberate omission contravenes accepted accounting practice and means that the accounts are not properly prepared.

**Auditor's opinion**

In our opinion, because of the significance of the matter discussed above, the financial statements do not give a true and fair view of the financial position of Snipe Co as at 31 January 20X2, and of its financial performance and cash flows for the year then ended in accordance with International Financial Reporting Standards.

**Required:**

**Critically appraise the extract from the proposed auditor's report of Snipe Co for the year ended 31 January 20X2.**

**Note: you are NOT required to re-draft the extract of the auditor's report. (9 marks)**

**(Total: 25 marks)**

 *Calculate your allowed time, allocate the time to the separate parts...............*

# OTHER ASSIGNMENTS

**34   JANSEN & CO**  *Walk in the footsteps of a top tutor*

**(a)**   You are an audit manager in Jansen & Co which offers a range of audit and other assurance services to its clients. One of your audit clients is Narley Co which operates a commercial haulage company. Narley Co has been an audit client for the last five years and is currently planning a significant expansion of its operations into a new geographical area and jurisdiction. In order to finance the planned expansion, Narley Co needs funds to purchase additional heavy goods vehicles, expand its warehousing facilities and recruit more drivers. The company is also planning a major advertising and marketing campaign targeted at potential customers in the new jurisdiction.

Narley Co's finance director, Suzanne Seddon, has approached you to ask if your firm will provide a report on the prospective financial information which has been prepared in support of a loan application. The application is for a new long-term loan of $22 million from the company's current lender which it intends to use exclusively to finance the planned expansion. The company currently has an existing long-term loan of $31 million from the same bank which is redeemable in five years' time.

Suzanne Seddon has provided you with the following extract from the prospective financial information which will form part of the company's loan application:

**Forecast statements of profit or loss**

| | Note | Year ended 31 August 20X8 | Year ending 31 August 20X9 | Year ending 31 August 20Y0 |
|---|---|---|---|---|
| | | Unaudited $000 | Forecast $000 | Forecast $000 |
| Revenue | 1 | 138,861 | 174,965 | 225,705 |
| Cost of sales | 2 | (104,862) | (124,786) | (157,230) |
| Administrative expenses | 3 | (22,936) | (21,984) | (20,743) |
| Operating profit | | 11,063 | 28,195 | 47,732 |
| Finance costs | 4 | (1,450) | (1,638) | (1,597) |
| Profit before tax | | 9,613 | 26,557 | 46,135 |

**Notes:**

1      Revenue represents the amounts derived from the provision of haulage services to commercial customers operating principally in the retail sector. Narley Co's board of directors believes that trade in both its existing and new markets will experience significant growth over the next two years.

2      Cost of sales comprises the costs of warehousing and distribution including relevant staff costs, maintenance and repair of vehicles and depreciation of property, equipment and vehicles.

3      Administrative expenses are mainly the costs of running Narley Co's central head office facility.

4      Finance costs represent the cost of servicing long-term finance from Narley Co's bankers.

**Required:**

**(i)      Explain the matters which should be considered by Jansen & Co before accepting the engagement to review and report on Narley Co's prospective financial information.      (6 marks)**

**(ii)      Assuming Jansen & Co accepts the engagement, recommend the examination procedures to be performed in respect of Narley Co's forecast statements of profit or loss.      (9 marks)**

**(b)**      One of your colleagues at Jansen & Co, Rodney Evans, has been taken ill at short notice and you have been temporarily assigned as audit manager on Watson Co, an IT consultancy company which is listed on a second tier investment market. The final audit of Watson Co for the year ended 30 June 20X8 is approaching completion and you are in the process of reviewing the audit working papers. The draft financial statements for the year recognise profit before taxation for the year of $54.2 million and total assets of $23.1 million.

The audit supervisor, who is a part-qualified chartered certified accountant, has sent you an email from which the following extract is taken:

'It's great to have you on board as I was beginning to worry that there would be no manager review of our working papers prior to the final audit clearance meeting next week. The audit assistant and myself have done our best to complete all of the audit work but we only saw Rodney on the first day of the audit about a month ago when I think he was already feeling unwell. We had a short briefing meeting with him at which he told us 'if in doubt, follow last year's working papers.'

One issue which I wanted to check with you is that Watson Co has introduced a cash-settled share-based payment scheme by granting its directors share appreciation rights (SARs) for the first time this year. This was not identified at planning as a high risk area. The SARs were granted on 1 July 20X7 at which date the client obtained a valuation of the rights which was performed by an external firm of valuers. I have filed a copy of the valuation report and I have looked up the valuers online and have found a very professional looking website which confirms that they know what they are doing. The cost of the SARs scheme based on this valuation is being appropriately recognised over the three-year vesting period and a straight line expense of $195,000 has been recognised in the statement of profit or loss on this basis. A corresponding equity reserve has also been correctly recognised on the statement of financial position.

The amount also seems immaterial and I can't see any need to propose any amendments to the financial statements in relation to either the amounts recognised or the disclosures made in the notes to the financial statements.'

**Required:**

**Comment on the quality of the planning and performance of the audit of Watson Co discussing the quality control and other professional issues raised.** **(10 marks)**

**(Total: 25 marks)**

### 35 VIZSLA  *Walk in the footsteps of a top tutor*

**(a)** You are an audit manager in Pointer & Co, a firm of Chartered Certified Accountants which offers a range of assurance services. You are responsible for the audit of Vizsla Co, a company which provides approximately 10% of your firm's practice income each year. The finance director of Vizsla Co has recently contacted you to provide information about another company, Setter Co, which is looking to appoint a provider of assurance services. An extract from the email which the finance director of Vizsla Co has sent to you is shown below:

*'One of my friends, Gordon Potts, is the managing director of Setter Co, a small company which is looking to expand in the next few years. I know that Gordon has approached the company's bank for finance of $6 million to fund the expansion. To support this loan application, Gordon needs to appoint a firm to provide a limited assurance review on the company's financial statements. He would also want the appointed firm to provide tax planning advice and to prepare both the company's and his personal tax computations for submission to the tax authorities. I have asked Gordon to contact you, and I hope that Pointer & Co will be able to provide these services to Setter Co for a low fee. If the fee you suggest is too high, and unacceptable to Gordon, then I will recommend that Gordon approaches Griffon & Co instead, and I would also consider appointing Griffon & Co to provide the audit of Vizsla Co.'*

Griffon & Co is a firm of Chartered Certified Accountants which has an office in the same town as Pointer & Co.

You have done some research on both Setter Co and Gordon Potts and have confirmed that the company is small enough to be exempt from audit. The company is owner-managed, with the Potts family owning 90% of the share capital. Gordon Potts is a director and majority shareholder of three other companies. An article in a newspaper from several years ago about Gordon Potts indicated that one of his companies was once fined for breach of employment law and that he had used money from one of the company's pension plans to set up a business abroad, appointing his son as the managing director of that business.

**Required:**

**In relation to Pointer & Co's potential acceptance of Setter Co as a client of the firm:**

**(i)** **Explain the ethical issues and other matters which should be considered; and.**

**(ii)** **Explain the importance of obtaining customer due diligence and recommend the information which should be obtained.** **(16 marks)**

**(b)** Pointer & Co has agreed to perform an assurance engagement for Vizsla Co; the engagement will be a review of prospective financial information which is needed to support the company's overdraft facilities. Vizsla Co had a financial year ended 30 September 20X7, and an unmodified opinion was issued on these financial statements last month. Pointer & Co's partner responsible for ethics has agreed that any threats to objectivity will be reduced to an acceptable level through the use of a team separate from the audit team to perform the work.

The operating profit forecast for the two years to 31 March 20Y0 prepared by a member of the accounting team of Vizsla Co is shown below, along with some accompanying notes.

| | Note | Six months to 30 September 20X8 $000 | Six months to 31 March 20X9 $000 | Six months to 30 September 20X9 $000 | Six months to 31 March 20Y0 $000 |
|---|---|---|---|---|---|
| Revenue | 1 | 12,800 | 16,900 | 13,700 | 18,900 |
| Gross profit % | | 34% | 45% | 36% | 46% |
| Operating costs: | | | | | |
| Staff costs | | (2,800) | (2,900) | (2,800) | (2,900) |
| Design costs | 2 | (1,200) | (1,200) | (1,250) | (1,250) |
| Marketing | | (900) | (1,000) | (1,100) | (1,100) |
| Interest on overdraft | 3 | (25) | (10) | – | – |
| Other expenses | 4 | (3,840) | (5,070) | (4,110) | (5,670) |
| Operating profit | | 4,035 | 6,720 | 4,440 | 7,980 |

**Notes:**

1 Vizsla Co is a producer of greetings cards and giftware, the demand for which is seasonal in nature.

2 Design costs are mostly payroll costs of the staff working in the company's design team, and the costs relate to the design and development of new product ranges.

3. Vizsla Co has agreed with its bank to clear its overdraft by 1 September 20X9, and the management team is confident that after that point the company will not need an overdraft facility.

4 The total 'Other expenses' is calculated based on 30% of the projected revenue for the six-month period.

**Required:**

**Recommend the examination procedures which should be used in the review of the profit forecast.** **(9 marks)**

**(Total: 25 marks)**

**36   ROPE**  *Walk in the footsteps of a top tutor*

 *Question debrief*

You are the manager responsible for the audit of Rope Co for the year ended 30 September 20X6. During a visit to the team performing the fieldwork, the audit senior shows you a cash flow forecast covering six-month periods to 30 September 20X8 as prepared by management as part of their assessment of the going concern status of the company. The audit senior asks whether any of the forecast cash flows disclosed require any further investigation during the audit fieldwork.

**The actual and forecast six-monthly cash flows for Rope Co for the periods ended:**

|  | Actual | | | Forecast | | |
|---|---|---|---|---|---|---|
|  | 31 March 20X6 | 30 Sept 20X6 | 31 March 20X7 | 30 Sept 20X7 | 31 March 20X8 | 30 Sept 20X8 |
|  | $000 | $000 | $000 | $000 | $000 | $000 |
| Operating cash flows |  |  |  |  |  |  |
| Receipts from customers | 13,935 | 14,050 | 14,300 | 14,700 | 14,950 | 15,400 |
| Payments to suppliers | (10,725) | (10,850) | (11,050) | (11,400) | (11,600) | (12,000) |
| Salaries | (1,250) | (1,300) | (1,275) | (1,326) | (1,301) | (1,353) |
| Other operating cash payments | (1,875) | (1,850) | (1,913) | (1,887) | (1,951) | (1,925) |
| Other cash flows |  |  |  |  |  |  |
| Sale of investments | – | – | – | – | – | 500 |
| Repayment of J Stewart loan | – | – | – | – | – | (500) |
| Repayment of bank loan | – | – | – | – | (1,500) | – |
| Receipt of bank loan | – | – | – | – | 1,500 | – |
| Cash flow for the period | 85 | 50 | 62 | 87 | 98 | 122 |
| Opening cash | (275) | (190) | (140) | (78) | 9 | 107 |
| Closing cash | (190) | (140) | (78) | 9 | 107 | 229 |

The following additional information has been provided in support of the forecasts:

•   Receipts from customers and payments to suppliers have been estimated based on detailed sales forecasts prepared by the sales director.

•   Salaries and overheads have been estimated as the prior year cost plus general inflation of 2%.

•   The bank loan expires on 5 January 20X8. The finance director expects to take out a matching facility with the current lender to pay off the existing debt.

•   On 1 October 20X5, the chief executive, Mr J Stewart, gave the company a three-year, interest free loan secured by a fixed charge over the operational assets of Rope Co. The audit team was unaware of this loan prior to obtaining the cash flow forecast.

•   The directors plan to sell some investments in listed shares to fund the repayment of the chief executive's loan. At 30 September 20X6, the investments were carried in the statement of financial position at their fair value of $350,000.

**Required:**

(a)   Evaluate the appropriateness of the cash flow forecast prepared by Rope Co and recommend the further audit procedures which should be performed.     **(14 marks)**

(b)   Comment on the matters to be considered in respect of the loan from Mr J Stewart and recommend the further audit procedures to be performed.     **(6 marks)**

(c)   Rope Co's chief executive, Mr Stewart, has requested that the audit engagement partner accompanies him to the meeting with the bank where the matching loan will be discussed. Mr Stewart has hinted that if the partner does not accompany him to the meeting, he will put the audit out to tender.

Identify and discuss the ethical and other professional issues raised by the chief executive's request, and recommend any actions that should be taken by the audit firm.     **(5 marks)**

**(Total: 25 marks)**

 *Calculate your allowed time, allocate the time to the separate parts...............*

### 37    HAWK  *Walk in the footsteps of a top tutor*

You are a manager in Lapwing & Co. One of your audit clients is Hawk Co which operates commercial real estate properties typically comprising several floors of retail units and leisure facilities such as cinemas and health clubs, which are rented out to provide rental income.

Your firm has just been approached to provide an additional engagement for Hawk Co, to review and provide a report on the company's business plan, including forecast financial statements for the 12-month period to 31 May 20X3. Hawk Co is in the process of negotiating a new bank loan of $30 million and the report on the business plan is at the request of the bank. It is anticipated that the loan would be advanced in August 20X2 and would carry an interest rate of 4%. The report would be provided by your firm's business advisory department and a second partner review will be conducted which will reduce any threat to objectivity to an acceptable level.

Extracts from the forecast financial statements included in the business plan are given below:

**Statement of profit or loss (extract)**

|  | Note | FORECAST 12 months to 31 May 20X3 $000 | UNAUDITED 12 months to 31 May 20X2 $000 |
|---|---|---|---|
| **Revenue** |  | 25,000 | 20,600 |
| Operating expenses |  | (16,550) | (14,420) |
| **Operating profit** |  | 8,450 | 6,180 |
| Profit on disposal of Beak Retail | 1 | 4,720 | – |
| Finance costs |  | (2,650) | (1,690) |
| **Profit before tax** |  | 10,520 | 4,490 |

**Statement of financial position**

| | Note | FORECAST<br>12 months to<br>31 May 20X3<br>$000 | UNAUDITED<br>12 months to<br>31 May 20X2<br>$000 |
|---|---|---|---|
| **Assets** | | | |
| **Non-current assets** | | | |
| Property, plant and equipment | 2 | 330,150 | 293,000 |
| **Current assets** | | | |
| Inventory | | 500 | 450 |
| Receivables | | 3,600 | 3,300 |
| Cash and cash equivalents | | 2,250 | 3,750 |
| | | 6,350 | 7,500 |
| **Total assets** | | 336,500 | 300,500 |
| | | | |
| **Equity and liabilities** | | | |
| **Equity** | | | |
| Share capital | | 105,000 | 100,000 |
| Retained earnings | | 93,400 | 92,600 |
| **Total equity** | | 198,400 | 192,600 |
| | | | |
| **Non-current liabilities** | | | |
| Long-term borrowings | 2 | 82,500 | 52,500 |
| Deferred tax | | 50,000 | 50,000 |
| **Current liabilities** | | | |
| Trade payables | | 5,600 | 5,400 |
| **Total liabilities** | | 138,100 | 107,900 |
| | | | |
| **Total equity and liabilities** | | 336,500 | 300,500 |

**Notes:**

(1)   Beak Retail is a retail park which is underperforming. Its sale is currently being negotiated, and is expected to take place in September 20X2.

(2)   Hawk Co is planning to invest the cash raised from the bank loan in a new retail and leisure park which is being developed jointly with another company, Kestrel Co.

**Required:**

**In respect of the engagement to provide a report on Hawk Co's business plan:**

(a)   **Identify and explain the matters that should be considered in agreeing the terms of the engagement.**

      **Note: You are NOT required to consider ethical threats to objectivity.      (6 marks)**

(b)   **Recommend the procedures that should be performed in order to examine and report on the forecast financial statements of Hawk Co for the year to 31 May 20X3.**

      **(15 marks)**

(c)   **Explain the difference between best estimate assumptions and hypothetical assumptions used in a forecast and discuss the relative level of risk of each.**

      **(4 marks)**

      **(Total: 25 marks)**

**38 CHEETAH**  *Walk in the footsteps of a top tutor*

(a)   You are a manager in one of the assurance departments of Leopard & Co, a large firm of Chartered Certified Accountants. You are currently assigned to a due diligence engagement for one of your firm's audit clients, Cheetah Co, a manufacturer of bespoke furniture. The audit of Cheetah Co is conducted by a team from a different department. You have never been involved in the audit of this client.

The engagement is to conduct a financial and operational due diligence review of Zebra Co, a company which has been identified as a potential acquisition target by Cheetah Co, due to the synergies offered and the potential to expand the existing production facilities. As part of the due diligence review, you have been asked to provide a valuation of Zebra Co's assets and liabilities and an analysis of the company's operating profit forecasts. This will assist Cheetah Co in determining an appropriate purchase price for Zebra Co.

During the engagement fieldwork your team identified two matters, which require your further consideration, as follows:

1    While reviewing correspondence with customers in relation to outstanding receivables, one of the team found a letter from a large retailer, for which Zebra Co produces a number of unique products, providing advanced notice that they are not renewing their purchasing agreement when the current one expires. The customer advised that they are switching to a new entrant to the market who is substantially cheaper than Zebra Co. A brief analysis identified that the customer provides, on average, almost 5% of Zebra Co's annual revenues.

2    Zebra Co owns a piece of land which was given to it as a gift by the local authorities ten years ago. The land surrounds the entrance to the main production premises and is designated as a nature reserve. Restrictions were imposed on the usage of the land which also limit who the owner is able to sell the land to in the future. The land has zero carrying value in the financial statements.

No additional matters have arisen for your consideration. You are also aware that the financial statements for the last ten years have been audited and no modifications have been made to the auditor's opinion during this period.

**Required:**

**In respect of the two matters identified above:**

(i)    **Explain why each matter requires further investigation as part of the due diligence review, and** **(7 marks)**

(ii)   **Recommend the investigation procedures to be performed.** **(10 marks)**

**(b)** The management team of Cheetah Co has also approached Leopard & Co to ask whether representatives of the firm would be available to attend a meeting with the company's bankers, who they are hoping will finance the acquisition of Zebra Co, to support the management team in conveying the suitability of the acquisition of Zebra Co.

For the meeting the bank requires the most up-to-date interim accounts of Cheetah Co with the accompanying auditor's independent interim review report. Your firm is due to complete the interim review shortly and the management team of Cheetah Co has requested that the interim review is completed quickly so that it does not hold up negotiations with the bank, stating that if it does, it may affect the outcome of the next audit tender, which is due to take place after the completion of this year's audit.

**Required:**

**Comment on the ethical and professional issues raised, and recommend any actions which should be taken in respect of the request from the management team of Cheetah Co.**

(8 marks)

(Total: 25 marks)

**39 SANZIO**  *Walk in the footsteps of a top tutor*

**(a)** You are a manager in Raphael & Co, a firm of accountants which has 12 offices and 30 partners, 10 of whom are members of ACCA. An advertisement has been drafted as part of the firm's drive to increase the number of clients. It is suggested that it should be placed in a number of quality national as well as local newspapers:

> Have you had enough of your accountant charging you too much for poor quality services?
>
> Does your business need a kick-start?
>
> Look no further. Raphael & Co provides the most comprehensive range of finance and accountancy services in the country as well as having the leading tax team in the country who are just waiting to save you money.
>
> Still not sure? We guarantee to be cheaper than your existing service provider and for the month of January we are offering free business advice to all new audit clients.
>
> Drop in and see us at your local office for a free consultation.
>
> Raphael & Co, Chartered Certified Accountants.

**Required:**

**Comment on the suitability of the advertisement discussing any ethical and professional issues raised.** (7 marks)

**(b)** As a result of advertising, Raphael & Co has been appointed by Sanzio Co to perform a due diligence review of a potential acquisition target, Titian Tyres Co. As part of the due diligence review and to allow for consideration of an appropriate offer price, Sanzio Co has requested that you identify and value all the assets and liabilities of Titian Tyres Co, including items which may not currently be reported in the statement of financial position.

Sanzio Co is a large, privately owned company operating only in this country, which sells spare parts and accessories for cars, vans and bicycles. Titian Tyres Co is a national chain of vehicle service centres, specialising in the repair and replacement of tyres, although the company also offers a complete range of engine and bodywork services as well. If the acquisition is successful, the management of Sanzio Co intends to open a Titian Tyres service centre in each of its stores.

One of the reasons for Titian Tyres Co's success is their internally generated customer database, which records all customer service details. Using the information contained on the database software, the company's operating system automatically informs previous customers when their vehicle is due for its next service via email, mobile phone text or automated letter. It also informs a customer service team to telephone the customer if they fail to book a service within two weeks of receiving the notification. According to the management of Titian Tyres Co, repeat business makes up over 60% of annual sales and management believes that this is a distinct competitive advantage over other service centres.

Titian Tyres Co also recently purchased a licence to distribute a new, innovative tyre which was designed and patented in the United States. The tyre is made of 100% recycled materials and, due to a new manufacturing process, is more hardwearing and therefore needs replacing less often. Titian Tyres Co paid $5 million for the licence in January 20X5 and the company is currently the sole, licenced distributor in this country.

During a brief review of Titian Tyres Co's financial statements for the year ended 30 June 20X5, you notice a contingent liability disclosure in the notes relating to compensation claims made after the fitting of faulty engine parts during 20X4. The management of Titian Tyres Co has stated that the fault lies with the manufacturer of the part and that they have made a claim against the manufacturer for the total amount sought by the affected customers.

**Required:**

(i)    Describe the purpose of a due diligence assignment and compare the scope of a due diligence assignment with that of an audit of historical financial statements. **(6 marks)**

(ii)   Recommend, with reasons, the principal additional information which should be made available to assist with your valuation of Titian Tyres Co's intangible assets. **(7 marks)**

(iii)  Explain the specific enquiries you should make of Titian Tyres Co's management relevant to the contingent liability disclosed in the financial statements. **(5 marks)**

**(Total: 25 marks)**

**40   BALTIMORE**  *Walk in the footsteps of a top tutor*

 *Question debrief*

You are a manager in the business advisory department of Goleen & Co. Your firm has been approached to provide assurance to Baltimore Co, a company which is not an audit client of your firm, on a potential acquisition. You have just had a conversation with Mark Clear, Baltimore Co's managing director, who made the following comments:

'Baltimore Co is a book publisher specialising in publishing textbooks and academic journals. In the last few years the market has changed significantly, with the majority of customers purchasing books from online sellers. This has led to a reduction in profits, and we recognise that we need to diversify our product range in order to survive. As a result of this, we decided to offer a subscription-based website to customers, which would provide the customer with access to our full range of textbooks and journals online.

On investigating how to set up this website, we found that we lack sufficient knowledge and resources to develop it ourselves and began to look for another company which has the necessary skills, with a view to acquiring the company. We have identified Mizzen Co as a potential acquisition, and we have approached the bank for a loan which will be used to finance the acquisition if it goes ahead.

Baltimore Co has not previously acquired another company. We would like to engage your firm to provide guidance regarding the acquisition. I understand that a due diligence review would be advisable prior to deciding on whether to go ahead with the acquisition, but the other directors are not sure that this is required, and they don't understand what the review would involve. They are also unsure about the type of conclusion that would be issued and whether it would be similar to the opinion in an auditor's report.'

Mark Clear has sent you the following information about Mizzen Co:

**Company background**

Mizzen Co was established four years ago by two university graduates, Vic Sandhu and Lou Lien, who secured funds from a venture capitalist company, BizGrow, to set up the company. Vic and Lou created a new type of website interface which has proven extremely popular, and which led to the company growing rapidly and building a good reputation. They continue to innovate and have won awards for website design. Vic and Lou have a minority shareholding in Mizzen Co.

Mizzen Co employs 50 people and operates from premises owned by BizGrow, for which a nominal rent of $1,000 is paid annually. The company uses few assets other than computer equipment and fixtures and fittings. The biggest expense is wages and salaries and due to increased demand for website development, freelance specialists have been used in the last six months. According to the most recent audited financial statements, Mizzen Co has a bank balance of $500,000.

The company has three revenue streams:

1    Developing and maintaining websites for corporate customers. Mizzen Co charges a one-off fee to its customers for the initial development of a website and for maintaining the website for two years. The amount of this fee depends on the size and complexity of the website and averages at $10,000 per website. The customer can then choose to pay another one-off fee, averaging $2,000, for Mizzen Co to provide maintenance for a further five years.

2    Mizzen Co has also developed a subscription-based website on which it provides access to technical material for computer specialists. Customers pay an annual fee of $250 which gives them unlimited access to the website. This accounts for approximately 30% of Mizzen Co's total revenue.

3    The company has built up several customer databases which are made available, for a fee, to other companies for marketing purposes. This is the smallest revenue stream, accounting for approximately 20% of Mizzen Co's total revenue.

**Extracts from audited financial statements**

**Statement of profit or loss**

|  | Year ended 30 September 20X3 $000 | Year ended 30 September 20X2 $000 | Year ended 30 September 20X1 $000 | Year ended 30 September 20X0 $000 |
|---|---|---|---|---|
| Revenue | 4,268 | 3,450 | 2,150 | 500 |
| Operating expenses | (2,118) | (2,010) | (1,290) | (1,000) |
| Operating profit/(loss) | 2,150 | 1,440 | 860 | (500) |
| Finance costs | (250) | (250) | (250) | – |
| Profit/(loss) before tax | 1,900 | 1,190 | 610 | (500) |
| Tax expense | (475) | (300) | (140) | – |
| Profit/(loss) for the year | 1,425 | 890 | 470 | (500) |

There were no items of other comprehensive income recognised in any year.

**Required:**

(a)    Discuss the benefits to Baltimore Co of a due diligence review being performed on Mizzen Co.    **(6 marks)**

(b)    Identify and explain the matters which you would focus on in your due diligence review and recommend the additional information which you will need to perform your work.    **(16 marks)**

(c)    Describe the type of conclusion which would be issued for a due diligence report and compare this to an auditor's report.    **(3 marks)**

(Total: 25 marks)

 *Calculate your allowed time, allocate the time to the separate parts..............*

**41 JACOB**  *Walk in the footsteps of a top tutor*

Jacob Co, an audit client of your firm, is a large privately owned company whose operations involve a repair and maintenance service for domestic customers. The company offers a range of services, such as plumbing and electrical repairs and maintenance, and the repair of domestic appliances such as washing machines and cookers, as well as dealing with emergencies such as damage caused by flooding. All work is covered by a two-year warranty.

The directors of Jacob Co have been seeking to acquire expertise in the repair and maintenance of swimming pools and hot-tubs as this is a service increasingly requested, but not offered by the company. They have recently identified Locke Co as a potential acquisition. Preliminary discussions have been held between the directors of the two companies with a view to the acquisition of Locke Co by Jacob Co. This will be the first acquisition performed by the current management team of Jacob Co. Your firm has been asked to perform a due diligence review on Locke Co prior to further discussions taking place. You have been provided with the following information regarding Locke Co:

Locke Co is owner-managed, with three of the five board members being the original founders of the company, which was incorporated thirty years ago. The head office is located in a prestigious building, which is owned by the founders' family estate. The company recently acquired a separate piece of land on which a new head office is to be built.

The company has grown rapidly in the last three years as more affluent customers can afford the cost of installing and maintaining swimming pools and hot-tubs. The expansion was funded by a significant bank loan. The company relies on an overdraft facility in the winter months when less operating cash inflows arise from maintenance work.

Locke Co enjoys a good reputation, though this was tarnished last year by a complaint by a famous actor who claimed that, following maintenance of his swimming pool by Locke Co's employees, the water contained a chemical which damaged his skin. A court case is ongoing and is attracting media attention.

The company's financial year end is 31 August. Its accounting function is outsourced to Austin Co, a local provider of accounting and tax services.

**Required:**

(a) Explain the potential benefits to Jacob Co of having an externally provided due diligence review. **(6 marks)**

(b) Recommend additional information which should be made available for your firm's due diligence review, and explain the need for the information. **(14 marks)**

Jacob Co is tendering for an important contract to provide subcontracting services to Burke Co. Burke Co is also an audit client of your firm and Jacob Co's management has asked your firm to provide advice on the tender it is preparing.

(c) Explain the ethical and professional matters your firm should consider in deciding whether to provide advice to Jacob Co on the tender. **(5 marks)**

**(Total: 25 marks)**

## 42   MOOSEWOOD HOSPITAL   *Walk in the footsteps of a top tutor*

>  *Question debrief*

**(a)** You are the manager responsible for the audit of Moosewood Hospital Co, for the year ended 31 March 20X7, working in the audit department of Fern & Co. Moosewood Hospital Co is a private sector medical facility, where patients undergo minor surgical procedures and receive treatments such as physiotherapy. You have recently visited the audit team, who are currently on site performing the fieldwork, to review the work performed to date and to discuss their progress. During your visit the audit senior informed you of the following matter:

During a review of the valuation of medical inventories, including medicines used in a variety of treatments at the hospital, it was noted that a number of items had passed their recommended use by dates. These were recorded on an inventory spreadsheet maintained by the financial controller and were easy to spot because they were highlighted in red. One of the audit team inspected a sample of the inventories in question and confirmed that their use by dates had expired. When asked about this, the financial controller stated that the audit team must be mistaken. The audit team requested to look at the spreadsheet again but he refused. The next day the finance director confronted the audit team accusing them of extending their investigations 'beyond their remit'. He also threatened to remove them from the premises if they continued to ask questions which were not relevant to the audit of the hospital's financial statements. Since then, the audit team has been unable to complete the audit of medical inventories. They have also noted that the room where the inventories were previously kept has been emptied.

**Required:**

**Identify and explain the ethical and professional issues raised and recommend any actions which should be taken in respect of the matter described by the audit senior.**

**(11 marks)**

**(b)** Fern & Co is also engaged to produce an assurance report on the performance information of Moosewood Hospital Co which is included in the company's integrated report. The integrated report will be published on the company's website later in the year, and is not part of the information published with the financial statements.

Fern & Co has a specialist team, independent from the audit department, which provides assurance on key performance indicators. Under the terms of the engagement, this team is required to provide assurance with regard to both the accuracy and completeness of the key performance indicators which are used to monitor the hospital's efficiency and effectiveness. Several of the key performance indicators included in the draft integrated report, all of which the Hospital claims to have met, are shown below:

1   To maintain an average patient to nurse ratio of no more than 6:1.

2   To achieve a minimum 75% annual usage of surgical rooms.

3   To ensure that the rate of admissions within 28 days for previously treated conditions does not exceed 3%.

**Required:**

(i)   Discuss the benefits of independent assurance being provided on the key performance indicators included in the integrated report of Moosewood Hospital Co to the company's management and to external users of the report.

(4 marks)

(ii)  Recommend the examination procedures which should be used in obtaining assurance relating to the key performance indicators of Moosewood Hospital Co.

(10 marks)

(Total: 25 marks)

---

 *Calculate your allowed time, allocate the time to the separate parts...............*

---

**43   NEWMAN & CO**  *Walk in the footsteps of a top tutor*

(a)   You are a manager in Newman & Co, a global firm of Chartered Certified Accountants. You are responsible for evaluating proposed engagements and for recommending to a team of partners whether or not an engagement should be accepted by your firm.

Eastwood Co, a listed company, is an existing audit client and is an international mail services operator, with a global network including 220 countries and 300,000 employees. The company offers mail and freight services to individual and corporate customers, as well as storage and logistical services.

Eastwood Co takes its corporate social responsibility seriously, and publishes social and environmental key performance indicators (KPIs) in a Sustainability Report, which is published with the financial statements in the annual report. Partly in response to requests from shareholders and pressure groups, Eastwood Co's management has decided that in the forthcoming annual report, the KPIs should be accompanied by an independent assurance report. An approach has been made to your firm to provide this report in addition to the audit.

To help in your evaluation of this potential engagement, you have been given an extract from the draft Sustainability Report, containing some of the KPIs published by Eastwood Co. In total, 25 environmental KPIs, and 50 social KPIs are disclosed.

**Extract from Sustainability Report:**

| Year ended 31 October | 20X5 Draft | 20X4 Actual |
|---|---|---|
| $CO_2$ emissions (million tonnes) | 26.8 | 28.3 |
| Energy use (million kilowatt hours) | 4,895 | 5,250 |
| Charitable donations ($ million) | 10.5 | 8.2 |
| Number of serious accidents in the workplace | 60 | 68 |
| Average annual spend on training per employee | $180 | $175 |

You have also had a meeting with Ali Monroe, the manager responsible for the audit of Eastwood Co, and notes of the meeting are given below:

---

**Notes from meeting with audit manager, Ali Monroe**

Newman & Co has audited Eastwood Co for three years, and it is a major audit client of our firm, due to its global presence and recent listing on two major stock exchanges. The audit is managed from our office in Oldtown, which is also the location of the global headquarters of Eastwood Co.

We have not done any work on the KPIs, other than review them for consistency, as we would with any 'other information' issued with the financial statements. The KPIs are produced by Eastwood Co's Sustainability Department, located in Fartown.

We have performed audit procedures on the charitable donations, as this is disclosed in a note to the financial statements, and our evidence indicates that there have been donations of $9 million this year, which is the amount disclosed in the note. However, the draft KPI is a different figure – $10.5 million, and this is the figure highlighted in the draft Chair's Statement as well as the draft Sustainability Report. $9 million is material to the financial statements.

The audit work is nearly complete, and the annual report is to be published in about four weeks, in time for the company meeting, scheduled for 31 January 20X5.

---

Your firm has recently established a specialist social and environmental assurance department based in Oldtown, and if the engagement to report on the Sustainability Report is accepted, it would be performed by members of that team, who would not be involved with the audit.

**Required:**

(i) Evaluate the matters which should be considered before your firm accepts the invitation to perform an assurance engagement on the Sustainability Report of Eastwood Co. **(8 marks)**

(ii) Recommend procedures that could be used to verify the number of serious accidents in the workplace and the average annual spend on training per employee. **(7 marks)**

**(b)** Your firm has also been engaged to perform an assurance engagement on Faster Jets Co's corporate social responsibility (CSR) report. Faster Jets Co is an airline company and is a new audit client of Newman & Co. This engagement will be performed by the specialist social and environmental assurance department and there are no ethical threats created by the provision of this service in addition to the audit. An extract from the draft CSR report is shown below.

| CSR objective | CSR target | Performance in 20X5 |
|---|---|---|
| Continue to invest in local communities and contribute to charitable causes | Make direct charitable cash donations to local charities | Donations of $550,000 were made to local charities |
| | Build relationships with global charities and offer free flights to charitable organisations | 800 free flights with a value of $560,000 were provided to charities |
| | Develop our Local Learning Initiative and offer free one day education programmes to schools | $750,000 was spent on the Local Learning Initiative and 2,250 children attended education days |
| Reduce environmental impact of operations | Reduce the amount of vehicle fuel used on business travel by our employees | The number of miles travelled in vehicles reduced by 5%, and the amount spent on vehicle fuel reduced by 7% |

**Required:**

**Recommend the procedures to be used to gain assurance on the validity of the performance information in Faster Jets Co's CSR report.** **(6 marks)**

(c) **Discuss the difficulties in measuring and reporting on social and environmental performance.** **(4 marks)**

**(Total: 25 marks)**

## 44 BEYER  *Walk in the footsteps of a top tutor*

(a) You are a manager in the forensic department of your firm, Kaffe & Co. You have received a request from Beyer Co about an inventory fraud which was brought to the attention of the company's audit committee by a whistle-blower. Beyer Co is not currently a client of your firm.

Beyer Co manufactures and sells parts used in the automotive industry to both car manufacturers and to garages specialising in the repair and servicing of cars. The audit committee would like Kaffe & Co to perform a forensic investigation to quantify the loss suffered as a result of the inventory fraud, and to recommend improvements in the company's internal controls to avoid similar issues in the future. In addition, the audit committee has mentioned that although the quantification of the loss is to form the basis of an insurance claim, the matter has been reported to the police who will be investigating the matter further.

**Required:**

**Evaluate the matters which should be considered before your firm accepts the invitation to perform a forensic investigation for Beyer Co.** **(8 marks)**

(b) Having accepted the engagement, the operations director provides you with the following summary of the allegations of the whistle-blower:

'The warehouse manager has been working with one of the sales representatives to dispatch goods to a fictitious customer which the warehouse manager has created on the dispatch system. The sales orders are input by the sales representative into the dispatch system which is not directly linked to the invoicing and accounting system. After the goods dispatch note is issued by the warehouse manager and the goods leave the warehouse for delivery to the fictitious customer, the sales representative cancels the original order. The warehouse manager reverses the dispatch immediately so that the daily report on inventory movement used to generate invoices in the sales system does not reflect movement of the goods. The sales representative takes delivery of the goods at the address of the fictitious customer and then sells the parts on the internet, splitting the proceeds with the warehouse manager. The warehouse manager supervises and participates in all inventory counts and this way ensures he is able to adjust the records of inventory to disguise the missing items.'

The operations director has informed you that no authorisation is required for either the cancellation of orders or the reversal of dispatch notes.

**Required:**

(i)   **Recommend the procedures which should be performed in order to quantify the inventory loss; and**                                                                 **(6 marks)**

(ii)  **Evaluate the deficiencies in Beyer Co's internal control system, and explain how they contributed to the fraud, together with recommendations to prevent such a fraud reoccurring.**                                                       **(6 marks)**

(c)   The audit committee members have expressed their dissatisfaction that the company's auditor did not identify the fraud.

**Required:**

**Explain the difficulties arising for management and for the auditor with respect to discovering fraud.**                                                                 **(5 marks)**

**(Total: 25 marks)**

---

**45   RETRIEVER**  *Walk in the footsteps of a top tutor*

 *Question debrief*

(a)   Kennel & Co, a firm of Chartered Certified Accountants, is the external audit provider for the Retriever Group (the Group), a manufacturer of mobile phones and laptop computers. The Group obtained a stock exchange listing in July 20X2. The audit of the consolidated financial statements for the year ended 28 February 20X3 is nearing completion.

You are a manager in the audit department of Kennel & Co, responsible for conducting engagement quality control reviews on listed audit clients. You have discussed the Group audit with some of the junior members of the audit team, one of whom made the following comments about how it was planned and carried out.

'The audit has been quite time-pressured. The audit manager told the juniors not to perform some of the planned audit procedures on items such as directors' emoluments and share capital as they are considered to be low risk. He also instructed us not to use the firm's statistical sampling methods in selecting trade receivables balances for testing, as it would be quicker to pick the sample based on our own judgment.

'Two of the juniors were given the tasks of auditing trade payables and going concern. The audit manager asked us to review each other's work as it would be good training for us, and he didn't have time to review everything.

'I was discussing the Group's tax position with the financial controller, when she said that she was struggling to calculate the deferred tax asset that should be recognised. The deferred tax asset has arisen because several of the Group's subsidiaries have been loss making this year, creating unutilised tax losses. As I had just studied deferred tax at college I did the calculation of the Group's deferred tax position for her. The audit manager said this saved time as we now would not have to audit the deferred tax figure.

'The financial controller also asked for my advice as to how the tax losses could be utilised by the Group in the future. I provided her with some tax planning recommendations, for which she was very grateful.'

**Required:**

**In relation to the audit of the Retriever Group, evaluate the quality control, ethical and other professional matters arising in respect of the planning and performance of the Group audit.** **(13 marks)**

**(b)** The audit committee of the Group has contacted Kennel & Co to discuss an incident that took place on 1 June 20X3. On that date, there was a burglary at the Group's warehouse where inventory is stored prior to despatch to customers. CCTV filmed the thieves loading a lorry belonging to the Group with boxes containing finished goods. The last inventory count took place on 30 April 20X3.

The Group has insurance cover in place and Kennel & Co's forensic accounting department has been asked to provide a forensic accounting service to determine the amount to be claimed in respect of the burglary. The insurance covers the cost of assets lost as a result of thefts.

It is thought that the amount of the claim will be immaterial to the Group's financial statements, and there is no ethical threat in Kennel & Co's forensic accounting department providing the forensic accounting service.

**Required:**

**In respect of the theft and the associated insurance claim:**

**(i)** **Evaluate the matters to be considered, and the steps to be taken in planning the forensic accounting service.**

**(ii)** **Recommend the procedures to be performed in determining the amount of the claim.**

**Note: The total marks will be split equally between each part.** **(12 marks)**

**(Total: 25 marks)**

 *Calculate your allowed time, allocate the time to the separate parts..............*

**46  LARK & CO**  *Walk in the footsteps of a top tutor*

You are an audit manager working for Lark & Co, a firm of Chartered Certified Accountants. You are currently working on several clients. Issues have recently arisen in relation to three different clients which require your attention.

**(a)**  Chestnut Co is a large company which provides information technology services to business customers. The finance director of Chestnut Co, Jack Privet, contacted you this morning, saying:

'I was alerted yesterday to a fraud being conducted by members of our sales team. It appears that several sales representatives have been claiming reimbursement for fictitious travel and client entertaining expenses and inflating actual expenses incurred. Specifically, it has been alleged that the sales representatives have claimed on expenses for items such as gifts for clients and office supplies which were never actually purchased, claimed for business-class airline tickets but in reality had purchased economy tickets, claimed for non-existent business mileage and used the company credit card to purchase items for personal use. I am very worried about the scale of this fraud, as travel and client entertainment is one of our biggest expenses.

All of the alleged fraudsters have been suspended pending an investigation, which I would like your firm to conduct. We will prosecute these employees to attempt to recoup our losses if evidence shows that a fraud has indeed occurred, so your firm would need to provide an expert witness in the event of a court case. Can we meet tomorrow to discuss this potential assignment?'

Chestnut Co has a small internal audit department and in previous years the evidence obtained by Lark & Co as part of the external audit has indicated that the control environment of the company is generally good. The audit opinion on the financial statements for the year ended 31 March 20X4 was unmodified.

**Required:**

**(i)**  **Assess the ethical and professional issues raised by the request for your firm to investigate the alleged fraudulent activity.**                                        **(6 marks)**

**(ii)**  **Explain the matters that should be discussed in the meeting with Jack Privet in respect of planning the investigation into the alleged fraudulent activity.**                **(6 marks)**

**(b)**  Heron Co is an owner-managed business which operates a chain of bars and restaurants. This is your firm's first year auditing the client and the audit for the year ended 31 July 20X5 is underway. The audit senior has sent a note for your attention:

'When I was auditing revenue I noticed something strange. Heron Co's revenue, which is almost entirely cash-based, is recognised at $5.5 million in the draft financial statements. However, the accounting system shows that till receipts for cash paid by customers amount to only $3.5 million. This seemed odd, so I questioned Ava Gull, the financial controller about this. She said that Jack Heron, the company's owner, deals with cash receipts and posts through journals dealing with cash and revenue. Ava asked Jack the reason for these journals but he refused to give an explanation.

'While auditing cash, I noticed a payment of $2 million made by electronic transfer from the company's bank account to an overseas financial institution. The bank statement showed that the transfer was authorised by Jack Heron, but no other documentation regarding the transfer was available.

'Alarmed by the size of this transaction, and the lack of evidence to support it, I questioned Jack Heron, asking him about the source of cash receipts and the reason for electronic transfer. He would not give any answers and became quite aggressive.'

**Required:**

**Discuss the implications of the circumstances described in the audit senior's notes and the nature of any reporting which should take place by the audit senior.**

(8 marks)

(c)     You are currently reviewing the working papers of the audit of Coot Co for the year ended 28 February 20X5. In the working papers dealing with payroll, the audit junior has commented as follows:

'Several new employees have been added to the company's payroll during the year, with combined payments of $125,000 being made to them. There does not appear to be any authorisation for these additions. When I questioned the payroll supervisor who made the amendments, she said that no authorisation was needed because the new employees are only working for the company on a temporary basis.

However, when discussing staffing levels with management, it was stated that no new employees have been taken on this year. Other than the tests of controls planned, no other audit work has been performed.'

**Required:**

**Discuss how professional scepticism should be applied to the audit of Coot Co's payroll and recommend any further actions that should be taken by the auditor.**

(5 marks)

(Total: 25 marks)

**47     SQUIRE**  *Walk in the footsteps of a top tutor*

 *Question debrief*

(a)     You are responsible for the audit of Squire Co, a listed company, and you are completing the review of its interim financial statements for the six months ended 31 October 20X7. Squire Co is a car manufacturer, and historically has offered a three-year warranty on cars sold. The financial statements for the year ended 30 April 20X7 included a warranty provision of $1.5 million and recognised total assets of $27.5 million. You are aware that on 1 July 20X7, due to cost cutting measures, Squire Co stopped offering warranties on cars sold. The interim financial statements for the six months ended 31 October 20X7 do not recognise any warranty provision. Total assets are $30 million at 31 October 20X7.

**Required:**

(i)     Explain the principal analytical procedures that should be used to gather evidence in a review of interim financial information. **(7 marks)**

(ii)    Assess the matters that should be considered in forming a conclusion on Squire Co's interim financial statements, and the implications for the review report. **(6 marks)**

**(b)**     You are also responsible for the audit of Gull Co, a large, private company which is currently owned by the Brenner family, who own the majority of the company's shares.

Following the completion of the audit this year, the finance director, Jim Brenner, contacted you and told you that the family is considering listing the company on the stock exchange. They would like to recruit one of your audit partners for a six-month period to help prepare for the listing. As the board is concerned that the necessary skills and personnel to support the listing are not currently present within the company, Jim Brenner has also requested that your firm assist them in identifying and recruiting new members to the board.

Currently, most of the executive director roles are performed by family members, except for the directors of operations and human resources, who are both long-serving employees. The board operates no audit committee and there is only one non-executive director, who works elsewhere as an IT consultant. Other than the recruitment of new board members, Gull Co is not planning on making any changes to its governance structure prior to or subsequent to listing.

Gull Co has a financial year ending 31 March 20X8, and audit planning is scheduled to take place in January 20X8.

**Required:**

**In relation to the information provided for Gull Co, comment on:**

(i)     The ethical and professional matters in relation to the recruitment requests made by Gull Co.

(ii)    The implications the governance structure and proposed listing may have on the audit process.

**Note: The total marks will be split equally between each part.** **(12 marks)**

**(Total: 25 marks)**

 *Calculate your allowed time, allocate the time to the separate parts...............*

# PROFESSIONAL AND ETHICAL CONSIDERATIONS

**48   THOMASSON & CO**  *Walk in the footsteps of a top tutor*

You are an audit manager in Thomasson & Co, a firm of Chartered Certified Accountants. You have recently been assigned to the audit of Clean Co for the year ended 30 September 20X8. Clean Co is an unlisted company and has been an audit client of your firm for a number of years.

Clean Co is a national distributor of cleaning products. The company buys the cleaning products from wholesalers and employs a team of approximately 750 sales staff around the country who sell the company's products to both domestic households and small to medium-sized businesses. Around 75% of Clean Co's sales transactions are cash-based and each of the company's sales staff prepares a cash sales report on a monthly basis. According to Clean Co's chief executive, Simon Blackers, and in order to foster 'an entrepreneurial spirit' amongst his staff, each staff member (including the senior management team) is encouraged to make cash sales and is paid on a commission basis to sell the company's products to friends and family. Mr Blackers leads the way with this scheme and recently sold cleaning products with a value of $33,000 to a business associate of his. He has transferred these funds directly into an off-shore bank account in the company's name on which he is the sole signatory.

**Review of audit working papers**

Your review of the audit working papers and an initial meeting with Mr Blackers have identified the following potential issues:

Following your review of the audit engagement letter and the working papers of the taxation section of the audit file, you have established that Thomasson & Co performed the taxation computation for Clean Co and completed the tax returns for both the company and Mr Blackers personally. All of the taxation services have been invoiced to Clean Co as part of the total fee for the audit and professional services. Mr Blackers' personal tax return includes a significant number of transactions involving the purchase and sale of properties in various international locations. The taxation working papers include a detailed review of a number of off-shore bank accounts in Mr Blackers' name which identified the property transactions.

During your initial meeting with Mr Blackers, he informed you that Clean Co is planning to develop a new website in order to offer online sales to its customers. He has asked Thomasson & Co to provide assistance with the design and implementation of the website and online sales system.

As a result of your audit review visit at the client's premises, you have learned that the audit team was invited to and subsequently attended Clean Co's annual office party. The client provided each member of the audit team with a free voucher worth $30 which could be redeemed at the venue during the party. The audit senior, Paula Metcalfe, who has worked on the audit for the last three years has informed you that the audit team has always been encouraged to attend the party in order to develop good client relations.

**Required:**

(a) (i) Discuss the policies and procedures which Thomasson & Co should have in place in relation to an anti-money laundering programme; and **(4 marks)**

(ii) Evaluate whether there are any indicators of money laundering activities by either Clean Co or its staff. **(6 marks)**

(b) Comment on the ethical and professional issues arising from your review of the audit working papers and recommend any actions which should now be taken by Thomasson & Co. **(15 marks)**

**(Total: 25 marks)**

**49 WESTON & CO**  *Walk in the footsteps of a top tutor*

 *Question debrief*

You are an audit manager in Weston & Co which is an international firm of Chartered Certified Accountants with branches in many countries and which offers a range of audit and assurance services to its clients. Your responsibilities include reviewing ethical matters which arise with audit clients, and dealing with approaches from prospective audit clients.

(a) The management of Jones Co has invited Weston & Co to submit an audit proposal (tender document) for their consideration. Jones Co was established only two years ago, but has grown rapidly, and this will be the first year that an audit is required. In previous years a limited assurance review was performed on its financial statements by an unrelated audit firm. The company specialises in the recruitment of medical personnel and some of its start-up funding was raised from a venture capital company. There are plans for the company to open branches overseas to help recruit personnel from foreign countries.

Jones Co has one full-time accountant who uses an off-the-shelf accounting package to record transactions and to prepare financial information. The company has a financial year ending 31 March 20X5.

The following comment was made by Bentley Jones, the company's founder and owner-manager, in relation to the audit proposal and potential audit fee:

'I am looking for a firm of auditors who will give me a competitive audit fee. I am hoping that the fee will be quite low, as I am willing to pay more for services that I consider more beneficial to the business, such as strategic advice. I would like the audit fee to be linked to Jones Co's success in expanding overseas as a result of the audit firm's advice. Hopefully the audit will not be too disruptive and I would like it completed within four months of the year end.'

**Required:**

(i) Explain the specific matters to be included in the audit proposal (tender document), other than those relating to the audit fee. **(8 marks)**

(ii) Assuming that Weston & Co is appointed to provide the audit service to Jones Co, discuss the issues to be considered by the audit firm in determining a fee for the audit including any ethical matters raised. **(6 marks)**

**(b)** Ordway Co is a long-standing audit client of your firm and is a listed company. Bobby Wellington has acted as audit engagement partner for seven years and understands that a new audit partner needs to be appointed to take his place. Bobby is hoping to stay in contact with the client and act as the engagement quality control reviewer in forthcoming audits of Ordway Co.

**Required:**

**Explain the ethical threats raised by the long association of senior audit personnel with an audit client and the relevant safeguards to be applied, and discuss whether Bobby Wellington can act as engagement quality control reviewer in the future audits of Ordway Co.** **(6 marks)**

**(c)** Banbury Co is a listed entity, and its audit committee has asked Weston & Co to perform an actuarial valuation on the company's defined benefit pension plan. One of the audit partners is a qualified actuary and has the necessary skills and expertise to perform the service. Banbury Co has a year ending 28 February 20X5, and the audit planning is due to commence next week. Its financial statements for the year ended 28 February 20X4, in respect of which the auditor's report was unmodified, included total assets of $35 million and a pension liability of $105,000.

**Required:**

**Identify and discuss the ethical and other professional issues raised, and recommend any actions that should be taken in respect of Banbury Co.** **(5 marks)**

**(Total: 25 marks)**

 *Calculate your allowed time, allocate the time to the separate parts...............*

**50    DRAGON GROUP**  *Walk in the footsteps of a top tutor*

**(a)** Explain the reasons why a firm of auditors may decide **NOT** to seek re-election as auditor. **(4 marks)**

The Dragon Group is a large group of companies operating in the furniture retail trade. The group has expanded rapidly in the last three years, by acquiring several subsidiaries each year. The management of the parent company, Dragon Co, a listed company, has decided to put the audit of the group and all subsidiaries out to tender, as the current audit firm is not seeking re-election. The financial year end of the Dragon Group is 30 September 20X4.

You are a senior manager in Unicorn & Co, a global firm of Chartered Certified Accountants, with offices in over 150 countries across the world. Unicorn & Co has been invited to tender for the Dragon Group audit (including the audit of all subsidiaries). You manage a department within the firm which specialises in the audit of retail companies, and you have been assigned the task of drafting the tender document. You recently held a meeting with Edmund Jalousie, the group finance director, in which you discussed the current group structure, recent acquisitions, and the group's plans for future expansion.

**Meeting notes – Dragon Group**

**Group structure**

The parent company owns 20 subsidiaries, all of which are wholly owned. Half of the subsidiaries are located in the same country as the parent, and half overseas. Most of the foreign subsidiaries report under the same financial reporting framework as Dragon Co, but several prepare financial statements using local accounting rules.

**Acquisitions during the year**

Two companies were purchased in March 20X4, both located in this country:

(i)    Mermaid Co, a company which operates 20 furniture retail outlets. The audit opinion expressed by the incumbent auditors on the financial statements for the year ended 30 September 20X3 was modified due to material misstatement as a result of non-disclosure of a contingent liability. The contingent liability relates to a court case which is still ongoing.

(ii)   Minotaur Co, a large company, whose operations are distribution and warehousing. This represents a diversification away from retail, and it is hoped that the Dragon Group will benefit from significant economies of scale as a result of the acquisition.

**Other matters**

The acquisitive strategy of the group over the last few years has led to significant growth. Group revenue has increased by 25% in the last three years, and is predicted to increase by a further 35% in the next four years as the acquisition of more subsidiaries is planned. The Dragon Group has raised finance for the acquisitions in the past by becoming listed on the stock exchanges of three different countries. A new listing on a foreign stock exchange is planned for January 20X5. For this reason, management would like the group audit completed by 31 December 20X4.

**Required:**

(b)    Recommend and describe the principal matters to be included in your firm's tender document to provide the audit service to the Dragon Group.            **(8 marks)**

(c)    Using the specific information provided, evaluate the matters that should be considered before accepting the audit engagement, in the event of your firm being successful in the tender.            **(6 marks)**

(d)    Discuss how transnational audits may differ from other audits of historical information and how this may contribute to a higher level of audit risk in relation to the audit of Dragon Group.            **(7 marks)**

            **(Total: 25 marks)**

**51   TONY GROUP**  *Walk in the footsteps of a top tutor*

**(a)**   A high-quality audit features the exercise of professional judgement by the auditor, and importantly, a mind-set which includes professional scepticism throughout the planning and performance of the audit.

**Required:**

**Explain the meaning of the term professional scepticism, and discuss its importance in planning and performing an audit.** **(6 marks)**

You are an audit manager in Soprano & Co, working on the audit of the Tony Group (the Group), whose financial year ended on 31 March 20X5. This is the first time you have worked on the Group audit. The draft consolidated financial statements recognise profit before tax of $6 million (20X4 – $9 million) and total assets of $90 million (20X4 – $82 million). The Group manufactures equipment used in the oil extraction industry.

Goodwill of $10 million is recognised in the Group statement of financial position, having arisen on several business combinations over the last few years. An impairment review was conducted in March 20X5 by Silvio Dante, the Group finance director, and this year an impairment of $50,000 is to be recognised in respect of the goodwill.

Silvio has prepared a file of documentation to support the results of the impairment review, including notes on the assumptions used, his calculations, and conclusions. When he gave you this file, Silvio made the following comment:

'I don't think you should need any evidence other than that contained in my file. The assumptions used are straightforward, so you shouldn't need to look into them in detail. The assumptions are consistent with how we conducted impairment reviews in previous years and your firm has always agreed with the assumptions used, so you can check that back to last year's audit file. All of the calculations have been checked by the head of the Group's internal audit department.'

Silvio has also informed you that two members of the sales team are suspected of paying bribes in order to secure lucrative customer contracts. The internal audit team were alerted to this when they were auditing cash payments, and found significant payments to several new customers being made prior to contracts being signed. Silvio has asked if Soprano & Co would perform a forensic investigation into the alleged bribery payments.

**Required:**

**(b)**   **(i)**   **Discuss how professional scepticism should be applied to the statement made by Silvio.** **(7 marks)**

**(ii)**   **Design the principal audit procedures to be performed on the impairment of goodwill.** **(7 marks)**

**(c)**   **Design the procedures to be used in performing a forensic investigation on the alleged bribery payments.** **(5 marks)**

**(Total: 25 marks)**

**52    SPANIEL**  *Walk in the footsteps of a top tutor*

(a)    According to ISA 240 *The Auditor's Responsibilities Relating to Fraud in an Audit of Financial Statements*:

'When identifying and assessing the risks of material misstatement due to fraud, the auditor shall, based on a presumption that there are risks of fraud in revenue recognition, evaluate which types of revenue, revenue transactions or assertions give rise to such risks.'

**Required:**

**Discuss why the auditor should presume that there are risks of fraud in revenue recognition and why ISA 240 requires specific auditor responses in relation to the risks identified.**                                                                 **(7 marks)**

(b)    You are a manager in Groom & Co, a firm of Chartered Certified Accountants. You have just attended a monthly meeting of audit partners and managers at which client-related matters were discussed. Information in relation to two clients, which were discussed at the meeting, is given below:

**Spaniel Co**

The auditor's report on the financial statements of Spaniel Co, a long-standing audit client, for the year ended 31 December 20X2 was issued in April 20X3, and was unmodified. In May 20X3, Spaniel Co's audit committee contacted the audit engagement partner to discuss a fraud that had been discovered. The company's internal auditors estimate that $4.5 million has been stolen in a payroll fraud, which has been operating since May 20X2. The audit engagement partner commented that neither tests of controls nor substantive audit procedures were conducted on payroll in the audit of the latest financial statements as in previous years' audits there were no deficiencies found in controls over payroll. The total assets recognised in Spaniel Co's financial statements at 31 December 20X2 were $80 million. Spaniel Co is considering suing Groom & Co for the total amount of cash stolen from the company, claiming that the audit firm was negligent in conducting the audit.

**Required:**

**Explain the matters that should be considered in determining whether Groom & Co is liable to Spaniel Co in respect of the fraud.**                                       **(12 marks)**

(c)    **Bulldog Co**

Bulldog Co is a clothing manufacturer, which has recently expanded its operations overseas. To manage exposure to cash flows denominated in foreign currencies, the company has set up a treasury management function, which is responsible for entering into hedge transactions such as forward exchange contracts. These transactions are likely to be material to the financial statements. The audit partner is about to commence planning the audit for the year ending 31 July 20X3.

**Required:**

**Discuss why the audit of financial instruments is particularly challenging, and explain the matters to be considered in planning the audit of Bulldog Co's forward exchange contracts.**                                                                        **(6 marks)**

**(Total: 25 marks)**

## UK SYLLABUS ONLY

**53    KRUPT**  *Walk in the footsteps of a top tutor*

Krupt Ltd is a family owned business which has been an audit client of Jansen & Co for many years and on which you have been the audit manager for the last two years. The audit for the year ended 30 June 20X8 is approaching completion and the audit supervisor has asked for your advice in relation to recent developments at the client.

Krupt Ltd is a wholesaler of electronic goods and is owned by Mr and Mrs Krupt who are both 50% shareholders and directors of the company. The company's principal source of finance is a loan from Hongclays Bank of £1.2 million which is secured by a floating charge over the company's inventory. The bank has also taken out personal guarantees on the domestic residence owned jointly by Mr and Mrs Krupt under the terms of which the bank has the right to take possession of the property in the event that it cannot recover its debts from the company.

As part of the going concern review, the audit supervisor, Jemma Jones, has scrutinised the management accounts for the first four months of the current reporting period and has identified that the company is making significant losses which she believes to be unsustainable. She has also inspected correspondence between the company and Hongclays Bank which indicates that the company has already breached key loan covenants.

Jemma has been informed by the company's procurement manager that Krupt Ltd has recently taken delivery of a large quantity of a new inventory line with a value of £0.75 million which it has purchased on credit from one of its suppliers. At present the company also has other inventory with a total value of approximately £0.5 million. Based on a review of the company's bank statements and cash flow forecasts, Jemma does not believe that there is any realistic prospect that the company will be able to pay this supplier for the foreseeable future and is concerned about the possible implications of this transaction for the directors of the company. Jemma has not come across these issues before. She has a clear sense that something is wrong and she has asked you to:

**Required:**

(i)    **Explain the concepts of fraudulent and wrongful trading and**

(ii)    **Evaluate the possible implications of the circumstances and transactions noted during the going concern review for the directors of Krupt Ltd.**            **(10 marks)**

**54 KANDINSKY**  *Walk in the footsteps of a top tutor*

Malevich & Co is a firm of Chartered Certified Accountants offering audit and assurance services to a large portfolio of clients. You are a manager in the audit department responsible for the audit of two clients, Kandinsky Ltd and Viola Ltd.

**(a)** Kandinsky Ltd is a manufacturer of luxury food items including chocolate and other confectionery which are often sold as gift items individually or in hampers containing a selection of expensive items from the range of products. The company has a financial year ended 31 July 20X5, much of the planned audit work has been completed, and you are reviewing issues which have been raised by the audit senior. Due to an economic recession sales of products have fallen sharply this year and measures have been implemented to support the company's cash flow. You are aware that the company only has £150,000 in cash at the year end.

Extracts from the draft financial statements and other relevant information are given below.

| | Note | July 20X5 (Draft) £000 | July 20X4 (Actual) £000 |
|---|---|---|---|
| Revenue | | 2,440 | 3,950 |
| Operating expenses | | (2,100) | (2,800) |
| Finance charge | | (520) | (500) |
| (Loss)/profit before tax | | (180) | 650 |
| Total assets | | 10,400 | 13,500 |
| Long-term liabilities – bank loan | 1 | 3,500 | 3,000 |
| Short-term liabilities – trade payables | 2 | 900 | 650 |
| Disclosed in notes to financial statements: | | | |
| Undrawn borrowing facilities | 3 | 500 | 1,000 |
| Contingent liability | 4 | 120 | – |

**Notes:**

1 The bank loan was extended in March 20X5 by drawing on the borrowing facilities offered by the bank. The loan carries a fixed interest rate and is secured on the company's property including the head office and manufacturing site. The first repayment of loan capital is due on 30 June 20X6 when £350,000 is due to be paid.

2 Kandinsky Ltd renegotiated its terms of trade with its main supplier of cocoa beans, and extended payment terms from 50 days to 80 days in order to improve working capital.

3 The borrowing facilities are due to be reviewed by the bank in April 20X6 and contain covenants including that interest cover is maintained at 2, and the ratio of bank loan to operating profit does not exceed 4:1.

4 The contingent liability relates to a letter of support which Kandinsky Ltd has provided to its main supplier of cane sugar which is facing difficult trading conditions.

**Required:**

**In respect of the audit of Kandinsky Ltd:**

**Identify and explain the matters which may cast significant doubt on the Kandinsky Ltd's ability to continue as a going concern, and recommend the audit procedures to be performed in relation to the going concern matters identified.** **(13 marks)**

**(b)** You are also responsible for the audit of Viola Ltd, a small engineering company located in the Midlands with a financial year ended 31 March 20X5. The auditor's report for the financial year then ended, which was issued in September 20X5, contained an Emphasis of Matter paragraph outlining the going concern issues facing the company, but was otherwise unmodified.

The finance director of Viola Ltd phoned you yesterday to discuss some recent developments at the company. His comments are shown in the note below:

'I am getting in touch to update you on our situation and to ask for your firm's advice.

As you know, in the last financial year the company lost several contracts and we had to make a number of staff redundant. In recent months further contracts have been lost and Viola Ltd has faced severe working capital problems, resulting in the sale of some of our plant in order to meet liabilities as they fall due. We are restricted on the assets which can be sold as the company's bank loan is secured by a floating charge over non-current assets. In November 20X5 the accounts recognised net liabilities of £500,000 and without securing further finance, the future of the company does not look good.

We are tendering for three new contracts to supply components to local car manufacturers. However, our bank is reluctant to extend our borrowing facilities until the contracts are secured, which may not be for another few months.

My fellow directors are becoming concerned about the possibility of our creditors applying for compulsory liquidation of the company, which we want to avoid if possible. We also wish to avoid a creditor's voluntary liquidation. Can you please advise me on the alternatives which are available given the company's precarious financial situation? I need you to explain the procedures involved with any alternatives which you can recommend, and describe the impact on the employees and directors of the company.'

**Required:**

**Respond to the instructions in the note from the finance director.** **(12 marks)**

**(Total: 25 marks)**

**55  HUNT & CO**  *Walk in the footsteps of a top tutor*

(a)  Coxon Ltd is a chain of high street stores selling books, CDs and computer games. Unfortunately, it has not been able to compete with internet sites selling the same goods at a much cheaper price, and for the last two years the company has been loss making. The company was placed into compulsory liquidation last week due to being unable to pay its debts as they fall due.

The finance director, James Corgan, has contacted your firm, Hunt & Co, seeking advice on several issues to do with the liquidation. His comments are shown in the note below:

'We had thought for some time that the company was in financial difficulties, having lost market share to competitors, but we hoped to turn the company around. Things came to a head in January 20X4 when the accounts showed a net liabilities position for the first time, and several loan covenants had been breached. However, we decided to continue to trade in order to maximise cash inflows, keep staff employed for a few months longer, and try to negotiate finance from new providers. During this period we continued to order goods from several suppliers. However, the cash position deteriorated and in May 20X4 creditors applied to the court for the compulsory winding up of the company. The court has appointed liquidators who are about to commence the winding up.

As you can imagine, myself and the other directors are very worried about the situation. We have heard that we may be personally liable for some of the company's debts. Is this correct, and what are the potential consequences for us? Also, can you explain the impact of the compulsory liquidation process for our employees and for creditors?'

**Required:**

**Respond to the instructions in the note from the finance director.**       **(12 marks)**

(b)  Hunt & Co also audits Jay Ltd, a company with a year ended 30 September. The auditor's report for the year ended 30 September 20X3 was issued in December 20X3 and was unmodified. Jay Ltd operates two separate divisions both of which manufacture food supplements – 'Jay Sport' manufactures food supplements targeted at athletes, and 'Jay Plus' is targeted at the general public.

One of the key ingredients used in the 'Jay Sport' range has been found to have harmful side effects, so very few sales from that range have been made in the current financial year. The company is struggling to manage its working capital and meet interest payments on loans.

The directors are anxious about the future of the company and the audit engagement partner, Bill Kingfisher, has been asked to attend a meeting with them tomorrow to discuss their concerns over the financial performance and position of Jay Ltd.

**Attachment: Extract from Jay Ltd's management accounts at 31 May 20X4 (unaudited)**

**Statement of financial position**

| | £000 |
|---|---|
| Property, plant and equipment | 12,800 |
| Inventory | 500 |
| Trade receivables | 400 |
| Cash | 0 |
| | _____ |
| Total assets | 13,700 |
| | _____ |
| Share capital | 100 |
| Retained earnings | (1,050) |
| Long-term borrowings (secured with a fixed charge over property, plant and equipment) | 12,000 |
| Trade payables (including employees' wages of £300,000) | 1,250 |
| Bank overdraft | 1,400 |
| | _____ |
| Total equity and liabilities | 13,700 |
| | _____ |

**Statement of profit or loss (extract)**

| | Jay Sport | Jay Plus | Total |
|---|---|---|---|
| | £000 | £000 | £000 |
| Revenue | 50 | 1,450 | 1,500 |
| Operating costs | (800) | (1,200) | (2,000) |
| | ____ | ____ | ____ |
| Operating loss/profit | (750) | 250 | (500) |
| Finance costs | | | (800) |
| | | | ____ |
| Loss before tax | | | (1,300) |
| | | | ____ |

**Required:**

(i)     Examine the financial position of Jay Ltd and determine whether the company is insolvent.                                                                      (4 marks)

(ii)    Evaluate, reaching a recommendation, the options available to the directors in terms of the future of the company.                                    (9 marks)

(Total: 25 marks)

## 56  BUTLER (A)   *Walk in the footsteps of a top tutor*

Butler Ltd is a new audit client of your firm. You are the manager responsible for the audit of the financial statements for the year ended 31 May 20X1. Audit work is due to commence this week. Butler Ltd designs and manufactures aircraft engines and spare parts, and is a subsidiary of a multi-national group. The future of the company is uncertain, as against a background of economic recession, sales have been declining, several significant customer contracts have been cancelled unexpectedly, and competition from overseas has damaged the market share previously enjoyed by Butler Ltd. The management of Butler Ltd is concerned that given the company's poor liquidity position, the company could be placed into compulsory liquidation. Management have prepared a cash flow forecast for the first three months of the next financial year, and are currently preparing the forecasts for the whole 12 month period.

Extracts from the draft financial statements are shown below:

| Statement of financial position | 31 May 20X1 | 31 May 20X0 |
|---|---|---|
| | *Draft* | *Actual* |
| **Assets** | £ million | £ million |
| Non-current assets | | |
| Intangible assets (note 1) | 200 | 180 |
| Property, plant and equipment (note 2) | 1,300 | 1,200 |
| Deferred tax asset (note 3) | 235 | 20 |
| Financial assets | 25 | 35 |
| | 1,760 | 1,435 |
| Current assets | | |
| Inventory | 1,300 | 800 |
| Trade receivables | 2,100 | 1,860 |
| | 3,400 | 2,660 |
| **Total assets** | 5,160 | 4,095 |
| **Equity and liabilities** | | |
| Equity | | |
| Share capital | 300 | 300 |
| Retained earnings | (525) | 95 |
| | (225) | 395 |
| Non-current liabilities | | |
| Long-term borrowings (note 4) | 1,900 | 1,350 |
| Provisions (note 5) | 185 | 150 |
| | 2,085 | 1,500 |

| | | |
|---|---|---|
| Current liabilities | | |
| Short-term borrowings (note 6) | 800 | 400 |
| Trade payables | 2,500 | 1,800 |
| | 3,300 | 2,200 |
| Total equity and liabilities | 5,160 | 4,095 |

**Notes to the statement of financial position:**

Note 1    Intangible assets comprise goodwill on the acquisition of subsidiaries (£80 million), and development costs capitalised on engine development projects (£120 million).

Note 2    Property, plant and equipment includes land and buildings valued at £25 million, over which a fixed charge exists.

Note 3    The deferred tax asset has arisen following several loss-making years suffered by the company. The asset represents the tax benefit of unutilised tax losses carried forward.

Note 4    Long-term borrowings include a debenture due for repayment in July 20X2, and a loan from Butler Ltd's parent company due for repayment in December 20X2.

Note 5    Provisions relate to warranties provided to customers.

Note 6    Short-term borrowings comprise an overdraft (£25 million), a short-term loan (£60 million) due for repayment in August 20X1, and a bank loan (£715 million) repayable in September 20X1.

**Attachment: Cash flow forecast for the three months to 31 August 20X1**

| | June 20X1 £ million | July 20X1 £ million | August 20X1 £ million |
|---|---|---|---|
| **Cash inflows** | | | |
| Cash receipts from customers (note 1) | 175 | 195 | 220 |
| Loan receipt (note 2) | | 150 | |
| Government subsidy (note 3) | | | 50 |
| Sales of financial assets | 50 | | |
| **Total cash inflows** | 225 | 345 | 270 |
| **Cash outflows** | | | |
| Operating cash outflows | 200 | 200 | 290 |
| Interest payments | 40 | 40 | 40 |
| Loan repayment | | | 60 |
| **Total cash outflows** | 240 | 240 | 390 |
| **Net cash flow for the month** | (15) | 105 | (120) |
| Opening cash | (25) | (40) | 65 |
| Closing cash | (40) | 65 | (55) |

**Notes to the cash flow forecast:**

This cash flow forecast has been prepared by the management of Butler Ltd, and is based on the following assumptions:

1    Cash receipts from customers should accelerate given the anticipated improvement in economic conditions. In addition, the company has committed extra resources to the credit control function, in order to speed up collection of overdue debts.

2    The loan expected to be received in July 20X1 is currently being negotiated with our parent company, Rubery Ltd.

3    The government subsidy will be received once our application has been approved. The subsidy is awarded to companies which operate in areas of high unemployment and it subsidises the wages and salaries paid to staff.

**Required:**

(a)    **Identify and explain any matters arising from your review of the draft statement of financial position, and the cash flow forecast, which may cast significant doubt on the company's ability to continue as a going concern.**    **(10 marks)**

(b)    **Recommend the principal audit procedures to be carried out on the cash flow forecast.**    **(8 marks)**

(c)    (i)    **Explain the procedures involved in placing a company into compulsory liquidation.**    **(4 marks)**

        (ii)    **Explain the consequences of a compulsory liquidation for Butler Ltd's payables (creditors), employees and shareholders.**    **(3 marks)**

**(Total: 25 marks)**

# INT SYLLABUS ONLY

## 57    KANDINSKY     *Walk in the footsteps of a top tutor*

Malevich & Co is a firm of Chartered Certified Accountants offering audit and assurance services to a large portfolio of clients. You are a manager in the audit department responsible for the audit of two clients, Kandinsky Co and the Rothko University, both of which have a financial year ended 31 July 20X5. The audits of both clients are being completed and you are reviewing issues which have been raised by the audit seniors.

(a)    Kandinsky Co is a manufacturer of luxury food items including chocolate and other confectionery which are often sold as gift items individually or in hampers containing a selection of expensive items from the range of products. Due to an economic recession sales of products have fallen sharply this year and measures have been implemented to support the company's cash flow. You are aware that the company only has $150,000 in cash at the year end.

Extracts from the draft financial statements and other relevant information are given below.

| | Note | July 20X5 (Draft) $000 | July 20X4 (Actual) $000 |
|---|---|---|---|
| Revenue | | 2,440 | 3,950 |
| Operating expenses | | (2,100) | (2,800) |
| Finance charge | | (520) | (500) |
| | | ——— | ——— |
| (Loss)/profit before tax | | (180) | 650 |
| | | ——— | ——— |
| Total assets | | 10,400 | 13,500 |
| Long-term liabilities – bank loan | 1 | 3,500 | 3,000 |
| Short-term liabilities – trade payables | 2 | 900 | 650 |
| Disclosed in notes to financial statements: | | | |
| Undrawn borrowing facilities | 3 | 500 | 1,000 |
| Contingent liability | 4 | 120 | – |

**Notes:**

1  The bank loan was extended in March 20X5 by drawing on the borrowing facilities offered by the bank. The loan carries a fixed interest rate and is secured on the company's property including the head office and manufacturing site. The first repayment of loan capital is due on 30 June 20X6 when $350,000 is due to be paid.

2  Kandinsky Co renegotiated its terms of trade with its main supplier of cocoa beans, and extended payment terms from 50 days to 80 days in order to improve working capital.

3  The borrowing facilities are due to be reviewed by the bank in April 20X6 and contain covenants including that interest cover is maintained at 2, and the ratio of bank loan to operating profit does not exceed 4:1.

4  The contingent liability relates to a letter of support which Kandinsky Co has provided to its main supplier of cane sugar which is facing difficult trading conditions.

**Required:**

**In respect of the audit of Kandinsky Co:**

(i)  **Identify and explain the matters which may cast significant doubt on the company's ability to continue as a going concern.**　　**(9 marks)**

(ii)  **Recommend the audit procedures to be performed in relation to the going concern matters identified.**　　**(6 marks)**

**(b)** The Rothko University, a public sector entity, is a small university with approximately 2,000 students, which was established 10 years ago and specialises in vocational study programmes leading to the award of degrees in business, accountancy, finance, law and marketing. The highest performing students achieve a distinction on completing their degree programme, indicating excellence in the knowledge and understanding of their subject. Students pay tuition fees of $10,000 per year, and the degree programme is typically three years long.

The audit work in respect of the year ended 31 July 20X5 is almost complete, but the audit senior has not yet completed the audit work in respect of performance information which is being published with the annual financial statements for the first time this year. It is a requirement in the jurisdiction in which the Rothko University is located that the performance information is audited as part of the external audit.

Details on the performance information are given below:

| Performance area | Performance measure | 20X5 result |
|---|---|---|
| Graduation rate | % of students who complete their degree programme | 85% |
| Academic performance | % of students achieving a distinction | 20% |
| Employability | % of students who on graduation obtain graduate level employment | 65% |
| Course satisfaction | % of students who rate their university experience as excellent or very good | 70% |

**Required:**

**(i)** Discuss the relevance and measurability of the reported performance information.

**(ii)** Recommend the examination procedures to be used in auditing the performance information.

**Note: The total marks will be split equally between each part.** (10 marks)

(Total: 25 marks)

**THE FOLLOWING QUESTION IS NOT EXAM STANDARD BUT HAS BEEN INCLUDED TO PROVIDE VALUABLE QUESTION PRACTICE.**

**58** **PUBLIC SECTOR ORGANISATIONS**  *Walk in the footsteps of a top tutor*

(a) Define the terms 'performance audit' and 'performance information'. (2 marks)

(b) Suggest performance targets that could be measured for each of the following public sector organisations:

    (i) Local police department (3 marks)

    (ii) Local hospital (3 marks)

    (iii) Local council. (3 marks)

(c) Identify the stakeholder groups which might rely on the performance information produced by the public sector organisations in part (b) and explain how they could use such information. (9 marks)

(d) Explain the difficulties encountered by auditors when auditing performance information. (5 marks)

(Total: 25 marks)

# Section 3

# ANSWERS TO PRACTICE QUESTIONS – SECTION A

1    RYDER GROUP   *Walk in the footsteps of a top tutor*

**Top tutor tips**

Part (a) asks you to evaluate the audit risks to be considered when planning the audit. Audit risk comprises the risk that the financial statements contain material misstatement and detection risk. Risk of material misstatement is usually due to non-compliance with an accounting standard, although it also includes control risk. Think about the requirements of the relevant accounting standards and what the client might be doing incorrectly. Detection risks include auditing a client for the first time or where there is a tight reporting deadline. The requirement specifically instructs you to consider risks relating to disclosure, therefore make sure you include these.

Part (b) asks for additional information to effectively audit the disposal of a subsidiary. Think about how the disposal should be accounted for and therefore what information you will need to confirm the client has accounted for it in accordance with the applicable financial reporting framework.

Part (c) asks for audit procedures in respect of the investment in Peppers Co and the government grant. The procedures should enable the auditor to obtain evidence to determine whether the relevant financial reporting standard has been complied with. Make sure your procedures are clear and provide enough detail that they can be easily followed by the audit team.

Part (d) covers ethical considerations of providing a listed audit client with additional services such as providing a partner to sit on the audit committee and designing internal controls over the revenue system. In addition, the ethical considerations of referring a client to another firm in return for a referral fee need to be discussed. For each issue, explain the ethical threat arising and state the actions the firm should take to manage or eliminate the threats. Where possible, discuss the significance of the threat.

**Briefing notes**

To: **Mo Iqbal, audit engagement partner**

From: **Audit manager**

Subject: **Audit planning in relation to the Ryder Group Introduction**

These briefing notes have been prepared to assist in planning the audit of the Ryder Group (the Group). The notes begin with an evaluation of the audit risks which should be considered in planning the audit. The notes then identify and explain the additional information required to plan the audit of a significant disposal which is expected to take place shortly after the financial year end. The notes also include the recommended principal audit procedures which have been designed in respect of an investment made in a joint arrangement and a government grant received in the year. Finally, the notes discuss several ethical matters arising from requests made by the Group audit committee.

**(a)   Evaluation of significant audit risks**

**Planned disposal of Primal Burgers Co and acquisition of Valentine Co – events after the reporting date**

The Group is planning a significant restructuring. The disposal of Primal Burgers Co is planned to take place shortly after the year end, and the disposal will have a material impact on the Group financial statements given that Primal Burgers Co accounts for 23.2% of projected Group total assets and 30.9% of projected Group revenue.

The acquisition of Valentine Co, which is planned to take place in the first quarter of the next financial year, will be material to the Group, with the anticipated cost of investment and the fair value of identifiable net assets of Valentine Co representing 21.1% and 17.9% of projected Group assets respectively.

Both events will fall under the scope of IAS® 10 *Events after the Reporting Period*, meeting the definition of a non-adjusting event. IAS 10 requires that non-adjusting events should be disclosed if they are of such importance that non-disclosure would affect the ability of users to make proper evaluations and decisions. The required disclosure is the nature of the event and an estimate of its financial effect or a statement that a reasonable estimate of the effect cannot be made. The audit risk is that incomplete or inaccurate disclosure relating to the acquisition and disposal is provided in the notes to the financial statements.

**Disposal of Primal Burgers Co – assets held for sale and discontinued operations**

The planned disposal should be accounted for under IFRS® 5 *Non-current Assets Held for Sale and Discontinued Operations*, which requires that once certain conditions are met, a disposal group of assets should be classified as held for sale. The conditions include:

- management is committed to a plan to sell

- the asset is available for immediate sale

- an active programme to locate a buyer is initiated

- the sale is highly probable, within 12 months of classification as held for sale

- the asset is being actively marketed for sale at a sales price reasonable in relation to its fair value

- actions required to complete the plan indicate that it is unlikely that plan will be significantly changed or withdrawn.

Assuming that the conditions are met, which seems likely given that the board approved the sale in March 20X5 and that potential purchasers have already expressed an interest, the assets held in the disposal group should be reclassified as assets held for sale and measured at the lower of carrying amount and fair value less costs to sell. The assets should not be depreciated after reclassification. IFRS 5 also requires that immediately prior to classifying an asset or disposal group as held for sale, impairment is measured and recognised in accordance with the applicable IFRS Standards, which in this case would be IAS 16 *Property, Plant and Equipment* and IAS 36 *Impairment of Assets.*

Several audit risks arise as a result of the disposal. First there is a risk that the assets are not treated as a disposal group for the purpose of IFRS 5 and have continued to be depreciated. Assets are possibly overvalued if an impairment review has not been performed or assets not measured at the lower of carrying amount and fair value less costs to sell. The fact that Primal Burgers Co's revenue is projected to fall by 3.9% indicates that impairment of assets could be an issue, increasing the risk of misstatement.

There is also a risk relating to disclosure, as assets and liabilities held for sale should be recognised separately from other assets and liabilities in the statement of financial position, and if they have not been appropriately reclassified, then non-current assets and liabilities will be overstated.

There is also an audit risk that Primal Burgers Co is not treated as a discontinued operation in accordance with IFRS 5. A discontinued operation is defined as a component of an entity which either has been disposed of or is classified as held for sale, and represents a separate major line of business or a geographical area of operations and is part of a single co-ordinated plan to dispose of a separate major line of business or geographical area of operations.

Given the materiality of Primal Burgers Co and its products being a separate line of business for the Group, it meets the definition of a discontinued operation. In accordance with IFRS 5, the post-tax profit or loss of the discontinued operation and the post-tax gain or loss recognised on the measurement to fair value less cost to sell or on the disposal of the disposal group should be presented as a single amount on the face of the statement of comprehensive income.

In addition, detailed disclosure of revenue, expenses, pre-tax profit or loss and related income taxes is required either in the notes or in the statement of comprehensive income in a section distinct from continuing operations. The risk is that the necessary disclosures are not made, leading to incorrect presentation of Group profit or loss and incomplete information in the notes to the Group financial statements.

**Disposal of Primal Burgers Co – potential for manipulation**

A further audit risk relating to the disposal of Primal Burgers Co is that the results of the subsidiary could be manipulated to make it look more favourable to any potential purchaser. The financial information indicates that this subsidiary's revenue has declined and therefore it could be that management attempts to manipulate the financial statements to present a healthier financial performance to potential buyers. For example, costs could be suppressed or shifted to other Group companies to maintain the profit of Primal Burgers Co and make it more attractive to purchasers.

*Tutorial note*

*Credit will be awarded for the evaluation of other relevant audit risks relating to the disposal, for example, in relation to the presentation of information in the Group statement of cash flows.*

### Investment in Peppers Co

The Group will be investing $48 million in Peppers Co; this represents 10.1% of projected Group assets and therefore is material to the Group financial statements.

From the information provided, it seems that the investment is a joint venture, with control of Peppers Co shared between the Group and Smiths Co. IFRS 11 *Joint Arrangements* defines a joint venture as a joint arrangement whereby the parties who have joint control of the arrangement have rights to the net assets of the arrangement.

IFRS 11 requires that a joint venturer recognises its interest in a joint venture as an investment and shall account for that investment using the equity method in accordance with IAS 28 *Investments in Associates and Joint Ventures*. Audit risk arises if the Group fails to apply equity accounting to the investment, which may lead to an under or overstated value of investment and incorrect presentation of income and expenses relating to the joint venture in the Group statement of profit or loss.

### Mondays Coffee drive-through – capital expenditure

During the year, there has been significant capital expenditure relating to 50 new drive-through coffee shops. The total amount capitalised is $43 million, of which $15 million relates to acquiring operating licences. The audit risk relates to the classification of the licences within property, plant and equipment, they should instead be recognised as intangible assets.

This error is material, with the $15 million cost of the licences representing 3.2% of projected Group assets. If the error is uncorrected, property, plant and equipment is overstated and intangible assets are understated.

A consequence of the misclassification is that the $15 million should be amortised over its specific useful life of three years, so assuming that a full year's worth of amortisation should have been expensed, this amounts to $5 million. Currently, the amount has been treated as property, plant and equipment and depreciated over a 20-year life, so $0.75 million has been expensed. Therefore expenses are understated by $4.25 million. This is material, representing 21.3% of Group profit before tax. There is therefore an audit risk that Group profit is significantly overstated.

*Tutorial note*

*Credit will be awarded for the evaluation of other relevant audit risks, for example, including the risk that revenue and capital expenditure incurred in establishing the coffee shops is not appropriately recognised, and that a 20-year estimated life appears long given the nature and usage of the assets involved.*

### Mondays Coffee drive-through – reportable operating segment

According to the Group finance director, revenue from the new drive-through coffee shops accounts for almost all of the increase in revenue from Mondays Coffee Co. The financial information shows that Mondays Coffee Co revenue is projected to increase by $45 million this year. Total Group revenue is projected to be $320 million; $45 million is 14.1% of this total.

The revenue from the drive-through coffee shops could be a reportable operating segment under IFRS 8 *Operating Segments*. An operating segment is a component of an entity:

- which engages in business activities from which it may earn revenues and incur expenses

- whose operating results are reviewed regularly by the entity's chief operating decision maker to make decisions about resources to be allocated to the segment and assess its performance, and

- for which discrete financial information is available.

IFRS 8 requires an entity to report financial and descriptive information about its reportable segments. Reportable segments are operating segments or aggregations of operating segments which meet specified criteria, including that its reported revenue is 10% or more of the combined revenue of all operating segments.

It seems that the drive-through coffee shops should be treated as a reportable segment given that discrete information is available through the Group's management information system, the results are reviewed, and it generates more than 10% of Group revenue. The audit risk is that disclosure is not provided at all in relation to this reportable segment, or that disclosure is incomplete in the final version of the financial statements.

***Tutorial note***

*Credit will also be awarded for evaluation of the significance of the increase in revenue from the new drive-through coffee shops, and whether this could indicate overstatement of revenue. Other relevant audit risks will be credited, for example, relating to possible system changes introduced to incorporate the drive-through coffee shops in the financial reporting system.*

### Government grant

The Group received a government grant of $20 million, representing 4.2% of projected Group assets and therefore material to the Group statement of financial position. In addition, if the $20 million grant receipt had not been recognised in full as income this financial year, the projected Group profit before tax would be $0. The recognition as income is therefore extremely significant to the Group financial statements.

The grant should be accounted for in accordance with IAS 20 *Accounting for Government Grants and Disclosure of Government Assistance* which requires government grants to be recognised in profit or loss on a systematic basis over the periods in which the entity recognises as expenses the related costs for which the grants are intended to compensate.

The two parts of the grant should be accounted for separately. The amount relating to capital expenditure should be deferred on the statement of financial position and assuming that the grant will be used to upgrade items of property, plant and equipment, the grant should then be recognised in profit or loss over the periods in which depreciation expense on the assets to which it relates is recognised. The part of the grant relating to promotional activity should be recognised in profit or loss in the same period as the relevant expenses – which may be this year, or could be the next financial year, depending on when the expenses relating to the advertising campaign are incurred.

It is likely that if funds are not used in the manner intended by the government, i.e. that half of it is used to make the assets more environmentally friendly, then some or all of the grant would be repayable. This would mean that a provision or contingent liability should be recognised, and there is an audit risk that liabilities are understated if any amount probable to be repaid is not accounted for as a provision, or that insufficient disclosure is made in the note to the financial statements if a contingent liability arises.

Therefore the audit risk is that Group profit is overstated by a maximum amount of $20 million, and liabilities understated by the same amount. The accounting treatment could be a deliberate attempt to enhance the appearance of the Group profit for the year, and this issue should be approached with a high degree of professional scepticism during the audit.

### Audit committee lack of financial reporting expert

Since January 20X5, the Group audit committee does not have a financial reporting expert. It is a requirement of best practice corporate governance principles that the board should satisfy itself that at least one member of the audit committee has recent and relevant financial experience and that the committee as a whole shall have competence relevant to the sector in which the Group operates. The Group is in breach of this principle, as there has not been a financial reporting expert member of the audit committee for a significant period during the financial year, and this represents a control risk.

One of the roles of the audit committee is to monitor the integrity of the financial statements of the Group and, in particular, to review significant financial reporting judgements contained in them. Without a financial reporting expert on the audit committee to provide this oversight, there is a risk that inappropriate judgements are made and a higher risk that errors or deliberate manipulation of the financial statements are not addressed.

**(b)** **Additional information required to plan the audit of the disposal of Primal Burgers Co**

- The individual financial statements of Primal Burgers Co, to ascertain the detail of the amounts recognised – this will assist the audit team in planning to audit the compliance with measurement and disclosure requirements of IFRS 5 and to confirm materiality of the balances involved.

- A copy of the vendor's due diligence report produced by Usami & Co, to ascertain key findings, e.g. valuations of assets and liabilities; this will help in planning to audit the measurement of the disposal group and whether any impairment should be recognised.

- Further information surrounding the reasons for disposal, from the Group board minutes at which approval was given for the disposal, to enable the auditor to develop an understanding of management's rationale and how the disposal fits in with the Group restructuring as a whole.

- Information regarding the potential acquirers of Primal Burgers Co and the stage of negotiations, this will help the audit team develop an expectation as to whether the disposal is likely to take place after the year end and the potential sales price.

- Any preliminary determination by management of the anticipated profit or loss on disposal and expectation of any impairment to the value of assets held in the disposal group.

- Obtain a copy of management's assessment/workings of the impact on the Group's financial position on the sale of Primal Burgers Co and the overall impact of the restructure of the Group.

(c) (i) **Principal audit procedures in respect of the classification of the investment in Peppers Co**

- Obtain the legal documentation supporting the investment and agree the details of the investment including:

    - The date of the investment

    - Amount paid

    - Number of shares purchased

    - The voting rights attached to the shares

    - The nature of the profit sharing arrangement between the Group and Smiths Co

    - The nature of access to Peppers Co's assets under the terms of the agreement

    - Confirmation that there is no restriction of the Group's shared control of Peppers Co.

- Review board minutes to confirm the approval of the investment and to understand the business rationale for the investment.

- Review minutes of relevant meetings between the Group and Smiths Co to confirm that control is shared between the two investors and to understand the nature of the relationship and the decision-making process.

- Obtain documentation such as Peppers Co's organisational structure to confirm that the Group has successfully appointed members to the board of the company and that those members have equal power to the members appointed by Smiths Co.

(ii) **Principal audit procedures in respect of the government grant received**

- Obtain the documentation relating to the grant and review to obtain an understanding of:

    - The terms of the grant including the amount received, and in particular requirements relating to the specific use of the funds

-   The date by which the funds must be used

-   Any clauses relating to repayment of some or all of the grant should certain conditions arise.

-   Agree the amount received to bank statements and Ryder Co's cash book.

-   Obtain and review the Group's capital expenditure forecast to confirm the amount planned to be spent on capital expenditure relating to environmental matters.

-   Discuss the use of the grant to fund an advertising campaign with an appropriate person, e.g. Group marketing director, and review any plans to use the funds for promotional purposes to confirm that recycling features in the campaign, as intended by the government.

-   Confirm, through agreement to marketing plans, whether any funds will be spent during this financial year.

-   Obtain a written representation from management that the grant received will be used for the specific purposes required by the government.

**(d) Ethical issues**

**Partner to serve on audit committee**

The Group audit committee has requested that a senior partner from Squire & Co could assume a role on the Group audit committee while a replacement for the financial reporting expert committee member is being sought. Should a partner from Squire & Co take this appointment, a self-review threat to objectivity arises because an audit committee member is in a position to exert influence over the financial statements, and the audit team would be less likely to challenge issues during the audit, thereby losing their professional scepticism.

A self-interest threat also arises because the audit firm's interests become closely aligned to the interests of the Group, impacting on auditor objectivity.

*Tutorial note*

*Credit will also be awarded for discussion of other relevant threats to objectivity including the familiarity threat, and threat of assuming management responsibility.*

For these reasons, the *IESBA International Code of Ethics for Professional Accountants (the Code)* states that a partner or an employee of the audit firm shall not serve as a director or officer of an audit client. Therefore, Squire & Co cannot provide a senior partner, or any other member of staff, to serve on the Group's audit committee.

**Referral fee**

The Group audit committee understands that Squire & Co cannot provide a corporate finance service, but could recommend another firm, Ranger Associates, for this work, for which the firm would earn a referral fee. The Code states that this creates a self-interest threat to objectivity and to professional competence and due care.

The self-interest threat arises from the income generated from the referral, and this may result in the audit firm recommending another firm for the work without proper consideration of their competence to perform the engagement.

The *Code* does not prohibit referral fees but the significance of the threats should be evaluated and safeguards applied to reduce the threats to an acceptable level. Safeguards may include:

- Disclosing to the Group in writing the arrangement for a referral fee to be received from Ranger Associates, and

- Obtaining advance agreement from the Group that the arrangement is acceptable.

Therefore the matter should be discussed again with the Group audit committee, and if the committee confirms agreement with the proposed referral fee, Squire & Co can recommend Ranger Associates to perform the corporate finance work for the Group.

### Internal audit

A further threat arises from the audit committee's request for Squire & Co to work with the Group internal audit team to design and evaluate internal controls relating to revenue. The Code suggests that providing an audit client with an internal audit service might create a self-review threat to objectivity. This is because in subsequent audits the audit team may use the internal audit work performed in their audit of revenue. They may over-rely on the internal controls designed and evaluated by the audit firm or will not apply an appropriate level of scepticism when assessing the work.

In addition, a threat of management responsibility arises, whereby the audit firm is making decisions and using judgement which is properly the responsibility of management. The Code states that taking responsibility for designing, implementing, monitoring and maintaining internal control is assuming management responsibility.

According to the Code, an audit firm must not assume management responsibility for an audit client because the threat to independence created is so significant that no safeguards could reduce it to an acceptable level.

Specifically in relation to public interest entities, the Code further states that an audit firm shall not provide internal audit services which relate to a significant part of controls over financial reporting, financial accounting systems which are significant to the financial statements or amounts or disclosures which are material to the financial statements.

Therefore, Squire & Co should politely decline the request made by the audit committee and ensure that the committee is fully aware of the ethical issues raised by their requests.

### Conclusion

These briefing notes indicate that there is a range of audit risks to be considered in planning the forthcoming Group audit, many of the more significant risks relate to the Group's plans to restructure. The notes contain recommended audit procedures which have been designed in relation to two material audit issues, and finally three ethical issues have been identified and evaluated. Our firm should not provide internal audit assistance to the Group, nor allow a partner to serve on the Group audit committee. However, a referral fee from Ranger Associates is acceptable, provided the Group agrees to the arrangement.

## Examiner's comments

This question was set at the planning stage of the audit for an existing client. The scenario revolved around a long established group of companies audited by the same audit firm. The group was undergoing restructuring with several proposed changes to group structure some of which would not occur until after the year end.

There are four professional marks available in Question One:

- 1 mark for a suitable heading
- 1 mark for an introduction – this need be no more than a short introductory paragraph
- 1 mark for the structure of the answer, including the use of headings and paragraphs
- 1 mark for the clarity of the candidate's explanation

Candidates should refer to published answers for section A questions to understand how to present a suitable heading.

Part (a) required candidates to describe audit risks arising in relation to the group audit and was similar to the requirements seen in many past questions. Candidates generally appeared well prepared for this question and were able to identify several audit risks and evaluate them in such a way as to obtain a pass mark. When evaluating risks, candidates are advised to always bring in specific references to the scenario, give the details of the accounting treatment required where possible and the financial statement implications arising as a result of the audit risk. Candidates should ensure they provide an appropriate calculation of materiality and a conclusion as to whether an item is material or not material. Both of these are required for credit to be awarded.

Common issues arising on this requirement were as follows:

- Candidates giving rote-learnt risks with no application to the scenario, for example stating that this was a new client (it was an existing client) or that a significant risk to a listed company is management bias without referring to any specific bias drivers from the scenario (e.g. to prove the success of a restructuring strategy, to maximise the sales price for a subsidiary being disposed of) or demonstrating where the bias might impact on the financial statements (e.g. the incorrect recognition of the grant received in profit or the under amortisation of a three-year licence). Candidates must relate the audit risks to the information provided which will be different in every examination.

- Candidates describing audit risks that were highly unlikely to be a genuine risk – for example many candidates thought there was an audit risk that an acquisition planned for next year might be included in this year's consolidation in error or that a disposal the group were hoping to make post year end required the company to entirely remove the assets and liabilities from the consolidated financial statements and replace it with the profit on disposal.

- Candidates not fully understanding the basic concepts of control or influence in the context of group accounts, for example stating that a 50% shareholding means a company must be a subsidiary. While a shareholding over 50% might be indicative that control exists or a shareholding in the region 20-50% may indicate influence exists, the principles underlying financial reporting are based on substance not just strict percentage rules.

Part (b) was a four-mark requirement regarding additional information required to plan the audit of a disposal. This was well answered by candidates who appreciated that this did not relate to the final audit procedures but information that could be requested in advance.

Part (c) required audit procedures regarding a government grant and the classification of an investment in a joint venture. Generally, this requirement was well answered although common errors with the requirement regarding the joint venture were to cover a wider scope than classification or instead to give procedures for a totally different transaction from the scenario (e.g. a common incorrect answer was to list procedures relating to the audit of the PPE investment in a different group company). These errors arose from a lack of attention to the specific requirement.

Part (d) was a ten-mark ethics requirement and candidates' answers tended to be weak here. Many candidates simply listed the names of ethical threats without any application to the specific scenario. This is disappointing given the specific guidance published on the ACCA website as to what is required in terms of description for credit to be awarded in this area. Here candidates demonstrated that they had learned a list of threats but failed to demonstrate that they understood them or knew how they applied to a question. This was particularly apparent with regard to the request that an audit partner take a temporary position on the audit committee. Many candidates said this was a self-interest threat however they described it as arising because the partner would be paid a fee rather than because the partner would then be involved in the choice of audit firm and setting of the audit fee. Candidates also demonstrated insufficient detailed knowledge of the IESBA International Code of Ethics for Professional Accountants. Candidates often incorrectly stated that referral fees are not permitted, but recommended the use of a separate team to devise and test controls over revenue as an internal audit assignment which, for a listed company, is prohibited as revenues are a material component of the financial statements.

| ACCA marking guide | | Marks |
|---|---|---|
| **(a)** | **Evaluation of audit risks** Up to 3 marks for each audit risk evaluated unless otherwise indicated. Marks may be awarded for other, relevant risks not included in the marking guide. In addition, ½ mark for each relevant trend or calculation which forms part of the audit risk evaluation (max 3 marks). Materiality calculations should be awarded 1 mark each (max 4 marks). <br>• Disclosure of events after the reporting period in respect of Group restructuring – risk of inadequate disclosure <br>• Assets held for sale in respect of planned disposal of Primal Burgers Co – risk assets not measured or recognised appropriately as assets held for sale (up to 4 marks) <br>• Discontinued operation – risk that Group statement of profit or loss does not reflect results of Primal Burgers Co as a discontinued operation <br>• Disposal of Primal Burgers Co – incentive for manipulation (2 marks) <br>• Joint arrangement in Peppers Co – risk that the investment is not equity accounted <br>• Misclassification of operating licence in respect of Mondays Coffee Co drive-throughs as PPE, impact on measurement of PPE and intangible assets and associated expenses <br>• Mondays Coffee Co drive-throughs likely to be a reportable segment – risk of incomplete disclosure of operating segments <br>• Government grant – risk that conditions will not be met and a liability should be recognised for repayment of the grant <br>• Audit committee – lack of financial reporting expert creates control risk (2 marks) | |
| | **Maximum** | **24** |

**(b)**    **Additional information required to plan the audit of the planned disposal of Primal Burgers Co**

Up to 1 mark for each piece of additional information recommended:

- The financial statements of Primal Burgers Co, to ascertain the detail of the amounts recognised
- A copy of the vendor's due diligence report to ascertain key findings, e.g. valuations of assets and liabilities
- Information surrounding the reasons for disposal, from the Group board minutes at which approval was given for the disposal
- Information regarding the potential acquirers of Primal Burgers Co and the stage of negotiations
- Any preliminary determination by management of the anticipated profit or loss on disposal and expectation of any impairment to the value of assets held in the disposal group
- Obtain a copy of management's assessment/workings of the impact on the Group's financial position on the sale of Primal Burgers Co and the overall impact of the restructure of the Group

|  | Maximum | 4 |

**(c)**    **Principal audit procedures**

Up to 1 mark for each well designed audit procedure.

**(i)    The 50% investment in Peppers Co**

- Obtain the legal documentation supporting the investment and agree the details of the investment including (max 2 marks):
  - The date of the investment
  - Amount paid
  - Number of shares purchased
  - The voting rights attached to the shares
  - The nature of the profit sharing arrangement between the Group and Smiths Co
  - The nature of access to Peppers Co's assets under the terms of the agreement
  - Confirmation that there is no restriction of the Group's shared control of Peppers Co
- Review board minutes to confirm the approval of the investment and to understand the business rationale for the investment
- Review minutes of relevant meetings between the Group and Smiths Co to confirm that control is shared between the two investors and to understand the nature of the relationship and the decision-making process
- Obtain documentation such as Peppers Co's organisational structure to confirm that the Group has successfully appointed members to the board of the company and that those members have equal power to the members appointed by Smiths Co

**(ii)    The government grant**

- Obtain the documentation relating to the grant and review to obtain understanding of:
  - The terms of the grant, in particular requirements relating to the specific use of the funds
  - The date by which the funds must be used
  - Any clauses relating to repayment of some or all of the grant should certain conditions arise
- Agree the amount received to bank statement and cash book of Ryder Co
- Obtain and review the Group's capital expenditure forecast to confirm the amount planned to be spent on capital expenditure relating to environmental matters

- Discuss the use of the grant to fund an advertising campaign with an appropriate person, e.g. Group marketing director, and review any plans to use the funds for promotional purposes to confirm that recycling features in the campaign, as intended by the government
- Confirm, through agreement to marketing plans, whether any funds will be spent during this financial year
- Obtain a written representation from management that the grant received will be used for the specific purposes required by the government

|  | |
|---|---|
| **Maximum** | 8 |

**(d)** **Ethical issues**

Up to 1 mark for each point explained:

- Audit firm partner serving on Group audit committee – self-review threat explained
- Audit firm partner serving on Group audit committee – self-interest threat explained
- Safeguards cannot reduce to an acceptable level so cannot provide partner to serve on audit committee
- Referral fee – self-interest threat to objectivity and professional competence explained
- Can earn referral fee as long as safeguards used – disclose to client and obtain agreement (up to 2 marks)
- Internal audit assistance – self-review threat explained
- Internal audit assistance – management responsibility threat explained
- No safeguards can reduce threat relating to management responsibility
- For PIE client cannot provide internal audit assistance in relation to material/significant matter
- Audit firm therefore cannot provide internal audit assistance

|  | |
|---|---|
| **Maximum** | 10 |

**Professional marks**

Generally 1 mark for heading, 1 mark for introduction, 1 mark for use of headings within the briefing notes, 1 mark for clarity of comments made.

|  | |
|---|---|
| **Maximum** | 4 |

| **Total** | 50 |
|---|---|

2    MARGOT  *Walk in the footsteps of a top tutor*

*Top tutor tips*

*Part (a) requires evaluation of risks of material misstatement. Here you need to explain how the financial statements might not have been prepared in accordance with the applicable financial reporting standard. Refer to the requirements of the relevant standards in your answer. Explain which balances or classes of transactions are at risk of over or understatement and why. Note that the requirement explicitly instructs you not to include risks relating to the **valuation** of bearer plants or biological assets. Other risks of material misstatement such as classification will be acceptable.*

*Part (b) asks audit procedures in respect of the impairment of the factory and the development costs. The procedures should enable the auditor to obtain evidence to determine whether the relevant financial reporting standard has been complied with. Make sure your procedures are clear and provide enough detail that they can be easily followed by the audit team.*

*Part (c) requires the matters to consider when using the work of an expert. This requires knowledge of the relevant auditing standard.*

*Part (d) deals with the auditor's responsibilities in relation to laws and regulations and the actions that should be taken when non-compliance is brought to the attention of the auditor. This requires knowledge of the relevant auditing standard.*

**Briefing notes**

**To: Ben Duval, Audit engagement partner**

**From: Audit manager**

**Subject: Audit planning for Margot Co Introduction**

These briefing notes are prepared in respect of audit planning for our client Margot Co, with a financial year ending 30 June 20X9. The notes begin with an evaluation of the significant risks of material misstatement which should be considered in planning the audit. The notes then contain the audit procedures which have been designed in relation to two matters – the impairment of property, plant and equipment and capitalised development costs. A discussion is provided on the use of an auditor's expert in the audit of the company's biological assets. Finally, a member of the client's staff has alerted us to some suspicious behaviour, which could indicate a breach of law and regulations. The notes discuss this issue and recommend actions to be taken by our firm.

(a)    **Evaluation of significant risks of material misstatement**

**Results from preliminary analytical procedures**

The limited analytical procedures which have been performed indicate several potential risks of material misstatement. First, the current ratio has increased significantly, from 1.4 in 20X8, to a projected figure of 2.6 in 20X9. Using the information provided, the current liabilities in 20X8 were $1.564 million ($2.19 million/1.4) and are projected to be $1.288 million in 20X9 ($3.35 million/2.6).

Current assets are projected to increase by 53% and current liabilities projected to reduce by 17.6%. Given that the management accounts show that the cash balance is relatively static, there is a risk that other current assets, presumably inventory and receivables, could be overstated. However, the increase in current assets can at least partly be explained by the inclusion of the $450,000 prepayment relating to restoring the damaged factory; this is discussed in more detail later in the briefing notes.

There is also a risk that the current liabilities are understated; this risk is particularly significant given that according to the finance director, current liabilities includes a provision of $450,000 in relation to restoring the damaged factory.

The projected movement in the gearing ratio is small, from 32% to 28%. This fall in the gearing ratio is inconsistent with the fact that the company has taken a loan of $375,000 to finance the research and development. The expectation would be for the gearing ratio to increase, unless there has been a repayment of finance of which we are unaware.

Looking at the operating margin and return on capital employed, both ratios have improved by a small amount. This trend is worthy of scrutiny during the audit as the offers and discounts offered to customers by the company should act negatively on margins and profitability, so the improvements in ratios could indicate a potential overstatement of operating profit.

Another trend which is worth further investigation relates to online sales, which are projected to increase by 90.5% in the year. This is a significant increase, and while the finance director has asserted that the increase in sales is due to the success of the advertising campaign, this needs to be corroborated further. There is a risk of overstatement of revenue in relation to online sales which is explored in more detail below.

There is also a risk that revenue from other sources is overstated. Excluding online sales, revenue from other sources is projected to increase by 5.3%, a significant increase, which could also indicate overstatement of revenue.

**Management bias**

This is a private company where a majority of shares are owned by the Margot family. This brings a risk of management bias, especially as one of the family members is the company's chief executive officer, who is in a position to influence the financial statements. The extract from the management accounts shows that a significant dividend payment is made each year, so there is an expectation from the family members that the company will make sufficient profit to be able to pay these dividends each year.

There is therefore a significant inherent risk at the financial statement level that profit will be overstated. The risk that the financial statements are being deliberately manipulated is indicated by the accounting treatment applied to impairment which is discussed in more detail below.

**Online sales**

The online sales make up an increasing proportion of the company's revenue – according to the management accounts online sales are projected to represent 7% of total revenue in 20X9 (4% – 20X8).

Online sales can bring a number risks of material misstatement, for instance, cut off and timing of revenue recognition can be problematical. In the case of Margot Co, risks attach to the discounts which are offered on online sales as the discounts offered to customers appear to change frequently. This brings some complexity into the accounting, and the company should ensure that internal controls are operating effectively so that the accounting system is updated whenever the level and range of discounts and offers to customers are changed. Revenue could be over or understated if discounts are not accounted for appropriately, either because a discount is not recorded at all by the accounting system or is applied to the wrong products.

*Tutorial note*

*Credit will be awarded for other risks relating to online sales, where relevant to the question scenario, for example, related to the launch of the new online sales portal, which implies a change to the system used to record revenue, with related control risks.*

**Research and development**

In this financial year, $220,000 of research and development costs have been capitalised as an intangible asset. This represents 1.8% of total assets and 10.5% of profit before tax, and would be considered material to the financial statements.

This relates to research and development into new plastic-free packaging. According to IAS® 38 *Intangible Assets*, a distinction has to be made between research costs, which must be expensed, and development costs, which should only be capitalised if certain criteria are met including that the technical and commercial feasibility of the asset has been established.

It appears that the full amount paid to ProPack has been capitalised, which indicates that no distinction has been made between research costs and development costs. Only development costs can be capitalised, so there is a potential overstatement of the intangible asset if it includes research costs, which should be expensed. This means that the entity must intend and be able to complete the intangible asset and either use it or sell it and be able to demonstrate how the asset will generate future economic benefits.

There is a further risk of material misstatement because costs which are development costs may have been capitalised but the necessary criteria demonstrating that an asset has been created have not been met. Given that ProPack is only at the stage of testing prototypes, it appears that there is not yet demonstrable evidence that the new packaging is technically feasible or that Margot Co will be able to use the packaging.

In addition, there may problems in demonstrating that Margot Co has control of the development of new packaging, given that the development has been outsourced to another company. In this case, the IAS 38 criteria for capitalisation do not appear to have been met; this will result in overstatement of intangible assets and understatement of operating expenses.

### Impaired factory

The carrying amount of the impaired factory is material to the statement of financial position, representing 7% of total assets.

The damage to the factory has triggered an impairment review, as required by IAS 36 *Impairment of Assets*. However, the finance director has not prepared the impairment calculations in accordance with IAS 36, specifically the recoverable amount has not been correctly determined. The recoverable amount is the higher of value in use and fair value less costs to sell the asset. However, a review of the calculation provided indicates that the determination of value in use is not correct.

According to IAS 36, the cash flow projections which are used to determine the value in use of the impaired asset should relate to the asset in its current condition – expenditures to improve or enhance the asset's performance should not be anticipated. The finance director's estimate of value in use is based on the assumption that the building is repaired and new machinery purchased – neither of these assumptions should be included in the determination of value in use.

It is likely that the value in use, when properly determined, is much lower than the finance director's estimate, meaning that the impairment loss to be recognised is greater than the $210,250 as per the finance director's calculations. There is also a risk that the fair value less cost to sell is overestimated – if the factory is damaged and the machinery needs to be completely replaced, then a value of $135,000 included in management's calculation may be over optimistic. Therefore there is a risk that the impairment loss is understated, and the carrying value of the asset is overstated.

*Tutorial note*

*Credit will be awarded for further development of the impairment issue, for example, whether the impairment loss has been appropriately allocated over the assets of the cash generating unit.*

### Provision for restoring the damaged factory and acquiring new machinery

Related to the point above, the financial statements include a provision of $450,000 for repairing the factory and buying new machinery. The amount recognised represents 3.6% of total assets and is material to the statement of financial position, though it has no impact on profit.

A provision should only be recognised if it meets the criteria of IAS 37 *Provisions, Contingent Liabilities and Contingent Assets*, including that there is a present obligation as a result of a past event, and that a probable future outflow of economic benefit which can be reliably estimated exists.

In this case there does not seem to be a present obligation, the company is not contractually obliged to repair the damage and there is no evidence that a constructive obligation exists. Neither does it appear appropriate to recognise a prepayment for an expense which has not yet been incurred.

Therefore, the provision and related prepayment should not be recognised, and unless an adjustment is made to the financial statements, both current assets and current liabilities are overstated.

### Software and advertising costs capitalised

During the year, software development costs of $30,000 and advertising costs of $225,000 are capitalised as intangible assets. The advertising costs are material, representing 1.8% of total assets and 10.7% of profit for the year.

The advertising costs have been incurred to support the 'Fructus Gold' brand name, and the finance director justifies the capitalisation on the grounds that the advertising expenditure has led to an increase in sales. However, IAS 38 specifically states that advertising and promotional costs must not be recognised as intangible assets and must be expensed. Therefore intangible assets are overstated and operating expenses understated by a material amount.

The software development costs represent less than 1% of total assets and only 1.4% of profit, so are not considered to be material to the financial statements, and therefore in isolation do not represent a significant risk of material misstatement in monetary terms, especially given that according to IAS 38, it is appropriate to capitalise internally developed software costs assuming that the costs incurred give rise to an asset.

However, this matter is being highlighted because the finance director has used a similar justification for capitalising the advertising costs, which are likely to be materially misstated, as discussed above, and therefore this gives rise to a general concern over whether all costs relating to intangible assets are being treated appropriately.

### Identification and potential misclassification of assets

There is a risk that the agricultural assets are not identified and/or classified appropriately, which will have an implication for the valuation of the assets. For example, it may be difficult to distinguish between bearer plants and fruit growing on the trees, and it might be hard to identify the stage of development of fruit on the trees. This potentially impacts on the valuation of the assets, because bearer plants are measured at cost and depreciated in accordance with IAS 16 *Property, Plant and Equipment*, whereas the fruit should be measured at fair value in accordance with IAS 41 *Agriculture*.

*Tutorial note*

*Credit will be awarded for other, relevant risks of material misstatement, for example, the risk that the storm may have damaged assets other than the factory, in particular the bearer plants, which may have suffered impairment, and the risk that inventory may be overstated due to perishable nature of the goods.*

**(b)** **Audit procedures**

**(i)** **Impaired factory**

- Obtain management's detailed calculations to gain understanding and allow evaluation of the methodology and assumptions used, e.g. the basis of determining the fair value and the future period over which value in use was determined and the discount rate used to calculate the present value of future cash flows.

- Discuss the methodology and assumptions with management to confirm their rationale.

- From the non-current asset register, confirm the carrying amount of the cash generating unit prior to any impairment being recognised, and confirm the carrying amount of each component of the cash generating unit.

- Obtain a copy of the company's insurance policy and review the terms and conditions to confirm whether the buildings and machinery are covered by insurance.

- Develop an auditor's estimate of the fair value less cost to sell and value in use, in accordance with the IAS 36 requirements (i.e. not including the restoration costs and replacement of machinery), and compare to management's estimate. Developing an auditor's estimate would involve the following procedures:

    – Obtain and review the reports from the engineer to confirm the nature and extent of damage caused to the factory.

    – Obtain and review any external valuation report which the company has used as a basis of the fair value less cost to sell, and evaluate the reasonableness of any assumptions used in the valuation.

    – For the value in use, discuss with management to obtain their view as to whether the factory has any value in use at all in its current state.

    – Visit the factory to view the extent of damage caused by the storm and evaluate whether it can be used without any further capital expenditure.

- Consider whether the use of an auditor's expert is necessary to provide sufficient and appropriate evidence given the materiality of the figures.

**(ii)  Research and development costs**

- Discuss the project to develop new packaging with management, to develop an understanding of matters such as how the company intends to use the new packaging, the stage of development reached by the year end and whether the project may need additional funding.

- Obtain and review progress reports and correspondence from ProPack which will indicate the progress made so far.

- Obtain and review the contract with ProPack to determine contractual terms and if the asset will be owned and controlled by Margot Co and that ProPack does not have any continuing interest in the development once it is complete.

- After receiving client's permission, arrange to discuss the project with ProPack, to obtain further understanding on a range of matters including technical feasibility and the results of the testing on the prototype.

- Discuss with the company's production and marketing directors to obtain understanding of how the company will use the new packaging.

- Obtain any financial budgets prepared in relation to the project, to confirm the amount of expenditure which has been approved, and that the costs are clearly distinguishable.

- By reference to the company's cash position and available finance, evaluate whether Margot Co has sufficient funds to complete the development.

- Obtain samples of the prototype packaging from ProPack, to confirm existence.

- Agree the amount spent to date to invoices submitted by ProPack, and to the company's cash records.

---

**Tutorial note**

*Credit will be awarded for other relevant audit procedures, for example, in relation to assessing whether there are any reasons to doubt whether ProPack can continue the development.*

---

**(c)    Matters to consider before placing reliance on the work of the auditor's expert**

ISA 620 *Using the Work of an Auditor's Expert* contains requirements relating to the objectivity, competence and capabilities of the auditor's expert, the scope and objectives of their work, and assessing their work.

**Objectivity**

According to ISA 620, the auditor shall evaluate whether the auditor's expert has the necessary objectivity and this should include inquiry regarding interests and relationships which may create a threat to the expert's objectivity. The audit firm will need to ensure that the expert has no connection to Margot Co, for example, that they are not a related party of the company or any person in a position of influence over the financial statements.

If the expert's objectivity is threatened, little or no reliance can be placed on their work, and the audit firm should not treat it as a reliable source of audit evidence.

**Competence**

ISA 620 also requires the competence of the expert to be considered; this should include considering the expert's membership of appropriate professional bodies. Any doubts over the competence of the expert will reduce the reliability of audit evidence obtained.

The expert should in this case have experience in valuing the fruit which are the agricultural assets recognised in the statement of financial position, and be familiar with the framework for measuring fair value of these assets in accordance with IAS 41 *Agriculture* and IFRS 13 *Fair Value Measurement*.

**Scope of work**

ISA 620 requires the auditor to agree the scope of work with the expert. This may include agreement of the objectives of the work, how the expert's work will be used by the auditor and the methodology and key assumptions to be used.

---

In assessing the work performed by the expert, the auditor should confirm that the scope of the work is as agreed at the start of the engagement. If the expert has deviated from the agreed scope of work, it is likely to be less relevant and reliable.

**Relevance of conclusions**

ISA 620 states that the auditor shall evaluate the relevance and adequacy of the expert's findings or conclusions. This will involve consideration of the source data which was used, the appropriateness of assumptions and the reasons for any changes in methodology or assumptions. The conclusion should be consistent with other relevant audit findings and with the auditor's general understanding of the business.

If the work involves using source data which is significant to their workings, the audit team should plan to assess the relevance, completeness and accuracy of that data. Any inconsistencies should be investigated as they may indicate evidence which is not reliable.

*Tutorial note*

*Credit will be awarded for more specific comments in relation to evaluating the expert's work, for example, reperformance of calculations, and establishing that assumptions are in line with the auditor's understanding of the entity.*

**(d)    Audit implications of email from Len Larch**

The alleged use of prohibited chemicals raises concerns that the company may not be complying with relevant law and regulations. The auditor needs to consider the requirements of ISA 250 *Consideration of Laws and Regulations in an Audit of Financial Statements*. ISA 250 states that while it is management's responsibility to ensure that the entity's operations are conducted in accordance with the provisions of laws and regulation, the auditor does have some responsibility in relation to compliance with laws and regulations, especially where a non-compliance has an impact on the financial statements.

There is also an ethical issue in that one of the production managers may have been bribed by one of the company directors. Clearly, if this is true, it indicates a lack of integrity and would seem to confirm that the chemicals which are being used are prohibited.

*Tutorial note*

*UK syllabus: There is a risk that the Bribery Act (2010) has been breached by the inducement offered by the production manager.*

The auditor is required by ISA 315 *Identifying and Assessing the Risks of Material Misstatement Through Understanding the Entity and its Environment* to gain an understanding of the legal and regulatory framework in which the audited entity operates. This will help the auditor to identify non-compliance and to assess the implications of non-compliance.

Therefore the auditor should ensure a full knowledge and understanding of the laws and regulations relevant to the use of chemicals in the company's farms, and the implications of non-compliance.

ISA 250 requires that when non-compliance is identified or suspected, the auditor shall obtain an understanding of the nature of the act and the circumstances in which it has occurred, and further information to evaluate the possible effect on the financial statements.

Therefore procedures should be performed to obtain evidence about the suspected non-compliance, for example, to speak to the company's farm managers to understand whether the allegations are founded in fact. In addition, the audit team could perform further procedures, for example, reviewing purchase invoices to establish if these chemicals are actually being purchased and used in the business, and if so, on whose authority.

ISA 250 requires the matter to be discussed with management and where appropriate with those charged with governance. Given the potential severity of the situation, and that the chemicals may be toxic, there is the risk of poisoning the company's employees or customers, and the matter should be communicated as soon as possible.

The auditor should attempt to find out whether any member of management had issued instructions for these chemicals to be used, i.e. that there is a deliberate breach of law and regulations. ISA 250 suggests that when the auditor suspects management or those charged with governance of being involved with the non-compliance, the matter should be communicated to the next level of 'higher authority' such as an audit committee or supervisory board.

Given the family-managed nature of Margot Co, it may be that no higher authority exists, in which case the audit firm should take appropriate legal advice if they think that the matter may not be communicated by the entity.

The auditor needs to consider the potential implications for the financial statements. The non-compliance, if proven to have taken place, could lead to regulatory authorities imposing fines or penalties on Margot Co, which may need to be provided for in the financial statements. Audit procedures should be performed to determine the amount, materiality and probability of payment of any such fine or penalty imposed.

In addition, there is a risk that the use of chemicals means that inventory of harvested fruit and the fruit trees are contaminated with poisonous chemicals and possibly will need to be destroyed. The assets could therefore need to be written down in value. If any necessary impairment of the assets is not recognised, then non-current assets and current assets could be misstated. The audit team should therefore plan procedures to determine the value of the contaminated assets.

There may be a going concern issue once the non-compliance and its implications has been established and the facts get out into the media. There would be considerable impact on the reputation of the company and its brand; customers may stop purchasing the products for fear of a health risk and this could affect the going concern of the business.

In terms of reporting non-compliance to the relevant regulatory authorities, ISA 250 requires the auditor to determine whether they have a responsibility to report the identified or suspected non-compliance to parties outside the entity.

In the event that management or those charged with governance of the company fails to make the necessary disclosures to the regulatory authorities, the auditor should consider whether they should make the disclosure. This will depend on matters including whether there is a legal duty to disclose or whether it is considered to be in the public interest to do so.

Confidentiality is also an issue, and if disclosure were to be made by the auditor, it would be advisable to seek legal advice on the matter. Further advice on disclosure in the public interest is given by the IESBA's pronouncement on *Responding to Non-Compliance with Laws and Regulations* (NOCLAR). The guidance gives examples of situations where disclosure might be appropriate such as an entity being involved in bribery and breaches of regulation which might impact adversely on public health and safety.

The standard also clarifies that in exceptional circumstances where the auditor believes there may be an imminent breach of a law or regulation, they may need to disclose the matter immediately.

The decision to disclose will always be a matter for the auditor's judgement and where the disclosure is made in good faith, it will not constitute a breach of the duty of confidentiality.

*Tutorial note*

*UK syllabus: ISA (UK) 250 A states that the auditor should discuss this with those charged with governance and if the entity does not voluntarily report the matter itself or is unable to provide evidence that the matter has been reported, the auditor reports it.*

*According to ISA (UK) 250 A, determination of where the balance of public interest lies requires careful consideration. An auditor whose suspicions have been aroused uses professional judgement to determine whether the auditor's misgivings justify the auditor in carrying the matter further or are too insubstantial to deserve reporting. The auditor is protected from the risk of liability for breach of confidence or defamation provided that the disclosure is made in the public interest, and such disclosure is made to an appropriate body or person, and there is no malice motivating the disclosure.*

### Conclusion

These briefing notes have indicated that there are several significant risks of material misstatement to consider while planning the audit of Margot Co. More information is needed to perform a detailed analytical review, which may highlight further potential risks. The briefing notes also recommend relevant audit procedures for two significant risks of material misstatement – the impaired factory and research and development costs. We will plan to use the work of an expert, following the requirements of ISA 620. Finally, we need to consider carefully the issues raised by Len Larch, as it seems that the company is operating in breach of relevant laws and regulations, and that this is a deliberate act involving bribery of company employees. There are implications for our audit planning in that we must plan to obtain detailed information about the situation, and consider our reporting responsibilities in light of the severity of the situation and its implications for public health.

**Examiner's comments**

Requirement (a), for 20 marks asked candidates to evaluate the risks of material misstatement arising from the scenario. This was generally well answered with the majority of candidates able to follow a structured approach of calculating materiality, stating the relevant accounting rule applied to the specifics of the scenario, describing the risk that arose and the resulting impact on the financial statements. It was pleasing to see that fewer candidates diverted to answering from a business risk perspective, but where this did occur, no marks could be awarded. Candidates are reminded to read the question requirements carefully and ensure they are answering the question set. As in previous sittings, the examining team highlighted within the scenario that there was an internally generated brand which had been accounted for correctly and should not be recognised within the statement of financial position. A significant number of candidates still described this as a risk of material misstatement, clearly wasting time on an area that was not a risk. Several candidates who did identify that the brand was correctly accounted for, continued to describe how the internally generated brand, while not recognised should be tested for impairment. This demonstrates an area of weakness regarding basic financial reporting knowledge. Candidates would benefit from refreshing their knowledge on reporting standards for intangible assets and taking note of the guidance provided in the scenario by the examining team. A further area of weakness was noted with regards to the family owned business having a lack of corporate governance, audit committee and lack of controls leading to a risk of material misstatement. A significant number of candidates discussed the risk in very general terms, not linking any risk of management bias to the specifics of the question and therefore failed to score what would be regarded as standard risk marks that are easily achievable.

Some other common issues noted in candidate answers for RoMM included:

- Discussing audit procedures to be performed which did not meet the question requirement and therefore no credit awarded. If required, this will normally form a separate requirement within the question and should be answered where applicable.

- Including detailed definitions of audit risk or risks of material misstatement. The briefing notes are prepared for the audit engagement partner and this type of information is not required.

- Lack of basic knowledge of double entry and assumption that every double entry has one under and one overstatement e.g. if liabilities are understated, then expenses must be overstated.

- Lack of correct direction of risk or not being precise in terms of the financial statement impact, e.g. "liabilities will be under/overstated".

Requirement (b), for 10 marks required candidates to design principal audit procedures for specific areas of risk identified within requirement (a). Candidate answers were weaker than the previous sitting in December 2018, with many candidates providing procedures which referred to a weak information source or poorly explained purpose and were often not detailed enough to score full marks.

Some common issues noted in candidate answers for this requirement included:

- Focusing on board meeting minutes where this was not an appropriate source for a procedure based on the requirement.

- Procedures which simply stated "obtain relevant documents" which is not specific or detailed enough to score full marks.

– Requests to obtain written representations from management without being specific regarding what should be confirmed, or were not relevant to the area for which procedures were being performed.

The final requirements required candidates to discuss considerations for the use of an auditor's expert and for candidates to discuss the audit implications and actions to be taken, regarding professional and ethical issues present in the scenario. There were many strong answers in response to considerations regarding the use of the auditor's expert, but some candidates failed to address the level of detail required in line with ISA 620 *Using the Work of an Auditor's Expert*. Weaker answers focussed on practical considerations, such as whether the expert had the time and resources to perform the work rather than the key areas of the standard such as objectivity, competence, scope of work and relevance of conclusions.

It is disappointing to note that answers to ethics requirements continue to be weak, with many candidates not sufficiently justifying how the threat has arisen in line with the specifics of the scenario or the implication that arises for the auditor. Both considerations are needed in order score marks. Candidates undoubtedly know the name of the ethical threats and have an assumed knowledge from previous studies at AA yet continue to score poorly at AAA level. Candidates would benefit from reading the exam technique article published on ACCA's website for detailed guidance on how to discuss ethical threats.

| ACCA marking guide | |
|---|---|
| | *Marks* |
| **(a) Risk of material misstatement** | |
| Up to 3 marks for each significant risk of material misstatement evaluated unless otherwise indicated. Marks may be awarded for other, relevant risks not included in the marking guide. | |
| In addition, ½ mark for each relevant trend or calculation which form part of analytical review (max 3 marks). | |
| Materiality calculations should be awarded 1 mark each (max 3 marks). | |
| – Current ratio – related audit risks, e.g. overstatement of inventory/receivables, understatement of current liabilities | |
| – Gearing ratio – indicates that long-term liabilities could be understated | |
| – Improvements in margin and ROCE – possible overstatement of profit given the discounts offered to customers | |
| – Online sales – trend indicates possible overstatement of revenue | |
| – Risk of management bias due to owner-management and desire for dividend payments | |
| – Discounts offered on online sales | |
| – Research and development – risk that expenditure should not have been capitalised and that research and development costs have not been distinguished | |
| – Impairment – risk that the value in use and therefore impairment loss is not correct (max 4 marks for detailed discussion) | |
| – Provision for restoration of the impaired property – provision should not have been made | |
| – Intangible assets – whether amounts should have been capitalised | |
| – Bearer plants/biological assets/inventory – potentially difficult to distinguish the assets, with implications for their valuation | |
| **Maximum marks** | 20 |

**(b)** **Audit procedures on impairment and research and development costs**

Up to 1 mark for each well described procedure:

**(i)** **Impairment**

– Obtain management's detailed calculations and discuss with management to gain understanding of the methodology and assumptions used

– From the non-current asset register, confirm the carrying value of the cash generating unit prior to any impairment being recognised, and confirm the carrying value of each component of the cash generating unit

– Obtain a copy of the company's insurance policy and review the terms and conditions to confirm whether the buildings and machinery is covered by insurance

– Develop an auditor's estimate of the fair value less cost to sell and value in use and compare to management's estimate, this will include performing the following procedures:

– Obtain and review the reports from the engineer to confirm the nature and extent of damage caused to the factory

– Obtain and review any external valuation report which the company has used as a basis of the fair value less cost to sell, and evaluate the reasonableness of any assumptions used in the valuation

– For the value in use, discuss with management to obtain their view as to whether the factory has any value in use at all in its current state

– Visit the factory to view the extent of damage caused by the storm and evaluate whether it can be used without any further capital expenditure

– Given the materiality of the figures, an auditor's expert could be used to provide evidence

**(ii)** **Research and development costs**

– Discuss the project to develop new packaging with management, to develop an understanding of matters such as how the company intends to use the new packaging, the stage of development reached by the year end and whether the project may need additional funding

– Obtain and review reports and correspondence from ProPack which will indicate the progress made so far

– Obtain and review the contract with ProPack to determine contractual terms and if the asset will be owned and controlled by Margot Co and that ProPack does not have any continuing interest in the development once it is complete

– Discuss the project with ProPack, to obtain further understanding on a range of matters including technical feasibility and the results of testing of the prototype

– Discuss with the company's production and marketing directors to obtain understanding of how the company will use the new packaging

– Obtain any financial budgets prepared in relation to the project, to confirm the amount of expenditure which has been approved, and that the costs are clearly distinguishable

– By reference to the company's cash position and available finance, evaluate whether Margot Co has sufficient funds to complete the development

– Obtain samples of the prototype packaging from Propack, to confirm existence

– Agree the amount spent to date to invoices submitted by ProPack, and to the company's cash records

|  |  |
|---|---|
| **Maximum marks** | 10 |

| | | |
|---|---|---|
| **(c)** | **Use of an auditor's expert** | |
| | Up to 2 marks for each well explained point: | |
| |   –   Objectivity | |
| |   –   Competence | |
| |   –   Scope of work | |
| |   –   Relevance of conclusions | |
| | **Maximum marks** | **6** |
| | | |
| **(d)** | **Impact of email on audit** | |
| | Up to 2 marks for each well explained point: | |
| |   –   Use of chemicals likely to be a breach of laws and regulations | |
| |   –   Bribe indicates lack of integrity and that the activity is a non-compliance | |
| |   –   Auditor needs to understand laws and regulations applicable to the Group | |
| |   –   Further evidence should be obtained and the matter discussed with management | |
| |   –   Issue of lack of 'higher authority' as Margot Co is family owned and need to take legal advice | |
| |   –   Provisions for fines and penalties | |
| |   –   Valuation of inventory and biological assets | |
| |   –   Potential going concern issue due to bad publicity and impact on reputation | |
| |   –   Auditor may have a legal duty to disclose, or consider disclosing in the public interest | |
| |   –   Discussion of how requirements of NOCLAR relate to the scenario | |
| |   –   The audit firm may wish to seek legal advice regarding the situation (1 mark) | |
| | **Maximum marks** | **10** |
| | | |
| | **Professional marks** | |
| | Generally 1 mark for heading, 1 mark for introduction, 1 mark for use of headings within the briefing notes, 1 mark for clarity of comments made. | |
| | **Maximum marks** | **4** |
| **Total** | | **50** |

**3     REDBACK SPORTS**  *Walk in the footsteps of a top tutor*

*Top tutor tips*

*Part (a) requires evaluation of business risks. When describing business risks remember to explain the impact it will have on the company i.e. impact on profit or cash flow. The business risks should be relatable to the financial statements as the auditor will only consider business risks which will also give rise to a risk of material misstatement.*

*Part (b) asks for risks of material misstatement. Here you need to explain how the financial statements might not have been prepared in accordance with the applicable financial reporting standard. Refer to the requirements of the relevant standards in your answer. Explain which balances or classes of transactions are at risk of over or understatement and why.*

*Part (c) asks for audit procedures in respect of the government grant. The procedures should enable the auditor to obtain evidence to determine whether the relevant financial reporting standard has been complied with. Make sure your procedures are clear and provide enough detail that they can be easily followed.*

*Part (d) focuses on acceptance considerations. The firm should only accept engagements of an acceptable level of risk, taking ethical, professional and practical matters into consideration.*

*Part (e) requires a discussion of whether an audit or limited assurance review could have uncovered a fraud. Discuss the limitations of each type of engagement including the types of procedures that are performed for each. Remember that fraud is an intentional act of deception which means it may be difficult to identify due to concealment.*

**Briefing notes**

To:          Stella Cross, audit engagement partner

From:      Audit manager

Subject:   Audit of Redback Sports Co and potential provision of an audit or limited assurance review to Emu Gyms Co

**Introduction**

The first part of these briefing notes has been prepared in relation to the audit of Redback Sports Co. The audit planning will commence shortly, and these notes evaluate the business risks and the risks of material misstatement to be considered in planning the audit. The notes then go on to recommend the principal audit procedures to be used in the audit of a government grant which the company received during the year.

The second part of the briefing notes focuses on Emu Gyms Co, in particular the request from the company's managing director for our firm to provide an audit or a limited assurance review of the company's financial statements.

The notes finish by discussing a question which has been raised by the company's managing director, in relation to a suspected fraud at the company.

(a) **Evaluation of business risks to be considered in planning the audit of Redback Sports Co**

**Corporate governance**

The company does not have to comply with corporate governance requirements as it is not a listed entity, and it is good to note that the board includes two non-executive directors who seem able to offer independent views on strategy and management. However, the company lacks an audit committee and the internal audit team is small and lacking in independence as they report directly to the finance director. This means that the scope of their work is likely to be quite limited due to insufficient resources, and any recommendations made could potentially be ignored by the finance director.

Overall, this could lead to deficiencies in controls and inefficiencies in business operations. In addition, given that the company is looking to achieve a stock market listing in the next few years, it would be good practice to implement stronger governance procedures sooner rather than later. For example, having two non-executive directors may not be enough to meet the corporate governance requirements in the company's jurisdiction.

**Health and safety regulations**

The company operates in a highly regulated industry, and the risk of non-compliance with various laws and regulations is high. The sport and leisure industry has strict health and safety regulations which must be complied with, and there are regular health and safety inspections to ensure that regulations are being adhered to.

If the company is found not to be in compliance with the relevant regulations, its operating licence could be revoked, which would have reputational consequences, and ultimately could impact on the company's going concern status.

In addition to the risk of non-compliance, it will be costly to reduce this risk to an acceptable level, for example, through regular staff training on health and safety, leading to cash flow and profit implications. This is particularly relevant to the more adventurous sporting activities such as scuba diving, which the company has recently started to offer.

**Capital expenditure and maintenance requirements**

The company's success relies on gyms being equipped with modern equipment, and the other facilities such as tennis courts being maintained to a high standard. This requires a high annual expenditure, for example, this year alone $5.5 million has been incurred on maintenance and repairs.

Such high annual expenditure is a big drain on cash, and the company could face liquidity problems if cash inflows from customers are not maintained.

**Liquidity and overtrading**

The company's cash position is projected to deteriorate significantly, with the level of cash falling from $5.6 million to $1.4 million in the year. At the same time, revenue and profit before tax are both projected to increase, by 17.8% and 50% respectively.

While there is some doubt over the integrity of the figures reported by management, which will be discussed in the next section of the briefing notes, the trends could indicate that the company is expanding too quickly and overtrading, focusing on generating revenue rather than on managing cash flows appropriately. This is particularly concerning given the company's plans for further expansion in the next few years.

### Capacity

There could be problems facing the company in terms of the capacity of its facilities. Membership has increased significantly during the year, by 12.4%, and the number of pay as you go visits has increased by 5.3%. Although two new sport and leisure centres have opened this year, this may not be sufficient expansion, and there may be times when the facilities are overcrowded.

This may deter members from renewing their membership, and pay as you go customers might prefer to use other sport and leisure providers if overcrowding becomes problematical. The 'Healthy Kids' programme, and the government initiative to provide free access to the unemployed will exacerbate this problem.

### Competition and marketing expenses

The industry is competitive, which itself is a business risk, meaning there is pressure on the company to maintain its market share and customer base. There may be pressure to cut membership or pay as you go prices, which will impact on profit margins and cash flow.

The company appears to spend a lot on marketing to support its brand. This year, $8.5 million has been spent on marketing, which equates to 16% of revenue. This is a huge drain on cash and will impact significantly on the company's liquidity position.

### Government initiative

While the company's involvement with the government initiative to promote a healthy lifestyle to unemployed people is commendable, it may not prove popular with the existing sport and leisure centre members and pay as you go customers.

The initiative will put pressure on the capacity of the gyms, and could lead to the facilities becoming crowded, especially at peak time. This could lead to memberships not being renewed, and pay as you go customers moving to other providers. There is also an opportunity cost issue for the company, as the $2 million grant receipt does not appear to be particularly profitable in terms of the number of hours of free access to the gyms which have to be provided for the next three years.

There is an associated risk in that the company's systems need to be capable of accurately recording the number of free hours which are provided under this initiative, as this has to be reported on a monthly basis. The risk is that the systems do not capture the necessary information accurately, which could lead to reporting false information to the government. There is evidence that this system of recording could be overstating the hours of free access, as according to the finance director, 33,900 free hours have already been provided, which in the three-month period since the start of the initiative in September 20X8 equates to 11,300 hours per month, which seems high as this implies that approximately 3,800 people have responded to the initiative.

### Expansion plans

The expansion plans could take management's attention away from running the business, especially if identification of potential target companies becomes a time consuming process over the next year. Management controls over existing operations could deteriorate while attention is focused on the planned expansion and possible future flotation.

If there is pressure from existing shareholders for the expansion to be successful and flotation to take place, management could be pressured into making unwise decisions to increase the pace of development of the company's activities.

**New data management system**

Introducing a new data management system can create a business risk in that insufficient training may have been provided and/or appropriate internal controls may not have been designed or implemented in relation to the new system, increasing the risk of inaccurate recording, processing and reporting of information.

This would have a negative impact on management's ability to monitor the company's performance. Given that the new system is linked to the company's accounting software, there is a related audit risk, which will be discussed in the next section of these briefing notes.

**(b)** **Risk of material misstatement evaluation**

**Management bias**

The company has ambitious expansion plans, and is aiming to achieve a stock market listing within five years. This can create significant pressure on management to report strong financial performance, and the risk of earnings management is high. This can lead to a range of inappropriate accounting treatments including early recognition of revenue and other income and deferral of expenses.

There is some indication that earnings management may have taken place this year, for example, revenue is projected to increase by 17.8%, whereas the number of members, who provide the majority of the company's revenue, has increased by only 12.4%. Profit before tax is projected to increase by 50%. These trends indicate that income could be overstated and expenses understated, the specific reasons for which are evaluated below.

**Corporate governance and internal controls**

As discussed in the previous section, the company lacks an audit committee and only has a small internal audit team which is not operating independently. This has implications for controls over financial reporting, which could be deficient, and increases control risk.

There is a high scope for errors in financial reporting processes and for deliberate manipulation of balances and transactions, as the internal audit team does not have sufficient resources for thorough monitoring and reporting.

**Revenue recognition**

With 85% of revenue being from members' subscriptions, there is a risk that revenue is recognised incorrectly. There is a risk that the timing of revenue recognition is not appropriate, for example, if an annual membership is recognised in full when it is received by the company, rather than being recognised over the period of membership, thereby overstating revenue.

There are multiple revenue streams which complicates the financial reporting process and increases the risk. As well as members paying an annual subscription, customers can pay for access under the pay as you go scheme. In addition, the free access to the unemployed should not result in revenue recognition, but must be properly recorded as it has to be reported to the government on a monthly basis.

As discussed above, it is possible that the system is not recording the free access provided to the unemployed accurately, and that figures may be overstated.

### Capital expenditure and maintenance costs

The company has high levels of both capital expenditure and maintenance costs. There is a risk of material misstatement that capital expenditure and operating expenditure have not been appropriately separated for accounting purposes.

For example, maintenance costs could be incorrectly capitalised into non-current assets, overstating assets and understating operating expenses. This could be indicated by maintenance costs representing 10.4% of revenue this year, compared to 11.7% in the previous year.

Capital expenditure is recorded at $32 million this year compared to $20 million in the previous year; this significant increase can be at least partly explained by two new centres being opened in the year, but audit work will need to focus on the possible overstatement of the capital expenditure.

### Government grant

The company has received a $2 million grant this year, which has been recognised as other operating income. The amount is material, representing 29% of projected profit before tax.

The risk of material misstatement relates to whether this should all have been recognised as income in the current accounting period. IAS® 20 *Accounting for Government Grants and Disclosure of Government Assistance* requires that government grants are recognised in profit or loss on a systematic basis over the periods in which the entity recognises expenses for the related costs for which the grants are intended to compensate.

Redback Sports Co has recognised all the income this year, however, the scheme is intended to run for three years. Therefore there is a risk that the company has recognised the income too early, and a proportion of it should remain as deferred income; this leads to overstated profit and understated liabilities.

There could be a further issue in that the terms of the grant may require complete or partial repayment if the required number of hours of free access to sport facilities is not met. If any such terms exist, the company should evaluate whether the terms are likely to be met, and if not, should consider whether it would be appropriate to recognise a provision or disclose a contingent liability in the notes to the financial statements.

The risk is therefore that this has not been considered by management, leading possibly to understated liabilities or inadequate disclosure as required by IAS 37 *Provisions, Contingent Liabilities and Contingent Assets.*

### Data management system

The introduction of new systems, especially those which interface with the accounting system, creates a risk of material misstatement. Errors could have been made in the transfer of data from the old to the new system, and as this system deals with membership information, it is likely to impact on how revenue is recorded and processed.

Not all staff may yet have been trained in operating the system, leading to a higher risk of error, and controls may not yet have been fully implemented. This all means that transactions and balances relating to members are at risk of misstatement.

**Fee paid to celebrity athlete**

The $1 million paid to the celebrity athlete is material, representing 14.4% of projected net profit for the year.

Given that the athlete is providing a service to the company for two years, the cost should be recognised over that two-year period, with an element of the cost deferred until the 20Y0 financial statements.

If all of the expense has been recognised this year, profit is understated and assets are understated.

**Operating expenses**

Operating expenses includes staff costs, which are projected to increase by 7%, marketing costs, which are projected to stay at the same amount compared to 20X8, and maintenance and repair costs which have increased by 3.8%.

Given the increase in revenue of 17.8%, and the scale of operations increasing by the opening of two new centres, these categories of expenses would be expected to increase by a larger amount this year.

It could be that expenses have been omitted in error, or have been deliberately excluded, thereby understating expenses and overstating profit. These trends should be discussed with management, especially the staff costs, as this alone is highly material, representing 28.9% of projected revenue.

**Bank loan**

During the year, the company took out a significant loan of $30 million; this is material as it represents 23.1% of total assets.

The loan has been issued at a deep discount and there is a risk of material misstatement in that the finance costs associated with this loan may not be accounted for in accordance with IFRS® 9 *Financial Instruments*. IFRS 9 requires that the finance cost associated with a deep discount – in this case the $4 million difference between the amount received by Redback Sports Co of $30 million, and the amount repayable on maturity of the debt of $34 million – should be amortised over the term of the loan.

The risk is that finance costs and non-current liabilities will be understated if the appropriate finance cost is not accrued in this financial year.

**Related party transaction**

The managing director of Redback Sports Co, Bob Glider, has made a loan to the company of $1 million. While this is not material in monetary terms, representing only 0.8% of total assets, it is material by nature and is a related party transaction according to IAS 24 *Related Party Disclosures* given that the loan to the company is from a member of key management personnel.

The relevant disclosures as required by IAS 24 must be made in the notes to the financial statements, and there is a risk that the disclosures are incomplete. The necessary disclosures include information on the nature of the related party transaction, its amount, and the relevant terms and conditions of the loan.

There is also a risk that interest will not be accrued on the loan. The loan was made on 1 July 20X8, so by the year end interest of $20,000 ($1m × 3% × 8/12) should be accrued. This is not material in monetary terms to the financial statements as it represents less than 1% of projected profit before tax, however, audit judgement may conclude that it is material given the related party nature of the transaction.

**(c)    Principal audit procedures to be used on the government grant**

- Obtain the documentation relating to the grant, to confirm the amount, the date the cash was transferred to the company, the period covered by the grant, and terms on which the grant was awarded.

- Review the terms to confirm whether they contain any conditions relating to potential repayment of part or all of the grant if a required number of hours of free access is not met in the period covered by the grant.

- Agree the amount of cash received to the bank statement and cash book.

- Perform tests of control on the system used to record the number of free hours of access which have been used by the unemployed, focusing on how the access is recorded, to ensure that the recording is complete and accurate and that revenue is not recorded.

- Review forecasts and budgets to evaluate the pattern of anticipated use of the initiative by the unemployed, and to confirm that repayment of the grant is not likely.

- Discuss with management the accounting policy used for the receipt of cash, to confirm understanding that it has all been recognised in full this year, and to understand management's rationale for this accounting treatment.

- Recalculate the amount which should have been recognised on the basis of recognising the grant over the three-year period of the government's initiative.

**(d)    Evaluation of the matters to be considered in deciding whether to accept an engagement to provide Emu Gyms Co with an audit or limited assurance review**

Requirements and guidance relevant to accepting and continuing client relationships is contained in ISQC 1 *Quality Control for Firms that Perform Audits and Reviews of Financial Statements and Other Assurance and Related Services Engagements*. The fundamental requirements are that a firm must consider:

- Whether it is competent to perform the engagement and has the capabilities, including time and resources to do so

- Whether the relevant ethical requirements can be complied with; and

- The integrity of the client, and whether there is information which would lead it to conclude that the client lacks integrity.

**Competence and resources**

In terms of competence, our firm should be competent to perform the audit of a small company or to conduct a limited assurance review of the company's financial statements. As a firm of chartered certified accountants, and performing the audit of Redback Sports Co – a much larger company in the same industry – means that the firm has the relevant knowledge and experience to perform a high quality audit or limited assurance review.

The deadline by which the work needs to be completed should be confirmed with Mick Emu. The bank manager has suggested that the loan could be made available within the next two months, meaning that the audit or limited assurance review on the financial statements needs to be carried out as soon as possible. Our firm may not have enough staff available at short notice to perform the work required.

The other matter relevant is the scope of work which is required, this can have a significant impact on the resources needed. An audit will require more work and is therefore more resource-intensive, so it may be more difficult for our firm to carry out an audit at short notice compared to a limited assurance review. In addition, we should clarify whether the bank manager expects any work to be performed, and conclusions drawn, on the cash flow and profit forecasts, in which case more resources will need to be available to complete the engagement.

**Ethics**

**Payroll service**

Huntsman & Co provides the payroll service to Emu Gyms Co. This would give rise to a self-review threat because our firm has determined the payroll figures which form part of the financial statements which would then be subject to audit or limited assurance review and may result in over reliance on the payroll figures included in the financial statements.

Huntsman & Co should consider whether the payroll figure is material to the financial statements, and whether safeguards can be used to reduce any ethical threats to an acceptable level, for example, through the use of separate teams to provide the audit or limited assurance review and the payroll services and by having an independent second partner to review the work performed. If safeguards do not reduce the threats to an acceptable level, then the payroll service should not be carried out in addition to the audit or limited assurance review.

Providing the payroll service could also be seen as acting on behalf of management, further impairing the objectivity of the audit or limited assurance review provided on the financial statements. However, if the payroll service is purely routine transaction processing in its nature, this is less of a threat.

According to the IESBA *International Code of Ethics for Professional Accountants*, in order to avoid the risk of assuming a management responsibility, prior to accepting the non-audit service the firm should satisfy itself that company management:

- has designated an individual who possesses suitable skill, knowledge and experience to be responsible for client decisions and oversee the services

- will provide oversight of the services and evaluate the adequacy of the results of the services performed; and

- accept responsibility for the actions, if any, to be taken arising from the results of the services.

**Prospective financial information**

There would also be ethical threats arising if our firm were to perform work on the prospective financial information and also attend the meeting at the bank – this could be perceived as management involvement and creates an advocacy threat whereby the audit firm is promoting the interests of the client.

There could also be a perception by the bank that by attending the meeting, our firm is not only supporting our client's loan application, but also confirming the ability of the client to repay the loan, which is not the case. A liability issue could arise for our firm, in the event of the client defaulting on the loan, unless our firm's position is made very clear to the bank.

If a member of our firm does attend the meeting with the bank manager, it should be a representative of the firm who has not been involved with the audit or limited assurance review, and Mick should acknowledge his responsibility with regard to the preparation of the financial statements.

**Conflict of interest**

A further potential ethical issue arises in that our firm audits Redback Sports Co, which could be a competitor of Emu Gyms Co despite their difference in size. This situation can create a conflict of interest. According to the IESBA *International Code of Ethics for Professional Accountants*, before accepting a new client relationship or engagement, the audit firm should identify circumstances which could give rise to a conflict of interest and evaluate the significance of any ethical threats raised.

In this case, Huntsman & Co should disclose to both Emu Gyms Co and Redback Sports Co that the firm acts for both companies and obtain consent from both companies. The firm should also use separate teams to carry out work for the two companies and establish appropriate review procedures by an independent member of the firm.

Huntsman & Co should also remain alert for changes in circumstances which may make the conflict of interest more of an issue, for example, if Redback Sports Co identified that Emu Gyms Co could be a potential target company to acquire as part of its planned growth strategy.

**Integrity**

Emu Gyms Co is already a client of our firm, as we provide the company with a payroll service, therefore all of the necessary client due diligence will have taken place. There is nothing in the note provided by Stella Cross to indicate that client integrity could be a problem.

**(e)   Suspected fraud**

An audit and a limited assurance review differ in their scope and in the nature of procedures which are performed. It is not the purpose of either an audit or a limited assurance review to detect or prevent fraud, this is the responsibility of management, but arguably the indicators of fraud may have been noticed earlier if either had been performed.

In an audit, there is a wide scope in the work performed. Audit procedures are comprehensive, including tests of detail and tests of control, and will cover all material aspects of the financial statements. Given that historically the revenue from shop and café sales represented 5% and 8% of the company's revenue, these would represent a material source of revenue, and there would have been audit testing of the revenue transactions, including tests of detail performed on a sample basis. Additionally, the change in gross margin from 32% to 26% would have alerted the auditor to an unusual trend, leading to additional audit procedures being performed.

Part of the audit process is documenting and evaluating internal controls, and this would have involved an assessment of the controls over sales in the shops and cafés and over inventory. It is likely that deficiencies in internal controls, which may be allowing fraud to be carried out unnoticed, would be detected by the audit process and then communicated to management.

However, it is possible that even with an audit being conducted, the fraud might not have been detected. This is because frauds are usually concealed, and particularly if the employees involved have been colluding to carry out the fraud, it would be difficult to detect, especially if there has been deliberate falsification of accounting records.

In addition, the amounts involved are not highly material, the amount of inventory held by the company is small, meaning that this may not have been classified as an area with a high risk of material misstatement if an audit had been conducted. The inventory held at the shops is not likely to be material, and the inventory count might not have been attended by the audit team. Also, the detailed testing of sales transactions may not have uncovered the fraud given that the fraud appears to be based on theft of inventory. It is possible that the fraud would only have been uncovered through detailed testing of the controls over movement of inventory.

If a limited assurance review had been carried out, again it may have uncovered the fraud, but it is less likely compared to an audit. This is because a limited assurance review has a narrower scope than an audit, and investigation procedures are usually limited to only enquiry and analytical review. Tests of controls and detailed tests of detail are not carried out and therefore control deficiencies would not be picked up or reported to management, and it is not likely that inventory in the shop and café would have been a priority for review.

In conclusion, Mick is correct in thinking that if the company's financial statements had been subject to audit or limited assurance review before now, the suspected fraud is likely to have been uncovered by the audit, and may have been uncovered by a limited assurance review. However, if the fraud was well concealed, it is possible that even an audit would not have uncovered the activities of the fraudsters.

**Conclusion**

The evaluation in relation to Redback Sports Co indicates that the company faces a range of business risks, for instance, possible overtrading and problems with liquidity. There are also a number of significant audit risks which will impact on our audit planning, for example, the accounting treatment which has been applied to a government grant, and possible understatement of expenses. There is a significant risk of management bias given the company's plans for expansion. In relation to Emu Gyms Co, our firm should be able to provide a limited assurance review or audit of the company, provided that safeguards are put in place to reduce ethical threats, in particular self-review in relation to payroll costs, to an acceptable level. Finally, a discussion has been provided which considers whether an audit or limited assurance review would have uncovered the fraud which Mick suspects is taking place.

---

**Examiner's comments**

This question was a compulsory 50-mark case study style question comprising five parts. Requirements (a) – (c) focused on audit planning for an existing audit client and requirements (d) and (e) related to a non-audit client and acceptance procedures. In addition, there were four professional marks available. One professional mark is awarded for each of; a suitable heading, a brief introduction, a structured answer and clarity of explanations. All candidates should be capable of scoring a minimum of three professional marks and should note that in this examination a brief introduction is all that is required and time should not be spent writing a full-page introduction or lengthy conclusion. For a structured answer, simple headed paragraphs are the easiest way to score these marks. Candidates need not worry about spending time underlining or numbering headings as long as it is clear to which question/sub-question the points relate. For clarity marks the markers will consider whether they understood what the candidate was trying to convey and whether the discussion addressed the requirement. This is not the same as a requirement to write in perfect English and candidates are not penalised for poor spelling and grammar if the marker can understand the point being made.

---

Requirement (a), for eight marks, asked candidates to evaluate the business risks arising from the scenario in the question which focused on an existing audit client which operated a number of sports and leisure centres. This requirement is historically one where candidates achieve a strong pass and this trend continued in the December 2018 exam. It was pleasing to see that most candidates focused on the risks arising from the scenario and avoided speculative or generic risks. There were two marks available for each business risk and it should be noted that factors from the scenario could be described in a number of different ways in order to attract credit for that risk. The key here is that candidates look for a variety of indicators within the scenario on which to base their evaluation. Some candidates could improve their time management and marks here by avoiding repeating the same risk from lots of different angles – failure of the expansion strategy for example could be discussed in terms of a stock exchange listing, new gyms opened, diversification of services offered or acquisition plans however there are only two marks available for a risk connected to this indicator so discussing all of those in depth meant candidates didn't' have the time to describe sufficient risks. Candidates that remained focused here often achieved full marks. Those that focused on solely expansion and health and safety compliance from several different angles tended to only score four out of the eight available marks. Although this requirement provided candidates with a strong start to the examination, there were a significant number of candidates who demonstrated a lack of understanding over the role of nonexecutive directors in relation to the scenario. Non-executive directors (NEDs) are typically brought onto a board for their knowledge and skill in a particular field.

One such director in the question had previously been the chairman of a rival company. This director brought industry specific business experience to the board and this practice is typical in the business world, however many candidates appeared to think that he would leak information back to the company where he had previously held a non-executive position, out of loyalty. Very few candidates identified the real weaknesses in the board, such as a lack of financial expertise amongst the NEDs and a lack of an audit committee. It is often the case in exam answers that candidates do not appear to understand the difference between executive directors/management and NEDs/those charged with governance (TCWG) and as a result use the terms management and TCWG interchangeably.

Part (b), for 18 marks required candidates to evaluate the risks of material misstatements (RoMM) arising from the scenario. This was generally well attempted by the majority of candidates and covered financial reporting issues such as revenue recognition, the treatment of government grants, related party transactions and loan finance, alongside control risks such as the lack of independence of the internal audit department and systems changes. Where RoMMs covered financial reporting issues, candidates who followed the process of calculating materiality, stating the relevant accounting rule and applying that to the scenario to show where the risk arose and the impact on the financial statements were able to score full marks on risks covered. Some common issues in candidate answers included:

- Interpreting the question as all audit risks rather than RoMM which meant time was lost discussing detection risks which could not attain marks

- Lack of knowledge of basic double entry and the subsequent impact on the financial statements

- Discussing speculative risks not present in the scenario such as brands and intangible assets

- Giving audit procedures for each risk which is not required and therefore attains no credit.

It should be noted that when the question asks for RoMM, it does not require the definition of risks, theory behind audit or the audit approach to address the risks. Candidates who have studied past exams will have noted that in planning questions where audit procedures are required this has been asked for as a separate requirement and only over specific areas of the scenario.

Requirement (c) for six marks, required candidates to state principal audit procedures to be used in the audit of a grant received from the government. Candidates generally described the audit procedures well, with a source and a purpose and were able to focus on confirming the details of the grant to the formal agreement and consider the output from the system to confirm that conditions were being met. In this case the majority of the candidates were able to attain a pass on this requirement. Two common mistakes were noted; the first was the inclusion of irrelevant or ineffective tests such as reviewing board minutes for approval of the grant and written representations from management that the company had received the grant. Candidates who followed the guidance on audit procedures provided in the recent technical article should have been well prepared for this type of requirement and it should be noted that for six marks candidates should expect to give six well described procedures.

Part (d) for eight marks, introduced another client into the scenario and covered specific acceptance considerations and overall the marks here were disappointing. When considering audit acceptance, candidates are expected to cover competence and capability, ethical requirements and client integrity as specified in ISQC 1 *Quality Control for Firms that Perform Audits and Reviews of Financial Statements and Other Assurance and Related Services Engagements* as well as the commercial aspects of the decision. The requirement specifically asked candidates to evaluate these considerations with respect to an engagement to provide either an audit or a limited assurance review for an existing non-audit client. While many candidates were able to state some of the areas to be considered most did not apply these to the scenario at all and made generic comments that did not demonstrate the skills required to evaluate the situation. In this exam it is unlikely that simply stating learnt knowledge without application will be sufficient to pass any question. For example for client integrity and customer due diligence considerations marks were available for stating that as an existing client this would already have been performed but may need updated not for stating the company should perform it prior to acceptance. It was also disappointing that while most candidates know the names of ethical threats the majority of candidates still do not sufficiently justify how they arise or the implication, both of which are needed to score the marks at this level. In this case, a self-review threat arose with respect to payroll work done at the client. The firm also provided tax advice to the owner but not the company. Typical answers that candidates wrote which would not attain any credit included:

- Providing other services gives rise to a self-review threat – this statement shows no appreciation of which services give rise to this threat nor any implication.

- Providing personal tax services to the owner is a self-review threat – this is incorrect, there is generally no financial statement/audit impact arising from the owner's personal tax (if there were it would be given in the scenario – see discussion of question 3b later).

- Providing payroll services gives rise to self-review – this answer is better but still does not demonstrate that candidates know that the threat arises because the payroll figure is a material figure in the financial statements and would therefore be subject to audit by the firm.

Often candidates who were able to link the self-review to the audit of the payroll figure would not describe the implication of the threat to enable them to score a full mark. Simply saying that self-review means the auditor is not objective does not demonstrate understanding of the concept – how that lack of objectivity manifests is also required. Detailed guidance on how to discuss ethical threats for the AAA examination is provided in a recent technical article which can be found here. Candidates often missed the conflict of interest between the first client in the question and the second client and the time pressure highlighted by the deadline in the scenario.

Finally requirement (e) for six marks asked candidates to discuss whether an audit or limited assurance engagement would have identified a fraud in a minor revenue stream at the second client in previous years. Candidates who discussed materiality, sampling and the different level of testing that the two alternatives would provide tended to score well. A common mistake from candidates was to discuss forensic audits to investigate fraud which was not something asked for in the requirement. Many candidates appeared to incorrectly think that a limited review of financial statements as an alternative to an audit is the same as a review of prospective financial information.

## Marking scheme

|  |  | Marks |
|---|---|---|
| **(a)** | **Business risk evaluation** | |
| | Up to 2 marks for each audit risk identified and explained. Marks may be awarded for other, relevant business risks not included in the marking guide. In addition, allow ½ mark for relevant trends which form part of the business risk evaluation, e.g. % increase in revenue and profit before tax. | |
| | – Deficiencies in corporate governance/internal audit arrangements | 2 |
| | – Health and safety regulations – risk of non-compliance | 2 |
| | – Capital expenditure and maintenance – drain on cash flow | 2 |
| | – Liquidity problems and possible overtrading | 2 |
| | – Capacity restraints – due to big increase in members and government initiative | 2 |
| | – Marketing expenses – drain on cash | 2 |
| | – Government initiative – may impact negatively on existing memberships and risk that reporting to the government is not accurate | 2 |
| | – Expansion plans – could distract management | 2 |
| | – New management information system – risk inaccurate recording | 2 |
| | **Maximum marks** | **8** |
| **(b)** | **Risk of material misstatement evaluation** | |
| | Up to 3 marks for each ROMM evaluated. Allow 1 mark per audit risk for relevant materiality calculations, to a maximum of 4 marks. In addition, ½ mark for relevant trends which form part of the audit risk evaluation (max 3 marks). | |
| | – Management bias – risk revenue/profit overstated, expenses understated | 3 |
| | – Deficiencies in internal controls – possibly ineffective audit committee (max 2 marks) | 2 |
| | – Revenue recognition – members' subscriptions and multiple streams of revenue | 3 |
| | – Capital expenditure and maintenance costs – risk of misclassification | 3 |
| | – Government grant – risk income recognised too early and provisions not recognised | 3 |
| | – Data management system – risk in transfer of data and lack of controls | 3 |
| | – Amount paid to celebrity athlete – risk cost not spread over two-year period (max 2 marks) | 2 |

| | | |
|---|---|---|
| – | Staff costs and maintenance costs – risk of understatement (max 2 marks) | 2 |
| – | Bank loan – risk that deep discount not treated as finance cost | 3 |
| – | Related party transaction – risk of inadequate disclosure and that finance costs not accrued | 3 |
| | **Maximum marks** | **18** |

**(c)** **Audit procedures on the government grant**
Up to 1 mark for each well described procedure:

| | | |
|---|---|---|
| – | Obtain the documentation relating to the grant, confirm the amount, the date the cash was transferred to the company, the period covered by the grant, and terms on which the grant was awarded | 1 |
| – | Review the terms to confirm whether they contain any conditions relating to potential repayment of part or all of the grant | 1 |
| – | Agree the amount of cash received to the bank statement and cash book | 1 |
| – | Perform tests of control on the system used to record the number of free hours of access which have been used by the unemployed | 1 |
| – | Review forecasts and budgets to evaluate the pattern of anticipated use of the initiative by the unemployed, and to confirm that repayment of the grant is not likely | 1 |
| – | Discuss with management the accounting policy used, to confirm understanding, and to understand management's rationale | 1 |
| – | Recalculate the amount which should have been recognised on the basis of recognising the grant over the three-year period of the government's initiative | |
| | **Maximum marks** | **6** |

**(d)** **Evaluation of the matters to be considered in deciding whether to provide Emu Gyms Co with an audit or limited assurance review**
Up to 2 marks for each issue evaluated:

| | | |
|---|---|---|
| – | Recognition that engagement evaluation is part of a quality control framework (1 mark) | 1 |
| – | Competence – our firm should be competent but deadline is a problem | 2 |
| – | More resources will be needed for an audit rather than limited assurance review | 2 |
| – | Self-review threat due to providing payroll service | 2 |
| – | Assessing management responsibility | 2 |
| – | Advocacy/management involvement if attend meeting with bank | 2 |
| – | Conflict of interest as act for Redback Sports Co | 2 |
| – | Safeguards/actions re potential conflict of interest (1 mark each) | 1 |
| | **Maximum marks** | **8** |

**(e)** **Suspected fraud**
Up to 2 marks for each point of discussion:

| | | |
|---|---|---|
| – | Audit has wider scope with tests of detail and tests of control being likely to have uncovered the fraud | 2 |
| – | Limited assurance review only includes enquiry and analytical review | 2 |
| – | Limited assurance review less likely to have uncovered the fraud | 2 |
| – | Even with audit, fraud could have been concealed and may not have been detected | 2 |
| | **Maximum marks** | **6** |

| | | |
|---|---|---|
| **Professional marks** | | |
| Generally 1 mark for heading, 1 mark for introduction, 1 mark for use of headings within the briefing notes, 1 mark for clarity of comments made. | | |
| | **Maximum marks** | 4 |
| **Total** | | 50 |

## 4 EAGLE GROUP  *Walk in the footsteps of a top tutor*

### Top tutor tips

*Part (a) asks you to evaluate the audit risks to be considered when planning the audit. Audit risk comprises the risk that the financial statements contain material misstatement and detection risk. Risk of material misstatement is usually due to non-compliance with an accounting standard, although it also includes control risk. Think about the requirements of the relevant accounting standards and what the client might be doing incorrectly. Detection risks include auditing a client for the first time or where there is a tight reporting deadline.*

*Part (b) asks for audit procedures in respect of goodwill. Make sure your procedures are clear and provide enough detail that they can be followed. Pay attention to the note which instructs you NOT to consider impairment testing or foreign currency retranslation. There will be no marks awarded for these points so do not waste time considering them.*

*Part (c) requires you to evaluate the planning and comment on any issues arising from the proposed audit strategy. This is essentially a quality control question but focused on the planning of the audit rather than the audit work that has been performed during the audit.*

*Part (d) covers a common ethical issue relating to provision of a non-audit service to an audit client. Your answer should explain the ethical threats that would arise, evaluate the significance of the threats and state the actions the firm should take to manage the threats.*

### Briefing notes

**To:**       Maya Crag, audit engagement partner

**From:**    Audit manager

**Subject:**  Eagle Group – audit planning

### Introduction

These briefing notes are prepared to assist with planning the audit of the Eagle Group (the Group) for the financial year ending 31 December 20X8. The notes contain an evaluation of the audit risks which should be considered in planning the Group audit. The notes also recommend the principal audit procedures to be used in the audit of the goodwill which has arisen in respect of a newly acquired subsidiary. The notes then go on to evaluate an extract from the audit strategy which has been prepared by a component auditor. Finally, the Group finance director has requested our firm to provide a non-audit service in relation to the Group's integrated report, and the notes discuss the professional and ethical implications of this request.

**(a)    Evaluation of audit risk**

**Selected analytical procedures and associated audit risk evaluation**

|  | 20X8 | 20X7 |
|---|---|---|
| Operating margin | 350/5,770 × 100 = 6.1% | 270/5,990 × 100 = 4.5% |
| Return on capital employed | (350/2,245 + 650) × 100 = 12.1% | (270/2,093 + 620) × 100 = 10% |
| Current ratio | 1,450/597 = 2.4 | 1,420/547 = 2.6 |
| Debt/equity | 550/2,245 × 100 = 24.5% | 500/2,093 × 100 = 23.9% |
| Interest cover | 350/28 = 12.5 | 270/30 = 9 |
| Effective tax rate | 64/322 × 100 = 19.9% | 60/240 × 100 = 25% |

**Operating margin and operating expenses**

The Group's operating margin has increased from 4.5% to 6.1% despite a fall in revenue of 3.7%. This is due to a reduction in operating expenses of 4.5% and increase in other operating income of 50%. Return on capital employed shows a similar positive trend, despite the fall in revenue. There is an audit risk that expenses are understated, with the reduction in expenses being proportionately more than the reduction in revenue.

Within operating expenses the trends for each component are different – cost of raw materials consumables and supplies has decreased by 3.1%, which appears reasonable given the decline in revenue of 3.7%. However, staff costs have increased slightly by 1.1% which seems inconsistent with the revenue trend and with the increased automation of operations which has led to 5,000 staff being made redundant, which presumably means lower payroll costs this year. Expenses could have been misclassified into staff costs in error.

Depreciation, amortisation and impairment has increased by 3.6%, which is not a significant change, but will need to be investigated to consider how each element of the category has changed in the year. The most noticeable trend within operating expenses is that the other operating expenses category has reduced very significantly. The amount recognised this financial year is only 7.4% of the amount recognised the previous year; this appears totally inconsistent with the other trends noted. It could be that some costs, for example, accrued expenses, have not yet been accounted for, or that the 20X7 figure was unusually high.

**Other operating income**

There is also an audit risk that other operating income is overstated. According to the information in note 6, during the year a credit of $60 million has been recognised in profit for reversals of provisions, this is 50% greater than the amount recognised in the previous year. In addition, a credit of $30 million has been recognised for reversals of impairment losses. There is a risk that these figures have been manipulated in order to boost profits, as an earnings management technique, in reaction to the fall in revenue in the year.

The risk of management bias is high given the listed status of the Group, hence expectations from shareholders for a positive growth trend. The profit recognised on asset disposal and the increase in foreign currency gains could also be an indication of attempts to boost operating profit this year.

## Current ratio and gearing

Looking at the other ratios, the current ratio and gearing ratio do not indicate audit risks; however, more detail is needed to fully conclude on the liquidity and solvency position of the Group, and whether there are any hidden trends which are obscured by the high level analysis which has been performed with the information provided.

The interest cover has increased, due to both an increase in operating profit and a reduction in finance charges. This seems contradictory to the increase in borrowings of $50 million; as a result of this an increase in finance charges would be expected. There is an audit risk that finance charges are understated.

## Effective tax rate

The effective tax rate has fallen from 25% to 19.9%. An audit risk arises in that the tax expense and associated liability could be understated. This could indicate management bias as the financial statements suggest that accounting profit has increased, but the profit chargeable to tax used to determine the tax expense for the year appears to have decreased. There could be alternative explanations, for instance a fall in the rate of tax levied by the authorities, which will need to be investigated by the audit team.

## Consolidation of foreign subsidiaries

Given that the Group has many foreign subsidiaries, including the recent investment in Lynx Co, audit risks relating to their consolidation are potentially significant. Lynx Co has net assets with a fair value of $300 million according to the goodwill calculation provided by management, representing 8.6% of the Group's total assets and 13.4% of Group net assets. This makes Lynx Co material to the Group and possibly a significant component of the Group. Audit risks relevant to Lynx Co's status as a foreign subsidiary also attach to the Group's other foreign subsidiaries.

According to IAS 21 *The Effects of Changes in Foreign Exchange Rates*, the assets and liabilities of Lynx Co and other foreign subsidiaries should be retranslated using the closing exchange rate. Its income and expenses should be retranslated at the exchange rates at the dates of the transactions. The risk is that incorrect exchange rates are used for the retranslations. This could result in over/understatement of the assets, liabilities, income and expenses which are consolidated, including goodwill. It would also mean that the exchange gains and losses arising on retranslation and to be included in Group other comprehensive income are incorrectly determined.

In addition, Lynx Co was acquired on 1 March 20X8 and its income and expenses should have been consolidated from that date. There is a risk that the full year's income and expenses have been consolidated, leading to a risk of understatement of Group profit given that Lynx Co is forecast to be loss making this year, according to the audit strategy prepared by Vulture Associates.

## Measurement and recognition of exchange gains and losses

The calculation of exchange gains and losses can be complex, and there is a risk that it is not calculated correctly, or that some elements are omitted, for example, the exchange gain or loss on goodwill may be missed out of the calculation.

IAS 21 states that exchange gains and losses arising as a result of the retranslation of the subsidiary's balances are recognised in other comprehensive income. The risk is incorrect classification, for example, the gain or loss could be recognised incorrectly as part of profit for the year, for example, included in the $28 million foreign currency gains which form part of other operating income, which would be incorrect. The amount recognised within other operating income has increased, as only $23 million foreign currency gains were recognised the previous year, indicating a potential risk of overstatement.

**Goodwill**

The total goodwill recognised in the Group statement of financial position is $1,100 million, making it highly material at 31.5% of total assets.

Analytical review shows that the goodwill figure has increased by $130 million during the year. The goodwill relating to the acquisition of Lynx Co is $100 million according to management's calculations. Therefore there appears to be an unexplained increase in value of goodwill of $30 million during the year and there is an audit risk that the goodwill figure is overstated, unless justified by additional acquisitions or possibly by changes in value on the retranslation of goodwill relating to foreign subsidiaries, though this latter point would seem unlikely given the large size of the unexplained increase in value.

According to IFRS 3 *Business Combinations*, goodwill should be subject to an impairment review on an annual basis. Management has asserted that while they will test goodwill for impairment prior to the financial year end, they do not think that any impairment will be recognised. This view is based on what could be optimistic assumptions about further growth in revenue, and it is likely that the assumptions used in management's impairment review are similarly overoptimistic. Therefore there is a risk that goodwill will be overstated and Group operating expenses understated if impairment losses have not been correctly determined and recognised.

**Initial measurement of goodwill arising on acquisition of Lynx Co**

In order for goodwill to be calculated, the assets and liabilities of Lynx Co must have been identified and measured at fair value at the date of acquisition. Risks of material misstatement arise because the various components of goodwill each have specific risks attached. The goodwill of $100 million is material to the Group, representing 2.9% of Group assets.

A specific risk arises in relation to the fair value of net assets acquired. Not all assets and liabilities may have been identified, for example, contingent liabilities and contingent assets may be omitted.

A further risk relates to measurement at fair value, which is subjective and based on assumptions which may not be valid. The fair value of Lynx Co's net assets according to the goodwill calculation is $300 million, having been subject to a fair value uplift of $12 million. This was provided by an independent firm of accountants, which provides some comfort on the validity of the figure.

There is also a risk that the cost of investment is not stated correctly, for example, that the contingent consideration has not been determined on an appropriate basis.

First, the interest rate used to determine the discount factor is 18% – this seems high given that the Group's weighted average cost of capital is stated to be 10%.

Second, the contingent consideration is only payable if Lynx Co reaches certain profit targets. Given that the company, according to Vulture Associate's audit strategy, is projected to be loss making, it could be that the contingent consideration need not be recognised at all, or determined to be a lower figure than that currently recognised, based on a lower probability of it having to be paid.

The results of the analytical review have indicated that the other side of the journal entry for the contingent consideration is not described as a component of the non-current liabilities and the accounting for this will need to be clarified as there is a risk that it has been recorded incorrectly, perhaps as a component of equity.

**Intangible assets**

In relation to expenditure on intangible assets during the year, which totals $60 million, there are several audit risks. First, there is a question over whether all of this amount should have been capitalised as an intangible asset. Capitalisation is only appropriate where an asset has been created, and specifically in relation to development costs, the criteria from IAS 38 *Intangible Assets* must all be met. There is a risk that if any criteria have not been met, for example, if there is no probable future economic benefit from research into the new technology, then the amount should be expensed. There is a risk that intangible assets are overstated and operating expenses understated.

There is also an unexplained trend, in that intangible assets has only increased by $30 million, yet expenditure on intangible assets, according to management information, is $60 million. More information is needed to reconcile the expenditure as stated by management to the movement in intangible assets recognised in the Group statement of financial position.

Second, there is a risk that the amortisation period is not appropriate. It seems that the same useful life of 15 years has been applied to all of the different categories of intangible assets; this is not likely to be specific enough, for example, the useful life of an accounting system will not be the same as for development of robots. Fifteen years also seems to be a long period – usually technology-related assets are written off over a relatively short period to take account of rapid developments in technology. In respect of amortisation periods being too long, there is a risk that intangible assets are overstated and operating expenses understated.

**Detection risk in relation to Lynx Co**

Lynx Co is the only subsidiary which is not audited by Bison & Co. This gives rise to a risk that the quality of the audit of Lynx Co may not be to the same standard as Bison & Co, as Vulture Associates may not be used to auditing companies which form part of a listed group and results in increased detection risk at the Group level. The risk is increased by the problems with the audit strategy prepared by Vulture Associates, which will be discussed in part (c) to these briefing notes, which indicate that the audit of Lynx Co has not been appropriately planned in accordance with ISA requirements. Since our firm has not worked with Vulture Associates previously, we are not familiar with their methods and we may have issues with the quality of their work; therefore the detection risk is high in relation to Lynx Co's balances which will form part of the consolidated financial statements.

**(b)** **Principal audit procedures on the goodwill arising on the acquisition of Lynx Co**

–   Obtain the legal documentation pertaining to the acquisition, and review to confirm that the figures included in the goodwill calculation relating to consideration paid and payable are accurate and complete. In particular, confirm the targets to be used as the basis for payment of the contingent consideration in four years' time.

–   Also confirm from the purchase documentation that the Group has obtained an 80% shareholding and that this conveys control, i.e. the shares carry voting rights and there is no restriction on the Group exercising their control over Lynx Co.

–   Agree the $80 million cash paid to the bank statement and cash book of the acquiring company (presumably the parent company of the Group).

–   Review the board minutes for discussions relating to the acquisition, and for the relevant minute of board approval.

–   For the contingent consideration, obtain management's calculation of the present value of $271 million, and evaluate assumptions used in the calculation, in particular to consider the probability of payment by obtaining revenue and profit forecasts for Lynx Co for the next four years.

–   Discuss with management the reason for using an 18% interest rate in the calculation, asking them to justify the use of this interest rate when the Group's weighted average cost of capital is stated at 10%.

–   Evaluate management's rationale for using the 18% interest rate, concluding as to whether it is appropriate.

–   Confirm that the fair value of the non-controlling interest has been calculated based on an externally available share price at the date of acquisition. Agree the share price used in management's calculation to stock market records showing the share price of Lynx Co at the date of acquisition.

–   Obtain a copy of the due diligence report issued by Sidewinder & Co, review for confirmation of acquired assets and liabilities and their fair values.

–   Evaluate the methods used to determine the fair value of acquired assets, including the property, and liabilities to confirm compliance with IFRS 3 and IFRS 13 *Fair Value Measurement*.

–   Review the calculation of net assets acquired to confirm that Group accounting policies have been applied.

**(c)** **Evaluation of the extract of the audit strategy prepared by Vulture Associates in respect of their audit of Lynx Co**

The extract from the audit strategy covers two areas – reliance on internal controls, and the use of internal audit for external audit work. In each area it appears that ISA requirements have not been followed, meaning that the quality of the audit planned by Vulture Associates is in doubt.

### INT & UK: Controls effectiveness

In relation to reliance on internal controls, ISA 330 *The Auditor's Responses to Assessed Risks* contains requirements in relation to relying on work performed during previous audits on internal controls. ISA 330 states that if the auditor plans to use audit evidence from a previous audit about the operating effectiveness of specific controls, the auditor shall establish the continuing relevance of that evidence by obtaining audit evidence about whether significant changes in those controls have occurred subsequent to the previous audit.

The auditor shall obtain this evidence by performing inquiry combined with observation or inspection, to confirm the understanding of those specific controls, and if there have been changes which affect the continuing relevance of the audit evidence from the previous audit, the auditor shall test the controls in the current audit.

If there have not been such changes, the auditor shall test the controls at least once in every third audit, and shall test some controls each audit to avoid the possibility of testing all the controls on which the auditor intends to rely on a single audit period with no testing of controls in the subsequent two audit periods.

Therefore, in order to comply with ISA 330, Vulture Associates needs to do more than simply accept management's assertion that there have been no changes to controls. There needs to be some observation or inspection of controls, to confirm that there have been no changes, and this work and an appropriate conclusion need to be documented in the audit working papers.

In addition, there should be some testing of internal controls each year, so Vulture Associates should plan to perform some test of controls each year, so that over a three-year cycle, all controls are tested to confirm that controls are still operating effectively and therefore can continue to be relied upon.

The Group audit team should discuss this issue with Vulture Associates to ensure that adequate controls testing is performed. If, for some reason, Vulture Associates does not amend its audit strategy, then the Group audit team may decide to perform additional testing, given that Lynx Co is material to the Group.

### INT: Internal audit

According to ISA 610 *Using the Work of Internal Auditors*, it is acceptable, in some circumstances, for the external audit firm to use the internal audit function of an audited entity to provide direct assistance to the external audit team. However, in some jurisdictions, due to local regulations, the external auditor is prohibited from using internal auditors to provide direct assistance, and therefore the Group auditor team will need to consider whether the prohibition also extends to component auditors and, if so, it would not be appropriate for Vulture Associates to use the internal audit function. Assuming that there is no local restriction, before deciding whether to use the internal audit function, the external auditor must evaluate a number of factors, including:

– The extent to which the internal audit function's organisational status and relevant policies and procedures support the objectivity of the internal auditors.

– The level of competence of the internal audit function.

– Whether the internal audit function applies a systematic and disciplined approach, including quality control.

Vulture Associates must therefore perform this evaluation before making any decision about whether they should instruct the internal audit team to perform audit procedures. For example, if they find that the internal audit function does not have a good quality control procedure, it would not be appropriate to use them in external audit work.

Using the internal audit function to perform audit procedures is direct assistance to the external auditor. ISA 610 requires that where direct assistance is being provided, the external auditor shall evaluate the existence and significance of threats to objectivity and the level of competence of the internal auditors who will be providing such assistance. The external auditor shall not use an internal auditor to provide direct assistance if there are significant threats to the objectivity of the internal auditor or the internal auditor lacks sufficient competence to perform the proposed work. Vulture Associates therefore needs to document and conclude upon their assessment of the internal auditors' objectivity and competence.

There is also an issue with regard to the type of work they are given to perform. Vulture Associates is planning to ask the internal auditors to perform specific audit procedures in relation to trade receivables but this is not likely to be appropriate. ISA 610 states that the external auditor shall make all significant judgements in the audit engagement. Performing a trade receivables circularisation and reviewing the allowance against trade receivables both involve judgements, in relation to sample selection and also in relation to measurement of the receivables. The trade receivables is also likely to be a material balance in the financial statements. Therefore it would not be appropriate for the internal audit team to complete the audit, though they could be used for performing routine procedures not involving the use of judgement.

A further issue is that ISA 610 specifically states that the external auditor shall not use internal auditors to provide direct assistance to perform procedures which relate to work with which the internal auditors have been involved and which has already been, or will be, reported to management or those charged with governance. From the audit strategy, it appears that the internal audit function has worked on trade receivables during the year, so it would not be appropriate for the internal auditors to provide direct assistance to the external audit firm in relation to this area due to the self-review threat which would be created.

It may be possible for the internal auditors to provide direct assistance on non-judgemental areas of the financial statements if they have not performed internal audit work relating to those areas during the year.

### UK: Pension plan valuation

In relation to the valuation of the pension plan, it is not appropriate for a partner in Vulture Associates to have provided the pension plan valuation, as this creates several significant threats to auditor objectivity. In particular, a self-review threat arises due to the pension plan forming part of the financial statements on which the auditor expresses an opinion as the audit team may be reluctant to highlight errors or concerns on the work carried out by the partner. Performing the valuation may also result in a management threat whereby the audit firm may be perceived to be taking on the responsibilities of management, resulting in the firm becoming closely aligned with the views and interest of management and the partner not applying an appropriate degree of scepticism to the valuation.

ISA 600 (UK) *Special Considerations – Audits of Group Financial Statements (Including the Work of Component Auditors)* requires the group auditor to obtain an understanding as to whether the component auditor understands and will comply with the ethical requirements which are relevant to the group audit and, in particular, is independent.

This is because when performing work on the financial information of a component for a group audit, the component auditor is subject to ethical requirements which are relevant to the group audit. Therefore, the audit of Lynx Co should be conducted subject to UK principles and requirements as contained in the FRC Ethical Standard.

The Ethical Standard prohibits the external auditor from providing valuation services where the valuation would have a material effect on the financial statements. The pension plan is in deficit by £11 million, and the deficit is material to Lynx Co's financial statements, representing 3.7% of its net assets (according to management's goodwill calculation). Therefore, if the FRC Ethical Standard is applied to the situation, Vulture Associates should not have performed the valuation service.

The audit strategy also indicates that other significant non-audit services are provided by Vulture Associates, with fees amounting to £100,000. This indicates that there could be a self-interest threat to the objectivity of the audit firm, due to fee dependency. This has implications for the quality of the audit work performed.

It could be that Vulture Associates follows a local ethical code or standard which permits such valuation services to be provided. However, the situation is not acceptable for the purpose of the Group audit. The Group audit committee should be made aware of the situation, and if a separate valuation is not provided at the level of the individual company, then the Group audit strategy should consider including additional, independent work on the valuation of Lynx Co's pension plan. On a net basis, the pension plan deficit is less than 1% of Group total assets, however, the plan assets and the plan liabilities on an individual basis represent 1.1% and 1.4% of Group total assets, so are borderline in terms of materiality to the Group.

In conclusion, from the evaluation of this extract from the audit strategy, it seems that Vulture Associates is planning to carry out the audit of Lynx Co in a manner which does not comply with ISA requirements (and ethical requirements in the UK). This is a concern, given the materiality of the subsidiary to the Group, and our firm should liaise with Vulture Associates as soon as possible to discuss their audit planning.

**(d)   Ethical and professional implications of the request to provide a non-audit service on the Group's integrated report**

There are several issues to consider with regard to providing this service.

A significant issue relates to auditor objectivity. The IESBA *International Code of Ethics for Professional Accountants* (the *Code*) provides guidance on situations where the auditor is asked by the client to provide non-assurance services. Bison & Co needs to evaluate the significance of the threat and consider whether any safeguards can reduce the threat to an acceptable level.

While the integrated report is not part of the audited financial statements, the report will contain financial key performance indicators (KPIs), and the Group has asked for input specifically relating to the reconciliations between these KPIs and financial information contained in the financial statements. There is therefore a potential self-review threat to objectivity in that the audit firm has been asked to provide assurance on these KPIs which are related to figures which have been subject to external audit by the firm. The team performing the work will be reluctant to raise queries or highlight errors which have been made during the external audit when assessing the reconciliations of KPIs to audited financial information.

It could also be perceived that Bison & Co is taking on management responsibility by helping to determine content to be included in the integrated report, which is a threat to objectivity. The *Code* states that the audit firm shall not assume management responsibility for an audit client and that the threats created are so significant that safeguards cannot reduce them to an acceptable level.

While the *Code* does not specifically state that helping the client to determine the content of its integrated report is taking on management responsibility, certainly there could be that perception as the auditor will be involved in setting measurements which the company will benchmark itself against.

Additionally, working with management on the integrated report could create a familiarity threat to objectivity whereby close working relationships are formed, and the auditor becomes closely aligned with the views of management and is unable to approach the work with an appropriate degree of professional scepticism.

There is a potential problem in terms of compliance with ISA 720 *The Auditor's Responsibilities Relating to Other Information*, should Bison & Co accept the engagement. ISA 720 requires that auditors read other information in order to identify any material inconsistencies between the financial statements and information in the other information.

ISA 720 applies only to other information in the annual report, and it is not stated whether the Group's integrated report will be included in the annual report, or as a standalone document. Based on the above, it would seem unlikely that Bison & Co can provide this service to the Group, due to the threats to objectivity created.

Should the firm decide to take on the engagement, safeguards should be used to minimise the threats. For example, a partner who is independent should be involved in reviewing the audit work performed.

Aside from ethical issues, Bison & Co must also consider whether they have the competence to perform the work. Advising on the production of an integrated report is quite a specialist area, and it could be that the audit firm does not have the appropriate levels of expertise and experience to provide a quality service to the Group.

The fact that the Group wants to highlight its technological achievements, and presumably will select a range of non-financial KPIs and technological issues to discuss in the integrated report, makes the issue of competence more significant, as the audit firm may not have the necessary technical knowledge to provide advice in this area.

Aside from competence, the firm should also consider whether it has resources in terms of staff availability to complete the work to the desired deadline and to perform appropriate reviews of the work which has been completed.

Finally, given that the Group is a listed entity, it should comply with relevant corporate governance requirements. This means that the audit firm may be prohibited from providing services in addition to providing the external audit to the Group. The audit committee should apply the Group's policy on the engagement of the external auditor to supply non-audit services, the objective of which should be to ensure that the provision of such services does not impair the external auditor's independence or objectivity.

The Group's audit committee will need to pre-approve the provision of the service, and in making this decision they should consider a number of matters, for instance, the audit committee should consider whether the skills and experience of the audit firm make it the most suitable supplier of the non-audit service, whether there are safeguards in place to eliminate or reduce to an acceptable level any threat to objectivity and the level of fees to be incurred relative to the audit fee.

### Conclusion

These briefing notes indicate that there are a large number of audit risks to be considered in planning the audit, and that management needs to supply the audit team with a range of additional information for more thorough audit planning to be carried out. The audit of goodwill, and in particular the goodwill arising on the acquisition of Lynx Co, is an area of significant audit risk, and the notes recommend the principal audit procedures which should be conducted. An evaluation of the audit strategy prepared by Vulture Associates indicates that their audit of Lynx Co might not be a high quality audit. Finally, our firm needs to discuss the request to assist in preparing the Group's integrated report with the Group audit committee, and it seems unlikely given the threat of management involvement that we would be able to carry out this work for the Group.

---

**Examiner's comments**

Question one was a 50-mark case study style question with four requirements. It was set at the planning stage for an audit in a similar style to the specimen exam and to question one under the old P7 examination structure. The client was a large international listed distribution company which had a new foreign subsidiary acquisition in the year. Consistent with previous sessions four professional marks were available.

The first requirement was to produce an analysis of audit risks using analytical review of financials and other information provided on specific issues arising during the year. The format was the same as in the specimen exam and the requirement was worth 24 marks. Of these, up to five marks were available for the calculations forming part of the analytical review and up to four marks could be obtained for relevant materiality calculations and conclusions. The majority of marks were available for the evaluation of significant audit risks, which is consistent with past requirements of this type. This requirement was generally well attempted by the majority of candidates who calculated relevant ratios, discussed the risks arising from unexpected trends and relationships, and then analysed the risks arising from the specific issues described in the question. Using this approach and providing an evaluation containing the required level of detail, well prepared candidates were able to identify the specific risks from the information provided and score a clear pass on this part of the question.

---

The model answers provided to recent past audit risk questions will illustrate how to structure answers to achieve maximum credit on this sort of requirement. It was pleasing to note that very few candidates spent time describing the theory of audit risk which is not required and should not be included in an answer unless the examiner has asked for it. Despite the good attempt made on this part of the examination there were some common exam technique issues which resulted in difficulties for candidates in terms of attaining marks and managing their time. The first of these was the approach taken by some candidates to the analytical review.

Common issues arising from the analytical review were:

- Calculating too many ratios and trends which were not then mentioned in the main body of the candidate's answer and were a waste of effort - candidates are expected to demonstrate the auditing skill of knowing which items are unlikely to give rise to an audit risk – for example an immaterial area of the statement of financial position that hasn't moved much since the previous year and is not referred to in the question scenario is less likely to contain an audit risk. Candidates should consider how many risks and calculations are likely to be needed to score full marks rather than calculate 30+ ratio/trends which they then do not have time to discuss. A few key ratios along the lines of those seen in the answers to past questions are most likely to direct candidates on where to focus.

- Calculating ratios and then not referring to them – an analytical review is not simply calculating ratios. The ability to calculate ratios is examined within earlier parts of the qualification. It is what the results show that is the applied skill in this area and candidates who do not use the results of their calculations to draw conclusions and identify risks will not be able to attain credit.

- Not calculating any ratios – ignoring the requirement to perform an analytical review will restrict the risks identified from the scenario and hence make scoring maximum credit very difficult. This was most apparent in scripts from candidates sitting the UK version of the examination where many scored very few marks on this section of the question.

Another common mistake candidates made on this requirement was to spend a lot of time discussing speculative risks which generally do not obtain credit. The fact that a company is multinational with many subsidiaries does not automatically result in a key audit risk regarding the inability of the company to know how to perform a consolidation, or to account for foreign currency. The fact that this is not a new client and the audit engagement partner did not raise any concerns in this regard past should be taken as a sign that these are things are not key issues. Candidates should instead focus on the details given in the scenario that the engagement partner thought relevant to highlight. In this case, the acquisition of a new subsidiary and the risks arising from what is a significant non-routine transaction, the significant spend during the year on research and development which has been capitalised, and the fact that management does not believe there is any impairment of assets despite falling revenues. Recent past question answers illustrate the sort of risks which are considered relevant to the accompanying scenarios. Speculative risks do not attract credit in the examination and it is surprising that candidates chose to evaluate such risks when there were so many specific risks contained within the scenario. This session it was disappointing how many candidates opened with speculative risks such as failure to cancel intercompany balances, failure to account for day-to-day foreign currency transactions, and the control risk arising from international subsidiaries.

Candidates would score better if they were to prioritise risks in their planning and to focus on the ones described in detail by the examiner in the scenario rather than reproducing a rote learnt list of general points which do not demonstrate any application of knowledge to the scenario itself. A related mistake made by candidates was to discuss operating segments and EPS disclosures despite the requirement stating that these should not be considered. This has been the case in several sessions where the examiner has requested candidates do not consider presentation risks. Other commonly seen technical errors arose in relation to provisions where candidates would assume that redundancies early in the financial year would give rise to a year-end redundancy provision.

Post year-end redundancies are those which may give rise to a provision. Similarly, candidates often thought that, because automation was introduced during the year, it was likely that a similar strategy would exist in the future therefore provisions should be made for more redundancies "just in case". Such reasoning demonstrates a lack of comprehension of the fundamental concept of a liability and the requirement for a constructive obligation to exist before a provision can be made. For up–to-date examples of how audit risk is examined and the sort of points the examiner expects to be raised from a given scenario, candidates should refer to the September 2018 examination, the specimen exam, the March/June 2018 and the September/December 2016 published sample questions and answers. Candidates should note however that these are illustrative and that not every risk covered in those examples will be relevant to future questions on audit risk. A helpful exercise might be to map back the areas covered in the model answers to the indicators in the specific scenario to better understand how the examiner's answers reflect the specific areas of the information provided. In particular the September 2018 exam should provide an illustration of the type and volume of calculations that the examiner considered appropriate based on the marks available and the information provided. In addition to these issues, otherwise capable candidates failed to attain a strong mark on this section of the examination by failing to address the requirement. Particularly common in the UK and Irish versions of the examination was candidates discussing issues in terms of business risk or audit procedures, which were not asked for, and not actually evaluating the audit risk. Often candidates referred to accounting standards by number but made no attempt to describe the accounting treatment or to apply it to the scenario to determine the risks of material misstatement or would simply say that areas might be misstated without reference to the balance or direction of misstatement.

The second requirement for six marks asked candidates to provide audit procedures on the goodwill figure at acquisition for the subsidiary purchased in the year. Where candidates focused on the specific requirement and addressed the acquisition figure they generally scored full marks or close to full marks. Some candidates limited their marks here by discussing impairment reviews and disclosures instead.

The third requirement was a 10-mark requirement asking candidates to review and evaluate specific parts of the component auditor's strategy. This was the area of Question one which caused candidates the most difficulty. The requirement asked candidates to specifically focus only on the two issues mentioned in isolation and that all other considerations were satisfactory. Despite this a majority of candidates wrote answers describing the assessment of independence and competence of the component auditor. The first part of the strategy related to the intention to audit using a controls-based strategy but without testing controls this year as prior year results were good. Those that did go so far as to appraise the component strategy often thought that a controls-based approach was not permitted, and substantive testing should be performed in all places. Very few candidates appeared to appreciate that controls may be tested on a three-year cycle rather than every year.

The second area to be considered differed in the UK/IRL version of the examination from the INT examination. INT candidates were asked to appraise the components strategy of obtaining direct assistance from internal audit. Reponses here were mixed, with many candidates simply stating that internal auditors are not competent or independent and therefore could not be used. Given that candidates should be expecting to earn five marks on this requirement it should have been clear that more than once sentence was required to pass this part of the question. UK and IRL candidates were told that the component auditor had performed a pension valuation for the new subsidiary.

Many appeared to think this was a signal that the figure could be relied upon rather than considering the materiality of the balance and the fact that external auditors are not permitted to provide valuation services for listed clients where the amounts would be material to the financial statements.

The final requirement related to the client's request for the auditor to be involved in choosing KPIs for inclusion in the client's integrated report and to provide assurance on the report. Many candidates realised that there were ethical issues arising from this but did not explain specifically how they would arise or what the implication would be. Candidates should be prepared to give such detail in order to demonstrate understanding rather than simply list without explanation every possible threat to independence.

Candidates should note that the presentation marks are awarded for a suitable heading, a brief introduction, a structured answer and clarity of explanations. All candidates should be scoring a minimum of three professional marks and should note that in this examination a brief introduction need be no more than a single sentence and time should not be spent writing a full-page introduction. For a structured answer, headed paragraphs are the easiest way to score these marks. For clarity marks the markers will consider whether they understood what the candidate was trying to convey and whether the discussion addressed the requirement. This is not the same as a requirement to write in perfect English and candidates are not penalised for poor spelling and grammar as long as the marker can understand the point being made.

For guidance on how to provide the required level of detail, students should refer to the technical articles on Exam Technique for Advanced Audit and Assurance on the ACCA website.

| | Marking scheme | Marks |
|---|---|---|

**(a)  Audit risk evaluation**

Up to 3 marks for each audit risk identified and explained. Marks may be awarded for other relevant audit risks not included in the marking guide.

In addition, 1 mark for relevant ratios and ½ mark for relevant trends which form part of analytical review to a max of 5 marks.

Materiality calculations should be awarded 1 mark each to a max of 4 marks.

- Operating margin and ROCE changes – risk understated expenses/ overstated revenue
- Trends within operating expenses and related audit risks, e.g. misclassification of expenses
- Other operating income – risk of overstatement
- Risk of management bias due to listed status (max 2 marks)
- Current ratio & gearing and related audit risks – understated finance costs
- Effective tax rate – understatement of tax expense (max 2 marks)
- Consolidation of foreign subsidiaries
- Recognition and measurement of foreign exchange gains and losses
- Goodwill –measurement risk – lack of impairment review
- Goodwill on acquisition of Lynx Co (max 4 for detailed discussion)
- Intangible assets – audit risks in relation to unexplained movement in the year, whether amounts should have been capitalised and amortisation period (max 5 marks)
- Increased detection risk regarding Lynx Co due to be audited by a component auditor

**Maximum  24**

**(b)  Audit procedures on the goodwill recognised on acquisition of Lynx Co**

Up to 1 mark for each well described procedure

- Obtain and review legal documentation, in particular confirm the targets used as the basis for payment of contingent consideration
- Confirm that the Group has obtained an 80% shareholding and that this conveys control
- Agree the $80 million cash paid to the bank statement and cash book of the acquiring company
- Review the board minutes for relevant discussions including the minute of board approval
- Obtain management's calculation of contingent consideration, and evaluate assumptions used
- Discuss the 18% interest rate used in determining the discount factor and evaluate the justification given by management
- Confirm that the fair value of the non-controlling interest has been calculated based on an externally available share price at the date of acquisition by agreeing to stock market records
- Obtain a copy of the due diligence report issued by Sidewinder & Co, review for confirmation of acquired assets and liabilities and their fair values
- Evaluation of the methods used to determine the fair value of acquired assets, including the property, and liabilities to confirm compliance with IFRS 3 and IFRS 13 *Fair Value Measurement*
- Review the calculation of net assets acquired to confirm that Group accounting policies have been applied

**Maximum  6**

| | | | |
|---|---|---|---|
| (c) | **Evaluation of Vulture Co's audit strategy**<br>Up to 2 marks for each issue evaluated<br>**Controls effectiveness**<br>–     Evidence needs to be obtained to confirm that controls have not changed<br>–     Controls should be tested in a three-year cycle in order to place continued reliance on them<br>–     Group audit team may decide to perform additional tests of control of Vulture Associates do not amend their strategy<br>**INT: Internal audit**<br>–     Evaluate status, competence and quality control approach of the internal audit department<br>–     Objectivity should be evaluated where direct assistance is provided<br>–     Consider the type of work – work on inventories and receivables is not appropriate due to subjective nature<br>–     Internal auditors have worked on inventories and receivables so not objective<br>**UK: Pension plan valuation**<br>–     Performing pension plan valuation creates self-review and management threat to objectivity<br>–     Audit of Lynx Co should comply with Group-wide ethical policies<br>–     Given materiality to the Group, additional audit work to be performed on the pension plan<br>–     Conclusion on audit quality (1 mark) | | |
| |                                              **Maximum** | **10** | |
| (d) | **Ethical issues relating to request to assist management in preparing an integrated report**<br>Up to 2 marks for each relevant point explained, and 1 mark for relevant safeguard or action<br>–     Explain the threats to objectivity created – self-review, familiarity and management involvement (1 mark each if fully explained)<br>–     Conclusion as to whether service can be provided, following on from justification<br>–     Suggest appropriate safeguards if engagement accepted, e.g. independent review (1 mark each)<br>–     Explain that audit committee would need to pre-approve the engagement<br>–     Bison & Co to consider competence and resource availability<br>–     Discuss with audit committee (1 mark) | | |
| |                                              **Maximum** | **6** | |
| | **Professional marks**<br>Generally 1 mark for heading, 1 mark for introduction, 1 mark for use of headings within the briefing notes, 1 mark for clarity of comments made. | | |
| |                                              **Maximum** | **4** | |
| **Total** | | **50** | |

**5    BASSETT GROUP**  *Walk in the footsteps of a top tutor*

*Top tutor tips*

*Part (a)(i) asks you to evaluate the audit risks to be considered when planning the audit. Audit risk comprises the risk that the financial statements contain material misstatement and detection risk. Risk of material misstatement is usually due to non-compliance with an accounting standard. Think about the requirements of the relevant accounting standards and what the client might be doing incorrectly. Detection risks include auditing a client for the first time or where there is a tight reporting deadline.*

*Part (a)(ii) requires a higher level of skill and judgment as it asks for matters which should be approached with a high degree of professional scepticism. These will be the areas with a greater risk of fraud, bias or manipulation by the client.*

*Part (b)(i) requires knowledge from the text book in terms of identifying a significant component. This knowledge should then be applied to the information provided to determine whether Borzoi Co is a significant component.*

*Part (b)(ii) requires you to apply the requirements ISA 600 for relying on the work of a component auditor. Remember that the opinion the firm issues is the full responsibility of the firm, you cannot blame others if you rely on their work and it is not up to standard.*

*Part (c) requires knowledge of the actions the audit firm should take at the acceptance stage. The audit firm should only take on clients and work of an appropriate level of risk. One way to identify potential risks is to obtain professional clearance from the previous audit firm. In this case, the previous auditor had encountered problems and communicated these to Whippet & Co, the in-coming audit firm. Explain how the audit firm should have acted on this information before making the decision to accept the audit.*

**Briefing notes**

To:         **Kerry Dunker, audit engagement partner**

From:       **Audit manager**

Subject:    **Bassett Group – audit planning**

**Introduction**

These briefing notes relate to the audit planning of the Bassett Group (the Group) for the year ending 30 April 20X8. As requested, the notes contain an evaluation of the audit risks which should be considered in planning the Group audit, including an initial assessment of specific areas where the audit team should exercise professional scepticism. The notes also assess whether Borzoi Co, the Group's foreign subsidiary, is a significant component of the Group. We will be working with a component auditor, Saluki Associates, and these notes discuss the extent of involvement which our firm should have with the audit risk assessment to be performed by Saluki Associates on Borzoi Co.

**(a)** **(i) and (ii)**

**Audit risk and application of professional scepticism**

**New audit client**

This is the first year that our firm has audited the Group. This gives rise to detection risk, as our firm does not have experience with the client, making it more difficult for us to detect material misstatements. However, this risk can be mitigated through rigorous audit planning, including obtaining a thorough understanding of the business of the Group.

In addition, there is a risk that opening balances and comparative information may not be correct. There is no reason for this to be a particularly high risk, as the previous auditor's opinions have been unmodified for the last four years. However, because the prior year figures were not audited by Whippet & Co, we should plan to audit the opening balances carefully, in accordance with ISA 510 *Initial Audit Engagements – Opening Balances*, to ensure that opening balances and comparative information are both free from material misstatement.

**Pressure on results**

The Group is a listed entity, and the results of the preliminary analytical review indicate that there is a reduction in total Group revenue of 3.2%. The book publication operating segment has the most significant reduction in revenue of 6.7%.

Pressure from shareholders for the Group to return a better performance creates an incentive for management bias, especially given the significant investment in new software which has been made – shareholders will want to see a return on that investment.

This means that management may use earnings management techniques, or other methods of creative accounting, to create a healthier picture of financial performance than is actually the case. This creates an inherent risk of material misstatement, at the financial statement level.

This means that the audit team should apply professional scepticism to areas of the audit where the accounting is subject to management's judgement, especially if the accounting treatment which has been applied results in the acceleration or inflation of revenue, or the deferral of expenditure.

**Operating segments**

As the Group is a listed entity, it will be required to disclose information in the notes to the financial statements in accordance with IFRS 8 *Operating Segments*. There is an audit risk that the disclosure may be inaccurate, or incomplete, or that it does not reflect the way information on financial performance is monitored internally by the chief operating decision maker, as required by IFRS 8. For instance, the fact that two of the three reported operating segments are showing a drop in performance while the other shows improvement could indicate inaccuracy in the information.

In addition, if management is monitoring separately the performance of digital and non-digital sources of income, and if digital sales become significant in their own right, then this may need to be disclosed as a separate operating segment.

Professional scepticism should be applied to the audit of operating segments; due to management bias, the allocation of revenue, expenses and assets between segments could be subject to manipulation, for example, to mask the declining performance of the book and newspaper and magazine operating segments. Allocation is determined by management, and this judgement should be approached with scepticism, especially given the potential lack of integrity displayed by the CFO as indicated by the communication from Grey & Co.

### Internally developed software

The group financial statements recognise $10 million which has been capitalised in respect of internally developed software. This is equivalent to 10.5% of Group assets and the amount is therefore material to the financial statements.

An audit risk arises in that the requirements of IAS 38 *Intangible Assets* might not have been followed. Software development costs can only be capitalised if they meet the capitalisation criteria, including that a future economic benefit can be demonstrated and that technical and commercial feasibility of the asset have been established.

If these criteria have not been met, then the development costs should be expensed. In addition, the Group may not have distinguished appropriately between research and development costs. If research costs have been included in the amount capitalised then it is overstated, because research costs must always be expensed.

This is an area where professional scepticism should be applied, both in relation to management's assertion that the software costs meet the necessary conditions for capitalisation, and in relation to the distinction, if any, which has been made between research and development costs. There is a risk that profit is overstated by a material amount if the accounting treatment is incorrect.

### Impairment

Management is not planning to test the cash generating units for impairment, giving rise to a significant audit risk. Regardless of impairment indicators, goodwill must be tested for impairment each year according to IAS 38, and given that the Group has over 20 subsidiaries, it is likely that there is goodwill recognised in the consolidated statement of financial position and allocated into the cash generating units, meaning that they must be tested for impairment on an annual basis.

In addition, the reduction in revenue for the Group as a whole, and for the newspapers and magazines and books operating segments specifically, is an indicator of potential impairment. This should trigger an impairment review even if there is no goodwill allocated to the cash generating units.

Management's justification for not conducting an impairment review is wholly inappropriate and if an impairment review is not conducted and any necessary impairment loss not recognised, then profit and assets will be overstated, possibly by a material amount.

Again, this is an area where the audit team will need to apply professional scepticism, and challenge management on their assumption that an impairment review is not needed. Management's reluctance to conduct an impairment review could be due to management bias and the pressure to return a healthy profit to shareholders.

**Publication rights**

The publication rights are recognised as an intangible asset with a carrying amount of $7.9 million, representing 8.3% of total assets. This is material to the financial statements.

It is appropriate that the publication rights are amortised, as they have a finite life. However, the period over which they are amortised may not be appropriate. The Group accounting policy is to amortise over an average of 25 years, but the actual period to which the rights relate varies from five to 30 years. Therefore while it may be appropriate to use an average for the basis of an accounting policy, it means that some rights are being amortised over much too long a period, overstating intangible assets and understating expenses.

Management could be using this 25-year average period as a way of smoothing profits and managing earnings. The accounting policy may not be appropriate, and the audit team will need to be sceptical in relation to the appropriateness of the policy, and challenge management on its use.

**Author royalty advances**

The royalty advances recognised within current assets amount to $3.4 million, which is material at 3.6% of total assets.

Deferring the cost and treating it as a prepayment, seems to be appropriate. However, the Group accounting policy should be challenged by the audit team. Releasing the cost over a ten-year period seems to have no suitable justification and appears to be quite simplistic.

While industry practice can be used to develop accounting policies, the Group must consider the specific period of amortisation relevant to its publications, and not shape its accounting policies simply based on the actions of its competitors in the market, who might have very different types of publications providing economic benefit over a different period. Presumably some books published by the Group will have a much shorter life than ten years, in which case the advance royalty payment should be spread over a shorter period.

Similar to the point raised previously in relation to the accounting treatment of the publication rights, management could be using this ten-year average period as a way of smoothing profits and managing earnings. Again, the accounting policy may not be appropriate, and the audit team will need to be sceptical in relation to the appropriateness of the policy, and challenge management on its use.

**Borzoi Co – foreign currency retranslation**

In order to be consolidated into the Group, the financial statements of Borzoi Co will need to be retranslated from its local currency, the Oska, into $, in accordance with IAS 21 *The Effects of Changes in Foreign Exchange Rates*. IAS 21 requires that assets and liabilities are translated at the closing exchange rate at the reporting date, while income and expenses are translated at the exchange rates at the dates of the transactions.

The fact that the currency has been volatile over the last six months and could remain volatile for the rest of the year means that the retranslation of income and expenses is problematical; it is potentially complex and prone to contain errors, giving rise to risk of material misstatement given that Borzoi Co is a significant component of the Group (this will be discussed in more detail later in these briefing notes).

**Transfer of software**

The transfer of software gives rise to several audit risks.

First, there is a risk that the software was overvalued when it was transferred from Bassett Co to Borzoi Co. The fair value which was recognised in the parent company accounts immediately prior to the transfer of the asset was determined by Group management, and while revaluation is permitted by IAS 38 where an active market for the asset exists, this fair value could be inappropriate. In the absence of an active market, it is unlikely the revaluation should have been recognised at all.

There is a significant difference between the carrying amount of the software and the fair value determined by management, $1 million and $5.4 million respectively, giving rise to a revaluation of $4.4 million which was recognised by Bassett Co immediately prior to the transfer. The audit risk is that in the parent company, the revaluation should not have been recognised, or, if revaluation is appropriate, the amount recognised was based on an inappropriate value. In the individual financial statements of Borzoi Co, the asset could be overstated in value. Any overstatement of the asset has implications for subsequent amortisation charges, which would also be overstated in the financial statements of Borzoi Co.

The audit team should approach this issue with appropriate professional scepticism – the revaluation of the software will need to be justified by management as it could be a mechanism being used by Group management to inflate the assets of Borzoi Co and the Group as a whole. The audit team should also challenge the assertion made by management that a sufficiently active market exists to enable a reliable and realistic fair value to be determined for the software.

At Group level the transfer is an intercompany transaction and the consolidated financial statements should be prepared as if the transaction had not occurred. This is an additional and separate audit risk from the risk that the valuation of the asset is not appropriate.

There is an audit risk if the elimination of the intercompany transaction does not take place as part of the consolidation process. Adjustments should be made to cancel out the intercompany payable and receivable in respect of the $5.4 million which is outstanding between Borzoi Co and Basset Co.

**Corporate governance arrangements**

The Group CFO blocking access to the audit committee is not acceptable. Corporate governance principles as well as ISA 260 *Communication With Those Charged With Governance* require that the external auditor should have unrestricted and effective communication with the audit committee and the CFO should not interfere with these communications. This situation could indicate that the CFO has something to hide, and that the control environment within the Group is not strong and this risk is augmented by the points already raised in relation to management bias.

Certainly there would not seem to be a good ethical culture if the CFO is acting in this way. In line with corporate governance guidelines, the audit committee is required to assess the effectiveness of the external audit process and a key part of this is likely to be done via the direct communication the auditor and the audit committee have. As such it would appear as though the CFO may lack integrity or possibly does not understand the relevant corporate governance principles and is potentially disrupting the audit committee's ability to discharge its responsibilities.

In addition, ISA 260 specifies that the auditor should determine the appropriate persons within the entity's governance structure with whom to communicate. Further as per ISA 210 *Agreeing the Terms of Audit Engagements*, providing unrestricted access to persons within the entity is one of the preconditions for the audit. As such, the CFO is potentially imposing a limitation on the scope of the audit by not facilitating unrestricted and effective communication with the audit committee and the CFO should therefore not interfere with these communications.

All of these issues increase audit risk and the need for approaching the audit with professional scepticism, especially when dealing with estimates and judgements which have been determined by the CFO.

**Tutorial note**

*Credit will be awarded for other relevant audit risks and associated matters relating to professional scepticism, for example, whether an appropriate amortisation policy has been applied to the software in which the Group had invested during the year, and whether Borzoi Co (and any other subsidiaries) has different accounting policies to the rest of the Group which would require adjustment at consolidation.*

**(b)    (i)    Assessment of whether Borzoi Co is a significant component of the Group**

ISA 600/ISA (UK) 600 *Special Considerations – Audits of Group Financial Statements (Including the Work of Component Auditors)* requires the Group auditor to determine whether a component is a significant component. One of the reasons for this is because it determines the type and extent of involvement which the Group auditor should have with the work of the component auditor.

ISA 600 defines a significant component as a component identified by the group engagement team which is of individual financial significance to the group, or which, due to its specific nature or circumstances, is likely to include significant risks of material misstatement of the group financial statements.

ISA 600 suggests that benchmarks such as profit and assets should be assessed when determining significance but it does not require a specific threshold to be used. The standard does suggest that 15% could be an appropriate cut-off point for determining significance.

The total assets of Borzoi Co are 68 million Oska and if retranslated using the current exchange rate of 4 Oska:1$, its assets are $17 million. This represents 17.9% of Group assets and therefore based on the information at today's date, Borzoi Co is a significant component of the Group.

It is important to note that given the volatility of the Oska currency, the value of the subsidiary may change by the reporting date meaning that it is no longer significant due to its size. However, Borzoi Co could be significant due to its specific nature or circumstances, being the Group's only foreign subsidiary, which brings specific risks of material misstatement as outlined earlier in these briefing notes. There may also be regulatory or economic issues specific to the company, especially due to the political difficulties in its jurisdiction, which also impact on the Group and give rise to risks. Therefore regardless of its monetary size, it is likely that Borzoi Co will be considered to be a significant component of the Group.

(ii)     **The extent of involvement which our firm should have with the work of Saluki Associates**

When working with a component auditor, the group engagement team should obtain an understanding on a number of matters as required by ISA 600. These matters include the competence of the component auditor, whether the component auditor understands the ethical framework relevant to the Group audit and is independent, and the regulatory environment in which the component auditor operates.

The extent of involvement which our firm will have with Saluki Associates depends to an extent on the evaluation of these matters. If there are concerns over the competence, independence or diligence of Saluki Associates or the jurisdiction in which they operate, the level of involvement with their work should be increased in response.

According to ISA 600, if a component auditor performs an audit of the financial information of a significant component, the group engagement team is required to be involved in the component auditor's risk assessment to identify significant risks of material misstatement of the group financial statements.

The nature, timing and extent of this involvement are affected by the group engagement team's understanding of the component auditor, but at a minimum should include the following:

–     Discussing with the component auditor or component management the component's business activities which are significant to the group.

–     Discussing with the component auditor the susceptibility of the component to material misstatement of the financial information due to fraud or error.

–     Reviewing the component auditor's documentation of identified significant risks of material misstatement of the group financial statements. Such documentation may take the form of a memorandum which reflects the component auditor's conclusion with regard to the identified significant risks.

–     Evaluating the component auditor's communication on matters relevant to the group audit and discuss any significant matters arising from that evaluation with the component auditor, component management or group management as appropriate.

–     Determining whether it is necessary to review other relevant parts of the component auditor's audit documentation.

The Group audit team may need to have further involvement in the audit of the component where significant risks of material misstatement of the Group financial statements have been identified in a component.

In this case, the Group audit team shall evaluate the appropriateness of the further audit procedures to be performed to respond to the identified significant risks of material misstatement of the Group financial statements. Based on its understanding of the component auditor, the Group audit team will then determine whether it is necessary to be involved in the further audit procedures.

**(c)** **Ethical and professional issues**

Communication from the previous Group auditor has identified that the Group CFO blocked access of the auditor to the Group audit committee. This is a management imposed limitation on scope. The CFO would appear to lack integrity as he may be trying to keep information secret, possibly from others within the Group as well as the public.

This will raise doubts over the reliability of information provided by the CFO including representations made by him during the audit. This could lead to the need for a disclaimer of opinion as the auditor would not have sufficient appropriate evidence to be able to form a conclusion on the financial statements. Given that the issue relates to the CFO, this is likely to be considered pervasive.

According to ISA 210/ISA (UK) 210 *Agreeing the Terms of Audit Engagements*, the management of a client should acknowledge their responsibility to provide the auditor with access to all information which is relevant to the preparation of the financial statements which includes unrestricted access to persons within the entity from whom the auditor determines it necessary to obtain audit evidence.

At the acceptance stage, Whippet & Co should have confirmed that the preconditions for an audit were in place otherwise they should have declined the engagement.

In addition, the firm should have assessed the level of management integrity and if there were any significant issues identified, it would have been sensible not to proceed.

As mentioned above, the audit should be approached with a high degree of professional scepticism to ensure the same restrictions are not placed on the audit team of Whippet & Co. Assuming Whippet & Co have access to the audit committee at this point in time, these concerns should be raised and assurance obtained from the audit committee that the issues encountered by Grey & Co will not be experienced by our firm.

**Conclusion**

These briefing notes indicate a range of audit risks to be considered in planning the Group audit. In particular, there are significant risks of misstatement in relation to intangible assets and a foreign subsidiary. There is also a significant risk of management bias, and the audit will need to be planned and performed with appropriate levels of professional scepticism, especially given that this is a new audit client. Borzoi Co, a foreign subsidiary, is a significant component of the Group and we must have involvement with risk assessment in relation to the planning of its audit.

---

**Examiner's comments**

This question presented the scenario of new, listed, publishing client who had some quite aggressive accounting policies.

Part (a)(i) required candidates to evaluate audit risks. Generally this was satisfactorily answered and it was evident that candidates had prepared well for this type of scenario. There were plenty of areas where marks could be accumulated quite quickly, such as internally-generated assets, accounting for publication rights, the need for impairment reviews and segmental reporting. An area less understood was the concept of making a royalty advance and amortising this over the expected period of sales; many candidates did not understand the underlying double entry. It was also noted that a number of candidates had gaps in their financial reporting knowledge in respect of accounting for intangible assets and did not realise that internally developed software could be capitalised if the criteria set out in IAS 38 were met.

Some candidates continue to refer to generic risks of consolidation such as arithmetical mistakes, or omission of a subsidiary, which are often too vague to attract marks. Others digressed into describing audit procedures rather than risks. Better candidates focused on the consolidation of the named foreign subsidiary and were awarded marks for identifying the appropriate accounting treatment of the subsidiary and the need to adjust for the specific transactions detailed in the scenario.

The second requirement referred to areas where professional scepticism should be used. Again, there were plenty of areas where it was indicated in the question scenario that management were deferring and smoothing costs through inappropriate amortisation policies or by capitalising expenditure, which might not meet the qualifying criteria to be recognised as a development cost. Better candidates highlighted that there were many impairment indicators with revenue overall being static but online revenue growing at 20% annually which had clear implications for the other areas of the business as their share of revenues were, by definition, declining. The sale of software at an inflated value to the foreign subsidiary experiencing currency volatility was another clear warning flag that management were looking to inflate assets to enhance the financial statements.

Part (b) started by requiring the candidates to determine whether the foreign subsidiary was a significant component. The subsidiary was significant by value as it represented more than 15% of the group's assets although this could vary depending on the exchange rate which was applied and which was a point made by stronger candidates. In addition the nature of its specialist business and the fact the subsidiary operated in a volatile country were additional indicators that it was significant. A concerning number of candidates could not recall the 15% threshold and others confused significance with materiality. Other candidates mistakenly thought that a significant component was an associate.

The nature and extent of involvement that the group auditor should have with the risk assessment of the auditor of the foreign subsidiary was also mostly well-answered. Most candidates were able to discuss the need to consider the regulatory framework, competence and independence of the component auditor and the need for discussion and review of their documentation.

There were four professional marks available for presentation, logic and clarity. Candidates who presented their answers in a structured and reasoned manner with sub-headings and references scored well. A concise paragraph is all that is required as an introduction, not a whole page. Candidates are advised to space out their work and start a new page for each sub-section.

---

| | | | Marks |
|---|---|---|---|
| | | **Marking scheme** | *Marks* |

**(a)** **(i)** **Audit risk evaluation**

**(ii)** **Identification and explanation of matters where professional scepticism should be applied**

Up to 3 marks for each audit risk evaluated

Up to 1½ marks for each identification and explanation of matters where professional scepticism should be applied.

Allow 1 mark for each correct calculation and comment on materiality to a maximum of 3 marks.

– Detection risk due to this being a new client
– Management bias due to pressure on results
– Operating segments – potential inaccurate or incomplete disclosure
– Decline in revenue – lack of impairment review means asset could be overstated
– Software development costs – risk that R&D not distinguished and that development inappropriately capitalised
– Publication rights – risk that amortisation is not appropriate affecting assets and profit
– Author royalty advances – risk that expenses are inappropriately deferred
– Borzoi Co – risk in retranslation of the income statement
– Software revaluation – risk that the fair value is not appropriate
– Transfer of software – risk that intercompany transaction is not eliminated on consolidation
– Corporate governance – principles not being followed, increased risk of management bias, need to be sceptical when dealing with the CFO
– Requirement for the auditor to evaluate the effectiveness of the communication process between audit firm and audit committee
– Management imposed limitation in scope and breach of pre-conditions for audit due to restriction on communication with audit committee

Maximum marks for (a)(i) **18**
Maximum marks for (a)(ii) **9**

**(b)** **(i)** **Assessment of whether Borzoi Co is a significant component**

Up to 2 marks for each relevant point/comment explained

– Explanation of significance based on either individual financial significance to the group, or due to specific nature or circumstances
– Application to the scenario – determine that Borzoi Co's total assets are above 15% threshold
– Explanation that Borzoi Co is also has specific circumstances which mean it is a significant component

Maximum **5**

(ii) **Extent of involvement of Group auditor with Saluki Associates**

Up to 2 marks for each relevant point/comment explained

– Evaluation of component auditor independence, competence and regulatory environment in which they operate

– Group auditor must be involved with assessment of risk of material misstatement of Group financial statements

– Involvement can include discussion with component auditor or review of their risk assessment

– Where significant risk of misstatement to the Group accounts is identified, the Group auditor may be involved with further audit procedures

|  | |
|---|---|
| Maximum | 7 |

(c) **Ethical and professional issues**

Up to 1½ marks for each point of discussion/appropriate action.

– Limitation in scope imposed by CFO

– Doubts over reliability of evidence possibly resulting in disclaimer of opinion

– Preconditions for an audit as per ISA 210

– At acceptance stage audit firm should have ensured preconditions were in place and assessed management integrity

– Discuss with audit committee, who should provide assurance that the same issues will not be experienced by Whippet & Co

|  | |
|---|---|
| Maximum | 7 |

**Professional marks**

Generally 1 mark for heading, 1 mark for introduction, 1 mark for use of headings within the briefing notes, 1 mark for clarity of comments made.

|  | |
|---|---|
| Maximum | 4 |

| Total | 50 |
|---|---|

**6    SUNSHINE HOTEL GROUP**  *Walk in the footsteps of a top tutor*

*Top tutor tips*

*This is a typical risk question within a group context. When describing business risks remember to explain the impact it will have on the company i.e. impact on profit or cash flow. For risks of material misstatement you need to explain how the financial statements may not have been prepared in accordance with the applicable financial reporting standard.*

*In part (c)(i) consider how the auditor should deal with the issue of being asked to only speak with the Group FD regarding the claim from Ocean Protection.*

*Part (c)(ii) asks for audit procedures in respect of the claim for environmental damage caused by hotel guests. Make sure your procedures are clear and provide enough detail that they can be followed.*

*Part (d) covers a current development in the auditing profession, that of data analytics. You should read the relevant sections of the study text in this area and look out for any articles published on the topic as this could be examined as a current issue.*

**Briefing notes**

**To:**         **John Starling, audit engagement partner**

**From:**       **Audit manager**

**Subject:**    **Sunshine Hotel Group – audit planning**

**Introduction**

These briefing notes relate to the initial audit planning for the Sunshine Hotel Group (the Group), for the year ending 31 December 20X7. As requested, the notes contain an evaluation of the business risks facing our client, and the significant risks of material misstatement to be considered in our audit planning. The notes contain a discussion of the impact which an email received from the Group finance director relating to a claim for damages will have on our audit planning, as well as the recommended actions to be taken by Dove & Co and principal procedures which should be carried out in relation to this claim. Finally, the notes discuss how data analytics could be used in future audits of the Sunshine Hotel Group.

**(a)    Evaluation of business risks**

**Luxury product**

The Group offers a luxury product aimed at an exclusive market. This in itself creates a business risk, as the Group's activities are not diversified, and any decline in demand will immediately impact on profitability and cash flows.

The demand for luxury holidays will be sensitive to economic problems such as recession and travel to international destinations will be affected by events in the transportation industry, for example, if oil prices increase, there will be a knock-on effect on air fares, meaning less demand for the Group's hotels.

### Business expansion – inappropriate strategy

It is questionable whether the Group has a sound policy on expansion, given the problems encountered with recent acquisitions which have involved expanding into locations with political instability and local regulations which seem incompatible with the Group's operations and strategic goals.

The Group would appear to have invested $98 million, accounting for 28% of the Group's total assets, in these unsuitable locations, and it is doubtful whether an appropriate return on these investments will be possible. There is a risk that further unsuitable investments will be made as a result of poor strategic decisions on where to locate new hotels.

The Group appears to have a strategy of fairly rapid expansion, acquiring new sites and a hotel complex without properly investigating their appropriateness and fit with the Group's business model.

### Business expansion – finance

The Group is planning further expansion with capital expenditure of $45 million planned for new sites in 20X8. This equates to 12.9% of the Group's total assets, which is a significant amount and will be financed by a bank loan. While the Group's gearing is currently low at 25%, the additional finance being taken out from the Group's lending facility will increase gearing and incur additional interest charges of $1.6 million per annum, which is 16% of the projected profit before tax for the year. The increased debt and finance charges could impact on existing loan covenants and the additional interest payments will have cash flow as well as profit implications.

A further $25 million is needed for renovating the hotels which were damaged following a hurricane. Despite the fact that the repair work following the hurricane will ultimately be covered by insurance, the Group's capital expenditure at this time appears very high, and needs to be underpinned by sound financial planning in order to maintain solvency, especially given that only half of the insurance claim in relation to repair work will be paid in advance and it may take some time to recover the full amount given the significant sums involved.

### Moulin Blanche agreement

$5 million has been spent on an agreement which allows the company to use the Moulin Blanche name. This represents a significant outflow of cash where the benefits may take time to materialise or may not materialise to the extent of the level of investment.

If there is any damage to the reputation of the Moulin Blanche chain, this may have an effect on the Moulin Blanche restaurants at the Sunshine Hotel Group resulting in a much lower return on investment than anticipated.

### Profit margins and cash management

The nature of the business means that overheads will be high and profit margins likely to be low. Based on the projected profit before tax, the projected margin for 20X7 is 8%, and for 20X6 was 8.2%.

Annual expenses on marketing and advertising are high, and given the focus on luxury, a lot will need to be spent on maintenance of the hotels, purchasing quality food and drink, and training staff to provide high levels of customer service.

Offering all-inclusive holidays will also have implications for profit margins and for managing working capital as services, as well as food and drink, will have to be available whether guests use or consume them or not. The Group will need to maintain a high rate of room occupancy in order to maintain cash flows and profit margins.

Cash management might be particularly problematic given that the majority of cash is received on departure, rather than when the guests book their stay.

Refunds to customers following the recent hurricane will also impact on cash flows, as will the repairs needed to the damaged hotels.

**International operations**

The Group's international operations expose it to a number of risks. One which has already been mentioned relates to local regulations. With any international operation there is risk of non-compliance with local laws and regulations which could affect business operations.

Additionally, political and economic instability introduces possible unpredictability into operations, making it difficult to plan and budget for the Group's activities, as seen with the recent investment in a politically unstable area which is not yet generating a return for the Group.

There are also foreign exchange issues, which unless properly managed, for example, by using currency derivatives, can introduce volatility to profit and cash flows.

**Hurricanes**

The hurricane guarantee scheme exposes the Group to unforeseeable costs in the event of a hurricane disrupting operations. The costs of moving guests to another hotel could be high, as could the costs of refunding customer deposits if they choose to cancel their booking rather than transfer to a different hotel.

The cost of renovation in the case of hotels being damaged by hurricanes is also high and while this is covered by insurance, the Group will still need to fund the repair work before the full amount claimed on insurance is received which as discussed above will put significant pressure on the Group's cash flow.

In addition, having two hotels which have been damaged by hurricanes closed for several months while repair work is carried out will result in lost revenue and cash inflows.

**Claim relating to environmental damage**

This is potentially a very serious matter, should it become public knowledge. The reputational damage could be significant, especially given that the Group markets itself as a luxury brand. Consumers are likely to react unfavourably to the allegations that the Group's activities are harming the environment. This could result in cancellation of existing bookings and lower demand in the future, impacting on revenue and cash flows.

The email relating to the claim from Ocean Protection refers to international legislation and therefore this issue could impact in all of the countries in which the Group operates. The Group is hoping to negotiate with Ocean Protection to reduce the amount which is potentially payable and minimise media attention, but this may not be successful, Ocean Protection may not be willing to keep the issue out of the public eye or to settle for a smaller monetary amount.

(b)     **Significant risks of material misstatement**

**Revenue recognition**

The Group's revenue could be over or understated due to timing issues relating to the recognition of revenue. Customers pay 40% of the cost of their holiday in advance, and the Group has to refund any bookings which are cancelled a week or more before a guest is due to stay at a hotel.

There is a risk that revenue is recognised when deposits are received, which would be against the requirements of IFRS 15 *Revenue from Contracts with Customers*, which states that revenue should be recognised when, or as, an entity satisfies a performance obligation.

Therefore, the deposits should be recognised within current liabilities as deferred revenue until the guest's stay.

There is the risk that revenue is overstated and deferred revenue and therefore current liabilities are understated if revenue is recognised on payment.

*Tutorial note*

*Credit will be awarded for discussion of further risk of misstatement relating to revenue recognition, for example, when the Group satisfies its performance obligations and whether the goods and services provided to hotel guests are separate revenue streams.*

**Foreign exchange**

The Group holds $20 million in cash at the year end, most of which is held in foreign currencies. This represents 5.7% of Group assets, thus cash is material to the financial statements.

According to IAS 21 *The Effects of Changes in Foreign Exchange Rates*, at the reporting date foreign currency monetary amounts should be reported using the closing exchange rate, and the exchange difference should be reported as part of profit or loss.

There is a risk that the cash holdings are not retranslated using an appropriate year end exchange rate, causing assets and profit to be over or understated.

**Licence agreement**

The cost of the agreement with Moulin Blanche is 1.4% of Group assets, and 50% of profit for the year. It is highly material to profit and is borderline in terms of materiality to the statement of financial position.

The agreement appears to be a licensing arrangement, and as such it should be recognised in accordance with IAS 38 *Intangible Assets*, which requires initial recognition at cost and subsequent amortisation over the life of the asset, if the life is finite.

The current accounting treatment appears to be incorrect, because the cost has been treated as a marketing expense, leading to understatement of non-current assets and understatement of profit for the year by a significant amount. If the financial statements are not adjusted, they will contain a material misstatement, with implications for the auditor's report.

As the restaurants were opened on 1 July 20X7, six months after the licence was agreed, it would seem appropriate to amortise the asset over the remaining term of the agreement of 9½ years as this is the timeframe over which the licence will generate economic benefit. The annual amortisation expense would be $526,316, so if six months is recognised in this financial year, $263,158 should be charged to operating expenses, resulting in profit being closer to $14.74 million for the year.

### Impairment of non-current assets due to political instability and regulatory issues

The sites acquired at a cost of $75 million represent 21.4% of total assets, and the hotel complex acquired at a cost of $23 million represents 6.6% of total assets; these assets are material to the Group financial statements.

There are risks associated with the measurement of the assets, which are recognised as property, plant and equipment, as the assets could be impaired. None of these assets is currently being used by the Group in line with their principal activities, and there are indications that their recoverable value may be less than their cost. Due to the political instability and the regulatory issues, it seems that the assets may never generate the value in use which was anticipated, and their fair value may also have fallen below cost.

Therefore, in accordance with IAS 36 *Impairment of Assets*, management should conduct an impairment review, to determine the recoverable amount of the assets and whether any impairment loss should be recognised.

The risk is that assets are overstated, and profit overstated, if any necessary impairment of assets is not recognised at the reporting date.

### Effect of the hurricane

Two of the Group's hotels are closed due to extensive damage caused by a recent hurricane. It is anticipated that the Group's insurance policy will cover the damage of $25 million and the terms of the policy are that half will be paid in advance and the remainder on completion of the repairs, although this will need confirming during our audit testing. The accounting for these events will need to be carefully considered as there is a risk that assets and profit are overstated if the damage and subsequent claim have not been accounted for correctly.

The damage caused to the hotels and resultant loss of revenue is likely to represent an indicator of impairment which should be recorded in line with IAS 36. IAS 16 *Property, Plant and Equipment* requires the impairment and derecognition of PPE and any subsequent compensation claims to be treated as separate economic events and accounted for separately in the period they occur. The standard specifically states that it is not appropriate to net the events off and not record an impairment loss because there is an insurance claim in relation to the same assets.

As such, this may mean that the Group has to account for the impairment loss in the current year but cannot recognise the compensation claim until the next financial period as this can only be recognised when the compensation becomes receivable. If it is indeed the case that the insurance company will pay half of the claim in advance, then it is likely that $12.5m could be included in profit or loss in the current year.

### Provision/contingent liability

The letter received from Ocean Protection indicates that it may be necessary to recognise a provision or disclose a contingent liability, in respect of the $10 million damages which have been claimed.

The amount is material at 2.9% of total assets, and 67.9% of profit before tax (adjusted for the incorrect accounting treatment of the licence agreement).

According to IAS 37 *Provisions, Contingent Liabilities and Contingent Assets*, a provision should be recognised if there is a present obligation as a result of a past event, and that there is a probable outflow of future economic benefits for which a reliable estimate can be made.

It remains to be seen as to whether the Group can be held liable for the damage to the coral reefs. However, the finance director seems to be implying that the Group would like to reach a settlement, in which case a provision should be recognised.

A provision could therefore be necessary, but this depends on the negotiations between the Group and Ocean Protection, the outcome of which can only be confirmed following further investigation by the audit team during the final audit.

A contingent liability arises where there is either a possible obligation depending on whether some uncertain future event occurs, or a present obligation but payment is not probable or the amount cannot be measured reliably.

There is a risk that adequate disclosure is not provided in the notes to the financial statements, especially given the finance director's reluctance to draw attention to the matter.

**Tutorial note**

*Credit would also be awarded for discussion of other relevant risks of material misstatements.*

**(c)  (i)  Implications for audit planning**

The finance director's requests which restrict the audit team's ability to obtain audit evidence in relation to the environmental damage claim are inappropriate. In particular, the finance director should not dictate to the audit engagement partner that the audit team may not speak to Group employees.

According to ISA 210 *Agreeing the Terms of Audit Engagements*, the management of a client should acknowledge their responsibility to provide the auditor with access to all information which is relevant to the preparation of the financial statements which includes unrestricted access to persons within the entity from whom the auditor determines it necessary to obtain audit evidence.

This would appear to be an imposed limitation on scope, and the audit engagement partner should raise this issue with the Group's audit committee. The audit committee should be involved at the planning stage to obtain comfort that a quality audit will be performed, in accordance with corporate governance best practice, and therefore the audit committee should be able to intervene with the finance director's demands and allow the audit team full access to the relevant information, including the ability to contact Ocean Protection and the Group's lawyers.

The finance director would appear to lack integrity as he is trying to keep the issue a secret, possibly from others within the Group as well as the public. The audit engagement partner should consider whether other representations made by the finance director should be treated with an added emphasis on professional scepticism, and the risk of management bias leading to a risk of material misstatement could be high. This should be discussed during the audit team briefing meeting.

There is also an issue arising in relation to ISA 250 *Consideration of Laws and Regulations in an Audit of Financial Statements*, which requires that if the auditor becomes aware of information concerning an instance of non-compliance or suspected non-compliance with laws and regulations, the auditor shall obtain an understanding of the act and the circumstances in which it has occurred, and further information to evaluate the possible effect on the financial statements.

Therefore, the audit plan should contain planned audit procedures which are sufficient for the audit team to conclude on the accounting treatment and on whether the auditor has any reporting responsibilities outside the Group, for example, to communicate a breach of international environmental protection legislation to the appropriate authorities.

**(ii)    Planned audit procedures**

–    Obtain the letter received from Ocean Protection and review to understand the basis of the claim, for example, to confirm if it refers to a specific incident when damage was caused to the coral reefs.

–    Discuss the issue with the Group's legal adviser, to understand whether in their opinion, the Group could be liable for the damages, for example, to ascertain if there is any evidence that the damage to the coral reef was caused by activities of the Group or its customers.

–    Discuss with the Group's legal adviser the remit and scope of the legislation in relation to environmental protection to ensure an appropriate level of understanding in relation to the regulatory framework within which the Group operates.

–    Discuss with management and those charged with governance the procedures which the Group utilises to ensure that it is identifying and ensuring compliance with relevant legislation.

–    Obtain an understanding, through enquiry with relevant employees, such as those responsible for scuba diving and other water sports, as to the nature of activities which take place, the locations and frequency of scuba diving trips, and the level of supervision which the Group provides to its guests involved in these activities.

–    Obtain and read all correspondence between the Group and Ocean Protection, to track the progress of the legal claim up to the date that the auditor's report is issued, and to form an opinion on its treatment in the financial statements.

–    Obtain a written representation from management, as required by ISA 250, that all known instances of non-compliance, whether suspected or otherwise, have been made known to the auditor.

- Discuss the issue with those charged with governance, including discussion of whether the Group has taken any necessary steps to inform the relevant external authorities, if the Group has not complied with the international environmental protection legislation.

- Review the disclosures, if any, provided in the notes to the financial statements, to conclude as to whether the disclosure is sufficient for compliance with IAS 37.

- Read the other information published with the financial statements, including chairman's statement and directors' report, to assess whether any disclosure relating to the issue has been made, and if so, whether it is consistent with the financial statements.

**(d)    Data analytics**

Data analytics is the science and art of discovering and analysing patterns, deviations and inconsistencies, and extracting other useful information in the data of underlying or related subject matter of an audit through analysis, modelling, visualisation for the purpose of planning and performing the audit.

Data analytics can allow the interrogation of 100% of the transactions in a population where the data set is complete and can be provided to the auditor.

Essentially data analytics is a progression from using computer assisted audit techniques to perform analytical procedures.

**How data analytics can improve audit quality**

As there is potential to audit 100% of the transactions, detection risk is significantly reduced.

Audit procedures can be performed more quickly resulting in more time being available to analyse the information and exercise professional scepticism.

There is likely to be greater interaction between the audit firm and the audit committee throughout the year which is likely to result in the firm's knowledge of the business being updated on a regular basis as compared with a traditional year-end audit where the understanding is updated during the planning stage.

Specifically in relation to the Sunshine Hotel Group, audit quality can be improved by improving the consistency of the audits of the subsidiaries within the group, irrespective of which office of the firm performs the audit.

This means the auditor is more likely to issue an appropriate audit opinion.

**How they can be used in the audit of Sunshine Hotel Group**

- Testing journals as required by ISA 240 *The Auditor's Responsibilities Relating to Fraud in an Audit of Financial Statements.*

- Analysing the performance of hotels against other hotels in the group to identify inconsistencies and potential misstatements (fraud or error) for further investigation.

- Analysing the performance of hotels against competitors to identify inconsistencies.

- Analysing occupancy rates of hotels to assist with analytics over revenue.

- Analysing the level of inventory write-offs for food, drink and toiletries which may indicate theft.

**Potential limitations**

The use of data analytics is still quite limited and our firm may not have started to use them yet. To introduce data analytics for one client is likely to be too costly. It should be considered whether other clients would be interested in us using them for their audits to increase cost-effectiveness of implementation.

In addition to acquiring or developing data analytic software, audit staff will need to be trained to use them and this will take time and money.

The size of the data sets may be too large for the audit firm to be able to retain as audit evidence for the required retention period.

Maintaining confidentiality of client information may be more of an issue as the audit firm will hold entire data sets rather than the amount which is required to provide sufficient appropriate evidence to support the audit opinion.

**Conclusion**

These briefing notes highlight that the Group faces significant and varied business risk, in particular in relation to its expansion strategy which is possibly unsound. There are a number of significant risks of material misstatement which will need to be carefully considered during the planning of the Group audit, to ensure that an appropriate audit strategy is devised. Several issues are raised by the claim from Ocean Protection, and our audit programme should contain detailed and specific procedures to enable the audit team to form a conclusion on an appropriate accounting treatment.

---

**Examiner's comments**

This question was set at the planning stage of the audit cycle and was set pre-year end. The question asked candidates to evaluate the business risks and risks of material misstatement from a scenario given on a luxury hotel company. Generally, candidates did well in these sections and were capable of producing explained answers that often scored close to maximum marks. When preparing for future exams candidates are advised to try and remain focused on the risks which arise from the scenario given for while there are additional risks which may be relevant and obtain credit outside of those there are adequate marks available for explaining the risks arising from the information given. In particular when addressing risks of material misstatements candidates are more likely to attract credit for the material issues described by the examiner than from those they hypothesise might be present and which may be considered immaterial. It should also be noted that when the examiner states that company brand is not capitalised because it was internally generated this means that it does not give rises to a risk of material misstatement that it should have been on the statement on financial position. Where brands are examined in planning questions the examiner will generally flag whether they are internally generated or purchased. One important piece of information candidates need to take note of is the year-end date. Planning questions are generally set prior to the year end. None of the events within the scenario were subsequent events as they had already taken place four months prior to the year end.

In part (c) candidates were asked to respond to an email from the finance director of the client. The first connected requirement asked for the implication of the director restricting access of the auditor to information regarding a legal claim and thus giving rise to a potential limitation of scope and some additional points on confidentiality and compliance with laws and regulations. Disappointingly the majority of candidates did not appear to identify that the requirement was specifically referenced to the finance director's email and discussed how to audit the risks identified in part b or made general points on auditing subsidiaries. Attention to the wording of requirements is vital to perform well in examinations in general. In the requirement where candidates were asked for audit procedures in relation to a legal case, this was well answered.

---

| | Marking scheme | | |
|---|---|---|---|
| | | | *Marks* |
| **(a)** | **Business risk evaluation** | | |
| | Generally up to 2 marks for each business risk evaluated, in addition allow ½ mark for each relevant calculation, e.g. profit margin. | | |
| |   –   Luxury product – sensitive to changes in consumer's disposable income | | |
| |   –   Inappropriate business strategy | | |
| |   –   Finance | | |
| |   –   Financial implications of business expansion including impact on gearing, interest cover and cash flows | | |
| |   –   Moulin Blanche agreement | | |
| |   –   Profit margins and cash flows | | |
| |   –   International operations | | |
| |   –   Hurricanes | | |
| |   –   Claim relating to environmental damage – reputational issue, loss of customers | | |
| | | Maximum | 10 |
| **(b)** | **Significant risks of material misstatement** | | |
| | Up to 3 marks for each risk evaluated which requires discussion of the accounting treatment and identification of the associated risk of misstatement. | | |
| | Up to 2 marks for materiality calculations | | |
| |   –   Revenue recognition | | |
| |   –   Cash/foreign exchange | | |
| |   –   Licence agreement | | |
| |   –   Impairment of property, plant and equipment – political instability and regulatory issues | | |
| |   –   Impairment of assets – effect of hurricane | | |
| |   –   Provision/contingent liability regarding legal claim | | |
| |   –   Repairs to properties damaged by hurricane | | |
| | | Maximum | 18 |
| **(c)** | **Implications for audit planning** | | |
| | Up to 1½ marks for each point of discussion/appropriate action. | | |
| |   –   Limitation in scope imposed by finance director, not in accordance with agreeing the terms of an audit engagement | | |
| |   –   Discuss with audit committee, who should intervene to remove the limitation | | |
| |   –   Finance director lacks integrity, increase application of professional scepticism and increased audit risk | | |
| |   –   Consider required response when an instance of non-compliance is suspected and the reporting responsibilities of the auditor | | |

| | | |
|---|---|---|
| **Audit procedures**<br>Up to 1 mark for each well described audit procedure.<br>– Obtain the letter received from Ocean Protection, review to understand the basis of the claim<br>– Discuss the issue with the Group's legal adviser, to understand whether in their opinion, the Group could be liable for the damages<br>– Discuss with legal advisers to obtain understanding of the remit and scope of the legislation in relation to environmental protection<br>– Discuss with management the procedures which the Group utilises to ensure that it is identifying and ensuring compliance with relevant legislation<br>– Obtain an understanding, through enquiry with relevant employees, such as those responsible for scuba diving and other water sports, as to the nature of activities which take place<br>– Obtain and read all correspondence between the Group and Ocean Protection up to the date that the auditor's report is issued<br>– Obtain a written representation from management<br>– Discuss the issue with those charged with governance<br>– Review the disclosures, if any, provided in the notes to the financial statements<br>– Read the other information published with the financial statements for consistency with the financial statements | | |
| **Maximum for part c** | **10** | |

**(d)** **Data analytics**
1 mark per point.
(i)    Explanation
– Analysing patterns, deviations and inconsistencies
– 100% interrogation of transactions
– Progression of CAATs
Improve quality
– 100% testing possible
– More time to apply professional scepticism
– More likely to issue appropriate opinion
(ii)    How they can be used during the audit
– Journal testing
– Sensitivity analysis
– Analysis of performance of hotels
– Analysis of performance against competitors
– Analysis of inventory write-offs
Limitations
– Need to be developed/acquired
– Needs to be cost-effective/use for other clients
– Staff need to be trained
– Storage and retention of information
– Maintaining confidentiality of large amounts of client data

| | |
|---|---|
| **Maximum for part d** | **8** |

**Professional marks**
Generally 1 mark for heading, 1 mark for introduction, 1 mark for use of headings within the briefing notes, 1 mark for clarity of comments made.

| | |
|---|---|
| **Maximum** | **4** |
| **Total** | **50** |

## 7    LAUREL GROUP  *Walk in the footsteps of a top tutor*

### Top tutor tips

*Part (a). When evaluating the risks of material misstatement include the relevant accounting treatment required for the balance being discussed and why the client might not be using the appropriate treatment. State the risk to the balance i.e. whether it is likely to be understated or overstated. Where numbers are provided you can calculate whether the balance is material as this helps assess the significance of the risk.*

*Additional information in part (b) is essentially the evidence you will need to help with the analytical review. In general, disaggregated data is more useful for analytical review than highly summarised data therefore think about how the data already provided could be broken down to make the analysis more useful.*

*Part (c) requires audit procedures to be performed in respect of the brand and acquisition of a subsidiary. Procedures should provide sufficient description of the evidence to be obtained and how the auditor should obtain it.*

*Part (d) requires discussion of the ethical issues arising from performing a valuation of a company that the client is looking to acquire. Make sure you explain the issues properly. Marks will be limited if only a brief explanation is given. At this level you should be able to discuss whether the threat is a significant threat. Make sure you give a conclusion on the actions that need to be taken by the audit firm.*

### Briefing notes

To:          Brigitte Sanders, audit engagement partner

From:      Audit manager

Subject:   Audit planning – Laurel Group

### Introduction

These briefing notes are intended for use in planning the audit of the Laurel Group (the Group). The notes contain an evaluation of risks of material misstatement, which have been identified using information provided by the client following a meeting with the Group finance director and performing selected analytical procedures. The notes also identify the additional information which should be requested from the Laurel Group to allow for a more detailed preliminary analytical review to be performed. The notes then recommend the principal audit procedures to be performed in respect of an impaired brand and a planned acquisition which will take place after the reporting date. Finally, the notes discuss the ethical issues that could arise if the firm performs a valuation service for the Laurel Group.

**(a)** **Evaluation of risk of material misstatement**

**(b)** **Additional information to help in performing analytical review**

Selected analytical procedures and associated evaluation of risk of material misstatement

|  | 20X7 | 20X6 |
|---|---|---|
| Operating margin | 35/220 × 100 = 15.9% | 37/195 × 100 = 19% |
| Return on capital employed | (35/229 + 110) × 100 = 10.3% | (37/221 + 82) × 100 = 12.2% |
| Interest cover | 35/7 = 5 | 37/7 = 5.3 |
| Effective tax rate | 3/28 × 100 = 10.7% | 3/30 × 100 = 10% |
| Current ratio | 143/19 = 7.5 | 107/25 = 4.3 |
| Gearing ratio | (100/100 + 229) × 100 = 30.4% | (80/80 + 221) × 100 = 26.6% |

**Revenue and operating expenses**

Revenue is projected to increase by 12.8% in the year, whereas operating expenses increased by 17.1%, explaining the reduction in operating margin from 19% in 20X6 to 15.9% in 20X7. The trend in return on capital employed is consistent, with the return falling from 12.2% to 10.3%.

The notes from the meeting with the finance director state that an impairment loss of $30 million has been recognised during the year. Assuming that this cost has been included in operating expenses, it would be expected that operating expenses should increase by at least $30 million. However, operating expenses have increased by only $27 million during the year. If the $30 million impairment loss is excluded, it would seem that operating expenses have actually decreased by $3 million, which is not in line with expectations given the substantial increase in revenue. There is therefore a risk that operating expenses are understated and consequently profit is overstated. Detailed audit procedures will need to be performed to investigate the possible omission of expenses from the statement of profit or loss.

Conversely, there is also the risk that revenue is overstated given the withdrawal of the Chico branded products, implying that revenue should decrease due to lost sales from this revenue stream.

To assist with the analytical review on operating profit, the following additional information should be obtained:

– A disaggregation of revenue to show the revenue associated with the key brands of the Group, in particular the level of sales and contribution from the withdrawn Chico brand.

– A breakdown of revenue month by month, to establish when sales of the Chico brand cease.

– A disaggregation of the main categories of expenses included in operating expenses, which would confirm that the impairment loss has been included.

**Finance costs**

The interest cover is stable and indeed the finance cost recognised is constant at $7 million each year. Given that the Group took out a $20 million loan in January 20X7, it would be expected that finance charges should increase to take account of interest accruing on the new element of the loan. There is therefore a risk that finance charges and the associated loan liability are understated.

Additional information to help the analytical review here would include:

– Details of the loan taken out, including a copy of the new loan agreement to establish the interest rate payable, repayment terms and whether any borrowing costs other than interest were incurred.

**Tax expense**

The Group's effective tax rate also appears stable, increasing from 10% to 10.7% in the year. However, given the significant movement in the deferred tax liability there should be a corresponding change in the tax expense, assuming that the additional deferred tax should be charged to profit or loss. Currently, it is unclear how this increase in the deferred tax liability has been recorded.

The deferred tax liability itself creates a risk of material misstatement, which will be discussed separately, and the audit plan must contain detailed responses to ensure that sufficient and appropriate evidence is obtained in respect of both the current and deferred tax recognised.

**Current assets**

The current ratio has increased sharply in the year from 4.3 to 7.5. This could indicate that current assets are overstated or current liabilities understated and the reasons for the significant change must be discussed with the client as part of audit planning, in order to identify any specific risks such as potential overstatement of inventory included in current assets, for example, if any Chico inventory is not yet written down in value.

Additional information to help with this analysis would be:

– A breakdown of current assets so the individual figures for inventories, receivables and cash (and any other current assets recognised in the statement of financial position) can be identified and trends established.

– A breakdown of current liabilities to establish the reasons for the decrease of 24% on the prior year.

**Loan**

Gearing has increased due to the $20 million loan taken out. It is noted that the Group is going to take out another significant loan of $130 million should the acquisition of Azalea Co go ahead as planned in early June. Recognition of this loan as a liability will result in the gearing ratio increasing significantly to 50.1%.

Several risks arise in respect of this additional loan. First, the timing of its receipt is important. If the deal is to take place in early June, the finance would need to be in place in advance, and therefore it is likely that the loan is taken out just prior to the year end on 31 May. In this case it would need to be recognised and disclosed in accordance with IFRS 9 *Financial Instruments* and IFRS 7 *Financial Instruments: Disclosures*, and there is a risk that the liability is not measured appropriately or that disclosure is incomplete. Given the potential materiality of the loan, at 36.3% of existing total assets, this is a significant risk.

There is also a risk that the increase in gearing will breach any existing loan covenants. While this is a business risk rather than an audit risk, the matter may require disclosure in the financial statements, leading to a risk of material misstatement if necessary disclosures are not made.

Additional information which will help with the assessment of this risk includes:

–       Copies of any agreements with the bank so that terms can be verified, in particular the anticipated date of the receipt of the funds, and the impact on the financial statements and on analytical review procedures confirmed.

### Development costs

According to note 5 to the forecast financial statements, the $20 million loan was used to finance a specific new product development project. However, development costs recognised as an intangible asset has increased by only $15 million. The difference of $5 million is not explained by analytical review on the draft financial statements, and there is a risk that not all the amount spent on development costs has been capitalised, meaning that the intangible asset could be understated.

Conversely, it could be the case that that $5 million of the amount spent was not eligible for capitalisation under the recognition rules of IAS 38 *Intangible Assets*. However, as discussed above, the movement in operating expenses does not suggest that $5 million of research costs has been expensed. It may also be that the company continues to hold the $5 million in cash and this may be supported by the significant increase in current assets in the year.

Additional information is required to explain how the $20 million raised from the loan has been utilised, whether it was all spent on research and development, and the nature of the development costs which were funded from the loan.

### Retained earnings

Finally, retained earnings have increased by $8 million. Projected profit for the year is $25 million, therefore there is an unexplained reconciling item between retained earnings brought forward and carried forward (98 + 25 – 106 = 17). The difference of $17 million could be due to a dividend paid in the financial year, but additional information including a statement of changes in equity is required in order to plan an appropriate audit response.

### Property, plant and equipment

The change to the estimated useful lives of property, plant and equipment has increased profit by $5 million, which represents 17.9% of profit before tax and is therefore material to the financial statements.

This change in accounting estimate is permitted, but the audit team should be sceptical and carefully consider whether the change is justified. If the change was found to be inappropriate it would need to be corrected, increasing operating expenses by $5 million, reducing operating profit to $30 million and the operating margin would fall to only 13.6%.

This would be a significant reduction in profit and it could be that management bias is a risk factor, especially given the sizeable loan which is about to be agreed meaning that the projected financial statements may have already been scrutinised by the Group's bank.

**Chico brand name and associated issues**

The Group finance director states that the Chico brand name has been impaired by $30 million. However, the brand name intangible asset has fallen by $35 million in the year, so there is an unexplained reduction of $5 million. This may have been caused by the impairment or sale of another brand, and additional information should be sought to explain the movement in the year.

The audit team will need to verify whether the $30 million impairment recognised in relation to the Chico brand name is a full impairment of the amount recognised in relation to that specific brand within intangible assets. Given that the branded products have been withdrawn from sale, it should be fully written off. If any amount remains recognised, then intangible assets and operating profit will be overstated.

The amount written off amounts to 8.4% of Group assets and 107% of profit before tax. It is a highly material issue which may warrant separate disclosure under IAS 1 *Presentation of Financial Statements*. It is a risk that the necessary disclosures are not made in relation to the discontinuance and/or the impairment of assets.

There is also a risk that other brands could be impaired, for example, if the harmful ingredients used in the Chico brand are used in other perfume ranges. Management has stated that it believes there is no effect on other brands, however, the audit team must be sceptical of this as it is unlikely that management would want to recognise an additional impairment charge given the loan application and the reduction in profit during the year. The impairment recognised in the financial statements could therefore be understated.

There is also a risk that inventories are overstated if there are any Chico items included in the amount recognised within current assets. Any Chico products should be written down to the lower of cost and net realisable value in accordance with IAS 2 *Inventories*, and presumably the net realisable value would be zero.

There is a possibility that some non-current assets used in the production of the Chico fragrance may need to be measured and disclosed in accordance with IAS 36 *Impairment of Assets* and/or IFRS 5 *Assets Held for Sale and Discontinued Operations*. This would depend on whether the assets are impaired or meet the criteria to be classified as held for sale, for example, whether they constitute a separate major line of business.

There may also be an issue relating to the health issues caused by use of the Chico products. It is likely that customers may have already brought legal claims against the Group if they have suffered skin problems after using the products. If claims have not yet arisen, they may occur in the future.

There is a risk that necessary provisions have not been made, or that contingent liabilities have not been disclosed in the notes to the financial statements in accordance with IAS 37 *Provisions, Contingent Liabilities and Contingent Assets*. This would mean that potentially liabilities are understated and operating profit is overstated, or that disclosures are incomplete.

**Goodwill**

Goodwill recognised in the statement of financial position represents 5% of total assets and is material.

An impairment review of goodwill must be carried out annually for each cash-generating unit in accordance with IAS 36 *Impairment of Assets*.

Goodwill has not been impaired this year; we shall need to carry out a review of management's annual impairment test to assess its appropriateness and whether any of the goodwill has been impaired by the media coverage of the Chico product allegations. This means that goodwill and operating profit could be overstated if any necessary impairment has not been recognised.

**Deferred tax liability**

The finance director states that the change in the deferred tax liability relates to the changes in estimated useful lives of assets and associated accelerated tax depreciation (capital allowances). However, the impact on profit of the change to estimated useful lives amounts to $5 million, so the $8 million increase in deferred tax seems inappropriate and it is likely that the liability is overstated.

The deferred tax liability has increased by five times, and the $10 million recognised in the year-end projection is material at 2.8% of total assets. The changes in deferred tax and the related property, plant and equipment therefore does not appear to be proportionate and the amount recognised could be incorrect.

**Acquisition of Azalea Co**

The acquisition is planned to take place in early June and assuming it takes place, it will be a significant event to be disclosed in accordance with IAS 10 *Events After the Reporting Period*. Details of the acquisition will also need to be disclosed to comply with IFRS 3 *Business Combinations* which requires disclosure of information about a business combination whose acquisition date is after the end of the reporting period but before the financial statements are authorised for issue. There is a risk that the necessary disclosures are not made which would be a significant risk of material misstatement given the materiality of the acquisition.

*Tutorial note*

*Credit will be awarded for evaluation of other relevant risks of material misstatement including management bias due to the loan of $130 million being provided, and the complex and acquisitive nature of the Group, which leads to inherent risk of misstatement in relation to business combinations.*

**(c)**    **Audit procedures**

**(i)**    **Impairment of Chico brand**

–    Obtain management's calculations relevant to the impairment and review to understand methodology, for example, whether the brand has been entirely or partly written off.

–    Evaluate the assumptions used by management in their impairment review and consider their reasonableness.

–    Confirm the carrying value of the Chico brand pre-impairment to prior year financial statements or management accounts.

–    From management accounts, obtain a breakdown of total revenue by brand, to evaluate the significance of the Chico brand to financial performance and whether it constitutes a separate line of business for disclosure as a discontinued operation.

–    If the brand is not fully written off, discuss with management the reasons for this treatment given that the brand is now discontinued.

–    Obtain a breakdown of operating expenses to confirm that the impairment is included.

–    Review the presentation of the income statement, considering whether separate disclosure of the impairment is necessary given its materiality.

**(ii)**    **Acquisition of Azalea Co**

–    Read board minutes to understand the rationale for the acquisition, and to see that the acquisition is approved.

–    Discuss with Group management the way that control will be exercised over Azalea Co, enquiring as to whether the Group can determine the board members of Azalea Co.

–    Review the minutes of relevant meetings held between management of the Group and Azalea Co to confirm matters such as:

•    That the deal is likely to go ahead

•    The likely timescale

•    The amount and nature of consideration to be paid

•    The shareholding to be acquired and whether equity or non-equity shares

•    The planned operational integration (if any) of Azalea Co into the Group.

–    Obtain any due diligence reports which have been obtained by the Group and review for matters which may need to be disclosed in accordance with IAS 10 or IFRS 3.

–    Obtain copies of the finance agreement for the funds used to purchase Azalea Co.

–    After the reporting date, agree the cash consideration paid to bank records.

**(d)    Oleander Co**

**Conflict of interest**

A conflict of interest arises when a firm provides a service in relation to two or more clients whose interests in respect of the matter are in conflict.

In this case, the interests of Laurel Group and Oleander Co will be conflicting. Laurel Group will want to purchase the shares for the lowest possible amount and the owner of Oleander Co will want to sell them for the highest possible amount. This creates a significant threat to the objectivity of Holly & Co, who may be seen to be acting in the interest of one party at the expense of the other.

The problem is exacerbated by the nature of the engagement; Laurel Group will use information about the company, including operational information, to bargain over the price. Holly & Co may be privy to private information gained during their time as auditor of Oleander Co which Laurel Group might not have become aware of during normal due diligence procedures. If Holly & Co were to divulge this to Laurel Group, it would give them a potentially unfair advantage over the other client and would be a breach of confidentiality.

**Self-review threat**

Performing the valuation service for Laurel Group would also create a self-review threat because Holly & Co would have a significant influence over the valuation of Oleander Co, which would consequently be used to consolidate their accounts into the new, enlarged group which Holly & Co would be responsible for auditing in the future.

**Actions**

It is possible to reduce both the conflict of interest and self-review threats by using different teams to conduct the various services provided.

The IESBA *International Code of Ethics for Professional Accountants* and the FRC Ethical Standard both stipulate that a firm should not provide valuation services for a listed client if the valuation has a material effect on the financial statements which are consequently audited.

Therefore, before accepting the assignment, Holly & Co should consider the potential impact of the transaction and, if they believe it will be material, they should politely decline the engagement.

**Conclusion**

These briefing notes indicate that there are many potentially significant risks of material misstatement to be considered in planning the Group audit. The Group should provide the additional information requested to enable a more thorough analytical review to be performed as part of our audit planning. A range of audit procedures have been designed, which should reduce our detection risk in relation to the impaired brand and the planned acquisition of Azalea Co after the year end. In respect of the request to perform a valuation service, we should decline this offer due to the significant threats arising.

**Examiner's comments**

This question presented the scenario of a large cosmetics group and candidates were presented with three requirements.

Part (a) required risks of material misstatement in the audit to be considered, including using analytical procedures, and a full statement of financial position and statement of profit or loss were provided. This was generally well-answered as there were lots of potential risks to discuss. Candidates that did not score well often concentrated on explaining audit procedures rather than evaluating risks. Disappointingly many candidates only calculated one or two ratios or trends even though the question asked for analytical procedures and contained a full page of numerical data to analyse. Candidates' inability to utilise all the information provided when evaluating risks continues to be an area of concern and continues to demonstrate that candidates must improve their exam technique in this regard.

Part (b) required candidates to highlight additional information to enable more detailed analytical review to be performed. Answers to this part were collectively disappointing with most candidates giving generic lists of additional items that may be required, such as board minutes or impairment reviews. These would be required as part of a wider audit plan but that was not what the question asked for. Very few candidates actually answered the question and highlighted what information was required for analytical review purposes, such as a breakdown of sales by product or market.

Part (c) was split into two sections, firstly the audit procedures related to the impairment of a brand. This was reasonably answered with some good procedures highlighted but many candidates erroneously digressed into seeking the original cost of the brand and discussing whether any claims were being made against the company which would have been better-included in part (a).

In part (c) (ii) the audit procedures related to a planned acquisition and were generally well-answered with sensible procedures such as reviewing the due diligence report, board minutes and discussions with management about the likelihood of success. Theorising about whether the acquisition would be a subsidiary or associate, or suggesting audit procedures for the enlarged group did not answer the requirement.

In part (d) candidates often missed either the conflict of interest or the listed status of the company.

There were four professional marks available for presentation, logic and clarity. Candidates who presented their answers in a logical and reasoned manner with sub-headings and references scored well. Again candidates are advised to consider their exam technique in this area, for example only one concise paragraph is necessary as an introduction, not a whole page. Candidates are advised to space out their work and start a new page for each sub-section.

| Marking scheme | | Marks |
|---|---|---|

**(a)** **Risk of material misstatement evaluation**

Up to 3 marks for each risk evaluated

Generally 1 mark for each ratio (including comparative) calculated, and ½ mark for relevant trends calculated, up to a maximum of 5 marks.

Allow 1 mark for each correct calculation and comment on materiality up to a maximum of 2 marks.

**Risks in relation to ratio analysis**

– Understatement of operating expenses excluding the impairment loss

– Understatement of finance costs

– Tax expense not in line with movement in deferred tax liability

– Overstatement of current assets/understatement of current liabilities

– Significant new loan liability to be taken on around the reporting date – recognition, measurement and disclosure risks

– Unexplained/ inconsistent movement in intangible assets/loan raised to finance development

– Unreconciled movement in retained earnings

**Other risks of material misstatement**

– New loan may breach existing loan covenants – risk that IFRS 7 disclosures not made

– Change to PPE useful lives may not be appropriate – overstated assets and profit

– Management bias risk due to new loan being taken out

– Impairment to Chico brand may be understated if full carrying value of brand not written off

– Impairment may need separate disclosure due to materiality – risk of inadequate disclosure

– Chico inventories will need to be written off – risk of overstated assets

– Risk that goodwill has not been tested for impairment

– A provision may be needed for customer claims – risk of understated liabilities

– Deferred tax liability appears incorrect and likely to be overstated

**Maximum** **24**

**(b)** **Additional information**

Generally up to 1 mark for each piece of information recommended.

– Disaggregation of revenue into major brands to identify significant trends by brand

– Monthly breakdown of revenue to assess date at which Chico products were withdrawn

– Disaggregation of operating expenses to determine main categories and inclusion of impairment expense

– Disaggregation of current assets to assess movements in inventories, receivables and cash

– Disaggregation of current liabilities to assess significant decrease

– Details of the $20 million loan taken out to evaluate appropriateness of finance charge

– Details of the new $130 million loan to build into projected gearing and other ratios

– Reconciliation of brought forward and carried forward intangible assets

– Statement of changes in equity

**Maximum** **6**

**(c)** **Audit procedures**
Up to 1 mark for each well described procedure.

**(i)** **Impairment of brand name**
- Obtain management's calculations relevant to the impairment and review to understand methodology
- Evaluate the assumptions used by management in their impairment review and consider their reasonableness
- Confirm the carrying value of the Chico brand pre-impairment to prior year financial statements or management accounts
- From management accounts, obtain a breakdown of total revenue by brand, to evaluate the significance of the Chico brand
- If the brand is not fully written off, discuss with management the reasons for this treatment given that the brand is now discontinued
- Obtain a breakdown of operating expenses to confirm that the impairment is included
- Review the presentation of the income statement, considering whether separate disclosure of the impairment is necessary given its materiality

**(ii)** **Acquisition of Azalea Co**
- Read board minutes to understand the rationale for the acquisition, and to see that the acquisition is approved
- Discuss with Group management the way that control will be exercised over Azalea Co, enquiring as to whether the Group can determine the board members of Azalea Co
- Review the minutes of relevant meetings held between management of the Group and Azalea Co to confirm matters such as:
    - That the deal is likely to go ahead
    - The likely timescale
    - The amount and nature of consideration to be paid
    - The shareholding to be acquired and whether equity or non-equity shares
    - The planned operational integration (if any) of Azalea Co into the Group
- Obtain any due diligence reports which have been obtained by the Group and review for matters which may need to be disclosed in accordance with IAS 10 or IFRS 3
- After the reporting date, agree the cash consideration paid to bank records

| | |
|---|---|
| **Maximum** | 10 |

**(d)** **Ethical issues**
Generally up to 1½ marks for each well explained matter and 1 mark for each well explained and relevant response to the matters identified.
Note: Only ½ mark will be awarded for brief identification of a matter. Further marks will be awarded for explaining why the threat/matter is relevant in this specific context. Likewise only ½ mark will be awarded for brief response. Only well explained responses should score a full mark.
- Conflict of interest with competing audit clients
- Potentially private information held by Holly & Co in relation to Oleander Co
- Self-review threat caused by valuation service
- Possible use of separate teams (max 1 mark)
- Not permitted to conduct valuation service for audit client (max 1 mark)

| | |
|---|---|
| **Maximum** | 6 |

| | | |
|---|---|---|
| **Professional marks** Generally 1 mark for heading, 1 mark for introduction, 1 mark for use of headings within the briefing notes, 1 mark for clarity of comments made | | |
| | Maximum | 4 |
| Total | | 50 |

**8    ZED COMMUNICATIONS GROUP**   *Walk in the footsteps of a top tutor*

*Top tutor tips*

*Part (a) asks for audit risks. This is the most frequently examined type of risk and students should be able to properly describe the risks as either risks of material misstatement or detection risks.*

*Additional information in part (b) is essentially the evidence you would gather to help assess whether the risk is significant. For example, to ascertain the appropriate revenue recognition policy, the terms of the contracts need to be read to identify the performance obligations within the contracts.*

*Part (c) requires matters to be considered before relying on the work of the client's internal audit department. This requires text book knowledge to be applied to the details of the scenario. Look out for information that indicates the internal audit department is experienced and qualified as this will indicate evidence of competence. The requirement also refers to assistance from the internal audit department.*

*This is different to relying on the work of the internal auditor as direct assistance is where the internal audit helps with the external audit procedures. There are many restrictions given in ISA 610 and your answer should cover the most important ones.*

*Part (d) asks for procedures in respect of the shareholding in the joint venture and the licence acquired during the year. Procedures are very regularly examined as a follow on from audit risks. Make sure the procedures are adequately described so that the person performing the procedure will know what to do.*

*Part (e) requires advantages and disadvantages of joint audits. This is rote-learned knowledge and should therefore be quite straightforward.*

**Briefing notes**

| To: | Vincent Vega, audit engagement partner |
| From: | Audit engagement manager |
| Subject: | Audit planning – ZCG |

**Introduction**

These briefing notes have been prepared to assist in the audit planning of ZCG, and contain an evaluation of audit risk and a discussion of the matters to be considered in determining whether to place reliance on the Group's internal audit department. The notes provide audit procedures to be performed on the classification of the investment in WTC and on the measurement of a licence acquired on 1 January 20X5. The notes also discuss the advantages and disadvantages of joint audits that may be relevant if ZCG acquires the company in Neverland.

**(a)    Evaluation of audit risks**

**Recognition of 50% equity shareholding in WTC**

The 50% equity shareholding is likely to give rise to a joint venture under which control of WTC is shared between ZCG and Wolf Communications Co.

IFRS 11 *Joint Arrangements* requires that an investor which has joint control over a joint venture should recognise its investment using the equity method of accounting in accordance with IAS 28 *Investments in Associates and Joint Ventures*.

Audit risk arises in that despite owning 50% of the equity shares of WTC, ZCG may not actually share control with Wolf Communications, for example, if Wolf Communications retains a right to veto decisions or if ZCG cannot appoint an equal number of board members in order to make joint decisions with board members appointed by Wolf Communications. If ZCG does not have joint control, then WTC should not be treated as a joint venture.

Assuming that there is shared control, an audit risk arises in that ZCG may not have correctly applied equity accounting, thereby potentially over or understating ZCG's investment and resulting in incorrect presentation in the consolidated statement of financial position and statement of profit or loss. The cost of the investment in WTC represents 7.5% of ZCG's total assets at 31 August 20X6, thus the investment is material to the Group.

**Amortisation of licence to operate in Farland**

The licence acquired on 1 January 20X5 should be recognised as an intangible asset and amortised on a systematic basis over its useful life.

According to IAS 38 *Intangible Assets,* the amortisation method should reflect the pattern of benefits, or if the pattern cannot be determined reliably, the straight-line method of amortisation should be used.

Amortisation should begin when the asset is available for use, meaning when it is in the location and condition necessary for it to be capable of operating in the manner which management intends. ZCG therefore should begin to amortise the licence on 1 July 20X6 and amortise over the remaining licence period of eight and a half years.

The audit risk is that amortisation did not commence at the right point in time or that it has been determined using an inappropriate useful life, leading to over or understatement of the amortisation charge to profit as well as the carrying value of the intangible asset.

Assuming that it is appropriate to use the straight-line method, amortisation for the year to 31 December 20X6 should be $3.8 million (65/8.5 × 6/12). This represents 1.3% of extrapolated revenue for the year of $297 million (198 × 12/8) and is therefore material, and the amortisation will be more material next year when a full year's charge to profit is made.

**Impairment of the Farland licence**

IAS 38 does not require an annual impairment review to be conducted for all intangible assets. However, management should consider whether there are indicators of impairment and if necessary perform an impairment review on the licence.

The competitor's actions which appear to have reduced customer demand to a level below that anticipated is an indicator of potential impairment, so management must calculate the recoverable amount of the licence and compare to its carrying value in order to determine if the asset is impaired.

Therefore there is a risk that the licence is overstated in value, and operating profit also overstated if any necessary impairment has not been recognised.

**Revenue recognition**

Given the significance of revenue recognition to the Group's financial statements, the potential misapplication of IFRS 15 Revenue from Contracts with Customers.

ZCG is supplying customers with a multiple-element contract and is providing access to a mobile phone network, a fixed landline and a broadband service, so there are multiple performance obligations. ZCG must allocate the revenue from each contract to each of these obligations, in line with IFRS 15, and therefore there is a significant audit risk that this is not done correctly.

ZCG should have robust systems in place to ensure that contracts can be 'unbundled', enabling the revenue relating to each obligation to be separately determined, otherwise there is a significant risk that the revenue element attributable to each component will be over or understated.

There is also a risk that the revenue will not be recognised in the correct period. Revenue should be recognised when a performance obligation is satisfied, which in this case is over a period of time. Contracts vary in length, lasting two or three years, so there is an audit risk that the timing of revenue recognition is not appropriate.

The fact that total revenue, when extrapolated for the 12-month period, is expected to increase by 35% could indicate that revenue is being recognised too early. This could indicate a misapplication of IFRS 15, possibly changes to accounting policies which have been made on adoption of IFRS 15 are not appropriate.

IFRS 15 contains significant disclosure requirements and there is a risk that ZCG fails to provide sufficient disclosure on a range of matters relevant to its contracts with customers, including the significant judgments made in applying IFRS 15 to those contracts and sufficient disaggregation of the necessary disclosures.

Given the significant volume of individual customer contracts and the complexity of the accounting treatment, revenue recognition is a significant audit risk.

**Right to use network capacity**

The payment of $17.8 million to acquire access to network capacity represents 3% of total assets and 6% of extrapolated revenue for the year, thus the amount is material.

It seems that risk and reward does not pass to ZCG in respect of the assets being used and the seller retains control over the use of its network assets. Therefore the network capacity should not be recognised as an intangible asset of ZCG and the Group is currently adopting an inappropriate accounting treatment which has resulted in intangible assets being overstated.

The accounting treatment for these rights should be discussed with ZCG as soon as possible. The most appropriate accounting treatment would seem to be for ZCG to record the cost of the right to use the network capacity as a prepayment and recognise the cost in profit or loss on a straight-line basis over the term of the agreements and this accounting treatment should be reflected in the financial statements as soon as possible.

The audit team will need to be made aware of the risk that prepayments and operating expenses are over or understated if the cost has not been treated as a prepayment and/or is not released to profit or loss over an appropriate period.

A further risk is the payment to the network provider is for a specified amount of access to the network provider's network. There is a risk is that ZCG has exceeded the allocated allowance and that any necessary additional payment due for excess usage is not recognised in the financial statements.

**Internal controls and fraud risk**

The internal audit department has reported that internal controls are 'working well'. This statement will need to be substantiated but gives the impression that control risk is likely to be low. The work of the internal control department will be discussed in more detail in the next section of the briefing notes.

However, it is worth noting that two frauds have been found to be operating during the year, giving rise to audit risk. Although the total monetary amount attributable to the frauds is less than 1% of revenue, therefore immaterial, the fact that the frauds have occurred indicates that there are significant internal control deficiencies which could mean that other frauds are operating. We will need to carefully plan our audit approach to expenses and payroll in light of the increased fraud risk.

The lack of approval and authorisation of expenses discovered by internal audit is concerning as this appears to involve higher level management and may call into question management integrity.

We should review the work of internal audit to establish if this is an area where controls have been overridden or if there are current gaps within the control framework. We should review and update our systems notes to identify where reliance can potentially be placed on controls and where there are deficiencies.

The issue uncovered by internal audit in relation to payroll suggests that there is inadequate control over the Group's IT system. Access controls, which form part of the Group's general IT controls, are weak which means that other areas of the system may be vulnerable.

This significantly increases control risk and as a result presents a significant area of audit risk. We will need to ensure that we carefully plan our approach as this may mean that there are areas of the system where no reliance can be placed on internal controls and appropriate alternative procedures will need to be applied.

**Segmental reporting**

Being a listed entity, ZCG should provide segmental information in the notes to the financial statements in accordance with IFRS 8 *Operating Segments*.

The audit risk is that the segmental information provided is not sufficiently detailed and/or not based on the information reported internally to the Group's chief operating decision maker.

There are some unusual trends in the segmental revenue figures from the management accounts. For example, revenue from south east Asia appears to have increased significantly – if the 20X6 revenue figure is extrapolated to a 12-month period, the projected revenue from that segment is $49.5 million, an increase of 65% compared to 20X5.

There is a risk that revenues have been misallocated between segments and that the disclosure is inaccurate.

(b)  **Additional information**

- Legal documentation for the purchase of WTC should be reviewed, including voting rights acquired, to determine the extent to which control can be exercised by ZCG as this will impact the treatment in the financial statements.

- A copy of licence to operate in Farland should be reviewed to identify the terms of the licence and the appropriate amortisation period to be used.

- A sample of contracts with customers should be reviewed to identify the performance obligations in respect of the contracts to determine how ZCG should recognise revenue in accordance with IFRS 15.

- Other internal audit reports should be reviewed to evaluate findings and determine whether the work of the internal audit department is adequate for audit purposes.

- Details of the internal auditor's qualifications and experience should be obtained and reviewed to assess their competence before relying on their work.

- Notes of discussions held with internal audit to assess whether there are any other fraud risks of which they are aware which could impact our audit approach.

- Due diligence report for the potential acquisition.

- Details of the potential acquisition of the company in Neverland such as the likely completion date. If the acquisition is completed before the auditor's report is signed it will need to be disclosed as a non-adjusting event and will therefore impact our subsequent events procedures.

(c)  **Matters which should be considered in determining the amount of reliance, if any, which can be placed on the work of ZCG's internal audit department**

According to ISA 610 *Using the Work of Internal Auditors*, the external auditor may decide to use the work of the audit client's internal audit function to modify the nature or timing, or reduce the extent, of audit procedures to be performed directly by the external auditor.

Note that in some jurisdictions the external auditor may be prohibited, or restricted to some extent, by law or regulation from using the work of the internal audit function. Therefore Tarantino & Co should consider whether it is prohibited by the law or regulations which it must adhere to from relying on the work of ZCG's internal audit department or using the internal auditors to provide direct assistance.

**Evaluate the internal audit function**

Tarantino & Co must evaluate the internal audit department to determine whether its work is suitable by evaluating:

- The extent to which the internal audit function's organisational status and relevant policies and procedures support the objectivity of the internal auditors

- The level of competence of the internal audit function, and

- Whether the internal audit function applies a systematic and disciplined approach, including quality control.

**Objectivity**

One of the key issues to be evaluated is objectivity – the internal audit department should be unbiased in their work and be able to report their findings without being subject to the influence of others. The fact that the latest internal audit report is addressed to ZCG's finance director could indicate that there is a conflict of interest, as the internal audit department should report directly to the audit committee or to those charged with governance in order to maintain their independence.

**Competence**

The internal audit team is managed by a qualified accountant who is presumably technically competent, though the nature and status of his qualification should be determined. Tarantino & Co should consider whether the rest of the internal audit department is staffed by professional accountants, whether ZCG has a training programme in place for the internal auditors, for example, to ensure that they are up to date with new IFRS requirements such as IFRS 15, and whether there are sufficient resources for the internal auditors to carry out their duties in a large multi-national organisation.

When assessing competency, consideration must also be given to the overall findings which were reported regarding the deficiencies in the current internal control system. The internal audit department has concluded that controls are working well despite there being two instances of fraud in the year which may have more serious ramifications than first suggested.

**Scope of work**

The scope of work carried out in this area and the resultant recommendations will need to be reviewed. This may further suggest that the internal audit department is not free to investigate or report their findings due to the current reporting chains.

If there are doubts over either the objectivity or the competence of the internal audit department, then Tarantino & Co should not rely on their work.

**Systematic and disciplined approach**

In order to determine whether the internal audit department works in a systematic and disciplined way, Tarantino & Co should consider matters including the nature of documentation which is produced by the department and whether effective quality control procedures are in place such as direction, supervision and review of work carried out.

**Direct assistance**

If Tarantino & Co wants to use the internal audit function to provide direct assistance, then the firm should:

- obtain written agreement from an authorised representative of the entity that the internal auditors will be allowed to follow the external auditor's instructions, and that the entity will not intervene in the work the internal auditor performs for the external auditor, and

- obtain written agreement from the internal auditors that they will keep confidential specific matters as instructed by the external auditor and inform the external auditor of any threat to their objectivity.

If these confirmations cannot be obtained, then the internal auditors should not be used to provide direct assistance.

**UK syllabus:** In the UK, ISA (UK) 610 prohibits the use of internal auditors in providing direct assistance to the external auditor. Direct assistance is the use of internal auditors to perform audit procedures under the direction, supervision and review of the external auditor. However, the internal auditors can be used to provide non-direct assistance, for example, we may review their reports on risk management as a way of obtaining business understanding and identifying business risks and risks of material misstatement.

(d) (i) **Audit procedures on the classification of the 50% shareholding in WTC**

- Obtain the legal documentation supporting the investment and agree the details of the investment including:

 − The date of the investment

 − Amount paid

 − Number of shares purchased

 − The voting rights attached to the shares

 − The nature of the profit sharing arrangement between ZCG and Wolf Communications

 − The nature of access to WTC's assets under the terms of the agreement

 − Confirmation that there is no restriction of ZCG's shared control of WTC.

- Read board minutes to confirm the approval of the investment and to understand the business rationale for the investment.

- Read minutes of relevant meetings between ZCG and Wolf Communications to confirm that control is shared between the two companies and to understand the nature of the relationship and the decision-making process.

- Obtain documentation such as WTC's organisational structure to confirm that ZCG has successfully appointed members to the board of WTC and that those members have equal power to the members appointed by Wolf Communications.

(ii) **Audit procedures on the measurement of the operating licence to operate in Farland**

- Obtain the licence agreement and confirm the length of the licence period to be 10 years from the date it was granted.

- Confirm whether the licence can be renewed at the end of the 10-year period, as this may impact on the estimated useful life and amortisation.

- Re-perform management's calculation of the amortisation charged as an expense in 20X6.

- Discuss with management the process for identifying an appropriate amortisation method and where relevant, how the pattern of future economic benefits associated with the licence have been determined.

- Confirm with management that the Farland network became operational on 1 July 20X6.

- Review a sample of contracts with customers in Farland to verify that contracts commenced from the operational date of 1 July 20X6.

- Enquire with management on the existence of any factors indicating that a shorter useful life is appropriate, for example, the stability of market demand in Farland or possible restrictions on the network capacity in Farland.

- Review management accounts and cash flow forecasts to confirm that Farland is generating an income stream and is predicted to continue to generate cash.

- Obtain a written representation from management confirming that there are no indications of impairment of the licence of which management is aware.

(e) **Joint audit**

**Advantages**

In a joint audit, two or more audit firms are responsible for conducting the audit and for issuing the audit opinion. The main advantage of a joint audit of is that the local audit firm's understanding and experience will be retained, and that will be a valuable input to the audit. At the same time, Tarantino & Co can provide additional skills and resources if necessary.

Neverland may have different regulations to the rest of the Group, for example, there may be a different financial reporting framework. It makes sense for the local auditors, therefore, to retain some input to the audit as they will have detailed knowledge of such regulations.

The fact that the company is located in a distant location means that from a practical point of view it may be difficult for Tarantino & Co to provide staff for performing the bulk of the audit work. It will be more cost effective for this to be carried out by local auditors.

Two audit firms can also stand together against aggressive accounting treatments. In this way, a joint audit can enhance the quality of the audit. The benchmarking that takes place between the two firms raises the level of service quality.

### Disadvantages

The main disadvantage is that for the Group, having a joint audit is likely to be more expensive than appointing just one audit firm. However, the costs are likely to be less than if Tarantino & Co took sole responsibility, as having the current auditors retain an involvement will at least cut down on travel expenses. The small local firm will probably offer a cheaper audit service than Tarantino & Co.

For the audit firms, there may be problems in deciding on responsibilities, allocating work, and they will need to work very closely together to ensure that no duties go underperformed, and that the quality of the audit is maintained.

### Conclusion

These briefing notes highlight that there are a number of audit risks to be addressed, in particular revenue recognition, and fraud risks appear to be significant issues requiring a robust response from the audit team. We will need to carefully consider whether it is appropriate to receive direct assistance from the internal audit department.

---

**Examiner's comments**

This question followed the pattern of previous examinations and was set at the planning stage of the audit/assurance cycle. The context of the question was a large company looking to expand its international presence through different means.

Part (a) was a standard audit risk requirement and should have been an area where candidates were able to score strong marks for identifying audit risks from the scenario and describing the effects on the financial statements and elements of audit risk. This part of the question was disappointingly answered by many candidates. There is a tendency for weaker candidates to produce long but irrelevant answers. There is no place in this requirement for describing the audit risk model or discussing ethical issues. If ethical issues were required this would be flagged as a separate requirement. In this scenario the client was not a new client and had pre-existing international revenue streams, demonstrated by the prior year segmental revenue comparatives, therefore discussing detection risk due to a lack of auditor knowledge of the client or inability to audit international revenue was not relevant. The risks in this type of question are flagged up in the scenario and should be addressed using up to date knowledge of financial reporting standards to describe appropriate accounting treatment and highlighting the potential impact of errors on the financial statements. Generally, the direction of the error will be required to score well, simply stating that intangibles may be over or understated will not gain full credit as this does not demonstrate the level of knowledge which is required. As in previous audit risk questions, there is credit available for calculating and concluding on the materiality of a balance in the financial statements. A majority of candidates are able to correctly select the appropriate benchmark for materiality (e.g. assessing an asset or liability in the context of total assets rather than on revenue or profits) but frequently answers were presented with materiality based on prior year rather than current year figures. Audit risk continues to be an area that candidates find difficult and particularly it continues to be noted that many candidates fail to engage with the information provided in enough depth, specifically when provided with extracts from financial statements. Candidates are again reminded that in order to provide a full answer in relation to audit risk they should utilise and analyse all the information that is provided.

---

Candidates were also required to discuss the considerations to be taken into account when assessing whether and how to use internal audit to assist the external auditor. The majority of candidates were able to list the criteria as per ISA 610 *Using the Work of Internal Auditors*, to assess against and relate that back to the scenario, which was an improvement on the last time this standard was examined.

Candidates were required to provide the principal audit procedures to obtain audit evidence in relation to the classification of a joint venture and the measurement of an intangible asset. The majority of candidates performed satisfactorily in this requirement but again many had not read the requirement carefully enough and described tests covering other financial statement assertions than those required – for example assessing the cost of the joint venture which was not relevant to the classification risk, or failing to take into account that the intangible had been purchased in the prior year so the cost would have been audited at that point so audit procedures should have focused on confirming the brought forward figure and any adjustments for amortisation or impairment.

Requirement (e) asked for a discussion of the advantages and disadvantages of a joint audit being performed on a soon to be acquired subsidiary. Most candidates could identify at least two advantages and two disadvantages, though often they were not discussed at all and the answer amounted to little more than a list of bullet points, which would not have attracted many marks.

Some answers seemed to confuse a joint audit with an audit involving component auditors, and some used the fact that the foreign audit firm was a small firm to argue that it could not possibly be competent enough to perform an audit or have a good ethical standing.

There were four professional marks available, and most candidates secured most of these marks by providing an introduction and using headings to create an appropriate structure for their answer. However, presentation was not always good and candidates are reminded to pay attention to determining an appropriate layout for their answer.

| **Marking scheme** | | |
|---|---|---:|
| | | *Marks* |
| **(a)** | **Evaluation of audit risk** | |
| | Generally up to 3 marks for each audit risk evaluated | |
| | In addition, 1 mark for each correct materiality calculation to a maximum of 2 marks and 1 mark for each relevant calculation such as trends. | |
| | – Recognition of 50% equity shareholding in WTC | |
| | – Amortisation of licence to operate in Farland | |
| | – Possible impairment of licence | |
| | – Right to use network capacity | |
| | – Revenue recognition – max 5 marks if discuss a range of issues specific to IFRS 15 including multiple element contracts, timing of recognition, disclosure requirements, volume of transactions | |
| | – Internal controls and fraud risk – up to 4 marks for a detailed discussion of fraud risk | |
| | – Segmental reporting | |
| | **Maximum** | 18 |
| **(b)** | **Additional information** | |
| | 1 mark for each piece of relevant information. Credit should be given for other relevant recommendations | |
| | – Legal documentation for purchase of WTC | |
| | – Copy of licence for terms | |
| | – Contracts with customers to identify contractual terms for revenue recognition | |
| | – Other internal audit reports to evaluate findings | |

|  |  |  |
|---|---|---|
| – | Details of qualifications and experience of internal auditors to determine competence | |
| – | Notes of discussions with internal audit to assess risk due to fraud | |
| – | Due diligence report for potential acquisition | |
| – | Details of potential acquisition for possible disclosure as a non-adjusting event | |
| | **Maximum** | 6 |

**(c)    Internal audit**

Generally up to 2 marks for discussion of each relevant matter:

|  |  |  |
|---|---|---|
| – | General introduction, comment on prohibition in some jurisdictions | |
| – | Objectivity | |
| – | Competence | |
| – | Disciplined and systematic approach | |
| – | Using the internal auditors to provide direct assistance | |
| | **Maximum** | 6 |

**(d)    Audit procedures**

Generally 1 mark for each well explained audit procedure:

**(i)    Investment in WTC**

- Obtain the legal documentation supporting the investment and agree the details of the investment (max 2 marks for details of items to be verified)
- Read board minutes for approval of the investment understanding of the business rationale for the investment
- Read minutes of relevant meetings between ZCG and Wolf Communications to confirm shared control and shared decision-making process
- Confirm that ZCG has successfully appointed members to the board of WTC and that board decisions are made equally

**(ii)    Amortisation of licence**

- Obtain the licence agreement and confirm the length of the licence period
- Confirm whether the licence can be renewed at the end of the 10-year period
- Re-perform management's calculation of the amortisation charged as an expense in 20X6
- Discuss with management the process for determining the method of amortisation
- Review management accounts to confirm that the Farland network became operational on 1 July 20X6 and that Farland is generating a revenue stream from that date
- Review customer contracts to confirm network operational from 1 July 20X6
- Enquire with management on the existence of factors indicating that a shorter useful life is appropriate
- Review management accounts and cash flow forecasts to confirm that Farland is generating an income stream and is predicted to continue to generate cash
- Obtain a management representation to confirm that there are no indications of impairment of the licence of which management is aware

|  |  |  |
|---|---|---|
| | **Maximum** | 10 |

**(e)    Joint audit**

Up to 1 mark for each advantage/disadvantage discussed:

Advantages

- Retain local auditors' knowledge of company
- Local auditors' knowledge of local regulations
- Tarantino & Co can provide additional skills and resources
- Cost effective – reduce travel expenses, local firm likely to be cheaper
- Enhanced audit quality

| | | |
|---|---|---|
| Disadvantages | | |
| – But employing two audit firms could be more expensive | | |
| – Problems in allocating work – could increase audit risk | | |
| | **Maximum** | 6 |
| Professional marks – generally 1 mark each for heading, introduction, structure and clarity of explanations | | 4 |
| **Total** | | 50 |

**9 VANCOUVER GROUP**  *Walk in the footsteps of a top tutor*

*Top tutor tips*

*Part (a) asks why analytical procedures are performed as part of risk assessment procedures. Some students may struggle with this so don't waste time thinking for too long on this requirement. There are plenty of other marks to be earned on other parts.*

*Part (b) asks for audit risks and analytical procedures. Students should be aware of the need to perform analytical procedures in the exam to help identify audit risks as this has been examined several times before. Calculators are an essential item for this exam and easy marks can be achieved for calculations. Audit risks should explain the risks of material misstatement or a detection risk. When explaining a risk of material misstatement, try and give a brief overview of the accounting requirements from the relevant standard and explain why the client may not be complying with the standard. You must demonstrate knowledge of the requirements of the standard. Comments such as 'there is a risk the requirements of the accounting standard are not being followed' are too vague therefore will not earn marks.*

*Part (c) asks for procedures in respect of goodwill and the modernisation of the warehouse. Procedures are very regularly examined as a follow on from audit risks. Make sure the procedures are adequately described so that the person performing the procedure will know what to do.*

*Part (d) asks for discussion of two ethical issues. Ethical issues can appear more than once on the same exam and students should not be surprised if this happens. In order to score well, explain the issues, consider the significance of the issues and suggest actions the audit firm should take to address the issues.*

**Briefing notes**

To:         Albert Franks, audit engagement partner

From:     Audit manager

Subject:  Vancouver Group – audit planning

**Introduction**

These briefing notes evaluate the audit risks to be considered when planning the audit of the Group. Analytical procedures have been used to identify several audit risks. Audit procedures in relation to goodwill and modernisation costs have also been included. The briefing notes explain why analytical procedures are required as part of risk assessment. Finally, the briefing notes discuss the ethical implications of suggestions made by the Group audit committee.

**(a)     Analytical procedures and risk assessment**

According to ISA 520/ISA (UK) 520 *Analytical Procedures*, analytical procedures are the evaluation of financial information through analysis of plausible relationships between both financial and non-financial data. Analytical procedures can involve comparisons of financial data including trend analysis and the calculation and comparison of ratios. Analytical procedures include comparisons of the Group's financial information with, for example:

- Comparable information for prior periods

- Anticipated results of the Group, such as budgets or forecasts

- Expectations of the auditor, or

- Comparable information from competitors.

Analytical procedures performed at the planning stage help the auditor to identify and respond appropriately to risk, and to assist the auditor in obtaining an understanding of the audited companies within the Group.

ISA 315/ISA (UK) 315 *Identifying and Assessing the Risks of Material Misstatement through Understanding the Entity and its Environment* requires the auditor to perform analytical procedures as part of risk assessment procedures at the planning stage of the audit to provide a basis for the identification and assessment of risks of material misstatement at the financial statement and assertion levels.

An example of how analytical procedures assist the auditor is that performing analytical procedures may alert the auditor to a transaction or event of which they were previously unaware, therefore prompting the auditor to investigate the matter, obtain understanding of the matter and plan appropriate audit procedures to obtain sufficient appropriate audit evidence. Therefore analytical procedures are an essential part of developing the audit strategy and audit plan.

Analytical procedures may also help the auditor to identify the existence of unusual transactions or events, such as significant one-off events. Unusual amounts, ratios, and trends might also indicate matters which indicate risk. Unusual or unexpected relationships which are identified by these procedures may assist the auditor in identifying risks of material misstatement, especially risks of material misstatement due to fraud.

Without performing analytical procedures, the auditor would be unable to identify risks of material misstatement and respond accordingly. This would increase detection risk, making it more likely that an inappropriate audit opinion could be issued.

(b)     **Audit risk evaluation including analytical procedures**

**Selected analytical procedures and associated audit risk evaluation**

|  | *20X6* | *20X5* |
|---|---|---|
| Operating margin | 27/375 × 100 = 7.2% | 38/315 × 100 = 12.1% |
| Return on capital employed | 27/66 + 181 = 10.9% | 38/67 + 153 = 17.3% |
| Interest cover | 27/4 = 6.8 | 38/3 = 12.7 |
| Effective tax rate | 10/33 × 100 = 30.3% | 15/35 × 100 = 42.9% |
| Receivables collection period | 62/375 × 365 = 60 days | 45/315 × 365 = 52 days |
| Current ratio | 97/120 = 0.8 | 83/95 = 0.9 |

**Operating costs**

Analytical procedures reveals that the Group's revenue has increased by 19%, but that operating expenses have disproportionately increased by 25.6%, resulting in the fall in operating margin from 12.1% in 20X5 to 7.2% in 20X6.

This is a significant change, and while the higher costs incurred could be due to valid business reasons, the trend could indicate operating costs are overstated or sales are understated.

There is a risk that some of the costs involved in modernising the Group's warehousing facilities have been incorrectly treated as revenue expenditure when this should have been capitalised.

The trend in operating margin is consistent with the change in return on capital employed which has also fallen. The treatment of the costs involved in the modernisation of the Group's warehouse facilities will need detailed investigation to ensure that costs have been classified appropriately.

**Revenue**

The increase in revenue of 19% seems surprising given the finance director's comment that operations have not changed significantly during the year. This is a significant increase and there is therefore a risk that revenue could be overstated.

Detailed testing of the Group's revenue recognition policies will be required to verify that revenue is appropriately stated and recorded in the correct period.

**Finance costs**

The Group's interest cover has declined sharply, and finance costs have increased by 33%. This could indicate that finance costs are overstated, however, given that the Group has taken out additional debenture finance during the year, and also now has an overdraft, an increase in finance costs is to be expected and is more likely to simply reflect the significant drop which the Group has experienced in its operating profit levels.

The debenture may contain a covenant in relation to interest cover, and if so, there is a risk that the covenant may have been breached. While this is a business risk rather than an audit risk, the matter may require disclosure in the financial statements, leading to a risk of material misstatement if necessary disclosures are not made.

**Tax expense**

The comparison of effective tax rates shows that the effective tax rate is much lower in 20X6. This could be due to the utilisation of Toronto Co's tax losses which seems to have taken place due to the reduction in the Group's deferred tax asset this year. However, this is a complex issue and there is a risk that the tax expense is understated in comparison with the previous year.

Given the ongoing tax investigation regarding potential underpayment of tax, this is a significant audit risk. Depending on the possible outcome of the tax investigation, there may be a need to provide for additional tax liabilities and any penalties which may be imposed by the tax authorities.

Details of the investigation and its findings so far will need to be considered and the probability of the tax authorities finding against the Group should be considered as part of our detailed audit testing to verify that liabilities are complete or that disclosures for contingent liabilities are complete.

**Receivables**

The receivables collection days figure has increased from 52 days in 20X5 to 60 days in 20X6. This could be due to poor credit control.

If this is a significant risk to the Group the issues involved may need to be disclosed according to IFRS 7 *Financial Instruments: Disclosure*, hence there is a risk of inadequate disclosure.

The increase in receivables collection period may also indicate an overstatement of receivables balances.

**Provisions**

The provision of $6 million represents 1.6% of total assets and is material. The provisions balance has halved in value from $12 million in 20X5 to $6 million in 20X6. This could indicate that the provisions balance is understated and operating profit overstated, if there is not a valid reason for the reduction in value of the liability.

Audit procedures will need to be performed to ascertain the reason for the provision and to establish whether the criteria of IAS 37 are present to justify the need for the provision. For example, if there is no obligation at the year-end that is probable to lead to payment in the future, the provision should not continue to be recognised.

**Modernisation of warehousing facilities**

Overall, property, plant and equipment has increased by $43 million or 23% which is a significant movement, representing 11.7% of total assets. A total amount of $25 million has been spent on modernising the warehousing facilities which is material, representing 6.8% of total assets.

The modernisation programme explains part of the increase in property, plant and equipment but given that depreciation would have been charged, the reasons for the large increase must be carefully considered. As part of our audit work we will need to ensure that we understand how all of this movement has occurred as there are several risks of material misstatement associated with the expenditure.

**Treatment of expenditure**

There is a risk that the amounts capitalised into non-current assets are not correct in that capital and revenue expenditure may not have been correctly identified and accounted for separately.

According to IAS 16 *Property, Plant and Equipment*, modernisation costs which give rise to enhanced future economic benefit should be capitalised where the costs are directly attributable, whereas costs which do not create future economic benefit should be expensed.

It would seem that costs such as replacing electrical systems should be capitalised, but other incidental costs which may have been incurred such as repairing items within the warehouses should be expensed.

### Depreciation

In addition, there is a risk that the various components of each warehouse have not been treated as separate components and depreciated over a specific useful life. IAS 16 requires that each part of an item of property, plant and equipment with a cost which is significant in relation to the total cost of the item must be depreciated separately.

Items such as computer systems are likely to be significant components of the warehouses and as such should be accounted for as discrete assets in their own right.

Failure to correctly determine the significant components of the capital expenditure could lead to misstatement of the assets' carrying values and depreciation expenses.

### Borrowing costs

There is also an issue with the finance costs in respect of the $5 million debenture taken out to finance the modernisation programme. If the criteria of IAS 23 *Borrowing Costs* are met, in particular if the modernisation of the warehouses meets the definition of a qualifying asset, then borrowing costs should be capitalised during the period of modernisation.

A qualifying asset is an asset which takes a substantial period of time to get ready for its intended use or sale, so depending on the length of time that the modernisation programme has taken, it may meet the definition so borrowing costs would need to be capitalised.

There is therefore a risk that borrowing costs have not been capitalised if the qualifying asset definition has been met, and equally a risk that borrowing costs may have been capitalised incorrectly if the definition has not been met. The borrowing costs, however, may not be material in isolation.

If any accounting errors have occurred in the amounts capitalised into property, plant and equipment, then non-current assets may be over or understated, as would be the depreciation charge calculated on the carrying value of those assets.

### Disposal of shares in Calgary Co

A comparison of the statement of profit or loss for both years shows that the profit made on the disposal of shares in Calgary Co has been separately disclosed as part of profit in the year ending 31 July 20X6. The profit recognised is material at 30.3% of profit before tax. Several errors seem to have been made in accounting for the disposal and in respect of its disclosure.

**Profit on disposal**

It is not correct that this profit on disposal is recognised in the statement of profit or loss. According to IFRS 10 *Consolidated Financial Statements*, changes in a parent's ownership interest in a subsidiary which does not result in the parent losing control of the subsidiary are treated as equity transactions. Any difference between the amount by which the non-controlling interests are adjusted and the fair value of the consideration paid or received is recognised directly in equity and attributed to the owners of the parent.

This appears to have been incorrectly accounted for as there should not be a profit on disposal within the statement of profit or loss. Therefore profit before tax is overstated by $10 million. The tax charge may be overstated if it has been calculated based on profit including the gain made on the share disposal.

**Non-controlling interest**

While the non-controlling interest has been recognised in equity, the Group's profit for the year has not been attributed and disclosed between the Group and the non-controlling interest.

There is also a risk that the disclosure requirements of IFRS 12 *Disclosure of Interests in Other Entities* are not followed, in particular in relation to the change in group structure which has taken place during the year, as IFRS 12 specifically requires disclosure relating to the consequences of changes in a group's ownership interest in a subsidiary which does not result in a loss of control.

**Goodwill**

IAS 38 *Intangible Assets* requires that goodwill is tested annually for impairment regardless of whether indicators of potential impairment exist.

The goodwill of $30 million recorded in the statement of financial position is unchanged from the prior year, indicating that no impairment has been recorded in the current financial year. It could be that management has performed an impairment review and concluded that no impairment is necessary.

There is a risk that management has not conducted a thorough review or not carried out a review and goodwill may be overstated. This will require investigation as part of our detailed audit procedures.

**Management bias**

The sale of shares to an institutional investor creates an inherent risk of management bias as management may feel under pressure to return favourable results.

This could explain the positive trends in revenue shown by the analytical review and could also explain the incorrect presentation of the profit on disposal which has incorrectly inflated profit by $10m.

**Deferred tax asset**

There is a risk that the deferred tax asset is overstated. According to IAS 12 *Income Taxes*, a deferred tax asset is recognised for an unused tax loss carry-forward or unused tax credit if, and only if, it is considered probable that there will be sufficient future taxable profit against which the loss or credit carry-forward can be utilised.

While it appears that some of the deferred tax asset has been utilised this year, there remains a risk that if it is no longer recoverable, then the amount would need to be written off. Audit work should be planned to confirm the recoverability of the amount recognised.

**Audit committee – lack of financial reporting expert**

Guidance on the composition of audit committees suggests that a financial reporting expert should be included in the committee. This is to ensure that the functions of the audit committee in relation to financial reporting are carried out effectively, for example, in ensuring that accounting policies are appropriate. The lack of an expert increases the risk that incorrect accounting treatments will occur, and is effectively a control risk.

**(c)   Audit procedures**

**(i)   Goodwill**

- Obtain management's impairment review, if performed, and evaluate the reasonableness of the assumptions used to determine that the goodwill figure should remain unchanged.

- If no impairment review has been performed, discuss reasons for this with management and request that a review is performed.

- Review board minutes for any issues which could indicate impairment of goodwill e.g. trading problems or bad publicity relating to Toronto Co and Calgary Co.

- Review forecasts of Toronto Co and Calgary Co and evaluate the reasonableness of the forecasts by reference to past forecasts and actual results to identify possible impairment of goodwill.

- Obtain written representation from management regarding goodwill confirming they believe the balance of $30m is not impaired.

**(ii)   Modernisation of warehouse**

- Obtain a breakdown of all modernisation costs incurred, recalculate the schedule and trace a sample of costs to invoices to ensure accuracy.

- Review the breakdown of costs for any which should be expensed, e.g. design costs.

- Obtain a breakdown of assets disposed as part of the modernisation and review the non-current asset register to ensure the disposals have been removed.

- Physically inspect the factory to verify existence of the modernisation upgrade.

- Review the repairs and maintenance account for modernisation costs which have been expensed but should be capitalised.

- Compare the depreciation rates of the new assets with the actual life of assets disposed to ensure the rates are appropriate.

- Recalculate the depreciation charge for the modernised factory to ensure arithmetical accuracy.

**(d)   Ethical matters to be considered by our firm**

**Tax investigation**

The IESBA's *International Code of Ethics for Professional Accountants* (the Code) and the FRC Ethical Standard both state that an advocacy or self-review threat may be created when the firm represents an audit client in the resolution of a tax dispute, for example, before a tribunal or court.

The advocacy threat arises because the audit firm will take a position to promote the client's interests at the tribunal, leading to a threat to objectivity.

The self-review threat arises where the matter which is the subject of the investigation and tribunal will have an impact on the financial statements on which the audit firm will express an opinion.

**Tutorial note**

**UK syllabus:** *A management threat to objectivity may also arise where the audit firm becomes so closely identified with management's arguments regarding the tax issue that the auditor is inhibited from forming an impartial view of the treatment of the issue in the financial statements.*

The existence and significance of any threat will depend on a number of factors including:

- Whether the firm has provided the advice which is the subject of the tax dispute

- The extent to which the outcome of the dispute will have a material effect on the financial statements on which the firm will express an opinion.

In this case the threat is lessened by the fact that it was another firm of accountants, Victoria & Co, which provided the tax planning advice to the Group, but the materiality of the matter will need to be carefully considered by Montreal & Co before they agree to take on the engagement to provide the necessary support to the Group.

The significance of any threat created shall be evaluated and safeguards applied when necessary to eliminate the threat or reduce it to an acceptable level. Examples of such safeguards include:

- Using professionals who are not members of the audit team to perform the service.

- Having a tax professional provide advice to the audit team on the Group's tax position, and review the financial statement treatment.

The *Code* states that where the taxation services involve acting as an advocate for an audit client before a public tribunal or court in the resolution of a tax matter and the amounts involved are material to the financial statements on which the firm will express an opinion, the advocacy threat created would be so significant that no safeguards could eliminate or reduce the threat to an acceptable level. Therefore, the firm shall not perform this type of service for an audit client.

What constitutes a 'public tribunal or court' shall be determined according to how tax proceedings are heard in the particular jurisdiction.

**Appointment as a non-executive director and serve on audit committee**

This would seem inappropriate as one of the functions of the audit committee is to oversee the external audit function, and it would not be possible for an audit partner of the firm to remain objective when evaluating matters such as determining the audit fee.

The Code and FRC Ethical Standard specifically state that if a partner or employee of the firm serves as a director or officer of an audit client, the self-review and self-interest threats created would be so significant that no safeguards could reduce the threats to an acceptable level. Accordingly, no partner or employee shall serve as a director or officer of an audit client.

Hence, Montreal & Co must explain to the Vancouver Group that unfortunately it will not be possible for an audit partner to be appointed to serve as a non-executive director of the Group.

The provision of the tax investigation service should also be discussed, and the audit committee's approval for Montreal & Co to provide the service should be obtained, depending on the materiality of the matter to the financial statements and the deployment of safeguards to reduce threats to an acceptable level.

### Conclusion

These briefing notes have provided an assessment of the audit risks to be considered in planning the audit of the Vancouver Group, including analytical procedures and an explanation of the need for these procedures to be performed. The audit plan should include the procedures described above as well as further procedures in respect of areas of risk identified. There are several significant threats to our firm's objectivity which need to be discussed with the client prior to the audit fieldwork commencing.

---

**Examiner's comments**

The question followed the pattern of previous examinations and was set at the planning stage of the audit and candidates were presented with three requirements, which covered the use of analytical procedures at planning, identifying audit risks and ethics.

Candidates were asked to explain why analytical procedures are a fundamental part of audit planning and this requirement was generally well-answered by the majority of candidates. Good answers were tailored to the specifics of the situation and provided relevant examples.

Candidates were then required to identify audit risks, including through the use of analytical procedures. The best answers demonstrated that a methodical approach had been applied to the information in the scenario, and strong candidates had clearly worked through the information logically, calculating the key ratios and trends from the information provided, identifying the risk factors from the calculations and the remaining information, assessing materiality before going on to explain the risk fully and specifically in terms of how the risk could impact the financial statements. Candidates are reminded that when discussing risk relating to a specific accounting treatment, well explained answers will include an evaluation of the potential impact of the risk factor on the financial statements. A disappointing number of candidates failed to calculate any ratios or trends from the information supplied and thus provided weak answers and were unable to identify an appropriate number of audit risks for the marks available. Conversely some candidates calculated every trend or ratio possible, which was excessive and demonstrated poor time management; for example there was insufficient information in the question to calculate inventory or trade payable days so these ratios did not add to their answer.

Audit risk continues to be an area that candidates find difficult and particularly it continues to be noted that many candidates fail to engage with the information provided in enough depth, specifically when provided with extracts from financial statements. Candidates are again reminded that in order to provide a full answer in relation to audit risk they should utilise and analyse all the information that is provided.

---

Candidates were required to discuss the ethical issues relevant to the audit firm and to recommend any necessary actions. Performance in this area was mixed and it was clear that many candidates did not know the requirements of the Code of Ethics. For example a sizeable number of candidates advised that the audit engagement partner could simultaneously become a non-executive director on the audit committee of the entity under audit and failed to identify that the Code expressly prohibits this due to the extent of the self-review and self-interest threats which would be created. This demonstrates a lack of knowledge of the ethical requirements and a lack of professional judgment. Candidates are reminded that they must revise and be comfortable with the content of the code of ethics. Most candidates were however, able to highlight that there was a potential advocacy and self-review risk from representing the client in a tax enquiry but did not condition this on either grounds of materiality or that the firm had not been previously involved in the client's tax affairs.

There were four professional marks available and most candidates were able to earn the presentation marks by providing a clear introduction and conclusion and using headings to create an appropriate structure for their answer. Many candidates did not articulate their points in a clear or logical order and therefore many missed out on the logical flow and clarity marks.

| Marking scheme | | |
|---|---|---|
| | | *Marks* |
| **(a)** | **Analytical procedures and risk assessment**<br>Generally up to 1½ marks for each point explained:<br>– Definition/examples of analytical procedure<br>– Helps to identify risk of material misstatement<br>– Helps to develop business understanding<br>– Helps in developing the audit strategy and audit plan | |
| | Maximum | 4 |
| **(b)** | **Audit risk evaluation**<br>Up to 3 marks for each risk evaluated<br>1 mark for each ratio (including comparative) calculated, and ½ mark for relevant trends calculated, up to a maximum of 5 marks.<br>Allow 1 mark for each correct calculation and comment on materiality<br>**Risks in relation to ratio analysis**<br>– Overstatement of operating expenses<br>– Overstatement of revenue due to finance director's comments<br>– Interest cover and risk relating to disclosure<br>– Change in effective tax rates and risk tax expense incorrect<br>– Ongoing investigation and risk of fines and penalties which need to be provided for<br>– Liquidity issues and risk relating to disclosure<br>– Increase in receivables collection period and overstatement of trade receivables<br>– Onerous contract provision has halved in value, risk of understatement of liability<br>**Other audit risks**<br>– Whether capital and revenue expenditure appropriately accounted for in respect of the modernisation programme<br>– Whether assets have been accounted for using the concept of significant components<br>– Treatment of borrowing costs and whether eligible for capitalisation<br>– The gain on disposal of shares in Calgary Co is incorrectly recognised in profit for the year<br>– Non-controlling interest has not been disclosed in respect of profit for the year | |

- Risk of inadequate disclosure regarding the rationale for, and consequences of, the share disposal
- Risk of overstatement of goodwill as no evidence of impairment review
- Management bias due to sale of shares to institutional investor
- Deferred tax – risk of overstatement if the amount is not a recoverable asset
- Lack of financial reporting expert on the Group audit committee increases the risk of incorrect accounting treatments

|  |  |
|---|---|
| Maximum | 24 |

**(c)** **Audit procedures**
Generally 1 mark for each well explained audit procedure:
**(i)** **Valuation of goodwill**
- Review management's impairment review
- Discuss impairment of goodwill with management
- Review board minutes
- Review forecasts to identify possible impairment
- Obtain written representation from management

**(ii)** **Modernisation of warehouse**
- Obtain breakdown and trace costs to invoices
- Review breakdown for costs which should be expensed
- Review NCA register to ensure disposals removed
- Physically inspect the modernised factory
- Review repairs and maintenance account
- Review depreciation rates for appropriateness
- Recalculate depreciation

|  |  |
|---|---|
| Maximum | 10 |

**(d)** **Ethical issues**
Generally up to 1 mark for each relevant matter discussed:
- Advocacy threat (1 mark where risk is explained)
- Self-review threat (1 mark where risk is explained)
- Extent of threat lessened because another firm provided the tax planning
- Consider the materiality of the matter to the FS
- If matter is immaterial, then the service can be provided as long as safeguards in place (1 mark for each safeguard suggested)
- Where matter is material, the service should not be provided
- Appointment of audit partner to audit committee creates objectivity threat
- Code prohibits appointment of audit firm member as director of audit client
- Matters to be discussed with client's audit committee and the audit firm's ethical partner

|  |  |
|---|---|
| Maximum | 8 |

**Professional marks**
Generally 1 mark for heading, 1 mark for introduction, 1 mark for use of headings within the briefing notes, 1 mark for clarity of comments made

|  |  |
|---|---|
| Maximum | 4 |

| Total |  | 50 |
|---|---|---|

10  DALI    *Walk in the footsteps of a top tutor*

### Top tutor tips

*Part (a) asks for audit risks and additional information needed to help evaluate audit risk. Audit risk comprises the risk that the financial statements contain material misstatement and detection risk. Risk of material misstatement is usually due to non-compliance with an accounting standard. Think about the requirements of the relevant accounting standards and what the client might be doing incorrectly. Detection risks include auditing a client for the first time or where there is a tight reporting deadline.*

*Additional information is essentially the evidence you would gather in respect of the risks. For example, with the government grant you would want a copy of the grant terms and conditions to assess whether the grant conditions had been met. Where there is a subsequent requirement for audit procedures as in part (b), these are areas of audit risk that should be included in your answer to part (a).*

*Part (b) asks for procedures in respect of work in progress and the government grant. Procedures should be specific in terms of what the auditor needs to do to obtain the evidence they need.*

*Part (c) asks for the ethical issues arising if the audit firm performs a review of the internal control systems. It is important here to recognise that Dali is a listed company and therefore greater restrictions apply.*

*Part (d) asks for the impact outsourcing of payroll will have on the audit. You need to suggest how the auditor will obtain sufficient appropriate evidence from the service provider performing the payroll service.*

**Briefing notes**

To:        Sam Hockney, audit engagement partner

From:      Audit manager

Subject:   Audit planning – Dali Co

**Introduction**

These briefing notes are prepared to assist in the audit planning meeting for Dali Co, our manufacturing client supplying machinery and equipment to the quarrying industry. The notes contain an evaluation of audit risk along with recommendations of the additional information which is relevant to audit risk evaluation. The notes also explain the principal audit procedures to be performed in respect of the valuation of work in progress, and the government grant received during the year. The notes discuss the ethical and professional issues which need to be addressed as a result of the comments made by the audit committee. Finally, the impact on next year's audit due to the outsourcing of payroll is discussed.

**(a)  (i)  Audit risk evaluation**

**Stock exchange listing and pressure on results**

The listing obtained during the year can create inherent risk at the financial statement level because management may feel under pressure to achieve good results in this financial year.

The flotation raised equity capital, so there will be new shareholders who will want to see strong performance in the expectation of a dividend pay-out.

In addition, the introduction of the cash-settled share-based payment plan motivates management to produce financial statements which show a favourable performance and position which is likely to lead to an increase in the company's share price.

There is a risk that revenue and profits may be overstated. Revenue has increased by 2.2% and profit before tax by 6.5%, which may indicate overstatement.

**Disclosure for listed companies**

This is the first set of financial statements produced since Dali Co became listed.

There is a risk that the new finance director will not be familiar with the requirements specific to listed companies, for example, the company now falls under the scope of IAS 33 *Earnings per Share* and IFRS 8 *Operating Segments* for the first time. There is a risk of incomplete or inaccurate disclosures in respect of these standards and also in respect of any listing rules in the jurisdiction in which the company is listed.

**Foreign exchange transactions**

Dali Co purchases many components from foreign suppliers and is therefore likely to be transacting and making payments in foreign currencies.

According to IAS 21 *The Effects of Changes in Foreign Exchange Rates*, transactions should be initially recorded using the spot rate, and monetary items such as trade payables should be retranslated at the year-end using the closing rate. Exchange gains and losses should be recognised within profit for the year.

The risk is that the incorrect exchange rate is used for the translation and retranslation, or that the retranslation does not happen at the year-end, in which case trade payables and profit could be over or understated, depending on the movement in the exchange rate. The company may have entered into hedging arrangements as a way to reduce exposure to foreign exchange fluctuations.

There is a risk that hedging arrangements are not identified and accounted for as such in line with IFRS 9 *Financial Instruments* which could mean incomplete recognition of derivative financial assets or liabilities and the inappropriate treatment of associated gains or losses.

**Payment in advance and revenue recognition under contract with customers**

For items where significant design work is needed, Dali Co receives a payment in advance. This gives rise to risk in terms of when that part of the revenue generated from a sale of goods is recognised.

According to IFRS 15 *Revenue from Contracts with Customers*, revenue should only be recognised as or when the entity has fulfilled its performance obligations within the contract. The performance obligations will be satisfied either over time or at a point in time.

*Bespoke machinery*

If the machines are so bespoke that they cannot be sold to an alternative customer, the revenue should be recognised over time. This would mean that some or all of the advance payment could be recognised before the machine is completed and the asset is transferred to the customer.

There is a risk that an inappropriate amount of revenue has been recognised at the reporting date.

There is additional audit risk created if a customer were to cancel a contract part way through its completion, the bespoke work in progress may be worthless and would need to be written off according to IAS 2 *Inventories*. There is therefore a risk of overstated work in progress.

*Generic machinery*

For generic machines which are likely to be able to be sold to an alternative customer for minimal additional cost, revenue should be recognised at a point in time. In this case the advance payment is more than likely in respect of the performance obligation of providing the customer with the manufactured product. Therefore, at the point when the payment is received, it should be treated as a contract liability as the conditions for recognition of revenue are unlikely to have been met at this point in time. The revenue should be deferred and recognised when the customer obtains control of the asset.

There is a risk that revenue is recognised too early, especially given the risk of management bias and the incentive to overstate revenue and profit as discussed above.

**New directors**

During the year several new non-executive directors were appointed, as well as a new finance director.

While this may serve to strengthen the corporate governance structure including the control environment, equally the introduction of new personnel could mean inexperience and a control risk, particularly if the finance director is lacking in experience.

Some of the suggestions and accounting treatments made by the finance director indicate that their knowledge of the applicable financial reporting framework is weak, signalling that errors may occur in the preparation of the financial statements.

**Cash-settled share-based payment scheme**

This falls under the scope of IFRS 2 *Share-based Payment* which states that the liability in respect of the plan should be measured at fair value at the year-end.

The increase in the share price from $2.90 at flotation to $3.50 (projected) at the year-end indicates that a liability should be recognised at 31 December 20X5 based on the fair value of the liability which has accrued up to that date, with the expense recognised in the statement of profit or loss.

This accounting treatment has not been followed leading to understated liabilities and overstated profit, and the disclosure in respect of the plan may not be sufficient to meet the requirements of IFRS 2 which requires extensive disclosures including the effect of share-based payment transactions on the entity's profit or loss for the period and on its financial position.

### Revaluation of property

The decision to revalue the company's manufacturing sites creates several risks. First, revaluation involves establishing a current market price or fair value for each property included in the revaluation, which can be a subjective exercise, leading to inherent risk that the valuations may not be appropriate.

A risk also arises in that IAS 16 *Property, Plant and Equipment* requires all assets in the same class to be revalued, so if any properties which are manufacturing sites have not been included in the revaluation exercise, the amounts recognised will not be correct.

There is also a risk that depreciation has not been recalculated on the new, higher value of the properties, leading to overstatement of non-current assets and understatement of operating expenses.

IAS 16 also requires a significant level of disclosure in relation to a policy of revaluation, so there is a risk that the necessary disclosures are incomplete. The revaluation gain recognised in equity represents 3.9% of total assets and is therefore material to the financial statements.

### Deferred tax recognition

IAS 12 *Income Taxes* requires deferred tax to be recognised in respect of taxable temporary differences which arise between the carrying amount and tax base of assets and liabilities, including the differences which arise on the revaluation of non-current assets, regardless of whether the assets are likely to be disposed of in the foreseeable future.

The finance director's suggestion that deferred tax should not be provided for is therefore incorrect, and at present liabilities are understated, representing an error in the statement of financial position. There is no profit impact, however, as the deferred tax would be recognised in equity.

Depending on the rate of tax which would be used to determine the necessary provision, it may not be material to the financial statements.

### Government grant recognition

The government grant represents 11.1% of total assets and is material to the financial statements.

A risk arises in relation to the recognition of the grant. IAS 20 *Accounting for Government Grants and Disclosure of Government Assistance* requires that a grant is recognised as income over the period necessary to match the grant received with the related costs for which they are intended to compensate.

Therefore, the $2 million relating to costs incurred this year should be recognised as income, but the remainder should be released to profit on a systematic basis; in this case it would seem appropriate to release on a straight line basis until July 20Y0.

The risk is that the grant has been recognised on an inappropriate basis leading to over or understated profit for the year. The part of the grant not recognised in profit should be recognised in the statement of financial position.

IAS 20 allows classification as deferred income, or alternatively the amount can be netted against the assets to which the grant relates. There is therefore also a risk that the amount is recognised elsewhere in the statement of financial position, leading to incorrect presentation and disclosure.

If the terms of the grant have been breached, the grant or an element of it may need to be repaid. There is therefore a risk that if there is any breach, the associated provision for repayment is not recognised, understating liabilities.

### Inventory valuation

Work in progress is material at 13.3% of total assets and has increased by 26.3% in the current year.

The valuation of work in progress is likely to be complex as many different jobs for different customers are ongoing at the year-end, and each will have a different stage of completion and cost base at the year-end.

There are also issues more generally with the valuation of inventory, due to the customer returns of items which have recently occurred showing that there are problems with the quality of the goods supplied.

For items which have been returned, the net realisable value is likely to be less than the cost of the item indicating that a write-off may be necessary to reduce the value of the inventory according to IAS 2.

The increase in the inventory holding period, shows that inventory has become more slow-moving during the year also indicating that inventory may be overstated.

### Provision in respect of returned goods

A provision should be recognised where a reliable estimate can be made in relation to a probable outflow of economic resources and an obligating event has taken place.

The fact that Dali Co replaces faulty products free of charge indicates that a provision should be recognised based on the best estimate of the future economic outflow.

The risk is that no provision or an insufficient provision in relation to the warranty has been recognised, leading to understated liabilities and operating expenses.

### Working capital

The preliminary analytical review reveals that Dali Co is struggling to manage its working capital. The liquidity ratios provided show that the operating cycle has increased from 165 days in 20X4 to 205 days in 20X5.

The company may be finding it difficult to collect cash from customers, as the receivables period has increased by 20 days, and in turn the payment period to suppliers has increased by five days.

If there is doubt over the collectability of receivables, then certain balances may need to be written off, and there is a risk of overstatement of receivables and understatement of operating expenses if bad debts are not recognised.

### Control risk

The new non-executive directors have expressed concern over the effectiveness of internal controls and the increased risk of fraud. Expenses may be processed which do not relate to the company, fictitious suppliers or employees could be set up on the systems in the absence of any related controls. The financial statements may be materially misstated due to either fraud or error which has not been prevented or detected by the internal control system.

Payroll costs in particular may be materially misstated as the management team are considering outsourcing the payroll function as a result of the control deficiencies.

**Tutorial note**

*Credit will be awarded for other relevant audit risks.*

(ii) **Recommended additional information**

- Details of the stock exchange listing during the year including the terms of the flotation, number of equity shares issued and amount of equity capital raised.

- Any information available in relation to the flotation, for example, investor prospectus, pre- and post-flotation press releases, communications with the stock exchange registrar.

- Information on the specific listing rules relevant to the stock exchange, for example, the corporate governance code and disclosures necessary in company annual reports and financial statements.

- Details on the planned foreign stock exchange listing in 20X6 including the jurisdiction, the strategic rationale for seeking the listing and proposed timescales.

- Information on the background and experience of the new non-executive directors and the new finance director, for example, their professional qualifications and previous employment or directorships held.

- A full set of forecast financial statements including a statement of cash flows to assess the working capital issues faced by the company.

- Details on the valuation of properties including the date of the revaluation and information on the valuer such as their professional qualification and relationship with the company and a copy of the valuation report.

- Documentation on the cash-settled share-based payment scheme to gauge the number of members of the scheme and its potential materiality to the financial statements.

**Tutorial note**

*Credit will be awarded for other relevant information which would be available at this stage of the audit to help in the evaluation of audit risk.*

(b) (i) **Audit procedures in respect of the valuation of work in progress**

- Obtain a schedule itemising the jobs included in work in progress at the year-end, cast it and agree the total to the general ledger and draft financial statements.

- Agree a sample of items from the schedule to the inventory count records.

- For a sample of jobs included on the schedule:
    - Agree costs to supporting documentation such as supplier's invoice and payroll records.
    - For any overheads absorbed into the work in progress valuation, review the basis of the absorption and assess its reasonableness.
    - Assess how the degree of completion of the job has been determined at the year-end and agree the stage of completion of the job to records taken at the inventory count.
    - Agree the details of the job specification to customer order.
    - Confirm that net realisable value is greater than cost by agreeing the contract price and cash received from the customer post year end.
- To assess the completeness of work in progress, select a sample of customer orders and trace through to the list of jobs included in work in progress.

(ii) **Audit procedures in respect of the recognition and measurement of the government grant**

- Obtain the documentation relating to the grant to confirm the amount, the date the cash was received, and the terms on which the grant was awarded.
- Review the documentation for any conditions attached to the grant, for example, is there a requirement that a certain number of people are employed at the manufacturing plant?
- Discuss with management the method of recognition of the amount received, in particular how much of the grant has been recognised in profit and the treatment of the amount deferred in the statement of financial position.
- For the part of the grant relating to wages and salaries, confirm that the grant criteria have been complied with by examining payroll records and timesheets to verify that $2 million has been spent on wages in the deprived area.
- For the part of the grant relating to continued operation of the manufacturing site, determine the basis on which this is being released into profit and recalculate to confirm accuracy of management's calculations.
- Review forecasts and budgets in relation to the manufacturing site to assess the likelihood of its continued operations until 20Y0.
- Using the draft financial statements, confirm the accounting treatment outlined by discussion with management has been applied and recalculate the amounts recognised.
- Confirm the cash received to bank statement and cash book.

(c)      **Review of internal controls**

Reviewing the internal controls of an audit client which are relevant to the financial reporting system would create a self-review threat as the auditor would consequently assess the effectiveness of the control system during the external audit.

The design, implementation and maintenance of internal controls are also management responsibilities. If the auditor were to assist in this process, it may be considered that they were assuming these management responsibilities. This creates potential self-review, self-interest and familiarity threat. The latter arises because the audit firm could be considered to be aligning their views and interests to those of management.

Threats caused by adopting management responsibilities are so significant that there are no safeguards which could reduce the threats to an acceptable level.

The only effective measures which could be adopted would be those which ensured the audit firm did not adopt a management responsibility, such as ensuring that the client has assigned competent personnel to be responsible at all times for reviewing internal control review reports and for determining which of the recommendations from the report are to be implemented.

Furthermore, if the client is listed and also an audit client, then the audit firm should not provide internal audit services which relate to a significant part of the internal controls relevant to financial reporting. Given that this is the main expertise of the audit firm, it is likely that they will be required to perform some work in this area and this service would therefore not be appropriate.

If Dali Co would like the firm to perform a review of internal controls not related to the financial reporting system, Mondrian & Co would need to consider whether they have the professional competencies to complete the engagement to the necessary standard of quality.

---

*Tutorial note*

**UK syllabus:** *Internal audit services must not be provided to listed audit clients, therefore the request must be declined.*

---

**Concerns regarding deterioration in controls**

One of the responsibilities of the auditor is to evaluate the design and implementation of the client's controls relevant to the audit in order to assist with the identification of risks of material misstatement. This includes the specific requirement to consider the risk of material misstatement due to fraud.

If deficiencies in internal controls are identified, the auditor has to assess the potential impact on the financial statements and design a suitable response in order to reduce audit risk to an acceptable level. The auditor is also responsible for communicating significant deficiencies in internal control to those charged with governance on a timely basis.

The audit committee has suggested that a number of internal control deficiencies have recently been identified which they were not previously aware of. This suggests that these were not issues identified or reported to those charged with governance by the auditor.

If these internal control deficiencies relate to systems relevant to the audit, it may suggest that the audit firm's consideration of the internal control system failed to detect these potential problems, which may indicate ineffective audit planning. If so, this increases the risk that the audit procedures designed were inappropriate and that there is a heightened risk that the audit team failed to detect material misstatements during the audit. In the worst case scenario this could mean that Mondrian & Co issued an inappropriate audit opinion.

The audit committee of Dali Co has not specified which controls appear to have deteriorated and whether these are related to the audit or not. There is also no indication of the potential scale of any fraud or inefficient commercial practice. It is possible that the risks resulting from the deficiencies are so small that they did not lead to a risk of material misstatement. In these circumstances, the audit team may have identified the deficiencies as not being significant and reported them to an appropriate level of operating management.

In order to assess this further, the manager should examine the audit file and review the documentation in relation to the evaluation of the internal controls of Dali Co and assess any subsequent communications to management and those charged with governance. The concerns raised by the audit committee should be noted as points to take forward into next year's audit, when they should be reviewed and evaluated as part of planning the audit.

Additionally, Mondrian & Co should contact the audit committee of Dali Co to seek further clarification on the nature and extent of the deficiencies identified and whether this has resulted in any actual or suspected acts of fraud.

**(d)** **Impact of outsourcing on the audit**

Outsourcing is when certain functions within a business are contracted out to third parties known as service organisations. It is common for companies to outsource one or more of it functions, with payroll, IT and human resources being examples of functions which are typically outsourced.

Outsourcing does have an impact on audit planning. ISA 402 *Audit Considerations Relating to an Entity Using a Service Organisation* requires the auditor to obtain an understanding of how the audited entity (also known as the user entity) uses the services of a service organisation in the user entity's operations, including the following matters:

- The nature of the services provided by the service organisation and the significance of those services to the audited entity, including the effect on internal control

- The nature and materiality of the transactions processed or accounts or financial reporting processes affected by the service organisation

- The degree of interaction between the activities of the service organisation and those of the audited entity

- The nature of the relationship between the audited entity and the service organisation, including the relevant contractual terms.

The reasons for the auditor being required to understand these matters is so that any risk of material misstatement created by the use of the service organisation can be identified and an appropriate response planned.

The auditor is also required under ISA 402 to evaluate the design and implementation of relevant controls at the audited entity which relate to the services provided by the service organisation, including those which are applied to the transactions processed by the service organisation. This is to obtain understanding of the control risk associated with the outsourced function, for example, whether the transactions and information provided by the service organisation is monitored and whether checks are performed prior to inclusion in the financial statements.

Information should be available from the audited entity to enable the understanding outlined above to be obtained, for example, through reports received from the service organisation, technical manuals and the contract between the audited entity and the service organisation.

The auditor may decide that further work is necessary in order to evaluate the risk of material misstatement associated with the outsourcing arrangement's impact on the financial statements. It is common for a report on the description and design of controls at a service organisation to be obtained.

A type 1 report focuses on the description and design of controls, whereas a type 2 report also covers the operating effectiveness of the controls. This type of report can provide some assurance over the controls which should have operated at the service organisation.

Alternatively, the auditor may decide to contact the service organisation to request specific information, to visit the service organisation and perform procedures, probably tests on controls, or to use another auditor to perform such procedures. All of these methods of evaluating the service organisation's controls require permission from the client and can be time consuming to perform.

The purpose of obtaining the understanding above is to help the auditor to determine the level of competence of the service organisation, and whether it is independent of the audited entity. This will then impact on the risk of material misstatement assessed for the outsourced function.

### Conclusion

These briefing notes indicate that there are many areas of potential audit risk to be considered when developing the audit strategy for Dali Co, and that additional information should be requested from the client to be obtained as soon as possible to facilitate a more in-depth evaluation of certain audit risks identified. The audit procedures designed in respect of work in progress and the government grant received will provide assurance on these significant issues.

In respect of the request to review the internal control systems, the firm should consider whether this is appropriate given the potential self-review threat. We should also consider whether our audit should have identified these control issues during our work and review the work performed over controls again to ensure there are no quality issues. The audit file should include a point forward in respect of the outsourcing of payroll to ensure the planning of next year's audit incorporates the need to obtain information from the service organisation.

**Examiner's comments**

Candidates were required to provide an analysis of audit risks for a manufacturer of bespoke and generic machines. Performance on this requirement was good with the majority of candidates correctly describing audit risks rather than business risks. This is an area that most candidates are well prepared on, however stronger answers were able to develop and apply the relevant accounting treatment. Those able to identify specific areas of the financial statements which would be affected and to correctly identify whether the risk was over or understatement tended to score the strongest marks. A significant minority of candidates thought that the client was new to the firm as opposed to simply having a change in manager and spent time addressing opening balances and new client procedures which were not relevant to the question. Candidates are again reminded to read the question carefully and consider the context of the scenario both in terms of client history and timeframe before answering the question.

Candidates were further required to provide additional information needed to effectively plan the audit and candidates showed a marked improvement over previous sittings where this requirement has been examined. This type of question requires candidates to identify information that would be available in advance of the audit that would assist in the planning of the audit. Such information would generally help in the identification or evaluation of risks rather than the information available at the year-end for performing audit procedures. This is particularly relevant as the question was set almost a month prior to the year-end so financial statements and year-end balances would not yet be available.

Candidates were further required to provide audit procedures for the valuation of work in progress (WIP) and a government grant. With respect to the former, candidates often cited the need for an expert to value WIP rather than focusing on the components of cost and NRV in the machines. Similarly, there were a number of candidates who requested written representations from management on WIP despite the figure not being an issue where the knowledge was confined to management or one of management's intentions. Candidates are once again reminded that a written representation is not a suitable substitute for sufficient appropriate evidence.

The audit procedures relevant to the grant were generally well described.

Candidates were also asked to advise the listed audit client asking for a review of their control systems due to concerns about weaknesses in controls. Few candidates recognised the potential implications on the accuracy of the previous auditor's report and that these potential weaknesses could undermine the opinion. Clearly further details were needed to establish if the deficiencies in control would have had any significant impact on those financial statements. Many candidates simply provided a discussion of the advantages to the client of having a review of the internal control system but failed to appreciate that undertaking such a review for a listed client would be prohibited by the Code, and this again demonstrated that many candidates did not have a good enough understanding of the requirement of the ethical guidelines. In such circumstances opting for a separate team is not an effective safeguard and the review should not be done.

Part (d) focused on outsourcing, and asked candidates to consider how the outsourcing would affect audit planning. There were some good attempts, with most answers identifying issues in relation to access to information, assessment of the internal controls at the service organisation, and the competence of the service organisation. Disappointingly, few answers mentioned type 1 and type 2 reports that are typically obtained in this situation, and many tried to focus on ethical matters such as independence, and therefore didn't specifically address the requirement.

There were four professional marks available, and most candidates secured most of these marks by providing an introduction and using headings to create an appropriate structure for their answer. However, presentation was not always good and candidates are reminded to pay attention to determining an appropriate layout for their answer.

| Marking scheme | | | Marks |
|---|---|---|---|
| (a) | (i) | **Evaluation of audit risks**<br>Up to 3 marks for each audit risk evaluated, and 1 mark for relevant calculations (e.g. materiality, trends):<br>– Stock exchange listing and pressure on results<br>– Disclosure for listed companies<br>– Foreign exchange transactions and potential derivatives (up to 3 marks)<br>– Payment in advance and revenue recognition<br>– Potential for cancelled contracts and implication for valuation of work in progress<br>– New directors<br>– Cash-settled share-based payment scheme<br>– Revaluation of property<br>– Deferred tax recognition<br>– Government grant recognition and potential for repayment if terms are breached<br>– Inventory valuation<br>– Provision in respect of returned goods<br>– Working capital<br>– Control risk | |
| | | **Maximum** | **20** |
| | (ii) | **Additional information**<br>1 mark for each piece of relevant information. The list below is indicative, and credit should be given for other relevant recommendations:<br>– Details of the stock exchange listing during the year<br>– Information on the specific listing rules relevant to the stock exchange<br>– Details on the planned foreign stock exchange listing<br>– Information on the background and experience of the new non-executive directors and the new finance director<br>– A full set of draft financial statements including a statement of cash flows<br>– Details on the valuation of properties such as date of valuation and name of the valuer<br>– Documentation on the cash-settled share-based payment scheme | |
| | | **Maximum** | **5** |
| (b) | (i) | **Audit procedures on the valuation of work in progress**<br>1 mark for each well explained audit procedure:<br>– Obtain a schedule itemising the jobs included in work in progress at the year-end, cast it and agree the total to the general ledger and draft financial statements<br>– Agree a sample of items from the schedule to the inventory count records<br>– For a sample of jobs included on the schedule:<br> • Agree costs to supporting documentation such as supplier's invoice and payroll records | |

- For any overheads absorbed into the work in progress valuation, review the basis of the absorption and assess its reasonableness
- Assess how the degree of completion of the job has been determined at the year-end and agree the stage of completion of the job to records taken at the inventory count
- Agree the details of the job specification to customer order
- Confirm that net realisable value is greater than cost by agreeing the contract price and cash received from the customer post year-end
  - To assess the completeness of work in progress, select a sample of customer orders and trace through to the list of jobs included in work in progress

(ii) **Audit procedures in respect of the government grant**

1 mark for each well explained audit procedure:
  - Obtain the documentation relating to the grant to confirm the amount, the date the cash was received, and the terms on which the grant was awarded
  - Review the documentation for any conditions attached to the grant, for example, is there a requirement that a certain number of people are employed at the manufacturing plant?
  - Discuss with management the method of recognition of the amount received, in particular how much of the grant has been recognised in profit and the treatment of the amount deferred in the statement of financial position
  - For the part of the grant relating to continued operation of the manufacturing plant, determine the basis on which this is being released into profit, assess its reasonableness and recalculate to confirm accuracy of management's calculations
  - Review forecasts and budgets in relation to the manufacturing plant to assess the likelihood of its continued operations until 20Y0
  - Using the draft financial statements, confirm the accounting treatment outlined by discussion with management has been applied and recalculate the amounts recognised
  - Confirm the cash received to bank statement and cash book

|  |  |
|---|---|
| **Maximum** | 10 |

(c) **Review of internal controls**

Generally 1 mark for each well explained ethical and professional threat;
½ mark available for each recommended safeguard:
  - Self-review threat
  - Management responsibility: self-interest and familiarity threat
  - No safeguards which can reduce management threat
  - Possible safeguards to avoid management threat
  - Restriction on internal audit services for listed clients
  - Competence if review is not related to financial controls
  - Responsibilities of auditor in relation to internal controls
  - Possible deficiency in external audit procedures
  - Nature/severity of deficiencies not clear

|  |  |
|---|---|
| **Maximum** | 7 |

| | | | |
|---|---|---|---|
| **(d)** | **Impact of outsourcing on audit** | | |
| | Up to 1½ marks for each comment/explanation/definition: | | |
| | – Need to assess significance of outsourced function on financial statements | | |
| | – Need to understand relationship and interaction between audited entity and service organisation | | |
| | – Obtain understanding of the service organisation including internal controls | | |
| | – Means of obtaining understanding – type 1 and type 2 reports | | |
| | – Other means of obtaining understanding – requesting information, performing tests on controls at the service organisation | | |
| | **Maximum** | | 4 |
| | Professional marks for headings, introduction, conclusion and quality of explanations provided | | 4 |
| **Total** | | | **50** |

## 11 TED  *Walk in the footsteps of a top tutor*

*Top tutor tips*

*Part (a) asks for matters to consider when developing the audit strategy for a new audit client. Think of the elements included in an audit strategy and then apply this knowledge to a new audit client.*

*Part (b) focuses on audit risk, i.e. the risk that the financial statements contain material misstatement which is not detected by the auditor. Risk of material misstatement is usually due to non-compliance with an accounting standard. Think about the requirements of the relevant accounting standard and what the client might be doing incorrectly. Detection risks include auditing a client for the first time or where there is a tight reporting deadline.*

*Additional information required in part (b)(ii) is the evidence you would gather to determine the significance of the risks. For example, there will be less risk in relation to the treasury management function if the staff employed are competent and experienced. Information will need to be obtained to assess the competence of the department to determine the level of risk.*

*Part (c) asks for procedures in respect of the portfolio of short term investments and EPS. Procedures should be specific in terms of what the auditor needs to do to obtain the evidence they need. Where there is a requirement asking for procedures, these are areas of potential risk and should therefore have been included in your audit risks.*

*Part (d) looks at the ethical issues arising if an audit firm audits two competing clients. To earn all of the marks available you must discuss the issues as well as suggest appropriate safeguards to manage the conflict.*

**Briefing notes**

To:       Jack Hackett, audit engagement partner

From:    Audit manager

Subject:   Audit planning – Ted Co

**Introduction**

These briefing notes are prepared for the use of the audit team in planning the audit of Ted Co, our firm's new audit client which develops and publishes computer games. The briefing notes discuss the planning matters in respect of this being an initial audit engagement; evaluate the audit risks to be considered in planning the audit; and recommend audit procedures in respect of short-term investments and the earnings per share figure disclosed in the draft financial statements. Finally, the briefing notes look at how the firm should manage a conflict of interest that has arisen in relation to Ted Co and another audit client, Ralph Co.

**(a)**     In an initial audit engagement there are several factors which should be considered in addition to the planning procedures which are carried out for every audit. ISA 300 *Planning an Audit of Financial Statements* provides guidance in this area.

    **Review of predecessor auditor's working papers**

    Unless prohibited by laws or regulation, arrangements should be made with the predecessor auditor, for example, to review their working papers. Therefore communication should be made with Crilly & Co to request access to their working papers for the financial year ended 31 May 20X4.

    The review of the previous year's working papers would help Craggy & Co in planning the audit, for example, it may highlight matters pertinent to the audit of opening balances or an assessment of the appropriateness of Ted Co's accounting policies.

    It will also be important to consider whether any previous years' audit opinions were modified, and if so, the reason for the modification.

    **Professional clearance**

    As part of the client acceptance process, professional clearance should have been sought from Crilly & Co. Any matters which were brought to our firm's attention when professional clearance was obtained should be considered for their potential impact on the audit strategy.

    There should also be consideration of the matters which were discussed with Ted Co's management in connection with the appointment of Craggy & Co as auditors. For example, there may have been discussion of significant accounting policies which may impact on the planned audit strategy.

    **Opening balances**

    Particular care should be taken in planning the audit procedures necessary to obtain sufficient appropriate audit evidence regarding opening balances, and procedures should be planned in accordance with ISA 510 *Initial Audit Engagements – Opening Balances*.

    For example, procedures should be performed to determine whether the opening balances reflect the application of appropriate accounting policies and determining whether the prior period's closing balances have been correctly brought forward into the current period.

### Understanding of the business

With an initial audit engagement it is particularly important to develop an understanding of the business, including the legal and regulatory framework applicable to the company. This understanding must be fully documented and will help the audit team to perform effective analytical review procedures and to develop an appropriate audit strategy. Obtaining knowledge of the business will also help to identify whether it will be necessary to plan for the use of an auditor's expert.

### Independent review partner

Craggy & Co may have quality control procedures in place for use in the case of initial engagements, for example, the involvement of another partner or senior individual to review the overall audit strategy prior to commencing significant audit procedures. Compliance with any such procedures should be fully documented.

### Audit team

Given that this is a new audit client, that it is newly listed, and because of other risk factors to be discussed in the next part of these briefing notes, when developing the audit strategy consideration should be given to using an experienced audit team in order to reduce detection risk.

(b)     (i)     **Management bias – stock market listing**

The first audit risk identified relates to Ted Co becoming a listed entity during the year. This creates an inherent risk at the financial statement level and is caused by the potential for management bias.

Management will want to show good results to the new shareholders of the company, in particular the institutional shareholders, and therefore there is an incentive for the overstatement of revenue and profit.

The analytical review shows a significant increase in profit before tax of 48.1%, indicating potential overstatement.

### Management bias – Dougal Doyle shareholding

There is a related risk of overstatement due to Dougal Doyle and his family members retaining a 30% equity interest in Ted Co, which is an incentive for inflated profit so that a high level of dividend can be paid.

### Weak corporate governance

It appears that governance structures are not strong, for example, there are too few non-executive directors, and therefore Dougal Doyle is in a position to be able to dominate the board and to influence the preparation of the financial statements. This increases the risk of material misstatement due to management bias.

### Lack of knowledge of listing requirements

There is also a risk that management lacks knowledge of the reporting requirements specific to listed entities, for example, in relation to the calculation and disclosure of earnings per share which is discussed later in these briefing notes.

## E-commerce

With 25% of revenue generated through the company's website, this represents a significant revenue stream, and the income generated through e-commerce is material to the financial statements. E-commerce gives rise to a number of different audit risks, including but not limited to the following.

For the auditor, e-commerce can give rise to detection risk, largely due to the paperless nature of the transactions and the fact there is likely to be a limited audit trail, making it difficult to obtain audit evidence.

For the same reason, control risk is increased, as it can be hard to maintain robust controls unless they are embedded into the software which records the transaction. The auditor may find it difficult to perform tests on the controls of the system unless computer assisted audit techniques are used, as there will be few manual controls to evaluate.

Ted Co also faces risks relating to the security of the system, for example, risks relating to unauthorised access to the system, and there is an increased risk of fraud. All of these risks mean that there is high audit risk in relation to the revenue generated from the company's website.

Where sales are made online, cut-off can be a problem as it can be difficult to determine the exact point at which the revenue recognition criteria of IFRS 15 *Revenue from Contracts with Customers* have been met. Hence, over or understatement of revenue is a potential risk to be considered when planning the audit.

## Licence income

The licence income which is deferred in the statement of financial position represents 13.4% of total assets and is therefore material.

It may be the case that the revenue from the sale of a licence should not be deferred at all. The revenue recognition criteria of IFRS 15 need to be applied to the transaction, and if, for example, it were found that Ted Co has no continuing management involvement and that the control of the asset had been transferred to the buyer, then the revenue should be recognised immediately as the performance obligations within the contract have been fulfilled. This would mean a significant understatement of revenue and profit.

If it is appropriate that the revenue is deferred, then the period over which the revenue is recognised could be inappropriate, resulting in over or understated revenue in the accounting period.

## Foreign exchange transactions

Ted Co's products sell in over 60 countries and the products are manufactured overseas, so the company is involved with foreign currency transactions which can be complex in nature. There is a risk that the requirements of IAS 21 *The Effects of Changes in Foreign Exchange Rates* have not been followed. For example, if transactions have not been retranslated to Ted Co's functional currency at the date of the transaction, then the amounts involved may be over or understated.

There is also a risk that outstanding receivables and payables have not been retranslated at the year-end closing exchange rate, leading to over or understatement of assets and liabilities and unrecorded exchange gains or losses.

### Forward exchange contracts

The treasury management function is involved with forward exchange contracts, meaning that derivatives exist and should be accounted for in accordance with IFRS 9 *Financial Instruments*. This is a complex accounting issue, and there are numerous audit risks arising.

There is a risk that not all forward exchange contracts are identified, leading to incomplete recording of the balances involved.

There is also a risk in determining the fair value of the derivative at the year-end, as this can be judgmental and requires specialist knowledge.

There is also a risk that if the company has decided to adopt the hedge accounting rules, that these rules have not been properly applied, or that inadequate disclosure of relevant risks is made in the notes to the financial statements.

### Portfolio of equity shares

The cost of the portfolio of investments represents 6% of total assets and is material to the statement of financial position. The fall in value of the portfolio of $2 million represents 25% of profit before tax, and is therefore material to the statement of profit or loss.

The investment portfolio is recognised at cost, but this is not the correct measurement basis. The investments should be accounted for in accordance with IFRS 9 which requires investments in equity to be classified and then measured subsequent to initial recognition at fair value through profit or loss. There is an alternative treatment, fair value through other comprehensive income for which an election can be made, but given that this investment is speculative in nature, this classification would not be appropriate. It seems that the current accounting treatment is incorrect in that assets are overstated, and it is significant that the draft profit for the year is overstated by $2 million.

### New treasury management team

Further, there is a new team dealing with these complex treasury management transactions involving financial instruments. There may be a lack of knowledge and experience which adds to the risks outlined above in relation to the foreign exchange transactions, derivatives and portfolio of equity shares.

### Earnings per share calculation

Ted Co must calculate and disclose its earnings per share figure (EPS) in accordance with IAS 33 *Earnings per Share*. It appears that the calculation has not been performed in accordance with the requirements of the standard and is incorrect. IAS 33 requires EPS to be calculated based on the profit or loss for the year attributable to ordinary shareholders as presented in the statement of profit or loss, but in the draft financial statements it has been calculated based on an adjusted profit figure.

This is not in accordance with IAS 33, which only allows EPS based on an alternative profit figure to be disclosed in the notes to the financial statements as an additional figure, and should not be disclosed on the face of the financial statements. The earnings figure used as the basis of the calculation should also not be based on profit before tax but on the post-tax profit.

It appears that the denominator used in the EPS calculation is incorrect. It should be based on the weighted average number of shares which were in issue during the financial year, but the calculation shows that it is based on the number of shares in issue at the year-end. Due to the share issue in December 20X4, the weighted average will need to be determined and used in the calculation.

### Earnings per share – disclosure

There is a risk relating to inadequate disclosure, for example, a diluted EPS needs to be presented, as does a comparative for the previous year. The incorrect calculation and disclosure of EPS is a significant issue, especially given the company becoming listed during the year, which will focus the attention of investors on the EPS this year.

### Rapid growth

The analytical review which has been performed indicates rapid growth has occurred during the year. Revenue has increased by 46.3%, and profit before tax by 48.1%. The growth in the number of transactions could indicate a control risk, in that systems and personnel may struggle to keep pace with the volume of transactions which are being processed, leading to accounting errors being made. This is exacerbated by the lack of an internal audit department to provide assurance on systems and controls.

### Profit margins

The trend in gross profit and operating profit margins could indicate a misstatement. The ratios are as follows:

|  | 20X5 |  | 20X4 |  |
|---|---|---|---|---|
| Gross margin | 65,000/98,000 | 66.3% | 40,000/67,000 | 59.7% |
| Operating margin | 12,000/98,000 | 12.2% | 9,200/67,000 | 13.7% |

The increase in the gross margin at the same time as the decrease in the operating margin could indicate that expenses such as depreciation and amortisation have been misclassified between cost of sales and other operating expenses. The disproportionate changes in the two margins could also indicate that cost of sales is understated, for example, due to incomplete recording of expenses.

### Intangible assets – development costs

There has been a significant increase in the amount of development costs capitalised as an intangible asset. There is a risk that this amount is overstated.

Development costs should only be recognised as an asset when the criteria for capitalisation from IAS 38 *Intangible Assets* have been met. For example, the ability of the development costs to generate economic benefit should be demonstrated, along with the existence of resources to complete the development.

As discussed earlier, there is an incentive for management to maximise profits, so it would be in management's interests to capitalise as much of the development costs as possible. The intangible asset currently recognised represents 43.3% of total assets, and is highly material to the financial statements.

**Inventory**

Any year-end inventory counts held at the overseas manufacturing locations will already have taken place, so the audit strategy should focus on alternative methods of obtaining evidence regarding the existence of inventories at the year-end.

Due to the overseas locations of inventory counts, a detection risk may be created from the fact that it may not be possible for the audit firm to attend any inventory counts which take place at a later date.

**Opening balances**

As this is an initial audit engagement, our firm should be alert to the fact that opening balances may be misstated. There is no evidence that the previous audit firm were lacking in competence, and the audit opinion for the prior year was unmodified, but there is the risk that inappropriate accounting policies have been used, and that opening balances may not be correct.

(ii) **Additional information**

- Revenue recognition policy to ensure appropriate recognition of online sales.

- Notes of discussion with the non-executive director ascertaining the degree of oversight exercised over Dougal Doyle, if any.

- Licence terms and conditions to assess whether the licence income should be deferred, and over what period.

- Details of experience and qualifications of the treasury management staff to assess competence.

- In respect of the overseas manufacturing locations, details of inventory count instructions followed, results of inventory counts, details from management of the monitoring of overseas inventory counts performed by them, and any issues encountered during the counts, to ascertain the risk of misstatement of inventory.

- Breakdown of cost of sales and operating costs to review for misclassification as the gross and operating profit margins have changed inconsistently.

- Copies of working papers from the previous auditor to perform testing on opening balances.

(c) (i) **Audit procedures on the portfolio of short-term investments**

- Agree the fair value of the shares held as investments to stock market share price listings at 31 May 20X5.

- Confirm the original cost of the investment to cash book and bank statements.

- Discuss the accounting treatment with management and confirm that an adjustment will be made to recognise the shares at fair value.

- Review the notes to the financial statements to ensure that disclosure is sufficient to comply with the requirements of IFRS 9.

- Enquire with the treasury management function as to whether there have been any disposals of the original shares held and reinvestment of proceeds into the portfolio.

- Review board minutes to confirm the authorisation and approval of the amount invested.

- Review documentation relating to the scope and procedures of the new treasury management function, for example, to understand how the performance of investments is monitored.

- For any investments from which dividends have been received, confirm the number of shares held to supporting documentation such as dividend received certificates or vouchers.

(ii) **Audit procedures on earnings per share**

- Discuss with management the requirements of IAS 33 and request that management recalculates the EPS in accordance with those requirements.

- Review board minutes to confirm the authorisation of the issue of share capital, the number of shares and the price at which they were issued.

- Inspect any other supporting documentation for the share issue, such as a share issue prospectus or documentation submitted to the relevant regulatory body.

- Confirm that the share issue complies with the company's legal documentation (e.g. the memorandum and articles of association).

- Recalculate the weighted average number of shares for the year to 31 May 20X5.

- Recalculate EPS using the profit as disclosed in the statement of profit or loss and the weighted average number of shares.

- Discuss with management the existence of any factors which may impact on the calculation and disclosure of a diluted EPS figure, for example, convertible bonds.

- Read the notes to the financial statements in respect of EPS to confirm that disclosure is complete and accurate and complies with IAS 33.

---

*Tutorial note*

*Credit will be awarded for other, relevant audit procedures.*

---

(d) **Ethical issues**

The acquisition of the accountancy firm by Craggy & Co creates a potential conflict of interest because Craggy & Co will become the auditor of both Ted Co and their competitor Ralph Co.

There is nothing ethically inappropriate having clients in the same industry; this is actually normal practice and allows firms of accountants to develop industry specialisms which allow them to offer high quality, expert services. It is therefore likely that firms will have clients which compete in the same industry.

Acting for two competing companies may give rise to ethical threats though. It may be perceived that the auditor cannot offer objective services and advice to a company where it also audits a competitor. The clients may also be concerned that commercially sensitive information may be inadvertently, or intentionally, passed on to the competitor via the auditor.

The main safeguard available is to disclose the potential conflict to all parties involved. If both Ted Co and Ralph Co accept the situation, it is appropriate for Craggy & Co to continue in its capacity as auditor to both as long as appropriate safeguards are put in place. These include:

- The use of separate engagement teams

- Issuing clear guidelines to the teams on issues of security and confidentiality

- The use of confidentiality agreements by audit team members

- Regular review of the safeguards by an independent partner.

Craggy & Co must also evaluate whether there are sufficient resources available to conduct the audits of both companies using separate teams. If not, the audit firm will not be able to accept the additional work into the department.

If either Ralph Co or Ted Co do not give their consent, then Craggy & Co must resign as the auditor of one of the companies.

If this is the case, a number of ethical and commercial considerations should be made before deciding which client should be rejected. Craggy & Co will need to consider the risk profile of both clients and should conduct appropriate acceptance/ continuance procedures for both clients prior to making any final decision. From a commercial perspective, Craggy & Co may also consider which of the two clients provides the highest audit revenue. Ted Co appears to be the larger company currently but Ralph Co is a rapidly expanding business which could be a more lucrative audit client in the future. In this case Craggy & Co should also consider if they will be able to offer the range of services required by the rapidly expanding Ralph Co without creating any self-interest or self-review threats to independence.

Craggy & Co should also consider if any non-audit services are currently offered to the clients and whether additional services could be offered to either of them in the future. As a rapidly expanding business, it is possible that Ralph Co will require more services than the established Ted Co.

**Conclusion**

These briefing notes have shown that the audit risk of this engagement is relatively high, largely due to the existence of potential management bias, rapid growth and a number of complex balances and transactions. As this is our firm's first audit of Ted Co, an audit strategy needs to be developed to focus on these areas, as well as dealing with the additional planning issues which arise on an initial audit engagement. The conflict of interest arising in relation to Ted Co and Ralph Co will have implications for staffing the audit as audit team members involved with the audit of Ralph Co should not be assigned to the audit team of Ted Co.

**Examiner's comments**

This question was set in the planning phase of the audit of a new audit client, Ted Co. The company was a computer games designer and publisher which had experienced significant growth in recent years, and had become listed in its home jurisdiction during the financial year. Information was provided on the company's financial background, its operations and corporate governance structure. Extracts from the financial statements were provided along with the Earnings per Share (EPS) figure calculated by the company's finance director.

The first requirement asked candidates to discuss the matters specific to an initial audit engagement which should be considered in developing the audit strategy. Given that Ted Co was a new audit client this was a very relevant requirement.

The answers were very mixed in quality, with the best answers concentrating on practical matters such as reviewing the previous audit firm's working papers, planning procedures to obtain evidence on opening balances, and ensuring that the audit team developed a thorough understanding of the business. Unfortunately the majority of candidates provided generic answers discussing whether or not the firm could take on the audit, engagement letters, fees, customer due diligence and checking to see if the previous auditors had been correctly removed from office. It was not relevant to discuss whether the audit firm should take on the client and associated acceptance issues as it was clearly expressed in the scenario that this decision had already been taken and consequently answers of this nature scored limited credit.

Other weaker answers discussed general audit planning matters such as the need to determine a materiality level. This was not tailored to the specifics of this scenario as this would be relevant for any audit. Candidates are reminded to answer the specific question that has been set, which in this case should have meant answers focusing on matters relevant to planning an initial audit engagement after the engagement has been accepted. Some candidates wrote a lot for the marks available. Candidates are reminded that the marks for each requirement are a guide as to how long should be spent on answering the question. In some cases the answers to part (a) ran to several pages, leading to time pressure on subsequent answers.

Requirement (b) asked candidates to evaluate the audit risks to be considered in planning the audit. There were some excellent answers to this requirement, with many responses covering a range of audit risks, all well explained, and all relevant to the scenario. The best answers demonstrated that a methodical approach had been applied to the information in the scenario, and the better candidates had clearly worked through the information logically, identifying the risk factors, then going on to explain them fully and specifically. The audit risks that were generally dealt with well included those relating to the foreign currency transactions and to the portfolio of short term investments. The risk relating to whether research and development costs could be capitalised was also identified by the majority of candidates, but the issue of amortisation was not often discussed. To achieve a good mark for this type of requirement, candidates should look for a range of audit risks, some of which are risks of material misstatement and some are detection risks. Candidates however do not need to categorise the risks they are discussing or to spend time explaining the components of the audit risk model. When discussing audit risks relating to a specific accounting treatment, well explained answers will include an evaluation of the potential impact of the risk factor on the financial statements, for example, in this scenario there was a risk that the short term investments were overstated in value and that profit also was overstated. Materiality should be calculated when possible, as this allows prioritisation of the risks identified. Strong candidates, as well as providing detailed analysis and explanation of the risks, also attempted to prioritise the various risks identified thus demonstrating appropriate judgment and an understanding that the audit partner would want to know about the most significant risks first. Candidates are reminded that it is those risks that could result in a material misstatement in the financial statements, which need to be identified and addressed. Weak answers included answer points that were too vague to be awarded credit. Comments such as 'there is a risk this has not been accounted for properly', 'there is risk that this is not properly disclosed' and 'there is a risk that the accounting standard has not been followed' are unfortunately too common and will not earn marks due to the lack of specificity. It would be beneficial for candidates to review their answers and to consider whether what they have written would provide the audit engagement partner with the necessary knowledge to understand the risk profile of the client in question.

Other common weaknesses in answers include the following points:

- Discussing business risks instead of audit risks – in particular business risks relating to theft of inventory, security issues in relation to e-commerce and exposure to foreign currency fluctuations were often discussed, sometimes in a lot of detail, but usually the related audit risk was not developed.

- Incorrect comments on accounting treatments – for example discussing that the licences granted by Ted Co should be treated as intangible assets.

- Lack of knowledge on some accounting issues – in particular many candidates clearly did not know how EPS should be calculated and therefore did not realise that the finance director's calculation was incorrect or how short term investments should be measured.

- Evaluation of the company's corporate governance structure, but not linking this to audit risk.

- Incorrect materiality calculations.

Requirement (c) asked candidates to design audit procedures to be performed on the portfolio of short term investments and on the EPS figure. Some candidates proved able to provide a good list of procedures, but this was the minority. Answers tended to be better in relation to the investment portfolio, with many candidates appreciating that determining the short-term nature of the investments was an important issue and that the fair value of the shares at the year-end could be agreed to stock market listings. However, most candidates could only provide vague suggestions such as 'discuss with the board' or 'agree to supporting documentation', and in relation to the fair value of the share many candidates could only suggest to 'rely on an expert' which was not necessary given that the investment relates to the shares of listed companies. Some candidates tried to make the procedures much too complicated, not fully appreciating that traded equity shares can be easily valued and documented.

The procedures in relation to EPS were often very vague, with many candidates only able to suggest a recalculation of components of the calculation provided, or check the board had approved the calculation, neither of which were relevant given that the calculation was incorrect. Very few candidates picked up on the fact that the weighted average number of shares would need to be verified given that the company had a share issue during the year.

The final part dealt with a conflict of interest between two competing clients arising after an acquisition of another firm and candidates attempting this question tended to score well.

There were four professional marks available, and most candidates secured most of these marks by providing an introduction and using headings to create an appropriate structure for their answer. However, presentation was not always good and candidates are reminded to pay attention to determining an appropriate layout for their answer.

| Marking scheme | | | Marks |
|---|---|---|---|

**(a)** Initial audit engagement

Generally up to 1½ marks for each point discussed, including:

- Communicate with the previous auditor, review their working papers
- Consider whether any previous auditor reports were modified
- Consider any matters which were raised when professional clearance was obtained
- Consider matters discussed with management during our firm's appointment
- Need to develop thorough business understanding
- Risk of misstatement in opening balances/previously applied accounting policies
- Firm's quality control procedures for new audit clients
- Need to use experienced audit team to reduce detection risk

Maximum    **6**

**(b)** **(i)** Evaluation of audit risk

Generally up to 3 marks for each risk evaluated, and 1 mark for each calculation of materiality.

- Management bias due to recent stock market listing – pressure on results
- Management bias due to owner's shareholding – incentive to overstate profit
- Weak corporate governance, potential for Dougal to dominate the board
- Management lacks knowledge and experience of the reporting requirements for listed entities
- E-commerce (allow up to 3 marks for discussion of several risks factors)
- Licence income – should the revenue be deferred
- Licence income – whether deferred income recognised over an appropriate period
- Foreign exchange transactions – risk of using incorrect exchange rate
- Forward currency contracts – risk derivatives not recognised or measured incorrectly
- Portfolio of investments – risk fair value accounting not applied
- New team dealing with complex issues of treasury management
- EPS – incorrectly calculated (allow 3 marks for detailed discussion)
- EPS – risk of incomplete disclosure
- Rapid growth – control risk due to volume of transactions
- Profit margins – risk expenses misclassified (also allow 1 mark for each margin correctly calculated with comparative)
- Development costs – risk of over-capitalisation of development costs
- Inventory – year-end counts already taken place, difficulties in attending inventory counts
- Opening balances (give mark here if not given in (a) above)

Maximum    **20**

(ii)   **Additional information**
1 mark for each piece of relevant information. Credit should be given for other relevant recommendations
- Revenue recognition policy
- Oversight of NED
- Licence terms and conditions
- Experience and qualifications of treasury management staff
- Inventory count controls and results
- Breakdown of cost of sales and operating costs
- Previous auditor's working papers

|  | **Maximum** | 5 |

(c)   (i)   **Procedures on portfolio of investments**
Generally 1 mark for each procedure explained:
- Agree the fair value of the shares held as investments to stock market share price listings
- Confirm the original cost of the investment to cash book and bank statements
- Discuss the accounting treatment with management and confirm that an adjustment will be made to recognise the shares at fair value
- Review the notes to the financial statements to ensure that disclosure is sufficient to comply with the requirements of IFRS 9
- Enquire with the treasury management function regarding disposals and reinvestment
- Review board minutes to confirm the authorisation and approval of the amount invested
- Confirm the number of shares held to supporting documentation such as dividend received vouchers
- Review documentation relating to the scope and procedures of the new treasury management function

(ii)   **Procedures on EPS**
Generally 1 mark for each procedure explained:
- Discuss with management the requirements of IAS 33 ad request that management recalculates the EPS in accordance with those requirements
- Review board minutes to confirm the authorisation of the issue of share capital, the number of shares and the price at which they were issued
- Confirm the share issue complies with the company's legal documentation such as the memorandum and articles of association
- Inspect any other supporting documentation for the share issue, such as a share issue prospectus
- Recalculate the weighted average number of shares for the year to 31 May 20X5
- Recalculate EPS using the profit as disclosed in the statement of profit or loss and the weighted average number of shares
- Discuss with management the existence of any factors which may impact on the calculation and disclosure of a diluted EPS figure, for example, convertible bonds
- Read the notes to the financial statements in respect of EPS to confirm that disclosure is complete and accurate and complies with IAS 33

|  | **Maximum** | 10 |

| (d) | **Ralph Co** | | |
|---|---|---|---|
| | – Conflict of interest | | |
| | – Normal to audit firms in the same industry | | |
| | – Threat to objectivity | | |
| | – Confidentiality threat | | |
| | – Full disclosure to both clients | | |
| | – Possible safeguards (½ each, 1 max) | | |
| | – Consideration of resources available | | |
| | – Possible resignation from one audit | | |
| | | Maximum | 5 |
| | **Professional marks** | | |
| | Overall presentation, structure and logical flow of the briefing notes and for the clarity of the evaluation and discussion provided. | | |
| | | Maximum | 4 |
| **Total** | | | **50** |

## 12 CONNOLLY  *Walk in the footsteps of a top tutor*

### Top tutor tips

*The majority of the marks for this question are for risk assessment. Business risks are the risk the company does not meet its strategic objectives i.e. the issues management are concerned about. Explain the impact of the issue to the company's profits or cash flows. You are then asked for risk of material misstatement, i.e. the risk that the financial statements contain material misstatement. This is usually due to non-compliance with an accounting standard. Think about the requirements of the relevant accounting standard and what the client might be doing incorrectly.*

*Part (c) asks for procedures in respect of the newly acquired brand name. Procedures should be specific in terms of what the auditor needs to do to obtain the evidence they need.*

*Part (d) requires discussion of ethical issues arising as a result of the loan guarantee and the request for advice. To earn the marks make sure you identify and explain the threats, discuss whether the threats are significant and finally suggest how to safeguard against them.*

*Don't forget to present your answer in a briefing note format and include an introduction and a conclusion as well as subheadings to get the professional marks.*

**Briefing notes**

To:             Ali Stone, audit engagement partner

From:          Audit manager

Subject:      Audit planning – Connolly Co

**Introduction**

These briefing notes are prepared to assist in planning the audit of Connolly Co, our client operating in the pharmaceutical industry. Specifically, the briefing notes will evaluate the business risks and risks of material misstatement to be considered when planning the audit of Connolly Co, recommend audit procedures in relation to a new brand acquired during the year, and finally explain the ethical threats to our firm.

**(a)    Business risks**

**Licensing of products**

A significant regulatory risk relates to the highly regulated nature of the industry in which the company operates. If any of Connolly Co's products fail to be licensed for development and sale, it would mean that costs already incurred are wasted. Research and development costs are significant. For example, in 20X4 the cash outflow in relation to research and development amounted to 7.5% of revenue, and the failure to obtain the necessary licences is a major threat to the company's business objectives.

**Patent infringements**

In developing new products and improving existing products, Connolly Co must be careful not to breach any competitor's existing patent. In the event of this occurring, significant legal costs could be incurred in defending the company's legal position. Time and effort must be spent monitoring product developments to ensure legal compliance with existing patents. Similarly, while patents serve to protect Connolly Co's products, if a competitor were found to be in breach of one of the company's patents, costs of bringing legal action against that company could be substantial.

**Advertising regulations**

The company risks running inappropriate advertising campaigns, and failing to comply with local variations in regulatory requirements. For example, if television campaigns to promote products occurred in countries where this is not allowed, the company could face fines and reputational damage, with consequences for cash flow and revenue streams.

**Skilled personnel**

The nature of Connolly Co's operations demands a skilled workforce with the necessary scientific knowledge to be able to develop new drugs. Loss of personnel, especially to competitors in the industry, would be a drain on the remaining resources and in the worst case scenario it could delay the development and launch of new products. It may be difficult to attract and retain skilled staff given the pending court case and potential reputational damage to the company.

**Diversification and rapid growth**

During the year Connolly Co has acquired a new brand name and range of products, and has also diversified into a new market, that of animal health products. While diversification has commercial and strategic advantages, it can bring risks. Management may struggle to deal with the increased number of operations which they need to monitor and control, or they may focus so much on ensuring the success of the new business segments that existing activities are neglected. There may also be additional costs associated with the diversification which puts pressure on cash and on the margins of the enlarged business. This may be the reason for the fall in operating profit of 10.8% and for the decline in operating margin from 24% to 20%.

**Cash flow and liquidity issues**

Connolly Co seems to be struggling to maintain its cash position, as this year its cash flow is negative by $1.2 million. Contributing factors to this will include the costs of acquiring the 'Cold Comforts' brand name, expenditure to launch the new animal-related product line, and the cash outflow in relation to ongoing research and development, which has increased by 7.1% in the year. The first two of these are one-off issues and may not create a cause for concern over long-term cash management issues, but the company must be careful to maintain a positive cash inflow from its operating activities to provide a sound foundation for future activities.

Companies operating in this industry must be careful to manage cash flows due to the nature of the product lifecycle, meaning that large amounts have to be expended long before any revenue is generated, in some cases the time lag may be many years before any cash inflow is derived from expenditure on research activities.

**Gearing**

The fact that the company has approached its bank to make cash available in the event of damages of $3 million having to be paid out indicates that the company is not very liquid, and is relying to some degree on external finance.

If the bank refuses to extend existing borrowing facilities, the company may have to find finance from other sources, for example, from an alternative external provider of funds or from an issue of equity shares, which may be difficult to achieve and expensive. The company has relatively high gearing, which may deter potential providers of finance or discourage potential equity investors.

**Future funding of research and development**

If finance is refused, the company may not be able to pay liabilities as they fall due, and other operational problems may arise, for example, an inability to continue to fund in-progress research and development projects. Ultimately this would result in a going concern problem, though much more information is needed to assess if this is a risk at this year-end.

**Court case and bad publicity**

The court case against the company will create reputational damage. Publicity over people suffering side effects while participating in clinical trials will undoubtedly lead to bad publicity, affecting market share especially if competitors take advantage of the situation. It is also likely that the bad publicity will lead to increased scrutiny of the company's activities making it more vulnerable should further problems arise.

### Risk of overtrading

The fall in operating margin and earnings per share is a worrying sign for shareholders, though for the reasons explained above this may not be the start of a long-term trend as several events in this year have put one-off pressure on margins. However, there could be a risk of overtrading, as the company's revenue has increased by 5.2%.

### Imported goods – exchange rate fluctuations

Connolly Co imports all of its packaging from overseas. This exposes the company to exchange rate volatility and consequentially cash flow fluctuations. The company chooses not to mitigate this risk by using forward exchange contracts. Exchange gains and losses can also cause volatility in profits.

### Imported goods – transportation issues

Heavy reliance on imports means that transportation costs will be high and this will put pressure on Connolly Co's margins. It is not just the cost that is an issue – reliance on imports is risky as supply could be disrupted due to aviation problems, such as the grounding of aircraft after volcanic eruptions or terrorist activities.

Reliance on imported goods increases the likelihood of a stock out. Unless Connolly Co keeps a reasonable level of packaging in inventory, production would have to be halted if supply were interrupted, creating idle time and inefficiencies, and causing loss of customer goodwill.

### Reliance on single supplier

All of Connolly Co's packaging is supplied by one overseas supplier. This level of reliance is extremely risky, as any disruption to the supplier's operations, for example, due to financial difficulties or political interference, could result in the curtailment of supply, leading to similar problems of stock outs and halted production as discussed above.

**(b)   Risks of material misstatement**

### Inherent risk of management bias

Connolly Co's management is attempting to raise finance, and the bank will use its financial statements as part of their lending decision. There is therefore pressure on management to present a favourable position. This may lead to bias in how balances and transactions are measured and presented.

For example, there is a risk that earnings management techniques are used to overstate revenue and understate expenses in order to maximise the profit recognised. Estimates included in the financial statements are also subject to higher risk. ISA 540 *Auditing Accounting Estimates, Including Fair Value Accounting Estimates, and Related Disclosures* states that auditors shall review the judgments and decisions made by management in the making of accounting estimates to identify whether there are indicators of management bias.

### Research and development costs – recognition

There is a significant risk that the requirements of IAS 38 *Intangible Assets* have not been followed. Research costs must be expensed and strict criteria must be applied to development expenditure to determine whether it should be capitalised and recognised as an intangible asset.

Development costs are capitalised only after technical and commercial feasibility of the asset for sale or use have been established, and Connolly Co must demonstrate an intention and ability to complete the development and that it will generate future economic benefits.

The risk is that research costs have been inappropriately classified as development costs and then capitalised, overstating assets and understating expenses.

A specific risk relates to the drug which was being developed but in relation to which there have been side effects during the clinical trials. It is unlikely that the costs in relation to this product development continue to meet the criteria for capitalisation, so there is a risk that they have not been written off, overstating assets and profit.

### Development costs – amortisation

When an intangible asset has a finite useful life, it should be amortised systematically over that life. For a development asset, the amortisation should correspond with the pattern of economic benefits generated from the sale of associated goods. The risk is that the amortisation period has not been appropriately assessed.

For example, if a competitor introduces a successful rival product which reduces the period over which Connolly Co's product will generate economic benefit, this should be reflected in a reduction in the period over which that product is amortised, resulting in an increased amortisation charge. The risk if this does not happen is that assets are overstated and expenses are understated.

### Patents – recognition and amortisation

The cost of acquiring patents for products should be capitalised and recognised as an intangible asset as the patent provides protection over the economic benefit to be derived. Once recognised, patents should be amortised over the period of their duration.

If patent costs have been expensed rather than capitalised, this would understate assets and overstate expenses. If amortisation has not been charged, this will overstate assets and understate expenses.

### Court case – provisions and contingent liabilities

The court case which has been brought against Connolly Co may give rise to a present obligation as a result of a past event, and if there is a probable outflow of economic benefit which can be measured reliably, then a provision should be recognised. The clinical trial took place before year end, so the obligating event has occurred. If the company agrees an out of court settlement with the individual before the year end , or it is expected that the individual will agree to a settlement, there will be a probable outflow of economic benefits and a provision should be recognised.

If the company decides not to try for an out of court settlement, an assessment of probability of the case going against Connolly Co will need to be made. If it is considered that there is a possible rather than probable outflow of economic benefit, a contingent liability will need to be disclosed.

The risk is that either a necessary provision is not recognised, understating liabilities and expenses, or that a contingent liability is not appropriately disclosed in the notes to the financial statements, in accordance with IAS 37 *Provisions, Contingent Liabilities and Contingent Assets*.

Legal fees relating to the court case should also be accrued if they have been incurred before the year-end, and failure to do so will understate current liabilities and understate expenses.

### Segmental reporting

The diversification into the new product area relating to animal health may warrant separate disclosure according to IFRS 8 *Operating Segments*. This requires listed companies to disclose in a note to the financial statements the performance of the company disaggregated over its operating or geographical segments, as the information is viewed by management.

As the new product area has been successful and contributes 15% to revenue, it could be seen as a significant operating segment, and disclosure of its revenue, profit and other figures may be required. The risk is non-disclosure or incomplete disclosure of the necessary information.

### Brand name

The company acquired the 'Cold Comforts' brand from a rival company during the year. The cost of the brand represents 2.5% of assets which is material to the financial statements.

Connolly Co must be confident that the Cold Comforts brand will generate economic benefits equivalent to or greater than the carrying value included in the financial statements either through sales of products carrying the Cold Comforts name or through sale of the brand name itself.

The risk is that the asset is overvalued if $5 million was not an appropriate fair value for the brand or if the amortisation period of 15 years is not appropriate.

### Foreign currency transactions – initial recognition

The majority of Connolly Co's packaging is imported, leading to risk in the accounting treatment of foreign currency transactions. According to IAS 21 *The Effects of Changes in Foreign Exchange Rates,* foreign currency transactions should be initially recognised having been translated using the spot rate, or an average rate may be used if exchange rates do not fluctuate significantly.

The risk on initial recognition is that an inappropriate exchange rate has been used in the translation of the amount, causing an inaccurate expense, current liability and inventory valuation to be recorded, which may be over or understated in value.

### Foreign currency transactions – exchange gains and losses

Further risk arises in the accounting treatment of balances relating to foreign currency at the year-end. Payables denominated in a foreign currency must be retranslated using the closing rate, with exchange gains or losses recognised in profit or loss for the year.

The risk is that the year-end retranslation does not take place, or that an inappropriate exchange rate is used for the retranslation, leading to over or understated current liabilities and operating expenses.

Risk also exists relating to transactions that are settled within the year, if the correct exchange gain or loss has not been included in profit. Inventory should not be retranslated at the year-end as it is a non-monetary item, so any retranslation of inventory would result in over or undervaluation of inventory and profit.

*Tutorial note*

*More than the required number of risks of material misstatement have been included in this answer for illustrative purposes. Credit will be awarded for the identification and explanation of other relevant risks.*

**(c)   Audit procedures**

- Review board minutes for evidence of discussion of the purchase of the acquired brand, and for its approval.

- Agree the cost of $5 million to the company's cash book and bank statement.

- Obtain the purchase agreement and confirm the rights of Connolly Co in respect of the brand.

- Discuss with management the estimated useful life of the brand of 15 years and obtain an understanding of how 15 years has been determined as appropriate.

- If the 15-year useful life is a period stipulated in the purchase document, confirm to the terms of the agreement.

- If the 15-year useful life is based on the life expectancy of the product, obtain an understanding of the basis for this, for example, by reviewing a cash flow forecast of sales of the product.

- Obtain any market research or customer satisfaction surveys to confirm the existence of a revenue stream.

- Consider whether there are any indicators of potential impairment at the year-end by obtaining pre year-end sales information and reviewing terms of contracts to supply the products to pharmacies.

- Recalculate the amortisation expense for the year and agree the charge to the financial statements, and confirm adequacy of disclosure in the notes to the financial statements.

**(d)   Ethical threats**

There are two ethical threats relevant to the audit firm.

**Guarantee in respect of bank loan**

The provision of such a guarantee represents a financial interest in an audit client, and creates a self-interest threat because the audit firm has an interest in the financial position of the client. The audit firm may be reluctant to request adjustments to the financial statements that would result in the firm having to honour the guarantee.

If an audit firm guarantees a loan to an audit client, the self-interest threat created would be so significant that no safeguards could reduce the threat to an acceptable level unless the loan or guarantee is immaterial to both the audit firm and the client.

In this case the loan would be material as it represents 5% of Connolly Co's total assets, and would also be considered material in nature because of the company's need for the additional finance.

**UK syllabus**: FRC Ethical Standard section 2 states that audit firms, persons in a position to influence the conduct and outcome of the audit and immediate family members of such persons shall not make a loan to, or guarantee the borrowings of, an audited entity or its affiliates unless this represents a deposit made with a bank or similar deposit-taking institution in the ordinary course of business and on normal business terms. An intimidation as well as a self-interest threat arises when an audit firm makes a loan to, or guarantees a loan in respect of, an audited entity.

**Advice on accounting and management information systems**

If advice is given, it would constitute the provision of a non-assurance service to an audit client. Services related to IT systems including the design or implementation of hardware or software systems may create a self-review threat. This is because when auditing the financial statements the auditor would assess the systems which they had recommended, and may be reluctant to criticise them if they are ineffective.

There is also a risk of assuming the responsibility of management, especially as Connolly Co has little experience in this area, so would rely on the auditor's suggestions and be less inclined to make their own decision.

In the case of an audit client which is a public interest entity, an audit firm shall not provide services involving the design or implementation of IT systems which form a significant part of the internal control over financial reporting or which generate information which is significant to the client's accounting records or financial statements on which the firm will express an opinion.

Therefore the audit firm should not provide a service to give advice on the accounting systems. With further clarification on the nature of the management information systems and the update required to them, it may be possible for the audit firm to provide a service to Connolly Co, as long as those systems are outside of the financial reporting system. However, it may be prudent for the audit firm to decline offering any advice on systems to the client.

These ethical issues should be discussed with those charged with governance of Connolly Co, with an explanation provided as to why the audit firm cannot guarantee the loan or provide the non-audit service to the company.

**UK syllabus:** FRC Ethical Standard section 5 states that the audit firm shall not undertake an engagement to design, provide or implement information technology systems for an audited entity where the systems concerned would be important to any significant part of the accounting system or to the production of the financial statements and the auditor would place significant reliance upon them as part of the audit of the financial statements; or for the purposes of the information technology services, the audit firm would undertake part of the role of management.

**Conclusion**

Connolly Co faces a variety of business risks, some of which are generic to the industry in which it operates, while others are more entity-specific. A number of risks of material misstatement have been discussed, and the audit planning must ensure that appropriate responses are designed for each of them. The purchase of a new brand will necessitate detailed audit testing. Two ethical issues have been raised by requests from the client for our firm to provide a loan guarantee and to provide advice on systems, both of which create significant threats to independence and objectivity, and the matters must be discussed with the client before advising that we are unable to provide the guarantee or to provide the systems advice.

**Examiner comments**

This question centred on planning the audit of a listed company operating in the pharmaceutical industry. Candidates were provided with background information about the company's products and the environment in which the company, Connolly Co, operated. In addition, information was provided in the form of minutes from a meeting with Connolly's finance director, covering several issues relevant to the audit. These included details of requests made to the company's bank for further finance, a successful diversification into a new market, the acquisition of a new brand during the year, an ongoing court case against the company following problems during a medical trial of its products, and an out of date management information system. Key financial information in the form of extracts from projected financial statements along with comparative information was also provided in the scenario.

The business risks faced by Connolly Co was generally well attempted, and in fact for many candidates this was the best attempted out of all of the question requirements. Most candidates proved able to identify and discuss many of the relevant business risks within their briefing notes and the risks surrounding non-compliance with stringent regulations, the risk of losing the licenses necessary to produce pharmaceutical products, the lack of cash to support ongoing product development, the risks attached to diversifying into a new market, and reputational risks associated with the court case against the company were generally well discussed. The best answers made full use of the information provided and performed analysis of the financial information, allowing for identification of the less obvious but often pertinent risks, such as that without the revenue derived from the new market entered into during the year the company's total revenue would have fallen by a significant amount. Furthermore strong candidates, as well as providing detailed analysis and explanation of the risks, also attempted to prioritise the various risks identified thus demonstrating appropriate judgment and an understanding that the audit partner would want to know about the most significant risks first. The key weakness present in many answers continues to be the poor quality of explanations. Weaker answers tended to just repeat facts given in the scenario with little attempt to discuss or evaluate them. Some answers began with a lengthy discussion of the definition of business risk and its components which was not necessary and demonstrates a lack of judgment when the briefing notes are being requested by an audit partner. Further many answers were very repetitive and did not consider the number of distinct business risks that would be required for the marks available. Many candidates discussed at length risks over going concern that were tenuous or lacked appropriate explanation. Many candidates also confused business risk and audit risk and therefore provided responses that were not relevant to the question.

The next requirement asked candidates to evaluate risks of material misstatement to be considered in planning the audit. Performance in this area was very mixed. There were some excellent answers to this requirement, with many candidates achieving close to full marks. Most candidates were able to identify the risks surrounding inappropriate accounting treatment which could lead to material misstatements, and were also able to quantify the materiality of the matters discussed. The risks that were most commonly discussed related to provisions, recognition of research and development costs, the valuation of potentially obsolete inventory, and the segmental reporting that would be likely required in relation to the new market entered into during the year. The best answers were well structured in how they explained the potential misstatement and included in their evaluation of each risk an identification of the risk factor from the scenario (e.g. the court case ongoing against the company), a determination of materiality where possible given the information in the question, a clear comment on the appropriateness of the accounting treatment where relevant, and the impact on the financial statements (e.g. non-recognition of a provision in relation to the court case could lead to an understatement of liabilities and an overstatement of operating profit). Only the better candidates identified that requesting additional finance from the bank to cover the damages from the court case implied that the outcome was probable rather than possible and should be provided for. Weaker answers failed to observe the number of risks of material misstatement that had been asked for, with a significant minority wasting valuable time by providing more risks than required.

Many candidates discussed a risk of material misstatement relating to accounting for the loan that had been applied for, but given that this had not yet been received it would not give rise to a risk of this nature in this reporting period. Other candidates discussed at length the issue of going concern and that the company's financial statements should be prepared on a break-up basis but there was certainly not enough evidence in the scenario to justify this as a risk of material misstatement. Other weaknesses in relation to this requirement included:

- Incorrect materiality calculations or stating that a balance was material with no justification.

- Lack of understanding of some accounting treatments, e.g. saying that intangible assets must be measured at fair value.

- Vague attempts to explain the risk of material misstatement along the lines of 'there is a risk it is not accounted for properly' or 'there is a risk the relevant accounting standard is not followed' – these points are too vague to score marks.

The next requirement asked candidates to design the principal audit procedures to be performed in respect of a brand name that had been acquired during the year. Answers to this requirement were very mixed, as is typical for requirements relating to audit procedures. The best answers provided well explained procedures that clearly set out how the test would be performed and where appropriate the documentation that would be used. Weaker answers contained vague or very brief lists that were not specific enough to constitute an audit procedure and therefore did not earn marks. Examples of weaker answer points include 'assess value of the brand' (this is not an audit procedure – how should the assessment take place?), 'discuss accounting treatment with management' (what specifically should be discussed?), 'look at the purchase contract' (what information should the auditor be looking for within the contract?). Candidates should ensure that procedures contain an actual instruction describing an action to be performed to satisfy a specific objective. A minority of candidates thought that rather than acquiring a specific asset i.e. the brand, as stated in the question, a company had been purchased. This led to candidates providing irrelevant audit procedures and wrongly discussing the accounting treatment for goodwill. Candidates are reminded to read the question extremely carefully.

The final requirement asked candidates to discuss the ethical issues arising from the engagement and to recommend appropriate actions. There were two matters present in the scenario that were appropriate to discuss – the fact that Connolly Co's bank had asked the audit firm to guarantee the loan extension that had been requested, and that the audit firm had been asked to give advice on the new management information system planned to be introduced the following year. This requirement was generally well attempted with the majority of candidates correctly identifying the two issues and providing some relevant discussion for each. Most candidates were able to explain the ethical threats associated with the issues and recognised that the significance of the threats would need to be determined. Many candidates appreciated that due to Connolly Co's listed status it qualified as a public interest entity, and therefore the threats to objectivity were heightened. Many candidates demonstrated sound judgment by concluding that the services should not be provided to the audit client as it would be unlikely that safeguards could reduce the threats to an acceptable level. However, credit was awarded where candidates mentioned the types of safeguards that could be considered. Weaker answers for this requirement identified the wrong ethical threats or failed to identify the significance of the company's listed status, concluding that it would be acceptable to provide the services. Other answers digressed into discussions on the general ethical issues surrounding the testing of medicines on animals or humans, which was not relevant to the question requirement.

There were four professional marks available, and most candidates secured most of these marks by providing an introduction and using headings and well-structured paragraphs to create an appropriate structure for their answer.

| Marking scheme | Marks |
|---|---|

**(a)** **Evaluation of business risks**

Generally up to 2 marks for each business risk evaluated. In addition, 1 mark for relevant trends calculated and used as part of the risk evaluation:

- Regulatory risk – licensing of products
- Regulatory risk – patent infringement
- Regulatory risk – advertising
- Skilled workforce
- Risk of diversification
- Cash flow issues – negative trend/cash management issues
- Cash flow issues – gearing
- Cash flow issues – future funding of R&D
- Cash flow issues – timing of cash flows
- Court case – bad publicity and further scrutiny
- Risk of overtrading
- Imported goods – exchange rate fluctuations
- Imported goods – transportation issues
- Reliance on single supplier

Maximum **12**

**(b)** **Risks of material misstatement**

Up to 3 marks for each risk evaluated

Allow up to ½ mark for each calculation which forms part of analytical review and 1 mark for appropriate and correct materiality calculations.

- Management bias
- Development costs – recognition
- Development costs – amortisation
- Patent costs
- Court case – provision or contingent liability
- Segmental reporting
- Brand name
- Initial translation of foreign exchange transactions
- Retranslation and exchange gains and losses

Maximum **20**

**(c)** **Procedures in relation to purchased brand name**

Generally 1 mark for each relevant, well described audit procedure:

- Review board minutes for approval
- Agree the cost of $5 million to the cash book and bank statement
- Obtain the purchase agreement and confirm the rights of Connolly Co
- Discuss with management the estimated useful life of the brand of 15 years and obtain an understanding of how 15 years has been determined as appropriate
- If the 15-year useful life is a period stipulated in the purchase document, confirm to the terms of the agreement
- If the 15-year useful life is based on the life expectancy of the product, review a cash flow forecast of sales of the product
- Obtain any market research or customer satisfaction surveys

– Consider whether there are any indicators of potential impairment
– Recalculate the amortisation expense for the year and confirm adequacy of disclosure in notes to the financial statements

| | Maximum | 7 |

**(d)** **Ethical matters**
Generally up to 1 mark for each point discussed:
– Loan guarantee is a financial self-interest threat
– The loan is material and guarantee should not be given
– The advice on systems would be a non-audit service
– Self-review threat created
– Threat of assuming management responsibility
– Can only be provided if systems unrelated to financial reporting
– In this case the advice relating to accounting systems must not be given
– Advisable not to provide the advice on MIS
– Discuss both matters with management/TCWG

| | Maximum | 7 |

**Professional marks**
Generally 1 mark for heading, 1 mark for introduction, 1 mark for use of headings within the briefing notes, 1 mark for clarity of comments made.

| | Maximum | 4 |

| Total | | 50 |

**13 GROHL**  *Walk in the footsteps of a top tutor*

*Top tutor tips*

*Parts (a) and (b) require evaluation of both business risks and risks of material misstatement. This is a common requirement as it enables the examiner to ensure that students understand both types of risks. Business risks should be considered from the perspective of the client i.e. risks to profit, cash flow, reputation, survival of the company. Risks of material misstatement are the risks to the financial statements. For risks of material misstatement it is important to identify the balances or disclosures that could be wrong and to explain why this might be the case. Risks of material misstatement result from non-compliance with accounting standards so try to remember the relevant accounting standard and what the accounting treatment should be. Vague answers stating that there is a risk that the relevant accounting standard might not have been followed will not earn marks. State the requirements of the standards.*

*In part (c) the procedures should be specific enough that another audit team member would know what to do if they were asked to perform the procedure. Be as specific as possible to ensure the marks are awarded.*

*Part (d) asks for discussion of ethical issues. A good approach to use here is to identify the type of threat, explain how the threat would affect the auditor's behaviour, evaluate whether the threat is significant, and finish off by suggesting safeguards or actions the audit firm should take to address the threat.*

*There are four professional marks available for the structure, presentation of the briefing notes and the clarity of the explanations. Your answer should be labelled 'Briefing Notes'. You should identify who the briefing notes are intended for. For the introduction, use the words from the requirement. The body of the answer should have a clear structure including headings for each risk. Don't forget to include a conclusion summarising the key points identified.*

*Part (e) covers the responsibilities of the auditor when non-compliance with laws and regulations is identified. Think about the requirements of ISA 250. There is also an ethical threat due to threatening behaviour by the client. Explain the actions the audit firm should take in such situations.*

**Briefing notes**

**To:** **Mia Vai, audit engagement partner**

**From:** **Audit manager**

**Subject:** **Audit planning – Grohl Co**

**Introduction**

These briefing notes evaluate the business risks facing Grohl Co, and evaluate the risks of material misstatement to be considered when planning the audit of the financial statements for the year ended 30 November 20X2. Audit procedures in relation to the product recall have also been included. In addition, two ethical issues are discussed and relevant actions recommended.

**(a)** **Business risks**

**Imported goods – exchange rate fluctuations**

Grohl Co relies on a key component of its production process being imported from overseas. This exposes the company to exchange rate volatility and consequentially cash flow fluctuations. The company chooses not to mitigate this risk by using forward exchange contracts, which may not be a wise strategy for a business so reliant on imports. Exchange gains and losses can also cause volatility in profits, and as the company already has a loss for the year, any adverse movements in exchange rates may quickly increase this loss.

**Imported goods – transportation issues**

Heavy reliance on imports means that transportation costs will be high, and with fuel costs continuing to increase this will put pressure on Grohl Co's margins. It is not just the cost that is an issue – reliance on imports is risky as supply could be disrupted due to aviation problems, such as the grounding of aircraft after volcanic eruptions or terrorist activities.

Reliance on imported goods increases the likelihood of a stock out. Unless Grohl Co keeps a reasonable level of copper wiring as inventory, production would have to be halted if supply were interrupted, creating idle time and inefficiencies, and causing loss of customer goodwill.

**Reliance on single supplier**

All of Grohl Co's copper wiring is supplied by one overseas supplier. This level of reliance is extremely risky, as any disruption to the supplier's operations, for example, due to financial difficulties or political interference, could result in the curtailment of supply, leading to similar problems of stock outs and halted production as discussed above.

### Quality control issues

Since appointing the new supplier of copper wiring, Grohl Co has subsequently experienced quality control issues with circuit boards, which could result in losing customers (discussed further below). This may have been due to changing supplier as part of a cost-cutting exercise. Given that the new supplier is overseas, it may make resolving the quality control issues more difficult. Additional costs may have to be incurred to ensure the quality of goods received, for example, extra costs in relation to electrical testing of the copper wiring. The company's operating margins for 20X2 are already low at only 4% (20X1 – 7.2%), and additional costs will put further pressure on margins.

### High-technology and competitive industry

Grohl Co sells into a high-technology industry, with computers and mobile phones being subject to rapid product development. It is likely that Grohl Co will need to adapt quickly to changing demands in the marketplace, but it may not have the resources to do this.

Grohl Co-operates in a very competitive market. With many suppliers chasing the same customer base, there will be extreme pressure to cut prices in order to remain competitive. As discussed above, the company's operating margins are already low, so competition based on price would not seem to be an option.

### Reliance on key customers

Grohl Co relies on only 20 key customers to generate its domestic revenue, which accounts for approximately half of its total revenue. In a competitive market, it may be difficult to retain customers without cutting prices, which will place further pressure on profit margins.

In addition, the product quality issue in November could mean that some contracts are cancelled, despite Grohl Co's swift action to recall defective items, meaning a potentially significant loss of revenue.

Furthermore, Grohl Co will have to refund dissatisfied customers or supply alternative products to them, putting strain on cash flows and operating margins.

### Regulatory issues

New regulations come into force within a few months of the year-end. It would appear that the existing production facilities do not comply with these regulations, and work has only recently begun on the new and regulation-compliant production line, so it is very unlikely that the new regulations can be complied with in time.

This creates a significant compliance risk for Grohl Co, which could lead to investigation by the regulatory authority, and non-compliance may result in forced cessation of production, fines, penalties and bad publicity. There may also be additional ongoing costs involved in complying with the new regulations, for example, monitoring costs, as well as the costs of the necessary capital expenditure.

### Additional finance taken out – liquidity/solvency issues

A loan representing 16.7% of total assets was taken out during the year. This is a significant amount, increasing the company's gearing, and creating an obligation to fund interest payments of $1.2 million per annum, as well as repayments of capital in the future.

Grohl Co does not appear to be cash-rich, with only $130,000 cash available at the year-end, and having built up an overdraft of $2.5 million in July, working capital management may be a long-term problem for the company. The current and quick ratios also indicate that Grohl Co would struggle to pay debts as they fall due.

**Profitability**

The draft statement of profit or loss indicates that revenue has fallen by 9.4%, and operating profit fallen by 50%. Overall, the company has made a loss for the year.

In 20X2 finance charges are not covered by operating profit, and it would seem that finance charges may not yet include the additional interest on the new loan, which would amount to $500,000 ($30m × 4% × 5/12). The inclusion of this additional cost would increase the loss for the year to $800,000. This may indicate going concern problems for the company.

**Change in key management**

The loss of several directors during the year is a business risk as it means that the company may lose important experience and skills. It will take time for the new directors to build up business knowledge and to develop and begin to implement successful business strategies.

**(b)** **Risks of material misstatement**

**Foreign currency transactions – initial recognition**

The majority of Grohl Co's copper wiring is imported, leading to risk in the accounting treatment of foreign currency transactions. According to IAS 21 *The Effects of Changes in Foreign Exchange Rates,* foreign currency transactions should be initially recognised having been translated using the spot rate, or an average rate may be used if exchange rates do not fluctuate significantly.

The risk on initial recognition is that an inappropriate exchange rate has been used in the translation of the amount, causing an inaccurate expense, current liability and inventory valuation to be recorded, which may be over or understated in value.

**Foreign currency transactions – exchange gains and losses**

Further risk arises in the accounting treatment of balances relating to foreign currency at the year-end. Payables denominated in a foreign currency must be retranslated using the closing rate, with exchange gains or losses recognised in profit or loss for the year.

The risk is that the year-end retranslation does not take place, or that an inappropriate exchange rate is used for the retranslation, leading to over or understated current liabilities and operating expenses.

Risk also exists relating to transactions that are settled within the year, if the correct exchange gain or loss has not been included in profit. Inventory should not be retranslated at the year-end as it is a non-monetary item, so any retranslation of inventory would result in over or undervaluation of inventory and profit.

**Product recall – obsolete inventory**

There is a quantity of copper wiring which appears to have no realisable value as it has been corroded and cannot be used in the production of circuit boards. This inventory should be written off, as according to IAS 2 *Inventories,* measurement should be at the lower of cost and net realisable value.

The risk is that inventory has not been reduced in value, leading to overstated current assets and overstated operating profit. The risk is heightened if Grohl Co has not adequately identified and separated the corroded copper wiring from the rest of its inventory. This is quite likely, given that the corrosion cannot be spotted visually and relies on the copper being tested.

**Product recall – refunds to customers**

Due to the faulty items being recalled, some customers may have demanded a refund instead of a replacement circuit board. If the customer had already paid for the goods, a provision should be recognised for the refund, as the original sale and subsequent product recall would create an obligation. If the customer had not already paid for the goods and did not want a replacement, then the balance on the customer's receivables account should be written off.

Depending on whether the customer had paid before the year-end, there is a risk of overstated profits and either understated provisions or overstated current assets if the necessary adjustment for any refunds is not made.

**Additional finance – capitalisation of new production line**

The new production process would appear to be a significant piece of capital expenditure, and it is crucial that directly attributable costs are appropriately capitalised according to IAS 16 Property, *Plant and Equipment* and IAS *23 Borrowing Costs.* Directly attributable finance costs must be capitalised during the period of construction of the processing line, and if they have not been capitalised, non-current assets will be understated and profit understated.

There is also a risk that due to the company's low level of profit, there is pressure on management to understate expenses. This could be achieved by treating items of revenue expenditure as capital expenditure, which would overstate non-current assets and overstate profit.

**New regulations – valuation of existing production facilities**

There is a risk that the existing production facilities are impaired. This is due to the new regulations which come into force next year, and may make at least part of the existing facilities redundant when the new production line is ready for use.

IAS 36 *Impairment of Assets* identifies adverse changes in the legal environment as an external indicator of potential impairment. If management does not perform an impairment review to identify the recoverable amount of the production facilities, then the carrying value may be overstated. Profit would also be overstated if the necessary impairment loss were not recognised.

**Additional finance – measurement and disclosure of loan**

The loan taken out is a financial liability and must be accounted for in accordance with IFRS *9 Financial Instruments,* which states that financial liabilities must be classified and measured at amortised cost using the effective interest method (unless an option is taken to measure at fair value).

The risk is that amortised cost has not been applied, meaning that finance costs have not accrued on the loan. The fact that the finance cost in the draft statement of profit or loss has remained static indicates that this may have happened, resulting in understated finance costs and understated liabilities.

There is also a risk that necessary disclosures under IFRS *7 Financial Instruments: Disclosures* have not been made. The notes to the financial statements should contain narrative and numerical disclosures regarding risk exposures, and given the materiality of the loan, it is likely that disclosure would be necessary.

*Tutorial note*

*More than the required number of risks of material misstatement have been identified and explained in the answer above. Credit will be awarded for any four relevant risks, such as cut-off problems in relation to overseas transactions.*

(c) **Audit procedures**

- Enquire of management whether any further complaints have been received post year-end which would indicate that the issue dates back to before November and would require further customers to be contacted.

- Obtain a list of customers contacted and compare this to the sales made in the period affected by the quality issue to ensure all customers likely to be affected have been contacted.

- Review correspondence received from customers to date to identify whether any further issues have occurred that indicates a wider recall of circuit boards is required.

- Obtain a breakdown of costs of repairing/replacing/refunding the circuit boards recalled and reconcile the entries to the number of customers affected to ensure completeness of costs.

- For any recalled items not repaired/replaced/refunded by the year-end agree the estimated cost to a provision in the financial statements.

- Review the cost of action taken post year-end and compare this to the provision at the year-end to ensure the provision is adequate.

- Enquire of management whether any further electrical testing of circuit boards has been performed and the results of those tests to ascertain whether any further inventory needs to be written down.

- Obtain written representation from management confirming the product recall is complete, the costs of resolving the issue are fully accounted for and the inventory is appropriately adjusted for the issue.

(d) **Ethical issues**

**Audit manager joining client**

An audit manager of Foo & Co is being interviewed for the position of financial controller at Grohl Co. Familiarity or intimidation threats may be created by employment with an audit client.

The familiarity threat is caused by the relationship that Bob Halen will have with the audit team, having worked at the firm. This may cause the audit team to fail to challenge him sufficiently and lose professional scepticism.

The more junior members of the audit team may also feel intimidated by him as his previous position was as audit manager. He will also be aware of the firm's audit methodology and procedures, making it easier for him to circumvent procedures.

If a former member of the audit team or partner of the firm has joined the audit client in a position that can influence the preparation of the financial statements, and a significant connection remains between the firm and the individual, the threat would be so significant that no safeguards could reduce the threat to an acceptable level.

It is crucial that Foo & Co ensures that no significant connection between the audit firm and Bob Halen remains, for example, by ensuring that he does not continue to participate or appear to participate in the firm's business or professional activities, and by making sure that he is not entitled to any benefits or payments from the audit firm. If a significant connection were to remain, then the threat to objectivity would be unacceptably high, and Foo & Co would have to consider resigning as auditors of Grohl Co.

In the event of Bob Halen accepting the position and no significant connection between him and the firm remaining, the existence and significance of familiarity and intimidation threats would need to be considered and appropriate safeguards, such as modifying the audit plan and changing the composition of the audit team, put in place.

There may have been a self-interest threat if Bob knew he was going to apply for the role at the same time as performing work for the client. Bob Halen may have avoided any conflict which would have affected his chances of getting the job.

Any work that Bob Halen may have recently performed on Grohl Co should be subject to review to ensure his objectivity has not been impaired. However, as audit planning has yet to commence, this may not be an important issue.

Foo & Co should have in place policies and procedures which require members of an audit team to notify the audit firm when entering employment negotiations with the client. The firm's policies and procedures should be reviewed to ensure they are adequate and they may need to be communicated again to members of staff.

**Tutorial note**

*It is not certain or even implied that Bob has deliberately tried to hide his intention to join Grohl Co – but credit will be awarded where candidates assume this to be the case. Equally, credit will be awarded for comments recognising that it is appropriate that Bob has been removed from the audit team.*

### Contingent fee

As to the comment regarding whether the audit can be conducted on a contingent fee basis, this is not allowed according to IESBA's *International Code of Ethics for Professional Accountants*. Contingent fee arrangements in respect of audit engagements create self-interest threats to the auditor's objectivity and independence that are so significant that they cannot be eliminated or reduced to an acceptable level by the application of any safeguards.

If the fee is contingent on the company's performance the audit firm may not request management to make adjustments to the financial statements which would result in lower profit as this would reduce the audit fee income.

The audit fee must not depend on contingencies such as whether the auditor's report on the financial statements is modified or unmodified. The basis for the calculation of the audit fee is agreed with the audited entity each year before significant audit work is undertaken.

**(e)** **Laws and regulations**

**Auditing standards requirements**

The storage of the potentially hazardous chemicals raises concerns that the Group may not be complying with regulations such as health and safety legislation. The auditor needs to consider the requirements of ISA 250 *Consideration of Laws and Regulations in an Audit of Financial Statements*, which states that while it is management's responsibility to ensure that the entity's operations are conducted in accordance with the provisions of laws and regulation, the auditor does have some responsibility in relation to compliance with laws and regulations, especially where a non-compliance has an impact on the financial statements.

The auditor is required by ISA 315 *Identifying and Assessing the Risks of Material Misstatement Through Understanding the Entity and its Environment* to gain an understanding of the legal and regulatory framework in which the audited entity operates. This will help the auditor to identify non-compliance and to assess the implications of non-compliance.

Therefore the auditor should ensure a full knowledge and understanding of the laws and regulations relevant to the storage of items in the Group's warehouses is obtained, focusing on health and safety issues and the implications of non-compliance.

ISA 250 requires that when non-compliance is identified or suspected, the auditor shall obtain an understanding of the nature of the act and the circumstances in which it has occurred, and further information to evaluate the possible effect on the financial statements.

Therefore procedures should be performed to obtain evidence about the suspected non-compliance, for example, to identify any further instances of non-compliance in the Group's other warehouses.

Management may not be aware that the warehouse manager is allowing the storage of these potentially hazardous items. ISA 250 requires the matter to be discussed with management and where appropriate with those charged with governance. The auditor must therefore ignore the warehouse manager's threats and communicate the suspected non-compliance as required by ISA 250.

Given the potential severity of the situation, and that the chemicals may not be safe, there is the risk of injury to the Group's employees or the general public, and the matter should be communicated as soon as possible. IESBA's ethical standard *Responding to Non-Compliance with Laws and Regulations* (NOCLAR) provides additional responsibilities for professional accountants to report non-compliance in situations such as this.

**Implications for the financial statements**

The auditor needs to consider the potential implications for the financial statements. The non-compliance could lead to regulatory authorities imposing fines or penalties on the Group, which may need to be provided for in the financial statements. Audit procedures should be performed to determine the amount, materiality and probability of payment of any such fine or penalty imposed.

### Reporting responsibilities

In terms of reporting non-compliance to the relevant regulatory authorities, ISA 250 and NOCLAR require the auditor to determine whether they should report the identified or suspected non-compliance to parties outside the entity. In the event that management or those charged with governance of the Group fail to make the necessary disclosures to the regulatory authorities, the auditor should make the disclosure. This will depend on matters including whether there is a legal duty to disclose or whether it is considered to be in the public interest to do so.

### Confidentiality

NOCLAR specifically addresses the confidentiality concerns Foo & Co may have and it is very unlikely to be considered a breach of confidentiality due to the safety concerns. If still concerned, the auditor could seek legal advice on the matter. This is very much a worst case scenario, however, as the Group's management is likely to make the necessary disclosures, and should be encouraged by the auditor to do so.

### Client behaviour

There is also an ethical issue arising from the warehouse manager's aggressive attitude and threatening behaviour. It would seem that the manager has something to hide, and that he was the only person who knew about the storage of the chemicals. He may have been bribed to allow the storage of the dangerous chemicals. His behaviour amounts to intimidation of the auditor, which is not acceptable behaviour, and those charged with governance should be alerted to the situation which arose. ISA 260 *Communication with Those Charged with Governance* requires the auditor to communicate significant difficulties encountered during the audit, which may include examples of lack of co-operation with the auditor, and imposed limitations on auditors performing their work.

### Control deficiency

The final issue is that the Group should review its policy of requiring limited documentation for contracts less than $10,000. This would seem to be inappropriate because it may lead to other instances of unknown items being stored in the Group's warehouses. This would seem to be a significant control deficiency, and should be reported to those charged with governance in accordance with both ISA 260 and ISA 265 *Communicating Deficiencies in Internal Control with Those Charged with Governance and Management*. The auditor could recommend improvements to the controls over the storage of items which should prevent any further non-compliance with laws and regulations from occurring.

### Conclusion

The audit of Grohl Co should be approached as high risk, due to the number of business risks and risks of material misstatement explained in these briefing notes. An audit strategy must be developed to minimise the overall level of audit risk, and strong quality control procedures must be adhered to throughout the audit. In addition, the ethical issue relating to Bob Halen must be brought to the attention of our firm's Ethics Partner as soon as possible so any further actions required can be performed such as review of any work performed by Bob Halen in respect of this year's audit. In respect of the Hawkins Group, the matter should be reported to those charged with governance and if appropriate action is not taken by the client, the matter should be reported to the appropriate authority by our firm.

**Examiner's comments**

The scenario and requirements involved the planning of the audit, and information was given on the business background and recent developments of the client company, as well as some financial information. There were also ethical issues embedded in the scenario.

It was clear that the majority of candidates were familiar with audit planning questions and seemed comfortable with the style of the question and with the amount of information that had been given in the scenario.

The first requirement asked candidates to evaluate the business risks faced by the company. This was by far the best answered requirement of the exam, with most candidates identifying and explaining a range of relevant business risks, which on the whole were developed in enough detail, with foreign exchange issues, the loss of several executives, reliance on a single supplier and too few customers, and the problems of operating in a high technology industry being the most commonly risks discussed. For candidates who achieved lower marks on this requirement, the problem was that they did not develop their discussion enough to achieve the maximum marks per point. Some of the answers just repeated the business issue as stated in the question without discussing any of the impact on the business at all. Most candidates discussed going concern, which was relevant, but instead of relating going concern to specific matters such as liquidity problems and the large loan, it was simply mentioned as a conclusion in relation to every business risk discussed, and therefore was not specific enough to earn credit. Many answers could have been improved in relation to business risk evaluation by including some simple analysis of the financial information made available, for example through the calculation of profit margins and trends. This would have been an easy way to develop the point that financial performance was suffering, as well as liquidity being poor.

Candidates were asked to evaluate the risks of material misstatement to be considered when planning the audit. Answers were very mixed for this requirement. Some candidates clearly understood the meaning of a risk of material misstatement, and could apply their knowledge to the question requirement, resulting in sound explanations. However, despite this being a regularly examined topic and the cornerstone of audit planning, the majority of answers were unsatisfactory. First, many candidates included a discussion about this being a first year audit which would result in a risk of material misstatement, but this was both incorrect and showed that the question had not been read carefully enough. Then, when attempting to explain a risk of material misstatement, many candidates could do little more than state a financial reporting rule, and then say the risk was that 'this would be incorrectly accounted for'. It was not clear if this type of vague statement was down to candidates being reluctant to come to a decision about whether a balance would be over or understated, or if they thought that their answer was specific enough. Very few answers were specific enough on the actual risk of misstatement to earn credit. The matters that tended to be better explained were the risks of misstatement to do with inventory obsolescence, impairment of property plant and equipment, and the finance costs associated with the new loan.

On a general note, many candidates seemed confused between a business risk and a risk of material misstatement, and some answers mixed up the two. Candidates are reminded that it is an essential skill of an auditor to be able to identify both types of risk, and that they are related to each other, but they are not the same thing.

The next requirement was to discuss the ethical issues raised in the scenario and to recommend actions to be taken by the audit firm. There were two ethical issues of relevance to planning the audit – the contingent fee that had been requested by the audit client, and the matter of the previous audit manager potentially gaining employment at the client. Answers here were mixed, and generally the answers in relation to the contingent fee were better than those in relation to employment at a client company. On the contingent fee most candidates seemed confident in their knowledge, and correctly identified that a contingent fee is not allowed for an audit engagement, and recommended sensible actions such as ensuring a discussion of the matter with those charged with governance. The majority of candidates had the correct knowledge here, and could apply appropriately to the question. As usual, candidates appear reasonably comfortable with the ethics part of the syllabus, but are reminded that to score well on ethical requirements, they must do more than just identify a threat. On the matter of the previous audit manager going to work at the audit client answers were unsatisfactory. Most could identify that it was an ethical threat, and could suggest which threat(s) arose, but were less competent at explaining why the threat arose in the first place. Most answers suggested at least one safeguard, usually involving reviews of work performed and ensuring that the manager has no further involvement with the audit, which were fine, but many also made inappropriate suggestions along the lines of 'forbidding' the manager to work at the client, 'prohibiting' the audit client from taking on the manager, and 'disciplining' the manager himself. Very few answers considered the key ethical issue of considering whether the audit manager retained any connection with the audit firm. Some answers had incorrectly assumed that the manager was being loaned to the client on a temporary basis, rather than taking up a permanent position, and some thought that he would be involved in both the audit and the preparation of financial statements. It is important to read the scenario carefully and to take time to think through the information that has been given before starting to write an answer.

The final requirements focused on laws and regulations. Information was provided about suspicious activity in the Group's storage facility warehouses, where it was implied that internal controls were deficient and that hazardous materials were being kept, possibly against relevant laws and regulations. An employee had threatened the audit senior when questioned about the situation. Candidates were asked to discuss the implications of this situation for the Group audit. Most candidates identified the obvious issues, namely that this was likely to be a breach of laws and regulations, internal controls were poor, and that an intimidation threat existed. Beyond this, the quality of answers varied dramatically. The best answers used a methodical approach to explain the auditor's responsibilities in relation to a suspected breach of laws and regulations; including the need to obtain more evidence, the auditor's reporting responsibilities, and the need to consider client confidentiality as well as possibly reporting the matter in the public interest. It was pleasing to see many candidates deal well with these issues, as well as the ethical threat raised by the employee's behaviour. Weaker answers focused solely on the potential money laundering implications, which while not irrelevant should not have been the only matter discussed. In addition, weaker answers simply stated facts without much attempt to apply the requirements of the relevant auditing standard to the scenario. Some candidates suggested that the audit firm was responsible for ensuring that the Group was complying with relevant laws and regulations, saying that the audit firm should 'ensure compliance', and there were occasionally suggestions that the audit senior should be 'disciplined' for not taking further action when threatened by the employee of the Group. These comments, especially the latter, demonstrate a lack of judgment or real understanding of the role of the auditor in this regard.

The question attracted a maximum of four professional marks. Generally candidates presented their answer in a logical and appropriate manner, and a significant number of answers included both an introduction and an appropriate conclusion. Most answers used headings to separate their answer points and generally the presentation was improved from previous sittings.

| | **Marking scheme** | | |
|---|---|---:|---:|
| | | | *Marks* |
| **(a)** | **Business risks** | | |
| | Up to 2 marks for each business risk evaluated | | |
| | – Exchange rate risk | | |
| | – Imports – transportation costs and potential for disrupted supply | | |
| | – Reliance on one supplier | | |
| | – Quality control issues | | |
| | – High-tech/competitive industry | | |
| | – Reliance on key customer contracts | | |
| | – Regulatory issues | | |
| | – Liquidity/solvency issues | | |
| | – Poor profitability | | |
| | – Change in key management | | |
| | | **Maximum** | 10 |
| **(b)** | **Risk of material misstatement** | | |
| | Up to 3 marks for each risk of material misstatement evaluated | | |
| | – Initial translation of foreign exchange transactions | | |
| | – Retranslation and exchange gains and losses | | |
| | – Obsolete inventory | | |
| | – Refunds to customers | | |
| | – Capitalisation of borrowing costs to new production line | | |
| | – Impairment of old production line | | |
| | – Loan classification, measurement and disclosure | | |
| | | **Maximum** | 14 |
| **(c)** | **Procedures** | | |
| | Generally 1 mark for each well explained audit procedure: | | |
| | – Enquire of management of any further complaints | | |
| | – Compare list of recalled items to sales | | |
| | – Review correspondence with customers | | |
| | – Reconcile breakdown of costs to customers affected | | |
| | – Agree outstanding costs to provision in FS | | |
| | – Review post year-end costs to assess adequacy of provision | | |
| | – Enquire of results of further electrical testing of inventory | | |
| | – Obtain written representation | | |
| | | **Maximum** | 6 |
| **(d)** | **Ethical issues** | | |
| | Generally 1 mark per comment: | | |
| | Audit manager joining client | | |
| | – Explain why familiarity threat arises | | |
| | – Explain why intimidation threat arises | | |
| | – Significant connections should be evaluated | | |
| | – If significant connections remain, firm should resign | | |
| | – If continue with audit, consider changing audit team | | |
| | – Review any work recently performed by Bob Halen | | |
| | – Consider firms policies and procedures | | |
| | Contingent fee | | |
| | – Explain why self-interest threat arises | | |
| | – Contingent fee not acceptable | | |
| | – The basis for calculation of the audit fee must be agreed with client | | |
| | | **Maximum** | 8 |

| | | |
|---|---|---|
| **(e)** | **Laws and regulations**<br>Generally up to 1½ marks for each point discussed:<br>– Storage of hazardous chemicals likely to be a breach of laws and regulations<br>– Auditor needs to understand laws and regulations applicable to the Group<br>– Further evidence should be obtained about the storage of chemicals<br>– Implications for the financial statements to be considered, e.g. provisions for fines and penalties<br>– Matter to be reported as soon as possible to those charged with governance<br>– Auditor may have a legal duty to disclose, or consider disclosing in the public interest<br>– Intimidation and threatening behaviour should be reported to those charged with governance<br>– Control deficiency and recommendation to be communicated to those charged with governance<br>– The audit firm may wish to seek legal advice regarding the situation | |
| | **Maximum** | 8 |
| | **Professional marks:**<br>Generally 1 mark for heading, 1 mark for introduction, 1 mark for use of headings within the briefing notes, 1 mark for clarity of comments made | |
| | **Maximum** | 4 |
| **Total** | | 50 |

## 14 CS GROUP  *Walk in the footsteps of a top tutor*

*Top tutor tips*

*Part (a) requires explanation of the implications of the acquisition of a subsidiary on the planning of the audit of CS Group. A good way to approach this requirement is to think about the planning aspects of a single company audit and apply them to the group situation e.g. risk assessment, materiality assessment, etc.*

*Part (b) asks for evaluation of the risks of material misstatement for both the individual financial statements of the parent and the consolidated financial statements. When explaining risks of material misstatement it is important to identify the balances or disclosures that could be wrong and explain why this might be the case. Risks of material misstatement result from non-compliance with accounting standards so try to remember the relevant accounting standard and what the accounting treatment should be. Vague answers stating there is a risk the relevant accounting standards have not been followed will not earn marks. State the requirements of the standards.*

*Part (c) asks for principal audit procedures to be performed in respect of goodwill. Procedures should be specific enough that another audit team member would know what to do if they were asked to perform the procedure. Be as specific as possible to ensure the marks are awarded.*

*In part (d) take care not just to identify and explain the issues but include the safeguards the firm should put in place to address the issues as this will provide a more complete evaluation. At this level you should also be able to discuss whether the threats are significant.*

**Briefing notes**

**To:** Jo Daw, audit engagement partner

**From:** Audit engagement manager

**Subject:** Audit planning – CS Group

**Introduction**

These briefing notes have been prepared to assist in the audit planning of CS Group, and identify and explain the impact of the acquisition of Canary Co for the planning of the individual company and Group audits. The notes then evaluate the risks of material misstatement to be considered when planning the audits and recommend audit procedures in respect of goodwill arising on the acquisition of Canary Co and a government grant received by Starling Co. Finally the notes will discuss the ethical and professional issues arising from complaints made by the finance director.

**(a)** **Implications of the acquisition of Canary Co for audit planning**

**Individual financial statement audit**

Our firm has been appointed auditor of the new subsidiary which was acquired on 1 February 20X2. This means that we must plan the audit of its individual financial statements, and then consider its implications for the audit of the consolidated financial statements.

**Obtaining an understanding of Canary Co, its environment and internal controls**

First, we must plan to develop an understanding of the company, including its environment and internal control, as required by ISA 315 *Identifying and* Assessing *the Risks of Material Misstatement through Understanding the Entity and Its Environment.* We must obtain an understanding of the relevant industry, regulatory and other external factors, the nature of the company's operations, ownership and governance structures, its selection and application of accounting policies, its objectives and strategies, and the measurement and review of its financial performance. Without this knowledge of the business we will be unable to properly perform risk assessment.

From our audit of the CS Group we will already have knowledge of the pottery industry, however, Canary Co's operations are different in that it specialises in figurines and makes some sales online.

The auditor should obtain an understanding of internal controls relevant to the audit. Therefore we must document our understanding of Canary Co's accounting systems and internal controls. This is important given that Canary Co has different IT systems to the rest of the group.

Canary Co makes sales online, and due to the likely complexity of the online sales system, consideration should be given as to whether the use of an expert is required, or whether automated tools and techniques can be used to obtain sufficient evidence on revenue.

It will take time to gain this knowledge and to properly document it. Given that the company's year end is less than one month away, it is important that we plan to begin this work as soon as possible, to avoid any delay to the audit of either the individual or the consolidated financial statements. We need to arrange with the client for members of the audit team to have access to the necessary information, including the accounting system, and to hold the necessary discussions with management. Once we have gained a thorough understanding of Canary Co we will be in a position to develop an audit strategy and detailed audit plan.

### Preliminary analytical review

We have been provided with the CS Group's forecast revenue and profit for the year, but need to perform a detailed preliminary analytical review on a full set of Canary Co's financial statements to fully understand the financial performance and position of the company, and to begin to form a view on materiality. This review will also highlight any significant transactions that have occurred this year.

### Communicate with predecessor auditor

As this is an initial audit engagement, we are required by ISA 300 *Planning an Audit of Financial Statements* to communicate with the predecessor auditor. If this has not yet occurred, we should contact the predecessor auditor and enquire regarding matters which may influence our audit strategy and plan. We may request access to their working papers, especially in respect of any matters which appear contentious or significant. We should also review the prior year audit opinion as this may include matters that impact on this year's audit.

### Opening balances

As the opening balances were audited by another firm, we should plan to perform additional work on opening balances as required by ISA 510 *Initial Audit Engagements – Opening Balances.*

### Consolidated financial statements audit

### Significant component

As Canary Co will form a component of the consolidated financial statements on which we are required to form an opinion, we must also consider the implications of its acquisition for the audit of the CS Group accounts. ISA 600 *Special Considerations – Audits of Group Financial Statements (Including the Work of Component Auditors)* requires that the group auditor must identify whether components of the group are significant components. Based on the forecast results Canary Co is a significant component, as it represents 11.9% of forecast consolidated revenue, and 23.5% of forecast consolidated profit before tax.

### Inter-company transactions

As our firm is auditing the individual financial statements of Canary Co, our risk assessment and planned response to risks identified at individual company level will also be relevant to the audit of the consolidated financial statements. However, we must also plan to obtain audit evidence in respect of balances and transactions which only become relevant on consolidation, such as any inter-company transactions that may occur.

**Non-coterminous year-end**

A significant matter which must be addressed is that of the different financial year end of Canary Co. We will have audited Canary Co's figures to its year end of 30 June 20X2, but an additional month will be consolidated to bring the accounts into line with the 31 July year end of the rest of the CS Group. Therefore, additional procedures will have to be planned to gain audit evidence on significant events and transactions of Canary Co which occur in July 20X2. This may not entail much extra work, as we will be conducting a review of subsequent events anyway, as part of our audit of the individual financial statements.

It may be that Canary Co's year end will be changed to bring into line with the rest of the CS Group. If so, we need to obtain copies of the documentary evidence to demonstrate that this has been done.

**Time apportionment of results**

When performing analytical procedures on the consolidated financial statements, we must be careful that when comparing this year's results with prior periods, we are making reasonable comparisons. This is because Canary Co's results are only included since the date of acquisition on 1 February 20X2 and comparative figures are not restated. Calculations such as return on capital employed will also be distorted, as the consolidated statement of financial position at 31 July 20X2 includes Canary Co's assets and liabilities in full, but the consolidated statement of profit or loss will only include six months' profit generated from those assets.

**Materiality**

Materiality needs to be assessed based on the new, enlarged group structure. Materiality for the group financial statements as a whole shall be determined when establishing the overall group audit strategy. The addition of Canary Co to the group during the year is likely to cause materiality to be different from previous years, possibly affecting audit strategy and the extent of testing in some areas.

**Additional time and resource**

Finally, we must ensure that sufficient time and resource is allocated to the audit of the consolidated financial statements as there will be additional work to perform on auditing the acquisition itself, including the goodwill asset, the fair value of assets acquired, the cash outflows, the contingent consideration, and the notes to the financial statements. As this is a complex area we should consider allocating this work to a senior, experienced member of the audit team. Relevant risks of material misstatement and audit procedures in respect of goodwill are discussed later in these notes.

**(b)    Risks of material misstatement**

**General matters**

Changes to corporate structure such as large acquisitions, moving into new lines of business and the installation of significant new IT systems related to financial reporting may indicate risks of material misstatement. The CS Group has been involved in all three of these during the financial year, so the audit generally should be approached as high risk.

### Goodwill

The client has determined goodwill arising on the acquisition of Canary Co to be $45 million, which is material to the consolidated financial statements, representing 8.2% of total assets. The various components of goodwill have specific risks attached. For the consideration, the contingent element of the consideration is inherently risky, as its measurement involves a judgment as to the probability of the amount being paid.

Currently, the full amount of contingent consideration is recognised, indicating that the amount is certain to be paid. IFRS 3 *Business Combinations* requires that contingent consideration is recognised at fair value at the time of the business combination, meaning that the probability of payment should be used in measuring the amount of consideration that is recognised at acquisition. This part of the consideration could therefore be overstated, if the assessment of probability of payment is incorrect.

Another risk is that the contingent consideration does not appear to have been discounted to present value as required by IFRS 3, again indicating that it is overstated.

The same risk factors apply to the individual financial statements of Crow Co, in which the cost of investment is recognised as a non-current asset.

The other component of the goodwill calculation is the value of identifiable assets acquired, which IFRS 3 requires to be measured at fair value at the date of acquisition. This again is inherently risky, as estimating fair value can involve uncertainty. Possibly the risk is reduced somewhat as the fair values have been determined by an external firm.

Goodwill should be tested for impairment annually according to IAS 36 *Impairment of Assets,* and a test should be performed in the year of acquisition, regardless of whether indicators of impairment exist. There is therefore a risk that goodwill may be overstated if management has not conducted an impairment test at the year-end. If the impairment review were to indicate that goodwill is overstated, there would be implications for the cost of investment recognised in Crow Co's financial statements, which may also be overstated.

### Loan stock

Crow Co has issued loan stock for $100 million, representing 18.2% of total assets, therefore this is material to the consolidated financial statements. The loan will be repaid at a significant premium of $20 million, which should be recognised as finance cost over the period of the loan using the amortised cost measurement method according to IFRS 9 *Financial Instruments.* A risk of misstatement arises if the premium relating to this financial year has not been included in finance costs.

In addition, finance costs could be understated if interest payable has not been accrued. The loan carries 5% interest per annum, and six months should be accrued by the 31 July year end, amounting to $2.5 million. Financial liabilities and finance costs will be understated if this has not been accrued.

There is also a risk of inadequate disclosure regarding the loan in the notes to the financial statements. IFRS 7 *Financial Instruments: Disclosures* requires narrative and numerical disclosures relating to financial instruments that give rise to risk exposure. Given the materiality of the loan, it is likely that disclosure would be required.

The risks described above are relevant to Crow Co's individual financial statements as well as the consolidated financial statements.

## Online sales

There is a risk that revenue is not recognised at the correct time, as it can be difficult to establish with online sales when the revenue recognition criteria of IFRS 15 *Revenue from Contracts with Customers* have been met. This could mean that revenue and profits are at risk of over or understatement. This is a significant issue as 30% of Canary Co's sales are made online, which approximates to sales of $4.8 million or 3.6% of this year's consolidated revenue, and will be a higher percentage of total sales next year when a full year of Canary Co's revenue is consolidated.

Prior to the acquisition of Canary Co, the CS Group had no experience of online sales, which means that there will not yet be a group accounting policy for online revenue recognition.

There may also be risks arising from the system not operating effectively or that controls are deficient leading to inaccurate recording of sales.

## Canary Co management

As this is the first time that Canary Co's management will be involved with group financial reporting, they will be unfamiliar with the processes used and information required by the CS Group in preparing the consolidated financial statements. There is a risk that information provided may be inaccurate or incomplete, for example in relation to inter-company transactions.

## Financial performance

Looking at the consolidated revenue and profit figures, it appears that the group's results are encouraging, with an increase in revenue of 8% and in profit before tax of 1.2%.

However, this comparison is distorted, as the 20X2 results include six months' revenue and profit from Canary Co, whereas the 20X1 results are purely Crow Co and Starling Co. A more meaningful comparison is made by removing Canary Co's results from the 202X figures, enabling a comparison of the results of Crow Co and Starling Co alone:

|  | $ million 20X2 forecast Crow Co | $ million 20X2 forecast Starling Co | $ million 20X2 forecast Crow Co and Starling Co | $ million 20X1 Actual Crow Co and Starling Co | % change |
|---|---|---|---|---|---|
| Revenue | 69.0 | 50.0 | 119.0 | 125.0 | (4.8%) |
| Profit before tax | 3.5 | 3.0 | 6.5 | 8.4 | (22.6%) |

The analysis reveals that Crow Co and Starling Co combined have a significantly reduced profit for the year, with revenue also slightly reduced. The apparent increase in costs may be caused by one-off costs to do with the acquisition of Canary Co, such as due diligence and legal costs. However there remains a risk of misstatement as costs could be overstated or revenue understated.

## Possible manipulation of financial statements

A risk of misstatement arises in relation to Canary Co as its financial statements have been prone to manipulation. In particular, its management may have felt pressure to overstate revenue and profits in order to secure a good sale price for the company. The existence of contingent consideration relating to the Group's post acquisition revenue is also a contributing factor to possible manipulation, as the Group will want to avoid paying the additional consideration.

### Grant received

Starling Co has received a grant of $35 million in respect of environmentally friendly capital expenditure, of which $25 million has already been spent. There is a risk in the recognition of the grant received. According to IAS 20 *Accounting for Government Grants and Disclosure of Government Assistance*, government grants shall be recognised as income over the periods necessary to match them with the related costs which they are intended to compensate. This means that the $35 million should not be recognised as income on receipt, but the income deferred and released to profit over the estimated useful life of the assets to which it relates. Alternatively, the cost of the asset could be reduced by the grant amount and subsequently a reduced depreciation charge should be recognised each year. There is a risk that the grant has been incorrectly treated and an inappropriate amount has been recognised in the statement of profit or loss this year.

A further risk arises in respect of the $10 million grant which has not yet been spent. Depending on the conditions of the grant, some or all of it may become repayable if it is not spent on qualifying assets within a certain time, and a provision may need to be recognised. $10 million represents 1.8% of consolidated assets, likely to be material to the CS Group financial statements. It is likely to form a much greater percentage of Starling Co's individual assets and therefore be more material in its individual financial statements.

### New IT system

A new system relevant to financial reporting was introduced to Crow Co and Starling Co which may indicate a risk of material misstatement. Errors may have occurred in transferring data from the old to the new system, and the controls over the new system may not be operating effectively.

Further, if Canary Co is not using the same IT system, there may be problems in performing its consolidation into the CS Group, for example, in reconciling inter-company balances.

### Starling Co finance director

One of the subsidiaries currently lacks a finance director. This means that there may be a lack of personnel with appropriate financial reporting and accounting skills, increasing the likelihood of error in Starling Co's individual financial statements, and meaning that inputs to the consolidated financial statements are also at risk of error. In addition, the reason for the finance director leaving should be ascertained, as it could indicate a risk of material misstatement, for example, if there was a disagreement over accounting policies.

(c) **Audit procedures**

(i) **Goodwill**

- Obtain the legal purchase agreement and confirm the date of the acquisition as being the date that control of Canary Co passed to Crow Co.

- From the legal purchase agreement, confirm the consideration paid, and the details of the contingent consideration, including its amount, date potentially payable, and the factors on which payment depends.

- Confirm that Canary Co is wholly owned by Crow Co through a review of its register of shareholders, and by agreement to legal documentation.

- Agree the cash payment of $125 million to cash book and bank statements.

- Review the board minutes for discussion regarding, and approval of, the purchase of Canary Co.

- Obtain the due diligence report prepared by the external provider and confirm the estimated fair value of net assets at acquisition.

- Discuss with management the reason for providing for the full amount of contingent consideration, and obtain written representation concerning the accounting treatment.

- Ask management to recalculate the contingent consideration on a discounted basis, and confirm goodwill is recognised on this basis in the consolidated financial statements.

---

*Tutorial note*

*Procedures relating to impairment testing of the goodwill at the year-end are not relevant to the requirement, which asks for procedures relating to the goodwill initially recognised on acquisition.*

---

**(ii) Government grant**

- Obtain the documentation relating to the grant to confirm the amount, the date the cash was received, and the terms on which the grant was awarded.

- Confirm the cash received to bank statement and cash book.

- Discuss with management the method of recognition of the amount received, in particular how much of the grant has been recognised in profit and the treatment of the amount deferred in the statement of financial position.

- For the $25 million spent on solar panels, inspect the purchase invoices to confirm the cost and description of items purchased.

- Review the grant documentation to ensure the intended upgrade to the production and packaging line will represent qualifying assets.

- Enquire of management when the $10 million will be spent and confirm that this is within the time frame specified in the grant conditions.

- Using the draft financial statements, confirm the accounting treatment outlined by discussion with management has been applied and recalculate the amounts recognised.

**(d) Ethical and professional issues**

Steve Eagle's threat that he will seek an alternative auditor unless the audit is cheaper and less intrusive than the prior year constitutes an intimidation threat to objectivity. This has arisen because Steve Eagle is trying to unduly influence the conduct of the audit.

The audit manager or partner should arrange a meeting with the senior management and the audit committee, if one exists, and they should explain how the audit has to be performed and how the fee is calculated.

They should take care to explain the professional standards which they have to comply with and the terms of the engagement which the client agreed to, specifically that management should provide all necessary documents and explanations deemed necessary by the auditor to collect sufficient appropriate evidence. It should be explained that due to the need to comply with these standards, they cannot guarantee to reduce either the volume of procedures or the audit fee.

Magpie & Co should also consider the integrity of Steve Eagle. If the audit firm considers any threat created too significant, then they may wish to resign from the engagement. If not, it may be necessary to use more senior, experienced staff on the assignment who are less likely to be intimidated by Steve Eagle while performing audit fieldwork.

If the audit proceeds, it should be ensured that the planning is performed by an appropriately experienced member of the audit team. This should be reviewed thoroughly by the audit manager and the partner to ensure that the procedures recommended are appropriate to the risk assessment performed. In this way Magpie & Co can ensure that any unnecessary, and potential time wasting, procedures are avoided.

The audit manager should then make sure that Steve Eagle is given adequate notice of the timing of the audit and provide him with a list of documentation which will be required during the course of the audit so that he may prepare for the visit by the audit team. The manager could also recommend that Steve Eagle and his team make specific time available to meet with the audit team and then request that the audit team use that time to ask all the necessary enquiries of the client. This should minimise any disruption experienced by the client during fieldwork.

The overdue fees create a self-interest threat. A self-interest threat may be created if fees due from an audit client remain unpaid for a long time, especially if not paid before the issue of the auditor's report for the following year.

The audit firm should determine the amount of fee which is unpaid, and whether it could be perceived to be a loan made to the client. It may be a relatively insignificant amount, and it may not be long overdue, in which case the threat to objectivity is not significant.

If the self-interest threat is significant, then no audit work should be performed until the fees are paid. This decision, and the reason for it, should be communicated to management or their audit committee, if possible.

**UK syllabus**: FRC Ethical Standard section 4 states that ordinarily, any outstanding fees for the previous audit period are paid before the audit firm commences any new audit work. Where they are not, it is important for the audit engagement partner to understand the nature of any disagreement or other issue.

### Conclusion

These briefing notes have shown that there are many risks of material misstatement largely due to the acquisition of Canary Co funded by an issue of loan stock. The audit strategy needs to be developed to focus on these areas. The ethical issues arising should be addressed as soon as possible to avoid causing delays and disputes for the forthcoming audit.

**Examiner's comments**

This question was based on the planning of a group audit when there had been a change in the group structure during the year. A wholly-owned subsidiary had been acquired, and candidates were given descriptions of some significant transactions and events, as well as limited financial information. It was obvious that the majority of candidates were familiar with this part of the syllabus. Candidates also seem comfortable with the style of the question and with the amount of information that had been given in the scenario.

Requirement (a) asked candidates to identify and explain the implications of the acquisition of the new subsidiary for the audit planning of the individual and consolidated financial statements. Most answers to this requirement identified the main planning implications, such as the determination of component and group materiality levels, the audit firm's need to obtain business understanding and assess the control environment in relation to the new subsidiary, and practical aspects such as the timings and resources needed for the group audit. Weaker answers to this requirement tended to just list out financial reporting matters, for example, that in the group financial statements related party transactions would have to be disclosed, and inter-company balances eliminated, but failed to link these points sufficiently well to audit planning implications.

The next part of the question dealt with risk assessment, requiring candidates to evaluate the risk of material misstatement to be considered in planning the individual and consolidated financial statements. The majority of answers focused on the correct type of risk (i.e. inherent and control risks), though some did discuss detection risks, which are irrelevant when evaluating the risk of material misstatement. Answers tended to cover a wide range of points but very often did not discuss the points in much depth. For example, almost all candidates identified that accounting for goodwill can be complex, leading to risk of misstatement, but few candidates explained the specific issues that give rise to risk. Similarly, most identified that the grant that had been received by one of the subsidiaries posed risk to the auditor, but most answers just suggested (often incorrectly) an accounting treatment and said little or nothing about the specific risk of misstatement. Many answers also went into a lot of detail about how particular balances and transactions should be audited, recommending procedures to be performed by the auditor, which was not asked for. Weaker answers simply stated an issue, for example, that a grant had been received, and said the risk was that it would not be accounted for properly. Clearly this is not an evaluation, as required, and will lead to minimal marks being awarded.

It was pleasing to see many candidates determining the materiality of the transactions and balances to the individual company concerned and to the group. However, candidates are reminded that materiality should be calculated in an appropriate manner. For example, the materiality of an asset or liability should usually be based on total assets and not on revenue. Candidates' understanding of the relevant financial reporting issues varied greatly. Most understood the basics of accounting for grants received, the revenue recognition issues caused by online sales, and that contingent consideration should be discounted to present value. However, knowledge on accounting for loan stock that had been issued by the parent company was inadequate, and very few properly discussed how the probability of paying the contingent consideration would affect its measurement at the reporting date.

Candidates attempting the UK and IRL adapted papers are reminded that the syllabus is based on International Financial Reporting Standards. References to, and discussions of, accounting treatments under UK GAAP are not correct and cannot be given credit. For example, a significant minority of answers discussed the amortisation of goodwill, which is not permitted under IFRS Standards (though it is correct under UK GAAP) and so could not be given any marks for this discussion.

The issues that were dealt with well included:

- The due diligence on Canary Co that had been provided by an external valuer

- The measurement of contingent consideration at present value

- Online sales creating risks to do with revenue recognition

- The control risks arising as a result of a new IT system

- The non-coterminous year end of Canary Co.

The issues that generally were inadequately evaluated included:

- The recognition and measurement of loan stock issued by Crow Co

- The classification and measurement of the grant received by Starling Co

- The financial information provided in relation to the group – very few answers performed any analytical review on the performance of the group and its components.

Requirement (c) asked candidates to design audit procedures to be performed. Generally candidates did well on this requirement, with many providing well described, relevant procedures. This represented a definite improvement from previous sittings.

The requirement covering ethical issues combined overdue fees with an intimidation threat and was well answered.

| Marking scheme | | |
|---|---|---|
| | | *Marks* |
| **(a)** | **Audit implications of Canary Co acquisition** | |
| | Up to 1½ marks for each implication explained (3 marks maximum for identification): | |
| | – Develop understanding of Canary Co business environment | |
| | – Document Canary Co accounting systems and controls | |
| | – Perform detailed analytical procedures on Canary Co | |
| | – Communicate with previous auditor | |
| | – Review prior year audit opinion for relevant matters | |
| | – Plan additional work on opening balances | |
| | – Determine that Canary Co is a significant component of the Group | |
| | – Plan for audit of intra-company transactions | |
| | – Issues on auditing the one month difference in financial year ends | |
| | – Impact of acquisition on analytical procedures at Group level | |
| | – Additional experienced staff may be needed, e.g. to audit complex goodwill | |
| | **Maximum** | **8** |

**(b)**     **Risk of material misstatement**

Up to 3 marks for each risk evaluated (unless a different maximum is indicated below):

–     General risks – diversification, change to group structure
–     Goodwill – contingent consideration – estimation uncertainty (probability of payment)
–     Goodwill – contingent consideration – measurement uncertainty (discounting)
–     Goodwill – fair value of net assets acquired
–     Goodwill – impairment
–     Identify that the issues in relation to cost of investment apply also in Crow Co's individual financial statements (1 mark)
–     Loan stock – premium on redemption
–     Loan stock – accrued interest
–     Loan stock – inadequate disclosure
–     Identify that the issues in relation to loan stock apply to cost of investment in Crow Co's individual financial statements (1 mark)
–     Online sales and risk relating to revenue recognition (additional 1 mark if calculation provided on online sales materiality to the Group)
–     No group accounting policy for online sales
–     Canary Co management have no experience regarding consolidation
–     Financial performance of Crow Co and Starling Co deteriorating
–     Possible misstatement of Canary Co revenue and profit
–     Grant received – capital expenditure
–     Grant received – amount not yet spent
–     New IT system
–     Starling Co – no finance director in place at year-end

|  |  |
|---|---|
| **Maximum** | 20 |

**(c)**     **Procedures**

Generally 1 mark per specific procedure:

**(i)     Goodwill**

–     Confirm acquisition date to legal documentation
–     Confirm consideration details to legal documentation
–     Agree 100% ownership, e.g. using Companies House search/register of significant shareholdings
–     Vouch consideration paid to bank statements/cash book
–     Review board minutes for discussion/approval of acquisition
–     Obtain due diligence report and agree net assets valuation
–     Discuss probability of paying contingent consideration
–     Obtain written representation regarding contingency
–     Recalculate goodwill including contingency on a discounted basis

**(ii)     Government grant**

–     Obtain and review grant documentation
–     Agree amount received to cash book and bank statement
–     Discuss method of recognition with management
–     Agree spend to invoices
–     Assess whether planned expenditure of remaining amount will be on qualifying assets
–     Enquire of management the time frame for additional spend
–     Review FS disclosure

|  |  |
|---|---|
| **Maximum** | 11 |

| | | | |
|---|---|---|---|
| **(d)** | **Ethical issues** | | |
| | – Intimidation threat to objectivity | | |
| | – Meet senior management and explain the terms of the audit | | |
| | – Explain need to follow professional standards | | |
| | – Consider integrity of Steve Eagle and implications for audit | | |
| | – Thorough performance and review of planning | | |
| | – Early notice of audit requirements and logistics | | |
| | – Self-interest threat created by overdue fees | | |
| | – Assess significance of outstanding fees | | |
| | – Delay audit until fees paid (1 max) | | |
| | | **Maximum** | **7** |

Professional marks for the overall presentation, structure and logical flow of the briefing notes, and for the clarity of the evaluation and discussion provided.

| | | | |
|---|---|---|---|
| | | **Maximum** | **4** |
| **Total** | | | **50** |

# Section 4

# ANSWERS TO PRACTICE QUESTIONS – SECTION B

## PLANNING AND CONDUCTING AN AUDIT OF HISTORICAL FINANCIAL INFORMATION

### 15    AWDRY

> **Top tutor tips**
>
> *Part (a) is a current issues and developments question relating to a revised auditing standard. Current issues and developments are usually highlighted in a technical article written by the examining team. Keep a look out for recent articles on the ACCA website.*
>
> *Part (b) asks for an evaluation of the client's accounting treatment, including the difficulties that might be encountered when auditing three accounting estimates. This requires a discussion of the subjectivity of the estimate and the extent to which the client will need to use their own judgment to determine the estimate. The question then asks for audit procedures in respect of the estimates. Audit procedures should be written in such a way that a member of the audit team can carry them out, therefore make sure they are sufficiently detailed. Audit procedures are used to obtain sufficient and appropriate evidence regarding the client's accounting treatment. Be clear about the source of the evidence and how the procedure should be carried out as vague procedures will not earn marks.*

**(a)    ISA 540 (Revised)** *Auditing Accounting Estimates and Related Disclosures*

The IAASB has issued International Standard on Auditing 540 (Revised) *Auditing Accounting Estimates and Related Disclosures* (ISA-540 (Revised)) which is effective for audits for periods beginning on or after 15 December 2019.

The IAASB has sought to make ISA-540 (Revised) scalable, recognising that the standard applies to all accounting estimates from the simplest depreciation calculation through to the most complex of derivative financial instruments and expected credit losses.

While the simpler accounting estimates will not generally give rise to high audit risk, many measurements based on estimates, including fair value measurements and impairments in relation to financial instruments, are imprecise and subjective in nature and will give rise to high inherent risk.

Such fair value and impairment assessments are likely to involve significant, complex judgments, for example, regarding market conditions, the timing of cash flows and the future intentions of the entity. The valuations will often involve complex models built on significant assumptions such as the predicted timing of cash flows, the most appropriate discount factor to use and judgments about probability weighted averages.

Management may not always have sufficient knowledge and experience in making these judgments. Moreover, there may even be a deliberate attempt by management to manipulate the value of an estimate in order to window dress the financial statements.

Professional scepticism is key to the audit of accounting estimates and ISA-540 (Revised) contains provisions which are designed to enhance the auditor's application of professional scepticism and a consideration of the potential for management bias.

Outreach activities with regulators and other key stakeholders pointed to the need for the IAASB to focus attention on revisions to ISA 540 *Auditing Accounting Estimates, Including Fair Value Accounting Estimates, and Related Disclosures*. Feedback from the IAASB's outreach projects revealed a perceived lack of consistency in the extent to which auditors obtained an understanding of accounting estimates together with evidence of insufficient and inappropriate work effort by auditors in this area.

The consultation process also identified a lack of professional scepticism being exercised by auditors and a need for more specific risk assessment requirements and more granular requirements regarding obtaining audit evidence.

It also identified a need to enhance communication between auditors and those charged with governance about accounting estimates and in particular the auditor's views about significant qualitative aspects of the entity's accounting practices.

The objective of ISA 540 is for the auditor to obtain sufficient appropriate evidence to evaluate whether accounting estimates and related disclosures are reasonable in the context of the relevant financial reporting framework or are misstated. Consequently, ISA-540 (Revised) aims to include enhanced risk assessment requirements and the draft standard emphasises that the risk of material misstatement in relation to the audit of accounting estimates is impacted by three key factors: complexity, the application of management judgment and estimation uncertainty.

The increased emphasis on the use of fair value measurement in IFRS Standards and the associated development of IFRS 13 *Fair Value Measurement* reflect the increasing complexity of the business environment. Furthermore, given the increased emphasis on the use of external sources in IFRS 13 and in making accounting estimates such as fair values, ISA-540 (Revised) aims to improve and clarify the requirements on the use of such information as it is in the public interest to do so.

These factors, together with the implementation of IFRS *9 Financial Instruments* and in particular its complex and highly subjective expected loss approach to the measurement of impairments and extensive disclosure requirements, highlighted a need to modernise ISA 540 for evolving financial reporting frameworks.

The risk that an entity's internal systems and controls fail to prevent and detect valuation errors needs to be assessed as part of the overall assessment of audit risk.

In relation to complex fair value and impairment estimates, a particular problem is that the measurement is likely to be performed infrequently for external reporting purposes and outside the normal accounting and management systems. This is especially true where the valuation is performed by an external specialist. As a non-routine event, therefore, the assessment of fair value is likely not to have the same level of monitoring or controls as a day-to-day business transaction and may give rise to high control risk.

The auditor should always seek to manage detection risk at an acceptable level through effective planning and execution of audit procedures. However, the audit team may lack knowledge and experience in dealing with the estimation technique in question and therefore may be unlikely to detect errors in the valuation and modelling techniques applied by the client. Any resulting over-reliance on an external specialist could also lead to errors not being identified.

**(b)    Difficulties in auditing accounting estimates and procedures**

**(i)     Cash-settled share-based payment scheme**

The expense recognised this year of $825,000 in respect of the cash-settled share-based payment scheme represents 11.1% of profit before tax and is therefore material to Awdry Co's statement of profit or loss for the year. The related liability of $825,000 which would be recognised on the statement of financial position is on the borderline of materiality to assets at 1.4%.

IFRS 2 *Share-Based Payment* requires that for cash-settled share-based payment transactions, the entity should measure the services acquired and the liability incurred at the fair value of the liability. Moreover, it states that until the liability is settled, the entity should remeasure the fair value of the liability at the end of each reporting period and at the date of settlement, with any changes in fair value recognised in profit or loss for the period.

In the case of Awdry Co, the expense and the associated liability has been calculated based on the fair value of the rights as at the reporting date and the treatment therefore complies with the requirements of IFRS 2 ($4.50 × 550,000 × 1/3 = $825,000).

IFRS 2 also requires that the amount recognised as an expense for cash-settled share-based payments should be based on the best available estimate of the number of awards which are expected to vest. The entity must therefore estimate the number of awards which are expected to vest.

In this case, management's estimate that all 55 staff will qualify for the rights appears to be based on a perception of good historic staff relations which may be inaccurate and the expectation that none of the eligible staff will leave over the three-year vesting period may prove to be unrealistic. The predictive nature of management's estimate in this regard represents a challenge to the auditor as it is difficult to obtain reliable evidence.

The fair value estimate of $4.50 is based on an options pricing models which is an example of a complex valuation model which, according to ISA-540 (Revised), is built on significant estimates and assumptions and is therefore challenging to audit. The initial choice of which option-pricing model to use is also a matter of judgment and whichever model is selected, it will incorporate judgmental inputs such as the current risk-free interest rate and measures of share price volatility.

**Procedures:**

- Obtain a copy of the contractual documentation for the share-based payment scheme and supporting file notes detailing principal terms and confirm:
  - grant date and vesting date
  - number of executives and senior employees awarded share appreciation rights
  - number of share appreciation rights awarded to each individual member of staff
  - conditions attaching to the share appreciation rights.

- Perform an assessment of the appropriateness of the model used to value the share appreciation rights and confirm that it is in line with the requirements of IFRS 2.

- Obtain details of the external expert used and assess the appropriateness of their appointment by considering their professional certification, experience, reputation and objectivity.

- Perform a review of the expert's valuation including an assessment of the assumptions used in order to determine the fair value of the share appreciation rights.

- Obtain details of historic staff turnover rates obtained from the human resources department including actual data for the first year of the vesting period and consider this in conjunction with the assumptions made by management.

- Perform a review of the forecast staffing levels through to the end of the vesting period including an assessment of the reasonableness of the assumptions used and their consistency with other budgets and forecasts.

- Discuss the basis of staff retention assumptions with management and challenge their appropriateness.

- Perform sensitivity analyses on both the valuation model and the staffing forecasts.

**(ii)     Regulatory penalties**

The expense recognised in this year's statement of profit or loss for the year of $1.3 million is material to both profit (17.6%) and assets (2.2%).

According to IAS 37 *Provisions, Contingent Liabilities and Contingent Assets*, the fine should be measured at its present value at the reporting date. IAS 37 states that where the effect of the time value of money is material, the amount of a provision should be the present value of the expenditures expected to be required to settle the obligation and that the discount rate used in the calculation should be a pre-tax rate which reflects current market assessments of the time value of money and the risks specific to the liability.

The cash flows for the repayment of the fine over the ten years should therefore be discounted at an appropriate rate to present value as at 28 February 20X9.

The audit of the provision represents a challenge for the auditor in a number of respects. First, it is difficult to estimate the amount payable as it has not yet been finalised and the amount currently recognised is an estimate based on management's judgment. These difficulties are compounded by IAS 37 requirements to measure the provision at present value.

The measurement process therefore also requires management to predict the payment dates and to identify an appropriate pre-tax rate to be applied as the discount factor. Both of these will require a significant level of management judgment which will be a challenge for the auditor to obtain sufficient relevant and reliable evidence on.

Moreover, there is also the possibility of other provisions being needed in relation to the costs of remedying the safety issues which the regulator has identified and in relation to other potentially unidentified safety problems. Here, addressing the completeness assertion will represent a key challenge to the auditor as it is inherently difficult to predict all of the costs to be incurred in the future especially when they have not yet been determined.

**Procedures:**

- Obtain a copy of the regulator's notice detailing the date of the issue and any indication of the amount of the penalty to be paid by Awdry Co.

- Obtain a copy of any draft instalment agreement detailing the timing and amount of each repayment.

- Review Awdry Co's correspondence with the regulator for evidence of the amount payable and details of the repayment schedule.

- Confirm to post year-end cash book and bank statements if any amounts have been paid after the year end.

- Inspect Awdry Co's correspondence with its lawyers in order to ascertain current status of negotiations and the views of its legal advisers.

- Review Awdry Co's cash flow statements and forecasts in order to assess the company's ability to pay the instalments.

- Enquire of management in relation to the current status of the negotiations; the need to measure the provision at present value and their non-compliance with IAS 37 (i.e. their failure to measure the provision at present value).

- Review the board minutes for evidence of management's discussion of the penalty, any planned remedial action to address safety issues and any other possible safety issues.

- Discuss with management the need for the company to perform a calculation of the present value of the provision (including identification of an appropriate discount rate).

**(iii)** **Property development**

The proposed valuation of the property at $4.9 million represents 8.4% of assets and is material to Awdry Co's statement of financial position as at 28 February 20X9.

According to IFRS 13 *Fair Value Measurement*, the fair value measurement of a non-financial asset should take into account a market participant's ability to generate economic benefits by using the asset in its highest and best use or by selling it to another market participant who would use the asset in its highest and best use.

The audit of the property development will be challenging for the auditor first because judgment will be required in order to identify the property's highest and best use per IFRS 13. The auditor must ensure, for example, that the valuation is compared to the property's fair value in its existing use as well as in any other potential uses. Indeed, there may be other potential uses which have not been considered.

IFRS 13 also states that the highest and best use of a non-financial asset such as a property must be:

– physically possible: this will therefore require independent expert confirmation that the conversion can be successfully undertaken

– legally permissible: this will require obtaining confirmation of formal permission from the local planning authority; and

– financially feasible: this will require a detailed assessment of whether Awdry Co will have sufficient cash flows in order to fund the development through to completion to complete development.

Overall therefore, the auditor will need extensive audit evidence, much of it from third parties, in order to confirm management's judgment that conversion into residential apartments represents the highest and best use of its former maintenance depot.

According to IFRS 13, when considering alternative uses for non-financial assets, the valuation should include all costs associated with the alternative uses. Hence, if the proposed development does represent the highest and best use of the property, the valuation should be adjusted for all of its associated costs.

The proposed valuation at $4.9 million is not therefore in compliance with IFRS 13 and on the basis of the information available, the valuation should be $3,527,000 (i.e. $4.9 million – $1.2 million – $173,000). If the additional costs are fairly stated therefore, the property is currently overstated by $1.373 million ($4.9 million – $3,527,000).

The auditor will, however, need external confirmation of the $173,000 in fees from the local building regulator and will also need to obtain sufficient appropriate audit evidence that the conversion costs of $1.2 million are fairly stated.

The conversion costs will present a particular challenge to the auditor as they will be based on the estimation of industry experts and the amounts will be inherently uncertain. There may be unforeseen additional costs payable to complete the conversion which will be difficult for the auditor to identify and quantify.

**Procedures:**

- Physically inspect the building to assess its condition and to perform an initial assessment of whether it might be suitable for conversion into residential apartments.

- Agree the carrying amount of the property to Awdry Co's non-current asset register.

- Obtain a valuation of the completed development by an independent external expert and agree the basis of valuation is in line with the requirements of IFRS 13.

- Obtain details of the external expert and assess their expertise and objectivity through assessment of their professional certification, experience, reputation and connections with Awdry Co.

- Inspect the quotation or contract with the building contractor to confirm the expected cost of $1.2 million.

- Inspect the planning permission documentation from the local authority in order to ensure that the proposed alternative use of property has been approved.

- Inspect correspondence with the local building regulator confirming the fees of $173,000.

- Discuss with management alternative uses of the property, explaining IFRS 13's valuation principles and confirming that no additional fees or costs will be payable.

- Review board minutes for evidence of management's discussion of the development.

- Review Awdry Co's cash flow statements and forecasts to ensure the project is financially feasible.

- Obtain written representations from management confirming all details and costs concerning development have been disclosed to the auditor.

---

**Examiner's comments**

This question was a 25-mark compulsory question which focused on the discussion of a published exposure draft and evaluation of accounting treatment for specific estimates given in the question scenario along with audit procedures to be performed.

Requirement (a) for 8 marks, required candidates to discuss accounting estimates as being an area of high risk and the reasons for the development of the exposure draft. Overall candidates had a good attempt at this requirement, and candidates that had read the article written by the examining team had the potential to score highly.

Requirement (b) for a total of 17 marks, was split into three sections and required candidates to evaluate the accounting treatment of three estimates given in the scenario. A large number of candidates demonstrated a weak understanding of the SBR syllabus and scored very poor marks. It was disappointing to note a lack of understanding of provisions. Only a limited number of candidates correctly stated the rule under IAS 37 *Provisions, Contingent Liabilities and Contingent Assets,* in relation to where the effect of the time value of money

---

is material the provision should be recognised at present value. There was a clear indication in the question that this was relevant and it was disappointing that more candidates did not identify this.

The quality of answers for this question was generally of a weaker standard and candidates were not able to demonstrate application of their knowledge of SBR in an audit context to the scenario.

| | ACCA marking guide | Marks |
|---|---|---|
| **(a)** | **ISA-540 (Revised) Auditing Accounting Estimates and Related Disclosures**<br>Generally 1 mark per point.<br>**Accounting estimates are source of high audit risk:**<br>– Inherent risk:<br>  – Subjectivity/uncertainty<br>  – Deliberate manipulation<br>  – Complexity<br>– Control risk:<br>  – Non-routine transactions<br>– Detection risk:<br>  – Audit team may lack knowledge/experience; and<br>  – May over rely on auditor's or expert<br>**Reasons for ISA-540 (Revised):**<br>– Lack of consistency in extent to which auditors obtained understanding of accounting estimates<br>– Insufficient and inappropriate work effort by auditors<br>– Lack of professional scepticism exercised by auditors<br>– Need for more specific risk assessment requirements and more granular requirements regarding obtaining audit evidence<br>– Need to modernise ISA 540 for evolving financial reporting frameworks<br>– Increasingly complex business environment and increased complexity in IFRS Standards<br>– Increased emphasis on use of fair value in IFRS Standards (related need for IFRS 13)<br>– IFRS 9's expected losses impairment model and related disclosures<br>– Need to enhance communication between auditors and TCWG about accounting estimates<br>– Professional scepticism is key in the audit of accounting estimates; ISA-540 (Revised) contains provisions designed to enhance auditor's application of professional scepticism and consideration of potential for management bias<br>– Given increased use of external sources in making accounting estimates, ISA-540 (Revised) aims to improve and clarify requirements on use of such information as it is in public interest to do so | |
| | **Maximum marks** | **8** |
| **(b)** | **Difficulties and procedures**<br>Generally up to 1 mark for each difficulty evaluated and each relevant procedure designed.<br>**(i)  Cash-settled share-based payments**<br>– Material expense to profit and borderline material to assets (with calculation(s))<br>– Treatment complies with IFRS 2 rules for accounting for cash settled share-based payments | |

Difficulties when performing audit:

- Management assumption of 100% staff retention may be unrealistic
- Predicted staff retention is estimation based on historic trends and future expectations; actual outcomes unlikely to correspond exactly
- Options pricing models are complex and challenging to audit
- Judgment involved in which option pricing model to use
- Option pricing models include judgmental inputs such as current risk-free interest rate and measures of share price volatility

Procedures:

- Obtain copy of share-based payments agreement and supporting file notes detailing principal terms (½ mark per term agreed)
- Perform assessment of appropriateness of model used to value rights/options
- Obtain details of external expert used including assessment of professional certification, experience, reputation and objectivity
- Critically review expert's valuation including assessment of assumptions used to determine fair value of the SARs
- Obtain details of historic staff turnover rates obtained from human resources/payroll department
- Review of forecast staffing levels through to end of vesting period including assessment of reasonableness of assumptions based on auditor's knowledge and understanding of client
- Discuss basis of staff retention assumptions with management and challenge their appropriateness
- Perform sensitivity analyses on valuation model and staffing forecasts

|  | |
|---|---|
| **Maximum marks** | 6 |

(ii) **Regulatory penalties**

- Material expense to profit and assets (with calculation)
- Expense and provision should have been recognised at present value per IAS 37

Difficulties when performing audit:

- Difficult to estimate final amount payable as not yet finalised; amount currently recognised is based on management's judgment
- Difficulties are compounded by need to measure at PV and therefore also predict payment dates and identify appropriate pre-tax rate; both require significant level of management judgment
- Also possibility of other provisions needed, e.g. for costs of correcting current issues and/or for other unidentified safety problems
- Addressing completeness assertion here is challenging and also difficult to predict as costs to be incurred in future and have not yet been determined

Procedures:

- Obtain copy of regulator's notice detailing date of issue and any quantification of amount of penalty payable by Awdry Co
- Obtain copy of any draft instalment agreement detailing the timing and amount of each repayment
- Review correspondence with regulator for evidence of amount payable and details of repayment schedule
- Confirm payment to bank statement
- Review correspondence with Awdry Co's lawyers to ascertain current status of negotiations and views of legal advisors
- Review of cash flow statements and forecasts to assess company's ability to pay instalments

|  |  |
|---|---|
| – Discuss with management the current status of negotiations; accounting treatment and non-compliance with IAS 37 (failure to measure at PV) | |
| – Review board minutes for evidence of discussion of penalty, remedial action to address safety issues and any other possible safety issues | |
| – Request client calculation of present value (including identification of appropriate discount rate) | |
| **Maximum marks** | **6** |

**(iii) Property development**
- Material to assets (with calculation)
- Incorrect valuation (non-compliance with IFRS 13); FV should be adjusted for all costs associated with alternative use

Difficulties when performing audit:
- Conversion costs will be based on estimation and will be inherently uncertain – hence challenge to obtain sufficient appropriate audit evidence that all costs have been identified and accurately quantified
- Judgment required to identify property's highest and best use per IFRS 13
- Per IFRS 13, highest and best use must be:

  physically possible – requires assessment of construction industry expert

  legally permissible – requires confirmation from local planning authority

  financially feasible – requires assessment of whether Awdry Co will have sufficient funds to complete development
- Valuation must be compared to the property's fair value in its existing use and other potential uses
- May be other potential uses which have not been considered.

Procedures:
- Physical inspection of building by auditor
- Agree carrying amount to non-current asset register
- Obtain valuation of completed development by independent external expert
- Obtain details of external expert including assessment of professional certification, experience, reputation and objectivity
- Inspect quotation/contract with building contractor to confirm cost of $1.2 million
- Inspect planning permission from local authority in order to ensure alternative use of property has been approved
- Inspect correspondence with local council confirming fees of $173,000
- Discuss with management all alternative uses of property, explaining IFRS 13 valuation principles and confirming no further fees/costs payable
- Review board minutes for evidence of discussion of development
- Review cash flow statements and forecasts to ensure project is financially feasible for Awdry Co
- Obtain written representations from management confirming all details and costs concerning development have been disclosed to auditor

| | |
|---|---|
| **Maximum marks** | **5** |
| **Total** | **25** |

# COMPLETION, REVIEW AND REPORTING

**16    LIFESON**  *Walk in the footsteps of a top tutor*

*Top tutor tips*

*Part (a) requires discussion of three accounting matters. First, consider the materiality of the issue. Next discuss the appropriate accounting treatment and give the risks of material misstatement that would arise if the appropriate treatment is not followed. Finally, the evidence is what you would expect to be recorded on the audit file when you come to review it. Be specific about the evidence in the same way as you would be specific when writing an audit procedure.*

*For part (b) you need to state the impact to the auditor's report if the client does not amend the financial statements. Consider the aggregate effect of the misstatements to assess whether there is a material misstatement. State the impact to both the report and opinion as a result of the issues. Don't waste time stating the reporting implications if the issues are corrected as this is not part of the requirement.*

**(a)    (i)    Sale and leaseback transaction**

**Matters**

**Transfer of control**

The auditor needs to consider the correct treatment of the sale and leaseback transaction as required by IFRS 16 *Leases* which requires that an assessment should be performed based on the criteria specified in IFRS 15 *Revenue from Contracts with Customers* as to whether control of the asset has been retained by the seller or whether it has passed to the buyer.

Control of an asset is defined by IFRS 15 as the ability to direct the use of and obtain substantially all of the remaining benefits from the asset. This includes the ability to prevent others from directing the use of and obtaining the benefits from the asset. The benefits related to the asset are the potential cash flows which may be obtained directly or indirectly.

**Right-of-use asset**

In this case, the lease term of ten years appears short compared to the asset's remaining life which is expected to exceed 50 years and given the demand for retail properties for rent in the area, it seems likely that Clive Co will direct the use of and obtain substantially all of the remaining benefits from the asset including the potential cash flows in the future.

On the basis of the information available, the proposed derecognition of the property in Lifeson Co's financial statements and the recording of the transaction as a sale in accordance with IFRS 15 appears to be correct. Lifeson Co should therefore derecognise the property and recognise a right-of-use asset based on the proportion of the previous carrying amount of the asset effectively retained under the terms of the lease.

In addition, it should recognise a financial liability based on the present value of the lease payments and any gain or loss arising on the transaction should be recognised in profit or loss for the year.

In this case, the asset has been correctly derecognised but the auditor should investigate whether the company has recognised the right-of-use asset at the correct amount.

**Evidence expected to be on file:**

- A copy of the sale and leaseback agreement reviewed to confirm the key details including in particular the rights of the lessee and the lessor to control the asset.

- A working paper detailing all key aspects of the agreement required to identify the detailed accounting treatment including the sale proceeds, rental amounts and timings, the lease term and the interest rate implicit in the lease.

- Agreement of the sale proceeds as per the sale agreement to the cash book and/or bank statement to confirm the correct calculation of the gain or loss on disposal.

- Notes of discussions with management in relation to the transfer of control to confirm whether the correct treatment of the sale and leaseback arrangement has been determined.

- A copy of any client working papers in relation to the calculation of the right-of-use asset to identify whether the client has recognised the right-of-use asset at the correct amount.

- A review of the board minutes for evidence of management's discussion of the sale and leaseback transaction and any evidence in relation to the transfer of control.

- A review of the local property market including trade journals, press articles, official statistics to confirm high demand for retail leases.

- A review of surveyor reports on the property to confirm the expected remaining life of the property.

- A copy of the client's working papers for the calculation of the present value of the lease payments and a recalculation of the present value of the lease payments by the auditor in order to form a basis for confirming the detailed accounting treatment of the lease.

- Agreement of the carrying amount of the property to the non-current asset register to determine whether the correct amount has been derecognised and whether the gain or loss on disposal has been recorded correctly.

- A schedule calculating any gain or loss on the transaction, recalculated by the audit team and confirming that it only represents the gain or loss on rights transferred to Clive Co.

- Review of the draft financial statements to confirm that details of the sale and leaseback transaction, such as the gain or loss arising on the transaction, have been disclosed in line with the requirements of IFRS 16.

(ii)    **Investment property**

**Matters**

**Materiality**

The carrying amount of the investment property represents 2.6% ($353,000/ $13.8 million) of Lifeson Co's total assets at the reporting date and is material to the financial statements.

**Classification as investment property**

The auditor should consider whether the requirements of IAS 40 *Investment Property* have been satisfied and confirm if the warehouse held by Lifeson Co is actually an investment property. IAS 40 defines an investment property as land and/or buildings held to earn rentals or for capital appreciation, or both.

Lifeson Co's warehouse has been held to earn rentals and for capital appreciation from 1 April 20X4 and therefore qualifies as an investment property from this date. The fact that the property has not yet been let by the reporting date does not impact on this classification. The end of owner-occupation of the warehouse is evidence of the change in use to an investment property.

**Fair value**

The warehouse is recognised at fair value of $353,000 and according to IAS 40, the fair value model is acceptable provided the treatment of any other investment property held by Lifeson Co is consistent.

On transfer of an owner-occupied property recognised at depreciated historical cost, which has not been previously impaired, to investment property carried at fair value, IAS 40 requires that any resulting increase in the carrying amount should be recognised in other comprehensive income as a revaluation surplus within equity. Thereafter, any further increase in fair value is recognised in profit or loss for the year.

In this case, Lifeson Co should recognise the initial increase of $25,000 ($348,000 – $323,000) in other comprehensive income rather than in its profit for the year and the additional increase of $5,000 ($353,000 – $348,000) which arises during the current year should be recognised in this year's profit or loss. Lifeson Co's recognition of the full $30,000 gain in its profit before tax for the current year is incorrect and therefore results in an overstatement of profit by $25,000.

**Evidence expected to be on file:**

*   Notes of discussions with management to confirm its intention to hold the property to earn rentals and for capital appreciation.

*   Inspection of title deeds held by Lifeson Co to confirm its ownership of the investment property.

*   Board minutes for evidence of management discussion of the change of use and for confirmation of the date when owner-occupation ceased.

*   Record of the physical inspection of the building by the auditor in order to confirm its general condition and that it is no longer occupied by Lifeson Co.

- Agreement of the accounting policy to the notes to the financial statements this year and in previous year, to confirm that the fair value model is to be adopted and is consistent with any other investment properties held.

- A market valuation of the building by an independent and external auditor's expert at the date of the change of use and at the reporting date to determine the respective fair values and the resulting gains.

- Details of the external expert valuer and a working paper detailing the assessment of their professional qualifications, experience, reputation, independence and objectivity.

- Agreement of the carrying amount at the date of the change of use to the non-current asset register to confirm the correct amount of the fair value gain.

- Written representations from management confirming the change of use, the relevant date and future intentions.

- Notes of discussions with management in relation to the incorrect recording of the gain and the need to include the error in the auditor's schedule of uncorrected misstatements.

- Review the disclosures made in the financial statements, such as details of the external valuation, to ensure they comply with the requirements of IAS 40.

**(iii)   Asset impairment**

**Matters**

**Materiality**

The carrying amount of the shopping mall represents 64.1% ($8.85 million/$13.8 million) of Lifeson Co's total assets at the reporting date and is therefore highly material to the company's financial statements.

**Value in use**

The auditor should consider whether the client's calculation of the shopping mall's recoverable amount based on value in use is in line with the requirements of IAS 36 *Impairment of Assets*. This should include an assessment of whether the client has used an appropriate discount factor for calculating value in use based on the rate which reflects current market assessments of the time value of money and the risks specific to the asset.

In line with IAS 36's definition of recoverable amount as the higher of its fair value less costs to sell and its value in use, the auditor should also consider whether the fair value less selling costs of the shopping mall exceeds its value in use.

**Reversal of impairment loss**

IAS 36 requires that the increased carrying amount of an asset, such as property, attributable to a reversal of an impairment loss should not exceed the carrying amount which would have been determined, net of depreciation, had no impairment loss been recognised for the asset in prior years. In this case, therefore, recognition of the reversal of the impairment loss should be calculated as follows.

|  | $million | $million |
|---|---|---|
| Carrying amount as at 31 March 20X5 prior to recognition of impairment reversal ($8.25m × 18/19) |  | 7.816 |
| Recoverable amount based on impairment review as at 31 March 20X5 | 8.850 |  |
| Capped to $9.5m × 18/20 = | 8.550 | 8.550 |
| Impairment reversal to be recognised |  | 0.734 |

As a result of Lifeson Co's failure to limit the impairment reversal to $0.734 million, profit and assets are overstated by $300,000 (1.034m – 0.734m).

**Evidence expected to be on file:**

- Agreement of the opening balances for the property to the non-current asset register as at 1 April 20X4 to confirm the correct amount has been brought forward in the client's working papers.

- Physical inspection of the shopping mall property to confirm its condition, occupancy level and to assess the reasonableness of the depreciation policy and forecast cash flows for the value in use calculation.

- Copy of the client working papers for impairment review giving evidence of the client's basis for assessing the fair value less selling costs of the mall and detailed calculations of its value in use.

- Copy of the client's cash flow forecasts and budgets supporting the value in use calculations.

- Notes of discussions with management in relation to the bases for the calculation of recoverable amount including an assessment of the reasonableness of the assumptions used by management in its forecasts and calculations and the appropriateness of the discount factor used in the value in use calculations.

- Written representations attesting to the reasonableness of its assumptions and other related management judgements.

- A recalculation of the value in use of the shopping mall by the auditor in order to confirm the accuracy of the client's calculation.

- Sensitivity analyses on the forecasts and the value in use calculations in order to assess the impact of any changes in the key assumptions.

- External confirmation of the shopping mall's net realisable value by an appropriately qualified, independent expert in order to ensure the recoverable amount has been correctly determined.

- Notes of discussions with management in relation to the incorrect recording of the impairment reversal and the need to include the error in the auditor's schedule of uncorrected misstatements.

**(b)** **Implications for the auditor's report**

Based on the analysis and discussion above, there are two misstatements in the financial statements in relation to the investment property and shopping mall which may have implications for this year's auditor's report.

**Investment property**

Lifeson Co has recorded the increase in the carrying amount of $30,000 on the warehouse in the statement of profit or loss for the year. The increase in fair value of $25,000 on transfer of the property to investment property should have been recorded in other comprehensive income and profit is therefore overstated by $25,000 in the year.

This overstatement represents 1.2% of profit before tax and therefore is immaterial in isolation. As this misstatement is immaterial, the auditor's report would not need to be modified and it will be at the discretion of management to make the adjustment.

If management intends to leave this as an uncorrected misstatement, written confirmation of its immaterial nature should be obtained via a written representation.

**Shopping mall**

Lifeson Co has incorrectly recognised the full impairment reversal of $1.034 million in profit for the year. As per IAS 36, the reversal of an impairment loss should not exceed the carrying amount which would have been determined had no impairment loss been recognised. Based on depreciation over a 20-year useful life, the carrying amount of the asset should be capped at $8.550 million and the reversal of the impairment to be recognised at $0.734 million ($8.550 million – $7.816 million).

Assets and profit are currently overstated by $300,000 representing 2.2% of total assets and 14% of profit before tax which is material to both the statement of financial position and statement of profit or loss.

**Overall impact on the auditor's report**

The misstatement in relation to the shopping mall is individually material and if management fails to amend the financial statements, the auditor's opinion should be modified due to the material, but not pervasive, misstatement of the shopping mall in relation to both the statement of financial position and the statement of profit or loss for the year.

The auditor's report should include a qualified 'except for' opinion paragraph at the start of report.

This paragraph should be followed immediately by a basis for qualified opinion paragraph which should explain the reasons for the qualified auditor's opinion and which should quantify the impact of the matters identified on the financial statements.

---

**Examiner's comments**

This question was set at the completion stage of an audit and proved difficult for many candidates. In part (a) three property-related issues were described for an audit client of the firm and candidates were required to analyse the matters to be considered (e.g. materiality, accounting treatments permitted, how that applied to the client in question, potential errors) and the evidence that would be expected on file in order to be able to conclude on the issues. Topics covered were a sale and leaseback, where control had passed to the lessor, an investment property and the reversal of an impairment relating to a property being used by the company.

---

Very few candidates appeared to understand the concept of control underpinning the sale and lease back – often candidates performed the appropriate test of considering the proportion of the life of the property that would be leased back but then incorrectly concluded that renting the property for one fifth of its life was effectively still owning the property. What was more concerning was that a significant minority of candidates were still discussing the concept of operating and finance leases and applying outdated accounting standards to a topic that has been examinable under IFRS16 *Leases* for several sessions.

The investment property requirement was handled better and many candidates were able to describe the option of holding the property at fair value with gains and losses being taken to the statement of profit and loss. Many candidates though then went on to say the property should then be depreciated or that it wasn't an investment property despite not being owner occupied or used within the business.

With regards to the impairment reversal, candidate performance was mixed. Many candidates realised that the reversal would be restricted and were able to obtain credit even if they didn't appreciate that the reversal was not restricted to the previous impairment charge but should be restricted to the written down value the asset would have had, had it not been impaired in the first place. Beyond that however many candidates suggested that the excess value of that amount could be recognised within Other Comprehensive Income which is not the case unless the company is using a revaluation model rather than a cost model for properties.

Many candidates were able to identify relevant audit procedures for the above accounting issues. In some instances this was the case even where they did not appear to fully understand the accounting issues themselves.

Part (b) required candidates to consider the effect of the misstatements in the investment property and the reversal of the impairment on the auditor's report. Here candidates often assessed the significance of the misstatement by reference to the entire asset value rather than the error amount, resulting in the conclusion that an immaterial misstatement would result in an adverse opinion. It was also common here that where a candidate calculated that the error was immaterial, they would go on to conclude that it was in fact material. It is vital that candidates appreciate the concept of materiality and are able to correctly apply it at this level. As noted in previous sessions, there was a significant minority of candidates who concluded that the immaterial misstatement should be disclosed in an emphasis of matter paragraph, again demonstrating a lack of understanding of the concept of materiality and when the use of an emphasis of matter paragraph is appropriate.

| ACCA marking guide | |
|---|---|
| | *Marks* |

**(a)** **Matters and evidence**

Generally up to 1 mark for each matter explained and each piece of evidence recommended (unless otherwise stated).

**(i)** **Sale and leaseback transaction**

**Matters**

- Consider treatment of sale and leaseback transaction as required by IFRS 16
- Assess whether control of asset has transferred to buyer
- Whether asset transfer is sale in line with IFRS 15
- IFRS 15 criteria based on transfer of control; ability to direct, use and obtain substantially all remaining benefits of asset
- Derecognise property and recognise right-of-use asset based on proportion of asset retained
- Recognise financial liability based on PV of lease payments
- Recognise gain/loss on transaction in P/L for year
- Reasoned conclusion that treatment appears to be correct on basis of information available

**Evidence**

- Copy of sale and leaseback agreement to confirm key details, e.g. rights of lessee and lessor to control asset; also: proceeds, rental amounts and timings, lease term, interest rate implicit in lease
- Discussions with management about transfer of control and correct treatment of sale and leaseback arrangement
- Board minutes for evidence of discussion of sale and leaseback transaction
- Review of local property market including trade journals, press articles, official statistics to confirm high demand for retail leases
- Review of surveyor reports on building to confirm expected life
- Agreement of carrying amount of property to non-current asset register
- Agreement of sale proceeds to cash book/bank statement
- Copy of client working papers for present value of lease payments
- Recalculation of PV of lease payments by auditor
- Review of financial statements to confirm that details of sale and leaseback transaction disclosed in line with IFRS 16 requirements

|  | |
|---|---|
| **Maximum** | **8** |

**(ii)** **Investment property**

**Matters**

- Materiality
- Discussion of whether it meets classification requirements from 1 April 20X4
- Property not let by 31 March 20X5 does not impact on this classification
- End of owner-occupation is evidence of change in use
- Fair value model is acceptable provided consistent treatment
- On transfer to investment property carried at fair value
- Increase of $25,000 should be recognised in other comprehensive income
- Resulting error: overstatement of profit by $25,000

**Evidence**

- Notes of discussions with management to confirm intention to hold property to earn rentals and for capital appreciation
- Inspection of title deeds to confirm ownership of investment property
- A copy of any client working papers in relation to the calculation of the right-of-use asset
- Accounting policy agreed to financial statements to confirm that fair value model is to be adopted and consistent
- Board minutes for evidence of management discussion of change of use and for confirmation of date when owner-occupation ceased
- Written representations from management confirming change of use, relevant date and future intentions
- Record of physical inspection of building in order to confirm its general condition and that it is no longer occupied by Lifeson Co
- Market valuation of building by independent and external auditor's expert at date of transfer and at reporting date to determine respective fair values and resulting gains
- Details of external expert valuer including an assessment of professional qualifications, experience, reputation, independence and objectivity
- Agreement of carrying amount on transfer to non-current asset register
- Notes of discussions with management in relation to incorrect recording of the gain and need to include error in auditor's schedule of uncorrected misstatements
- Review disclosures made in the financial statements to ensure they comply with the requirements of IAS 40

|  |  |
|---|---|
| **Maximum** | **6** |

**(iii)  Shopping mall – asset impairment**

**Matters**

- Materiality
- Whether client's calculation of recoverable amount based on value in use is in line with requirements of IAS 36
- Discussion of whether client has used appropriate discount factor for calculating value in use
- Whether NRV of shopping mall exceeds its value in use (at both dates)
- Reversal of impairment loss should be capped to depreciated historic cost had no impairment loss been recognised
- Resulting error: overstatement of profit and assets by $300,000

**Evidence**

- Agreement of opening balances for property to non-current asset register
- Physical inspection of shopping mall to confirm condition, occupancy level and reasonableness of depreciation policy and of management's cash flow forecasts
- Copy of client working papers for impairment review giving details of NRV of mall and value in use calculations
- Copy of client cash flow forecasts and budgets supporting value in use calculations
- Notes of discussions with management and assessment of reasonableness of assumptions used in forecasts and appropriateness of discount factor used in value in use calculations
- Management representations attesting to the reasonableness of assumptions and other related management judgements

- Recalculation of value in use by auditor
- Sensitivity analyses on forecasts and value in use calculations
- External confirmation of the shopping mall's net realisable value by an appropriately qualified, independent expert
- Notes of discussions with management in relation to incorrect recording of impairment reversal and need to include error in auditor's schedule of uncorrected misstatements

|  | Maximum | 6 |
| --- | --- | --- |

**(b)**      **Auditor's report**

**Investment property**
- Misstatement is immaterial
- No modification needed
- Written representation if not amended

**Shopping mall**
- Material misstatement due to inappropriate application of IAS 36
- Matter is not pervasive
- Qualified audit opinion
- Basis of qualified opinion paragraph

|  | Maximum | 5 |
| --- | --- | --- |
| Total |  | 25 |

## 17    KILMISTER      *Walk in the footsteps of a top tutor*

### Top tutor tips

*Part (a) asks for a critical appraisal of the draft auditor's report extracts. Don't just focus on whether the opinion is appropriate. You should also think about the titles of the paragraphs included and whether the names are correct, the order they appear in, whether the required information that should be included has been included and whether the wording used is professional and appropriate.*

*Part (b) asks for the matters which should be reported to those charged with governance at the end of the audit. In accordance with ISA 260, the auditor must report matters relating to significant control deficiencies, uncorrected misstatements which may impact the auditor's report and matters affecting independence for listed clients. In your answer you should explain why any control deficiencies are significant and the implications for the company, explain why the financial statements are misstated as a result of the client's accounting treatment and explain the ethical issues arising and the actions that will need to be taken to mitigate or eliminate the threats.*

**(a)** **Kilmister Co – Critical appraisal of extract from draft auditor's report**

**Presentation and structure of auditor's report extract**

The structure and format of the auditor's report is prescribed by ISA 700/ISA (UK) 700 *Forming an Opinion and Reporting on Financial Statements*. The auditor's report should be addressed solely to the shareholders of the reporting entity and the title should not include any reference to the directors of Kilmister Co. In addition, the first two paragraphs are presented in the incorrect order, the Opinion paragraph should precede the Basis for Opinion paragraph.

**Reference to ethical code**

ISA 700 requires that in the Basis for Opinion paragraph, the auditor should identify the relevant ethical code, naming the IESBA *International Code of Ethics for Professional Accountants*/FRC Ethical Standard. The draft auditor's report does not specifically refer to the ethical code which has been applied during the audit and is therefore not in compliance with the requirements of ISA 700.

**Material uncertainty regarding going concern**

ISA 570/ISA (UK) 570 *Going Concern* provides guidance on how an auditor should report uncertainties regarding going concern in the auditor's report. According to ISA 570, if adequate disclosure about the material uncertainty is not made in the financial statements, the auditor should express a qualified opinion or adverse opinion as appropriate.

The use of a 'material uncertainty regarding going concern' paragraph in the draft auditor's report extract is therefore incorrect. This paragraph should only be used when adequate disclosure has been made by the directors in the financial statements and would include a cross reference to this disclosure. Given that this disclosure has not been made, this is therefore not appropriate in this case.

In this case, therefore, the absence of any disclosure in the financial statements in relation to the uncertainties regarding going concern is grounds for a modification of the auditor's opinion. The modification is due to a material misstatement in relation to the absence of this key disclosure.

If, in the auditor's professional judgment, the impact of this non-disclosure on the financial statements is material but not pervasive, a qualified 'except for' opinion should be issued. In this case, the opinion paragraph should be headed 'qualified opinion' and this should be followed immediately by a 'basis for qualified opinion' paragraph.

If, on the other hand, the auditor believes that the impact on the financial statements of the non-disclosure is both material and pervasive, an adverse opinion should be given. The opinion paragraph should then be headed 'adverse opinion' and should be followed immediately by a 'basis for adverse opinion' paragraph.

In addition, details of the uncertainty regarding going concern should be given in the basis for qualified or adverse opinion paragraph.

**Long-term contracts**

The use of the 'other information' section in this context is inappropriate. This section should be used to describe the auditor's responsibilities for 'other information' (e.g. the rest of the annual report, including the management report) and the outcome of fulfilling those responsibilities.

The disclosure regarding long-term contracts is more in line with the requirements of ISA 701/ISA (UK) 701 *Communicating Key Audit Matters in the Independent Auditor's Report*, where key audit matters are those which in the auditor's professional judgment were of most significance to the audit. In determining which matters to report, the auditor should take into account areas of significant auditor attention in performing the audit, including:

–   Areas of higher assessed risk of material misstatement, or significant risks identified in accordance with ISA 315 (Revised) *Identifying and Assessing the Risks of Material Misstatement through Understanding the Entity and Its Environment.*

–   Significant auditor judgments relating to areas in the financial statements which involved significant management judgment, including accounting estimates which have been identified as having high estimation uncertainty.

–   The effect on the audit of significant events or transactions which occurred during the period.

The extract from the draft auditor's report states that significant judgment is applied in assessing the percentage of completeness of material long-term contracts and that this percentage is then applied in calculating the revenue for the year. This is a matter of high risk requiring significant auditor attention and given that Kilmister Co is a listed entity, it would be appropriate for this to be disclosed in the KAM section of the auditor's report.

The KAM section of the auditor's report should begin with an introductory paragraph explaining what a KAM is.

The KAM section should then explain why this matter is considered to be a KAM due to the significant judgment involved in assessing the percentage completeness of the long-term contracts and the high risk of material misstatement associated with this judgment process.

The KAM section should also include an explanation of how the KAM was addressed by the audit process. In this case, this might include, for example, an evaluation of the controls designed and implemented by Kilmister Co to monitor the progress of and the amounts owing on service and construction contracts; a review of the financial performance of key contracts against budgets and historical trends; and challenging management's estimates and judgments in respect of the progress to date on the contracts.

**(b)     Taylor Co – Report to those charged with governance**

A report to those charged with governance (TCWG) is produced to communicate matters relating to the external audit to those who are ultimately responsible for the financial statements. ISA 260/ISA (UK) 260 *Communication With Those Charged With Governance* requires the auditor to communicate many matters including independence and other ethical issues and the significant findings from the audit. In the case of Taylor Co, the matters to be communicated would include the following:

**Revaluation of property portfolio**

According to ISA 260/ISA (UK) 260, the significant findings from the audit include the auditor's views about significant qualitative aspects of the entity's accounting practices including accounting policies and any circumstances which affect the form and content of the auditor's report.

In the case of Taylor Co, the significant findings from the audit would relate to the changes in the accounting policy in relation to the revaluation of property and related material misstatements and the following matters should be communicated:

IAS 16 *Property, Plant and Equipment* states the revaluation policy should be consistent across a class of assets.

Four properties, which are material to the statement of financial position at 2.1% of total assets, are still carried at depreciated historic cost. This therefore represents a breach of IAS 16 and a material misstatement, which will impact on the form and content of the auditor's report.

According to ISA 260/ISA (UK) 260, the significant findings from the audit also include significant difficulties encountered during audit such as information delays.

The independent external valuation reports requested by Eddie & Co at the planning stage were not available when requested by the auditor and it took three weeks before they were received by the audit team.

The auditor should report this delay to those charged with governance, detailing its impact on the efficiency of the audit process together with any resulting increase in the audit fee.

**Renovation of car parking facilities**

The renovation expenditure on the car parking facilities at Taylor Co's properties should be recognised as an asset according to IAS 16 if it is probable that future economic benefits associated with the item will flow to the entity and the cost of the item can be measured reliably.

In Taylor Co's case, the cost has been quantified as $13.2 million and it has already derived economic benefits in the form of a significant increase in customer numbers and revenue at each of these locations. The expenditure should therefore be capitalised and its inclusion in operating expenses is not in compliance with IAS 16.

The amount of $13.2 million is also material to the statement of financial position at 2.5% of total assets.

The incorrect application of IAS 16 and the material misstatement should be included in a report to TCWG as a significant finding from the audit which will impact on the form and content of the auditor's report.

ISA 265/ISA (UK) 265 *Communicating Deficiencies in Internal Control to Those Charged With Governance and Management* requires the auditor to communicate appropriately to those charged with governance deficiencies in internal control which the auditor has identified during the audit and which, in the auditor's professional judgment, are of sufficient importance to merit their respective attentions.

The audit working papers include minutes of discussions with management which confirm that authorisation had not been gained for this expenditure. The lack of authorisation indicates a lack of management oversight and a serious weakness in control which could allow fraud to occur.

Furthermore, the lack of integrity shown by management in going ahead with the renovation works without the necessary permission is an example of management override and could be indicative of the tone set throughout the organisation.

This therefore represents a high risk matter and they may wish to implement controls and procedures to prevent further breaches.

The report to those charged with governance should include full details on this significant deficiency in internal control and should include recommendations to management in order to reduce the associated business risk.

**Long association of audit partner**

As discussed above, ISA 260/ISA (UK) 260 requires the auditor to communicate matters in relation to auditor independence. Bryony Robertson has acted as audit engagement partner for Taylor Co for eight (INT)/six (UK) consecutive years.

According to the IESBA International Code of Ethics for Professional Accountants (the Code)/FRC Ethical Standard, her long association with the audit client creates both familiarity and self-interest threats to auditor independence.

The familiarity threat arises due to the long and potentially close relationship which she has with the staff of Taylor Co leading to her being too sympathetic to their interests or too accepting of their work.

This in turn gives rise to a self-interest threat in that her long association and close relationship with the client create a personal interest which may inappropriately influence her professional judgment or behaviour.

In order to address these risks, the Code/FRC Ethical Standard requires that an audit partner in a listed entity should be rotated at least every seven years/five years and therefore her eight-year (INT)/six year (UK) tenure as the audit partner of Taylor Co appears to be in clear breach of this provision.

INT: The Code does allow for an engagement partner to serve for an additional year if the required rotation is not possible due to unforeseen circumstances such as the illness of the intended engagement partner, in this case Philip Campbell.

UK: The FRC Ethical Standard does allow for an engagement partner to serve for an additional two years if the client's audit committee decides that a degree of flexibility over the timing of rotation is necessary to safeguard the quality of the audit. This could arise if the audit firm has no other partners with the necessary knowledge and experience who are able to take over as engagement partner, in this case due to the illness of Phil Campbell.

In these circumstances, safeguards should be applied such as the independent review of the engagement which is being performed and this should be communicated to those charged with governance.

INT: Going forward beyond the current year, if it remains impossible to rotate the audit partner due to a lack of alternative expertise within the firm, it may be possible for Bryony Robertson to continue as the audit partner if special dispensation is received from the relevant regulator and the necessary safeguards are applied such as the engagement is subject to regular review by an independent, external expert.

---

**Examiner's comments**

This question was a 25-mark compulsory question which focused on completion and reporting and was in two sections.

Requirement (a) for 10 marks, asked candidates to critically appraise an extract from an auditor's report which had been incorrectly prepared and required amendment. The majority of responses were extremely disappointing and generally reflects weak knowledge of auditor reporting requirements. There remain a number of candidates who continue to show a lack of understanding of basic ISA requirements such as incorrectly suggesting that an unmodified opinion should have 'unmodified' in the title of the opinion or that a material uncertainty

---

related to going concern should be included within an emphasis of matter paragraph. Many candidates suggested that the use of "we believe" in the auditor's report is not appropriate wording, or that the use of "in our opinion" suggests that the auditor is not independent from the client and therefore a familiarity threat is present. This demonstrates a significant lack of understanding of auditor's reports and ISA 700 *Forming an Opinion and Reporting on Financial Statements*. Candidates were not expected to discuss what would or would not be present in a full report. Where candidates discussed, for example, "the signature of the partner is missing" or "responsibilities of the auditor are missing", this was not relevant to the requirement, which asked candidates to specifically critique the extract as presented. Discussion of given extracts of auditor's reports, again, should follow a structured approach and practising questions of this nature should allow candidates to score strong marks in these requirements. Candidates would benefit from increased knowledge of ISA 700, and in particular should review the appendices which show real examples of auditor's report and typical wording which is appropriate.

Requirement (b) for 15 marks, required candidates to discuss, along with reasons for discussion, specific matters raised in the scenario which should be reported to those charged with governance. Generally, candidates identified the "matters to be included" and used an approach of calculating the materiality of the issue, discussing the relevant accounting standard and how the matter had been dealt with incorrectly. However, candidates were vague on why matters should be included within a report to those charged with governance and continued to answer the question as if it were asking about the impact on the audit opinion. This demonstrates a lack of understanding of the question requirement by a number of candidates.

| ACCA marking scheme | |
|---|---|
| | *Marks* |
| **(a) Kilmister Co** | |
| **Critical appraisal of extract from draft auditor's report** | |
| Up to 1 mark per issue explained | |
| – Addressee should be shareholders (not directors) | |
| – Incorrect order – opinion paragraph should be before basis for opinion | |
| – Lack of specific reference to ethical code | |
| **Material uncertainty re going concern:** | |
| – Opinion paragraph should be headed 'qualified/adverse opinion' followed by 'basis for qualified/adverse opinion' | |
| – Modification due to material misstatement re absence of disclosure – 'except for' or adverse depending on auditor's professional judgment re level of impact on financial statements | |
| – Incorrect use of 'material uncertainty regarding going concern' paragraph – this paragraph should be used when adequate disclosure has been made by directors in financial statements | |
| – Details of uncertainty re going concerns should be given in basis for qualified/adverse opinion paragraph | |
| **Long term contracts:** | |
| – Incorrect use of 'other information' paragraph – should be used to describe auditor's responsibilities for 'other information' (e.g. rest of the annual report, including management report) and outcome of fulfilling those responsibilities | |
| – Issue is area of significant auditor judgment which should be considered for inclusion as KAM which as a listed company, Kilmister Co should disclose in separate KAM section of auditor's report | |

|  |  |
|---|---|
| – KAM section should include explanation of what is a KAM | |
| – KAM section should explain why matter is considered to be KAM | |
| – KAM section should also explain how KAM was addressed by audit process | |
| **Maximum** | **10** |

**(b)** **Taylor Co**
**Report to those charged with governance**
Generally up to 1 mark for each matter identified and explained
**Revaluation of property portfolio**
– Significant findings from audit should be reported to TCWG
– These include significant changes in accounting policy and material misstatements
– Revaluation of PPE should be consistent across a class of assets (IAS 16), four properties still carried at depreciated historic cost
– Four properties are material to SOFP (2.1% assets)
– Significant findings from audit also include significant difficulties encountered during audit such as information delays
– Delay makes audit less efficient and may result in increase in audit fee

**Renovation of car parking facilities**
– Taylor Co has derived economic benefits from expenditure, should be capitalised
– Material to SOFP (2.5% of assets)
– Incorrect application of IAS 16 and potential material misstatement should be included in report to TCWG as significant finding from audit
– Lack of authorisation indicates lack of management oversight and serious weakness in control which could allow fraud to occur
– Lack of integrity shown by management going ahead with renovation works without the necessary permission is an example of management override and could be the tone set throughout organisation
– Therefore this is a high risk matter and they may wish to implement controls and procedures to prevent further breaches
– Report to TCWG should include recommendations to management to reduce business risk

**Long association of audit partner**
– Matters to be communicated to TCWG include ethical issues in relation to auditor independence
– Long association creates familiarity and self-interest threats
– INT: Audit partner in listed entity should be rotated at least every seven years per IESBA Code
UK: Audit partner in listed entity should be rotated at least every five years per FRC Ethical Standard
– INT: IESBA Code allows for an additional year if required rotation not possible due to unforeseen circumstances
– UK: FRC Ethical Standard allows for an additional year if required to safeguard the quality of the audit
– INT: After current year, may still be possible for Bryony Robertson to continue as audit partner if engagement is subject to regular review by independent, external expert
– Safeguards should be applied including independent internal or external review of engagement (as per scenario)

| | |
|---|---|
| **Maximum** | **15** |
| **Total** | **25** |

18   DALEY  *Walk in the footsteps of a top tutor*

*Top tutor tips*

*Part (a) requires indicators of going concern issues. Going concern means the company is likely to be able to continue trading for the foreseeable future. The company will have difficulty continuing to trade if it does not have enough cash to pay its liabilities when they fall due. Look for the indicators in the scenario which could mean the cash inflows are not sufficient to cover the cash outflows.*

*Part (b) requires audit evidence on the cash flow forecast. Evidence needs to be obtained to assess the reasonableness of the assumptions used to prepare the forecast. The transactions have not yet occurred so limited supporting documentation will be available, for example, invoices will not exist at this point. However, some evidence will exist to support management's assumptions and this is what the auditor will need to obtain.*

*Part (c) asks for the reasons why the directors may not want to make disclosure of the going concern difficulties and the reporting implications if they do not make adequate disclosure. When suggesting an audit opinion you must state the wording of that opinion and justify your choice as this will be where the majority of the marks will be awarded.*

(a)   **Going concern indicators**

There are a range of matters which cast doubt on Daley Co's ability to continue as a going concern. In particular, the company appears to be exhibiting many of the indicators of a business which is overtrading.

**Revenue and profitability**

Daley Co has experienced a significant increase in revenue of 28.4% which may not be sustainable in the short to medium term without additional external sources of finance.

The company is also experiencing a significant decline in its operating profit margin and net profit margin. It is notable that even after taking account of the provision, other operating expenses have increased by more than 4.3 times $((9.1 - 3.5)/1.3)$ resulting in an overall loss of $3.4 million in the current reporting period.

It is possible that the company has had to reduce its selling prices in order to achieve the high level of sales growth and that this has resulted in a negative net profit margin this year of (30.1%).

**Liquidity and working capital**

Daley Co has also suffered a decline in liquidity as evidenced by a fall in its current ratio from 2.4 to 1.6 and in its acid test ratio from 1.1 to 0.6.

A review of the company's working capital ratios indicates long and worsening inventory holding periods (481 days in 20X8 compared to 466 days in 20X7) and overall inventory has increased by 57% which may be indicative of problems in relation to the saleability of inventory which is in breach of domestic regulations.

The company is currently taking on average 120 days to collect its trade debts (108 days in 20X7) and requires an average of 348 days in 20X8 (365 days in 20X7) to pay its trade payables. Although this is a fall in the average payment period compared to the prior year, it still appears to be a long period which may be related to ongoing payment disputes in relation to the regulatory breaches noted previously.

Overall, trade payables have increased by 44.8% on the prior year and the company may struggle to settle this liability given its worsening cash position, which may in turn result in a loss of goodwill with its suppliers and a refusal to supply or to withdraw credit in the future which would severely restrict the company's operations.

The poor working capital management and declining liquidity have resulted in Daley Co's cash position deteriorating from a positive position of $0.6 million in 20X7 to an overdraft of $1.8 million in 20X8 which is significant at 7.8% of total assets.

### Gearing and finance

In addition to problems with short-term finance and liquidity, Daley Co is also exhibiting a significant increase in gearing as evidenced by the increase in debt to equity from 2.3 in 20X7 to 6.4 in 20X8 and a fall in interest cover from 6.6 times to (1.5) times over the same period, indicating that the business is unable to service its current levels of finance.

The company's finance costs as a percentage of long-term borrowings have increased from 5.6% in 20X7 to 13.4% in 20X8. This may be due at least in part to the interest on the overdraft proving to be an expensive way of financing the entity's operations and if the overdraft has not been agreed with the bank, the company may be incurring additional penalties and charges thereby putting additional strain on the company's cash flows.

The increasing finance costs may also reflect lenders already perceiving Daley Co to be a high credit risk. It is also notable that non-current assets have decreased by 7.5% this year which suggests that the business is also struggling to replace and renew its existing capital expenditure levels. If this is the case, it may cast further doubt on the feasibility of the planned expansion of its operations.

### Legal claim

Given Daley Co's current financial position, it seems unlikely that the business will be able to settle the legal claim of $3.5 million which threatens to place severe demands on the company's cash flow. Indeed, if there is a prospect of more claims arising in the future, the problems with the saleability of inventory and management of working capital as a result of the regulatory breaches discussed earlier may worsen further leading to a greater deterioration in the company's cash flow position.

### Cash flow forecast

Overall, Daley Co's ability to continue to trade appears to be dependent on obtaining the new bank finance which it has assumed in its cash flow forecast. The bank financing is needed to meet existing liabilities and it is doubtful whether sufficient funding will be available in order to finance the proposed expansion.

Moreover, the forecast itself appears to be unrealistic in its other assumptions. In particular, the assumption that the business's revenue will grow by 25% seems optimistic given the arrival of a major competitor in its market place and the projected trade receivable collection period of 60 days may well be unachievable on the basis of the historic ratios identified above.

A return to a positive cash position is dependent on these assumptions and obtaining the new bank finance which may not be forthcoming based on the bank's assessment of the business's current financial position and performance.

**(b)** **Audit evidence on the cash flow forecast**

The audit working papers should include sufficient evidence that appropriate audit procedures have been conducted in relation to the assumption that Daley Co is a going concern at the reporting date, including the following:

- Evidence of agreement of the opening cash position to the cash book and bank reconciliation.

- Reperformance by the audit team of the client's calculations in preparing the forecast in order to check its arithmetic accuracy.

- Details of a review of the results of any market research which has been conducted by Daley Co for the next 12 months in order to assess the potential impact of the new competitor.

- Notes from meetings with management detailing discussion of the key assumptions made by management in the preparation of the forecast (including the growth rate and receivables collection period) and an assessment of the consistency of the assumptions with the auditor's knowledge of the business and with management's intentions regarding the future of the company and corroborating evidence of assumptions.

- Evaluation by the audit team of previous profit and other financial forecasts and their outcome in order to assess the consistency of the cash flow forecast with other prospective information prepared by management.

- A comparison of the cash flow forecast for the period October to November 20X8 with management accounts for the same period in order to assess the accuracy of the forecast compared to actual data to date.

- Results of analytical review of the items included in the cash flow forecast including, for example, a detailed review of the breakdown of different categories of expenses in order to identify any items which may have been omitted.

- A review of correspondence with Daley Co's lawyers in relation to the legal claims in order to assess the likelihood of losing the actions, the likely cost and the possibility of further claims arising in the future.

- Based on the review of legal correspondence, confirmation that the settlement of the legal claims has been appropriately included in the cash flow forecast.

- A review of correspondence with Daley Co's bankers and supporting documentation for both the company's existing loan facilities and the proposed new loan.

- Minutes of discussions with management in relation to the likelihood of obtaining the new loan.

- Based on these reviews and discussions, a recalculation by the auditor of the finance cost and confirmation that the finance cost and the receipt of the loan have been accurately reflected in the cash flow forecast.

- Working paper detailing the review of the documentation in relation to the new warehousing agreeing the cost and checking that the cash outflow is included in the forecast at the correct amount and at the correct date.

- A review of board minutes in relation to the company's current trading position and the ongoing negotiations for the proposed new bank finance.

- A consideration of the impact on cash flows and liquidity when the company is incurring the additional costs of compliance with all laws and regulations.

**(c)** **Reasons for non-disclosure and implications for the auditor's report**

**Motives for directors not wishing to make going concern disclosures**

The directors' motives for non-disclosure of uncertainties in relation to going concern seem likely to reflect a desire to present the company in a positive light to investors and other third parties. This is a particularly sensitive issue at a time when the company is planning a major expansion and is seeking to raise significant new finance while struggling to manage its liquidity and working capital.

The disclosure of uncertainties in relation to going concern may well deter the bank from lending the new finance and may lead to a loss of confidence and goodwill with key suppliers and customers.

Operational difficulties with suppliers and customers may prove to be particularly problematic with the arrival of the major new competitor in Daley Co's market in October 20X8.

**Implications for the auditor's report**

ISA 705/ISA (UK) 705 *Modifications to the Opinion in the Independent Auditor's Report* requires the auditor to modify the opinion in the auditor's report when they conclude that, based on the audit evidence obtained, the financial statements as a whole are not free from material misstatement.

The failure to include disclosures regarding material uncertainties in relation to going concern in Daley Co's financial statements represents a material omission which will therefore require a modification of the auditor's opinion. In this case, the auditor must exercise professional judgment and assess whether the absence of this disclosure is material but not pervasive to the financial statements or whether it is material and pervasive to the financial statements.

**Material but not pervasive**

If the auditor concludes that the omission of the required disclosures in relation to the going concern uncertainties is material but not pervasive to the financial statements, a qualified audit opinion on the grounds of material misstatement is appropriate, as the directors have failed to include required disclosures.

The auditor will include a 'Qualified Opinion' paragraph at the start of the auditor's report which will state that the financial statements are presented fairly in all material respects 'except for' the absence of this disclosure.

The qualified opinion paragraph will be followed immediately by a 'Basis for Qualified Opinion' paragraph which will give details of the going concern uncertainties in relation to Daley Co and explain that the financial statements do not adequately disclose these uncertainties.

**Material and pervasive**

If the auditor concludes that the omission of the required disclosures in relation to the going concern uncertainties is material and pervasive to the financial statements, an adverse audit opinion on the grounds of material misstatement is appropriate as in the auditor's opinion the lack of these disclosures will have a fundamental impact on the users' understanding of the financial statements.

The auditor will include an 'Adverse Opinion' paragraph at the start of the auditor's report which will state that the financial statements are not presented fairly in all material respects.

The adverse opinion paragraph will be followed immediately by a 'Basis for Adverse Opinion' paragraph which will give details of the going concern uncertainties in relation to Daley Co and explain that in the opinion of the auditor, the omission of key disclosures in this respect are fundamental and pervasive to the financial statements and therefore require an adverse opinion.

*Tutorial note*

*Key audit matters (KAM) disclosures are not relevant for Daley Co as it is not listed.*

**Examiner's comments**

This was a 25-mark question covering the going concern assessment for a non-listed client and was set at the completion stage of the audit.

Requirement (a) for ten marks asked candidates to evaluate matters which cast doubt on a client's ability to continue as a going concern (GC). Candidates were directed to analytical review of a cash flow forecast to aid in their evaluation and those who used the quantitative and discursive parts of the scenario to describe the GC risk indicators with an explanation of how that impacted on the company's future tended to score high marks on this question. Candidates who merely calculated ratios and stated the direction of movement or simply stated that an increase in the receivables collection period showed going concern issues attained very few marks. It is important candidates demonstrate their knowledge of how each matter gives rise to an issue for trading as a going concern. For example a fuller explanation would be that the increase in the receivables collection period may mean that there are irrecoverable debts which should be written off, increasing losses further, or that slow collection would decrease liquidity and therefore put pressure on the ability of the company to make payments as they fell due. A technique candidates could employ here would be to ask themselves why as they get to the end of a sentence, allowing them to add a second sentence demonstrating their understanding. A minority of candidates appeared to lack focus on the question requirement and answered this as a RoMM discussion, covering risks of material misstatements in the forecast rather than relating the scenario to the GC issues required.

Part (b) for nine marks requested an explanation of the audit evidence which would be needed with respect to the forecast and candidates scored best when they remembered this was future/prospective information, not historical, and where they related it specifically to the information given. For example, candidates who looked for specific assumptions in the information provided and devised sources of evidence to support each of those assumptions were able to attain far more marks than candidates who simply said evaluate the assumptions used by management in preparing the forecast. It is important that candidates appreciate that no two questions are the same and that the information given in the question should always be used to drive their answer.

Finally part (c) for six marks required candidates to explain why the directors may wish to exclude disclosures relating to going concern uncertainties in the notes to the financial statements and the possible implications on the auditor's report. Candidates were generally able to identify the reasons for non-disclosure but performed very poorly on the auditor's report implications. Many candidates wrongly stated that the directors omitting a required disclosure would not constitute a material misstatement. Many therefore went on to conclude that the opinion would be unmodified but that going concern disclosures would be made in the auditor's report instead of in the notes to the financial statements. This is not the case and candidates should ensure they are familiar with the reporting requirements in ISA 570 *Going Concern*. Some candidates suggested including such disclosures in the Key Audit Matters section or to include an Emphasis of Matter paragraph both of which would be inappropriate.

---

**Marking scheme**

|  |  | *Marks* |
|---|---|---|
| **(a)** | **Going concern indicators**<br>Up to 2 marks for each well-explained going concern indicator discussed<br>Up to 3 marks for calculation of relevant ratios and trends.<br>**Revenue and profitability**<br>– Significant increase in revenue of 28.4% (potential overtrading indicator) – Declining profit margins<br>– Increase in effective interest rate on long-term debt (lenders perceive as higher risk)<br>– Loss-making<br>**Liquidity and working capital**<br>– Declining liquidity<br>– Cash position has moved from positive to negative (overdraft) during year – Poor working capital management<br>**Gearing and finance**<br>– Increased gearing<br>– Decline in interest cover<br>– Failure to replace non-current assets (7.5% decrease in year)<br>**Legal claim**<br>– Significant legal claim, company does not appear to have cash to settle it<br>**Cash flow forecast**<br>– Cash flow forecast indicates improving liquidity and working capital, however, this appears optimistic (e.g. growth rate, receivable collection period assumptions)<br>– New competitor threatens to reduce market share<br>– Return to positive cash dependent on these assumptions and obtaining new bank finance which may not be forthcoming<br>– Company is dependent on obtaining new bank finance |  |
|  | **Maximum** | **10** |
| **(b)** | **Audit evidence on cash flow forecast**<br>Generally 1 mark for each well described source of audit evidence:<br>– Agreement of the opening cash position to cash book and bank reconciliation<br>– Accuracy check – recalculation<br>– Review of the results of any market research which has been conducted for next 12 months assessing impact of new competitor<br>– Discuss key assumptions made by management in preparation of forecast (including growth rate and receivables collection period), assess consistency with auditor's knowledge of the business and with management's intentions regarding the future of the company |  |

- Agreement that the cash flow forecast is consistent with profit and other financial forecasts which have been prepared by management
- Comparison of the cash flow forecast for the period October–November 20X8 with management accounts for the same period
- Analytical review of the items included in the cash flow forecast, for example, categories of expenses, to look for items which may have been omitted
- Review legal correspondence in relation to legal claims and assess likelihood of losing actions, likely cost and likelihood of further actions in future
- If appropriate, ensure settlement of legal claims has been included in forecast
- Review correspondence with bank and supporting documentation for existing and proposed loan facilities
- Discuss with management likelihood of obtaining new finance
- Check calculation of finance cost and inclusion in forecast
- Ensure amount and timing of receipt of new finance is accurately reflected in forecast
- Inspect documentation in relation to new warehousing agreeing cost and check that cash outflow is included in forecast at correct amount and timing
- Review of board minutes re company's current trading position and ongoing negotiations with bankers
- Consideration of impact on cash flows and liquidity when company is incurring additional costs of compliance with all laws and regulations

|                                            |     |
|--------------------------------------------|-----|
| **Maximum**                                | 9   |

(c) **Directors' reasons for non-disclosure and implications for auditor's report**

Generally up to 1 mark for each point discussed:

**Possible reasons for non-disclosure**
- Desire to present company in positive light to investors and other third parties
- Particularly significant given current position of company, e.g. seeking to raise new finance; struggling to manage liquidity and working capital; need to maintain confidence with suppliers and customers especially with arrival of new competitor

**Implications for auditor's report**
- Auditor must assess whether absence of disclosure is material but not pervasive to financial statements or whether it is material and pervasive to financial statements

**Material but not pervasive**
- Qualified opinion due to material misstatement ('except for' incomplete disclosure)
- Basis for qualified opinion paragraph to be included giving details of going concern uncertainties and that financial statements do not adequately disclose these uncertainties

**Material and pervasive**
- Adverse opinion due to material misstatement where the financial statements 'do not present fairly'
- Basis for adverse opinion paragraph explaining grounds for adverse opinion
- Position of opinion and basis for (qualified/adverse) opinion paragraphs
- Well reasoned conclusion on whether issue is pervasive

|                                            |     |
|--------------------------------------------|-----|
| **Maximum**                                | 6   |
| **Total**                                  | 25  |

19    CORAM & CO     *Walk in the footsteps of a top tutor*

*Top tutor tips*

*Part (a) provides you with the schedule of uncorrected misstatements for an audit client and asks for the matters to be discussed with management. Calculate whether the proposed adjustment is material. If it is material the adjustment must be made in order to avoid a modified opinion. You also need to explain the accounting treatment that they should have applied. Finish off by explaining the impact on the auditor's opinion if management does not make the proposed adjustments. The requirement only asks for the impact on the opinion, not the report, so do not waste time expanding beyond the opinion section. This is a typical completion and reporting question seen on many recent past papers which emphasises the importance of practising past papers to prepare for the exam.*

*Part (b) is an ethical and professional issues question. There are two separate issues and you should deal with them in turn. Identify the type of threat, explain how the threat could influence the audit, discuss whether the threat is significant and finish off by explaining the safeguards the firm should take to reduce the threat to an acceptable level.*

**(a)    Clark Co**

**Matters to be discussed with management in relation to the audit supervisor's proposed adjustments**

**(i)    Lease of testing equipment**

The lease at Clark Co's largest site is material to the statement of financial position at 2.2% of total assets. The leases at the other two sites are also material at 2.8% of total assets.

The general recognition and measurement requirements of IFRS 16 *Leases* require lessees to recognise a right-of-use asset and a lease liability at the commencement date of the lease at the present value of the lease payments. The standard defines the commencement date as the date the asset is available for use by the lessee. Given that the commencement date is 31 May 20X8 therefore, it is appropriate on this basis to recognise the lease on the statement of financial position as at this date.

It is significant, however, that IFRS 16 also contains an optional exemption for short-term leases of less than 12 months' duration with no purchase option. If Clark Co elects to apply this exemption, it does not recognise the leased assets or lease liabilities on the statement of financial position but rather, it recognises the lease payments associated with those leases as an expense in the statement of profit or loss for the year on either a straight-line basis over the lease term or another systematic basis.

However, IFRS 16 also requires that if this exemption is taken, it must be applied consistently by each class of underlying asset. Hence in this case, the client must either capitalise the leases across all three of the sites or apply the exemption consistently and not capitalise the leases across any of the sites. On either of these bases, as the commencement date of the lease coincides with the reporting date, there would not yet be any impact on Clark Co's statement of profit or loss for the year.

The audit manager should discuss the option of taking the short-term lease exemption with the finance director at tomorrow's meeting:

(i)     if the client elects not to take the exemption across the three sites, assets and liabilities will be materially understated. Hence the audit supervisor's proposed adjustment is correct and a right-of-use asset and lease liability of $475,000 should be recognised on the statement of financial position.

(ii)    Alternatively, if the client does elect to take the exemption across all three sites, then assets and liabilities are materially overstated and right-of-use assets and lease liabilities of $625,000 should be derecognised on the statement of financial position.

**Impact on audit opinion:**

If the client does not make any adjustment to the financial statements, the statement of financial position is materially misstated on the basis of misapplication of an accounting standard and the audit opinion should be qualified on this basis with an 'except for' opinion.

(ii)    **Legal claim**

The legal claim is material to the statement of financial position being 5.5% of Clark Co's total assets.

Following the requirements of IAS 37 *Provisions, Contingent Liabilities and Contingent Assets*, a provision should be recognised when: an entity has a present obligation (legal or constructive) as a result of a past event; it is probable that an outflow of resources embodying economic benefits will be required to settle the obligation; and a reliable estimate can be made of the amount of the obligation.

In this case the customer has already won the action against the company, the amount of the claim has been agreed by the courts and settlement is still outstanding at the reporting date. Hence, a provision of $1.2 million should be recognised on the statement of financial position.

IAS 37 also states that contingent assets are not recognised in financial statements since this may result in the recognition of income which may never be realised. However, the standard continues by stating that when the realisation of income is virtually certain, then the related asset is not a contingent asset and its recognition is appropriate. With respect to Clark Co's insurance claim therefore and the verified letter dated 25 May 20X8, the settlement of the claim as at the reporting date is virtually certain and an asset should be recognised separately on the statement of financial position.

The audit supervisor's proposed adjustment is correct and the finance director should therefore be requested to adjust the financial statements to include the separate recognition of the asset and the provision. If the adjustment is not made, both assets and liabilities will be materially misstated. There is no net impact on the statement of profit or loss for the year.

The finance director should also be advised that the financial statements should include full disclosure of the facts and amounts surrounding the provision for the legal claim together with full details of the expected reimbursement from the insurance company recognised as an asset.

**Impact on audit opinion:**

If the client does not make any adjustment to the financial statements, the statement of financial position is materially misstated and the audit opinion should be qualified on this basis with an 'except for' opinion.

**(iii)   Asset impairment**

The asset impairment of $85,000 is not material in isolation to either the statement of financial position (0.4% of total assets) or the statement of profit or loss for the period (3.7% of profit before taxation).

According to IAS 36 *Impairment of Assets*, an entity should assess at the end of each reporting period whether there is any indication that an asset or a cash generating unit may be impaired. If any such indication exists, the entity shall estimate the recoverable amount of the asset. The standard states that potential impairment indicators include external sources of information such as significant changes in the market in which the entity operates. As each of Clark Co's sites is considered a cash generating unit for impairment review purposes it seems appropriate therefore for the company to have conducted an impairment review at this site.

IAS 36 states that an asset or cash generating unit is impaired when the carrying amount exceeds the recoverable amount and it defines recoverable amount as the higher of the fair value less costs of disposal and the value in use. In the case of Clark Co, the auditor has agreed figures for carrying value and value in use and the key issue is the correct calculation of fair value less costs of disposal. Following IAS 36, the costs of disposal should include legal costs, transaction taxes and the costs of removing the assets but should exclude the costs associated with reorganising a business. The correct amount for fair value less costs of disposal is therefore $3,515,000 ($3.9 million – $126,000 – $174,000 – $85,000).

Given that this is higher than the value in use of $2.9 million, the recoverable amount of the assets is also $3,515,000 and therefore the assets are impaired by $85,000 ($3.6 million – $3,515,000). The client appears to have incorrectly omitted the costs of removing the assets from its calculation of fair value less costs of disposal and as a result the statement of financial position and the statement of profit or loss for the year are both overstated by $85,000.

The audit supervisor's proposed adjustment is therefore correct and the finance director should be advised of this error at tomorrow's meeting. Even though the amount is immaterial to both the statement of financial position and statement of profit or loss for the year, it is appropriate to request that the adjustment is made to the financial statements.

**Impact on audit opinion:**

Given that assets and profits are both immaterially overstated, if no adjustment is made to the financial statements, it follows that there will be no impact on the audit opinion in relation to this matter in isolation.

**(b)** **Turner Co**

**Ethical and professional issues and actions to be taken by the audit firm**

**Loan to member of the audit team**

According to the IESBA *International Code of Ethics for Professional Accountants* (the *Code*) and the FRC Ethical Standard, a loan to a member of the audit team may create a threat to the auditor's independence. If the loan is not made under normal lending procedures, and terms and conditions, a self-interest threat would be created as a result of Janette Stott's financial interest in the audit client. The self-interest threat arises because of the potential personal benefit derived which may motivate the audit team member to behave in a manner aimed at protecting that benefit.

Such a threat would be so significant that no safeguards could reduce the threat to an acceptable level. It follows therefore that the audit team member should not accept such a loan or guarantee. The *Code*, however, also states that a loan from an audit client which is a bank or similar institution to a member of the audit team which is made under normal lending procedures, is acceptable. Examples of such loans include home mortgages, car loans and credit card balances.

In addition, an intimidation threat to objectivity may arise where a loan is made from the audit client to a member of the audit team. The threat arises because of a fear that the audit client may, for example, change the terms of the loan or recall the loan, thus influencing the behaviour of the auditor.

It is possible therefore that the secured loan may be ethically acceptable and the key issue is whether 'the very best terms which the bank can offer' fall within Turner Co's normal lending procedures, and terms and conditions. The bank's standard lending terms and conditions should be obtained and reviewed alongside the documentation for Janette Stott's loan.

Ultimately, the audit engagement partner is responsible for ensuring that ethical principles are not breached, so the partner should be involved with the discussions.

The matter should be discussed with Janette and the client's business manager in order to establish whether the loan is to be made under the bank's normal lending procedures.

Janette should be advised of the outcome of the review and Turner Co's business manager should be advised of this decision, explaining the rationale and ethical rules behind it.

**Temporary staff assignment**

The *Code* states that the lending of staff to an audit client may create a self-review threat to auditor independence. The self-review threat arises when an auditor reviews work which they themselves have previously performed – for example, if the external auditor is involved in the process of preparing the payroll figures for inclusion in the financial statements and then audits them. As a result, there is a risk that the auditor would not be sufficiently objective in performing the audit and may fail to identify any shortcomings in their own work.

In addition, there is a risk of the staff member assuming management responsibilities if they are involved in making judgments and decisions which are the remit of management.

Such assistance can only therefore be given for a short period of time and the audit firm's staff must not assume management responsibilities and must not be involved in any activities specifically prohibited.

### Tutorial note

*According to the FRC Ethical Standard, a short period of time is generally expected to be no more than a small number of months. The client has requested staff for six months, which may be considered too long a period to avoid ethical threats from arising.*

### INT syllabus:

According to the *Code*, an audit firm cannot provide accounting and bookkeeping services (including payroll) to an audit client which is a public interest entity unless the services relate to matters which are collectively immaterial to the financial statements.

In this case Turner Co is a listed bank and is therefore a public interest entity. The assignment of a qualified member of staff as a supervisor on the client's main payroll system is likely to be material to the financial statements of a service industry client such as a bank and, in addition, may also involve management responsibilities. The audit manager should therefore discuss details of the proposed role of the seconded member of staff with the payroll manager and other key client contacts in order to establish the significance of the role and its materiality to the financial statements. Assuming that the role is material, the audit manager should decline the proposed staff assignment.

### UK syllabus:

According to the FRC Ethical Standard, payroll services must not be provided to a public interest entity. Therefore, the audit manager should decline the proposed staff assignment in relation to payroll services, explaining to the client the reasons why the Ethical Standard prohibits the provision of this service.

### Examiner's comments

Part (a) was worth 17 marks and was presented as a list of proposed audit adjustments and was very similar to the reporting requirement in the specimen exam. In this case, the requirement was more straightforward and asked for the matters to discuss with management and the impact on the audit opinion should management fail to adjust the errors. Candidates often did not remain focused on the requirement and detailed effects elsewhere in the auditor's report and the other actions they would take if management did not agree to amend the errors. In this question the correct accounting treatment was described for leases in addition to presenting the correctly calculated audit adjustments. Candidates often scored well in this requirement if they explained why the proposed treatments by the directors were not compliant with accounting standards (requirement for consistency in accounting policies, the requirement not to net off assets and liabilities and the relevant costs for calculating asset fair value less costs to sell in an impairment review). Common mistakes made in this question arose where candidates determined the directors were right and the auditors wrong or where they proposed to include a qualified audit opinion for an immaterial misstatement. Candidates should not assume that every issue in a reporting question will lead to a qualified opinion. An immaterial misstatement does not give rise to a modification to the opinion and conversely modifications cannot be avoided for material errors by including an emphasis of matter paragraph instead. Candidates should also note that when presenting audit opinions, it is not sufficient to say the opinion would be modified as this could mean any of four possibilities. Candidates should state the type of modification proposed e.g. qualified on the basis of material misstatement to score the mark. Simply writing qualified will not attract full marks as this could refer to either a material misstatement or an inability to obtain sufficient evidence. Similarly, when justifying the severity of a modified opinion candidates should justify whether something is pervasive or simply material to obtain the full mark. Simply stating something is not pervasive will only receive ½ a mark. This is consistent with the way audit reporting is marked in the Audit and Assurance paper and candidates should be used to this approach. Candidates who struggle with the format of auditor's reports should refer to the exam technique article which describes the key components and how to make a decision as to whether an item is pervasive or not.

Another weakness in answers provided here was to use out-of-date accounting standards to produce an answer. The examinable documents for Strategic Business Reporting are also examinable for this examination. While the majority of answers correctly applied IFRS 16 *Leases* to the question (the relevant parts of the standard were described within the scenario) a significant portion of the UK and IRL candidates continued to reference outdated treatment based on the definitions of operating and finance leases. It is important to note that the examinable versions of standards are those listed in the examinable documents area of the ACCA website and often this is in advance of the implementation in some jurisdictions.

Part (b) was less well answered. Candidates were presented with two ethical issues for eight marks and often were unable to describe how the threats arose. In particular, other than the common mistake of not adequately explaining the threats to objectivity that were present specific to the scenario, candidates appeared unable to differentiate between a loan from any audit client and a loan on normal commercial terms from a client that happened to be a financial institution. Similarly, candidates did not appear to be able to differentiate between the safeguards appropriate for a non-listed client and one which was. This was particularly the case on the UK and IRL exams where local regulations prohibit the provision of the service in question as it would form a material component of the financial statements.

| Marking scheme | | |
|---|---|---|
| | | *Marks* |
| (a) | **Clarke Co** | |
| | **Matters to be discussed and individual impact on financial statements** | |
| | Generally up to 2 marks for full discussion of each matter and impact on opinion. | |
| | – Lease at largest site is material to SOFP at 2.2% of total assets; leases at other two sites are also material at 2.8% of total assets (max 1 mark) | |
| | – General requirement of IFRS 16 to capitalise all leases on SOFP as right-of-use assets at PV of lease payments from commencement date (i.e. date asset is available for use) | |
| | – IFRS 16 exemption (optional) for short-term leases of less than 12 months with no purchase option hence if client elects, no need to recognise lease on SOFP (n.b. no P/L effect yet as commencement date at year end) | |

- Short-term lease exemption must be made by class of underlying asset, hence treatment across three sites must be consistent
- To discuss exemption with FD at meeting: if elects not to take exemption across the three sites, assets and liabilities are materially understated; hence the proposed adjustment is correct and a right-of-use asset and lease liability of $475,000 should be recognised
- Alternatively, if client does elect to take exemption across all three sites, then assets and liabilities are materially overstated and right-of-use assets and lease liabilities of $625,000 should be derecognised

**Impact on audit opinion:**
If client makes no adjustment, the statement of financial position is materially misstated and the audit opinion should be qualified on this basis with an 'except for' opinion

|                |   |
|----------------|---|
| Maximum        | 7 |

**Legal claim**
- Claim is material to SOFP at 5.5% of total assets (max 1 mark)
- Provision should be recognised per IAS 37 as unpaid, probable liability at reporting date
- Asset should also be recognised as payment by insurance company is virtually certain
- The asset and liability should be shown separately on the SOFP and not offset; there is no net impact on P/L; as a result both assets and liabilities are materially understated
- Full details of both provision and contingent asset should be disclosed in notes to financial statements

**Impact on audit opinion:**
If client makes no adjustment, the statement of financial position is materially misstated and the audit opinion should be qualified on this basis with an 'except for' opinion

|                |   |
|----------------|---|
| Maximum        | 5 |

**Asset impairment**
- Impairment of $85,000 is not material in isolation to either SOFP or P/L (max 1 mark)
- New competitor is significant change in site's market and therefore impairment indicator; site is CGU and therefore appropriate to conduct impairment test at this level
- Recoverable amount is higher of value in use and fair value less selling costs; fair value less costs of disposal is $3,515,000 and therefore asset is impaired by $85,000 (client appears to have incorrectly excluded cost of removing assets from calculation but correctly excluded the costs of business reorganisation)

**Impact on audit opinion:**
Assets and profits are both (immaterially) overstated; hence if no adjustment made, there will be no impact on the audit opinion in relation to this issue in isolation

|                    |    |
|--------------------|----|
| Maximum            | 5  |
| Maximum for part a | 17 |

(b) **Turner Co**
**Ethical and professional issues and actions to be taken by audit firm**
Generally up to 1 mark for each issue and action.
**Loan to member of the audit team**
Issues:
- Potential self-interest threat to auditor independence
- Key issue is whether 'the very best deal which the bank can offer' is made under normal lending procedures, terms and conditions

|  |  |  |
|---|---|---|
| – | If not, self-interest threat created would be so significant that no safeguards could reduce it to acceptable level and Janette should be told not to take loan | |
| – | If it is made under bank's normal lending procedures, terms and conditions, the loan does not create a threat to auditor's independence and Janette may accept the loan | |

Actions:

| | | |
|---|---|---|
| – | Discuss terms and conditions of loan with Janette and business manager | |
| – | Obtain draft loan documents and review details in order to establish whether under normal lending procedures, terms and conditions | |
| – | Inform audit engagement partner, who is responsible for ethical compliance | |
| – | Advise Janette on outcome of review and whether she can accept loan and advise business manager of decision explaining rationale/ethical rules | |
| | **Maximum** | **4** |

**Temporary staff assignment**

Issues:

| | | |
|---|---|---|
| – | Potential self-review threat to auditor independence | |
| – | Must not assume management responsibilities or provide non-assurance services prohibited by the *Code* | |
| – | Cannot provide accounting and bookkeeping services (including payroll) to audit client which is a public interest entity | |
| – | Exception if services relate to matters which are collectively immaterial to financial statements | |

Actions:

| | | |
|---|---|---|
| – | Discuss details of proposed role of seconded member of staff with payroll manager/other key client contacts in order to establish significance/materiality of role to financial statements | |
| – | Advise client of outcome of these enquiries/decision; seems likely that will have to decline assignment of staff member as payroll supervisor as role appears to be material/significant to financial statements – listed/public interest entity, supervisory/management role requiring qualified member of staff on main payroll system | |
| | **Maximum** | **4** |
| | **Maximum for part b** | **8** |
| **Total** | | **25** |

20   **BREARLEY & CO**    *Walk in the footsteps of a top tutor*

*Top tutor tips*

*Part (a) asks for the matters to be considered and the audit evidence that should be on file during your review of the audit file. Use the 'MARE' approach. First, consider the materiality of the issue. Next discuss the appropriate accounting treatment and give the risks of material misstatement that would arise if the appropriate treatment is not followed. Finally, the evidence is what you would expect to be recorded on the audit file when you come to review it.*

> *Part (b) asks for a critical appraisal of the draft auditor's report extracts. Don't just focus on whether the opinion is appropriate. You should also think about the titles of the paragraphs included and whether the names are correct, the order they appear in, whether the required information that should be included has been included and whether the wording used is professional and appropriate.*

**(a)** **Dilley Co**

**Matters**

The key matter to be considered is the status of the investment in Dilley Co in the consolidated financial statements of the Group. Although the 40% holding falls within the usual percentage presumption range for an associate following IAS 28 *Investments in Associates and Joint Ventures*, the existence of the share options over the remaining 60% is indicative of control following IFRS 10 *Consolidated Financial Statements*. IFRS 10 contains specific guidance on situations where control may exist when the investor does not hold a majority of the voting rights.

According to IFRS 10, control and therefore status as a subsidiary may be based on potential voting rights provided such rights are substantive. In the case of Dilley Co, the potential voting rights are exercisable in the near future (within one month of the reporting date) and the 10% discount on market price makes them commercially attractive to the Group. The options therefore represent substantive potential voting rights and Dilley Co's statement of profit or loss should be consolidated line by line from the date of acquisition.

The 40% holding in Dilley Co has been held for 11 months of the current reporting period. The time apportioned revenue of $82.5 million ($90 million × 11/12) is therefore material to the consolidated financial statements at 1.1%.

On the same basis, the time apportioned loss before tax is $11 million ($12 million × 11/12) which is $6.6 million greater than the loss recognised under the equity method of $4.4 million.

The difference is also material to the financial statements at 12% of the Group's profit before tax. Given the loss making status of Dilley Co, there is an incentive not to consolidate the entity. The auditor should exercise professional scepticism and consider whether there are any implications in relation to management integrity.

**Evidence**

- A copy of the legal documents supporting the acquisition of the shares and the options including the voting rights and the terms of exercise for the options.
- A review of the audit working papers for Dilley Co, including details of the issued share capital and the associated voting rights attached to shares.
- The group board minutes relating to the acquisition and the intentions of management in relation to Dilley Co.
- Written representations from management on the degree of influence exercised over Dilley Co and the future intentions of management in relation to the share options.

**(b)** **Willis Co**

**Matters**

The fair value of the derivatives of $6.1 million is material to consolidated profit before tax at 11.1% but in isolation, it is immaterial to consolidated assets at 0.4%.

IFRS 9 *Financial Instruments* requires the recognition of derivatives on the statement of financial position at fair value with the associated gains and losses being recognised in profit or loss for the period.

The fair value of $6.1 million should therefore be included in current assets on the Group's consolidated statement of financial position and given that the options were entered into in the last three months of the period at no initial net investment, a fair value gain of $6.1 million should also be recorded in the Group's consolidated statement of profit or loss for the year.

The treatment of the derivatives under local GAAP is acceptable in Willis Co's individual entity financial statements. For group purposes, however, accounting policies must be consistent and the profit before tax in the draft consolidated financial statements is materially understated.

The auditor must also exercise professional scepticism with regard to whether the directors have the required expertise to value the derivatives and should consider the need for independent, external evidence of the fair value of the options at the reporting date.

**Evidence**

– Details of the fair value of the options based on prices derived from an active market or if this is not available, an independent expert valuation.

– Audit documentation of the review of derivative contracts and confirmation of the terms and maturity dates.

– Notes of a discussion with management in relation to the basis of their valuation and the accounting treatment required in the consolidated financial statements.

**(b) Critical appraisal of the draft auditor's report**

There are a number of issues to consider in critically appraising the auditor's report extract which has been drafted by the audit senior. These include the following:

**Key audit matters (KAM)**

The section should include an introductory paragraph explaining the concept of KAM in order for users of the auditor's report to understand its importance and significance. The introduction should also clearly state that the auditor is not forming a separate opinion on the items identified as KAM.

**Valuation of financial instruments**

This is an area of significant audit judgment with a high risk of material misstatement, hence inclusion as KAM is appropriate although the disclosure should explain the factors which led the auditor to determine the matter was a KAM. It would also aid user understanding further if the auditor's report quantified the size and significance of the issue and explained its impact on the nature and extent of the audit effort.

The auditor should describe how the KAM was addressed in the audit, and although this is a matter for auditor judgment, the auditor may describe aspects of the auditor's response or approach, provide a brief overview of the procedures performed and an indication of the outcome of the procedures. Based on the current wording, the users of the auditor's report would have no clear indication of how the auditor has gathered evidence over this key area.

There are also several issues in relation to the detailed drafting of the paragraph. The report should not refer to the Group's finance director by name and should not imply criticism of him as result of his inexperience. The use of the word 'guesswork' is inappropriate and undermines the credibility of the audit and financial reporting process.

**Customer liquidation**

The amount owed by the customer of $287,253 is material to the loss before tax at 13.1% and to assets at 2%. The 'except for' qualification on the grounds of material misstatement is therefore appropriate. However, the details of the material misstatement should not be included in the KAM section at all but should be given in the basis for qualified opinion paragraph.

This should also be clearly cross referenced within the opinion paragraph itself. Furthermore, the wording of the report currently references reducing the profit before tax when it should refer to increasing the loss before tax.

**Opinion paragraph**

This is incorrectly positioned and incorrectly titled. It should be at the start of the auditor's report and should simply be titled 'Qualified Opinion'. The opinion paragraph should be clearly cross referenced to the 'Basis for Qualified Opinion' paragraph which should be placed immediately below the opinion paragraph and should clearly describe the issue which has given rise to a qualified opinion. As above, the 'except for' qualification on the grounds of materiality is appropriate.

**Going concern – Emphasis of matter**

Following ISA 570 *Going Concern*, the use of an emphasis of matter paragraph to refer to uncertainties in relation to going concern disclosures in the financial statements is no longer appropriate. The auditor's report should now include a specific section headed 'Material Uncertainty Related to Going Concern' immediately after the basis for opinion paragraph and before the KAM section. The material uncertainty related to going concern should be cross referenced clearly to the disclosure note where the directors have given details of the uncertainty. If the matter has not been adequately disclosed by the directors in the financial statements, the auditor should give full details of the uncertainties in relation to going concern and the audit opinion should be qualified 'except for' the material misstatement in relation to this lack of disclosure.

---

**Examiner's comments**

This question was centred on the review of a Group of companies and required candidates to consider the matters outlined and to explain what audit evidence would be required.

The first scenario described the accounting treatment of a new acquisition in which the client company had acquired 40% of the voting shares but with an option to acquire the remaining 60% at a discount to the market value. IFRS 10 *Consolidated Financial Statements* contains specific guidance on such situations when the investor may have control even when a majority of the shares are not held. In this case as the options were exercisable in the near future the acquisition should have been treated as a subsidiary rather than an associate. This question tended to produce poor answers as the majority of candidates proved to be unfamiliar with the relevant accounting standard and hence did not realise the accounting for the acquisition was incorrect.

---

The second scenario included a foreign subsidiary that used local GAAP rather than IFRS. The subsidiary had forward commodity options with a fair value of $6.1m that had been disclosed at the year-end rather than included on the statement of financial position. Stronger candidates were able to recognise that on consolidation the subsidiary accounts should be aligned with IFRS and the derivatives recognised on the consolidated statement of financial position at fair value with the associated gains or losses being recognised in the consolidated statement of profit or loss. Further credit was then available for considering the evidence required to support the value of the derivatives. A number of weaker candidates disappointingly discussed the need to translate the year-end financial statements of the subsidiary although the question had specifically stated that the subsidiary had the same functional and presentational currency as the parent.

The second requirement was to critically appraise an extract from an auditor's report, which had been incorrectly prepared and needed amendment. It was clear that the candidates had read the relevant article and were able to identify that the sections were in the wrong order, contained inappropriate wording and that the key audit matters and emphasis of matters paragraphs had been incorrectly used. Good candidates were able to explain when an issue should be included as a key audit matter or if the issue would result in a qualification and hence needed to be part of the basis of opinion paragraph. Other candidates correctly commented that it would be inappropriate to include an emphasis of matter paragraph but that the report should include a section headed material uncertainty related to going concern.

| Marking scheme | | Marks |
|---|---|---|
| **(a)** **Matters to consider and evidence on file**<br>Generally up to 1½ marks for each matter and up to 1 mark for each evidence point explained.<br>**(i)** **Dilley Co**<br>**Matters**<br>– Materiality<br>– IFRS 10 definition of subsidiary is based on control and contains specific guidance on situations where control may exist when investor does NOT hold majority of voting rights<br>– Control and subsidiary status may be based on potential voting rights; following IFRS 10 rights do not have to be currently exercisable but must be 'substantive'<br>– Here potential voting rights are exercisable in near future and are 'in the money', hence likely to be subsidiary; consolidated SOCI should therefore include line by line consolidation for 11 months and a loss of $11 million in relation to Dilley Co<br>– Difference of $6.6 million is material to group SOCI; management have incentive not to consolidate (especially in light of declining profitability)<br>– Group revenue should include $82.5 million for Dilley Co and will therefore also be materially understated<br>**Evidence**<br>– Copy of legal documents supporting acquisition of shares and options including voting rights and terms of exercise for options<br>– Audit working papers for Dilley Co confirming details of issued share capital and associated voting rights<br>– Board minutes relating to acquisition and management intentions in relation to Dilley Co<br>– Management representations on degree of influence and future intentions<br>– Copy of the adjusting journal required to reflect the correct treatment in the financial statements | | |
| Maximum | | 7 |

**(ii)    Willis Co**

**Matters**

- Materiality
- Group accounting policies should be consistent
- Treatment is acceptable in individual entity financial statements but not for Group accounts
- IFRS 9 requires recognition of derivatives on SOFP at fair value with gains and losses in profit or loss for period
- Fair value of derivatives is material to group profit (with supporting calculation)
- Directors may not have expertise required for valuation of the options
- Need for external independent evidence of fair value at reporting date

**Evidence**

- Fair value based on market prices or if not available, independent expert valuation
- Audit documentation of review of derivative contracts and confirmation of terms and maturity dates
- Notes of discussion with management in relation to the basis of their valuation and the accounting treatment
- Copy of the adjusting journal required to reflect the correct treatment in the financial statements

| | |
|---|---:|
| **Maximum** | **6** |

**(b)    Critical appraisal of the draft auditor's report**

In general up to 1 mark for each well explained point:

**KAM section**

- KAM section should include introductory paragraph explaining what KAMs are
- Auditor not forming separate opinion on KAM

**Valuation of financial instruments**

- Area of significant audit judgment with high risk of material misstatement, hence inclusion as KAM potentially appropriate
- Would aid user understanding if:
  - quantified size/significance of issue
  - explained impact on nature and extent of audit effort
- Inappropriate drafting of paragraph:
  - should not refer to FD by name
  - should not imply criticism of him as result of inexperience
  - choice of language 'guesswork' undermines credibility of audit and financial reporting process

**Customer liquidation**

- Material to profit and assets (with calculation)
- Details of material misstatement should not be included in KAM section at all but should be given in basis for qualified opinion paragraph and should be clearly cross referenced to opinion paragraph
- Wording refers to reducing profit before tax when it should refer to increasing the loss before tax

**Opinion paragraph**

- Incorrectly positioned, should now be at start of auditor's report and should be clearly cross referenced to basis of opinion paragraph below which details the material misstatement
- Incorrect title, it should be headed simply 'Qualified Opinion'
- Except for qualification appropriate on grounds of material misstatement

| | | |
|---|---|---|
| **Going concern** | | |
| – Following ISA 570 (revised), use of an EoM paragraph no longer appropriate | | |
| – Auditor's report should now include section headed 'Material Uncertainty Related to Going Concern' | | |
| – Section should be immediately after basis for opinion but before KAM section | | |
| – Should cross reference clearly to disclosure note where directors have given details of uncertainty | | |
| – If not adequately disclosed by directors, opinion should be qualified 'except for' lack of disclosure | | |
| | Maximum | 12 |
| **Total** | | 25 |

## 21 BASKING  *Walk in the footsteps of a top tutor*

*Top tutor tips*

*Part (a) is a knowledge requirement covering the three types of misstatement and why the auditor should consider the type of misstatement when evaluating the further actions to be taken. You either know this or you don't. If you don't know it, move on to part (b) which is a more common requirement and come back to part (a) once you've got the easier marks.*

*Part (b) asks for matters to be discussed with management followed by the reporting implications. This is a typical question seen on almost every recent past paper which emphasises the importance of practising past papers to prepare for the exam.*

*Part (c) requires knowledge and application of the key audit matter section within an auditor's report for a listed company. You need to know the types of matters that would be referred to in a KAM and be able to describe the information that would be included in the KAM.*

**(a)** **Types of misstatement**

ISA 450 *Evaluation of Misstatements Identified During the Audit* identifies three types of misstatement:

1   Factual misstatements

2   Judgmental misstatements, and

3   Projected misstatements.

It is important for the auditor to consider the type of misstatement as the nature of an identified misstatement will have a significant impact on the auditor's evaluation of the misstatement and any consequent further actions necessary in response.

**Factual misstatements**

When the auditor discovers a factual misstatement, where there can be no doubt over the error, there is little room for discussion with management. Once a factual misstatement, such as a miscalculation of depreciation, has been established, management should be asked to correct it.

**Judgmental misstatements**

With regard to judgmental misstatements, the validity of the auditor's opinion and any consequent corrections recommended by the auditor are more open to debate. It is therefore vital that in such matters the auditor compiles sufficient evidence to justify why they believe management's judgment is inappropriate in a specific circumstance. Without this weight of evidence to support their position, it is unlikely that management will accept the auditor's view.

Even with sufficient evidence, management may still disagree with the auditor's opinion and refuse to accept their judgment in a specific matter. This heightens the risk that the auditor makes an inappropriate conclusion and, ultimately, that they issue an incorrect auditor's report.

If material matters of this nature are identified, it is vital that they are considered by a suitably senior member of the audit team.

**Projected misstatements**

Projected misstatements assume that an error identified in a sample may be repeated throughout the whole population. The smaller the size of the population originally tested, the lower the validity of this assumption. Clearly the auditor should not recommend the correction of a projected misstatement. These should be used by the audit team to determine the potential for a material misstatement in the wider population being tested and this should guide their decisions as to whether they need to extend their testing.

(b) (1) **Depreciation charge**

**Matters**

The error identified in the sample represents less than 0.001% of total assets and less than 0.02% of profits. In isolation the error is therefore immaterial.

The error is, however, limited to the sample audited, which represents only 3.6% of total vehicles. If the error is extrapolated to the whole population, it could potentially lead to a total error of $9.7million (0.35m/4.5m × 125m). This represents 0.03% of total assets and 0.4% of profits; and it would seem that the potential error is therefore also not material to the financial statements. The auditor should ensure that they understand how the error has occurred and if the error is isolated, for example, to a certain category of asset, as there is scope for the error to be greater depending on how the miscalculation has occurred.

Regardless of the immateriality of the projected misstatement, there is still a factual, known error in the financial statements. Management should be asked to correct the error in relation to the depreciation of newly acquired assets.

Management should be asked to make the corrected non-current asset register available to the audit team so that they are able to audit the revised register to determine its accuracy.

Furthermore, the auditor should seek evidence that, as well as correcting the error in the financial statements, the relevant system has been corrected to ensure that all new non-current asset purchases are correctly depreciated in the future so that it does not affect subsequent periods.

**Opinion**

If management refuses to amend the valuation of motor vehicles, then assets and depreciation will both be misstated by an immaterial amount.

As long as the auditor is satisfied that the source of the error has been corrected and this is not an ongoing issue which will effect subsequent periods, the auditor would issue a standard, unmodified audit opinion, stating that the financial statements are fairly presented in all material respects.

**(2)    Loan**

**Matters**

The loan represents a related party transaction as it is between the company and one of its key management personnel.

The value of the loan may be trivial; it certainly is not material to the financial statements by value. Regardless, related party transactions are material by nature.

In these circumstances, the directors of the company may be abusing their position and power for their own personal gain and it is likely that the loan is being provided to Mrs Angel on favourable or non-commercial terms.

For this reason, details relating to the loan must be disclosed in the financial statements, including the amount of the loan, who the loan has been made to and the amount outstanding at the end of the year.

The auditor in this circumstance will disagree with the judgment applied by management in their application of IAS 24 *Related Party Transactions* and the auditor should request that the additional disclosures are added to the financial statements.

**Opinion**

If management refuses to make the recommended adjustments to the financial statements, then the auditor will conclude that the financial statements are materially misstated due to a lack of appropriate disclosure. While the adjustment is material by nature, a lack of disclosure is unlikely to be considered to be pervasive to the financial statements as a whole.

In these circumstances the auditor should issue a qualified opinion, stating that 'except for' the matters identified the financial statements are fairly presented.

**(3)    Provision**

**Matters**

A provision for 7% of one month's sales would total $328 million ($56,360m/ 12 × 7%). Reducing it to 4% would create a provision of $188 million ($56,360m/12 × 4%). As a result of the change in calculation, the amount of the provision would be reduced by $140 million.

As well as reducing the provision recognised on the statement of financial position, the release of the provision would also increase the profit reported by $140 million. At 5.5% of profit and 0.37% of total assets, the adjustment is material to the statement of profit or loss but not to the statement of financial position.

This is clearly a matter of judgment. The change must, however, be reasonable and supported by evidence that it is more appropriate to the circumstances of the business. The audit team has found no evidence to support the change made by management.

The risk associated with this is heightened because the release of provisions is a known earnings management technique and Basking Co has suffered a reduction in profits this year. The auditor must apply professional scepticism in these circumstances and be aware that management may be using this as a device to restore profits to help achieve their annual targets.

In these circumstances, it would be appropriate to ask the management team of Basking Co for some form of evidence that the change to their system will lead to a lower rate of refunds. In the absence of any evidence the auditor should explain that the change is purely speculative and as it appears to be unjustified at the present time, that Basking Co should revert back to the original provision until there is evidence of improved effectiveness.

**Opinion**

If management refuses to amend the provision, it is likely that the auditor will conclude that the financial statements are materially misstated. In isolation it is unlikely that the auditor will conclude that this is a pervasive matter as it has limited impact on the financial statements as a whole.

In these circumstances, the auditor should issue a qualified opinion, stating that 'except for' the matters identified the financial statements are fairly presented.

**(c)    New computer system**

Basking Co is a listed entity therefore a Key Audit Matters (KAM) section will be required in the auditor's report.

These are matters that, in the auditor's professional judgment, were of most significance in the audit and required significant attention during the audit.

KAM are selected from matters communicated with those charged with governance.

Examples of matters to be included in a KAM are areas of significant audit risk and areas requiring significant auditor judgment relating to areas of the financial statements.

In the auditor's report of Basking Co, the KAM section should include a reference to the audit risk related to accuracy and completeness of revenue as a result of the new computer system.

The KAM should detail why this was considered to be an area of significance in the audit and therefore determined to be a KAM.

It should also explain how the matter was addressed in the audit and the auditor should provide a brief overview of the audit procedures adopted such as tests of controls over the new system and substantive tests over revenue.

**Examiner's comments**

Candidates who had read the examiner's article prior to the examination and who have a good understanding of materiality should have found this question straightforward. Candidates were asked for a discussion on the three types of misstatement described in ISA 450 *Evaluation of Misstatements Identified During the Audit*. Candidates were expected to define the types of misstatement (factual, judgmental and projected) and could get full marks by describing how to address each of those with management or through further audit work.

The second part of the scenario had an example of each type of misstatement and required application of the knowledge demonstrated in the first part of the question, requiring candidates to cover what should be discussed with management and the effect on the audit opinion. This was well answered by well-prepared candidates however a significant portion of candidates failed to calculate materiality correctly and concluded an immaterial depreciation error was material. There was also a lack of appreciation that related party transactions are material by nature. Candidates should note that the requirement specifically asked for the effect on the audit opinion not the full auditor's report so there was no credit available for describing the basis of opinion or Key Audit Matters in part (b). There are still a number of candidates who show a lack of understanding of misstatements and propose emphasis of matter paragraphs as an alternative to qualifying the report for factual misstatements or to explain immaterial/trivial items.

---

## Marking scheme

|  |  | *Marks* |
|---|---|---|
| **(a)** | **Types of misstatement** | |
| | In general up to 1½ marks for each relevant and adequate point of explanation. Award ½ mark for identification of a relevant matter and up to a further 1 mark for appropriate discussion. ½ mark should be awarded for relevant points which are either too brief or poorly explained. | |
| | – Identification and discussion of types of misstatement (max 1) | |
| | – Impact on evaluation of impact on financial statements | |
| | – Subjectivity involved in judgmental matters | |
| | – Potential inaccuracy of projected misstatements | |
| | **Maximum** | **5** |
| **(b)** | In general up to 1 mark for each relevant and adequate point of explanation. ½ mark should be awarded for relevant points which are either too brief or poorly explained. | |
| | **(1) Depreciation** | |
| | – Error in isolation immaterial (max ½ mark) | |
| | – Error also immaterial when projected to total population | |
| | – Client should be requested to amend the error | |
| | – Auditor should investigate revised non-current asset register | |
| | – If management refuses, there is still no material misstatement | |
| | – Unmodified opinion | |
| | **Maximum** | **5** |

|  |  |  |  |  |
|---|---|---|---|---|
| (2) | **Loan** | | | |
| | – | Related party transaction | | |
| | – | Material by nature | | |
| | – | Requires full disclosure in the financial statements | | |
| | – | Failure to adjust leads to a material but not pervasive misstatement | | |
| | – | Qualified opinion | | |
| | | | **Maximum** | 5 |
| (3) | **Provision** | | | |
| | – | Calculation of potential provision values and value of adjustment | | |
| | – | Adjustment is material to statement of profit or loss | | |
| | – | Matter of judgment – must be reasoned and supported with evidence | | |
| | – | Potential for earnings management | | |
| | – | Request management to reinstate full provision | | |
| | – | Failure to adjust leads to a material but not pervasive misstatement | | |
| | – | Qualified opinion | | |
| | | | **Maximum** | 5 |

| (c) | **New computer system** | | | |
|---|---|---|---|---|
| | – | Listed company therefore KAM required | | |
| | – | KAM – matters of significance during the audit requiring extra attention | | |
| | – | Selected from those charged with governance | | |
| | – | Examples of matters to be included in a KAM section | | |
| | – | KAM should detail audit risk related to revenue | | |
| | – | KAM should detail why it was an area of significance | | |
| | – | KAM should detail how the matter was addressed | | |
| | | | **Maximum** | 5 |
| **Total** | | | | 25 |

## 22 MAGNOLIA GROUP  *Walk in the footsteps of a top tutor*

*Top tutor tips*

*Part (i) of the requirement asks for quality control and other professional issues raised in relation to three scenarios. Quality control is a common topic in the exam. Consider whether the audit has been performed in accordance with professional standards and whether the auditor has conducted the work with due professional care. Consider how you would have audited the matters described and whether the auditor has performed those procedures. If not, suggest them in your answer to part (ii).*

*For part (d) you need to state the impact to the auditor's report if the client does not amend the financial statements. State the impact to both the report and opinion as a result of the issues. When considering the impact to the group auditor's report you must consider whether the issue affecting the subsidiary is material to the group as a whole.*

(a)     **Hyacinth Co – internal controls and results of control testing**

(i)     **Audit planning and performance**

Where assessment of internal controls at the initial stage of the audit concludes that controls are ineffective there is no necessity to perform tests of controls, which was an incorrect response in the Group audit. Tests of controls should not be performed in order to confirm that controls are not effective.

According to ISA 330/ISA (UK) 330 *The Auditor's Response to Assessed Risks*, the auditor should only use tests of control as a method of gathering evidence where there is an expectation that controls are operating effectively.

The correct response should have been to increase substantive audit procedures around the area of intra-group transactions. Given that the Group companies supply each other with chemical products to use in their manufacturing processes, the volume and monetary amount of the intra-group transactions could be significant. Related party transactions are often an area of significant risk and intra-group balances can be an easy way to manipulate the individual company accounts.

The comment made by the audit manager that 'no further work is necessary' on the intra-group transactions seems to be based on the concept that intra-group balances are cancelled in the Group financial statements at consolidation. This is true, but audit work should be performed on these transactions because they will still be recognised in the individual financial statements and audit evidence should be obtained to support the value of the transactions and balances. Further, if these balances have not been appropriately reconciled, this could create significant issues on consolidation.

In addition, if no audit work is performed on the intra-group transactions then no assurance can be obtained over the value of adjustments made during the consolidation process to eliminate them. Also audit work should be performed to determine the validity of any provision for unrealised profit recognised in the Group financial statements. There does not appear to be any audit evidence at all to support the necessary consolidation adjustments which is a significant deficiency in the quality of the group audit. It seems that the communications between Group and component auditors is not robust. The instructions given by Crocus & Co to the component auditors seem to lack detail, for example, Crocus & Co should be instructing the component auditors to carry out specific procedures on intra-group balances and transactions.

In relation to controls over capital expenditure, it is not appropriate to conclude that controls will be effective across the Group just because they are effective in one of the Group components. Testing the controls in one component cannot provide assurance that the control risk in the other components is at the same level. This is particularly the case for Geranium Co, which is a recent acquisition, and Crocus & Co has no previous knowledge of its control environment and processes.

It is possible that the audit of capital expenditure in the Group components other than Hyacinth Co is not of acceptable quality due to over-reliance on controls over which no assurance has been obtained. The instructions given to the component auditors may not have been based on an appropriate audit strategy in relation to the audit of capital expenditure.

Crocus & Co, in its evaluation of the work performed by the component auditors, should have assessed the level of testing which was performed on Daisy Co and Geranium Co's internal controls over capital expenditure, and the conclusions which were drawn. Sufficient and appropriate audit evidence may not have been obtained, leading to a risk of material misstatement of property, plant and equipment.

**(ii)** **Further actions to be taken**

The deficiencies in internal control over intra-group transactions should be brought to the attention of Group management. ISA 600 / ISA (UK) 600 *Special Considerations – Audits of Group Financial Statements (Including the Work of Component Auditors)* requires that the group engagement team shall determine which identified deficiencies in internal control to communicate to those charged with governance and group management. This should include group-wide controls and controls over the consolidation process.

The audit working papers for the component companies should be reviewed to establish if any audit procedures on intra-group balances and transactions have been performed at the company level.

Further audit procedures should be performed on intra-group transactions including:

- Discuss with the Group finance director the process used to determine the value of intra-group transactions and balances which are adjusted at consolidation.

- Using automated tools and techniques, such as audit software, determine the monetary value of intra-group balances and agree to the finance director's estimate and amounts in the consolidation schedule.

- Perform substantive analytical procedures to form an evaluation of the expected level of intra-group sales and purchases.

- Obtain copies of the individual company accounts and agree all relevant group balances and disclosures.

- Agree a sample of intra-group sales and purchases to source documentation including orders and invoices.

- Determine the basis of any provision for unrealised profit recognised through review of the finance director's calculations, and re-perform the relevant calculations.

In respect of the audit work on capital expenditure, the Group audit team should firstly determine the materiality of capital expenditure in each component and if material ensure that further substantive audit procedures are performed or have been performed by the component auditor, including:

- Agreeing a sample of capital expenditure items to source documentation including capital expenditure budget, supplier invoice and order or requisition form.

- Physical verification of a sample of items.

- Obtaining relevant insurance documents for significant assets acquired.

**(b)** **Geranium Co – new subsidiary**

**(i)** **Audit planning and performance**

The audit manager's conclusion that Geranium is immaterial to the Group financial statements is based on the profit to be consolidated, which amounts to 2% of Group profit before tax. However, the assets of Geranium Co amount to 23.1% of Group total assets and therefore the subsidiary is material to the Group on that basis.

The Group audit team should give further consideration to whether Geranium Co is a significant component of the Group. It is likely that representing nearly one quarter of Group assets makes the company a significant component.

According to ISA 600, depending on the nature and circumstances of the group, appropriate benchmarks for determining whether a component is a significant component might include a threshold based on group assets, liabilities, cash flows, profit or turnover. For example, the group engagement team may consider that components exceeding 15% of the chosen benchmark are significant components.

Assuming therefore that Geranium Co is a significant component of the group, obtaining audit evidence purely based on analytical procedures is not sufficient. ISA 600 allows that for components which are not significant components, the group engagement team can perform analytical procedures at group level. However, for a component which is significant due to its individual financial significance to the group, the group engagement team, or a component auditor on its behalf, shall perform an audit of the financial information of the component using component materiality.

The audit evidence obtained by the group audit team in respect of Geranium Co therefore needs to be more robust in order for the Group audit manager to reach a conclusion on its balances which will be consolidated.

The lack of audit working papers indicates that there has been no communication with the component auditors. This is a significant quality control problem and a breach of ISA 600 which requires that the group audit team obtain an understanding of the component auditor, and be involved with the component auditor's risk assessment to identify risks of material misstatement. This is especially the case given that Geranium Co is a new component of the group, and this is Crocus & Co's first experience of working with their auditors.

**(ii)** **Further actions to be taken**

The component auditor's independence and competence should be evaluated and procedures should be performed to evaluate whether the component auditor operates in a regulatory environment which actively oversees auditors. These could be achieved through a discussion with the component auditor and requesting them to complete a questionnaire on these matters for evaluation by the group audit team.

The Group audit team should liaise with the component auditor as soon as possible in order to discuss their audit findings, obtain access to their working papers, and ultimately decide on the specific nature of the further procedures to be performed, which should be based on component materiality.

(c) **Daisy Co – restriction on international trade**

(i) **Audit planning and performance**

Based on monetary values, Daisy Co does not appear to be a significant component, its assets represent 6.2% of consolidated assets, and its profit is less than 1% of group profit and immaterial on that basis. As discussed above, a normal threshold for a significant component is 15% of group assets or profit.

However, due to the new government regulations and their potential impact on the operations of Daisy Co, the component could be evaluated as significant due to its specific circumstances which may create a risk of material misstatement at group level.

One risk arises in relation to the goodwill balance, which is material at 2.3% of group assets. The government regulation is an indicator that goodwill could be impaired, but an assessment of goodwill is required regardless of the existence of such indicators. The audit working papers will need to be carefully reviewed to ascertain the extent of work, if any, which has been performed on the goodwill of Daisy Co. The audit manager's comment that the issue has no impact on the consolidated accounts implies that this matter may not have been factored into any goodwill assessment which has taken place as part of audit procedures. Therefore the quality of the audit evidence to support the goodwill balance of $3 million is in doubt.

It is not sufficient to rely solely on the audit opinion issued by Foxglove & Co. ISA 600 requires that for a component which is significant because it is likely to include significant risks of material misstatement of the group financial statements due to its specific nature or circumstances, the group engagement team, or a component auditor on its behalf, shall perform one or more of the following:

–   An audit of the financial information of the component using component materiality.

–   An audit of one or more account balances, classes of transactions or disclosures relating to the likely significant. risks of material misstatement of the group financial statements.

–   Specified audit procedures relating to the likely significant risks of material misstatement of the group financial statements.

There is a risk that not all of the implications of the government regulations have been addressed by Foxglove & Co during their audit. For example, they should have considered the overall going concern status of the company, and the impact on the valuation of property, plant and equipment as well as inventories.

There is also a risk that does not appear to have been considered by the Group audit manager in that the government regulation may affect other components of the group due to Daisy Co's role in the group of developing and providing products to the other group companies, and therefore any restrictions on Daisy Co's operations may affect all the other components of the group. This issue may also raise concerns over the work which has been conducted in relation to ISA 250/ISA (UK) 250 *Consideration of Laws and Regulations in an Audit of Financial Statements* and there is a risk that the Group auditor's assessment of the legal and regulatory framework that affects the Group has not been sufficiently understood or documented.

The fact that the Group's board members have not mentioned the regulation to the Group audit manager could indicate that the Group's management is trying to hide the situation from the auditor. The audit manager should exercise professional scepticism and enquire further into the matter, as discussed below. If the Group's management were genuinely unaware of the new regulations then corporate governance, especially in relation to risk monitoring and assessment would appear to be deficient. This impacts on the audit by increasing the risk of management bias and actions of management which may deliberately mislead the auditor.

In summary, this situation indicated a lack of quality in the group audit due to the over reliance on the audit findings of the component auditor. In addition, the group audit manager seems not to have considered the wider implications of the government regulation on the risk assessment for the group as a whole.

(ii)     **Further actions to be taken**

Request the audit working papers from Foxglove & Co and review the work performed on the government regulation and its impact on the financial statements and going concern. The group audit team should confirm the materiality level which was used in audit procedures is in line with their assessment of an appropriate component materiality, and should ensure that appropriate methods were used to identify and respond to the risks of material misstatement.

The group audit team may decide that additional audit procedures are necessary, for example:

- Obtain the assessment of going concern performed by the management of Daisy Co and review the reasonableness of the assumptions used, especially those relating to future revenue streams and cash inflows.

- Obtain a copy of the government regulation to understand the exact nature of the restrictions imposed and implications for the going concern of Daisy Co.

In addition, the group assessment of going concern will need to be re-evaluated, taking into account the impact of the government regulation on the other Group companies. Given that the Group sells products in over 50 countries, it is likely that it is not just Daisy Co which is affected by this new regulation, and additional audit work should be performed on evaluating the going concern status of each company and of the Group as a whole.

Additional procedures should be performed on the $3 million goodwill balance recognised in respect of Daisy Co, to include a determination of the value in use of Daisy Co, based on future cash flows taking into account the likely impact of the government regulations.

**Conclusion**

Overall, the problems noted in the Group audit indicate that the Group audit manager lacks competence, and that inappropriate judgments have been made. There are several instances of ISA requirements not being followed and the audit has not been performed with sufficient due care for professional standards. The Group audit manager should receive training on Group accounting and Group audit issues in order to resolve the deficiencies identified in the planning and performance of this audit, and to ensure that future audits are managed appropriately.

**(d)    Auditor's opinion and report**

**Daisy Co**

The financial statements of Daisy Co will be materially misstated if the required disclosure is not made.

The auditor must use professional judgment to determine whether the effect is material but not pervasive or material and pervasive.

Assuming it is material but not pervasive, a qualified opinion should be expressed, with the auditor stating in the opinion that except for the effects of the matters described in the basis for qualified opinion paragraph, the financial statements show a true and fair view.

The basis for qualified opinion should contain a description of the matters giving rise to the qualification.

**Magnolia Group**

The impact to the group auditor's report will depend on whether the going concern status of the group as a whole is affected.

If there are no material uncertainties affecting the group's status, an unmodified opinion and report will be issued.

If the going concern issues affect the group, group management may make adequate disclosure which will result in an unmodified opinion. The auditor's report would need to include a Material Uncertainty Related to Going Concern section which would draw the user's attention to the client's disclosure note.

If management do not make the required disclosure in the consolidated financial statements, the auditor's opinion would be modified in the same way as for Daisy Co, with a qualified opinion.

---

**Examiner's comments**

This question focused on a group audit with component auditors and audit issues in each of the subsidiaries. This question was not well-answered overall with many candidates appearing not to understand the concept of the level of control required by the group auditor and the amount of instruction and interaction required with component auditors.

Part (a) considered a poorly-planned audit where the audit manager had concluded at the interim audit that intercompany balances which were not being properly accounted for did not matter "as they were eliminated on consolidation" yet he repeated the same tests and reliance on controls at the final audit. Candidates seemed unable to grasp that, because of the control failures, substantive work (such as reconciliations) was required and that this control failure should be highlighted to management at the interim stage so they could take steps to resolve these issues in advance of the final audit. Additionally, the manager tested capital expenditure controls in only one subsidiary and concluded that those results could be applied to the rest of the group without further testing. Many candidates discussed generically how to audit capital expenditure and did not consider the relevant issues raised in the scenario and that it would be necessary to evaluate the work of the component auditors and identify what additional procedures might be required.

---

Part (b) concerned a subsidiary acquired during the year which had a different auditor. Candidates generally failed to recognise that the role of the component auditor is firstly to audit the subsidiary for its whole financial year, regardless of the change of ownership. Most did not appreciate that the group auditor needs to issue instructions to the component auditor, assess their competence and independence and review and document their work as part of the group audit. Incorrectly blaming the component auditor for a poorly-planned group audit showed a lack of knowledge of the fundamentals of how a group audit works.

Requirement (c) presented another subsidiary which had a potential going concern issue but the component auditors had concluded that there was not a significant risk. Strong answers proposed a more detailed review of the component auditor's work and conclusions along with an assessment of their competence and then considered the impact on the group as a whole. It is evident that there is poor understanding that goodwill arising in the consolidated accounts is held in the consolidated statement of financial position and not in the financial statements of the subsidiary and that assessing any potential impairment is the role of the group auditor, not the component auditor. Candidates are advised to make sure that they are knowledgeable of the requirements of the ISAs in this area.

| **Marking scheme** | |
|---|---|
| | *Marks* |
| Generally up to 1½ marks for each relevant point identified and explained. Allow maximum 1½ marks for comments on the competence of the Group audit manager and the need for additional training. These marks can be awarded in any section of the question | |
| **(a)**    **Internal controls** | |
|     **(i)**    **Quality of audit work** | |
|         –   Performing tests of controls not an appropriate response where controls are deficient | |
|         –   Intra-group balances and transactions should be audited even if cancelled on consolidation | |
|         –   If not performed then the cancellation and determination of provisions for unrealised profit may not be correct | |
|         –   Inappropriate assumption on the strength of group-wide controls. The work of component auditors on capex controls should have been evaluated | |
|         –   Audit evidence may be lacking on capex and property, plant and equipment | |
|     **(ii)**    **Further actions or procedures** | |
|         –   Communicate with those charged with governance on the control deficiency | |
|         –   Review working papers on components for evidence on intra-group balances | |
|         –   Perform additional audit procedures on intra-group balances (max 3 marks for specific procedures) | |
|         –   Perform additional procedures on capex (max 2 marks for specific procedures) | |
|                                                   **Maximum** | **8** |
| **(b)**    **Geranium Co** | |
|     **(i)**    **Quality of audit work** | |
|         –   Determine that Geranium Co is a significant component | |
|         –   Not sufficient to perform analytical review only for a significant component | |
|         –   Audit evidence is insufficient to support group audit opinion | |
|         –   Understanding of the component auditor should have been obtained | |

**(ii) Further actions or procedures**
- Obtain understanding of independence, competence and regulatory framework of Fern & Co
- Liaise with Fern & Co in order to:
  - Obtain their working papers for review
  - Understand their risk assessment procedures and responses to risks identified
  - Plan further audit procedures if considered necessary

**Maximum**     5

**(c) Daisy Co**
**(i) Quality of audit work**
- Determine that Daisy Co is significant due to special circumstances
- Goodwill relating to Daisy Co likely to be overstated – not identified by audit manager
- Cannot rely solely on component auditor's opinion
- Further work required by ISA 600 including additional work on the balance identified as high risk
- Further impacts may not have been identified e.g. impairment of other assets
- Impact on other group components and group going concern should be evaluated
- Lack of audit manager's professional scepticism and increased audit risk

**(ii) Further actions or procedures**
- Request working papers of Foxglove & Co for review
- Perform additional procedures relating to the regulations and potential impairment in individual financial statements of Daisy Co (max 2 marks for specific procedures)
- Extend audit procedures at group level on goodwill impairment and going concern (max 2 marks for specific procedures)

**Maximum**     7

**(d) Auditor's opinion and report**
Generally up to 1 mark for each relevant point explained
Daisy Co
- Lack of disclosure – material misstatement
- Discussion of whether it is pervasive
- Qualified opinion
- Basis for qualified opinion paragraph
Magnolia Group
- Depends on whether going concern of group is affected
- Unmodified opinion if not affected
- Unmodified opinion with additional communication if disclosure made
- Qualified opinion if disclosure not made

**Maximum**     5

**Total**     25

**23 OSIER**  *Walk in the footsteps of a top tutor*

---

***Top tutor tips***

*For 'Matters and evidence' questions, use the 'MARE' approach to make it easier to score the required number of marks. First, consider the materiality of the issue. Next discuss the appropriate accounting treatment and give the risks of material misstatement that would arise if the appropriate treatment is not followed. Finally, the evidence is what you would expect to be recorded on the audit file when you come to review it. Be specific about the evidence, don't just say 'supporting documentation', suggest what that documentation would be and what it would show. Assume that half of the marks will be for matters and half of the marks will be for evidence.*

*In part (b) you need to assess the aggregate of the adjustments suggested by the auditor to determine whether or not the audit opinion should be modified. Identify the type of opinion required considering whether the misstatement is not material; material but not pervasive; or material and pervasive. Then go on to discuss any other impact to the auditor's report such as an explanation as to why the opinion is modified or any additional communications required.*

---

**(a)    (i)    Cost of inventory**

**Matters**

**Materiality**

Inventory costs represent 1.1% of total assets and 19.6% of profit. Inventory is therefore material to both the statement of financial position and the statement of profit or loss.

**Risk of material misstatement**

The calculation of the cost of inventory is complex. This complexity increases the risk of error in the calculation, which increases the risk of misstatement.

The calculation is also subject to a number of estimates; the average production time per unit, the forecast annual wage cost, the scheduled hours of production and the forecast units of production are all estimates. These estimates increase the risk of both error and manipulation of the calculation to suit management's bias.

Given both the complexity and subjectivity involved in the calculation there is a significant risk that the inventory cost may be misstated.

**Evidence expected to be on file:**

–    Documentation of the system for obtaining the data used in the costing exercise and calculating the final cost. This should identify the key controls that operate in this system and there should be evidence on file that these controls have been appropriately tested.

–    A copy of the summary of inventory purchase costs. A sample of the purchase costs, including the additional costs of transport and handling, should have been confirmed through inspection of original purchase invoices, copies of which should also be on file.

- Documentation of the results of a discussion with the production manager to ascertain how they estimate the average production time per unit of inventory. Any calculations referred to by management should have been re-performed by the audit team to confirm their mathematical accuracy and agreed to corroborating documentation.

- A copy of the calculation of the forecast annual wage cost. The initial staffing levels should have been confirmed through inspection of current human resource records and for a sample of the staff their initial wages should have been confirmed through inspection of payroll records.

- Forecast wage increments should have been agreed to either post year end confirmation issued by human resources or minutes of board meetings approving pay rises.

- Documentation of the results of a discussion with management regarding how the forecast is made and who is ultimately responsible for reviewing and approving the forecast.

- A copy of the calculation of forecast units of production. This should have been analytically reviewed in comparison to the previous year's production levels. Where there are significant differences explanations should have been sought from management.

- A copy of the calculation of forecast production overheads. This should have been analytically reviewed by category of overhead in relation to the previous year to identify any significant variances. Corroborating evidence, such as rental and utilities agreements, should have been obtained where possible.

- Evidence on all management's schedules that the figures have been recalculated by the audit team to confirm the mathematical accuracy of management's calculations.

**(ii)  Impairment**

**Matters**

**Materiality**

The impairment of $9 million represents 0.47% of total assets and 8.41% of profit. While it is not material to the statement of financial position it is material to the statement of profit or loss.

**Calculation of recoverable amount**

The fair value of the retail outlets, the disposal costs and the value in use are all management estimates. This increases the risk of material misstatement through both error and management manipulation of the reported figures.

In particular, while the estimate for the fair value appears to have a reasonable basis, the estimate of value in use appears to be too basic. The assumption that the cash flows attributable to the whole of the retail division will grow at 1% per annum is too simplistic and appears to lack commercial justification. It is likely that each retail outlet will be subject to regional variations in growth and growth rates will also be subject to annual fluctuations based upon economic variables. There is also no justification as to why 1% growth has been selected to represent 'poor performance', at the very least this should be benchmarked to more widespread and reliable growth forecasts, e.g. national forecasts of economic growth.

**Allocation of the impairment**

The impairment has been allocated against all of the tangible assets in the cash generating unit. This is incorrect; as a cash generating unit the impairment should firstly be allocated against any goodwill relating to the cash generating unit in accordance with IAS 36 *Impairment of Assets*. It should then be allocated against the remaining assets on a pro-rata basis bearing in mind that an asset should not be impaired below the highest of either its fair value less costs of disposal or its value in use.

**Evidence expected to be on file:**

– Copies of the offers received to purchase the retail outlets, confirming the amounts offered. These should have been used to recalculate the average used for the estimate of fair value.

– Documentation of enquiries with management with regard to how they estimated the disposal costs and what experience they have had with the sale of similar operations.

– A copy of the forecast cash flows attributable to the retail outlets. This should contain evidence of analytical review in comparison to the year ended 31 March 20X7 to confirm the accuracy of the base cash flows.

– Evidence of a recalculation of the future cash flows using management's estimates of 1% growth to confirm the mathematical accuracy of management's calculation.

– Evidence of a recalculation of the value in use using a range of growth rates to assess the sensitivity of management's calculations to economic variables. The differences between these valuations and management's valuation should have been reviewed to assess the likelihood of a material under or overvaluation.

– Evidence of an analytical review of performance by retail outlet or geographical area of operations, referenced to sales and cash flow records where available, to confirm whether growth rates are consistent across the brand or whether there are variances.

– Documentation of enquiries with management relating to their expectations for specific retail outlets or areas of operations and whether there are any specific matters which they are aware of which may affect regional performance, e.g. the opening of new out-of-town shopping facilities or competitors setting up in the same location.

– A schedule of any goodwill included in the statement of financial position with analysis of its various components to assess whether any part is attributable to the retail outlets as a cash generating unit. This is specifically relevant to any acquired brands which may be sold through the retail stores or any retail brands acquired by Osier Co.

– A recalculation of the allocation of the impairment by the auditor, firstly against any goodwill determined to be attributable to the cash generating unit, then against the remaining assets pro rata.

– Copies of previous forecasts. Where the retail outlets forecast performance exceeds the 1% currently predicted by management there should be evidence of discussion with management to ascertain the reasons for changing their outlook.

(iii) **Warranty provision**

**Matters**

**Materiality**

The year-end provision represents 0.36% of total assets and 6.54% of profit. It is not, therefore, material to the statement of financial position but it is material to the statement of profit or loss.

**Estimates**

The estimate of returns is clearly subject to significant subjectivity. This increases the risk of material misstatement due to both error and manipulation.

The estimate is made by the sales director; while this may be the best person to forecast sales they may not be the best person to predict returns. Returns are likely to be influenced more heavily by product quality, which the production or quality control manager may be better placed to predict. This implies that the forecast amount is based on simplistic, general estimates using sales levels rather than consideration of specific product quality issues.

**Evidence of prior overstatement**

The risk of misstatement is amplified by the evidence of large overstatements in the past. The reversal of unutilised provisions suggests that previous estimates were too high, which indicates inaccuracy in the forecasting process. The reversal of unutilised provisions represents 2.9% of profit so is not individually material to the financial statements.

**Possible creative accounting**

Provisions can be used to smooth profits; i.e. a provision made in a year where profits are high and reversed in future years (i.e. released back to the statement of profit and loss) when earnings targets are not being met.

The reversal of unutilised provisions in the year has increased Osier Co's profits by $3.1 million. While this is not a material amount on its own, with other creative accounting devices, such as the manipulation of estimates of the cost of inventory and impairments, this could lead to a material overstatement of profits.

This should be considered a particular risk for Osier Co as their profits have declined during the year, despite a 5.5% increase in revenue during the year. The decline in performance provides an increased incentive for management to adopt manipulative accounting practices to help achieve targets and smooth profits.

**Evidence expected to be on file:**

– Copies of the terms of sale offered to customers to confirm the length of the warranty period.

– Notes of a discussion with the sales director confirming the basis of the calculation for forecast returns. These should specifically note any general rates of return applied to the calculation and any specific matters the director has taken into consideration, such as known faults or poor quality.

- A copy of the calculation of the provision. The components of the calculation should have been recalculated and analytically reviewed in comparison to previous years and any fluctuations should have been corroborated to supporting evidence.

- A schedule analysing the total returns received following the year-end. A sample of these returns should have been matched to the original sales invoice, confirming the date upon which the goods were first sold.

- This schedule should also have been analytically reviewed in comparison to the same period in previous years to identify whether returns levels were consistent. Any significant fluctuations should have been corroborated with evidence or management enquiry.

- A schedule confirming the calculation of the total unutilised provisions reversed during the year. These should be accompanied with the notes of a meeting with management identifying the reasons why these provisions were not needed and, where possible, what time period the original provision related to.

- Notes of a discussion with the production or quality control manager identifying whether there are any known problems with goods sold during the warranty period, and what products were affected. If any such matters exist there should be evidence that these have been traced through to the provision calculation.

**(b)    Auditor's report and opinion**

The misstatement of $9 million represents 0.5% of total assets and 8.4% of profit before tax. It is not, therefore, material to the statement of financial position but it is material to the statement of profit or loss.

The opinion will therefore be modified as a result of material misstatement.

The matter is unlikely to be considered pervasive as the required adjustment would not lead to a reported profit being restated as a loss and only the retail assets will be affected.

In these circumstances the auditor would issue a qualified audit opinion stating that 'except for' this matter the financial statements are fairly presented.

The auditor should also include a 'Basis for Qualified Opinion' paragraph below the opinion paragraph. This should describe and quantify the financial effects of the misstatement.

**Examiner's comments**

There were three scenarios where candidates were asked to describe the key matters and audit evidence that would be expected in each. Overall there appeared to be a poor understanding of the accounting issues raised by the scenarios.

Part (a) concerned the audit of manufactured inventory and the appropriate inclusion of overhead and labour costs. Most identified the need to check the components back to source documentation and review the reasonableness of the process but many candidates concentrated on discussing auditing and accounting standards rather than detailing the evidence that should have been gathered. However this was the best answered of the three sections.

Part (b) related to a topical subject – an impairment review of a retailer's property portfolio caused by diminishing shop sales countered by growing internet sales. Many candidates simply discussed whether or not an impairment review should be carried out as there were indicators of impairment (falling retail sales) but this was a given from the question as the review had already been undertaken. Few questioned whether it was reasonable to base the value in use on the assumption that sales would grow by 1% a year when in reality they were falling. Candidates appeared unwilling to challenge this underlying assumption which actually lacked commercial justification.

Part (c) related to the audit of a warranty provision. Candidates spent a lot of time discussing IAS 37 with only a minority correctly questioning why the warranty provision was decreasing when the revenues were actually increasing, thus the majority of candidates demonstrated a lack of professional scepticism. Evidence and therefore the procedures to audit the provision were generally sound, such as looking at sales volume and historic claims rates by product group and basing the provision on these. Very few candidates questioned if there was the potential for management bias as there was a substantial release of the provision without explanation when the company's profits were falling despite increasing revenues. Candidates are reminded here that the application of professional scepticism is a key component of the auditor's skillset.

| **Marking scheme** | |
|---|---|
| | *Marks* |
| Generally up to 1½ marks for each well explained matter and 1 mark for each well explained piece of evidence recommended.<br>Note: Marks will be awarded for explanations of why calculations and balances are complex or subjective and how this affects their accuracy. Simple statements that calculations and balances are complex or subjective will be awarded a maximum of ½ mark each, where relevant.<br>**(a)   (i)   Inventory**<br>        **Matters**<br>        –   Materiality<br>        –   Complexity of calculation<br>        –   Subjectivity in calculation<br>        **Evidence**<br>        –   Documentation of systems and controls<br>        –   Summary of purchase costs and matching to purchase invoices<br>        –   Calculation of forecast wages matched to underlying HR and payroll records<br>        –   Confirmations of wage increments/rises<br>        –   Calculation of forecast production units reviewed in comparison to prior year<br>        –   Calculation of forecast overheads corroborated to new agreements | |
| **Maximum** | 6 |

| | | | |
|---|---|---|---:|
| | (ii) | **Impairment** | |

**(ii) Impairment**

**Matters**
- Materiality
- Uncertainty relating to estimates
- Growth rate assumption in relation to value in use
- Allocation of impairment does not seem to be correct

**Evidence**
- Copies of offers for retail outlets
- Copy of forecast cash flows relating to retail outlets
- Recalculation of forecasts using management's predictions
- Analytical review by unit/geographical region to assess appropriateness of general growth rate
- Notes re discussion about retail prospects by area
- Schedule of goodwill analysed by division
- Recalculation of allocation of impairment
- Copies of previous forecasts

**Maximum**      **8**

**(iii) Warranty provision**

**Matters**
- Materiality
- Uncertainty relating to estimates
- Competence of sales director to make estimates
- Evidence of prior overstatement
- Possible creative accounting/profit smoothing

**Evidence**
- Copies of terms of sale
- Notes re basis of forecasting returns levels
- Breakdown of provision calculation
- Schedule listing post year end returns
- Notes re the reason for the unutilised provision
- Notes re known production/quality problems

**Maximum**      **7**

**(b) Auditor's opinion and report**

Generally up to 1 mark for each relevant point explained
- Materiality calculation of misstatement
- Discussion of whether it is pervasive
- Qualified opinion
- Basis for qualified opinion paragraph

**Maximum**      **4**

**Total**      **25**

**24 ROCKET**  *Walk in the footsteps of a top tutor*

***Top tutor tips***

*Requirement (a) requires knowledge of the most recent changes to the current format of the auditor's report. The verb 'discuss' allows for a balanced argument to be presented. In this case the question asks for a discussion of the benefits so whilst there may be many benefits of the new auditor's report you can also state the disadvantages that arise from the longer report or how the intended benefits may not necessarily materialise.*

*Requirement (b) requires discussion of the relevant accounting treatment in the same way as you would approach a 'Matters and evidence' question. To finish off, you need to explain the impact on the auditor's report if the issues are not resolved.*

*Part (c) is slightly unusual in that you are required to critically appraise an assurance report rather than an auditor's report. Use the same approach as you would take if it was an auditor's report. Work your way through the report methodically identifying where the wording is not as per the relevant professional standard wording and explain why the wording given is not appropriate.*

**(a)  Extended auditor's report**

The extended auditor's report that is given in ISA 700 *Forming an Opinion and Reporting on Financial Statements* differs from the previous version of the report in the following ways:

The opinion is given at the start of the report rather than towards the end of the report where users previously had to search for it. The opinion is likely to be the section that users will be most interested in and therefore it is sensible to include this early on. By including the opinion in a more prominent place it reflects its importance.

An Other Information section is included which explains the auditor's responsibility to read the other information that is published for consistency with the financial statements and the knowledge of the auditor. If there is an inconsistency it will be described in the Other Information section. This responsibility was not referred to in the previous version of the report unless there was an inconsistency and potentially resulted in some users believing the entire annual report had been audited. Any inconsistencies were previously referred to in an Other Matter paragraph which users potentially did not pay much attention to.

The section on auditor responsibilities is much more detailed than the previous version of the auditor's report. There has always been an expectation gap in that users think the auditor has a greater responsibility than they actually have for detecting fraud and error and what the audit involves. By including more detail about the audit process it should be more evident to users that an audit involves a significant amount of judgment about subjective matters which means it is not a straightforward exercise and different auditors may reach different conclusions about the same issue.

For listed companies a Key Audit Matters section is included which describes matters the auditor considers to be of importance to the user to aid their understanding of the audit. These matters are selected from the matters communicated with those charged with governance and include areas of higher assessed risk of material misstatement and areas which involve significant management judgment. This again is intended to highlight to users the difficulties faced when auditing a company and how the audit addressed the matters. If users have a greater understanding about the complexities of an audit they should be more sympathetic towards the auditor and recognise that not every fraud and error can be detected during the audit.

Whilst the changes described above appear to provide much better communication between the auditor and users and therefore should go some way to reduce the expectation gap, the benefits may not be seen by everyone.

The report is much longer, extending onto several pages as compared with one or two pages previously. Users may not be inclined to read through that amount of detail.

Even with an understanding that the audit is a subjective exercise users may still believe the auditor's main responsibility should be to detect fraud as they are professionally qualified and should know what to look for.

For those who understand more about the process and recognise the issues of subjectivity and complexity they may see the audit as a pointless exercise which may affect the credibility of the audit process and the profession as a whole.

In conclusion there are many benefits from the introduction of the extended auditor's reports and the increased level of detail should improve the understanding of users of the financial statements and the auditor's report. However, the reports may provide too much detail which may not be read at all or which may result in users focusing more on the limitations of an audit which may reduce the credibility of the audit process.

**(b)** **(i)** **Matters**

**Materiality**

The revenue of $17 million recognised in relation to the highlighted transactions represents 1.2% of revenue and 12.2% of profit before tax. The sales are, therefore, material to the financial statements.

**Bill and hold arrangement**

IFRS 15 *Revenue from Contracts with Customers* specifies that an entity shall recognise revenue only when it has satisfied its performance obligations by transferring the goods (or services) to its customer.

Rocket Co believes that they have satisfied their performance obligations by having the goods available for the customers by the specified date. The situation, however, represents a 'bill and hold' arrangement, whereby Rocket Co has billed the customer but has yet to physically transfer the goods to them.

**Transfer of control**

IFRS 15 specifies that in these circumstances it should be determined when the customer obtains control of the goods. The contracts specify that the goods have to be delivered for inspection and 'acceptance;' implying that the customer will not accept control until they have satisfactorily completed their inspections. Rocket Co has, therefore, not fulfilled their performance obligations and should not recognise the revenue in relation to these two contracts.

### Revenue recognition

Given Rocket Co's listed status, management may be under pressure to report better results. Revenue has fallen by 3.5% based on the draft financial statements.

If the $17 million relating to the bill and hold arrangement is excluded from the 20X7 financial statements, then the reduction in revenue is greater, at 4.6%.

### Further actions

Thyme & Co should request that the client adjusts their financial statements to reverse the revenue recognised in relation to the goods being stored at the third party facility.

If they refuse to adjust the financial statements, Thyme & Co should communicate the misstatement to those charged with governance. They should repeat the request to adjust the financial statements and inform them of the modifications that will be made to the auditor's report if the adjustments are not made.

If the client still refuses to amend the financial statements, Thyme & Co should request a written representation from the client confirming their intention to proceed without amending the financial statements and that they are aware of the potential repercussions.

## (ii) Auditor's report

### Material but not pervasive misstatement

If management refuses to reverse the $17 million of revenue recognised in relation to these transactions the auditor will conclude that the financial statements are materially misstated.

The matter is material to the statement of profit or loss but it is unlikely to be considered pervasive; the required adjustment would not lead to a reported profit being restated as a loss and the only captions of the financial statements affected will be revenue and receivables.

### Qualified opinion

In these circumstances the auditor would issue a qualified audit opinion stating that 'except for' these matters the financial statements are fairly presented.

The auditor should also include a 'Basis for Qualified Opinion' paragraph below the opinion paragraph. This should describe and quantify the financial effects of the misstatement.

## (c) Assurance report on examination of forecast

### Addressee

The report is currently addressed to the shareholders of Tulip Co which is not appropriate. The intended users for the report are more likely to be the board of directors, who wishes to use it in conjunction with a loan application, and the report should be addressed as such.

### Type of forecast

The report fails to specify what forecast the assurance relates to. Companies can forecast various elements of financial performance, position and cash flow. It is vital to identify specifically which forecast, and which elements of the forecast, are covered by the assurance report.

**Period covered**

The assurance report fails to specify the period covered by the forecast. This is important because it is plausible that only part of the forecast is covered by the assurance report, particularly if it is a long range forecast.

**Specific document and page reference**

The assurance report simply refers to the forecast 'contained in the loan proposal'. This is not specific enough. This increases the risk that the same forecast can be reissued with the assurance report in other loan proposals. The assurance report should state the title of the document the forecast is included in and the page numbers upon which assurance is being provided.

**Relevant standards**

The report simply refers to 'relevant standards;' it should state which standards have been followed during the engagement. Given the nature of the assignment the report should state that it has been conducted in accordance with International Standard on Assurance Engagements 3400 *The Examination of Prospective Financial Information*.

**Responsibility for preparation**

The content of the report in relation to setting out the respective responsibilities of the practitioner and the responsible party are not in line with the relevant standards. Rather than stating that the practitioner is not responsible for the preparation of the forecast, ISAE 3400 specifies that the assurance report should state that management is responsible for the information provided and the assumptions upon which it is based.

**Detail regarding the relevant assumptions**

The assurance report should make it clear what assumptions the forecast is based upon and what assumptions the assurance report relates to. To this end the report should refer to the note in the forecast where the underlying assumptions are presented.

**Negative statement of assurance needed**

The assurance provided in the draft assurance report is worded positively. ISAE 3400 requires that for an examination of prospective financial information a statement of negative assurance is provided.

For an unmodified conclusion, such as that presented in the draft, the wording used should state that 'based upon our examination of the evidence supporting the assumptions, nothing has come to our attention which causes us to believe............'

**International Financial Reporting Standards**

The report should refer to 'International Financial Reporting Standards' rather than 'IFRS.'

**Inappropriate caveat**

The caveat at the end of the report should be reworded as it somewhat undermines the credibility of the forecast and the assurance provided by stating that the forecast is unlikely to be accurate.

A more appropriate statement would refer to the uncertainty in relation to the nature of a forecast and that the actual results may vary from those anticipated.

### Reference to the purpose and distribution of the report

It is common practice for a report on prospective financial information to include a reference to the purpose of the information and on its distribution. Thyme & Co should consider including this reference as a means of limiting the distribution of the report to the intended parties.

---

**Examiner's comments**

Part (a) concerned revenue recognition. Many candidates gave a good summary of the IFRS 15 *Revenue from Contracts with Customers*, conditions that revenue cannot be recognised until the goods have been delivered, control transferred and all performance obligations have been met. However some candidates demonstrated out-of-date financial reporting knowledge by referencing the superseded IAS 18 *Revenue*. For the most part candidates usually correctly identified that the sale had not actually occurred before year end and should be adjusted for. However, many candidates digressed into visiting and inspecting the goods in a third-party warehouse when it was clear that the performance obligations had not yet been met. Most highlighted that they should ask management to amend the accounts and that the matter should be referred to those charged with governance.

The impact on the auditor's report if no adjustment was made was mostly well-answered with candidates explaining that the accounting treatment was factually incorrect and would result in an 'except for' qualification. Candidates were good at highlighting the sequencing of matters in the auditor's report and it is refreshing to see that this area was clearly understood. Stronger candidates additionally examined whether the matter was pervasive (which would result in a disclaimer of opinion) based on the fact that the issue focused on the timing of revenue recognition.

Part (b) involved reviewing a non-audit assurance report which had been prepared in conjunction with seeking a bank loan. Good answers highlighted that the report had been poorly written (in that it was not correctly addressed, provided positive assurance, was not time-bound and was self-contradictory) and explained how each of these should be remedied. Poorer answers only concentrated on omissions, such as the lack of a date on the report.

---

| Marking scheme | | | |
|---|---|---|---|
| | | | *Marks* |
| **(a)** | Generally up to 1½ marks for each well explained point | | |
| | **Extended auditor reports** | | |
| | – Opinion at the start which reflects importance | | |
| | – Inclusion of Other Information section | | |
| | – Auditor responsibilities explained in more detail | | |
| | – Inclusion of Key Audit Matters section for listed companies | | |
| | – Limitations | | |
| | – Conclusion | | |
| | | **Maximum** | 5 |
| **(b)** | Generally up to 1½ marks for each well explained matter and 1 mark for each well explained action recommended. | | |
| | **(i) Revenue recognition** | | |
| | **Matters** | | |
| | – Materiality | | |
| | – IFRS 15 – Satisfaction of performance obligations | | |
| | – Control not yet passed to client | | |
| | – Revenue recognition and management bias | | |
| | – Revenue recognised too early and, therefore, misstated | | |

**Actions**
- Request adjustment to financial statements
- If refused communicate with those charged with governance
- Obtain written representation

|  |  |
|---|---|
| **Maximum** | 7 |

(ii)     **Auditor's report**
- Financial statements materially misstated
- Matter is not pervasive
- Qualified auditor's report
- 'Except for' opinion
- Basis of qualified opinion paragraph

|  |  |
|---|---|
| **Maximum** | 5 |

(c)     **Critique of assurance report**
- Addressee inappropriate
- Type of forecast reviewed
- Period covered by the forecast
- Document forecast is included in and page references
- Assurance standards complied with
- Responsibility for preparation
- Reference to assumptions
- Negative statement of assurance
- International Financial Reporting Standards
- Inappropriate caveat
- Reference to purpose and distribution of the report

|  |  |
|---|---|
| **Maximum** | 8 |
| **Total** | 25 |

**25     BOSTON**  *Walk in the footsteps of a top tutor*

*Top tutor tips*

*Part (a) is a current issues question relating to exposure drafts issued by the IAASB on quality management. Exposure drafts are examinable to the extent there is an examiner's article published on the topic therefore students are advised to keep checking the ACCA website in the weeks before the exam in case any articles are published.*

*Part (b) asks for matters to be discussed with management in relation to four uncorrected misstatements. You can take the same approach as a 'matters' question i.e. state whether the issue is material, the accounting treatment required and the risk to the financial statements.*

*For part (c) you need to state the impact to the auditor's report if the client does not amend the financial statements. Consider the aggregate effect of the misstatements to assess whether there is a material misstatement. State the impact to both the report and opinion as a result of the issues. Don't waste time stating the reporting implications if the issues are corrected as this is not part of the requirement.*

(a) **Quality management**

**The need for change**

The main objectives for an accountancy firm in respect of quality control are to:

–    Perform work in accordance with professional standards and applicable legal and regulatory requirements, and

–    Issue engagement reports which are appropriate in the circumstances.

Quality management is an area of increasing importance due to the accounting scandals that have been widely publicised in recent years.

The accountancy profession has always tried to maintain confidence in the work of professional accountants and recent scandals such as Carillion, Patisserie Valerie, BHS and Ted Baker are likely to cause confidence in the profession to plummet.

The IAASB is seeking to increase the robustness of quality systems applied by accountancy firms to reduce the risk of failures of this scale and frequency occurring by introducing a range of quality management standards to replace and revise existing standards in this area.

**Current guidance**

Currently there are two quality control standards providing guidance:

–    ISQC 1 *Quality Control for Firms that Perform Audits and Reviews of Financial Statements, and Other Assurance and Related Services Engagements*

–    ISA 220 *Quality Control for an Audit of Financial Statements.*

**Proposed guidance**

There will now be 3 quality standards providing guidance for firms:

1    ISQM 1 – *Quality Management for Firms that Perform Audits or Reviews of Financial Statements or Other Assurance or Related Services Engagements* (currently ISQC 1)

This standard enhances the current requirements of ISQC 1 and requires a more proactive approach for identifying risks to quality and responding to them appropriately.

2    ISQM 2 – *Engagement Quality Reviews* (currently included within ISA 220 and ISQC 1)

This standard extracts the requirements for engagement quality control reviews from the existing standards of ISQC 1 and ISA 220. This has been done to emphasise the need for engagement quality control reviews and to differentiate the responsibilities of the engagement quality control reviewer from those of the firm.

3    ISA 220 (Revised) – *Quality Management for an Audit of the Financial Statements*

The revised standard aims to keep ISA 220 fit for purpose in a wide range of circumstances and in a complex environment by emphasising the importance of professional scepticism, enhancing the documentation of the auditor's judgment, and reinforcing the need for robust communications during the audit.

**Improvements/benefits of the proposed changes**

The changes are being proposed to improve quality of engagements by:

– Bringing the standards up to date to take account of the evolving environment and keeping them fit for purpose.

– Improving the governance of the accountancy firm by increasing leadership responsibilities including enhancing the engagement partner's responsibilities.

– Greater monitoring of the firm's quality management systems.

– More thorough engagement quality reviews.

**Scalability**

The new standards requires firms to proactively identify and respond to risks affecting quality. This allows for the standards to be applied proportionately to the size of the accountancy firm as smaller firms will not necessarily need to implement the same policies and procedures as larger firms. Firms will need to customize the design, implementation and operation of its quality management system based on the nature and circumstances of the firm and the engagements it performs.

**(b)    Matters to discuss at meeting**

During the completion stage of the audit, the effect of uncorrected misstatements must be evaluated by the auditor, as required by ISA 450/ISA (UK) 450 *Evaluation of Misstatements Identified during the Audit*. This requires that the auditor obtains an understanding of management's reasons for not making recommended adjustments to the financial statements and that they take this into account when evaluating whether the financial statements as a whole are free from material misstatement.

In order to maintain accurate accounting records, management should be encouraged to record all misstatements to ensure that the risk of material misstatements in future periods is reduced due to the cumulative effect of immaterial uncorrected misstatements.

ISA 450 also requires that the auditor communicates with those charged with governance about uncorrected misstatements and the effect that they, individually or in aggregate, may have on the opinion in the auditor's report. Each of the matters included in the summary of uncorrected misstatements will be discussed below and the impact on the auditor's report considered individually and in aggregate.

**(i)    Impairment**

When performing an impairment test, in accordance with IAS 36 *Impairment of Assets*, the carrying value of the asset (or cash generating unit) in question is compared to the recoverable amount of the asset. If the recoverable amount is lower than the carrying value an impairment loss should be recognised, reducing the asset down from its carrying value to the recoverable amount.

The recoverable amount is calculated as the higher of the fair value less costs to sell and value in use. In relation to the cash generating unit, Boston Co estimated that the greater of these two figures was the value in use at $3.5 million. This was compared to the carrying value of $3.6 million and the asset has been impaired by $100,000 accordingly.

The findings of audit procedures carried out suggest that an inappropriate estimate was used in the calculation of value in use. Boston Co applied the company's annual growth rates when estimating the cash flows attributable to the cash generating unit. A more relevant estimate for the growth rates, specific to the cash generating unit, was available and should have been used.

This would have generated a value in use of $3.1 million which is still higher than fair value less cost to sell of $3 million, and should be used as the recoverable amount. As management already impaired the asset to $3.5 million, a further impairment of $400,000 is required to value it appropriately at $3.1 million.

At the meeting management should be asked why they used the company's forecast growth rates, rather than the factory's growth rates and whether any matters have arisen since the audit to suggest that the growth rates used by the audit team are now inappropriate.

The adjustment represents 6.25% of profit and 0.4% of total assets. While not material to the statement of financial position, it is material to profit.

If management does not adjust for this or provide justifications as to why their valuation is more appropriate, this will lead to a material misstatement of the financial statements.

(ii) **Borrowing costs**

Interest charges are borrowing costs. The borrowing costs relating to the construction of qualifying assets, such as property and plant, should be capitalised during the construction period, in accordance with IAS 23 *Borrowing Costs*.

As the manufacturing plant is not due for completion until November 20X6, it is still a qualifying asset and the interest should have been capitalised. Boston Co has incorrectly expensed the interest as part of the finance charges for the year.

The correcting adjustment is therefore to reduce finance charges and to add the interest to the cost of the asset on the statement of financial position.

The charges of $75,000 represent 1.2% of profit and 0.07% of assets so are not material to either profit or the statement of financial position.

(iii) **Cleveland Co**

At the year-end Boston Co would have recognised a net receivable of $95,000 as being due from their customer Cleveland Co. Although $30,000 has been received after the year-end, the request to have the company liquidated indicates that any further payment is unlikely to be received.

In accordance with IAS 10 *Events After the Reporting Period*, this is an adjusting event indicating that management's assessment of the recoverability of the balance is inaccurate and that the remainder of the outstanding balance should be written off as an irrecoverable debt.

As Boston Co has previously provided for $5,000 management should provide for the remaining $65,000 in the financial statements for the year ended 31 December 20X5. This will reduce net trade receivables on the statement of financial position and profit before tax by $65,000.

At the meeting enquiries should be made as to whether any further correspondence has been received from either the management of Cleveland Co or the liquidators offering any form of reimbursement to Boston Co. If not, then the proposed adjustment should be encouraged.

The adjustment represents 1.0% of profit and 0.06% of total assets so is not material individually to either profit or the statement of financial position.

**(iv)    Investment in Nebraska**

The investment in Nebraska has been designated as fair value through profit or loss. As per IFRS 9 *Financial Instruments*, the value at the year-end must be adjusted to reflect the fair value of the investment, and any gain or loss recognised in the statement of profit or loss.

The fair value of the investment at the year-end is $643,500 (150,000 shares × $4.29). This represents an increase in the fair value of $43,500, which should be taken to the statement of profit or loss as a gain. The carrying value of the investment should also be increased by this amount.

$43,500 represents 0.7% of profit and 0.04% of total assets. It is therefore not material individually to either profit or the statement of financial position.

**(c)    Impact on the audit opinion and auditor's report**

When considering their opinion, the auditor must conclude whether the financial statements as a whole are free from material misstatement. In order to do this, they must consider whether any remaining uncorrected misstatements are material, either on an individual basis or in aggregate.

The aggregate effect of the misstatements would be to overstate Boston Co's profit by $346,500 ($465,000 – $118,500). Total assets on the statement of financial position would also be overstated by this amount.

This represents 5.4% of profit and 0.3% of total assets. The overstatement would therefore be material to the statement of profit or loss on an aggregate basis but not to the statement of financial position.

However, as the necessary adjustment regarding the impairment of the factory building is individually material, management should be informed that if the valuation calculated by the audit team is more appropriate then failure to incorporate this adjustment will result in the auditor concluding that the financial statements are materially misstated. Based upon this, a modification to the audit opinion in accordance with ISA 705 *Modifications to the Opinion in the Independent Auditor's Report* will be required.

The type of modification depends on the significance of the material misstatement. In this case, the misstatement regarding the impairment is material to the financial statements, but is unlikely to be considered pervasive. This is supported by the fact that the adjustment is not material to the statement of financial position and it is therefore unlikely that the auditor will conclude that the financial statements as a whole are misleading.

Therefore a qualified opinion should be expressed, with the auditor stating in the opinion that the financial statements show a true and fair view 'except for' the effects of the matters described in the basis for qualified opinion paragraph.

The basis for qualified opinion paragraph should include a description of the matter giving rise to the qualification, including quantification of the financial effects of the misstatement.

The remaining uncorrected misstatements are, individually and in aggregate, immaterial to the financial statements and it will be at the discretion of management to amend and will have no impact on the auditor's report.

---

**Examiner's comments**

The question set out four potential audit adjustments and candidates were required to discuss each, considering the individual and aggregate impact on the auditor's report. The values of each potential adjustment were given in the question so there were materiality marks available and many candidates scored these but performed less well in discussing the associated issues. Most of the adjustments were relatively straightforward such as the capitalisation of loan interest, allowance for a bad debt and revaluation of investments and the issues around these were reasonably answered. The issue of impairment was less well answered.

There was significant inconsistency in answers where candidates concluded that an issue was not material but concluded that the auditor's report required modification. Furthermore candidates need to ensure that they understand what Emphasis of Matter and Other Matters paragraphs are. They are not a substitute for a modified opinion and should only be used where there are significant issues that the auditor wants to bring to the attention of the users of the accounts.

---

| Marking scheme | | Marks |
|---|---|---|
| **(a)** | **Quality management** | |
| | Generally up to 1 mark for each point explained: | |
| | –   Objectives of a quality management system | |
| | –   Recent accounting scandals affecting the reputation of the profession has created a need for guidance to change | |
| | –   Current guidance provided by ISA 220 and ISQC 1 | |
| | –   Proposed guidance will see the introduction of three standards – ISQM 1, ISQM 2 and ISA 220 (Revised) | |
| | –   ISQM 1 – requires a more proactive approach to risk identification | |
| | –   ISQM 2 – emphasises the importance of engagement quality reviews | |
| | –   ISA 220 – emphasises the need for professional scepticism and documentation of auditor judgement | |
| | –   Benefits of the new guidance include keeping the standards fit for purpose, increased robustness, greater monitoring and improved governance (2 marks) | |
| | –   Allows for firms to apply the requirements proportionately to the size and nature of the firm and engagements performed | |
| | **Maximum** | **6** |
| **(b)** | **Summary of uncorrected misstatements** | |
| | In general up to 1 mark for each point of explanation and up to ½ mark for each appropriate calculation: | |
| | General comments | |
| | –   Obtaining an understanding of management's reasons | |
| | –   Encourage management to amend all misstatements | |
| | –   Communicate effect of misstatements to TCWG | |

---

| | | |
|---|---|---|
| **(i)** | **Impairment** | |
| | – Explanation of original calculation | |
| | – Inappropriate estimates used | |
| | – Revised impairments | |
| | – Justification of the proposed adjustment | |
| | – Request further clarification at meeting | |
| | – Matter is material individually | |
| **(ii)** | **Borrowing costs** | |
| | – Capitalisation rules | |
| | – Qualifying asset | |
| | – Identification of incorrect treatment of interest costs | |
| | – Explanation of adjustment | |
| | – Not material individually | |
| **(iii)** | **Cleveland** | |
| | – Liquidation is indication of further impairment | |
| | – Adjusting event after the reporting period | |
| | – Need to write off remainder of outstanding balance | |
| | – Request evidence of any further correspondence | |
| | – Not material individually | |
| **(iv)** | **Nebraska** | |
| | – Need to revalue investment to fair value at year end | |
| | – Calculation of fair value (½ max) and adjustment (½ max) | |
| | – Gain taken to statement of profit and loss | |
| | – Not material individually | |
| | **Maximum** | 14 |
| **(c)** | **Auditor's report** | |
| | – Aggregate impact on financial statements | |
| | – Material to profit | |
| | – Impairment individually material | |
| | – Modification of opinion due to a material misstatement | |
| | – Discussion of whether it is pervasive | |
| | – Qualified opinion | |
| | – Basis for qualified opinion paragraph | |
| | – Remaining misstatement immaterial – no impact on the opinion | |
| | **Maximum** | 5 |
| **Total** | | 25 |

**26 MACAU & CO**  *Walk in the footsteps of a top tutor*

*Top tutor tips*

*Part (a) requires evaluation of quality control, ethical and other professional matters arising. This is a regularly examined topic. Typical issues to look out for in such a question are: whether the work has been assigned to the appropriate level of staff, whether sufficient time has been allocated for the audit, whether sufficient appropriate evidence has been obtained (e.g. have the ISAs been followed), whether any ethical threats have been addressed appropriately and whether adequate quality control procedures have been performed in respect of the engagement such as adequate levels of supervision and review.*

> *Part (b) is a typical completion requirement asking for 'matters and evidence'. This is examined very frequently and the 'MARE' approach can help to provide structure to answers. MARE stands for:*
>
> *Materiality – calculate whether the issue is material.*
>
> *Accounting treatment – state the required treatment and why the client's treatment is wrong.*
>
> *Risk – to the financial statements and the impact on the audit opinion if not corrected.*
>
> *Evidence – the evidence that would have been documented on the audit file by the person who audited the section being reviewed.*

**(a)    Quality control, ethical and professional matters**

The audit of Stanley Co does not seem to have been performed with a high regard for the quality of the audit and there appear to be several ways in which the ISA requirements have been breached.

**Materiality**

First, it is not appropriate that the materiality level was determined at the planning stage of the audit but has not been reviewed or adjusted since. ISA 320/ISA (UK) 320 *Materiality in Planning and Performing an Audit* requires the auditor to determine materiality for the financial statements as a whole at the planning stage of the audit, and to revise it as the audit progresses as necessary where new facts and information become available which impact on materiality. It may be the case that no revision to the materiality which was initially determined is necessary, but a review should have taken place and this should be clearly documented in the audit working papers.

**Audit of property, plant and equipment**

The audit of the packing machine has not been properly carried out, and there seems to be a lack of sufficient, appropriate audit evidence to support the audit conclusion. The cost of the asset is material, based on the initial materiality, therefore there is a risk of material misstatement if sufficient and appropriate evidence is not obtained. By the year end the asset's carrying value is less than materiality, presumably due to depreciation being charged, but this does not negate the need for obtaining robust audit evidence for the cost and subsequent measurement of the asset.

The packing machine should have been physically verified. Obtaining the order and invoice does not confirm the existence of the machine, or that it is in working order. In addition, without a physical verification, the audit team would be unaware of problems such as physical damage to the machine or obsolescence, which could indicate impairment of the asset.

Relying on the distribution company to provide evidence on the existence and use of the asset is not appropriate. ISA 500/ISA (UK) 500 *Audit Evidence* states that audit evidence obtained directly by the auditor is more reliable than audit evidence obtained indirectly or by inference. External confirmations can be used to provide audit evidence but in this case the external confirmation should corroborate evidence obtained directly by the auditor, rather than be the only source of evidence. The relationship between Stanley Co and Aberdeen Co should also be understood by the auditor, and evidence should be obtained to confirm whether or not the two companies are related parties, as this would impact on the extent to which the external confirmation can be relied upon as a source of evidence.

**Inventory count**

In respect of the inventory count attendance, the audit team should have discussed the discrepancies with management as they could indicate more widespread problems with the inventory count. Given the comment that the inventory count appeared unorganised, it is possible that count instructions were not being followed or that some items had not been included in the count.

One of the requirements of ISA 501/ISA (UK) 501 *Audit Evidence – Specific Considerations for Selected Items* is that while attending an inventory count, the auditor shall evaluate management's instructions and procedures for recording and controlling the results of the entity's physical inventory counting.

It is not clear from the conclusion of the audit work whether the problems noted at the inventory count have been discussed with management. The auditor attending the inventory count should have raised the issues at the time and assessed whether a recount of all of the inventory was required.

Training may need to be provided to audit staff to ensure that they understand the auditor's role at an inventory count and can deal with problems which may arise in the appropriate manner.

The discrepancies noted at the inventory count should be subject to further audit work. The results of the test counts should be extrapolated over the population in order to evaluate the potential misstatement of inventory as a whole. The results should then be evaluated in accordance with ISA 450/ISA (UK) 450 *Evaluation of Misstatements Identified during the Audit* which requires that the auditor shall accumulate misstatements identified during the audit, other than those which are clearly trivial, and that misstatements should be discussed with management.

The issues raised by the way in which the inventory count was performed could represent a significant control deficiency and should be raised with those charged with governance in accordance with ISA 265 *Communicating Deficiencies in Internal Control to Those Charged with Governance and Management*.

**Working paper review**

The audit senior's comments in relation to the review by the manager and partner indicate that elements of ISA 220/ISA (UK) 220 *Quality Control for an Audit of Financial Statements* have been breached. ISA 220 requires that the engagement partner shall, through a review of the audit documentation and discussion with the engagement team, be satisfied that sufficient appropriate audit evidence has been obtained to support the conclusions reached and for the auditor's report to be issued.

It appears that in this case the partner has not properly reviewed the working papers, instead relying on the audit senior's comment that there were no problems in the audit work. ISA 220 does state that the audit partner need not review all audit documentation, but only a 'quick look' at the working papers could indicate that areas of risk or critical judgment have not been reviewed in sufficient detail.

There is also an issue in that the manager and partner reviews took place at the same time and near the completion of the audit fieldwork. Reviews should happen on a timely basis throughout the audit to enable problems to be resolved at an appropriate time. Reviews should also be hierarchical and it appears that the audit partner has not reviewed the work of the audit manager.

**Ethical considerations**

Finally, there appears to be a potential threat to objectivity due to the audit engagement partner's brother providing a management consultancy service to the audit client. This amounts to a self-interest threat in that the partner's brother receives income from the audit client. The audit partner's objectivity is therefore threatened, and this is a significant risk due to his position of influence over the audit. He may even receive an introducer's commission from his brother.

The matter should be investigated further, and a senior member of the audit firm or the firm's partner responsible for ethics should discuss the comments made in Stanley Co's board minutes with Joe Lantau in order to evaluate the ethical threat and determine any necessary actions. The amount which is being paid to Mick Lantau should be made known, as well as whether the amount is a market rate, and whether other providers of management advice were considered by the company.

The partner's comments to the audit junior indicate a lack of integrity, and indicate that the partner may have something to hide, which increases the threat to objectivity. The audit partner may need to be removed from the audit and his work reviewed.

**(b) (i) Matters to consider and actions to take**

The work in progress represents 4.7% of total assets and is therefore material to the statement of financial position. The deferred income is also material at 2.7% of total assets.

Even though the correspondence with BMC is dated after the end of the reporting period, BMC was suffering from financial problems during the year ending 31 December 20X5 which was notified to Kowloon Co before the year end. Therefore the cancellation of the contract appears to meet the definition of an adjusting event under IAS 10 *Events after the Reporting Period* because it confirms conditions which existed at the year end.

Management must consider whether it is still appropriate to recognise the work in progress as an asset. According to IFRS 15 *Revenue from Contracts with Customers*, costs incurred to fulfil a contract are recognised as an asset if and only if all of the following criteria are met:

- The costs relate directly to a contract (or a specific anticipated contract)

- The costs generate or enhance resources of the entity which will be used in satisfying performance obligations in the future

- The costs are expected to be recovered.

The cancellation of the contract indicates that the costs of the work in progress are not recoverable from BMC, in which case the balance should be written off. Management is not planning to amend the balances recognised at the year end, and the audit team should investigate the reasons for this. Possibly management is asserting that the machine design costs could be utilised for a different contract, despite the fact that the machine was developed specifically for BMC.

Audit work should focus on the contractual arrangements between Kowloon Co and BMC, particularly in relation to the ownership of the rights to the design work which has taken place. If the design work has been based on an innovation by BMC, then it needs to be determined if this information can still be used.

If the design work which has been undertaken to date can be used by Kowloon and results in an ability to develop a new type of product for other customers, there is the possibility that the costs (excluding any research costs) could be capitalised in line with IAS 38 *Intangible Assets*. This should be discussed with the project manager and finance director to assess if this has been considered and if the capitalisation criteria of IAS 38 can be satisfied.

The accounting treatment of the deferred income also needs to be considered. Depending on the terms of the contract with BMC, the amount could be repayable, though this may not be the case given that it is BMC which has cancelled the contract. If part or all of the amount is repayable, it can remain recognised as a current liability. If it is not repayable, it should be released to the statement of profit or loss.

If the costs cannot be capitalised, then there is a loss which needs to be recognised. Assuming that the advance payment is non-refundable, the net position of the development cost and the deferred income balances result in a loss of $150,000. This represents 15.8% of profit for the year and is material.

If any necessary adjustments are not made there will be implications for the auditor's report, which would contain a modified opinion due to material misstatement.

Due to the significance of the matter to the financial statements, the contract cancellation and loss of BMC as a customer should be discussed in the other information to be issued with the financial statements, in this case in the integrated report.

The audit firm must consider its responsibilities in respect of ISA 720 *The Auditor's Responsibilities Relating to Other Information in Documents Containing Audited Financial Statements*. ISA 720 requires the auditor to read the other information to identify material inconsistencies, if any, with the audited financial statements.

Depending on the wording used in the integrated report when referring to the company's activities during the year and its financial performance, omitting to mention the cancellation of the contract could constitute a material misstatement of fact or a material inconsistency.

The matter should be discussed with management, who should be encouraged not only to amend the financial statements but also to discuss the cancellation of the contract in the integrated report. If management refuses to make the necessary amendments and disclosures, the matter should be discussed with those charged with governance and/or the company's legal counsel.

(ii)     **Evidence**

- A copy of the contract between Kowloon Co and BMC reviewed for terms, in particular on whether the cancellation of the contract triggers a repayment of the payment in advance and in relation to ownership of the rights to the development which has so far taken place.

- Copies of correspondence between Kowloon Co and BMC reviewed for implications of the cancellation of the contract.

- Written confirmation from BMC that the contract has been cancelled and the date of the cancellation.

- Written representation from the project manager confirming that BMC contacted him regarding their financial difficulties in December 20X5.

- Notes of a discussion with the project manager to confirm if the work in progress could be used for a different contract or the feasibility of the design work leading to a new type of product which could be produced by Kowloon Co.

- Correspondence with legal counsel regarding the ownership of the machine and whether there are any legal implications following the contract cancellation and potential proposal to sell the machine to a different customer.

- Review of post year-end orders/board minutes to assess if any conclusion regarding completion of the machine has been made and if it can be sold to an alternative customer, whether any potential customer has been identified.

- Extracts from the financial statements and journals to confirm that the necessary adjustments have been made.

- A copy of the integrated report, reviewed to confirm whether the cancellation of the contract and loss of BMC as a customer has been discussed.

---

**Examiner's comments**

This question combined two familiar formats by asking candidates to comment on the quality of the audit work performed and discuss the quality control, ethical and professional issues raised in part (a) and to comment on the matters arising and evidence expected to be found in relation to a number of financial reporting issues in part (b).

In part (a), there was tendency to re-write statements of fact from the question which scored no marks but stronger candidates discussed the issues and explained why the firm's actions were clearly inappropriate. Very few candidates were able to discuss the need for materiality to be constantly reviewed throughout the audit in light of changing circumstances. However, most candidates picked up that a significant addition to property, plant and equipment sited at a supplier's premises needed to be physically verified and that reliance on third party evidence for existence was inappropriate in the circumstances. The inventory count had been poorly performed but few candidates developed this to consider where the real audit risks may lie and the need to inform management of the weakness in internal controls and for the auditors to investigate the discrepancies and extend their testing. Improper manager/ partner review was highlighted by the majority of candidates but the implications of the partner's cursory review were not always followed through to a logical conclusion. In relation to the matters to consider, candidates were faced with a situation where the client had encountered a cancelled manufacturing contract. Most candidates scored the materiality marks for both the value of WIP and deferred income. A significant number of candidates discussed how WIP should have been calculated and its composition without realising that this was irrelevant as it needed to be recognised at nil unless a further use for it could be validly identified. Stronger candidates identified that the client may be able to levy a compensation claim for breach of contract. A worrying number of candidates also believed that writing off a deferred income creditor was a cost rather than a credit to the statement of profit or loss which shows a more fundamental lack of accounting knowledge. Likewise, many candidates confused WIP with R&D contracts and raised irrelevancies such as depreciation. The question stated that going concern was not an issue yet many candidates discussed this in depth as part of their answer. Candidates must realise that if the question makes a statement of this nature then marks will not be awarded for discussion, regardless of the quality of their answer and are again reminded to read the question scenario carefully. Audit evidence required was generally well-answered and there were some straightforward marks achieved by a majority of candidates, specifically the needs to obtain the relevant contract, board minutes, the cancellation letter and evidence of funds received. Some candidates were over reliant on written representations from management which are never as compelling as third-party evidence.

| | | **Marking scheme** | *Marks* |
|---|---|---|---|
| (a) | | **Quality control, ethical and other professional issues** | |
| | | Generally up to 1 mark for each point explained: | |
| | | – Materiality should be reviewed as the audit progresses | |
| | | – Insufficient audit evidence obtained in relation to packing machine: | |
| | | 1 mark for comment on materiality | |
| | | 1 mark for comment on physical verification | |
| | | 1 mark for comment on external confirmation | |
| | | 1 mark for comment on whether the distribution company is a related party | |
| | | 1 mark for comment on assertions/inappropriate audit conclusion | |
| | | – Lack of organisation at inventory count should have been discussed with management | |
| | | – Extrapolate test count discrepancies over the population | |
| | | – Audit staff may need training on inventory count attendance | |
| | | – Accumulate misstatements and discuss with management | |
| | | – The inaccuracy of the client's test counts should be reported to management as a control deficiency | |
| | | – Insufficient review performed by audit manager | |
| | | – Review left too late and should be ongoing during the audit | |
| | | – Potential self-interest threat regarding audit engagement partner's brother | |
| | | – Matter should be investigated and notified to audit firm's ethical partner | |
| | | – The audit partner lacks integrity, maybe has something to hide | |
| | | – The partner may need to be removed from the audit and his work reviewed | |
| | | **Maximum** | **13** |
| (b) | (i) | **Matters and actions to take** | |
| | | Generally 1 mark per comment/recommended action explained: | |
| | | – Calculation and determination of materiality (1 mark for each of the work in progress and the deferred income) | |
| | | – Contract cancellation is an adjusting event after the reporting period | |
| | | – The work in progress should be written off and charged to profit unless it can be used on a different contract | |
| | | – The deferred income may be repayable, if not it should be released to profit | |
| | | – Reporting implications if necessary adjustments not made | |
| | | – Integrated report may be inconsistent with financial statements or contain a misstatement of fact | |
| | | – Auditor's responsibility to read the integrated report to identify inconsistencies/misstatements | |
| | | – Matters to be discussed with management/those charged with governance | |
| | | **Maximum** | **7** |

|       |       |                                                                                                                                                                                                                                                                                                                                                              |       |
| ----- | ----- | ------------------------------------------------------------------------------------------------------------------------------------------------------------------------------------------------------------------------------------------------------------------------------------------------------------------------------------------------------------ | ----- |
|       | (ii)  | **Evidence**                                                                                                                                                                                                                                                                                                                                                 |       |
|       |       | Generally 1 mark for a well explained audit evidence point:                                                                                                                                                                                                                                                                                                  |       |
|       |       | – A copy of the contract between Kowloon Co and BMC reviewed for terms, in particular on whether the cancellation of the contract triggers a repayment of the payment in advance and in relation to ownership of the rights to the development which has so far taken place                                                                                    |       |
|       |       | – Copies of correspondence between Kowloon Co and BMC reviewed for implications of the cancellation of the contract                                                                                                                                                                                                                                           |       |
|       |       | – Written confirmation from BMC that the contract has been cancelled and the date of the cancellation                                                                                                                                                                                                                                                        |       |
|       |       | – Written representation from the project manager confirming that BMC contacted him regarding their financial difficulties in December 2015                                                                                                                                                                                                                   |       |
|       |       | – Notes of a discussion with the project manager to confirm if the work in progress could be used for a different contract or the feasibility of the design work leading to a new type of product which could be produced by Kowloon Co                                                                                                                       |       |
|       |       | – Correspondence with legal counsel regarding legal implications of selling to alternative customer                                                                                                                                                                                                                                                           |       |
|       |       | – Review of orders/board minutes to identify if course of action has been determined and alternative customer identified                                                                                                                                                                                                                                     |       |
|       |       | – Extracts from the financial statements and journals to confirm that the necessary adjustments have been made                                                                                                                                                                                                                                               |       |
|       |       | – A copy of the integrated report, reviewed to confirm whether the cancellation of the contract has been discussed                                                                                                                                                                                                                                           |       |
|       |       | **Maximum**                                                                                                                                                                                                                                                                                                                                                  | 5     |
| Total |       |                                                                                                                                                                                                                                                                                                                                                              | 25    |

## 27 DARREN  *Walk in the footsteps of a top tutor*

*Top tutor tips*

*Requirements (a) and (b) requires discussion of the relevant accounting treatment in the same way as you would approach a 'Matters and evidence' question. To finish off, you need to explain the impact on the auditor's report if the issues are not resolved.*

*Requirement (c) deals with a limitation of scope being imposed by management. Your answer should cover how the auditor should respond when they cannot obtain sufficient appropriate evidence.*

*In part (d) you need to discuss how the auditor should address inconsistencies between the unaudited information in the integrated report and the audited financial statements including the reporting implications.*

**(a) Bridge contract**

The total estimated profit of $5 million which has been recognised in the statement of profit or loss represents 22.2% of profit for the year and is therefore material.

In accordance with IFRS 15 *Revenue from Contracts with Customers,* revenue is recognised when or as the performance obligations within the contract are satisfied.

*Performance obligations fulfilled over time*

In the case of the construction of a bridge, the performance obligations are likely to be fulfilled over time as the bridge is unlikely to have an alternative use, i.e. it is unlikely to be able to be sold to another customer if Flyover Co were to cancel the contract part way through.

Where revenue is recognised over time the revenue recognised should be based on progress towards the satisfaction of the performance obligation. Revenue can be measured according to inputs such as time elapsed or costs incurred, or output, such as surveys.

Darren Co has recognised 100% of the contract profit even though the contract is not yet complete. The contract period is 15 months, and by the year-end the contract has been ongoing for seven months only. Therefore the profit has been recognised too early and is overstated.

Based on the time period in months, it appears that the contract is 7/15 complete, and therefore profit in the region of $2.3 million ($5 million × 7/15) can be recognised, and that profit is overstated by $2.7 million. The overstatement is material at 12% of profit before tax.

**Tutorial note**

*This calculation provides a rough guide only and is included for the purposes of assessing whether the possible misstatement might be material. Alternative progress measures can be used and the entity should select a method that best measures progress towards the performance obligations. Other methods may be more appropriate.*

*Performance obligations fulfilled at a point in time*

If the revenue should be recognised at a point in time then the revenue should only be recognised when the control of the bridge asset is transferred to Flyover Co. The $5 million recognised at the reporting date should be reversed as profit is overstated.

The audit firm should needs to clarify Darren Co's revenue recognition policy and confirm whether the revenue should be recognised over time or at a point in time.

Further evidence should be obtained to determine the amount of revenue which can be recognised, including:

- Discuss with management the methods available to measure progress towards performance obligations and assess the reasonableness of the method used.

- Scrutinise the contract terms to ensure all performance obligations within the contract have been identified.

- Review surveys of work performed by 31 January 20X5 to estimate progress towards the satisfaction of each performance obligation at the reporting date.

- Read correspondence with the customer to confirm that the contract is progressing in a satisfactory way.

If any necessary adjustment is not made, then profit is overstated by a material amount. This gives rise to a material misstatement, and the audit opinion should be modified.

A qualified 'except for' opinion should be given, and the Basis for Qualified Opinion paragraph should explain the reason for the qualification, including a quantification of the misstatement.

This is only one contract, and Darren Co typically works on three contracts at a time. Therefore further audit work is likely to be needed in respect of any other contracts which are currently being carried out. If the same accounting treatment has been applied to other contracts, the misstatement may be even greater, and could potentially result in an adverse opinion if the accumulated misstatements were considered by the auditor to be both material and pervasive to the financial statements.

In addition, Darren Co may have been using an inappropriate accounting treatment in previous years, and therefore there may be misstatements in the opening balances. This should be discussed with management to determine how contracts have been accounted for historically. Any errors which may be discovered should be corrected retrospectively, leading to further adjustments to the financial statements.

**(b)    Legal action**

The amount claimed by Newbuild Co is material to the financial statements, representing 10.8% of total assets and 178% of profit before tax. It is also likely to be considered material by nature, as the possible payment is much larger than the amount of cash recognised in the financial statements at the year-end.

The implications for the going concern status of Darren Co should be considered. The matter should be discussed with management to obtain an understanding of how Darren Co could meet any necessary cash payment. Due to the potential for such a sizeable cash payment, management should confirm that should the amount become payable, the company has adequate resources to fund the cash outflow, for example, through the existence of lending facilities.

The correct accounting treatment seems to have been applied. According to IAS 37 *Provisions, Contingent Liabilities and Contingent Assets*, if an amount is possible, rather than probable to be paid, then it is treated as a contingent liability, and a note to the accounts should be provided to describe the nature of the situation, an estimate of the possible financial effect and an indication of any uncertainties.

To ensure that IAS 37 has been complied with, the auditor should review the contents of the note for completeness and accuracy. Events after the reporting date should also be considered, for example, legal correspondence should be reviewed, to confirm that the probability of payment has not changed by the time of the auditor's report being signed.

Due to the size of the potential cash outflow, the auditor should consider including a Material Uncertainty Related to Going Concern section in the auditor's report.

The going concern section should include a clear reference to the note to the financial statements where the matter is disclosed. The paragraph should also make it clear that the audit opinion is not modified in respect of this matter.

**(c)    Military building**

The expenses represent 31.1% of profit for the year so they are material to the financial statements.

Nidge & Co is unable to obtain sufficient appropriate evidence relating to the expenses. Given the limitation imposed by management, the auditor will be unable to form a conclusion about the occurrence, completeness, accuracy or classification of the associated expenses.

ISA 705 *Modifications to the Opinion in the Independent Auditor's Report* requires that when management imposes a limitation on the scope of the audit, the auditor should request that they remove the limitation.

If management refuses, the auditor should communicate the matter to those charged with governance, explaining the implications of the matter and the impact on this year's audit opinion.

In addition, as this is a matter which is likely to arise again in future audits, the auditor should stress that the compound effect of this in the future may give rise to both a material and pervasive matter, which would give rise to a disclaimer of opinion.

As well as the implications on the auditor's report, those charged with governance should be informed that in accordance with ISA 210 *Agreeing the Terms of Audit Engagements,* the auditor may not be able to continue with the audit engagement in the future if management continues to impose the limitation on the scope of the auditor's work and the auditor believes that it may result in them disclaiming their opinion.

In the current year under these circumstances, it will be necessary to issue a modified opinion. Given the claimed value of the expenses, it is likely that the matter will be considered material but not pervasive to the financial statements and a qualified opinion will be issued.

The 'Basis for Qualified Opinion' paragraph should describe the matter giving rise to the modification.

**(d)   KPI**

The key performance indicators (KPIs) included in an integrated report are by definition 'other information' according to ISA 720 *The Auditor's Responsibilities Relating to Other Information in Documents Containing Audited Financial Statements*.

Other information is defined as financial and non-financial information included in a document containing audited financial statements and the auditor's report.

The requirement of ISA 720 is that the auditor shall read the other information, in order to identify any information contained within any of the financial or non-financial information in the annual report that is apparently materially incorrect based on, or materially inconsistent with, the knowledge acquired by the auditor in the course of performing the audit.

There appears to be an inconsistency because the KPI states that profit before tax has increased by 20%, but the increase shown in the financial statements is 12.5%. The auditor must use professional judgment to determine if this is a material inconsistency.

Assuming that this is deemed to be a material inconsistency, the auditor should consider whether the financial statements or the other information should be amended.

The audit completion procedures, including final analytical review and review of all working papers will determine whether the profit before tax figure as stated in the financial statements needs to be amended. From the discussion above, it is likely that some adjustment to profit before tax will be needed regardless of the inconsistent KPI.

It is most likely that the KPI included in the integrated report should be changed in agreement with the movement in profit shown in the adjusted financial statements, and management should be asked to make the necessary change to the KPI.

The auditor may seek legal advice if management refuses to amend the KPI to remove the material inconsistency. All of the matters affecting the auditor's report should be discussed with those charged with governance.

If management refuse to change the other information, then the auditor's report should provide a description of the inconsistency in the 'Other Information' section of the report.

Alternatively the auditor may withhold the auditor's report or withdraw from the engagement.

**UK syllabus:** Further actions are also available to auditors in the UK who have the right to speak at general meetings of company members, and could therefore highlight the inconsistency to shareholders in this way, if it remains unresolved.

These actions are very much a last resort, however, and management is likely to resolve the inconsistency rather than facing these consequences.

---

**Examiner's comments**

This question was based on the audit of Darren Co, a company operating in the construction industry and a new client of Nidge & Co. Information was provided in respect of several issues at the completion stage of the audit, and for each issue candidates were required to discuss the implication for the completion of the audit and for the auditor's report, and to recommend further actions to be taken. Generally the question was well attempted by many candidates who seemed well prepared for a question of this type.

Part (a) described how Darren's financial statements recognised all of the profit relating to a long-term construction contract even though it was only part completed at the year-end. Candidates performed well on this requirement, providing answers which confidently discussed both the inappropriate accounting treatment and the implications for the audit opinion if the material misstatements identified were not corrected by management. Some candidates missed out on marks by not recommending any further actions or by only discussing the impact for the audit opinion itself and not the overall impact on the auditor's report, failing to mention the need for a Basis for Opinion paragraph within the auditor's report. Only the strongest candidates realised that this incorrect accounting treatment may have been applied to other contracts and that opening balances may be incorrect given that this was a new audit client.

Part (b) provided information on a completed contract in respect of which Darren Co was facing legal action due to problems that had arisen following completion. The scenario stated that disclosure on the matter had been made in the notes to the financial statements and that the audit evidence on file concluded there to be a possibility of Darren Co having to pay the damages claimed. Candidates again seemed confident of the accounting rules, yet many suggested that a provision should be made for the damages. This may be because candidates assumed that there should be some implication for the auditor's opinion given the facts of the scenario, but this was not the case. The other significant issue was that Darren Co could not afford to pay the damages given its small cash balance, and this could raise a threat to the going concern status of the company. Only the strongest candidates made this connection and were able to explain clearly the implications for the auditor's report. In this scenario the issue was that a disclosure would be sufficient, as long as there was only a possibility that the claim would need to be paid, but the crucial aspect was that audit firm would need to audit the disclosure carefully to obtain evidence as to its sufficiency especially given the potential impact on going concern. As in part (a), the further actions were generally not given, other than a generic suggestion to "discuss with management".

Part (d) briefly outlined that Darren Co had included as a key performance indicator in its integrated report the percentage increase in profit before tax. Candidates were provided with the information to calculate that the indicator was incorrect. It was unfortunate that a significant minority of candidates were unable to work out a simple percentage increase despite the information being clearly presented in the question scenario. Despite this, almost all answers identified that the stated key performance indicator was incorrect. The best answers explained that management should be asked to amend the figure in the integrated report, and the impact on the auditor's report. Weaker answers suggested that the opinion should be modified due to material misstatement which is incorrect. Again, there were few suggestions of further action to be taken other than "discuss with management". The main weakness in answers to this question was a lack of specificity in the actions that had been recommended, and in many answers no actions were provided at all, severely limiting the marks that could be awarded.

## Marking scheme

| | Marks |
|---|---|
| Generally up to 1½ marks for each relevant point explained, with 1 mark for correct determination of materiality. | |

**(a)** **Bridge contract**
– Profit recognised is material
– Profit should be recognised by reference to stage of completion
– Profit appears to be overstated/recognised too early
– Further actions (1 mark each):
  • Review company's stated accounting policy
  • Review contract terms for revenue recognition trigger points
  • Verify stage of completion using surveyor's reports
  • Correspondence with customer to confirm contract progress
– Material misstatement leading to qualification of audit opinion
– Basis for Qualified Opinion paragraph
– Other contracts need to be reviewed
– Opening balances could also be materially misstated

|  | Maximum | 8 |
|---|---|---|

**(b)** **Legal action**
– Possible cash payment material by monetary amount and by nature
– Going concern implication due to size of possible cash outflow
– Treatment as a contingent liability appears correct
– Further actions (1 mark each):
  • Review post year-end legal correspondence
  • Confirm financing in place if amount becomes payable
  • Read note to accounts to ensure complete and accurate
– Material uncertainty related to going concern paragraph to highlight the significant uncertainty
– Content of the Material uncertainty related to going concern paragraph

|  | Maximum | 6 |
|---|---|---|

**(c)** **Military building**
– Expenses are material (must include relevant calculation)
– Management imposed limitation on scope
– Auditor should request that management removes the limitation
– Communication of potential impact to those charged with governance
– Impact on future audits

|  |  |  |
|---|---|---|
| | – If limitation is not removed, audit opinion will be modified<br>– Matter is material but not pervasive - qualified opinion<br>– Basis for qualified opinion paragraph | |
| | **Maximum** | 5 |
| **(d)** | **KPI**<br>– KPIs included in integrated report are other information<br>– Read other information to identify material inconsistencies<br>– The profit increase KPI is not the same as reported in the financial statements giving rise to material inconsistency<br>– Further actions (1 mark each):<br> • Consider whether the FS or KPI should be amended<br> • Request amendment of the KPI once audit finalised<br>– Reporting implications<br>– Auditor should seek legal advice (1 mark)<br>– All matters should be discussed with those charged with governance (1 mark) | |
| | **Maximum** | 6 |
| **Total** | | 25 |

## 28 THURMAN  *Walk in the footsteps of a top tutor*

### Top tutor tips

*This question examines the review stage of the audit but in a different way to the usual 'matters and evidence' questions seen in past exams. The question asks for comment on whether the evidence obtained is sufficient and appropriate. Has enough work been done? Has the most reliable form of evidence been obtained? Enquiries and written representations are the least reliable forms of evidence so ideally there will be better evidence than this on file. Think about what evidence you would expect to be on file. Compare this with the evidence that has been obtained. Any difference between what you would do and what has been done indicates that sufficient appropriate evidence has not been obtained. This should then form your answer to the next part of the requirement which asks for further procedures.*

**(a)  Assets held for sale**

**(i)  Audit evidence obtained**

The evidence does not appear to be sufficient to draw a conclusion on the appropriateness of classifying the property and any other related assets and liabilities as held for sale.

A discussion with management regarding the accounting treatment is relevant, as the audit team will need to understand management's rationale. However, management's explanation should not be accepted at face value and should be corroborated through further audit procedures.

It is not sufficient to simply put management's justification for the accounting treatment on the audit file and conclude that it is correct. For example, the factory can only be classified as held for sale if it is available for immediate sale in its current condition, which may not be the case.

In terms of the manual journal, checking that it is arithmetically correct, while relevant, is not sufficient evidence. Further evidence should be obtained in order to conclude that the basis of the calculation is in accordance with IFRS 5 *Non-current Assets Held for Sale and Discontinued Operations* and there should be consideration as to whether other requirements of the standard other than those related to the reclassification and measurement of the asset have been complied with.

For example, the results specific to the factory may need to be disclosed as a discontinued operation in the statement of profit or loss and the statement of cash flows. No audit evidence appears to have been obtained in respect of these issues.

**(ii)** **Further audit procedures**

- Review board minutes to confirm that the sale of the factory has been approved and to agree the date of the approval to the board minutes and relevant staff announcements.

- Obtain correspondence with estate agents to confirm that the factory is being actively marketed.

- Obtain confirmation, for example, by a review of production schedules, inventory movement records and payroll records, that production at the factory has stopped and thus it is available for immediate sale.

- Use an auditor's expert to confirm the fair value of the property and agree that this figure has been used in the impairment calculation.

- Using management accounts, determine whether the factory is a separate major line of business in which case its results should be disclosed as a discontinued operation.

**(iii)** **Report to those charged with governance**

ISA 265/ISA (UK) 265 *Communicating Deficiencies in Internal Controls to Those Charged with Governance and Management* requires the auditor to communicate significant deficiencies in internal control to those charged with governance and management. In deciding whether a control deficiency is significant, one of the matters which should be considered is the importance of the control to the financial reporting process.

Controls over the period-end financial reporting process such as controls over non-recurring journal entries can be important as they often deal with one-off material matters which are being accounted for outside the normal accounting system.

Therefore the journal posted by the finance director should be subject to some form of internal control, for example, approval by the board or the audit committee. The report to those charged with governance should recommend that controls are established over period-end journals posted to ensure their accuracy and validity.

In addition, the finance director should not be asking the audit team to check his figures. This could be perceived as a self-review threat to independence. This should potentially be flagged to the audit committee.

The fact that there is, according to the finance director, no one else at the company with relevant knowledge is concerning. The audit committee should be made aware of this and appropriate steps taken to ensure that sufficiently knowledgeable personnel are hired or appropriate training is provided to existing staff.

**(b)    Capital expenditure**

**(i)    Audit work performed**

The audit work has revealed that internal controls have not been operating and this should have led to more extensive testing of capital expenditure, rather than the audit programme being completed as planned. Generally, the audit team should extend audit testing on capital expenditure, for example, by extending sample testing and reducing the level of materiality applied in audit tests.

The audit team should also investigate why the controls are not operating, considering whether they are being deliberately ignored or overridden, whether time pressure or lack of resources is making the controls difficult to operate, or if there is a suspicion of collusion and possible fraud.

The procedures on the purchase of the vehicles do not appear to cover all relevant assertions, for example, there is nothing to confirm that Thurman Co has correctly depreciated the vehicles or that they are actually owned and being used by the company, or even that they exist.

**(ii)    Further audit procedures**

- Obtain the insurance documents to confirm that Thurman Co is paying the relevant insurance for the vehicles.

- Physically verify the vehicles and confirm that they are being used by employees on company business.

- Obtain the log book/vehicle registration document and other relevant ownership documents such as those issued by the vehicle licensing body, to confirm the right of Thurman Co to recognise the vehicles.

- Trace the vehicles to the company's non-current asset register.

- Recalculate the depreciation which should have been charged on the vehicles and agree to the statement of profit or loss for the year.

**(iii)    Report to those charged with governance**

The auditor should report to those charged with governance that there appears to be a deficiency in internal controls. While the audit team's findings do not indicate that a fraud is taking place, the lack of segregation of duties and the failure to obtain appropriate authorisation makes it easy for assets to be misappropriated and creates a significant fraud risk.

The audit firm should explain the implications of the control deficiencies to management and recommend improvements. For example, authorisation should be a pre-requisite for any order over a certain monetary amount. Thurman Co should also be encouraged to improve the control environment, for example, by training staff on the importance of controls and setting an appropriate tone at the top so that there is no tolerance of controls being ignored or deliberately circumvented.

**(c)** **Payroll**

**(i)** **Audit work**

The audit work in respect of the payroll needs to be much more thorough. Simply agreeing the amounts to the reports issued by Jackson Co provides no evidence on the completeness, accuracy or validity of the payroll figures recognised in the financial statements.

The audit team seems to have relied on Jackson's year-end reports as being accurate and the requirements of ISA 402/ISA (UK) 402 *Audit Considerations Relating to an Entity Using a Service Organisation* do not appear to have been followed.

The audit team needs to obtain assurance on the controls which Jackson Co has implemented in order to assess the risk of material misstatement in the payroll figures and to respond to the risk with appropriate audit procedures. The controls which Thurman Co uses to verify the information received from Jackson Co also need to be understood.

With the permission of Thurman Co, the audit team should contact Jackson Co with the objective of obtaining more information which can be used to assess how the payroll has been processed, and the controls which are in place. The controls in place at Thurman Co should be documented and tested.

It is recommended that further substantive procedures should be carried out to provide a wider range of evidence on the payroll expense recognised in the financial statements.

In relation to the casual employees, the fact that the amount involved is immaterial means that the audit team does not need to perform any further detailed audit procedures as there is no risk of material misstatement. However, as there is a risk over the completeness of these costs, the controls in place to ensure this process is effectively managed should be discussed with management and documented.

**(ii)** **Further audit procedures**

- Review the service agreement between Thurman Co and Jackson Co to understand the exact work which is conducted by Jackson Co as a service organisation.

- Read all reports made by Jackson Co during the year to identify any risks of misstatement in the payroll figure.

- Discuss and document relevant controls in place at Thurman Co over the information received from Jackson Co and the management of casual employees, and perform tests of controls on a sample basis.

- The amount of unpaid taxes in respect of the casual workers should be quantified by recalculations of the amounts due.

- Read any user manuals or systems overviews to assess the efficacy of controls in place over the processing of payroll.

- If necessary, obtain a type 1 or type 2 report from Jackson Co to obtain further assurance on the controls which the service organisation has in place.

- Perform a substantive analytical review on payroll, preparing an auditor's expectation of the payroll figures and comparing it to that recognised in the financial statements and discussing any variance with management.

- Perform test of detail by selecting a sample from the payroll records and agreeing the amounts to payslips and HR records.

### (iii) Report to those charged with governance

The fact that casual employees are being paid from petty cash without being put onto the company's payroll indicates that Thurman Co may not be complying with relevant regulations, for example, that appropriate payroll taxes are not being paid. Despite the amounts involved being immaterial, the potential non-compliance should be reported to those charged with governance, along with a recommendation that all employees, whether casual or not, should be processed through the company's payroll system. There may be implications for the financial statements if fines or penalties are imposed by the tax authorities in respect of the non-compliance.

---

**Examiner's comments**

This question was set in the completion stage of the audit and as is generally the case with completion questions, it was focused on the accounting treatment and audit evidence obtained on three issues. In this case, candidates were also required to discuss the impact of the issues found on the report to those charged with governance. Candidates generally demonstrated a good knowledge of the financial reporting implications of the areas and were often able to identify that the evidence obtained was insufficient and suggest further procedures. For many candidates the control weaknesses in the company and the implication of a deficiency in controls on further audit strategy and testing was not always identified. Candidates' responses to the matters to include in the report were variable with some candidates discussing auditor's report qualifications (despite no errors being flagged) or giving general answers to the contents of the report with no reference to the scenario in the exam.

---

| Marking scheme | Marks |
|---|---|
| Generally 1 mark for each relevant point of discussion and well explained audit procedure:<br>**(a)    Asset held for sale**<br>    **(i)    Audit evidence**<br>        – Discussion is relevant but management's assertions must be corroborated<br>        – Discussion alone is not sufficient to reach an audit conclusion<br>        – Evidence not obtained on whether IFRS 5 classification criteria have been met<br>        – Evidence not obtained on whether disclosure of discontinued operations is necessary<br>    **(ii)    Further procedures**<br>        – Review board minutes to confirm the sale approval and date<br>        – Correspondence with estate agents to confirm that the factory is being actively marketed<br>        – Confirmation, for example, by a review of production schedules, inventory movement records and payroll records that production at the factory has stopped<br>        – Auditor's expert to confirm the fair value of the property<br>        – Determine whether the factory is a separate major line of business and should be disclosed as a discontinued operation | |

(iii) **Report to those charged with governance**
- Should be controls in place over year-end journals (2 marks for detailed discussion)
- Finance director should not have to ask the audit team to check his work

|  |  |
|---|---|
| **Maximum** | 9 |

(b) **Capital expenditure**
(i) **Audit evidence**
- Testing should have been extended after the control deficiency was identified
- Reason for the controls not operating effectively should be investigated
- Increases the fraud risk in relation to capital expenditure
- Not all assertions have been covered by audit testing in respect of the vehicles purchased

(ii) **Further audit procedures**
- Obtain the insurance documents to confirm that Thurman Co is paying the relevant insurance for the vehicles
- Physically verify the vehicles and confirm that they are being used by employees on company business
- Obtain the log book and other relevant ownership documents to confirm the right of Thurman Co to recognise the vehicles
- Trace the vehicles to the company's fixed asset register
- Recalculate the depreciation which should have been charged on the vehicles

(iii) **Report to those charged with governance**
- Explain the deficiencies and the implications, i.e. increased fraud risk
- Recommend improvements to specific controls and to the general control environment

|  |  |
|---|---|
| **Maximum** | 7 |

(c) **Payroll**
(i) **Audit work**
- Agreeing payroll to the service organisation's report does not provide sufficient evidence on completeness, accuracy or validity of the amounts
- The controls at the service organisation must be assessed for their adequacy
- No further work needed on the petty cash payments to casual workers as the amount is not material

(ii) **Further audit procedures**
- Review the service agreement between Thurman Co and Jackson Co to understand the exact work which is conducted by Jackson Co as a service organisation
- Read all reports made by Jackson Co during the year to identify any risks of misstatement in the payroll figure
- Discuss and document relevant controls in place at Thurman Co over the information received from Jackson Co and the management of casual employees, and perform tests of controls on a sample basis
- Recalculate the amount of any unpaid tax which may be due to the tax authorities
- Read any user manuals or systems overviews to assess the efficacy of controls in place over the processing of payroll
- If necessary, obtain a type 1 or type 2 report from Jackson Co to obtain further assurance on the controls which the service organisation has in place
- Perform a substantive analytical review on payroll, preparing an auditor's expectation of the payroll figures and comparing it to that recognised in the financial statements and discussing any variance with management

|  |  |  |
|---|---|---|
| | – Perform test of detail by selecting a sample from the payroll records and agreeing the amounts to payslips and HR records | |
| (iii) | **Report to those charged with governance** | |
| | – There is not a significant control deficiency as the amounts involved are immaterial | |
| | – Potential non-compliance with regulations, e.g. tax regulation should be reported | |
| | – Recommend that all workers are put through payroll to ensure compliance | |
| | **Maximum** | 9 |
| **Total** | | 25 |

## 29 ADDER GROUP  *Walk in the footsteps of a top tutor*

### Top tutor tips

*For 'Matters and evidence' questions, use the 'MARE' approach to make it easier to score the required number of marks. First, consider the materiality of the issue. Next discuss the appropriate accounting treatment and give the risks of material misstatement that would arise if the appropriate treatment is not followed. Finally, the evidence is what you would expect to be recorded on the audit file when you come to review it. Be specific about the evidence, don't say 'supporting documentation', suggest what that documentation would be and what it would show. Assume that half of the marks will be for matters and half of the marks will be for evidence.*

*Part (b) asks for a critical appraisal of the draft report extracts. This is a common reporting question seen several times in previous exams and should not cause problems for students who are familiar with the format of an auditor's report and who have practised this style of question before. Work your way through the auditor's report and think about whether the wording is appropriate, the order of the paragraphs is correct, the names of the paragraphs are correct and ultimately, whether you agree with the opinion suggested.*

**(a)** **(i)** The sale and leaseback transaction is material to the Group statement of financial position. The proceeds received on the sale of the property, equivalent to the fair value of the assets, represents 23.3% of Group assets, and the carrying value of the assets disposed of were $27 million ($35 million – $8 million), representing 18% of Group assets. In addition, the profit recognised on the disposal represents 40% of the Group's profit for the year, so it is highly material to the statement of profit or loss.

The accounting treatment does not appear to be in accordance with IFRS 16 *Leases*. IFRS 16 says the accounting treatment of a sale and leaseback depends on whether a performance obligation, as defined in IFRS 15 *Revenue from Contracts with Customers,* has been satisfied. Adder Group will be obtaining substantially all of the asset's remaining benefits, suggesting that control has not passed to the buyer.

Therefore, the transfer of the asset does not represent a 'sale'. As such, the asset should remain recognised in the statement of financial position, and the proceeds received from the sale should be recognised as a financial liability.

Therefore the Group's profit is materially overstated, and the total assets and liabilities are materially understated.

The following adjustments should be recommended to management:

| | | |
|---|---|---|
| DR | Property, plant and equipment | $27 million |
| DR | Profit or loss | $8 million |
| CR | Financial liability | $35 million |

The complex should be depreciated over the final four months of the year, giving rise to depreciation of $0.5 million ($27 million/20 years × 4/12). The adjustment required is:

| | | |
|---|---|---|
| DR | Profit or loss | $0.5 million |
| CR | Property, plant and equipment | $0.5 million |

The finance charge on the financial liability which has accrued since the transfer of the asset should be quantified, its materiality determined, and the appropriate adjustment communicated to management.

If the adjustments are not made, the Group financial statements will contain a material misstatement, with implications for the auditor's opinion, which would be modified due to a material misstatement following the misapplication of IFRS 16 to the sale and leaseback transaction.

**Evidence:**

- A copy of the lease, signed by the buyer-lessor, and a review of its major clauses to confirm that control of the asset remains with the Group.

- Review of forecasts and budgets to confirm that economic benefit is expected to be generated through the continued use of the property complex.

- Agreement of the $35 million cash proceeds to the bank statement and cash book.

- Physical inspection of the property complex to confirm that it is being used by the Group.

- Confirmation of the fair value of the property complex, possibly using an auditor's expert, in which case the expert's report should be included in the audit working papers.

- Where fair value has been established using an auditor's or management expert, evaluation of the expert's work including confirmation that the fair value is determined according to the applicable financial reporting framework, and that all assumptions are reasonable.

- Minutes of a discussion with management regarding the accounting treatment and including an auditor's request to amend the financial statements.

- A copy of insurance documents stating that the Group is responsible for insuring the property complex.

- Recalculation of finance charge and depreciation expense in relation to the leased asset.

**(ii)**   The Group's interest in Baldrick Co is material, as the company's assets are equivalent to 12% of total Group assets, and its loss is equivalent to 25% of the Group's profit.

It is questionable whether Baldrick Co should have been accounted for as an associate. An associate arises where there is significant influence over an investee, according to IAS 28 *Investments in Associates and Joint Ventures*. Significant influence is typified by an equity shareholding of 20 – 50%, so the Group's shareholding of 52% would seem to indicate that the Group exercises control, rather than significant influence.

However, it may be that even with a 52% shareholding, the Group cannot exercise control, for example, if it is prevented from doing so due to agreements between other shareholders, or because it cannot appoint members to the board of Baldrick Co. This would be unusual though, so audit evidence must be sought on the nature of the shareholding in Baldrick Co and whether the Group actually exercises control or significant influence over the company. Baldrick Co not having been integrated into the Group's activities is not a valid reason for its non-consolidation as a subsidiary.

If the Group does have a controlling interest, and Baldrick Co remains recognised as an associate, the Group financial statements will be materially misstated, with implications for the auditor's opinion, which would be modified due to the application of an inappropriate accounting treatment.

If Baldrick Co should be treated as a subsidiary rather than an associate, then the company's loss for the year should be consolidated from the date of acquisition which was 1 January 20X5. Therefore, a loss of $1.25 million ($5 million × 3/12) should be consolidated into Group profit. The loss which has already been recognised, assuming that equity accounting has been correctly applied, would be $650,000 ($5 million × 3/12 × 52%), therefore an additional loss of $600,000 needs to be recognised.

In addition, there are presentation issues to consider. Equity accounting requires the investment in the associate to be recognised on one line in the statement of financial position, and the income from the associate to be disclosed on one line of the statement of profit or loss.

Treating Baldrick Co as a subsidiary will require a line-by-line consolidation, which will have a significant impact on numerous balances within the financial statements.

The combination of adjustments in relation to the sale and leaseback transaction and the consolidation of Baldrick Co as a subsidiary may be considered pervasive to the Group financial statements, and if so, and the necessary adjustments are not made, then the audit opinion could be adverse.

**Evidence:**

*   Agreement of the cash paid to acquire Baldrick Co to cash book and bank statements.
*   Review of board minutes for discussion of the change in Group structure and for authorisation of the acquisition.
*   Review of legal documentation pertaining to the acquisition of Baldrick Co, to confirm the number of equity shares acquired, and the rights attached to the shareholding, e.g. the ability to appoint board members.
*   Inspection of other supporting documentation relating to the acquisition such as due diligence reports.

- Notes of discussion with management regarding the exercise of control over Baldrick Co, e.g. the planned level of participation in its operating and financial decisions.

- Review of forecasts and budgets to assess the plans for integrating Baldrick Co into the Group.

- Ensure that correct time apportionment has been applied in calculating the amount of losses recognised in the consolidation of Baldrick Co.

- Evaluation and recalculation of amounts recognised in Group equity in respect of Baldrick Co, in particular the determination of pre- and post-acquisition results.

**(b)** **Opinion and basis for opinion paragraphs not separate**

In terms of structure, the basis for opinion and opinion paragraphs should not be combined together. When the auditor modifies the opinion on the financial statements, the auditor shall include a paragraph in the auditor's report which provides a description of the matter giving rise to the modification. Therefore the auditor's report needs to be amended to include two separate paragraphs.

The auditor should use the heading 'Basis for Qualified Opinion', 'Basis for Adverse Opinion', or 'Basis for Disclaimer of Opinion', as appropriate.

**'Proven conclusively'**

The paragraph states that audit procedures have 'proven conclusively' in respect of trade receivables. This term is misleading, implying that every transaction has been tested. Audit procedures provide a reasonable, but not absolute, level of assurance on the financial statements, and conclusive proof is not an appropriate term to be used in the auditor's report.

**Quantification of potential adjustment**

The amount of the potential adjustment to trade receivables and its financial impact should be included in the paragraph. If there is a material misstatement of the financial statements which relates to specific amounts in the financial statements (including quantitative disclosures), the auditor shall include in the basis for modification paragraph a description and quantification of the financial effects of the misstatement, unless impracticable. The relevant financial reporting standard should also be referred to.

**Unprofessional wording**

The paragraph uses unprofessional wording by naming the finance director. The auditor's report should refer to management collectively and not single out one person as being responsible for the financial statements. In addition, it should not state that she 'refused' to make an adjustment.

**Type of opinion**

The incorrect type of modified audit opinion seems to have been given. The trade receivables balance is material at $2.5 million, which is in excess of the materiality threshold of $1.5 million used in the audit and so a qualification due to material misstatement seems necessary. The auditor's report uses a disclaimer of opinion, which is used when the auditor cannot form an opinion, usually due to lack of audit evidence, which does not appear to be the case here.

### Level of modification

In addition, the level of modification seems incorrect. The matter is material at 22.7% of profit but is unlikely to be pervasive to the financial statements. Therefore a qualified 'except for' opinion is sufficient.

### Emphasis of matter paragraph

The use of an Emphasis of Matter paragraph in respect of the court case is not appropriate. An Emphasis of Matter paragraph is used to refer to a matter appropriately presented or disclosed in the financial statements which, in the auditor's judgment, is of such importance that it is fundamental to users' understanding of the financial statements.

The court case and its potential legal consequences are not material, being well below the materiality threshold of $1.5 million. The matter is certainly not fundamental to users' understanding of the financial statements. Due to the immaterial nature of the matter it need not be referred to in the auditor's report at all.

The auditor has reached the conclusion that the court case has not been accounted for correctly. The Emphasis of Matter paragraph should only be used to highlight matters which have been appropriately accounted for and disclosed within the financial statements, and its use to describe non-compliance with the relevant financial reporting standard is not appropriate.

---

**Examiner comments**

The first requirement asked candidates to comment on the matters to be considered and explain the audit evidence they would expect to find in a review of the working papers relating to the audit of the Adder Group. Candidates who have practised past exam papers will be familiar with requirements of this type, and with scenarios set in the completion stage of the audit.

The first issue related to a sale and leaseback arrangement. The Adder Group had derecognised the asset and recognised a profit on disposal. Candidates had to discuss whether the accounting treatment appeared appropriate. Answers on the whole were good. Most candidates proved able to confidently discuss whether the lease had been appropriately classified and accounted for. In addition almost all candidates correctly determined the materiality of the balances and could provide some specific and well explained points on audit evidence.

The second issue related to the acquisition of a 52% shareholding in Baldrick Co, which had been accounted for as an associate in the consolidated financial statements. Again, candidates were able to identify that the accounting treatment seemed incorrect, and could explain their reasoning. Fewer candidates appreciated that the loss-making status of Baldrick Co was the possible explanation for the Group's reluctance to consolidate it as a subsidiary and therefore that the Group's profits were overstated. Most candidates could provide some evidence points, with the most commonly cited being the board approval of the acquisition and agreeing the cash paid to bank statements. Fewer candidates could suggest how the audit firm should obtain evidence on the exercise of control by the parent company or on the mechanics of the consolidation that should have taken place. It was encouraging that so many scripts discussed financial reporting matters with confidence, and crucially, were able to link those matters to relevant audit evidence points; for requirement.

---

Requirement (b) asked for a critical appraisal of a proposed auditor's report. The report contained many errors of fact and of judgment, and well prepared candidates scored highly here. There were some quite obvious matters that most candidates discussed, for example that the structure of the report was not correct, the wording was not professional, the basis for opinion paragraph lacked sufficient detail, and the nature of the modification was wrong in the circumstances described in the scenario. Most candidates also commented on the incorrect use of the Emphasis of Matter paragraph and correctly determined the materiality of the two issues described in the scenario. Overall however, answers to this requirement were often too short for the marks available, and while most issues had been identified, they were not always well explained.

| Marking scheme | |
|---|---|
| | *Marks* |
| Generally up to 1½ marks for each matter discussed, and 1 mark for each well explained procedure: | |
| **(a)**     **(i)**    **Sale and leaseback** | |
|                **Matters:** | |
|                –   Correct determination of materiality | |
|                –   IFRS 16 treatment | |
|                –   Assets and liabilities understated, profit overstated | |
|                –   Adjustment recommended | |
|                –   Depreciation should be re-measured | |
|                –   Finance charge accrual | |
|                –   Implications for auditor's report if not adjusted | |
|                **Evidence:** | |
|                –   A copy of the lease | |
|                –   Forecasts and budgets | |
|                –   Physical inspection of the property complex | |
|                –   Confirmation of the fair value of the property | |
|                –   Evaluation of the expert's work | |
|                –   Bank statement and cash book | |
|                –   Minutes of a discussion with management | |
|                –   A copy of insurance documents | |
|                –   Recalculation of finance charge and depreciation | |
|       **(ii)**   **Baldrick Co** | |
|                **Matters:** | |
|                –   Correct determination of materiality of Baldrick Co | |
|                –   If Group exercises control, Baldrick Co is a subsidiary | |
|                –   Need to determine nature of the Group's interest in Baldrick Co | |
|                –   Impact on audit opinion is at least qualification due to material misstatement | |
|                –   Discussion of impact on Group profit | |
|                –   Presentation issues | |
|                –   Impact could be pervasive in combination with the sale and leaseback | |
|                **Evidence:** | |
|                –   Cash book and bank statements | |
|                –   Board minutes for authorisation | |
|                –   Legal documentation for the acquisition of Baldrick Co | |
|                –   Due diligence reports | |
|                –   Notes of discussion with management regarding control | |
|                –   Plans for integrating Baldrick Co into the Group | |
|                –   Ensure that losses from the date of acquisition only are consolidated | |
|                –   Evaluation and recalculation of amounts recognised in Group equity in respect of Baldrick Co | |
| **Maximum** | **16** |

| (b) | **Evaluation of draft auditor's report** | | |
|---|---|---|---|
| | In general up to 1½ marks for each relevant point of evaluation: | | |
| | – Incorrect presentation and combining of Opinion and Basis for Opinion paragraphs | | |
| | – Wording regarding 'proven conclusively' is inappropriate | | |
| | – Description of material misstatement should include quantification and impact on financial statements | | |
| | – The relevant financial reporting standard should be referred to | | |
| | – Unprofessional wording regarding the finance director | | |
| | – Inappropriate opinion given – should be modified due to material misstatement not due to disclaimer of opinion | | |
| | – Level of modification incorrect – it is material but not pervasive | | |
| | – Court case not fundamental so not appropriate to include in Emphasis of Matter paragraph | | |
| | – Emphasis of Matter should only be used for matters appropriately accounted for which is not the case | | |
| | | **Maximum** | 9 |
| **Total** | | | **25** |

## 30 FRANCIS GROUP  *Walk in the footsteps of a top tutor*

### Top tutor tips

*This question is a typical 'matters and evidence' question. Use the 'MARE' approach. First, consider the materiality of the issue. Next discuss the appropriate accounting treatment and give the risks of material misstatement that would arise if the appropriate treatment is not followed. Finally, the evidence is what you would expect to be recorded on the audit file when you come to review it. Be specific about the evidence, don't say 'supporting documentation', and suggest what that documentation would be and what it would show.*

*There are three issues to deal with and each has its own mark allocation therefore deal with both matters and evidence for the acquisition of Teapot, then the property complex, and finally the intercompany balances. Don't deal with matters for all three then evidence for all three as the structure of the requirements and the mark allocations indicates that this is not the appropriate presentation.*

### (a)  (i)  Measurement of goodwill on acquisition

The goodwill arising on the acquisition of Teapot Co is material to the Group financial statements, representing 6% of total assets.

The goodwill should be recognised as an intangible asset and measured according to IAS 38 *Intangible Assets* and IFRS 3 *Business Combinations*.

The purchase consideration should reflect the fair value of total consideration paid and payable, and there is a risk that the amount shown in the calculation is not complete, for example, if any deferred or contingent consideration has not been included.

The non-controlling interest has been measured at fair value. This is permitted by IFRS 3, and the decision to measure at fair value can be made on an investment by investment basis. The important issue is the basis for measurement of fair value.

If Teapot Co is a listed company, then the market value of its shares at the date of acquisition can be used and this is a reliable measurement.

If Teapot Co is not listed, then management should have used estimation techniques according to the fair value hierarchy of inputs contained in IFRS 13 *Fair Value Measurement*. This would introduce subjectivity into the measurement of non-controlling interest and goodwill and the method of determining fair value must be clearly understood by the auditor.

The net assets acquired should be all identifiable assets and liabilities at the date of acquisition. For such a significant acquisition some form of due diligence investigation should have been performed, and one of the objectives of this would be to determine the existence of assets and liabilities, even those not recognised in Teapot Co's individual financial statements.

There is a risk that not all acquired assets and liabilities have been identified, or that they have not been appropriately measured at fair value, which would lead to over or understatement of goodwill and incomplete recording of assets and liabilities in the consolidated financial statements.

The fair value adjustment of $300,000 made in relation to Teapot Co's property is not material to the Group accounts, representing less than 1% of total assets. However, the auditor should confirm that additional depreciation is being charged at Group level in respect of the fair value uplift. Though the value of the depreciation would not be material to the consolidated financial statements, for completeness and accuracy the adjustment should be made.

The auditor should also consider if any further adjustments need to be made to Teapot Co's net assets to ensure that Group accounting policies have been applied. IFRS 3 requires consistency in accounting policies across Group members, so if the necessary adjustments have not been made, the assets and liabilities will be over or understated on consolidation.

**Evidence:**

- Agreement of the purchase consideration to the legal documentation pertaining to the acquisition, and a review of the documents to ensure that the figures included in the goodwill calculation are complete.

- Agreement of the $75 million to the bank statement and cash book of the acquiring company (presumably the parent company of the Group).

- Review of board minutes for discussions relating to the acquisition, and for the relevant minute of board approval.

- A review of the purchase documentation and a register of significant shareholders of Teapot Co to confirm the 20% non-controlling interest.

- If Teapot Co's shares are not listed, a discussion with management as to how the fair value of the non-controlling interest has been determined and evaluation of the appropriateness of the method used.

- If Teapot Co's shares are listed, confirmation that the fair value of the non-controlling interest has been calculated based on an externally available share price at the date of acquisition.

- A copy of any due diligence report relevant to the acquisition, reviewed for confirmation of acquired assets and liabilities and their fair values.

- An evaluation of the methods used to determine the fair value of acquired assets, including the property, and liabilities to confirm compliance with IFRS 3 and IFRS 13.
- Review of depreciation calculations, and recalculation, to confirm that additional depreciation is being charged on the fair value uplift.
- A review of the calculation of net assets acquired to confirm that Group accounting policies have been applied.

**Impairment of goodwill**

IAS 38 requires that goodwill is tested annually for impairment regardless of whether indicators of potential impairment exist. The goodwill in relation to Teapot Co is recognised at the same amount at the year-end as it was at acquisition, indicating that no impairment has been recognised. It could be that management has performed an impairment review and has concluded that there is no impairment, or that no impairment review has been performed at all.

However, Group profit has declined by 30.3% over the year, which in itself is an indicator of potential impairment of the Group's assets, so it is unlikely that no impairment exists unless the fall in revenue relates to parts of the Group's activities which are unrelated to Teapot Co.

There is a risk that Group assets are overstated and profit overstated if any necessary impairment has not been recognised.

**Evidence:**

- Discussion with management regarding the potential impairment of Group assets and confirmation as to whether an impairment review has been performed.
- A copy of any impairment review performed by management, with scrutiny of the assumptions used, and re-performance of calculations.
- The auditor's impairment evaluation and calculation compared with that of management.

**(ii)** **Property complex**

The carrying value of the property complex is material to the Group financial statements, representing 3.6% of total assets.

The natural disaster is a subsequent event, and its accounting treatment should be in accordance with IAS 10 *Events After the Reporting Period*. IAS 10 distinguishes between adjusting and non-adjusting events, the classification being dependent on whether the event provides additional information about conditions already existing at the year-end. The natural disaster is a non-adjusting event as it indicates a condition which arose after the year-end.

Disclosure is necessary in a note to the financial statements to describe the impact of the natural disaster, and quantify the effect which it will have on next year's financial statements.

The demolition of the property complex should be explained in the note to the financial statements and reference made to the monetary amounts involved. Consideration should be made of any other costs which will be incurred, e.g. if there is inventory to be written off, and the costs of the demolition itself.

The contingent asset of $18 million should not have been recognised as per IAS 37 *Provisions, Contingent Liabilities and Contingent Assets*. Even if the amount were virtually certain to be received, the fact that it relates to the non-adjusting event after the reporting period means that it cannot be recognised as an asset and deferred income at the year-end.

The financial statements should be adjusted to remove the contingent asset and the deferred income. The amount is material at 4% of total assets. There would be no profit impact of this adjustment as the $18 million has not been recognised in the statement of profit or loss.

**Evidence:**

- A copy of any press release made by the Group after the natural disaster, and relevant media reports of the natural disaster, in particular focusing on its impact on the property complex.

- Photographic evidence of the site after the natural disaster, and of the demolished site.

- A copy of the note to the financial statements describing the event, reviewed for completeness and accuracy.

- A schedule of the costs of the demolition, with a sample agreed to supporting documentation, e.g. invoices for work performed and confirmation that this is included in the costs described in the note to the financial statements.

- A schedule showing the value of inventories and items such as fixtures and fittings at the time of the disaster, and confirmation that this is included in the costs described in the note to the financial statements.

- A copy of the insurance claim and correspondence with the Group's insurers to confirm that the property is insured.

- Confirmation that an adjustment has been made to reverse out the contingent asset and deferred income which has been recognised.

(iii) **Intercompany trading**

The intercompany receivables and payables balances represent 4.4% of Group assets and are material to the consolidated statement of financial position. The inventory is also material, at 11% of Group assets.

On consolidation, the intercompany receivables and payables balances of $20 million should be eliminated, leaving only balances between the Group and external parties recognised at Group level.

There is a risk that during the consolidation process the elimination has not happened, overstating Group assets and liabilities by the same amount.

If the intercompany transaction included a profit element, then the inventory of $50 million needs to be reduced in value by an adjustment for unrealised profit. This means that the profit made by Marks Co on the sale of any inventory still remaining in the Group at the year-end is eliminated. If the adjustment has not been made, then inventory and Group profit will be overstated.

**Evidence:**

- Review of consolidation working papers to confirm that the intercompany balances have been eliminated.

- A copy of the terms of sale between Marks Co and Roberts Co, scrutinised to find out if a profit margin or mark-up is part of the sales price.

- A reconciliation of the intercompany balances between Roberts Co and Marks Co to confirm that there are no other reconciling items to be adjusted, e.g. cash in transit or goods in transit.

- Copies of inventory movement reports for the goods sold from Marks Co to Roberts Co, to determine the quantity of goods transferred.

- Details of the inventory count held at Roberts Co at the year-end, reviewed to confirm that no other intercompany goods are held at the year-end.

**(b)    Implications for the auditor's report**

The contingent asset should not be recognised. The event is a non-adjusting event therefore disclosure is required but no accounting entries.

Even if the event had occurred before the year-end, the correspondence received from the insurance company provides evidence that the insurance company will not pay the claim therefore there will be no future receipt of economic benefits.

The auditor should review the financial statements to identify whether any disclosure has been made of the issue. If no disclosure has been made the financial statements will be materially misstated due to lack of disclosure of the non-adjusting event and overstatement of contingent assets.

The issue is likely to be considered material but not pervasive as the misstatement only represents 4% of total assets. Going concern is not affected.

The audit opinion should be modified with a qualified opinion. The opinion will state 'except for' this matter the financial statements give a true and fair view.

Within the auditor's report the basis for opinion will be changed to a basis for qualified opinion. This will include an explanation of the reason for issuing a qualified opinion.

The basis for qualified opinion will also describe the financial impact the misstatement has on the financial statements in respect of the current year and accumulated reserves.

---

**Examiner's comments**

This question contained information relevant to the audit completion of the Francis Group. Specifically, three issues had been highlighted by the audit senior, and candidates were asked in respect of each issue to comment on the matters to be considered and explain the audit evidence they should expect to find during a review of the audit working papers. This type of requirement is common in this paper, and it was encouraging to see that many candidates had obviously practised past exam questions containing similar requirements. Most candidates approached each of the issues in a sensible manner by firstly determining the materiality of the matters involved, considering the appropriate financial reporting treatment and risk of misstatement, and then providing some examples of appropriate audit evidence relevant to the matters discussed. However, the question was not well attempted by all, and it was usually a lack of knowledge of financial reporting requirements, and/or an inability to explain the relevant audit evidence that let some candidates down.

Requirement (a)(i) related to an acquisition of a subsidiary that had taken place during the year. A goodwill calculation had been provided, along with information regarding a fair value adjustment relevant to the net assets of the subsidiary at acquisition. Candidates were able to achieve a good mark here if they tackled each component of the information provided in turn and used that approach to deliver a structured answer.

In relation to the goodwill calculation, many candidates identified that no impairment had been recognised, and therefore that the goodwill balance may be overvalued. Only the strongest candidates mentioned that a significant drop in the Group's profit for the year meant that it would be very likely that an impairment loss should be recognised. It was worrying to see how many candidates referred to the need for goodwill to be amortised over a useful life – a practice that has not been allowed under IFRS 3 *Business Combinations* for many years. Fewer candidates touched on the measurement issues in relation to the non-controlling interest component of goodwill, which was usually ignored in answers. Looking at the fair value adjustment to net assets, most candidates recognised that this would be a subjective issue and that ideally an independent valuer's report or due diligence report would be required as audit evidence to justify the adjustment. Weaker candidates thought that the accounting treatment of goodwill was incorrect and set about correcting the perceived errors.

Some incorrect accounting treatments frequently discussed included:

- Goodwill should be amortised over an estimated useful life (discussed above)

- Goodwill only needs to be tested for impairment when indicators of impairment exist

- Non-controlling interest should not be part of the goodwill calculation

- Fair value adjustments are not required and are an indication of fraudulent financial reporting.

The evidence points provided by candidates for this requirement tended to revolve around recalculations of the various balances, and confirming figures to supporting documentation such as the purchase documentation and due diligence reports. These were all valid evidence points but it would benefit candidates to consider a wider range of evidence that may be available especially in relation to the more subjective and therefore higher risk elements, for example a discussion with management regarding the need for an impairment review of goodwill or a review and assessment of the methods used to determine the fair value of the non- controlling interest.

Requirement (a)(ii) related to a natural disaster that had taken place two months after the year-end, resulting in the demolition of the Group's head office and main manufacturing site. The Group had claimed under its insurance an amount in excess of the value of the demolished property, and the whole amount of the claim was recognised in the statement of financial position as a current asset and deferred income. This requirement was generally well answered, with almost all candidates correctly determining the materiality of the property complex and the contingent asset. Most candidates also appreciated that the auditor should consider the event to be a non-adjusting event after the reporting date, requiring disclosure in the notes to the financial statements, in line with the requirements of IAS 10 *Events After the Reporting Period*. The audit evidence suggested was usually relevant and sensible, tending to focus on the insurance claim, discussing the need for demolition with management, and evidence from documents such as health and safety reports on the necessity for the demolition. Many answers identified that a key part of the audit evidence would be in the form of a review of the sufficiency of the required notes to the financial statements describing and quantifying the financial implications of the non-adjusting event. In a minority of scripts candidates suggested that the event was actually an adjusting event and that impairment of the property complex should be recognised in this financial year. Weaker answers to this requirement suggested that the event should be recognised by impairing the property complex and recognising the contingent asset. However, encouragingly even where candidates had discussed the incorrect accounting treatment, the evidence points provided were generally appropriate to the scenario.

Requirement (a)(iii) briefly described the details of intercompany trading that had taken place between components of the Group resulting in intercompany receivables and payables in the individual financial statements of the components, and inventory within the recipient company including a profit element. Most candidates correctly determined that at Group level the intercompany transactions should be eliminated and that a provision for unrealised profit would be necessary to remove the profit element of the transaction. Most candidates also correctly calculated the relevant materiality figures and could provide a couple of evidence points. The main concern with responses to this requirement was that they were often brief, with the audit evidence described usually amounting to little more than recalculations and 'check the elimination has happened'.

In summary the question was well attempted by many candidates, with the matters to consider element of the requirements usually better attempted than the audit evidence points. It was clear that many candidates had practised past questions of this type and were well prepared for the style of question requirement.

The UK and IRL adapted papers were slightly different in that the requirements were not broken down and therefore marks were not allocated to each separate issue. This did not seem to affect how candidates approached the question, and again it was generally well attempted. It was however much more common to see references to incorrect financial reporting requirements, specifically that goodwill must be amortised over an estimated useful life.

Candidates are reminded that if they choose to attempt the UK or IRL adapted paper, the financial reporting requirements are still based on IFRS Standards, as in the INT paper, and therefore discussing financial reporting requirements of UK and Irish GAAP will not score credit.

| Marking scheme | |
|---|---|
| | *Marks* |
| Generally 1 mark for each matter considered/evidence point explained: | |
| (a) (i) **Teapot Co** | |
| **Matters:** | |
| – Materiality of the goodwill | |
| – Purchase price/consideration to be at fair value | |
| – Risk of understatement if components of consideration not included | |
| – Non-controlling interest at fair value – determination of fair value if Teapot Co is listed | |
| – Non-controlling interest at fair value – determination of fair value if Teapot Co is not listed | |
| – Use of fair value hierarchy to determine fair value | |
| – Risk that not all acquired assets and liabilities have been separately identified | |
| – Risk in the measurement of acquired assets and liabilities – judgmental | |
| – Additional depreciation to be charged on fair value uplift | |
| – Group accounting policies to be applied to net assets acquired on consolidation | |
| – Impairment indicator exists – fall in revenue | |
| – Impairment review required regardless for goodwill | |
| – Risk goodwill and Group profit overstated if necessary impairment not recognised | |
| **Evidence:** | |
| – Agreement of the purchase consideration | |
| – Agreement of the $75 million to the bank statement and cash book | |
| – Review of board minutes for discussions relating to the acquisition | |
| – A review of the purchase documentation and a register of significant shareholders of Teapot Co to confirm the 20% NCI | |

|  |  |
|---|---|
| – If Teapot Co's shares are not listed, a discussion with management as to how the fair value of the non-controlling interest has been determined | |
| – If Teapot Co's shares are listed, confirmation that the fair value of the non-controlling interest has been calculated based on an externally available share price at the date of acquisition | |
| – A copy of any due diligence report relevant to the acquisition | |
| – An evaluation of the methods used to determine the fair value of acquired assets | |
| – Review of depreciation calculations, and recalculation | |
| – A review of the calculation of net assets acquired | |
| – Discussion with management regarding the potential impairment of Group assets | |
| – A copy of any impairment review performed by management | |

|  |  |
|---|---|
| **Maximum** | 9 |

**(ii)    Property complex**

**Matters:**
- Materiality of the asset (calculation) and significance to profit
- Identify event as non-adjusting
- Describe content of note to financial statements
- Consider other costs, e.g. inventories to be written off
- Contingent asset/deferred income should not be recognised

**Evidence:**
- A copy of any press release/media reports
- Photographic evidence of the site after the natural disaster and of the demolished site
- A copy of the note to the financial statements describing the event
- A schedule of the costs of the demolition, with a sample agreed to supporting documentation
- A schedule showing the value of inventories and items such as fixtures and fittings
- A copy of the insurance claim
- Confirmation of the removal of the contingent asset from the financial statements

|  |  |
|---|---|
| **Maximum** | 6 |

**(iii)   Intercompany trading**

**Matters:**
- Materiality of the intercompany balance and the inventory
- At Group level the intercompany balances must be eliminated
- If they are not eliminated, Group current assets and liabilities will be overstated
- A provision for unrealised profit may need to be recognised in respect of the inventory

**Evidence:**
- Review of consolidation working papers to confirm that the intercompany balances have been eliminated
- A copy of the terms of sale scrutinised to find out if a profit margin or mark-up is part of the sales price
- A reconciliation of the intercompany balances between Roberts Co and Marks Co to confirm that there are no other reconciling items to be adjusted, e.g. cash in transit or goods in transit
- Copies of inventory movement reports for the goods sold from Marks Co to Roberts Co to determine quantity of goods transferred
- Details of the inventory count held at Roberts Co at the year-end, reviewed to confirm that no other intercompany goods are held at the year-end

|  |  |
|---|---|
| **Maximum** | 5 |

| (b) | **Auditor's report** | | |
|---|---|---|---|
| | Generally up to 1 mark for each point explained | | |
| | – Contingent asset should not be recognised | | |
| | – Insurance company refusing to pay out therefore no receipt | | |
| | – Review financial statements for disclosure of event | | |
| | – Material but not pervasive | | |
| | – Qualified 'except for' | | |
| | – Basis for qualified opinion explains the misstatement | | |
| | – Basis for qualified quantifies the misstatement | | |
| | | Maximum | 5 |
| **Total** | | | 25 |

## 31 COOPER  *Walk in the footsteps of a top tutor*

### Top tutor tips

*Part (a) is a typical 'matters and evidence' question. Use the 'MARE' approach. First, consider the materiality of the issue. Next discuss the appropriate accounting treatment and give the risks of material misstatement that would arise if the appropriate treatment is not followed. Finally, the evidence is what you would expect to be recorded on the audit file when you come to review it. Be specific about the evidence, don't say 'supporting documentation', suggest what that documentation would be and what it would show.*

*Part (b) asks for a critical appraisal of the draft report extracts. Don't just focus on whether the opinion is appropriate. You should also think about the titles of the paragraphs included and whether the names are correct, the order they appear in, whether the required information that should be included has been included and whether the wording used is professional and appropriate.*

**(a) (i) Matters to consider:**

**Factories**

The factories are a class of assets which is material to the statement of financial position, representing 25% of total assets. The factories manufacturing the chemical which is to be phased out are half of the total class of assets, representing 12.5% of total assets and therefore material.

The new government regulation indicates that the products made in these factories will be phased out by 20X7. According to IAS 36 *Impairment of Assets*, this is an indicator of potential impairment of the assets. IAS 36 gives examples of indicators that an asset may be impaired in value, one of which is significant adverse changes which have taken place or are expected to take place in the technological, market, economic or legal environment in which the entity operates.

Management should have conducted an impairment review to determine the recoverable amount of the factories, which would be the greater of the fair value less cost to sell and the value in use of the assets.

The new government regulation is potentially going to detrimentally affect the revenue generating ability of the factories, and hence their value in use to Cooper Co. This means that the recoverable amount of the factories may be less than their carrying value of $30 million, and that an impairment loss should be recognised. If any necessary impairment loss is not recognised, then property, plant and equipment, and operating profit will be overstated.

However, sales are still buoyant and may continue to be so until the product is discontinued, so an impairment test may reveal that there is no impairment to be recognised. This is likely to be the case if the factories can be used to produce an alternative product, possibly the new product which is being researched.

**Feasibility study**

The $1 million which has been spent on the feasibility study represents 6.7% of profit before tax and 0.4% of assets. It is material in relation to the statement of profit or loss but not material in relation to the statement of financial position.

There is a risk that management has capitalised the expenditure as an intangible asset, which is not appropriate. Under IAS 38 *Intangible Assets*, research costs must be treated as an operating expense.

In the longer term, if a replacement chemical cannot be developed to replace the one being discontinued, there may be going concern issues for Cooper Co. However, this does not impact the financial statements for this year.

**Evidence:**

- A copy of the government regulation stating that the product made by the factories is to be phased out in 20X7.

- Agreement of the carrying value of the factories making this product to the non-current asset register and general ledger at an amount of $30 million.

- A review of forecast financial statements and management accounts to confirm the amount of revenue still being generated by the factories.

- A copy of management's impairment test, including an assessment of the validity of any assumptions used and confirmation that they are in line with auditor's understanding of the business.

- A discussion with management regarding the potential future use of the factories, and whether the potential new product can be produced by them.

- Confirmation that the research costs are included in operating expenses, and have not been capitalised.

(ii) Hannah Osbourne is a related party of Cooper Co. This is according to IAS 24 *Related Party Disclosures*, which states that a member of key management personnel is a related party of the reporting entity. ISA 550/ISA (UK) 550 *Related Parties* requires that the auditor evaluates whether identified related party relationships and transactions have been appropriately accounted for and disclosed in accordance with the applicable financial reporting framework. In addition, ISA 550 requires that where a significant related party transaction outside of the entity's normal course of business is identified, the auditor shall inspect the underlying contracts or agreements, if any, and evaluate whether:

- The business rationale (or lack thereof) of the transactions suggests that they may have been entered into to engage in fraudulent financial reporting or to conceal misappropriation of assets

- The terms of the transactions are consistent with management's explanations; and

- The transactions have been appropriately accounted for and disclosed in accordance with the applicable financial reporting framework.

The auditor shall also obtain audit evidence that the transactions have been appropriately authorised and approved.

IAS 24 states that a related party transaction should be disclosed if it is material. Based on monetary value the amount of the transaction is not material, based on either the book value or the market value of the car, as it represents less than 1% of total assets and of profit using either measure of value.

However, the materiality should also be judged based on the significance of the transaction to the person involved. The car's market value of $75,000 could be deemed significant to Hannah, especially if she is not going to settle the amount, meaning effectively that she has been given the car for free by the company.

As the transaction is with a member of key management personnel, it is effectively material by nature, regardless of monetary amount. Therefore disclosure of the transaction in the notes to the financial statements will be necessary to avoid a material misstatement.

In relation to a material related party transaction, IAS 24 requires disclosure of the nature of the related party relationship along with information about the transaction itself, such as the amount of the transaction, any relevant terms and conditions, and any balances outstanding.

If the related party transaction has not been disclosed, the auditor should consider the implications for the auditor's report, which may require a modified opinion due to material misstatement.

Finally the auditor should consider the recoverability of the $50,000 outstanding, given that the invoice was raised several months before the year-end and the amount has not yet been paid. If the amount is not recoverable and needs to be written off, this will not be material in monetary terms for Cooper Co but an adjustment would be advisable to avoid overstatement of receivables and operating profit.

**Evidence:**

- A review of the notes to the financial statements to confirm that sufficient disclosure has been made to comply with the requirements of IAS 24.

- A copy of the invoice raised, and agreement to the receivables ledger to confirm the amount of $50,000 which is outstanding.

- A copy of any contract or other document pertaining to the sale of the car to Hannah, and a review of its terms and conditions, e.g. specification of when the amount is due for payment.

- A post year-end review of the bank statement and cash books to confirm if the amount has been received in the subsequent events period.

- Confirmation that the carrying value of $50,000 has been removed from the non-current asset register and general ledger.

- Confirmation that any profit or loss recognised on the disposal has been recognised in profit for the year.
- A review of board minutes to confirm the transaction was appropriately authorised.
- A written representation from management stating that management has disclosed to the auditor the identity of the entity's related parties and all the related party relationships and transactions of which they are aware, and that management has appropriately accounted for and disclosed such relationships and transactions in accordance with the requirements of IAS 24.

**(b)    Critical appraisal of the draft report**

**Type of opinion**

When an auditor issues an opinion expressing that the financial statements 'do not give a true and fair view', this represents an adverse opinion. The paragraph explaining the modification should, therefore, be titled 'Basis for Adverse Opinion' rather than simply 'Basis of Modified Opinion'.

An adverse opinion means that the auditor considers the misstatement to be material and pervasive to the financial statements of the Hopper Group. Pervasive matters are those which affect a substantial proportion of the financial statements or fundamentally affect the users' understanding of the financial statements.

It is unlikely that the failure to recognise contingent consideration is pervasive. The main effect would be to understate goodwill and liabilities. This would not be considered a substantial proportion of the financial statements, neither would it be fundamental to understanding the Hopper Group's performance and position.

However, there is also some uncertainty as to whether the matter is even material. If the matter is determined to be material but not pervasive, then a qualified opinion would be appropriate on the basis of a material misstatement. If the matter is not material, then no modification would be necessary to the audit opinion.

**Inadequate description of issue**

The auditor's reference to 'the acquisition of the new subsidiary' is too vague. The Hopper Group may have purchased a number of subsidiaries to which this phrase could relate. It is important that the auditor provides adequate description of the event and in these circumstances it would be appropriate to name the subsidiary referred to.

**No quantification of the issue**

The auditor has not quantified the amount of the contingent element of the consideration. For the users to understand the potential implications of any necessary adjustments, they need to know how much the contingent consideration will be if it becomes payable. The auditor should quantify the financial effects of any misstatements, unless it is impracticable to do so.

In addition to the above point, the auditor should provide more description of the financial effects of the misstatement, including full quantification of the effect of the required adjustment to the assets, liabilities, incomes, revenues and equity of the Hopper Group.

### Reference to the financial statement note

The auditor should identify the note to the financial statements relevant to the contingent liability disclosure rather than just stating 'in the note'. This will improve the understandability and usefulness of the contents of the auditor's report.

### Unprofessional wording

The use of the term 'we do not feel that the treatment is correct' is too vague and not professional. While there may be some interpretation necessary when trying to apply financial reporting standards to unique circumstances, the expression used is ambiguous and may be interpreted as some form of disclaimer by the auditor with regard to the correct accounting treatment. The auditor should clearly explain how the treatment applied in the financial statements has departed from the requirements of the relevant standard.

*Tutorial note*

*As an illustration to the above point, an appropriate wording would be: 'Management has not recognised the acquisition-date fair value of contingent consideration as part of the consideration transferred in exchange for the acquiree, which constitutes a departure from International Financial Reporting Standards.'*

The ambiguity is compounded by the use of the phrase 'if this is the case, it would be appropriate to adjust the goodwill'. This once again suggests that the correct treatment is uncertain and perhaps open to interpretation.

### Relevant standard

If the auditor wishes to refer to a specific accounting standard they should refer to its full title. Therefore instead of referring to 'the relevant standard' they should refer to IFRS 3 *Business Combinations*.

### Title of opinion paragraph

The opinion paragraph requires an appropriate heading. In this case the auditors have issued an adverse opinion and the paragraph should be headed 'Adverse Opinion'.

### Uncertainty over whether the issue is material

As with the basis paragraph, the opinion paragraph lacks authority. Suggesting that the required adjustments 'may' materially affect the financial statements implies that there is a degree of uncertainty. This is not the case as the amount of the contingent consideration will be disclosed in the relevant purchase agreement, so the auditor should be able to determine whether or not the required adjustments are material.

Regardless, the sentence discussing whether or not the balance is material is not required in the auditor's report as to warrant inclusion in the report the matter must be considered material. The disclosure of the nature and financial effect of the misstatement in the basis paragraph is sufficient.

### Emphasis of matter paragraph

Finally, the emphasis of matter paragraph should not be included in the auditor's report. An emphasis of matter paragraph is only used to draw attention to an uncertainty/matter of fundamental importance which is correctly accounted for and disclosed in the financial statements.

An emphasis of matter is not required in this case for the following reasons:

- Emphasis of matter is only required to highlight matters which the auditor believes are fundamental to the users' understanding of the business. An example may include an uncertainty relating to the future outcome of exceptional litigation. That is not the case with the Hopper Group and the contingent liability does not appear to be fundamental.

- Emphasis of matter is only used for matters where the auditor has obtained sufficient appropriate evidence that the matter is not materially misstated in the financial statements. If the financial statements are materially misstated, in this regard the matter would be fully disclosed by the auditor in the basis for qualified/adverse opinion paragraph and no emphasis of matter is necessary.

---

**Examiner's comments**

The first requirement presented information on two separate issues uncovered during the audit that have been brought to your attention by the audit senior – factories that are producing a chemical that would be phased out in three years' time and a vehicle that was sold to the company's finance director. The wording of this requirement would have been familiar to candidates who had practised past exam papers, and specifically candidates were required to comment on the matters to be considered in relation to each of the issues, and the audit evidence that should be found during a review of the audit working papers. There were some excellent answers here, with many candidates achieving close to the maximum marks. Most candidates correctly identified that possible impairment was the main matter to consider in relation to the factories, and discussed the issue well.

However, there were two common problems visible in answers. Firstly, there was an over emphasis on going concern issues, even though the scenario explicitly stated that sales of output from the factories was still buoyant. While it was correct to identify that without a replacement for the product there would be an impact on the company's revenue in the future, this was not a pressing issue for this year's audit. Secondly, in relation to the feasibility study into a replacement chemical, many candidates spent time detailing the capitalisation criteria for development costs, even when they had already stated in their answer that the amounts would have to be expensed as a research cost. This wasted valuable time as the capitalisation criteria were not relevant to their answer. Worryingly, a significant minority of answers commented on the need for a provision to be made for the loss of revenue that would happen in future years, which displays a lack of understanding over some fairly basic accounting principles.

The second issue was often well dealt with, with many answers correctly identifying the related party transaction and explaining the associated issues, including the necessary disclosure of the transaction in the financial statements. However there were often errors in the calculation of materiality, with candidates thinking that the vehicle had been sold for $50 million to the finance director, indicating that they had failed to read the question carefully. Weaker answers often stated that the sale was 'illegal' or 'unethical', or that the accounting treatment was wrong, and that assets should always be revalued to fair value immediately prior to sale.

---

For both issues, while the comments on the matters to consider were often good, the evidence points were usually weaker. Candidates lost marks by not providing an explanation of why the evidence would be necessary, which was a specific requirement of the question. For example while most candidates suggested a review of management's impairment calculations, this was rarely expanded upon. Similarly it was often recommended that a copy of the government regulation should be on file and reviewed, but the purpose of this review was seldom explained. In relation to the related party transaction, few procedures other than checking the invoice and obtaining written representations were usually given, and while these are relevant again the purpose of the evidence was not usually explained.

In part (b) candidates were required to critically appraise a draft auditor's report. This approach to a reporting question has been seen many times in the past and answers were generally good in this area. A minority of candidates however incorrectly spent time discussing the accounting treatment for contingent liabilities rather than contingent consideration in an acquisition context. This often led to the conclusion that there was no requirement to modify the auditor's report therefore the shortcomings of the report were overlooked.

### Marking scheme

|  | | | Marks |
|---|---|---|---|
| (a) | (i) | **Factories**<br>Generally up to 1½ marks for each matter and up to 1 mark for each evidence point explained:<br>**Matters:**<br>– Materiality of factories to statement of financial position<br>– Government regulation is an indicator of impairment<br>– Management need to conduct an impairment review<br>– Implication for financial statements if factories are overstated<br>– Impairment review may reveal that factories are not overstated<br>**Feasibility study**<br>– Materiality calculation<br>– Research costs may not be capitalised<br>– No going concern issues this year but could be a longer term problem<br>**Evidence:**<br>– A copy of the government regulation<br>– Agreement of the carrying value of the factories making this product to the non-current asset register and general ledger<br>– A review of forecast financial statements and management accounts to confirm the amount of revenue still being generated by the factories<br>– A copy of and assessment of management's impairment test<br>– A discussion with management regarding the potential future use of the factories, and whether the potential new product can be produced by them<br>– Confirmation that the research costs are included in operating expenses, and have not been capitalised | |
|  |  | Maximum | 8 |

(ii) **Related party transaction**

Generally up to 1½ marks for each matter and up to 1 mark for each evidence point explained:

**Matters:**
-   Hannah is a member of key management personnel and therefore a related party
-   Auditor required to review documents and to consider whether transaction authorised
-   Materiality should not be based solely on monetary calculations – it is material by nature
-   The amount is outstanding and may need to be written off
-   Disclosure needed in notes to financial statements
-   Implications for auditor's report if appropriate disclosure not made

**Evidence:**
-   A review of the notes to the financial statements to confirm that sufficient disclosure has been made
-   A copy of the invoice raised, and agreement to the receivables ledger
-   A copy of any contract or other document pertaining to the sale of the car to Hannah, and a review of its terms and conditions
-   A post year-end review of the bank statement and cash books to confirm if the amount has been received subsequent to the year-end
-   Confirmation that the carrying value of $50,000 has been removed from the non-current asset register and general ledger
-   Confirmation that profit or loss on disposal has been included in profit or loss
-   Board minutes to confirm authorisation
-   Written representation from management

|  |  |
|---|---|
| Maximum | 7 |

(b)  **Critical appraisal of auditor's report**

Generally up to 1½ mark for each relevant point of appraisal.
-   Heading of 'basis  paragraph' (1 max)
-   Vagueness of description of subsidiary
-   Quantification of contingent consideration
-   Identification of note in financial statements
-   Vagueness in relation to correct accounting treatment
-   Quantification of the effects on the financial statements
-   Vague reference to 'relevant accounting standard' (1 max)
-   Opinion paragraph heading (1 max)
-   Reference to materiality
-   Pervasiveness of the matter
-   Appropriate opinion qualified or unmodified
-   Use of emphasis of matter paragraph

|  |  |
|---|---|
| Maximum | 10 |
| **Total** | 25 |

**32   POODLE GROUP**  *Walk in the footsteps of a top tutor*

---

*Top tutor tips*

*This question focuses on completion and reporting implications in a group context. There are three issues which need to be discussed. Deal with each issue in turn.*

*When considering the implications for the auditor's report, remember that the aggregate effects of the misstatements should be considered. Remember also to consider not just the opinion but any other impacts to the report.*

---

(a)   **Audit completion, adjustments necessary, additional audit procedures**

**Toy Co**

The amount claimed against Toy Co is material to consolidated profit, representing 25% of consolidated profit before tax. The amount is not material to consolidated total assets, representing less than 1% of that amount.

The same accounting policies should be applied across the Group in the consolidated financial statements. Therefore in accordance with IAS 37 *Provisions, Contingent Liabilities and Contingent Assets*, a provision should be recognised in the consolidated financial statements if the amount is probable to be paid. The adjustment needed is:

DR Operating expenses                    $500,000

CR Current liabilities – provisions       $500,000

The audit evidence obtained by the component auditors is insufficient. Verbal evidence is not a reliable source of evidence. Further audit procedures should be performed, including:

- Obtain written evidence from Toy Co's legal advisors including a statement that in their opinion the damages are probable to be paid, and the basis of that opinion.

- Review the claim itself to confirm that $500,000 is the amount claimed by the ex-employee.

- Inspect the board minutes of Toy Co for evidence of discussion of the claim, to obtain an understanding as to the reason for the claim and whether it has been disputed by Toy Co.

These further audit procedures may be performed by the component auditor, or by the Group audit team.

If, having obtained evidence to confirm that the damages are probable to be paid, the consolidated financial statements are not adjusted to include the provision, the consolidated statement of profit or loss will be materially misstated.

---

### Trade receivable

The trade receivable is material to the consolidated financial statements, representing 2.8% of total assets and 80% of profit before tax. The amount that is potentially irrecoverable is 90% of the total balance outstanding, i.e. $1.44 million. This amount is also material, representing 2.5% of total assets and 72% of profit before tax.

IFRS 9 *Financial Instruments* requires that impaired trade receivables are recognised at fair value, which is the present value of estimated cash inflows. According to the information provided by Terrier Co's administrators, it is likely that 10% of the amount outstanding will be paid and the remaining 90% should be written off.

The adjustment needed is:

DR Operating expenses (irrecoverable debts expense) $1,440,000

CR Trade receivables $1,440,000

The amount should be adjusted in the financial statements for the year ended 31 March 20X3, even though notice was not received until May 20X3. This is because according to IAS 10 *Events After the Reporting Period*, an adjusting event is one that provides additional information about conditions existing at the year-end.

*Tutorial note*

*Credit will be awarded for comments relating to whether separate disclosure on the face of the statement of profit or loss is appropriate, due to the material and unusual nature of the item.*

The auditor should perform additional procedures as follows:

- Obtain the notice from Terrier Co's administrators confirming that the company is insolvent and that only 10% of amount outstanding is likely to be paid.

- Obtain a written confirmation from the administrators stating the expected timing of the payment.

- Inspect post year-end cash receipts to see if any of the outstanding balance has been received from Terrier Co.

- Recalculate the impairment losses and trace the posting of the impairment into the general ledger and the financial statements.

If the consolidated financial statements are not adjusted for the irrecoverable amount, current assets will be overstated and profits overstated by $1.44 million. This is a very significant matter as the adjustment to profit is highly material.

### Chair's statement

The chair's statement contains an inconsistency, as according to the consolidated financial statements, revenue has increased by 5.9%, but the chair states that revenue has increased by 20%.

The chair's statement does not form part of the financial statements therefore is not subject to audit and not covered by the auditor's opinion.

However, ISA 720/ISA (UK) 720 *The Auditor's Responsibilities Relating to Other Information in Documents Containing Audited Financial Statements* requires the auditor to read the other information, in order to identify any information contained within any of the financial or non-financial information in the annual report that is apparently materially incorrect based on, or materially inconsistent with, the knowledge acquired by the auditor in the course of performing the audit.

The auditor needs to determine whether it is the financial statements or chair's statement that needs to be revised, so that the inconsistency is removed.

The audit work performed on revenue should be reviewed to ensure that sufficient and appropriate evidence has been gained to support the figures in the financial statements.

The matter should be discussed with management, who should be asked to amend the disclosure in the chair's statement. Management should be presented with the results of the audit work, to justify, if necessary, that the amendment needs to be made. The inclusion of the incorrect figure in the draft chair's statement could be a genuine mistake, in which case management should be happy to make the change.

If management refuse to remove the inconsistency, the auditor should communicate this to those charged with governance.

In extreme situations, where a material inconsistency remains uncorrected by management, it may be necessary for the audit firm to withdraw from the audit. In such cases legal advice should be sought, to protect the interests of the audit firm.

**(b)**   **Implications for auditor's report**

**Amendments to the financial statements**

Individually, the provision and irrecoverable debt are material and would require adjustment otherwise a qualified 'except for' opinion would be required.

The materiality and overall significance of the provision and irrecoverable receivable should be considered in aggregate. When combined, the adjustment needed to net assets and to operating expenses is $1.94 million. This adjustment would reduce the draft consolidated profit before tax to only $60,000.

The auditor should discuss the need for the adjustment with the client (including those charged with governance), and explain that a qualified or adverse opinion will result from the material misstatements.

The combined misstatement could be considered both material and pervasive to the financial statements as the profit figure is significantly impacted by the adjustments necessary.

In this case, the auditor should express an adverse opinion, stating that the financial statements do not give a true and fair view.

The basis for opinion section will be changed to 'Basis for Adverse Opinion', which will describe the reason for the adverse opinion and provide quantification of the financial impact of the misstatements.

**Amendments to the chair's statement**

If the inconsistency is not resolved, the impact to the auditor's report depends on whether it is the other information, or the financial statements that have not been corrected.

If the financial statements have not been revised, and therefore contain an item which the auditor believes to be materially misstated, then the audit opinion should be modified.

If management refuses to change the other information, the auditor should provide a description of the inconsistency in the 'Other Information' section of the auditor's report.

Alternatively the auditor may withhold the auditor's report or withdraw from the engagement.

**UK syllabus:** Further actions are also available to auditors in the UK who have the right to speak at general meetings of company members, and could therefore highlight the inconsistency to shareholders in this way, if it remains unresolved.

---

**Examiner's comments**

This question focused on audit completion and auditors' reports. Performance tended to be weak on this question overall. The question was based in a Group audit scenario, in which three matters pertaining to the completion of the audit were described. The scenario made it clear that management was reluctant to adjust the consolidated financial statements in respect of the matters described.

The first scenario described the situation in relation to Toy Co, an overseas subsidiary of the Group that was audited by local auditors and reported under the local financial reporting framework, not International Financial Reporting Standards. The main issue was that under the local financial reporting rules a claim against the company would not result in the recognition of a provision, but under IFRS Standards the provision should be recognised. The amount was correctly identified by almost all as material to the Group financial statements, and answers were generally satisfactory, despite the slightly complex scenario. Most candidates explained how an adjustment should be made at Group level. Some answers insisted, incorrectly, that the adjustment should be made in the subsidiary's individual financial statements. The fact that the audit evidence so far obtained was insufficient was not always identified, and only a minority of answers suggested the further audit procedures that should be conducted.

The second scenario provided a short description relating to a receivables balance outstanding in the parent company's financial statements for which payment was unlikely to be received due to the insolvency of the company owing the amount. Many candidates correctly identified this as an adjusting event after the reporting period, and determined that the amount was highly material. Some answers tended to focus on the going concern status of both companies, or suggested that the matter should be disclosed in both sets of financial statements but not adjusted for.

The third scenario briefly described how the chair's statement to be published in the Group's annual report, contained a statement that the Group's revenue had increased by 20%. The vast majority of answers correctly determined that this was incorrect as revenue had actually increased by 5.9%. While there were some sound answers here from candidates who clearly understood the implications, unfortunately in many answers there was little else to be said, indicating a lack of knowledge of the auditor's responsibilities in relation to other information published with the financial statements, or the impact of such a misstatement on the auditor's report.

---

There are two comments to make in relation to how candidates dealt with the reporting implications of the issues. The first point is that very few candidates considered the issues in aggregate. This was important because in aggregate the potential adjustments had a significant impact on Group results, and a discussion of whether this would result in an adverse opinion was relevant. Candidates are encouraged to always look at the bigger picture and even though the scenarios are described separately, they should at some point in the answer be considered collectively. The second issue is that very few answers went beyond discussing the impact on the audit opinion. However the question asked for impact on the auditor's report, so marks were available for describing the structure and content of the basis for opinion paragraph as well as the opinion itself.

| | Marking scheme | | |
|---|---|---|---|
| | | | *Marks* |
| (a) | **Audit completion, adjustments necessary, additional audit procedures** | | |
| | Generally up to 1 mark for each point assessed/procedure recommended: | | |
| | **Toy Co** | | |
| | – Materiality calculation | | |
| | – Group accounting policy should be applied | | |
| | – Adjustment needed to operating profit and current liabilities | | |
| | – Verbal evidence is not reliable. Further procedures required. | | |
| | – Written correspondence from legal advisors | | |
| | – Review claim | | |
| | – Inspect board minutes | | |
| | – Other valid additional procedures (1 mark each) | | |
| | – If damages are probable to be paid, FS will be materially misstated | | |
| | **Trade receivable** | | |
| | – Materiality calculation of adjustment | | |
| | – 90% should be written off | | |
| | – Double entry of adjustment required | | |
| | – Account for as an adjusting event | | |
| | – Obtain notice from administrators | | |
| | – Obtain confirmation of timing of payment from administrators | | |
| | – Inspect post year-end cash receipts | | |
| | – Recalculate impairment loss | | |
| | – Other valid additional procedures (1 mark each) | | |
| | – Overstatement of operating profit and current assets | | |
| | **Chair's statement** | | |
| | – Chair's statement contains a misstatement regarding revenue | | |
| | – Chair's statement not part of FS therefore not audited | | |
| | – Auditor required to read other information for consistency | | |
| | – Determine whether FS or chair's statement needs revising | | |
| | – Review audit work performed on revenue | | |
| | – Request draft chair's statement to be amended | | |
| | – If management refuse, communicate to TCWG | | |
| | – If inconsistency remains uncorrected consider withdrawal | | |
| | | **Maximum** | **18** |

| | | |
|---|---|---|
| **(b)** | **Implications for auditor's report** | |
| | Generally up to 1 mark for each point assessed | |
| | **Amendments to the financial statements** | |
| | – Individually, misstatements are material requiring a qualified opinion | |
| | – Aggregate effect of provision and irrecoverable debt | |
| | – Discuss adjustment with client | |
| | – Material and pervasive due to significance of impact | |
| | – Adverse opinion – do not give TFV | |
| | – Basis for adverse opinion | |
| | **Amendments to the chair's statement** | |
| | – Impact on auditor's report depends on whether FS or chair's statement requires amendment | |
| | – If FS – modify audit opinion | |
| | – If chair's statement – provide description in Other Information section of auditor's report | |
| | – Alternatively, withhold auditor's report or withdraw from engagement | |
| | **Maximum** | 7 |
| **Total** | | 25 |

## 33 SNIPE  *Walk in the footsteps of a top tutor*

### Top tutor tips

*Part (a) is a typical 'matters and evidence' question. First, consider the materiality of the issue. Next discuss the appropriate accounting treatment and give the risks of material misstatement that would arise if the appropriate treatment is not followed. Finally, the evidence is what you would expect to be recorded on the audit file when you come to review it. Be specific about the evidence, don't say 'supporting documentation', suggest what that documentation would be and what it would show.*

*Part (b) asks for a critical appraisal of the draft report extracts. Don't just focus on whether the opinion is appropriate. You should also think about the titles of the paragraphs included and whether the names are correct, the order they appear in, whether the required information that should be included has been included and whether the wording used is professional and appropriate.*

### (a) New processing area

#### Matters to consider

The total cost of the new processing area of $5 million represents 2.9% of total assets and is material to the statement of financial position. The borrowing costs are not material to the statement of financial position, representing less than 1% of total assets; however, the costs are material to profit representing 10% of profit before tax.

The directly attributable costs, including borrowing costs, relating to the new processing area should be capitalised as property, plant and equipment. According to IAS 23 *Borrowing Costs,* borrowing costs that are directly attributable to the acquisition, construction or production of a qualifying asset should be capitalised as part of the cost of that asset. The borrowing costs should be capitalised only during the period of construction, with capitalisation ceasing when substantially all the activities necessary to prepare the qualifying asset for its intended use or sale are complete.

In this case, the new processing area was ready for use on 1 September, so capitalisation of borrowing costs should have ceased at that point. It seems that the borrowing costs have been appropriately capitalised at $100,000, which represents six months' interest on the loan ($4m × 5% × 6/12).

The new processing area should be depreciated from 1 September, as according to IAS 16 *Property, Plant and Equipment,* depreciation of an asset begins when it is in the location and condition necessary for it to be capable of operating in the manner intended by management.

There should therefore be five months' depreciation included in profit for the year ended 31 January 20X2, amounting to $138,889 ($5m/15 years × 5/12).

### Evidence

- A breakdown of the components of the $4.9 million capitalised costs (excluding $100,000 borrowing costs) reviewed to ensure all items are eligible for capitalisation.

- Agreement of a sample of the capitalised costs to supporting documentation (e.g. invoices for tangible items such as cement, payroll records for internal labour costs).

- A copy of the approved budget or capital expenditure plan for the extension.

- An original copy of the loan agreement, confirming the amount borrowed, the date of the cash receipt, the interest rate and whether the loan is secured on any assets.

- Documentation to verify that the extension was complete and ready for use on 1 September, such as a building completion certificate.

- Recalculation of the borrowing cost, depreciation charge and carrying value of the extension at the year-end, and agreement of all figures to the draft financial statements.

- Confirmation that the additions to property, plant and equipment are disclosed in the required note to the financial statements.

### Assets held for sale

### Matters to consider

The properties classified as assets held for sale are material to the financial statements as the year-end carrying value of $24 million represent 13.7% of total assets.

Assets can only be classified as held for sale if the conditions referred to in IFRS 5 *Non-current Assets Held for Sale and Discontinued Operations* are met. The conditions include the following:

- Management is committed to a plan to sell

- The assets are available for immediate sale

- An active programme to locate a buyer is initiated

- The sale is highly probable, within 12 months of classification as held for sale (subject to limited exceptions)

- The asset is being actively marketed for sale at a sales price reasonable in relation to its fair value

- Actions required to complete the plan indicate that it is unlikely that the plan will be significantly changed or withdrawn.

There is a risk that the assets have been inappropriately classified if the above conditions have not been met.

IFRS 5 requires that at classification as held for sale, assets are measured at the lower of carrying value and fair value less costs to sell. This appears to have been correctly accounted for when classification occurred in October 20X1. Though not specifically required by IFRS 5, an impairment review should take place at 31 January 20X2, to ensure that there is no further impairment of the properties to be recognised at the year-end. If an impairment review has not taken place, the assets may be misstated in value.

The assets should not be depreciated after being classified as held for sale, therefore audit procedures should confirm that depreciation has ceased from October 20X1.

Disclosure is needed in the notes to the financial statements to include a description of the non-current assets classified as held for sale, a description of the facts and circumstances of the sale and its expected timing, and a quantification of the impairment loss and where in the statement of profit or loss and other comprehensive income it is recognised.

**Evidence**

- A copy of the board minute at which the disposal of the properties was agreed by management.

- Details of the active programme in place to locate a buyer, for example, instructions given to real estate agency, marketing literature.

- A copy of any minutes of meetings held with prospective purchasers of any of the properties, or copies of correspondence with them.

- Written representation from management on the opinion that the assets will be sold within 12 months.

- Subsequent events review, including a review of post year-end board minutes and a review of significant cash transactions, to confirm if any properties are sold in the period after the year-end.

- Details of any impairment review conducted by management on the properties at 31 January 20X2.

- A copy of the client's depreciation calculations, to confirm that depreciation was charged up to October 20X1 but not subsequent to the reclassification of the assets as held for sale.

(b) The **description and explanation** provided for the adverse opinion is not sufficient, for a number of reasons. Firstly, the matter is not quantified. The paragraph should clearly state the amount of $10.5 million, and state that this is material to the financial statements.

The paragraph does not say whether the pension plan is in surplus or deficit, i.e. whether it is an asset or a liability which is omitted from the financial statements.

There is **no description of the impact of this omission** on the financial statements. Wording such as 'if the deficit had been recognised, total liabilities would increase by $10.5 million, and shareholders' equity would reduce by the same amount' should be included.

It is **not clear whether any accounting for the pension plan has taken place** at all. As well as recognising the plan surplus or deficit in the statement of financial position, accounting entries are also required to deal with other items such as the current service cost of the plan, and any actuarial gains or losses which have arisen during the year. Whether these have been omitted as well, and their potential impact on profit or equity is not mentioned.

**No reference is made to the relevant accounting standard** IAS 19 *Employee Benefits*. Reference should be made in order to help users' understanding of the breach of accounting standards that has been made.

The **use of the word 'deliberate'** when describing the omission of the pension plan is not professional, sounds accusatory and may not be correct. The plan may have been omitted in error and an adjustment to the financial statements may have been suggested by the audit firm and is being considered by management.

It is **unlikely that this issue alone would be sufficient to give rise to an adverse opinion**. An adverse opinion should be given when misstatements are both material and pervasive to the financial statements. The amount of the deficit, and therefore the liability that should be recognised, is $10.5 million, which represents 6% of total assets. The amount is definitely material, but would not be considered pervasive to the financial statements.

The **titles and positioning of the two paragraphs** included in the extract are not appropriate. In this case, the titles are incorrect, and the paragraphs should be switched round, so that the basis for modification is provided **after** the opinion.

The opinion paragraph should be entitled 'Adverse Opinion'.

When the auditor modifies the opinion, the 'Basis for Adverse Opinion', should describe the matter giving rise to the modification.

*Tutorial note*

*Where a misstatement is confined to specific elements of the financial statements, it would only be considered pervasive if it represents a substantial proportion of the financial statements.*

**Examiner's comments**

Part (a) described the self-construction of new property, plant and equipment at a client. A loan had been taken out to help finance the construction, and financial information was provided in relation to the asset and the loan. Candidates were asked to comment on the matters that should be considered, and the evidence that should be found when conducting a file review of non-current assets. Candidates should have been familiar with this type of question requirement, as it commonly features in the exam. Sound answers contained a calculation and explanation of the materiality of the asset and of the borrowing costs that had been capitalised, followed by a discussion of the appropriate accounting treatment, including whether the borrowing cost should be capitalised, and when depreciation in relation to the asset should commence. There were some sound answers here, with candidates demonstrating sound knowledge of the relevant financial reporting standard requirements, and going on to provide some very well described and relevant audit procedures. Weaker answers said that it was not possible to capitalise borrowing costs, or incorrectly thought that the construction should be accounted for as some kind of long-term construction contract. The audit evidence points in the weaker answers tended to rely on representations from management and recalculations of every figure provided in the question. The second issue described a number of properties that had been classified as held for sale. Information was given on the carrying value and fair value less cost to sell of the properties. Most answers were satisfactory, largely because candidates were confident in explaining the relevant financial reporting requirements and applying them to the brief scenario.

The audit evidence points were sometimes a little vague, for example 'discuss with management', 'get management representation', 'review board minutes', and only a limited amount of credit could be awarded for such comments.

Part (b) involved the critique of an extract from an auditor's report. The report contained an adverse opinion, which most candidates spotted, in relation to the non-recognition of a defined benefit pension deficit on the company's statement of financial position. There were some sound answers here, and candidates' performance in questions of this type has shown a definite improvement. Some answers not only identified but also provided an explanation of the problems with the auditor's report. The majority of answers suggested that an 'except for' qualification may be more suitable than an adverse opinion, and correctly calculated the materiality of the pension plan deficit to support their discussion. A significant proportion of answers picked up on the order of the paragraphs in the report and on the incorrect wording used in the headings, and on the lack of explanation that had been provided in the report regarding the material misstatement. Fewer answers discussed the inappropriate use of the phrase 'deliberate omission'. The weaker answers tended to just list out bullet points with no explanation, limiting the amount of marks that could be awarded. Other weaker answers attempted to discuss the appropriate accounting treatment for the pension, often incorrectly.

| | Marking scheme | |
|---|---|---|
| | | *Marks* |
| **(a)** | Generally 1 mark for each matter/evidence point explained: | |
| | **New processing area** | |
| | **Matters:** | |
| | –  Materiality calculation | |
| | –  Borrowing costs are directly attributable to the asset | |
| | –  Borrowing costs should be capitalised during period of construction | |
| | –  Amounts are correctly capitalised | |
| | –  Depreciate from September 20X1 | |
| | –  Additions to non-current assets should be disclosed in note | |
| | **Evidence:** | |
| | –  Review of costs capitalised for eligibility | |
| | –  Agreement of sample of costs to supporting documentation | |
| | –  Copy of approved capital expenditure budget/discuss significant variances | |
| | –  Agreement of loan details to loan documentation | |
| | –  Recalculation of borrowing costs, depreciation, asset carrying value | |
| | –  Confirmation of completeness of disclosure in notes to FS | |
| | **Maximum** | **8** |
| | | |
| | **Assets held for sale** | |
| | **Matters:** | |
| | –  Assets held for sale are material (calculation) | |
| | –  Conditions required to classify assets as held for sale (up to 2 marks) | |
| | –  Re-measurement at classification appears correct | |
| | –  Further impairment review may be needed at year-end | |
| | –  Depreciation should not be charged after reclassification | |
| | –  Disclosure in notes to financial statements | |
| | **Evidence:** | |
| | –  Board minute at which the disposal of the properties was agreed | |
| | –  Details of the active programme in place to locate a buyer | |
| | –  A copy of any minutes of meetings held with prospective purchasers of any of the properties | |
| | –  Written representation from management that the assets will be sold within 12 month | |
| | –  Subsequent events reviews | |
| | –  Confirm depreciation ceased on reclassification | |
| | –  Details of any impairment review conducted by management | |
| | **Maximum** | **8** |
| | | |
| **(b)** | **Auditor's report** | |
| | Generally 1½ marks per comment: | |
| | –  Amounts not quantified | |
| | –  Impact on financial statements not described | |
| | –  Unclear from report if any accounting taken place | |
| | –  No reference made to relevant accounting standard | |
| | –  Use of word 'deliberate' not professional | |
| | –  Materiality calculation | |
| | –  Discuss whether adverse opinion appropriate | |
| | –  Inappropriate headings | |
| | –  Paragraph order | |
| | **Maximum** | **9** |
| **Total** | | **25** |

# OTHER ASSIGNMENTS

**34    JANSEN & Co**  *Walk in the footsteps of a top tutor*

---

*Top tutor tips*

*Part (a)(i) requires matters to consider before accepting a PFI engagement. The firm should only take on work of an acceptable level of risk so think about the risks that could arise by providing the assurance requested.*

*In part (a)(ii) the examination procedures need to focus on assessing the reasonableness of the assumptions used to prepare the forecast. Remember that these transactions have not happened as of yet so you will not be able to inspect invoices, etc. Instead, think about how the client determined the forecast figures and assess whether this is reasonable. Include some of the more general procedures that apply to every client for some easy marks.*

*Part (b) requires evaluation of the quality of the planning and performance of the audit. Typical issues to look out for in such a question are: whether the work has been assigned to the appropriate level of staff, whether the audit team have demonstrated competence and professional judgment, whether the ISAs been followed, whether the timing and frequency of reviews is appropriate.*

---

**(a)    (i)    Matters to be considered before acceptance of engagement**

When considering acceptance of the engagement to review Narley Co's prospective financial information (PFI), Jansen & Co must consider whether it is ethically acceptable to perform the review.

The review of the PFI represents a non-assurance service and the IESBA *International Code of Ethics for Professional Accountants* (the *Code*) states that providing this service in addition to the audit may create an advocacy threat. An advocacy threat arises when the auditor is asked to promote or represent their client in some way. In this situation there is a risk of the auditor being seen to promote the interests of the client with a third party such as a bank. As a result, there is a danger that the auditor will be biased in favour of the client and therefore cannot be fully objective.

Accepting the assignment may also create a self-interest threat as a result of the auditor being perceived to have an interest in the outcome of negotiations with a third party and which may motivate the auditor to behave in order to protect that interest.

A self-review threat may also arise because the negotiations may result in facts and amounts which will form part of the audited financial statements. As a result, the auditor will be auditing financial statements which in part at least represent work which they themselves have performed. It follows that there is a risk that the auditor will not be sufficiently objective in performing the audit and may fail to identify any shortcomings in their own work.

In the case of Narley Co, the advocacy threat appears to be particularly significant as the audit firm could be seen to be promoting the interests of the audit client to the bank. The auditor should therefore only accept the engagement if adequate safeguards can be put in place to manage the threat to independence to an acceptable level.

Potential safeguards might include the following:

– The use of separate teams of suitably experienced staff for the audit and the review of the PFI.

– Independent senior review of the PFI working papers.

– Discussion of the potential ethical issues and threats to auditor independence with those charged with governance at Narley Co.

It should be noted, however, that it would not be possible to manage a significant advocacy threat through such safeguards and in such a case the appointment should not be accepted.

ISAE 3400 *The Examination of Prospective Financial Information* provides further guidance on the issues which the auditor should consider before accepting an engagement to examine PFI. According to ISAE 3400, the auditor should consider amongst other things:

– The intended use of the information – for example, whether it will be used solely for the purpose of the proposed loan finance.

– Whether the information will be for general or limited distribution – the auditor needs to consider who will receive the report and potentially rely upon it.

– The nature of the assumptions, that is, whether they are best-estimate or hypothetical assumptions – in this case it seems likely that they will be best estimate assumptions as Narley Co expects to obtain finance in order to fund its planned expansion.

– The elements to be included in the information – Jansen & Co needs to clarify the exact content of the PFI which they are being asked to report on, for example, whether it only includes the forecast statements of profit or loss or whether it also includes forecast statements of financial position and forecast cash flow statements; and

– The period covered by the information – shorter term forecasts are likely to be more reliable than projections over a longer period.

Jansen & Co must also consider whether the firm has sufficient staff available with the appropriate skills and experience to perform the review engagement in line with the client's required reporting deadlines.

Overall, the auditor must assess the risks associated with the review engagement and should not accept an engagement when the assumptions are clearly unrealistic or when the auditor believes that the prospective financial information will be inappropriate for its intended use.

**(ii)**    **Examination procedures to be performed**

The examination procedures which should be performed in respect of Narley Co's forecast statements of profit or loss include the following:

–    Recalculation of the forecast statements of profit or loss to confirm arithmetic accuracy.

–    Confirmation that the accounting policies used in the forecast statements are consistent with those used in the audited financial statements and that they comply with IFRS.

–    Discuss the key assumptions which have been made by the client in the preparation of the forecast statements with management assessing their reasonableness and consistency with the audit firm's cumulative knowledge and understanding of the client.

–    Review of market research documentation in Narley Co's existing markets and the new market and discuss it with management to assess whether the growth patterns being forecast in revenue represent reasonable and realistic expectations.

–    Obtain copies of any new customer contracts for existing and new markets to confirm the reasonableness of the projected growth in revenue.

–    Obtain a written representation from management confirming the reasonableness and completeness of the assumptions they have made in preparing the forecasts.

–    The competence and experience of the client staff who have prepared the forecasts should be assessed; the assessment should include the accuracy of PFI which has been prepared in previous periods and the reasons for any significant variances compared to actual outcomes.

–    Recalculation of depreciation to ensure the correct inclusion of depreciation on the new HGVs and warehousing facilities within the forecast statements.

–    Obtain and review a breakdown of operating expenses in order to ensure that all items have been appropriately included, for example: advertising and marketing costs for the campaign in the new jurisdiction; additional staff costs for the new drivers including recruitment expenses; any trading tariffs relevant to operating in the new market and any foreign currency and exchange implications.

–    Recent utility bills should be inspected and an assessment of the reasonableness of forecast utility overheads should be performed.

–    Obtain and review the supporting documentation for Narley Co's existing loan agreements with the bank as well as the draft documentation for the new loan; the forecast finance costs should be recalculated and agreed to the forecast statements.

- Perform analytical review, followed by discussion with management to seek corroborating evidence of key trends and ratios including:

    - Growth in revenue (26% from 20X8 to 20X9; 29% from 20X9 to 20Y0)

    - Cost of sales as a percentage of revenue (75.5% in 20X8; 71.3% in 20X9; 69.7% in 20Y0)

    - The declining trend in administrative expenses (decrease of 4.2% from 20X8 to 20X9; 5.6% from 20X9 to 20Y0)

    - The increase in the net profit margin (6.9% in 20X8; 15.2% in 20X9; 20.4% in 20Y0).

**(b)**   **Watson Co**

**Quality control issues raised by the audit supervisor's email**

ISA 220 *Quality Control for an Audit of Financial Statements* requires the auditor to implement quality control procedures at the engagement level which provide reasonable assurance that the audit complies with professional standards and applicable legal and regulatory requirements and that the auditor's report is appropriate in the circumstances.

The overall quality of each audit assignment is the responsibility of the audit engagement partner and effective engagement performance entails adequate direction, consultation, supervision and review.

In this case, the conduct of the audit raises a number of quality control issues in relation to the effective performance of the audit of Watson Co's financial statements, including the following:

**Share-based payment scheme:**

The failure to identify the new cash-settled share-based payment scheme as a potentially high risk area indicates inadequate planning and a lack of consultation with the client. The share-based payment scheme is a complex and judgmental area and given that the scheme was only introduced in the year, it should have been identified as a key area of audit risk.

The assignment of a part-qualified supervisor to the audit of a listed entity is also indicative of poor audit planning. The audit supervisor appears to have inadequate skills and expertise to audit this public interest entity. This is evidenced by the incorrect treatment of the share-based payment scheme and the audit supervisor's comment that basing the expense in the profit or loss account on the valuation at the date of grant is appropriate and that the recognition of an equity reserve on the statement of financial position is correct in the email to the audit manager.

According to IFRS 2 *Share-based Payments*, the valuation of the share appreciation rights for a cash-settled scheme should be updated at the reporting date and the standard requires recognition of the cumulative cost of the scheme as a liability, not as an equity reserve.

The audit supervisor also fails to recognise that a share-based payment scheme with the directors of Watson Co constitutes a related party transaction. While the supervisor is correct in saying that the cost of the scheme this year of $195,000 is immaterial on a quantitative basis (it represents only 0.36% of profit before taxation and 0.84% of total assets), as a related party transaction with directors, the scheme should be considered to be material by nature and should be fully disclosed in the notes to the financial statements in accordance with IAS 24 *Related Party Disclosures*.

The related party disclosures are particularly important for a listed entity such as Watson Co. In line with ISA 450 *Evaluation of Misstatements Identified During the Audit*, all misstatements should be accumulated and therefore the error should also have been included in the audit working papers and adjustment should have been requested.

Other quality control issues include:

–   The staffing levels on the audit also appear to be inadequate given that there are only two audit team members. This is again indicative of poor audit planning.

–   In addition, it is clear that the audit manager should have been replaced earlier and that Watson Co has failed to provide adequate direction and supervision of the audit.

–   The original audit manager, Rodney Evans, has also provided an inadequate briefing meeting prior to the commencement of the audit work. The advice to follow last year's working papers is inappropriate as the auditor must always be on the look-out for new situations and issues such as the new share-based payment scheme.

–   Jansen & Co has also failed to monitor the progress of the audit and therefore to update and change the audit plan as necessary during the course of the audit as required by ISA 300 *Planning an Audit of Financial Statements*. This is evidenced by the fact that the audit clearance meeting is scheduled for next week and the initial manager review is only just taking place.

    In addition, there appears to be no evidence of engagement partner oversight over the course of the audit fieldwork and it is the engagement partner's responsibility to ensure that they have reviewed the documentation to ensure that sufficient appropriate evidence has been obtained and that the auditor's report issued in the circumstances is appropriate.

–   There appears to be a lack of audit evidence in relation to the firm of external valuers which has been used to value the share options. ISA 500 *Audit Evidence* requires the auditor to obtain sufficient and appropriate audit evidence that the valuation work performed by the management expert is adequate for the purposes of the audit.

    The auditor must therefore evaluate whether management's expert possesses the necessary competence, capabilities and objectivity to perform the valuations and whether the scope of their work is satisfactory for audit purposes. The 'checking out' of the expert online with reference to a website is clearly inadequate for audit purposes and this again reflects the inexperience and lack of expertise of the audit supervisor and poor audit planning with respect to the staffing on the audit.

**Examiner's comments**

Part (a) was very similar to Question three in the specimen exam and asked for the considerations for an audit firm when deciding whether it could provide assurance on prospective financial information. Candidates could score well on this requirement if they had prepared by reviewing similar past requirements, the specimen exam or if they were aware of the content of ISAE 3400 The Examination of Prospective Financial Information. The main weaknesses in answers on this requirement was where candidates did not tailor their answer to an existing client and hence lost time giving detail on customer due diligence, or where candidates did not give detail on the ethical threats arising. This is a common area where candidates lose marks. Another area of this requirement where candidates limited their capacity to score well was by focusing on post-acceptance issues such as the production of an engagement letter rather than the pre-acceptance decision issues.

Candidates were then asked to describe procedures to be performed on the profit forecast. The majority of candidates scored well on this section and a large number of answers provided a much clearer description of audit procedures than that seen in previous sessions. A minority of candidates made bland comments about agreeing opening balances and loan covenants which were not relevant to the statement of profit or loss.

The final requirement for INT candidates was a 10-mark quality control question which was similar to past exams where candidates are required to describe quality control failings. While few candidates scored full marks here the answers provided were generally good if candidates had allocated sufficient time to this requirement.

| | | **Marking scheme** | **Marks** |
|---|---|---|---|
| (a) | (i) | **Matters to be considered before acceptance of engagement**<br>Up to 2 marks for each matter explained<br>– Auditor independence including potentially significant advocacy threat and possible self-review and self-interest threats<br>– Intended use of report, e.g. solely for bank or wider distribution<br>– Nature of assumptions and time period covered (in this case two years)<br>– Availability of experienced, competent staff and time frame for assurance work<br>– Appropriate safeguards to reduce risks to acceptable level<br>– Details of PFI to be given to bank, e.g. forecast P/L only | |
| | | **Maximum** | 6 |
| | (ii) | **Examination procedures**<br>Generally up to 1 mark for each described procedure. Also allow 1 mark for each relevant analytical procedure used to max of 3 marks<br>**General procedures**<br>– Re-cast the forecast to ensure it is arithmetically correct<br>– Confirm the consistency of accounting policies applied<br>– Discuss key assumptions with management and assess reasonableness<br>– Obtain written representations from management on reasonableness and completeness of assumptions<br>– Assess competence and experience of client staff preparing forecasts including accuracy of PFI prepared in previous periods and reasons for any significant variances | |

|  | |  |
|---|---|---|
| | **Specific procedures** | |
| | – Review market research documentation and discuss with management | |
| | – Obtain and review customer contracts for new customers to confirm projected growth in revenue | |
| | – Perform analytical review of key trends; up to 3 marks for analysis of key trends by candidates including: | |
| | • Growth in revenue | |
| | • Cost of sales as % of revenue | |
| | • Declining trend in admin expenses | |
| | • Increase in net profit margin | |
| | – Review of capex forecasts and agreement to invoices/supplier quotations | |
| | – Recalculate depreciation and ensure correct inclusion of depreciation on new HGVs and warehousing facilities | |
| | – Obtain and review breakdown of operating expenses; ensure all items appropriately included, e.g. advertising/marketing costs; additional staff costs for new drivers including recruitment expenses; any trading tariffs with overseas market and any forex implications | |
| | – Inspect recent utility bills and assess reasonableness of forecast utility overheads | |
| | – Obtain and review documentation for existing loan agreements with bank and draft documentation for new loan and recalculate finance costs | |
| | **Maximum** | **9** |
| **(b)** | **Watson Co** | |
| | Generally up to 1 mark for each issue discussed | |
| | – Inadequate planning/consultation with client re SBP scheme (ISA 220) | |
| | – Complex judgmental area, should have been identified as high risk | |
| | – Part-qualified supervisor, inadequate skills and expertise for this listed client | |
| | – Treatment of SBP is incorrect, valuation should have been updated at year end for cash-based scheme | |
| | – Recognition as equity reserve is also incorrect, IFRS 2 requires recognition as liability for cash-based scheme | |
| | – SBP is immaterial quantitatively (extra 1 mark for relevant calculation and comment) but scheme is RPT with directors which is material by nature especially for listed entity | |
| | – Error should have been calculated and adjustment requested | |
| | – The matter should have been included in the related party disclosure notes in accordance with IAS 24 | |
| | – Inadequate staffing levels – only two-member team and audit manager should have been replaced earlier | |
| | – Inadequate briefing meeting, poor quality advice to follow last year's working papers – should always be on look-out for new situations and issues | |
| | – Insufficient monitoring and supervision by audit manager | |
| | – No evidence of partner oversight during course of audit work | |
| | – Failure to update and change audit plan as necessary during course of audit (ISA 300); clearance meeting is next week and manager review is only just taking place | |
| | – Lack of audit evidence re external valuer – competence, capabilities, objectivity, scope of work; reference to website is inadequate and reflects inexperience and lack of expertise of supervisor (up to 2 marks for development of discussion) | |
| | | **10** |
| **Total** | | **25** |

**35    VIZSLA**  *Walk in the footsteps of a top tutor*

*Top tutor tips*

*Part (a) requires knowledge of money laundering responsibilities. This is straightforward knowledge from the study text.*

*In part (b) the examination procedures need to focus on assessing the reasonableness of the assumptions used to prepare the forecast. Remember that these transactions have not happened as of yet so you will not be able to inspect invoices, etc. Instead, think about how the client determined the forecast figures and assess whether this is reasonable. Include some of the more general procedures that apply to every client for some easy marks.*

**(a)    (i)    Ethical and other matters to be considered before accepting Setter Co as a client of the firm**

Requirements and guidance relevant to accepting and continuing client relationships is contained in ISQC 1 *Quality Control for Firms that Perform Audits and Reviews of Financial Statements and Other Assurance and Related Services Engagements*. The fundamental requirements are that a firm must consider:

– Its competence to perform the engagement and whether the firm has the capabilities, including time and resources to do so.

– Whether the relevant ethical requirements can be complied with.

– The integrity of the client, and whether there is information which would lead it to conclude that the client lacks integrity.

**Competence and resources**

Looking at each consideration in turn, there seems no reason why Pointer & Co would not have the competence to carry out the assignment, which is a limited assurance review of historical financial statements. Being a firm of Chartered Certified Accountants, and performing assurance services such as the audit of Vizsla Co, means that the firm has the relevant knowledge and experience to perform a high quality limited assurance review.

However, the pressure to perform the audit for a low fee could impact on Pointer & Co's ability to perform a high quality limited assurance review if insufficient resources are made available, given the potential restriction on the fee which can be charged to provide the service. ISQC 1 also mentions that where the client is aggressively concerned with maintaining the firm's fees as low as possible, this can indicate a lack of integrity of the client.

**Ethical issues**

In terms of ethics there are several matters to consider. First, it appears that Vizsla Co is putting pressure on Pointer & Co to accept the engagement. Vizsla Co is a relatively significant client of Pointer & Co, providing 10% of the firm's annual practice income, and there is an intimidation threat in that Vizsla Co has threatened to move to another audit provider if Pointer & Co does not accept Setter Co as a client and perform the work for a low fee. This could also be perceived as a self-interest threat in that Pointer & Co has a financial interest in maintaining a good relationship with Vizsla Co.

A further ethical issue arises from the suggestion that Pointer & Co should provide tax planning advice to Setter Co and prepare its tax submissions. This would give rise to a self-review threat because Pointer & Co would have some input to the tax figures which form part of the financial statements which would then be subject to the limited assurance review. Providing the tax planning advice could also be seen as acting on behalf of management, further impairing the objectivity of the limited assurance provided on the financial statements.

Pointer & Co should consider whether safeguards can be used to reduce any ethical threats to an acceptable level, for example, through the use of separate teams to provide the limited assurance review and the tax services and by having an independent second partner to review the work performed. If safeguards do not reduce the threats to an acceptable level, then the tax service should not be carried out in addition to the limited assurance review.

**Client integrity**

Preparing the personal tax computations of Gordon Potts is less of an ethical issue in terms of objectivity as his personal tax is a separate issue and not reflected in the company's financial statements, but there may be other issues with providing this advice, linked to integrity, which will be discussed next.

The integrity of Gordon Potts will need to be carefully evaluated. There is nothing wrong with him having business interests in several companies, though information about each of these will need to be obtained. The key issues with integrity relate to the breach of employment law and his taking money from a company pension plan to set up a business which is managed by his son. The breach of employment law indicates that Gordon Potts has a questionable reputation and possibly that he has been involved in criminal activity, depending on what laws have been breached, and the seriousness of the non-compliance. The information comes from a newspaper article, so it may not be very credible and may not even be true, so more information will need to be sought on this issue.

Taking money from the company pension plan is likely to be a breach of the relevant regulations, and it would seem that this was done for the benefit of his son. The fact that this business is located in a foreign country makes the business arrangements complicated, and while it could be completely innocent, it could also mean that there is something more sinister behind the connections between the companies, for example, it could be an arrangement to facilitate money laundering.

Pointer & Co must obtain sufficient information to carefully evaluate the appropriateness of accepting Setter Co as a client, and they must document the acceptance decision in accordance with ISQC 1.

**(ii)** **The importance of obtaining customer due diligence and the information which should be obtained**

Customer due diligence (CDD), also called know your client procedures, is needed as part of anti-money laundering regulations, which all audit firms should have in place when accepting new clients. It refers to the firm obtaining information to be able to identify who the prospective client is and verify identity by reference to independent and reliable source material. This is a crucial part of risk assessment when taking on a new client and allows the firm to understand not only the identity of the prospective client, but also the nature of the business and its source of funds.

Specifically, the firm should address the following as part of customer due diligence:

– Identify the customer and verify their identity using documents, data or information obtained from a reliable and independent source.

– Confirm the identities of all shareholders, including the specific family members who collectively own 90% of the company's share capital, and the other shareholder(s) who own the remaining 10%.

– Identify any beneficial owner who is not the client. This is the individual (or individuals) behind the client who ultimately own or control the client or on whose behalf a transaction or activity is being conducted.

– Where a business relationship is established, understand the purpose and intended nature of the relationship, for example, details of the customer's business or the source of the funds.

Businesses must also conduct ongoing monitoring to identify large, unusual or suspicious transactions as part of CDD. All of the documents obtained for the purpose of carrying out CDD checks must be retained for a minimum of five years from the end of the business relationship.

In this scenario, the information which should be obtained includes:

– To confirm the identity of Gordon Potts, photographic evidence, for example his passport, should be seen and a copy taken, along with other means of identification showing his address, for example, recent utility bills or bank statements.

– In relation to Setter Co, the company certificate of incorporation should be seen, to confirm its legal status and the date and place of incorporation.

– A Companies House search (or equivalent) on Setter Co should take place. This will confirm the existence of the company, the shareholders and directors and will provide some financial information. This will confirm that Gordon Potts is the 'beneficial owner' of the entity – i.e. that he is the person who owns or controls, directly or indirectly, more than 25% of the shares or voting rights or who otherwise exercises control over the directors.

– The identity of the other companies controlled by Gordon Potts should also be found, and searches on them conducted, to confirm their existence and the nature of the relationship with Setter Co.

– The latest financial statements of Setter Co, and the other companies in which Gordon Potts has an interest should be reviewed. This will help Pointer & Co to understand the businesses and their relationship with each other, identify the sources of income and whether there are significant transactions between the companies.

– Identify the source of funding for the company, whether there are bank loans or other providers of finance, and the nature of the finance provided in terms of when it is repayable, whether any company assets are provided as collateral for the debt, and whether Gordon Potts or other shareholders have made personal guarantees in respect of any sources of company finance.

– While not strictly part of confirming the identity of Gordon or his companies, Pointer & Co would clearly need to obtain further information about the breach of employment law, and confirm the facts surrounding the situation. Currently the only information available is from a newspaper article and this may not be a credible source.

**(b)** **Examination procedures on the operating profit forecast of Vizsla Co**

**General procedures:**

• Enquire as to the identity of the preparer of the operating profit forecast, and assess their competence, especially given that interest costs have been included as part of operating profit which is incorrect.

• Obtain an understanding as to the procedures and controls which have been followed in the preparation of the forecast, for example, has the forecast been approved by a senior member of the company's accounting team.

• Confirm that the accounting policies applied in Vizsla Co's financial statements have been consistently applied in the preparation of the operating profit forecast, for example, that design costs are expensed rather than capitalised as a development cost.

• Confirm that the assumptions underpinning the forecast are in line with knowledge of the business obtained from performing the company's audit, for example, the seasonality of the sales can be confirmed by looking at the audit evidence obtained in the audit of revenue.

• Re-cast the forecast to ensure it is arithmetically correct.

**Specific procedures:**

• Enquire whether a more detailed profit forecast is available, or ask management to prepare one, for example, detailing out cost of sales and other expenses. In addition, request a forecast statement of financial position and statement of cash flows.

*Tutorial note*

*There could be matters which make the profit forecast unachievable revealed through assessment of the statement of financial position and statement of cash flows, e.g. the timing of the working capital cycle may make achieving the profit forecast unachievable if funds are not available at certain points of time especially given the seasonal nature of the business.*

- Request that management prepares a profit forecast in the same format as audited financial statements and in accordance with IFRS Standards, i.e. the interest cost should be shown below the operating profit line.

- Having obtained the cost of sales figure for each six-month period, recalculate the gross profit figures given in the forecast.

- Compare this to gross profit margins in the prior year audited financial statements and investigate any anomalies.

- Having obtained a break down showing the components of cost of sales and other expenses, for each significant category of expense, perform analytical review to confirm that the forecast costs appear to be in line with expectations, and discuss any unusually high or low forecast costs with management.

- Based on the above, assess whether there are any missing categories of expenditure which have not been included in the forecast, e.g. there is no depreciation included in the forecast.

- For revenue, which is forecast to increase by a significant amount (e.g. 11.8% increase comparing the six months ending 31 March 20X9 and 31 March 20Y0), consider whether the forecast appears overly optimistic. For instance, there is not a corresponding increase in marketing costs to support the forecast increase in revenue.

- Compare revenue in the year forecast to 30 September 20X9 with revenue from prior years' audited financial statements.

- Investigate any unusual trends through discussion with management.

- Review any marketing plans and discuss with an appropriate senior member of staff, for example, the sales director, to establish the rationale for forecasting a significant increase in revenue, for example, there may be plans to introduce new product lines. Consider this in light of the fact that design costs and marketing are not forecast to increase by a significant amount.

- Review the design costs as they appear to be fairly static with just a small increase to achieve a much bigger % increase in revenue. Discuss with management and assess if such an increase in revenue can be achieved with such a small increase in design costs.

- Confirm costs to appropriate supporting documentation, e.g. staff costs to human resources projected costs, marketing costs to advertising budgets.

- Assess whether the overdraft is likely to be repaid in September 20X9, for example, by obtaining and reviewing the cash flow forecast prepared for the same period as the operating profit forecast.

- Discuss with management the rationale for using 30% of revenue as a basis for determining the amount of other expenses. In addition, compare this to the results of audit procedures performed on expenses to gauge whether 30% appears to be a reasonable basis.

**Examiner's comments**

Part (a) related to the ethical issues and other matters which should be considered in respect of the acceptance of a potential new client. The introduction was made through an existing client who sought to intimidate the auditor into taking on the new client of doubtful reputation.

A number of candidates had obviously studied a recent article on the ACCA website on how to answer ethics questions and were able to earn good marks. Candidates are reminded that they need to identify the indicator in the scenario, what the relevant ethical threat is, to describe why this is the case and further explain the implication to the auditor if relevant safeguards aren't then put in place.

Most candidates highlighted the key area of intimidation but there was a tendency to diverge into potential advocacy issues with the new client seeking a bank loan, which was beyond the scope of the question. The need for safeguards was usually well explained but candidates need to be able to explain, for example, what a self-review threat is (reviewing their own work which causes a loss of scepticism) rather than just stating that there is a self-review threat.

The potential new client had a questionable history and not enough candidates explored this in sufficient detail.

The importance of new customer due diligence was also a requirement of this question and this was poorly answered as many confused this with a due diligence review. Many candidates talked about initial acceptance procedures such as reviewing accounts and contacting the previous auditor rather than concentrating on the main Customer Due Diligence (CDD) procedures such as money laundering, sources of client funds, the identity of the beneficial owner, any shadow directors and other companies owned by the prospective client. Other candidates incorrectly discussed procedures, which would be undertaken when performing audit planning. Most, however, did pick up on needing photographic identification, Companies House searches and Certificates of Incorporation as proof of identification as well as wanting to understand the previous issues of alleged pension fund misappropriation & breach of employment laws.

Part (b) required candidates to recommend examination procedures to be used when reviewing a profit forecast and was generally well answered with all of the main areas covered. Candidates were able to include the need to identify who prepared the forecast and their competence, unusual trends in revenue, revenues growing quicker than costs and the risk of management bias while the objective of the forecast was to procure a bank loan. Marks were also available for calculating relevant trends and good candidates were able to earn extra credit here.

| | | | Marks |
|---|---|---|---|
| | | **Marking scheme** | *Marks* |

**(a)** **(i)** **Ethical and other matters to be considered before accepting Setter Co as a client of the firm**

Up to 1½ marks for each ethical or professional issue explained

- General requirements of ISQC 1
- Competence to perform the work – this should not be a problem
- Intimidation and self-interest threat from Vizsla Co
- Low fees potentially impair quality of work
- Pressure on fees from Setter Co indicates lack of integrity
- Self-review and management threat from performing tax planning for the company
- Safeguards should be used to reduce threats to an acceptable level, if this is not possible that tax planning should not be performed
- Providing personal tax advice not ethically wrong but may not want to accept work due to integrity issues
- Breach of employment law and taking money from pension plan indicates lack of integrity/criminal activity/poor reputation

**(ii)** **Customer due diligence – reasons and recommended information**

Up to 1½ marks for each point explained/recommended

- Part of anti-money laundering regulations (up to 3 marks for detailed explanation of regulations)
- Identity of Gordon Potts – passport, recent utility bills or bank statements
- Identity of other shareholders including the other family members and other 10% shareholders
- Setter Co – the company certificate of incorporation, to confirm legal status, date and place of incorporation
- A Companies House search (or equivalent) on Setter Co – confirm the existence of the company, the shareholders and directors, beneficial owners
- Other companies controlled by Gordon Potts – confirm their existence and the nature of the relationship with Setter Co
- Review of the latest financial statements of Setter Co, and the other companies in which Gordon Potts has an interest should be reviewed
- Identify the source of funding, when funding is repayable and the existence of any security provided by the company or by personal guarantee of owners
- Facts surrounding the breach of employment law as reported by the newspaper

|  | Maximum | **16** |
|---|---|---|

**(b)** **Examination procedures**

Up to 1 mark for each procedure explained. In addition, ½ mark for relevant calculations, e.g. trend analysis, up to a maximum of 2 marks

**General procedures**

- Identity of the preparer of the operating profit forecast, and assess their competence
- Understanding the procedures/controls which have been followed in the preparation of the forecast
- Confirm the consistency of accounting policies applied
- Confirm that the assumptions underpinning the forecast are in line with knowledge of the business obtained from performing the company's audit
- Re-cast the forecast to ensure it is arithmetically correct

**Specific procedures**

– Ask management to prepare a more detailed profit forecast in an appropriate format and to provide forecast statement of financial position and statement of cash flows
– Recalculate the gross profit margins and compare with gross profit margins from audited financial statements
– Obtain a break down showing the components of cost of sales and other expenses; perform analytical review and discuss results
– Assess whether there are any missing categories of expenditure
– For revenue, consider whether the forecast appears overly optimistic – allow credit for calculation of appropriate trends from the forecast
– Compare revenue forecast with revenue from prior years' audited financial statements. Investigate any unusual trends through discussion with management
– Review any marketing plans and discuss with an appropriate senior member of staff, for example, the sales director
– Review design costs, discuss with management and assess if such an increase in revenue can be achieved with such a small increase in design costs
– Confirm costs to appropriate supporting documentation, e.g. staff costs to human resources projected costs, marketing costs to advertising budgets
– Obtain and review the cash flow forecast prepared for the same period as the operating profit forecast
– Discuss with management the rationale for using 30% of revenue as a basis for determining the amount of other expenses

|  | |
|---|---|
| Maximum | 9 |
| **Total** | 25 |

**36    ROPE**  *Walk in the footsteps of a top tutor*

---

*Top tutor tips*

*The wording of this question is more unusual than previous prospective financial information questions. In this question, some of the assumptions used to prepare the forecast have been provided and the requirement is to evaluate the appropriateness of the forecast. Consider whether the assumptions are reasonable. The question also asks for procedures which should be performed which is a more typical requirement.*

*When dealing with ethical and professional issues remember to consider the significance of the issues as well as identifying them and explaining them. Safeguards should also be included in your answer.*

---

**(a)    The cash flow forecast of Rope Co**

When a company has prepared a cash flow forecast as part of their assessment of going concern, in accordance with ISA 570 *Going Concern* the auditor needs to evaluate the reliability of the underlying data used to prepare the forecast and to determine whether there is adequate support for the assumptions underlying the forecast. There are a number of issues relating to the forecast which raise concerns about the assessment of Rope's going concern status and therefore warrant further investigation.

**Receipts from customers**

There was little growth in cash receipts in the second half of the year ended 30 September 20X6 (0.8%), yet in each consequent six-month period management predicts a significant rise in receipts of between 1.7% and 3.0%.

This could be based on overly optimistic forecasts in relation to sales growth for the same period. If sales forecasts are too optimistic, this could eliminate the forecast small positive cash flows, which could leave the company in a net overdraft position for the entire two-year period.

The movement in relation to customer receipts is a key assumption underpinning the return to a positive cash position and needs to be scrutinised further.

**Salaries and other payments**

While **annual** receipts from customers and payments to suppliers are forecast to rise during the forecast period by 8.5% and 9.4%, respectively, the amounts attributable to salaries and other operating payments are only forecast to rise by 4.1%.

**Workings**

| $000's | Annual receipts | Annual payments | Salaries and other payments |
|---|---|---|---|
| **20X8** | 14,950 + 15,400 = 30,350 | 11,600 + 12,000 = 23,600 | 1,301 + 1,353 + 1,951 + 1,925 = 6,530 |
| **20X6** | 13,935 + 14,050 = 27,985 | 10,725 + 10,850 = 21,575 | 1,250 +1,300 + 1,875 + 1,850 = 6,275 |
| **Difference** | 2,365 | 2,025 | 255 |
| **% increase** | 8.5% | 9.4%. | 4.1% |

This is based on management's simple assumption of a general 2% annual inflation in these costs. This seems to be overly simplistic and will require further investigation. Salary costs could be forecast using a more sophisticated methodology based on required employee numbers and average wages/salaries.

The significant forecast increase in sales suggests that operating activities will increase over the next two years and it might be expected that staff requirements may increase in line with this. For similar reasons, it is likely that a larger increase in other operating costs would be required to match the increased administrative burden of producing and selling more goods and/or services.

### Sale of investments

Management is planning to sell some investments in listed shareholdings for $500,000 to repay a loan to the chief executive. At 30 September 20X6, however, the fair value of the investments was only $350,000. As the fair value of these investments is revalued at the end of each year based upon the current share price, this is assumed to reflect the amount at which the shares were trading at the end of September. Management is therefore expecting the shares to increase in value by $150,000 in the space of two years, which represents a 43% rise. This is an extremely optimistic assumption in comparison to average rates of growth across most stock markets.

It therefore appears likely that there will be a shortfall in the amount raised to repay Mr Stewart. Rope Co will therefore have to supplement the amount received from selling investments with cash from other sources, which will lead to a reduction in the cash position in comparison to the forecasts.

### Repayment of the bank loan

The bank loan is due for repayment 15 months after the year end. Management is assuming that they will be able to fund the repayment with a new loan facility from the same finance provider. Without any agreement in place from the provider, this represents a significant assumption.

Without a new facility Rope Co will have no means with which to repay their obligation, which could lead to the lender taking action to recover the loan amount. This could include seizing assets which were provided as security over the loan or commencing insolvency proceedings.

In either case, this could have a significant impact on Rope's ability to trade into the foreseeable future and, therefore, the loan repayment event represents a material uncertainty which may need to be fully disclosed in the financial statements of Rope Co in accordance with IAS 1 *Presentation of Financial Statements*.

### Missing cash flows

There seems to be a lack of consideration of a number of non-operating cash flows which one might expect to see in a two-year forecast. For example, most companies maintain a practice of regular replacement of old, inefficient tangible non-current assets as opposed to making larger, less regular replacements which may create a significant drain on cash resources in one particular year. The forecast currently has no allocation for capital investment. In a similar fashion, there are no cash flows related to tax and dividend payments. It is possible that such transactions have been overlooked in the preparation of the forecast.

### Further audit procedures

- Obtain a copy of the latest interim financial statements and compare the actual post year-end sales performance with the forecast sales upon which the cash flow forecast is based.

- Discuss with management the rationale for the expected increase in customer receipts and where possible confirm this to customer correspondence, orders or contracts.

- Inspect the documentation detailing the terms of the loan with Mr Stewart to confirm the amount outstanding and the agreed date of repayment.

- Inspect the terms of the bank loan to confirm the final amount due for repayment, the date of repayment and whether any assets have been accepted as security for the loan.

- Enquire of management whether they have entered into any negotiations with their bank, or any other financial institution, to provide a replacement loan in January 20X8. If so, request corroborating evidence such as signed agreements, agreements in principle or correspondence with the financial institutions.

- Enquire of management whether they have any contingency plans in place to repay both loans on time should they not be able to raise the required amount through selling investments and obtaining new loan agreements.

- Perform an analytical review of actual monthly payroll costs incurred obtained from the payroll department. Include any available payment periods after 30 September 20X6 to help ascertain whether management's assumptions regarding salaries are appropriate. Seek corroborating evidence for any fluctuations in cost such as HR records confirming pay awards and changes in staff.

- Perform an analytical review of actual other operational costs and consider the level of other costs as a percentage of sales. Compare this to the levels included in the forecast. Investigate any significant differences.

- Corroborate the lack of investment in new tangible non-current assets by performing an analytical review of the levels of additions and disposals over the last, say, five years to see if this supports the absence of any allocation for this in the short-term future and consider this in light of our understanding of the entity and its production process.

- Compare the cash flow forecasts to any capital expenditure forecasts prepared by Rope Co to ensure that the cash flow forecast is consistent with this. Ask management to explain any differences identified.

- Review the non-current asset register and identify any assets with a zero or negligible carrying value which could indicate that the assets have fulfilled their useful lives and are due for replacement.

- Inspect the cash book post year end to see if there are any significant cash transactions which do not appear to have been included in the forecasts, in particular cash transactions relating to purchases or disposals of assets and dividend payments.

- Review the outcome of previous forecasts prepared by management to assess how effective management has been in the past at preparing accurate forecasts.

- Obtain written representations from management confirming that they have no intention to either purchase or dispose of non-current assets or to pay dividends over the next two years.

**(b)** **Matters relating to the loan from Mr J Stewart**

**Related party transaction**

As a key member of staff at Rope Co, the loan from the chief executive represents a related party transaction. As such, the transaction and related outstanding balances must be fully disclosed in the financial statements in accordance with IAS 24 *Related Party Disclosures*.

This means that the nature of the related party relationship, the nature and the amount of the loan, the amounts outstanding at the year end and the terms and conditions of the loan, including a description of the fixed charge, must be disclosed in the notes to the financial statements.

**Interest free loan measurement**

The loan was received during the current year ended 30 September 20X6. The loan liability should have been initially recorded at its fair value, which would normally be the transaction price of $500,000. IFRS 9 *Financial Instruments*, however, states that in the case of an interest free loan, the fair value should be measured as the present value of all future cash flows discounted using the prevailing market rates for similar instruments.

While it will be difficult to identify a similar instrument due to the nature of the relationship between the lender and the company, a similar instrument should be identified based upon the currency used, the loan term and any other similar factors, for example, a three-year, $ loan from a bank.

At the year end, the outstanding loan liability should have been measured using the amortised cost method and the effective interest calculated should be recognised as a finance charge in the statement of profit or loss.

**Further audit procedures**

- Inspect the loan agreement to confirm the amounts loaned to the company, and the other relevant terms including the rate of interest, the repayment date and the associated penalties for late payment.

- Inspect the related party disclosures in the financial statements to ensure that they provide sufficient information and accurately reflect the terms and amounts relating to the transaction.

- Additional procedures will need to be performed regarding the completeness of related party transactions as the loan with Mr Stewart was not identified through normal audit procedures.

- The market rate used in the calculation of the fair value of the loan should be compared to a range of suitable instruments, e.g. three-year bank loans, to ascertain its appropriateness. Following this, the calculation should be checked for arithmetical accuracy.

- The amount recorded for the initial loan value and the year-end value should be recalculated using the appropriate discount factor and market rate to confirm the arithmetical accuracy of management's calculations.

- Review the loan liability recognised in the financial statements to ensure that the appropriate, discounted figure has been used.

- Reconcile the effective interest rate for 20X6 from the amortised cost calculation to the finance charges in the statement of profit or loss to confirm that this is appropriately included in profits.

(c)    **Ethical and professional issues**

The request to attend a meeting with the company's bank can give rise to an advocacy threat to objectivity. An advocacy threat is the threat that a professional accountant will promote a client's or employer's position to the point that the professional accountant's objectivity is compromised.

In this case, the chief executive may want the audit engagement partner to support a view that Rope Co will be able to continue as a going concern and that the loan ultimately will be repaid. This means that the audit partner is promoting the client which leads to the creation of an advocacy threat.

In addition, from a legal perspective, the audit firm must be careful not to create the impression that they are in any way guaranteeing the future existence of the company or providing assurance on the draft financial statements. In legal terms, attending the meeting and promoting the interests of the client could create legal 'proximity', which increases the risk of legal action against the auditor in the event of Rope Co defaulting on any loan provided by the bank.

It may be possible for a partner other than the audit engagement partner to attend the meeting with the bank, which would be a form of safeguard against the ethical threat.

The audit firm's partner responsible for ethics should consider the severity of the threat and whether this, or another safeguard, could reduce the threat to an acceptable level.

An audit firm being threatened with dismissal from a client engagement represents an intimidation threat. The chief executive's actions should also lead to questions over his integrity.

The audit firm may wish to consider resigning from the audit if the threat becomes too severe.

---

**Examiner's comments**

Part (a) required candidates to appraise the forecast and suggest further procedures in assessing the use of the report as part of the going concern review during the audit. This was generally well answered by the majority of candidates attempting the question.

In part (b) candidates were required to discuss a loan from the chief executive to the company. This had been provided during the year being audited and the audit was still ongoing. Stronger candidates appropriately recognised this as a related party transaction and commented on the materiality and disclosure requirements before going on to describe procedures to perform. There were a significant number of candidates who had failed to take in to account the date the loan was provided and assumed it was missed in the prior year audit so instead focused their answers on a perceived lack of integrity of the directors, inappropriate levels of disclosure in prior year financial statements and audit qualifications.

Requirement (c) outlined the situation where the audit engagement partner had been asked to accompany the chief executive to a meeting with the bank where additional finance would be sought, and there was an intimidation threat in that the client had threatened to put the audit out for tender. Again, candidates generally did well on this requirement, identifying and explaining the correct ethical threats, and on the whole recommending appropriate courses of action. The only problem in some scripts was a focus on the lack of integrity of the chief executive, rather than discussing specific ethical threats raised.

---

| | | Marks |
|---|---|---|
| **Marking scheme** | | |

Generally up to 1½ marks for each well explained matter and 1 mark for each well explained procedure recommended:

**(a)    Cash flow forecast**

**Matters**

- Potential overestimation of cash receipts from customers
- Lower than forecast sales may lead to net overdraft
- Potential underestimation of salary and other operating payments
- Simplistic assumption of cost inflation
- Investments do not match management's forecast disposal valuation
- Assumption of growth in value of investments is very optimistic
- Ability to repay loans dependent upon other assumptions
- Lack of specific consideration of non-operating cash flows

**Procedures**

- Review latest interim financial statements
- Discuss forecast sales and customer receipts with management
- Inspect J Stewart loan agreement
- Inspect terms of bank loan
- Enquire of management whether they have begun renegotiations regarding bank loan facility
- Enquire with management about contingency plans
- Perform analytical review of payroll costs
- Perform analytical review of other operating costs
- Inspect non-current asset registers
- Inspect post year-end cash book
- Review outcomes of previous management forecasts
- Obtain written representations from management (max ½ mark)

|  | Maximum | 14 |
|---|---|---|

**(b)    J Stewart loan**

**Matters**

- Provision of the loan represents a related party transaction
- Disclosure requirements of RPT
- Calculation of fair value for an interest free loan
- Determination of market rates for a similar instrument
- Valuation of loan at end of year using amortised cost method

**Procedures**

- Inspect terms of loan agreement
- Inspect related party disclosures in the financial statements
- Additional procedures in relation to potential other RPTs
- Compare market rate used to range of suitable instruments
- Recalculate initial and year-end loan amounts
- Reconcile effective interest rate from amortised cost calculation to statement of P&L

|  | Maximum | 6 |
|---|---|---|

**(c)    Ethical and professional issues**

Generally 1 mark for each point identified and discussed:

- Advocacy threat created by attending meeting
- Chief executive may want the engagement partner to support the going concern status of the company
- Legal proximity may be created by attending meeting
- Different partner should attend the meeting
- Ethics partner should consider severity of threat
- Intimidation threat from threat of removal from office
- Integrity of the chief executive questionable
- Consider resignation

|  | Maximum | 5 |
|---|---|---|

| **Total** | | **25** |

**37    HAWK**  *Walk in the footsteps of a top tutor*

### Top tutor tips

*Part (a) asks for matters to be considered in agreeing the terms of engagement for an examination of a forecast. These are the matters that need to be included in the engagement letter for this assignment. A good approach to take for this question is to identify matters that could lead to misunderstandings in future which the firm would want to clarify in writing to avoid such misunderstandings. Knowledge of audit engagement letters can also be used and adapted to this type of engagement.*

*Part (b) requires the procedures to be performed on the forecast. It is important to remember that these events and transactions have not yet happened and therefore cannot be agreed to supporting documentation in the same way as historical figures. You need to generate procedures which will help you assess whether the assumptions used in the forecast are reasonable.*

*Part (c) requires an understanding of the different types of assumption that can be used to prepare a forecast. Common sense can be applied here if you don't know the answer.*

**(a)    Management's responsibilities**

The terms of the engagement should set out management's responsibilities for the preparation of the business plan and forecast financial statements, including all assumptions used, and for providing the auditor with all relevant information and source data used in developing the assumptions. This is to clarify the roles of management and of Lapwing & Co, and reduce the scope for any misunderstanding.

**The intended use of the business plan and report**

It should be confirmed that the report will be provided to the bank and that it will not be distributed or made available to other parties. This will establish the potential liability of Lapwing & Co to third parties, and help to determine the need and extent of any liability disclaimer that may be considered necessary. Lapwing & Co should also establish that the bank will use the report only in helping to reach a decision in respect of the additional finance being sought by Hawk Co.

**The elements of the business plan to be covered by the engagement**

The extent of the engagement should be agreed. Lapwing & Co need to determine whether they are being asked to report just on the forecast financial statements, or on the whole business plan including any narrative descriptions or explanations of Hawk Co's intended future business activities. This will help to determine the scope of the work involved and its complexity.

**The period covered by the forecasts**

This should be confirmed when agreeing the terms of the engagement, as assumptions become more speculative as the length of the period covered increases, making it more difficult for Lapwing & Co to substantiate the acceptability of the figures, and increasing the risk of the engagement. It should also be confirmed that a 12-month forecast period is sufficient for the bank's purposes.

**The nature of the assumptions used in the business plan**

It is crucial that Lapwing & Co determine the nature of assumptions, especially whether the assumptions are based on best estimates or are hypothetical. This is important because ISAE 3400 *The Examination of Prospective Financial Information* states that the auditor should not accept, or should withdraw from, an engagement when the assumptions are clearly unrealistic or when the auditor believes that the prospective financial information will be inappropriate for its intended use.

**The planned contents of the assurance report**

The engagement letter should confirm the planned elements of the report to be issued, to avoid any misunderstanding with management. In particular, Lapwing & Co should clarify that their report will contain a statement of negative assurance as to whether the assumptions provide a reasonable basis for the prospective financial information, and a conclusion as to whether the prospective financial information is properly prepared on the basis of the assumptions and is presented in accordance with the relevant financial reporting framework. The bank may require the report to be in a particular format and include specific wordings in order to make their lending decision.

**(b)** **General procedures**

- Recalculate the forecast financial statements to confirm the arithmetic accuracy.

- Agree the unaudited figures for the period to 31 May 20X2 to management accounts, and agree the cash figure to bank statement or bank reconciliation.

- Confirm the consistency of the accounting policies used in the preparation of the forecast financial statements with those used in the last audited financial statements.

- Consider the accuracy of forecasts prepared in prior periods by comparison with actual results and discuss with management the reasons for any significant variances.

- Perform analytical procedures to assess the reasonableness of the forecast financial statements. For example, finance charges should increase in line with the additional finance being sought.

- Discuss the extent to which the joint venture with Kestrel Co has been included in the forecast financial statements.

- Review any agreement with Kestrel Co, or minutes of meetings at which the joint venture has been discussed to understand the nature, scale, and timeframe of the proposed joint business arrangement.

- Review any projected financial information for the joint venture, and agree any components relating to it into the forecast financial statements.

**Forecast statement of profit or loss**

- Consider the reasonableness of forecast trends in the light of auditor's knowledge of Hawk Co's business and the current and forecast economic situation and any other relevant external factors.

- Discuss the reason for the anticipated 21.4% increase in revenue with management, to understand if the increase is due to the inclusion of figures relating to the joint venture with Kestrel Co, or other factors.

- Discuss the trend in operating profit with management – the operating margin is forecast to improve from 30% to 33.8%. This improvement may be due to the sale of the underperforming Beak Retail Park.

- Obtain a breakdown of items included in forecast operating expenses and perform an analytical review to compare to those included in the 20X2 figures, to check for any omissions.

- Using the cost breakdown, consider whether depreciation charges have increased in line with the planned capital expenditure.

- Request confirmation from the bank of the potential terms of the $30 million loan being negotiated, to confirm the interest rate at 4%. Consider whether the finance charge in the forecast statement of profit or loss appears reasonable. (If the loan is advanced in August, it should increase the company's finance charge by $1 million ($30 million × 4% × 10/12).)

- Discuss the potential sale of Beak Retail with management and review relevant board minutes, to obtain understanding of the likelihood of the sale, and the main terms of the sale negotiation.

- Recalculate the profit on the planned disposal, agreeing the potential proceeds to any written documentation relating to the sale, vendor's due diligence report, or draft legal documentation if available.

- Agree the potential proceeds on disposal to management's cash flow forecast, and confirm that operating cash flows relevant to Beak Retail are not included from the anticipated date of its sale.

- Discuss the reason for not including current tax in the profit forecast.

**Forecast statement of financial position**

- Agree the increase in property, plant and equipment to an authorised capital expenditure budget, and to any plans for the joint development with Kestrel Co.

- Obtain and review a reconciliation of the movement in property, plant and equipment. Agree that all assets relating to Beak Retail are derecognised on its disposal, and that any assets relating to the joint development with Kestrel Co are recognised in accordance with capital expenditure forecasts, and are properly recognised per IFRS 11 *Joint Arrangements*.

- Discuss the planned increase in equity with management to understand the reason for any planned share issue, its date and the nature of the share issue (rights issue or issue at full market price being the most likely).

- Perform analytical procedures on working capital and discuss trends with management, for example, the receivables collection period is forecast to reduce from 58 to 53 days, and the reason for this should be obtained.

---

*Tutorial note*

*Credit will be awarded for other examples of ratios calculated on the figures provided such as inventory turnover and average payables payment period.*

---

- Agree the increase in long-term borrowings to documentation relating to the new loan, and also to the forecast cash flow statement (where it should be included as a cash flow arising from financing activities).

- Discuss the deferred tax provision with management to understand why no movement on the balance is forecast, particularly given the planned capital expenditure.

- Obtain and review a forecast statement of changes in equity to ensure that movements in retained earnings appear reasonable. (Retained earnings are forecast to increase by $800,000, but the profit forecast for the period is $10.52 million – there must be other items taken through retained earnings such as a planned dividend.)

- Agree the movement in cash, and the forecast closing cash position to a cash flow forecast.

**(c)** **Best estimate and hypothetical assumptions**

Best estimate assumptions relate to future events that management expects to take place and the actions management expects to take.

Management may have already implemented a plan which incorporates these assumptions and as such there may be some evidence available to support them.

This makes it easier for the auditor to validate the reasonableness of the assumptions used to prepare the forecast which may reduce engagement risk.

Hypothetical assumptions relate to future events and management actions that are not necessarily expected to take place.

Hypothetical assumptions generally relate to events and actions further into the future therefore are more uncertain and less evidence, if any, will be available to support them.

This makes it more difficult for the auditor to validate the reasonableness of the assumptions used to prepare the forecast which may increase engagement risk.

---

**Examiner's comments**

The question related to an audit client, Hawk Co that had requested its auditor to provide a report on forecast financial statements included in a business plan, which would be used to help secure a loan. The scenario contained extracts from a forecast statement of profit or loss and a forecast statement of financial position.

Requirement (a) asked candidates to identify and explain the matters that should be considered in agreeing the terms of engagement. Candidates were specifically told not to consider ethical threats to objectivity. Answers varied greatly in quality for this requirement. The best answers focused on matters that should be discussed with the client, such as management's responsibilities, the nature of the assumptions used in the forecasts and the planned contents of the report and explained why those matters should form part of the terms of the engagement. Most answers discussed that negative assurance should be given, and explained the importance of determining the intended user of the report including issues to do with the use of a liability disclaimer. A significant number of candidates achieved high marks on this requirement. Weaker answers discussed only matters such as fee arrangements and deadlines, which, while relevant, are not enough to score well. Some answers discussed ethical issues, which specifically were not required, and others explained matters that would be more relevant to the initial acceptance of the engagement rather than agreeing terms with the client, such as whether the firm had the competence to perform the work.

---

Requirement (b) asked candidates to recommend the procedures that should be used to examine and report on the forecast financial statements to be included in the business plan. The best answers made good use of the forecast financial statements that had been provided, and gave procedures that were both well described and relevant to the specific content of the financial statements. Many candidates also performed analytical procedures to determine unusual trends and relationships in the figures and information provided, which helped to generate very exact procedures. Sound answers had a range of procedures, some general, some focused on income and expenses, some focused on assets, liabilities and equity. Weaker answers tended to state simple enquiries, for example 'ask management who prepared the forecasts', or 'ask why sales has increased' without any further development. Another problem arose in answers that seemed not to realise that the figures were forecasts, so source documentation would not be available in the same way that it is for an audit of historical information. For example, many answers suggested agreeing assets purchased to invoices from suppliers, or the forecast increase in share capital to share certificates, but these items would not yet exist as they relate to future transactions. The one area that was missing from almost all answers was the need to ensure internal consistency in all forecast figures, so for example cross-checking from the forecast financial statements to a capital expenditure budget and to cash flow forecasts. Another problem with weaker answers was that they tended not to always provide procedures. For example, some answers contained a lengthy discussion as to whether a part of the business that was planned to be sold should be accounted for as a held-for-sale group of assets, which is not very relevant to the question requirement. These answers seemed to be drifting into an assessment of potential material misstatements, which was not asked for.

| Marking scheme | | Marks |
|---|---|---|
| **(a)** | **Matters to be included in the terms of agreement** | |
| | Up to 1½ marks for each matter identified and explained (2 marks maximum for identification): | |
| | – Management's responsibilities | |
| | – Intended use of the information and report | |
| | – The contents of the business plan | |
| | – The period covered by the forecasts | |
| | – The nature of assumptions used in the forecasts | |
| | – The format and planned content of the assurance report | |
| | **Maximum** | **6** |
| **(b)** | **Procedures on forecast financial information** | |
| | Up to 1 mark for each procedure (brief examples below): | |
| | – Re-calculate forecast | |
| | – Consistency of accounting policies used | |
| | – Discuss how joint venture has been included | |
| | – General analytical procedures | |
| | – Discuss trends – allow up to 3 marks for calculations performed and linked to procedures | |
| | – Review and compare breakdown of costs | |
| | – Recalculate profit on disposal, agreement of components to supporting documentation | |
| | – Agree increase in property, plant and equipment to capital expenditure budget | |
| | – Discuss working capital trends – allow 2 marks for calculations performed and linked to procedures | |
| | – Agree movement in long-term borrowings to new loan documentation | |
| | – Obtain and review forecast statement of changes in equity and confirm validity of reconciling items | |
| | **Maximum** | **15** |

**(c)**     **Best estimate and hypothetical assumptions**
Generally 1 mark per point:
–     Best estimate – actions expected to be taken
–     Best estimate – more certain, more evidence likely to be available
–     Best estimate – creates less engagement risk
–     Hypothetical – actions which may or may not be taken
–     Hypothetical – unlikely to be any reliable evidence
–     Hypothetical – higher risk

|  | Maximum | 4 |
| --- | --- | --- |
| Total | | 25 |

**38     CHEETAH**  *Walk in the footsteps of a top tutor*

**Top tutor tips**

*Part (a) requires an explanation of why the issues require further attention. Here you need to look at how the issues could impact the value of the company and therefore the price to be paid for the company.*

*Part (b) looks at the ethical and professional issues of conducting a review of interim financial information in a short time frame with the report being relied on by the bank providing the finance for the acquisition. This is quite a straightforward ethical situation. Make sure you explain the issues. Stating the name of a threat is not an explanation. You must say how this could affect the behaviour of the auditor or the outcome of the audit.*

**(a)     (i)     Why the matters require further investigation**

**Termination of contract**

**Impact on forecasts**

The loss of the customer may lead to a reduction in forecast revenue by as much as 5% per year. This may also lead to a reduction in costs specifically relevant to servicing the customer. For example, sales staff specifically allocated to servicing this client.

This is significant because the forecast future cash flows of Zebra Co will be critical in determining the value of the company and the price offered by Cheetah Co. It is therefore vital to establish all of the potential revenue and cost implications of the loss of the customer to ascertain the impact on the purchase price.

**Wider implications of new competitor**

The customer referred to has switched to a new, cheaper supplier. This may have wider implications if the new supplier is directly targeting the customers of Zebra Co. It is possible that other customers may switch to the new supplier in the future, which would have further implications on future revenue and cost forecasts.

It may not be possible to determine the potential impact of the new supplier at this point, which increases the level of uncertainty associated with the potential acquisition. Cheetah Co may be able to use this uncertainty as a tool for bargaining with the owners of Zebra Co over the final agreed price.

### Possible impairment of other assets

The loss of a major customer may be an indication of impairment of the assets of Zebra Co. This will be particularly relevant if Zebra Co holds specific assets for manufacturing the unique furniture products made for this client.

As well as production assets, Zebra Co may also be holding inventories which are specifically relevant to the customer which cannot be re-used elsewhere or sold to other customers. If this is the case, these inventories will almost certainly be impaired.

If not performed at the year end, it may now be appropriate to conduct an impairment review to ensure that the valuation of the assets, as presented in the financial statements, is still appropriate in the circumstances.

### Gifted land

### Possible restriction on sale

The restriction on the sale of the land may mean that Zebra Co is prohibited from including the land as part of the acquisition by Cheetah Co. It is likely that following acquisition, Cheetah Co will not be able to initiate a sale of the land to an external company or develop or change its current use. This may act as a deal breaker if Cheetah Co is not able to obtain control over the land surrounding the entrance to the production facilities.

If Zebra Co is not permitted to include the land as part of the deal with Cheetah Co, then this may also have an impact on the purchase price as the owners of Zebra Co may have attributed some value to the land in their expectation of the price which they can achieve. If so, it will be important to ascertain the value attributed to the land by the owners to negotiate the reduction of the purchase price.

### Possible limitation on future usage

If the land can be included as part of the acquisition deal, the restrictions may also mean that Cheetah Co is not able to use the land for their intended purpose, such as the future expansion of production facilities, resulting in the acquisition of Zebra Co not being an appropriate strategic fit for Cheetah Co if one of the key aims is future expansion. If this is the case, then this will severely limit the value of the land to the company.

If the land can be acquired but cannot be developed, it is likely that there will be ongoing maintenance costs and potentially other requirements and conditions regarding the upkeep of the nature reserve set out by the local authority, which need to be understood as part of the review. The cost of maintenance may result in a net annual cost to the business and this needs to be quantified as part of the due diligence work.

It will be vital to ascertain what restrictions are in place and whether the directors of Cheetah Co believe they can extract any value from the use of the land.

Based upon this, the directors of Cheetah Co may wish to try and negotiate the purchase of Zebra Co without the associated land or they may wish to negotiate a lower price based on the restricted usage.

**Uncertainty regarding valuation**

It may be difficult to accurately value the piece of land. The value attributed to it in the financial statements is zero, so this may not provide an appropriate basis for estimating the resale value. A land valuation expert may be able to provide an estimation of the current market value of the land without restriction on its use but they may find it difficult to accurately value how much it is worth with the local authority restrictions. It may also be difficult to value the land based on the future cash flows attributable to it if it is not currently in use and its future usage is uncertain.

As a result, the valuation of the land may become a point of significant negotiation between the directors of Cheetah Co and Zebra Co. This may also become a deal breaker if the two parties are unable to reach agreement on the matter.

**(ii)    Procedures**

**Termination of contract**

- Analytically review the total historic value of revenue earned from the customer to help determine an appropriate estimate for the potential loss of future revenues and cash inflows.

- Enquire of management whether the loss of the customer will have any other repercussions, such as the sale of specific assets or the redundancy of staff and the costs associated with this if such action was required.

- Perform an analytical review to identify other major customers by value of revenue contributions to the business. For all major customers identified, review any supply agreements/contracts in place to determine when they expire.

- If any contracts with major customers are due to expire within the next few years, enquire of management whether any discussions have taken place with those customers in relation to renegotiating the terms.

- Obtain any correspondence available with the identified major customers to identify whether there is any indication that they may attempt to either renegotiate the terms of their agreements or switch them to a new supplier.

- Enquire of a relevant manager, such as a production manager or sales manager, whether there is any specific inventory which has been produced in relation to the customer who is not renewing their agreement. If this is the case, obtain a breakdown of the total inventories produced for this client and discuss with management whether they will be able to sell this inventory at full price given the notice to terminate the contract.

- Inspect the forecasts prepared by management to ensure that the changes to the revenue and cost streams identified above have been appropriately incorporated.

### Gifted land

- Review the terms supplied when the land was originally gifted to Zebra Co. Identify the specific restrictions in relation to how the land may be used and who the land may be sold to in the future.

- Enquire of a legal adviser whether this will have any impact in relation to the sale of the land to Cheetah Co and their consequent usage of it.

- Engage a land valuation expert to provide a valuation of the land. Ask them to consider the implications of the restrictions imposed upon the land in the valuation.

- If Zebra Co is not permitted to sell the land, or the restrictions imposed on the usage of the land are too restrictive, seek legal advice in relation to the potential options, including whether the land can be gifted back to the local authority prior to the acquisition.

- Inspect the forecasts prepared by the management of Zebra Co to identify the specific forecast costs and revenues associated with the usage of the land. Prepare a revised version of the forecasts which excludes these revenues and costs to identify the potential implications on the forecasts if the deal is conducted excluding the gifted land.

**(b)** **Ethical and other professional issues**

### Advocacy threat

Accompanying the client to a meeting with their bankers will create an advocacy threat to objectivity as Leopard & Co may be perceived to be representatives of Cheetah Co.

This is particularly relevant as the bank may wish to establish a number of facts relating to the suitability of providing finance to Cheetah Co. For example, they may ask for representations that the company will continue as a going concern and that any forecast cash flows presented are accurate.

As Cheetah Co's auditor, these questions may be directed at the firm's representatives and the bank may take any response provided to their questions as assurance over these matters.

### Management responsibility

Leopard & Co must also be careful that in providing services relating to the potential acquisition of Zebra Co and the associated financing arrangements that the firm is not assuming a management responsibility.

Although the terms of the engagement have not yet been confirmed, it is likely that by attending the meeting with the client, the audit firm will give the impression of supporting the acquisition of Zebra Co and therefore give credit to the decision.

The IESBA *International Code of Ethics for Professional Accountants* (the Code)/FRC Ethical Standard specifically states that the firm shall not assume a management responsibility for an audit client as the threats created would be so significant that no safeguards could reduce the threats to an acceptable level.

### Self-review threat – loan transaction

Providing assistance in finance raising transactions for audit clients also creates a self-review threat to objectivity. A self-review threat arises where the outcome or consequences of a corporate finance service provided by the audit firm may be material to the financial statements under review.

This is a particular problem as the transaction will directly affect the financial statements, which the audit team will be responsible for auditing in consequent financial periods and therefore the audit team is likely to be more accepting of information provided or may not investigate issues as thoroughly, as the team may feel that much of this has been done via the due diligence.

### Self-review threat – interim review

Reviewing the work of the team engaged in the interim financial statements review would also create a self-review threat to objectivity as the audit team would be reviewing the work of another team within the audit firm.

It may be perceived externally that the purpose of reviewing the progress of the interim review is to ensure that any output from this does not impact the attempt by Cheetah Co to secure the loan finance.

### Intimidation threat

The request by Cheetah Co to ensure that the interim review does not impede the application for a loan may be perceived as intimidation by the client. It appears as though they are putting pressure on Leopard & Co to finish the work based on the deadlines imposed by the bank, rather than those originally agreed with the client.

This may force the auditor into changing their approach to any remaining procedures which would be considered to be undue influence of the client over the procedures performed.

This appears to be supported by a further threat relating to the upcoming tender for the audit. The management team of Cheetah Co appears to be suggesting that failing to ensure the interim review is completed on time for the loan decision may have an adverse impact on any consequent tender bid.

### Purpose of meeting

It is not clear why representatives of Leopard & Co have been invited to attend the meeting with the bank. The purpose of both the due diligence service and the interim review is to report to the directors and owners of Cheetah Co, respectively. The firm has no responsibility to report to any third party, including potential lenders.

There may be an expectation for Leopard & Co to provide assurances to the bank in relation to the accuracy of forecasts presented or the financial position of Cheetah Co. If this is the case, it is outside the scope of any of the current engagements and Leopard & Co would not be in a position to provide this assurance.

### Actions

The firm should ascertain the purpose of attending the meeting with the bank; if there is any expectation that it will provide assurances to the bank, then the request should be declined, explaining to Cheetah Co that the firm's responsibilities extend to reporting to the management and the owners of the company and not to any third parties.

If there is no expectation to provide any assurances and the firm is expected to attend the meeting solely in regard to the role of providing due diligence services to Cheetah Co and assisting them in determining a purchase price, then it may be possible for representatives of Leopard & Co to attend.

It must be made clear, however, that no members of the audit team/ interim audit team will be able to attend and the firm will not be permitted to make any representations to the bank. A written representation should be obtained from management clarifying these points.

In order to reduce the risk of Leopard & Co assuming a management responsibility, the representation should also state that Cheetah Co has assigned responsibility for the final decisions relating to the acquisition and financing to a suitably experienced individual within the company.

Further, that Cheetah Co's management will provide oversight of the services performed, will evaluate the adequacy of the outcome of the services for the purposes of Cheetah Co, and accept responsibility for the actions to be taken as a result of the services performed by Leopard & Co.

On balance, Leopard & Co may consider that the threats, both real and perceived, are too great and it would be most prudent not to attend the meeting. If this is the case, Leopard & Co should politely decline the invitation, explaining the reasons why it is inappropriate.

Leopard & Co should communicate with the directors of Cheetah Co explaining that the firm is unable to be involved in the interim review or to review any of the working papers. Leopard & Co should explain the reasons to the client.

The firm should also explain that, if the client has any concerns, they should communicate with the interim review engagement partner to ascertain a reasonable timeframe for conclusion of this engagement.

---

**Examiner's comments**

This question focused on due diligence where a separate team from the firm were working on due diligence at an audit client. Here two issues had been identified and candidates had to explain why they warranted further investigation and what procedures they would perform. Stronger candidates here were able to see the future implication for the valuation of the target company from both the loss of a major customer and a new entrant into the market, and from the ownership of land with restricted use. Candidates should try to remain focused on the future value of the company in such questions and not dwell on the financial reporting aspects. Here there was a piece of land recorded in the accounts at its historical cost of zero as it had been gifted. A significant portion of candidates spent time on this fact and stated that it was in breach of accounting rules not to revalue PPE. This is not the case. A revaluation model may be adopted by companies but is not required. The market value of the land was important in valuing the company but its carrying amount was not for the purposes of this question.

Part (b) of this question addressed ethical issues which would arise if the firm was to attend a meeting with the bank regarding financing for this acquisition and this requirement was well answered with well-prepared candidates being able to recognise advocacy and intimidation threats. Candidates often missed the point that a separate team was already preparing the due diligence, as detailed in the scenario and incorrectly recognised the use of separate teams as a safeguard, which was not relevant. It should be noted that to attract credit for ethical threats candidates should not simply state the name of the threat, they should explain what it means and relate it to the scenario. Simply listing the name of ethical threats does not attract credit. An example of wording required to attract the full credit for advocacy is: 'The client's request for the auditor to attend the meeting with the bank would create an advocacy threat to objectivity, as the auditor would be perceived to be representing the client to the bank, and therefore the bank may take assurance from the auditors' response regarding the suitability of providing finance.'

---

**Marking scheme**

|  |  |  |  | Marks |
|---|---|---|---|---|
| (a) | (i) | **Due diligence investigation** | | |
| | | Up to 1½ marks for each matter discussed. Award ½ mark for identification of a relevant point up to a further 1 mark for appropriate discussion of the relevance of this point to the specific case. | | |
| | | **Termination of contract** | | |
| | | – Impact on forecast revenues, costs and cash flows | | |
| | | – Wider implications of a new, cheaper supplier entering the market | | |
| | | – Potential impairment of assets employed specifically for the client | | |
| | | **Gifted land** | | |
| | | – Possible restriction on sale to Cheetah Co | | |
| | | – Possible restriction on how land is used if purchased | | |
| | | – Uncertainty regarding how to value the land | | |
| | | | Maximum | 7 |
| | (ii) | **Procedures** | | |
| | | Up to 1 mark for each adequately explained procedure. Award ½ mark for relevant procedures which are poorly explained. | | |
| | | – Analytically review historic sales to customer | | |
| | | – Enquire of management about further repercussions | | |
| | | – Analytically review sales by customer to identify other major ones | | |
| | | – Review trade contracts/agreements with other major customers | | |
| | | – Inspect correspondence with major customers | | |
| | | – Identify inventories produced specifically for customer | | |
| | | – Inspect forecasts to ensure adequate adjustment made | | |
| | | – Inspect terms of gifted land | | |
| | | – Enquire of legal adviser re. impact of restrictions | | |
| | | – Seek a valuation from an expert | | |
| | | – Identify potential options for land | | |
| | | – Prepare revised forecast excluding land | | |
| | | | Maximum | 10 |

---

| **(b)** | **Enquiries** | | |
|---|---|---|---|
| | Generally 1 mark per point: | | |
| | – Advocacy threat | | |
| | – Management responsibility | | |
| | – Self-review: loan transaction | | |
| | – Self-review: interim review | | |
| | – Intimidation threat | | |
| | – Purpose/scope of meeting | | |
| | – Ascertain purpose of attending meeting | | |
| | – Obtain written representation | | |
| | – Politely decline to attend | | |
| | – Explain that you are unable to review interim engagement progress | | |
| | | **Maximum** | **8** |
| **Total** | | | **25** |

**39   SANZIO**      *Walk in the footsteps of a top tutor*

*Top tutor tips*

*Part (a) requires an assessment of the suitability of a proposed advertisement. Advertisements must not contain any content which would reflect adversely on the profession or other members. They must not contain misleading information which mispresents the firm or the services the firm offers.*

*Part (b)(i) asks for the purpose of a due diligence assignment. This is the reason for performing a due diligence review i.e. what benefits can be generated for the client. The requirement also asks for a comparison of the scope of a due diligence assignment and an audit. Here you should identify not just the differences but the similarities as well.*

*Part (b)(ii) asks for the information you would require to assist in your valuation of the Titian Tyres' intangible assets, primarily the customer database and the licence. The customer database is an internally generated asset therefore won't be included in the financial statements of Titian Tyres. Remember that the value of an asset is dependent on the expected future cash flows so identify information that would help assess the level of future cash flows that could be generated from the assets.*

*Part (b)(iii) asks for enquiries to be made regarding the contingent liability included in the notes to the financial statements. Here you should be trying to assess the likelihood of payment and the potential amount of the payment.*

**(a)** **Advertisement**

**Accountant charging you too much for poor quality services**

Accountants are permitted to advertise subject to the requirements in the ACCA Code of Ethics and Conduct that the advert should 'not reflect adversely on the professional accountant, ACCA or the accounting profession'. The advert does not appear to be in keeping with this principle as it suggests that other firms of accountants charge inappropriately high fees and that the quality of their services is questionable. This discredits the services offered by other professional accountants as well as implying that the services offered by Raphael & Co are far superior.

**Most comprehensive range of services**

The advert states that the firm offers 'the most comprehensive range of finance and accountancy services in the country'. This is misleading. With 12 offices and only 30 partners, Raphael & Co is unlikely to be one of the largest accountancy firms in the country and is therefore unlikely to offer the most comprehensive range of services. If it is misleading, this statement must be withdrawn from the advertisement.

**Leading tax team**

The advert also implies that they have the country's leading tax team. It is not possible to substantiate this claim as it is not possible to measure the effectiveness of tax teams and even if it were, no such measure currently exists. This is, therefore, also potentially misleading and should be withdrawn from the advert.

**Tax team waiting to save you money**

The suggestion that the tax experts are waiting to save the client money is inappropriate. No such guarantees can be made because tax professionals must apply relevant tax legislation in an objective manner. This may lead to a reduction in a client's current tax expense or it may not. Any failure to apply these regulations appropriately could raise questions about the professional behaviour of the practitioner.

**Guarantee to be cheaper than your existing service provider**

Guaranteeing to be cheaper than other service providers is often referred to as 'lowballing'. This could create a potential self-interest threat to objectivity and it could also threaten professional competence and due care if the practitioner is unable to apply the appropriate professional standards for that level of fee.

[**UK syllabus:** FRC Ethical Standard section 4 states that the audit engagement partner shall be satisfied and able to demonstrate that the audit engagement has assigned to it sufficient partners and staff with appropriate time and skill to perform the audit in accordance with all applicable auditing and ethical standards, irrespective of the audit fee to be charged.]

**Business advice to audit clients**

Offering business advice to audit clients creates a potential self-review threat to objectivity. It depends on the sort of advice offered but it is possible that the auditor in consequent years may have to audit aspects of the business affected by the advice given. This would be particularly relevant if the practitioner provided advice with regard to systems design. It would be possible to offer both services if Raphael & Co can use different teams to provide each service. Given that they have 12 offices, it may be possible to keep these services completely separate and they may be able to offer both.

[**UK syllabus**: According to FRC Ethical Standard section 5, offering a non-audit service such as business advice to audit clients potentially creates self-interest, self-review, management and advocacy threats to objectivity.]

### Free advice

Offering services for free as part of a promotion is not prohibited but, similar to lowballing, this increases the threat to competence and due care if sufficient time and resources are not allocated to the task. This may also devalue the services offered by Raphael & Co as they may be perceived as being a promotional tool as opposed to a professional service.

Firms of accountants are permitted to offer free consultations, so this does not create any specific threats. The phrase 'drop in and see us' may cause a problem with potential clients though as it may not always be possible to expect to see senior staff members without an appointment. To avoid damaging the professional profile of the firm, Raphael & Co would need to make sure they had a dedicated member of staff available to meet potential customers who is available without prior notice.

### Chartered Certified Accountants

Finally, Raphael & Co is not permitted to use the term 'Chartered Certified Accountants' because fewer than 50% of the partners of the firm are ACCA members. This reference should be removed.

**(b) (i) The purpose of due diligence**

**Information gathering**

Due diligence is the process of fact finding to help reduce the risk involved in investment decisions. It is used when gathering information about a target company, for the purpose of ensuring that the acquirer has full knowledge of the operations, financial performance and position, legal and tax situation, as well as the general commercial background of the target. In particular, due diligence helps to uncover potential problems before a decision regarding the acquisition is made.

**Verification of management representations**

During a sale, the vendor may make representations to the potential acquirer which it is essential to verify. As an example, the vendor may state that the company has recently had a health and safety or fire safety investigation or that since their last year end they have replaced ageing property, plant and equipment. Due diligence can be used to substantiate such claims.

**Identification of assets and liabilities**

One of the key reasons for performing due diligence is to identify the assets and liabilities of the target company, which is vital when trying to value the target company. It is particularly important to attempt to identify and value the intangible assets of the target company, including their brands, customer databases and development costs. Internally generated intangibles will not be included on the statement of financial position and are particularly difficult to assess.

The valuation of liabilities is also critical because the acquirer will have to settle these in the future. This must be appropriately planned for and considered during the negotiation of the acquisition price. Contingent liabilities are particularly significant because, by their nature, the amount required to settle them and the likelihood of settlement are uncertain.

**Operational issues**

As well as the risk associated with the valuation of a business, the acquirer must also consider operational implications which could jeopardise a proposed acquisition, such as high staff turnover, the need to renegotiate supplier or customer contracts or contracts with lenders, and future changes in the product mix of the target company. Any of these could lead to operational problems in the future and could be considered potential 'deal breakers' or, at the very least, be used to negotiate the acquisition price.

**Acquisition planning**

Due diligence will also assess the potential commercial benefits and drawbacks of the acquisition. For example, it could be used to calculate the potential economies of scale from aligning the supply chains of the buyer and the target company. On the other hand, there are post-acquisition costs to consider, such as the costs of reorganisation and the potential staff turnover which may be experienced.

**Scope of a due diligence assignment compared to an audit**

With due diligence, the scope is focused primarily on fact finding, which means that the investigation will draw on a much wider range of sources than those connected with the current financial statements. These include:

- Several years' worth of historical financial statements

- Management accounts

- Profit and cash flow forecasts

- Recent business plans and internal strategies/objectives

- Employee contracts, particularly those of management

- All binding contracts, such as supply contracts, lease agreements and loan agreement

- Discussions with management, employees and third parties.

While many of these items may be reviewed during an audit of historical financial statements, it is likely that due diligence will require a much wider range of information.

The objective of an audit is to provide reasonable assurance that the financial statements are free from material misstatement. In contrast, the aim of due diligence is to provide the acquirer with a set of information which has been collated and, most likely, reviewed by the practitioner. Unless requested by the client, the practitioner will not express any conclusion with regard to the accuracy of the information provided. In this case, due diligence is performed as an 'agreed upon procedures' assignment.

If the practitioner is requested to provide assurance regarding the accuracy of the information provided, the due diligence service would be performed as a limited assurance review engagement. This is a lower level of assurance than that provided in an audit due to the reduced procedures performed during due diligence.

The type of work performed during due diligence is quite different to an audit, as a due diligence investigation uses, primarily, analytical procedures and enquiry as a means of gathering information. Very few, if any, substantive procedures are carried out, unless they are specifically requested by the client or there are specific issues which cause concern and therefore need more detailed investigation. This is in contrast to an audit, where a comprehensive range of tests of control and substantive tests are performed.

Due diligence is much more 'forward looking' than an audit. Much of the time during a due diligence investigation will be spent assessing forecasts and predictions. This is in contrast to an audit, where procedures only tend to consider future events if they are directly relevant to the year-end financial statements, for example, contingencies, or going concern problems.

In contrast to an audit, when it is essential to evaluate systems and controls, the due diligence investigation will not conduct detailed testing of the accounting and internal control systems, unless specifically requested to do so.

### (ii) Intangible assets

**Customer database**

- A copy of the financial statements for the year ended 30 June 20X5 to identify the current carrying value of any purchased intangibles relating to the database, such as computer software.

- A copy of the original purchase agreement for the software to identify the age of the software and when any product licences expire.

- A copy of the original purchase/ongoing maintenance contracts for the software to identify the continuing costs of maintaining the system at its current level of efficiency.

- Historic records of sales by customer to verify management's statement that repeat customers make up over 60% of annual sales.

- Copies of a sample of recent automated customer communications traced to customer bookings/sales records to confirm the current efficacy of the system.

- Sales forecasts for the foreseeable future to assess the potential future cash flows attributable to the customer database system to assess its value when determining the potential purchase price.

- Confirmation of the current price of similar database software to assess the market value/fair value of the asset.

**Licence**

- A copy of the original purchase agreement for the licence to confirm the $5 million cost and the exclusivity of the agreement.

- The original purchase agreement can also be used to identify whether any further incremental/contingent considerations or royalties are due in the future.

- A copy of the licence agreement to confirm whether the licence is for a fixed period of time or not and to confirm the exclusivity of the licence.

- A breakdown of the sales figures relating to the new tyres to enable comparison of the performance of the new tyres to existing brands.

- Forecasts showing the expected future sales attributable to the new tyres to confirm the continued inflow of economic benefit from the asset.

**(iii)** **Contingent liabilities**

The following enquiries should be made of the management of Titian Tyres Co:

- Enquire of management and ascertain if any legal advice has been sought to determine who is liable to pay compensation in these cases, Titian Tyres Co or the supplier of the parts.

- Enquire whether or not management has sought any legal advice with regard to the likelihood of having to settle the claims.

- Enquire if management has records showing how many vehicles have been fitted with the faulty parts and whether these have been used in any estimates of the likely settlement costs.

- Discuss with management the level of claims which have been settled since the year end. Compare this with the original estimation to establish how effective management has been in making these estimates.

- Enquire of management for how long the company used the faulty parts and for what portion of this time period the known claims relate to.

- Discuss with management the details of any new claims which have been made since the year end which were not included in any estimations of the cost of settlement included in the contingent liability disclosure in the financial statements.

- Discuss with management their assessment of any risk that further claims will be made of which they are currently unaware.

- Enquire of management if other quality problems have been experienced with other parts from the same supplier.

---

**Examiner's comments**

Part (a) required students to critique the appropriateness of advertising being utilised by the firm. The majority of students were well prepared to answer this question with a format that has been used before, and were able to confidently identify and evaluate the ethical issues associated with the proposed advertisement.

In part (b) candidates were required to provide a description of the purpose of a due diligence assignment and to demonstrate an understanding of the purpose of due diligence by providing a comparison with a statutory audit of financial statements. The majority of candidates attempting this part of the question scored well demonstrating sound knowledge of this area of the syllabus.

---

The remainder of the question focused on the work that may be performed during a due diligence assignment and specifically around the valuation of specific assets and liabilities within a target company. The question here asked for further information that may be required and enquiries that would be made in order to provide assurance on such items. Candidates produced the strongest answers with respect to the valuation of a purchased licence albeit often focusing on initial recording rather than current values/impairment. The valuation of an internally generated database proved harder as many candidates quoted the financial reporting rules and concluded it should not be presented within the financial statements. This was often despite having previously described the purpose of due diligence as a method of identifying assets and liabilities not included in the financial statements which nevertheless would form part of the fair values at acquisition. Candidates would benefit from reviewing the question as a whole in order to consider how the different sections and requirements fit together. More effective planning, prior to writing, would allow candidates to demonstrate a better understanding of these connections.

The final item related to a contingent liability that was presented in the target company's financial statements. Answers to this were of mixed quality but it was disappointing how many candidates again lost sight of the assignment being one of due diligence and made comments regarding the financial statements disclosure requirement. Candidates are reminded that more effective reading and planning would allow a clearer understanding of what is being asked for and that time should be spent ensuring that answers are tailored to the specifics of the question.

| Marking scheme | | | Marks |
|---|---|---|---|
| **(a)** | **Advertisement** | | |
| | Up to 1½ marks for each point of evaluation and up to 1 mark for each response recommended. | | |
| | – Advert reflects adversely on other professional accountants | | |
| | – Misleading with regards to size of firm | | |
| | – Misleading comments regarding expertise of tax team | | |
| | – Threat to professional behaviour by guaranteeing to save tax | | |
| | – Lowballing – self-interest threat and threat to professional competence and due care | | |
| | – Potential self-review threat from business advice | | |
| | – Free consultations permitted | | |
| | – Remove misleading claims from advert | | |
| | – Separate teams for audit and other services advertised | | |
| | | Maximum | 7 |
| **(b)** | **(i)** | **Purpose and scope of due diligence** | |
| | | Generally up to 1 mark for each description of the purpose of due diligence and up to 1 mark for each point of comparison with an audit. | |
| | | **Purpose:** | |
| | | – Gathering information to reduce risk of investment decisions | |
| | | – Verification on management representations | |
| | | – Identification and valuation of assets and liabilities | |
| | | – Identification of operational concerns and synergies | |
| | | – Assistance with acquisition planning | |
| | | **Scope:** | |
| | | – Range of sources used | |
| | | – Level of assurance/type of engagement | |
| | | – Types of procedure performed | |
| | | – Forward looking v mainly historical | |
| | | – No controls testing | |
| | | Maximum | 6 |

| | | | |
|---|---|---|---|
| (ii) | **Additional Information** | | |
| | Up to 1 mark for each piece of information recommended and adequately explained. | | |
| | – Database: | | |
| | – 30 June 20X5 financial statements (carrying value) | | |
| | – Original software purchase agreement | | |
| | – Software maintenance contract | | |
| | – Historic records of sales by customer | | |
| | – Sample customer communications | | |
| | – Sales forecasts | | |
| | **Licence:** | | |
| | – Original purchase agreement (cost) | | |
| | – Original purchase agreement (incremental/contingent consideration) | | |
| | – Licence terms and conditions | | |
| | – Sales figures for new brand | | |
| | – Forecast sales for new brand | | |
| | | Maximum | 7 |
| (iii) | **Enquiries** | | |
| | Up to 1 mark for enquiry recommended and adequately explained. | | |
| | – Legal advice regarding who bears the liability | | |
| | – Legal advice regarding likelihood of settlement | | |
| | – Basis of estimation of liability | | |
| | – Settlement of claims since year end | | |
| | – How long faulty parts used for | | |
| | – New claims since year end | | |
| | – Risk of further claims | | |
| | – Quality problems with other parts | | |
| | | Maximum | 5 |
| **Total** | | | **25** |

## 40 BALTIMORE  *Walk in the footsteps of a top tutor*

*Top tutor tips*

*Part (a) requires discussion of the benefits of a due diligence review being performed prior to the acquisition of a company. There were indications in the scenario that the client did not have the skill to do this and you are expected to identify these points and use them in your answer.*

*Part (b) asked for matters to focus on during the due diligence review. A due diligence review is performed to find information relevant to the client's decision regarding the acquisition. Therefore you should identify the matters that might deter them from going ahead with the acquisition or might encourage them to go ahead with the acquisition.*

*Part (c) is a straightforward requirement asking for the type of conclusion, i.e. level of assurance, to be issued on the due diligence review and to compare this to an audit.*

(a)    **Three benefits of due diligence to Baltimore Co**

**Identification of assets and liabilities**

One of the objectives of a due diligence review is for the assets and liabilities of the target company to be identified and valued. Therefore a benefit of due diligence to Baltimore Co is to gain an understanding of the nature of assets and liabilities which are being acquired, as not all assets and liabilities of Mizzen Co are recognised in its financial statements. For example, Mizzen Co has built up several customer databases, which, being internally generated, will not be recognised as assets in its statement of financial position, but these could be valuable assets to Baltimore Co.

**Identification of operational issues**

The due diligence review should uncover more information about operational issues, which may then help Baltimore Co's management to decide whether to go ahead with the acquisition. For example, only one of Mizzen Co's revenue streams appears to be directly relevant to Baltimore Co's expansion plans, so more information is needed about the other operations of Mizzen Co to determine how they may be of benefit to Baltimore Co. The due diligence review should cover a wide range of issues, such as reviews of the company's legal and tax positions, which may uncover significant matters.

**Expertise**

An externally provided due diligence review, as opposed to a review conducted by management of Baltimore Co, is likely to provide information in a time-efficient, impartial manner. Baltimore Co's management has not previously dealt with an acquisition, whereas the audit firm has the financial and business understanding and expertise to provide a quality due diligence review. A review report issued by Goleen & Co will add credibility to the planned acquisition, which may help secure the bank loan which is needed to fund the acquisition.

*Tutorial note*

*Credit will be awarded for other relevant benefits which are discussed.*

(b)    **Matters to focus on in the due diligence review**

**Equity owners of Mizzen Co and involvement of BizGrow**

The nature of the involvement of the venture capitalist company, BizGrow, is a crucial issue which must be the starting point of the due diligence review. Venture capitalists provide equity when a company is incorporated, and typically look for an exit route within three to seven years. Mizzen Co was incorporated four years ago, so it will be important to determine whether BizGrow retains its original equity holding in Mizzen Co, and if so, whether the acquisition of BizGrow's shares by Baltimore Co would be compatible with the planned exit route.

**Key skills and expertise**

It appears that the original founders of Mizzen Co, Vic Sandhu and Lou Lien, are crucial to the success of Mizzen Co and it would be in Baltimore Co's interests to keep them involved with the business. However, Vic and Lou may wish to focus on further work involving IT innovation rather than Baltimore Co's planned website and without Vic and Lou's expertise the acquisition may be much less worthwhile. However, there could be other employed personnel with the necessary skills and experience to meet Baltimore Co's needs, or much of the skill and expertise could be provided from freelancers, who will not be part of the acquisition.

**Internally generated intangible assets**

Mizzen Co is likely to have several important internally generated intangible assets, which will not be recognised in its individual accounts but must be identified and measured as part of the due diligence review. First, Vic and Lou have innovated and developed new website interfaces, and the review must determine the nature of this intellectual property (IP), and whether it belongs to Vic and Lou or to Mizzen Co. The measurement of this asset will be very difficult, and it is likely to form an important part of the acquisition deal if Baltimore Co want to acquire the IP to use in its new website.

There are also several customer databases which need to be measured and included in the list of assets acquired, which again may be difficult to measure in value. It is important for the due diligence review to confirm the relevance of the databases to Baltimore Co's operations, and that the databases contain up-to-date information.

**Premises**

Mizzen Co currently operates from premises owned by BizGrow and pays a nominal rent for this. Presumably if the acquisition were to go ahead, this arrangement would cease. The due diligence review should consider the need for new premises to be found for Mizzen Co and the associated costs. Possibly there is room for Mizzen Co to operate from Baltimore Co's premises as the operations do not appear to need a large space. The rental agreement may be fixed for a period of time and cancellation may incur a penalty.

**Other tangible assets**

Mizzen Co appears to own only items such as computer equipment and fixtures and fittings. It needs to be clarified whether these assets are owned or held under lease, and also whether any other tangible assets, such as vehicles, are used in the business. Any commitments for future purchases of tangible assets should be reviewed.

**Accounting policy on revenue recognition**

Mizzen Co has some fairly complex revenue streams, and the due diligence review should establish that the accounting policies in place are reasonable and in line with IFRS 15 *Revenue from Contracts with Customers*. The revenue generated from website development and maintenance should be split into two components, with the revenue for website development recognised once the website has been provided to the customer, but the revenue for maintenance spread over the contract period. There is a risk that revenue is recognised too early, inflating Mizzen Co's profit.

The revenue recognition policy for annual subscriptions should also be scrutinised, with revenue relating to future periods being deferred.

### Sustainability and relevance of revenue streams

The financial statements indicate that revenue has increased each year, and that in the last year it has increased by 23.7%. This is an impressive growth rate and work must be done to analyse the likelihood of revenue streams being maintained and further growth being achieved. For example, the proportion of website development and two year maintenance contracts which are renewed should be investigated. Not all of Mizzen Co's revenue streams seem very relevant to Baltimore Co's operations, so how these may be managed post-acquisition should be considered.

### Operating expenses

The financial extracts indicate a potentially unusual trend in relation to operating expenses. In 20X1 and 20X2, operating expenses represented 60% and 58.3% of revenue respectively. In 20X3, this had reduced to 49.6%. This may be due to economies of scale being achieved as the company grows, or possibly expenses are understated or revenue overstated in 20X3. As freelance web designers have been used in 20X3, operating expenses may have been expected to increase in proportion to revenue. The due diligence review should perform detailed analysis on the operating costs incurred by the company to gain assurance that expenses are complete and accurately recorded.

With the exception of 20X0, the finance cost has remained static at $250,000 per annum. The due diligence review must uncover what this finance cost relates to, and whether it will continue post-acquisition. It may be a bank loan or it could be a payment made to BizGrow, as venture capitalist companies often impose a management charge on companies which they have invested in. Baltimore Co will need to understand the nature of any liability in relation to this finance charge.

### Cash position and cash management

Mizzen Co's cash position should be confirmed. Given that the company appears to have limited need for capital expenditure and working capital, and given the level of profits which has been made in the last three years, it could be expected that the company would be cash-rich. The due diligence review should confirm how the cash generated by the company since incorporation has been used, for example, in dividend payments to BizGrow and to Vic and Lou.

### Additional information required

- Contract or legal documentation describing the nature of the investment which BizGrow made when Mizzen Co was incorporated, and detailing the planned exit route.

- A register of shareholders showing all shareholders of Mizzen Co.

- An organisational structure, in order to identify the members of management and key personnel and their roles within Mizzen Co.

- A list of employees and their roles within the company, and their related obligations including salary, holiday entitlements, retirement plans, health insurance and other benefits provided by Mizzen Co, and details of compensation to be paid in the case of redundancy.

- A list of freelance web designers used by Mizzen Co, and a description of the work they perform.

- The key terms of contracts or agreements with freelance web designers.

- A list of all IT innovations which have been created and developed by Mizzen Co, and details of any patent or copyright agreements relating to them.

- Agreements with employees regarding assignment of intellectual property and confidentiality.

- Copies of the customer databases showing contact details of all people or companies included on the list.

- A list of companies which have contracts with Mizzen Co for website development and maintenance.

- A copy of all contracts with customers for review of the period for which maintenance is to be provided.

- A breakdown of the revenue which has been generated from making each database available to other companies, and the dates when they were made available.

- A summary of the controls which are in place to ensure that the database details are regularly updated.

- A copy of the rental agreement with BizGrow, to determine whether any penalty is payable on cancellation.

- Non-current asset register showing descriptions and values of all assets used in the business.

- Copies of any lease agreements, for example, leases of computer equipment, photocopiers, etc.

- Details of any capital expenditure budgets for previous accounting periods, and any planned capital expenditure in the future.

- Mizzen Co's stated accounting policy on revenue recognition.

- Systems and controls documentation over the processing of revenue receipts.

- An analysis of expenses included in operating expenses for each year and copies of documentation relating to ongoing expenses, such as salaries and other overheads.

- Copies of management accounts to agree expenses in the audited accounts are in line and to perform more detailed analytical review.

- The full set of financial statements and auditor's reports for each year since the company's incorporation, to:

  - Confirm the assets and liabilities recognised

  - Agree the level of dividends paid each year

  - Review all of the accounting policies used in preparing the financial statements

  - Find the details of any related party transactions that have occurred

  - Review the statement of cash flows for each year.

- Any agreements with banks or other external providers of finance, including finance advanced and relevant finance charges, or confirmation that no such finance has been provided to Mizzen Co.

**Tutorial note**

*Credit will be awarded for other relevant information which would be required as part of the due diligence review.*

**(c)    Due diligence conclusion**

Due diligence is a specific example of a direct reporting assurance engagement. The form of the report issued in this type of engagement is covered by ISAE 3000 *Assurance Engagements other than Audits or Reviews of Historical Financial Information*, and ISRE 2400 *Engagements to Review Historical Financial Statements* also contains relevant guidance.

The main difference between a review report and an auditor's report is the level of assurance that is given. In a review report a conclusion is expressed in a negative form. The conclusion would start with the wording 'based on our review, nothing has come to our attention...'

This type of conclusion is used because the nature of a due diligence review is that only limited assurance has been obtained over the subject matter. The procedures used in a review engagement are mainly enquiry and analytical review which can only provide limited assurance.

**Tutorial note**

*Credit is equally awarded where answers discuss the due diligence assignment as being based on agreed upon procedures, in which case no assurance is provided.*

In comparison, in an audit of historical information, the auditor will use a wide variety of procedures to obtain evidence to give reasonable assurance that the financial statements are free from material misstatement. This means that an opinion expressed in a positive form can be given.

**Examiner's comments**

This question focused on due diligence, a topic that has appeared several times previous to this sitting. The scenario described a due diligence assignment to be performed on the target company Mizzen Co, at the request of Baltimore Co. The history and activities of the target company was described in some detail, and some financial information provided for the last four years. For Baltimore Co this would be their first acquisition, and was being considered as a means to diversify the company's operations.

Requirement (a) asked candidates to discuss the benefits to Baltimore Co of a due diligence review being performed on Mizzen Co. While some reasonable answers were given, possibly by candidates who had practiced the past exam question containing a similar requirement, on the whole answers were unsatisfactory. The following factors contributed to inadequate performance in relation to this requirement.

- Writing answers that were much too brief for the marks available – it was common to see three sentences given as an answer to this requirement, which cannot be enough for a 6 mark requirement.

- At the other extreme, some very lengthy answers were given that usually failed to answer the question requirement and instead either simply wrote in detail on how a due diligence assignment should be performed, or suggested in some detail the operational benefits to Baltimore Co of acquiring Mizzen Co.

Requirement (b) was the main part of the question, and asked candidates to identify and explain the matters that the due diligence review would focus on, and to recommend the additional information needed. The answers provided to this requirement were extremely mixed in quality. There were some exceptionally sound answers, explaining relevant matters in sufficient depth, and using the financial information provided to come up with reasonable points. These answers also provided relevant requests for additional information. However, the majority of answers were unsatisfactory. Most candidates picked up at least a few marks by identifying some of the matters that the review would focus on, but many candidates let themselves down by failing to explain the matters that they had identified in any real depth. It was common for answers to simply contain a list of bullet points with very little explanation at all, and only a limited amount of marks can be awarded to answers of this type.

Some points were better dealt with, including the following:

- Most answers picked up on the fact that Mizzen Co used premises owned by the venture capitalist company, and the fact that this arrangement would probably cease on the acquisition.

- Many candidates realised that the two founders of Mizzen Co were crucial to the company's success and that without them the acquisition would probably be pointless.

- Many candidates used the financial information to some extent, though sometimes only in a very limited way, but most picked up on the fact that Mizzen Co was paying finance charges, and so information would be needed to understand what those charges relate to.

- Many answers considered that revenue recognition would be a matter to focus on due to the relatively complex nature of the company's revenue streams.

- Some answers performed a little analytical review on the financial information to reveal that expenses were not increasing in line with revenue, and that this would need to be investigated.

The answers that were unsatisfactory, as well as containing inadequately explained points as mentioned above, also tended to focus too much on financial reporting matters, for example giving very lengthy discussions on the calculation of goodwill. While the accounting treatment of some items certainly was relevant to the answer, just focusing on these matters meant that candidates did not provide a broad enough range of comments to score well. Another factor leading to poor marks for this requirement was that many candidates simply failed to recommend any additional information at all that would be needed in the review. Many candidates missed out on marks here, for example for recommending that a statement of financial position, management accounts and cash flow forecasts would be needed. Some candidates supplied a lengthy discussion of matters relating to the acceptance of the due diligence assignment, such as agreeing fees and clarifying deadlines, which was not asked for.

Requirement (c) required candidates to describe the type of conclusion that would be issued for a due diligence report and to compare this to an auditor's report. This was well answered by most candidates, who compared the type of assurance that could be offered for a due diligence assignment with that given in an auditor's report, and linked this to the type of work that is carried out. Credit was awarded for different types of answers, as some discussed due diligence as being performed as agreed upon procedures rather than a review engagement, either of which is appropriate.

| Marking scheme | | Marks |
|---|---|---|
| **(a)** **Benefit of due diligence** | | |
| Up to 2 marks for each benefit discussed | | |
| – Identification of assets and liabilities | | |
| – Valuation of assets and liabilities | | |
| – Review of operational issues | | |
| – Examination of financial position and performance | | |
| – Added credibility and expertise | | |
| – Added value for negotiation of purchase price | | |
| – Other advice can be given, e.g. on obtaining finance | | |
| | Maximum | 6 |
| **(b)** **Areas to focus on and additional information** | | |
| Generally up to 1½ marks for each explanation of area to focus on: | | |
| – Equity owners of Mizzen Co and involvement of BizGrow | | |
| – Key skills and expertise | | |
| – Internally generated intangible assets | | |
| – Premises | | |
| – Other intangible assets | | |
| – Accounting policy on revenue recognition | | |
| – Sustainability and relevance of revenue streams | | |
| – Operating expenses | | |
| – Finance charges | | |
| – Cash management | | |
| 1 mark for each specific additional information recommended: | | |
| – Contract or legal documentation dealing with BizGrow's investment | | |
| – A register of shareholders showing all shareholders of Mizzen Co | | |
| – An organisational structure | | |
| – A list of employees and their role within the company, obligations and compensation | | |
| – A list of freelance web designers used by Mizzen Co, and a description of the work they perform | | |
| – The key terms of contracts or agreements with freelance web designers | | |
| – A list of all IT innovations which have been created and developed by Mizzen Co, and details of any patent or copyright agreements relating to them | | |
| – Agreements with employees regarding IP and confidentiality | | |
| – Copies of the customer databases | | |
| – A list of companies which have contracts with Mizzen Co for website development and maintenance | | |
| – A copy of all maintenance contracts with customers | | |
| – A breakdown of the revenue that has been generated from making each database available to other companies, and the dates when they were made available | | |
| – A summary of the controls which are in place to ensure that the database details are regularly updated | | |
| – A copy of the premises rental agreement with BizGrow | | |
| – Non-current asset register | | |

|  |  |  |
| --- | --- | --- |
| – Copies of any lease agreements | | |
| – Details of any capital expenditure budgets for previous accounting periods, and any planned capital expenditure in the future | | |
| – Mizzen Co's stated accounting policy on revenue recognition | | |
| – Systems and controls documentation over the processing of revenue receipts | | |
| – Analysis of expenses included in operating expenses for each year | | |
| – Copies of management accounts | | |
| – The full set of financial statements and auditor's reports | | |
| – Any agreements with banks or other external providers of finance | | |
| | Maximum | 16 |

(c) **Conclusion on due diligence**

Generally 1 mark for each discussion point:

|  |  |  |
| --- | --- | --- |
| – Due diligence report to express conclusion of negative assurance | | |
| – Limited assurance due to nature of work performed | | |
| – Audit opinion is a positive opinion of reasonable assurance | | |
| | Maximum | 3 |
| **Total** | | **25** |

## 41 JACOB  *Walk in the footsteps of a top tutor*

*Top tutor tips*

*Part (a) asks for benefits of externally provided due diligence prior to the acquisition of a company. Try and think of reasons why the client might not be able to do the due diligence for themselves.*

*Part (b) requires the information you would require for your due diligence review. Think about the information that would help you identify whether there are any financial, operational, tax or legal issues with the company being acquired. Is there anything happening that would deter the client from purchasing the company? Is there anything that would impact the price that they would be prepared to pay for the company?*

*Part (c) covers the ethical issues arising from a conflict of interest. Explain the ethical issues and actions the firm should take to manage the conflict effectively.*

(a) **Benefits of a due diligence review**

**Identification of assets and liabilities**

One benefit is that by conducting a due diligence review, the assets and liabilities of Locke Co can be identified and a potential value placed on them. Without a due diligence review it will be difficult for management to negotiate a fair price for Locke Co, as the price paid should include consideration of assets and liabilities not necessarily shown in the accounts, for example, any contingent liabilities which may exist in connection with warranties provided to customers of Locke Co.

### Gather information on the court case

Locke Co is currently involved in a court case which is attracting media attention. This negative publicity may affect Locke Co's reputation and could have an impact on future revenues which will in turn affect the value of the company. In addition, any liabilities arising as a result of the court case will further impact the value of the company and the price that Jacob Co may be willing to pay. The due diligence review will look at the latest information available on the case which may help Jacob Co decide whether or not they want to take the risk of purchasing a company which is experiencing such problems.

### Identification of operational issues

The due diligence review should uncover more information about operational issues, which may then help Jacob Co's directors in deciding whether to go ahead with the acquisition. For example, Locke Co may need to relocate its head office, as it is currently located on the owners' family estate. If this is the case, significant expense could be involved in building or purchasing new premises, or the head office function could be merged with that of Jacob Co. Either way, it is a practical operational issue that will need to be planned for, if the acquisition were to go ahead.

### Expertise

Another benefit is that an externally provided due diligence review, as opposed to a review conducted by management of Jacob Co, is likely to provide information in a time-efficient, impartial manner. The audit firm has the financial and business understanding and expertise to provide a quality due diligence review. The management of Jacob Co can focus their attention on operational issues, for example, considering how best to merge the acquired business into existing operations, leaving the detailed due diligence review to be performed by independent experts.

### Enhanced credibility

It is not stated how Jacob Co intend to finance the acquisition. If finance is to be obtained externally from a bank or other investor the external due diligence review may provide more assurance than due diligence performed by management who are pursuing the acquisition. Externally provided due diligence will be more objective. The providers of finance may have greater confidence that the investment will be less risky and therefore be more likely to lend money to finance the acquisition.

### Liquidity of Locke Co

Locke Co has a significant bank loan and relies on an overdraft for cash flow in winter months. The due diligence review will assess the terms and conditions of these arrangements and assess the potential impact on the future liquidity profile of Lock Co. If Locke Co is unlikely to be able to sustain itself financially Jacob Co may need to inject cash to keep it going. This will make the investment a less attractive proposition and may be a deciding factor in whether to go ahead with the purchase.

**(b)    Further information to be requested**

**Directors, and any other key management personnel's contracts of employment –** these will be needed to see if there are any contractual settlement terms if the contract of employment is terminated after the acquisition. The family members who founded the company may be looking for an exit route and may not wish to be involved with the company after acquisition, so sizeable amounts could be payable to them on termination of their contracts.

**An organisational structure** should be obtained, in order to identify the members of management and key personnel and their roles within Locke Co. After acquisition, Jacob Co may wish to retain the services of some members of key management, while others may be made redundant as activities with Jacob Co are streamlined.

**Details of any legal arrangement**, such as a lease, covering the use of the family owned property by the company. Jacob Co's management may wish to relocate and/or merge Locke Co's head office function. If there is a formal lease arrangement currently in place, there could be early termination penalties to be paid on early termination of the lease.

**Purchase documentation regarding the land obtained for the purpose of building a new head office**. This will provide information on the location and size of the land. Jacob Co may wish to consider an alternative use for this land, or its sale, or possibly not including the land in the acquisition deal, if it does not wish to go ahead with the construction of the new premises. A copy of planning permission, if any has been sought, regarding the planned construction of a new head office should also be obtained.

**Prior-year audited financial statements, and management accounts for this financial year** – this information can be used to verify the assertion that Locke Co has enjoyed rapid growth. The financial statements will also provide useful information regarding contingent liabilities, the liquidity position of the company, accounting policies, and the value of assets. Further information should be sought regarding the market value of assets if the financial statements have been prepared using the historical cost convention.

**The most recent management accounts** for the current year should be analysed. They will reveal any significant change in the company's position or performance since the last audited accounts, for example, if revenue has decreased significantly, or further finance taken out.

**Forecasts and budgets for future periods** will enable an analysis of the future prospects of the company. Attention should be paid to the cash flow forecast in particular, given that the company has seasonal cash inflows, and uses an overdraft for several months of the year. Expansion in the past should not lead to an assumption that expansion will continue, and the assumptions underpinning the forecasts and budgets should be carefully considered for validity.

**The signed loan agreement** should be reviewed. Jacob Co will need to know the exact amount and terms of the loan, including the interest rate, any other finance charges, whether the loan is secured on company assets, the repayment terms, and any covenants attached to the loan. The amount is described as significant, and Jacob Co should be wary of taking on this amount of debt without a clear understanding of its associated risk exposure.

**Details should also be obtained regarding the overdraft facility**, such as the maximum facility that is extended to the company, the interest rate, when the facility is due for renewal or review, and how many months on average the facility is used in a financial year. If the acquisition were to go ahead, Locke Co could prove to be a cash drain on the group. Jacob Co may plan to alleviate this by an inter-company loan of cash during the winter months, but the seasonality of the cash flows must be clearly understood before an acquisition decision is made.

**Legal correspondence pertaining to the court case** should be obtained. This should show the amount of damages claimed against the company, and the timescale as to when the case should go to court. The correspondence should also show the amount of legal fees incurred so far, and give an indication as to the future amount of fees likely to be paid. A review of the board minutes of Locke Co may indicate the likelihood of the court case going against the company. Jacob Co will need a detailed understanding of the financial consequences of this legal matter if they are to acquire the company.

**Information should also be sought regarding the bad publicity caused by the court case**. A copy of any press statements made by company representatives would be useful background information.

It is stated that Locke Co enjoys a 'good reputation'. Information to substantiate this claim should be sought, such as the results of customer satisfaction surveys, or data showing the level of repeat customers. Any exaggeration of the claim regarding the company's reputation could mean that Jacob Co can negotiate a lower purchase price, and will need to consider the impact of Locke Co's reputation on its own operations.

**Details of warranties offered to customers** should be obtained, including the length of period covered by the warranty, and any limits on the amount that can be claimed under warranty, to consider the level of contingent liability they may represent. If significant potential warranty claims exist, this should be reflected in the price offered to acquire Locke Co.

**The contract between Locke Co and Austin Co** should be obtained and scrutinised. It is essential to understand exactly what services are performed by the service organisation – which could include bookkeeping, payroll, preparation of management accounts and dealing with tax issues. The cost of the outsourcing should also be considered, as well as the reputation of Austin Co. These are important considerations, as Jacob Co may wish to bring the accounting function back in-house, most likely to streamline Locke Co's accounting systems with that of Jacob Co.

(c)     **Conflict of interest**

A potential conflict between the interest of two audit clients arises from our firm offering advice to Jacob Co on the tender being presented to Burke Co. A conflict of interest may create potential threats to objectivity, confidentiality or other threats to compliance with the fundamental ethical principles.

The firm faces the problem of potentially giving advice to one audit client in relation to another audit client, which threatens objectivity. There may also be problems to do with confidentiality of information, as either party could benefit from information obtained from the audit firm about the other party.

In dealing with conflicts of interest, the significance of any threats should be evaluated, and safeguards must be applied when necessary to eliminate the threats or reduce them to an acceptable level. The most important safeguard is disclosure by the audit firm. The audit firm should notify both Jacob Co and Burke Co of the potential conflict of interest and obtain their consent to act.

Other possible safeguards could include:

*   The use of separate engagement teams.

*   Procedures to prevent access to information (for example, strict physical separation of such teams, confidential and secure data filing).

- Clear guidelines for members of the engagement team on issues of security and confidentiality.

- The use of confidentiality agreements signed by employees and partners of the firm.

- Regular review of the application of safeguards by a senior individual not involved with relevant client engagements.

The firm may decide, having evaluated the threats and available safeguards, that the threats cannot be reduced to an acceptable level, in which case the firm should decline from giving advice to Jacob Co regarding the tender.

---

**Examiner's comments**

This question focused on due diligence. The scenario described a potential acquisition being planned by an audit client of your firm.

Requirement (a) required an explanation of the benefits of an externally provided due diligence review to the audit client. This was reasonably well answered, though many answers were not made very specific to the scenario and tended to discuss the benefits of any due diligence review rather than an externally provided one.

Requirement (b) asked for additional information to be made available for the firm's due diligence review. Answers were satisfactory, and the majority of candidates did not struggle to apply their knowledge to the scenario, usually providing some focused answers dealing well with the specifics of the question scenario. Most answers seemed to use a logical approach – working through the information provided to generate answer points, and this meant that on the whole most of the key issues from the scenario were covered in the answer. A small proportion of answers also included irrelevant discussions of the type of report that would be provided to the client, or a discussion of ethical issues which were not asked for.

Requirement (c) was about a potential conflict of interest between two audit clients and confidentiality of information. The audit firm had been asked to provide advice on a tender for an important contract that one audit client was preparing in relation to a different audit client. Many candidates did correctly determine that a conflict of interest would arise and could recommend appropriate safeguards. However, many answers failed to identify the potential issues surrounding the confidentiality of client information. Some candidates tried to include a comment on every one of the ethical principles – many of which were irrelevant. It is a better exam technique to focus on the most relevant of the ethical threats, and not to try to cover all of them.

---

| | **Marking scheme** | |
|---|---|---|
| | | *Marks* |
| **(a)** | **Benefits of due diligence** | |
| | Up to 2 marks for each benefit explained | |
| | • Identify and value assets and liabilities to be acquired | |
| | • Assessment of potential impact of court case | |
| | • Identify and allow planning for operational issues | |
| | • Provision by external experts – technically competent and time efficient | |
| | • Enhanced credibility provided by an independent review | |
| | • Evaluation of the liquidity position of Locke Co | |
| | **Maximum** | **6** |
| **(b)** | **Information required** | |
| | Generally ½ mark for identification and up to 1 further mark for explanation (maximum 3 marks for identification): | |
| | • Service contracts of directors | |
| | • Organisational structure | |
| | • Lease/arrangement regarding head office | |
| | • Details of land purchased | |
| | • Planning permission for new head office | |
| | • Prior year accounts and management accounts | |
| | • Forecasts and budgets | |
| | • Loan agreement | |
| | • Overdraft facility details | |
| | • Legal correspondence | |
| | • Customer satisfaction surveys | |
| | • Details of warranty agreements | |
| | • Outsourcing agreement | |
| | **Maximum** | **14** |
| **(c)** | **Conflict of interest** | |
| | • Identify/explain the conflict of interest | |
| | • Threats to objectivity and confidentiality created | |
| | • Safeguard of disclosure to both parties | |
| | • Other safeguards (½ mark each), e.g. | |
| |    – separate teams | |
| |    – confidentiality agreements | |
| |    – review of situation by independent partner | |
| | • If threats too significant the advice should not be given | |
| | **Maximum** | **5** |
| **Total** | | **25** |

**42   MOOSEWOOD HOSPITAL**  *Walk in the footsteps of a top tutor*

> *Top tutor tips*
>
> *This question covers performance information. In the context of the question produced in this exam kit, the performance information forms part of the integrated report of a private hospital i.e. a company. In the context of an INT variant exam, the hospital in the scenario is likely to be a public sector organisation. You would attempt the question in the same way, irrespective of whether the hospital is private or a public sector organisation.*
>
> *Part (a) deals with ethical and professional issues arising from the client being in breach of laws and regulations. Draw on your knowledge of the relevant auditing standard and explain the auditor's responsibilities when such issues arise.*
>
> *Part (b)(i) requires benefits of an assurance report on KPIs being included in the integrated report. Think of the benefits of assurance and apply them to the scenario.*
>
> *Part (b)(ii) requires procedures to be performed in relation to the KPIs given in the scenario. Think of the documentation that would be produced and kept by the hospital that would help you verify the KPIs. Where you need a better understanding of the KPI an enquiry might be needed to obtain that understanding.*

**(a)   Ethical and professional issues**

**Compliance with laws and regulations**

It appears that Moosewood Hospital Co is storing and possibly using medicines which have passed their recommended use by date. This may be illegal, it may breach the terms of agreement with their suppliers and, most significantly, this may lead to patient harm or ineffective treatment.

ISA 250 *Consideration of Law and Regulations in an Audit of Financial Statements* requires that in the event of a suspected non-compliance with law and regulations, the auditor should document the findings and discuss them with management.

The audit team should attempt to obtain more information about the suspected non-compliance, though this will be difficult given the actions of the financial controller, who is denying access to the relevant source of information and the attempt to intimidate the audit team by the finance director.

The audit team should seek appropriate legal advice in relation to the use of out of date medicines. If this is a breach of regulations, then the auditor may have a statutory or public duty to report this incident to the relevant regulator, such as the UK's General Medical Council.

**Reporting non-compliance to those charged with governance**

If Fern & Co believes that non-compliance with relevant law and regulation is taking place, then according to ISA 250, the matter should be reported to those charged with governance of Moosewood Hospital Co. This communication should happen without delay given that it appears to be deliberate and owing to the potential seriousness of the use of expired medical inventory.

At present it is unclear whether those charged with governance are aware of these practices. The auditor should request that those charged with governance make any necessary disclosure to the relevant authorities, clearly state the reasons why Moosewood Hospital Co should make the disclosure and that if the board fails to comply, that Fern & Co will be compelled to make the disclosure themselves.

If the auditor suspects that members of senior management including the board of directors are involved with the non-compliance, then the auditor should report the matter to the next higher level of authority, such as the audit committee.

### Confidentiality

Reporting the incident to a regulator would require the auditor to report information about a client to a third party, which is a breach of client confidentiality. In these circumstances, however, legal and regulatory responsibilities, as well as acting in the public interest would be considered to outweigh the confidentiality requirement.

Fern & Co should seek legal advice before they act to minimise the risk of legal dispute with their client or legal action from the regulator due to inaction.

### Impact on the financial statements

It is not correct for management to assert that the issue with out of date inventory is not relevant to the audit, because if any of the inventory is obsolete, then it should be written off in the financial statements.

By restricting the audit team's ability to audit inventory, management has imposed a limitation on the scope of the audit. If the auditor is unable to obtain satisfactory evidence relating to inventories, then this may lead to a modification of the auditor's report.

Fern & Co should report this matter to those charged with governance and request that they provide access to the necessary evidence. They should also explain what repercussions this will have on the auditor's report if they fail to comply.

If Moosewood Hospital Co has failed to comply with any legal, regulatory or contractual requirements, they may incur fines or other financial penalties. The audit approach should now be modified to include additional procedures aimed at investigating the potential implications of the use of out of date medicines and the potential value of fines and penalties.

### Intimidation threat

The aggressive actions of the finance director amount to an intimidation threat to objectivity. The finance director has tried to influence the conduct of the audit with threatening behaviour.

Fern & Co should inform those charged with governance, explaining the significance of the matter and that it cannot be tolerated. Fern & Co should explain the reasons for the enquiries made by the audit team and the significance of being allowed to complete these procedures.

**Management integrity**

While the intentions of management are not clear, it does appear that they are trying to conceal a matter of some significance from the auditor.

The audit team must increase their scepticism of all evidence provided by management, particularly written representations obtained from management as they may be subject to bias and evidence which they could potentially manipulate, such as internal spreadsheets. In particular, if the audit team is given access to the inventory valuation spreadsheet, they must remain vigilant for any indication that this has been subsequently altered.

**Withdrawal from engagement**

If the audit team believes that management is complicit in any significant illegal activity and/or attempt to manipulate the financial statements, they may reconsider their position as auditor. Fern & Co may wish to resign from the audit engagement to protect their reputation and to protect them from being implicated in any ensuing legal case.

Before taking any action, the matter should be discussed by the senior partners of the audit firm and an appropriate legal adviser.

**(b)   (i)   Benefits of independent assurance**

Obtaining an independent assurance report on the integrated report, and specifically on the key performance indicators (KPIs) contained within the report, is a way to enhance the credibility of the integrated report. Information provided by an organisation without any external assurance being obtained may not be perceived as trustworthy or accurate.

The integrated report is outside the scope of the audit, other than being read as part of 'other information' if it is published alongside the audited financial statements, which is not the case for Moosehead Hospital Co, and therefore without any assurance report being obtained, the contents of the integrated report including the KPIs could be seen as lacking in credibility.

Therefore, for users of the integrated report, a review report by Fern & Co can provide some assurance that the KPIs are relevant, derived from reliable source information and accurate. It is important to note, however, that only a low level of assurance is provided, and that the nature of the assurance will depend on the terms of the engagement between Fern & Co and Moosehead Hospital Co, for example, the engagement may be restricted to certain agreed upon procedures on specific KPIs.

Operating in a regulated industry makes the assurance even more important, as the KPIs may need to be reported to the authorities.

For management, the assurance report will also help in providing some assurance on how the KPIs have been determined, including that the systems and controls are sufficient to produce the necessary information. Management will presumably be using the KPIs to monitor performance and therefore having assurance on the accuracy of the KPIs should provide comfort to management that appropriate decisions are being made.

**(ii)** **Procedures**

**General**

- Document the systems which are in place for recording the information relevant to the performance measures, noting the key controls which should operate to ensure the accuracy of the information which is captured, recorded and reported. Evidence of the operating effectiveness of these controls throughout the period should be obtained.

- In particular, the auditor should obtain an understanding of the level of scrutiny of the performance measures by senior management, including: the frequency of their reviews; the level of detail which is provided; and their responses should the reported performance measures differ from their expectations.

- Each of the calculations of the performance measures should be obtained. Using the figures supplied by management, these should be recalculated by the audit team to ensure mathematical accuracy.

- The performance measures should be analytically reviewed against historic performance levels, on a monthly basis if such information is available, to identify any significant fluctuations in reported performance levels. Where fluctuations occur reasons should be sought through management enquiry, which should then be corroborated with evidence wherever possible.

---

*Tutorial note*

*Other, relevant general procedures will also be awarded credit but will only be awarded credit once, i.e. candidates will not be given credit for repeating the same general procedure for each performance measure.*

---

**Patient/nurse ratio**

- Obtain copies of the original document in which the basis for calculating the performance measures were agreed. This may be in the form of a strategic document agreed with the National Health Service or it may even be the minutes of the executive board. From this identify whether any specific definition is provided of the term 'average' or whether a specific formula is provided. In particular, it is important to ascertain over what period the average must be calculated.

- From the same document ascertain which patients must be included in the calculation, i.e. should this include emergency patients or just patients admitted for treatment by appointment.

- Confirm the calculation of the number of patients treated through inspection of underlying treatment and appointment records.

- Confirm the calculation of the number of nurses through inspection of underlying staff rotas and records of hours worked supplied to human resources and payroll departments.

**Surgical room usage**

- Enquire of the manager responsible for planning and co-ordinating surgical operations what the 'normal' period of time (i.e. excluding emergencies) is during which surgical procedures may be performed, i.e. which hours during the day and whether there are any days where scheduled procedures would not be performed.

- Obtain and inspect the hospital plans to identify the total number of surgical rooms available.

- Using the information above, calculate the total number of surgical hours available to the hospital. Compare the figure calculated to the figure used in management's calculation to identify any significant variances.

- Obtain a schedule of the total hours of surgery performed during the year. Confirm a sample of the times recorded to underlying hospital records to confirm the accuracy of the figures used in this calculation.

**Admissions for previously treated conditions**

- Enquire of management how they define a 'previously treated condition'. For example, does this depend upon the underlying symptoms or the diagnosis of the medical practitioner?

- Obtain a copy of the patient admissions records. Use computer assisted audit techniques to identify patients admitted to the hospital within 28 days of a previous admission. If possible, inspect the underlying patient records to identify whether the patient was treated for either the same or a similar condition. If not, enquire of the medical practitioners responsible for their care during their admission.

- Where the above procedure identifies patients admitted for the same condition, ensure that these patients are recorded in management's calculation of the performance measure to ensure the completeness of the information used in the calculation.

---

**Examiner's comments**

This question focused on the audit of a hospital and was generally not well-answered.

Part (a) focused on a potential breach of laws and regulations through the potential use of out-of-date medicines and an intimidating client. Most candidates discussed the implication for inventory valuation reasonably and some suggested highlighting the issues and lack of co-operation from the finance director to those changed with governance and the potential for a limitation on the scope of the audit. Disappointingly only a minority of candidates identified that there was a wider issue that using out-of-date medication could have severe or fatal health consequences and were able to discuss the balance between the auditor's duty of confidentiality to the client compared with their wider ethical duty to notify the appropriate regulators and after seeking legal advice.

---

Part (b) asked about the benefits of independent assurance provided on key performance indicators for both management and external users. Candidates mostly correctly commented that this would provide greater credibility to the information and so would be relied on more by external users. Fewer candidates identified that this would also provide management with assurance that the systems and controls in place to produce the information was sufficient and operating satisfactorily.

In part (c) candidates were required to explain how to audit some performance KPIs and although some good points were made a number of candidates stretched their imagination as to how these could be verified and were simply impractical in the nature of their procedures.

## Marking scheme

| | Marks |
|---|---|
| Generally up to 1½ marks for each well explained point and 1 mark for each well explained procedure recommended: | |
| **(a) Ethical and professional issues** | |
| – Suspected non-compliance with laws and regulations | |
| – Attempt to obtain more evidence for discussion with management | |
| – Reporting non-compliance to those charged with governance | |
| – Confidentiality threat | |
| – Report to regulator | |
| – Limitation on scope of audit | |
| – Impact on the financial statements | |
| – Intimidation threat | |
| – Management integrity | |
| – Withdrawal from engagement | |
| **Maximum** | **11** |
| **(b) (i) Benefits of an assurance report on the KPIs included in the integrated report** | |
| – Assurance report enhances credibility of the integrated report generally and specifically the KPIs | |
| – Integrated report outside scope of audit | |
| – Important to gain assurance given regulated nature of the industry | |
| – Management use KPIs to monitor performance so credibility enhances management decision making processes | |
| **Maximum** | **4** |
| **(ii) Procedures in relation to key performance indicators** | |
| **General:** | |
| – Document systems and test controls | |
| – Identify level of senior management scrutiny of KPIs | |
| – Recalculate KPIs to confirm mathematical accuracy | |
| – Analytical review to historic performance | |
| **Patient/nurse ratio:** | |
| – Obtain definition of 'average' for patient/nurse ratio | |
| – Identify which patients to include | |
| – Confirm patient numbers to patient records | |
| – Confirm staff numbers to HR records | |
| **Surgical rooms:** | |
| – Discuss normal levels of room usage | |
| – Obtain hospital plans to identify number of surgical rooms | |
| – Recalculate number of surgical hours available | |
| – Confirm surgical times to underlying surgery/treatment records | |

| | |
|---|---|
| **Admissions for previously treated conditions:**<br>–    Enquire how a previously treated condition is identified<br>–    Inspect patient admission records to identify readmissions within 28 days<br>–    Inspect underlying patient records to identify if conditions match | |
| Maximum | 10 |
| Total | 25 |

## 43    NEWMAN & CO        *Walk in the footsteps of a top tutor*

*Top tutor tips*

*This question deals with social and environmental reporting.*

*In part (a)(i) take a methodical approach to the scenario and think of the matters that should be considered before accepting this type of engagement. Remember that the firm should only take on work of an acceptable level of risk.*

*In parts (a)(ii) and (b), apply your knowledge of audit procedures to this type of engagement.*

*Part (c) is a common requirement for this topic. This is rote-learned knowledge from the text book which can be applied to the specific KPIs mentioned in the scenario to make it more relevant.*

**(a)    (i)    Matters that should be considered in making acceptance decision**

**Objectivity**

The proposed assurance engagement represents a non-audit service. IESBA's *International Code of Ethics for Professional Accountants* does not prohibit the provision of additional assurance services to an audit client, however, the audit firm must carefully consider whether the provision of the additional service creates a threat to objectivity and independence of the firm or members of the audit team.

For example, when the total fees generated by a client represent a large proportion of a firm's total fees, the perceived dependence on the client for fee income creates a self-interest threat. Due to the nature of the proposed engagement, self-review and advocacy threats may also be created, as the Sustainability Report is published with the audited financial statements, and the audit firm could be perceived to be promoting the interests of its client by providing an assurance report on the key performance indicators (KPIs).

Newman & Co should only accept the invitation to provide the assurance engagement after careful consideration of objectivity, and a review as to whether safeguards can reduce any threat to objectivity to an acceptable level. As Eastwood Co is a 'major client', the fee level from providing both the audit and the assurance services could breach the permitted level of recurring fees allowed from one client. The fact that the company is listed means that the assessment of objectivity is particularly important and a second partner review of the objectivity of the situation may be considered necessary.

[**UK syllabus:** FRC Ethical Standard section 5 suggests that the audit engagement partner should assess the significance of any threat to objectivity created by the potential provision of the non-audit service and should consider whether there are safeguards that could be applied and which would be effective to eliminate the threat or reduce it to an acceptable level. If such safeguards can be identified and are applied, the non-audit service may be provided. However, where no such safeguards are applied, the only course is for the audit firm either not to undertake the engagement to provide the non-audit service in question or not to accept (or to withdraw from) the audit engagement.]

The fact that a separate team, with no involvement with the audit, will be working on the KPIs strengthens the objectivity of the assignment.

**Eastwood Co's requirements**

Assurance engagements can vary in terms of the level of work that is expected, and the level of assurance that is required. This will clearly impact on the scale of the assignment. For example, Eastwood Co may require specific procedures to be performed on certain KPIs to provide a high level of assurance, whereas a lower level of assurance may be acceptable for other KPIs.

Newman & Co should also clarify the expected form and content and expected wording of the assurance report itself, and whether any specific third party will be using the Sustainability Report for a particular purpose, as this may create risk exposure for the firm.

**Competence**

The audit firm's specialist social and environmental assurance department has only been recently established, and the firm may not have sufficient experienced staff to perform the assurance engagement. The fundamental principle of professional competence and due care requires that members of an engagement team should possess sufficient skill and knowledge to be able to perform the assignment, and be able to apply their skill and knowledge appropriately in the circumstances of the engagement.

Some of Eastwood Co's KPIs appear quite specialised – verification of $CO_2$ emissions for example, may require specialist knowledge and expertise. Newman & Co could bring in experts to perform this work, if necessary, but this would have cost implications and would reduce the recoverability of the assignment.

**Scale of the engagement**

The Sustainability Report contains 75 KPIs, and presumably a lot of written content in addition. All of these KPIs will need to be verified, and the written content of the report reviewed for accuracy and consistency, meaning that this is a relatively large engagement.

Newman & Co should consider whether the newly established sustainability reporting assurance team has enough resources to perform the engagement within the required time scale, bearing in mind the time pressure which is further discussed below.

### Time pressure

Given that the financial statements are scheduled to be published in four weeks, it is doubtful whether the assurance assignment could be completed, and a report issued, in time for it to be included in the annual report, particularly given the global nature of the assignment.

Newman & Co may wish to clarify with Eastwood Co's management whether they intend to publish the assurance report within the annual report, as they have done previously, or whether a separate report will be issued at a later point in time, which would allow more time for the assurance engagement to be conducted.

### Fee level and profitability

Such a potentially large scale assignment should attract a large fee. Costs will have to be carefully managed to ensure the profitability of the engagement, especially considering that overseas travel will be involved, as presumably much of the field work will be performed at Eastwood Co's Sustainability Department in Fartown.

The fee level would need to be negotiated bearing in mind the specialist nature of the work, and the urgency of the assignment, both of which mean that a high fee could be commanded.

### Global engagement

The firm's sustainability reporting team is situated in a different country to Eastwood Co's Sustainability Department. Although this does not on its own mean that the assignment should not be taken on, it makes the assignment logistically difficult.

Members of the assurance department must be willing to travel overseas to conduct at least some of their work, as it would be difficult to perform the engagement without visiting the department responsible for providing the KPIs. Other locations may also need to be visited. There are also cost implications of the travel, which will need to be built into the proposed fee for the engagement. Language may also present a barrier to accepting the engagement, depending on the language used in Fartown's location.

### Risk

Eastwood Co is a large company with a global presence. It is listed on several stock exchanges, and so it appears to have a high public profile. In addition, pressure groups are keen to see the added credibility of an assurance report issued in relation to the KPIs disclosed. For all of these reasons, there will be scrutiny of the Sustainability Report and the assurance report.

Newman & Co should bear in mind that this creates a risk exposure for the firm. If the assignment were taken, the firm would have to carefully manage this risk exposure through thorough planning of the engagement and applying strong quality control measures.

The firm would also need to ensure that the fee is commensurate with the level of risk exposure. Given the inconsistency that has come to light regarding one of the draft KPIs, which appears to overstate charitable donations made by the company, we may need to consider that management are trying to show the company's KPIs in a favourable way, which adds to the risk of the engagement.

**Commercial consideration**

If Newman & Co does not accept the assurance engagement, the firm risks losing the audit client in future years to another firm that would be willing to provide both services. As Eastwood Co is a prestigious client, this commercial consideration will be important, but should not override any ethical considerations.

(ii)    **Procedures to verify the number of serious accidents in the workplace**

- Review records held by human resources, which summarise the number and type of accidents reported in the workplace.

- Review the accident log book from a sample of locations.

- Discuss the definition of a 'serious' accident (as opposed to a 'minor' accident) and establish the nature of criteria applied to an accident to determine whether it is serious.

- Review correspondence with legal advisors which may indicate legal action being taken against Eastwood Co in respect of serious accidents in the workplace.

- Review minutes of board meetings for discussions of any serious accidents and associated repercussions for the company.

- Ascertain through discussion with management and/or legal advisors, if Eastwood Co has any convictions for health and safety offences during the year (which could indicate that serious accidents have occurred).

- Enquire as to whether the company has received any health and safety visits (the regulatory authority would usually perform one if an employee has a serious accident). Review documentation from any health and safety visits for evidence of any serious accidents.

- Consider talking to employees to identify if any accidents have not been recorded in the accident book.

**Procedures to verify the annual training spend per employee**

- Review Eastwood Co's approved training budget in comparison to previous years to ascertain the overall level of planned spending on training.

- Obtain a breakdown of the total training spend and review for any items misclassified as training costs.

- Agree significant components of the total training spend to supporting documentation such as contracts with training providers and to invoices received from those providers.

- Agree the total amount spent on significant training programmes to cash book and/or bank statements.

- Using data on total number of employees provided by the payroll department, recalculate the annual training spend per employee.

**(b)**    **Faster Jets Co**

**Procedures to gain assurance on the validity of the performance measures**

- Obtain a summary of all amounts donated to charitable causes and agree a sample to the cash book.

- For large donations above a certain limit (say $10,000) confirm that authorisation for the payment has been made, e.g. by agreeing to minutes of management meetings.

- Review correspondence with charities for confirmation of the amounts paid.

- Review relevant press releases and publicity campaigns, e.g. the free flight scheme and the local education schemes are likely to have been publicised.

- For the $750,000 spent on the local education scheme, obtain a breakdown of the amounts spent and scrutinise to ensure all relate to the scheme, e.g. payments to educators.

- Obtain a sample of classroom registers to confirm attendance of children on certain days.

- For the free flights donated to charity, perform analytical review to confirm that the average value of a flight seems reasonable – the average being $700 ($560,000/800).

- For a sample of the 800 free flights, obtain confirmation that the passenger was a guest of Faster Jets Co, e.g. through correspondence with the passenger and relevant charity.

- Agree a sample of business miles travelled in vehicles to a mileage log, and fuel costs to employee expenses claims forms and the general ledger.

**(c)**    **Difficulties measuring and reporting on social and environmental performance**

It is common for companies to produce a report on corporate social responsibility (CSR), and in some countries this is a requirement. CSR reports contain a wide variety of key performance indicators (KPIs) relating to the social and environmental targets which the company is aiming to achieve. It can be difficult to measure and report on social and environmental KPIs for a number of reasons.

**Difficult to define**

Measurements of social and environmental performance are not always easy to define. For example, Faster Jets Co aims to develop an education programme, which is vague in terms of measurement. The measurement only becomes precisely defined when a KPI which is capable of being quantified is attached to it, for example, the number of free education days provided in a year. It can also be difficult to identify key stakeholders and the KPIs which each stakeholder group is interested in.

**Difficult to quantify**

Targets and KPIs may be difficult to quantify in monetary terms. For example, Faster Jets Co's provision of free flights to charitable organisations can be quantified in terms of the number of flights donated, but the actual value of the flights is more questionable as this could be measured at cost price or market value. The monetary value may not even be very relevant to users of the CSR report.

### Lack of systems to capture data

In addition, systems and controls are often not established well enough to allow accurate measurement, and the measurement of social and environmental matters may not be based on reliable evidence. However, this is not always the case, for example, the accounting system should be able to determine accurately the amount of cash donated to charity and the amount spent on vehicle fuel.

### Difficult to make comparisons

Finally, it is hard to compare these targets and KPIs between companies, as they are not strictly defined, so each company will set its own target. It will also be difficult to make year on year comparisons for the same company, as targets may change in response to business activities.

---

**Examiner's comments**

Requirement (a)(i) asked candidates to identify and explain the matters that should be considered in evaluating whether the audit firm should perform an assurance engagement on the client's Sustainability Report. It was clear that most candidates knew the matters that should be considered (ethical constraints, resources, knowledge, timescale, fees etc.), and most candidates took the right approach to the question, by working through the various 'matters' and applying them to the question. The fact that this was not an audit engagement did not seem to faze candidates, and there were many sound answers to this requirement. Some answers evaluated the many ethical problems with taking on the assurance engagement as well as providing the audit for 'a major client', and appreciated that with only four weeks to complete the work, it would probably be impossible to ensure quality work could be performed on a global scale to such a tight deadline by an inexperienced team. Some answers also picked up on the fact that the client's listed status would probably prevent the audit firm from conducting the assurance engagement, and certainly the situation would need to be discussed with, and approved by the audit committee. However, some answers were much too brief for the marks available, amounting to little more than a bullet point list of matters to be considered but with no application to the scenario. Without application it was not possible to pass this requirement. Other common mistakes included:

- Ignoring the fact that the client was already an existing audit client, so discussing the need to contact its auditors for information.

- Not reading the question and thinking that you had been approached to perform the audit.

- Only discussing the potential problems and not identifying the benefits of providing the service (e.g. it would provide experience for the newly established assurance team).

- Ignoring information given in the question (e.g. saying that the firm would need to ask about the use of the assurance report – when the question clearly states that it would be published in the annual report with the financial statements).

Requirement (a)(ii) asked for procedures that could be used to verify two key performance indicators (KPIs) – the number of serious accidents in the workplace, and the average annual spend on training per employee. A fair proportion of answers were sound, with precise procedures recommended, but, many recommended procedures relied too much on observation and enquiry, and ignored the fact that the client was a global company with 300,000 employees which led to some bizarre and meaningless procedures being given.

---

Examples included 'observe a serious accident', 'inspect the location of a serious accident', 'ask how much is spent on training', and 'look at the training room to see how many chairs are there'. None of these could verify the KPIs and are pointless.

In requirement (b) the audit firm had been asked to perform an assurance engagement on Faster Jets Co's corporate social responsibility (CSR) report, and a number of CSR objectives and targets were provided along with the performance indicators to be included in the CSR report. The main weakness in responses was that candidates simply repeated the same procedures for each of the performance measures given, even if they weren't appropriate. For example, one of the performance measures related to free flights that had been donated to charities, and many candidates recommended that this should be agreed to bank statements or cash book even though it is not a cash transaction. Candidates are encouraged to think about whether the procedures they are recommending are sensible in the context of the scenario. As is often the case when presented with a requirement to detail procedures, many candidates provided procedures that were not well explained, and in many cases weren't procedures at all, e.g. 'review the free flights', 'inspect the education days', 'confirm the vehicle fuel'. This type of comment cannot be given credit as it is too vague and does not answer the question requirement.

Part (c) asked for a discussion of the difficulties in measuring and reporting on social and environmental performance. This short requirement was well attempted by many candidates, with most identifying that it can be difficult to define and quantify CSR measures, that systems are often not in place to capture the relevant information and that comparisons are difficult due to the lack of a regulatory framework.

| Marking scheme | | | | Marks |
|---|---|---|---|---|
| (a) | (i) | **Acceptance matters** <br> ½ mark for each matter identified (to max 4 marks) and up to 1½ further marks for explanation <br> – Objectivity (up to 3 marks allowed) <br> – Client's specific requirements <br> – Competence <br> – Large scale engagement <br> – Fee level and profitability <br> – Time pressure <br> – Global engagement <br> – Risk <br> – Commercial consideration | | |
| | | Maximum | | 8 |
| | (ii) | **Procedures on number of serious accidents** <br> 1 mark per specific procedure <br> – HR records review <br> – Accident book review <br> – Determine criteria for serious accident <br> – Review legal correspondence <br> – Review board minutes <br> – Review documentation of health and safety inspections <br> – Ascertain any convictions for breach of health and safety rules <br> **Procedures on average training spend** <br> 1 mark per specific procedure <br> – Review approved training budget <br> – Review components of total spend for mis-classified items | | |

|  |  |
|---|---|
| – Agree sample of invoices/contracts with training providers | |
| – Agree sample to cash book/bank statement (½ only) | |
| – Recalculate average | |

| | Maximum | 7 |
|---|---|---|

**(b)** **Procedures on Faster Jets Co's performance measures**

Generally 1 mark for a well explained procedure:

– Obtain a summary of all amounts donated to charitable causes and agree to cash book

– For large donation confirm that authorisation for the payment has been made

– Review correspondence with charities

– Review relevant press releases and publicity campaigns

– For the $750,000 spent on the local education scheme, obtain a breakdown of the amounts spent and scrutinise to ensure all relate to the scheme, e.g. payments to educators

– Obtain a sample of registers to confirm attendance of children on certain days

– For the free flights donated to charity, perform analytical review to confirm that the average value of a flight seems reasonable – the average being $700

– For a sample of the 800 free flights, obtain confirmation that the passenger was a guest of Faster Jets Co

– Agree a sample of business miles travelled in vehicles and fuel costs to employee expenses claims forms

| | Maximum | 6 |
|---|---|---|

**(c)** **Difficulties measuring and reporting on social and environmental performance**

Up to 1½ marks for each point discussed:

– Measures are difficult to define

– Measures are difficult to quantify

– Systems not set up to capture data

– Hard to make comparisons

| | Maximum | 4 |
|---|---|---|

| **Total** | | 25 |
|---|---|---|

**44    BEYER**  *Walk in the footsteps of a top tutor*

*Top tutor tips*

*Part (a) requires professional considerations before accepting a forensic investigation. A forensic investigation is a specialist assignment and this must be considered when deciding whether to accept the invitation. General acceptance considerations which are applicable to all types of engagement can also be included such as whether the firm has the resource and competence to perform the work.*

*Part (b)(i) requires the procedures to be performed to quantify the loss. A common sense approach can be taken here. Also think about the audit procedures which will help quantify the inventory stolen.*

*In part (b)(ii) consider how the fraud was able to occur, i.e. which controls were missing or ineffective. Explain how, if they had been in place, the fraud could have been prevented. Where controls are missing, these should form the basis of your recommendations to prevent the fraud from occurring again in the future.*

**(a)    Beyer Co**

**Scope of the investigation**

Kaffe & Co should establish the specific work which Beyer Co expects them to perform. It is likely that the quantification of the loss represents an agreed upon procedures engagement and these would need to be confirmed with Beyer Co in advance.

The identification and recommendation on controls issues is more likely to be of a consulting nature and the process and outcomes agreed with the client. The assignment may require specific competencies, such as the use of specialists in the use of automated tools techniques and this should be identified prior to acceptance of the engagement.

Kaffe & Co would also need to establish the time period Beyer Co would like them to investigate. This will all have an impact on the total fee charged.

**Establishing how Kaffe & Co's investigation relates to the criminal investigation**

If the quantification of the loss were to become a criminal investigation, then the relevant authorities would take the lead. It is not clear whether the authorities would require additional, professional support in their investigation and, if so, what sort of assistance they would require. For example, it is possible that they would gather their own evidence, but they may require the use of an expert witness to verify their findings in court.

It is therefore vital that, before any terms are agreed or engagement contracts are signed, Kaffe & Co speaks to the authorities to ascertain whether there will be any criminal investigation and, if so, what their role might be in the investigation, and how they might interact with any other experts appointed by the authority to assist in the investigation.

### Confidentiality

Firms providing professional services must always ensure that information relating to clients is not given to third parties without the permission of the client. In preparing the report for the insurance company, Kaffe & Co will need permission from Beyer Co to disclose the information to the insurance company. In an investigation such as this, it is highly likely that all of the evidence collected will have to be submitted to the authorities to assist with their criminal investigation. It is therefore vital that before Kaffe & Co accepts the assignment, they obtain permission to do so from the board of Beyer Co.

### The types of reports and prospective users

The firm must confirm with Beyer Co what types of report they would expect as a result of the engagement and whom the reports would be distributed to. In forensic engagements, the procedures to be performed would normally be agreed and then the results of those procedures would be reported.

It may be that the insurance company expects an opinion to be given on the results of the investigation and if this is the case, then the assurance issued would be limited to negative assurance. Kaffe & Co would usually expressly state that the report is not intended for use by third parties.

In this investigation, it is possible that the relevant authorities would want to use the results of the procedures to compile evidence for their case. It would, if this were the case, be important to establish if additional reports would be required for this.

Management also wants additional reports relating to the deficiencies identified in the control environment and systems recommendations on how to strengthen controls in this area. The form and content of such a report must be agreed upon in advance of accepting the assignment.

### Professional competence

Before they can accept the role, Kaffe & Co must be certain that they have staff with the requisite competencies to be able to conduct the investigation effectively.

If this were conducted as a criminal investigation, it is also vital that the staff used have sufficient experience in relation to the gathering and safeguarding of evidence. Any failure to follow the relevant protocol may render the evidence useless to the legal case.

### Time pressure, deadlines and resource availability

As well as having staff with the requisite competencies to conduct the engagement, it is also vital that those staff are available to be able to conduct the investigation in the time frame suggested. The insurance company is likely to set the time frame for any initial investigation. If the relevant authorities conduct an additional criminal investigation, Kaffe & Co must consider the extent of the possible investigation and whether they are able to commit the necessary resources without adversely affecting their other client commitments.

### Client due diligence

As Beyer Co is a new client, Kaffe & Co may be required to perform client identification procedures as part of local anti-money laundering regulations. If this is the case, the firm must explain the need to obtain information about the company and its directors before Beyer Co can be accepted as a client. If Beyer Co is unable, or refuses, to do this, then Kaffe & Co would not be able to take on Beyer Co as a client or proceed with the engagement.

**(b)** **(i)** **Procedures to be performed to quantify the inventory loss**

- Meet with the audit committee and members of management to understand and document what they know about the fraud and who might be involved.

- Discuss with the company's legal team what is known about the fraud at present and the source of the information.

- If possible, interview the whistle-blower to identify the potential staff involved and the timescales over which the fraud has been perpetrated.

- Obtain the prior year report to management from the auditor and inspect auditor's reports to identify any deficiencies or discrepancies in inventories identified by the auditors.

- Obtain/prepare a reconciliation of all orders placed including cancelled orders to all invoices raised to identify the total of all orders placed but not invoiced to establish the maximum potential value of the theft.

- Arrange to conduct a full inventory count to identify discrepancies between the inventory records and physical inventory.

- Investigate records of inventory written off to identify possible attempts to disguise the missing items.

- Interview sales, warehouse and accounting staff to identify the system in place for creating a sales order and for setting up customers within the sales and inventory systems.

- Use data analytics tools to identify the total of cancelled orders within the inventory records system and any addresses which are associated with large volumes of cancellations.

- Identify which cancelled orders are assigned to the sales representative identified by the whistle-blower.

- Identify which customers those orders are assigned to and verify their existence within the invoicing system and, where possible, their registered business address to ensure they are genuine customers.

- From this, identify fictitious customers and reconcile their cancelled orders to the inventory discrepancies identified.

- Assess if the amounts ordered by the fictitious customers agree to the total discrepancies or if there is a further difference to be investigated.

- Obtain inventory listing to identify the cost of the parts stolen and calculate the cost of the inventory identified as relating to the fictitious customer orders.

- Using data analytics tools, identify any other sales staff with unusual levels of cancelled sales dispatches to see if this is a wider issue.

(ii)    **Control deficiencies and recommendations**

**Lack of segregation of duties and monitoring of order cancellations**

There is a lack of internal control over the warehouse team, particularly in relation to authorisation and approval of transactions. The warehouse manager having the ability to create new customers on the system without authorisation has allowed fictitious customers to be created.

The ability of the sales representative to cancel orders and the ability of the warehouse manager to reverse dispatches without authorisation gives rise to a lack of segregation of duties. These processes should require authorisation from a senior member of staff, for instance, sales cancellations should be approved by the sales manager and reversed goods dispatches by the operations manager.

Additionally, the lack of reconciliation of the sales orders to the amounts invoiced allowed the cancellation of deliveries to avoid detection from any invoicing process. The consistent cancellation of dispatches relating to one customer from one sales representative may have drawn attention within the sales system had the transaction made it that far.

The existence of the inventory system in isolation from the invoicing and accounting system allowed for incomplete information to be relayed further up within the business. While this in itself is not an issue, it did mean that any management review of accounting and invoicing reports does not act as a means of review of the inventory management and dispatch system.

In many businesses, a system which linked the inventory movements with the accounting and management information system would allow reports to be generated to monitor for unusual levels of returns and cancellations. In the absence of the ability to merge the two systems, it may be possible for additional reporting functions to be added to the inventory system to allow reports of returns and cancellations to be generated for review at a higher level than the warehouse manager to provide oversight of this area.

A proper monitoring system would have flagged that one sales representative in particular had higher than usual cancellation levels which could have been investigated and monitored by management.

It would also be possible to implement a system where all cancelled orders and reversed dispatches are processed outside of the sales and warehouse team, for example, by the accounts department.

**Lack of segregation of duties in the warehouse counts**

The lack of segregation of duties between warehouse staff and inventory count staff allowed the fictitious sales orders to pass unnoticed as the inventory discrepancy which would have flagged the issue was ineffective. An independent inventory count process using an external company or using staff from outside the warehouse to perform counts and reconcile the inventory amounts to inventory records would have identified missing inventory sooner.

**Additional implications of the fraud**

In addition to the value of the inventory stolen by the warehouse manager and sales representative, the business is not holding accurate records of its inventory, meaning that it may be in breach of the requirement to keep proper records of assets and liabilities and its assets are overstated. This may or may not be a material amount.

There is also a business risk arising from inaccurate inventory in that inventory believed to be on hand to satisfy genuine orders may not exist, causing delays and disruption to the ability of Beyer Co to satisfy customer orders in a timely manner causing customer satisfaction issues and potential loss of customers if the delays become unacceptable.

**Recommendations**

- Integration of the sales order and invoicing systems into the management information system.

- New customers should be created by the accounts department not the sales/dispatch teams.

- Authorisation process for cancelled orders/returns.

- Creation and regular review of exception reports and unusual trends including cancellation reports by higher level management to identify irregular or suspicious patterns.

- Regular inventory counts to be performed by staff independent of the warehouse and sales staff.

**(c)    Difficulty identifying fraud**

According to ISA 240 *The Auditor's Responsibilities Relating to Fraud in an Audit of Financial Statements*, management of the company and those charged with governance are responsible for the prevention and detection of fraud and error within the company through the provision of a sound system of internal controls and a strong control environment. However, even when controls are in place, fraud can be difficult to detect. By its nature, fraud is hidden, and controls intended to reduce the risk of fraud may be insufficient to prevent or detect fraud.

In many cases, the detection of fraud is made difficult because the perpetrator will deliberately conceal their activity. In the case of Beyer Co, the missing inventory was concealed by the falsifying of inventory count records. This meant that the amounts stolen were not apparent from the control in place to detect inventory anomalies.

Frauds such as this one are made harder to detect by the collusion of more than one person. This can mean that segregation of duties controls which are in place to prevent or detect fraud can be circumvented.

Frauds are also often performed in small enough amounts that the losses are immaterial in comparison to the size of the company which means that high level controls such as monitoring of KPIs related to profit margins may not detect the fraud until the fraud reaches a scale which affects the business significantly.

Given the difficulties faced by companies in identifying fraud, it is often the case that fraud is discovered by accident or through whistle-blowers and when this happens, it is common for companies to ask why auditors did not discover the fraud during their audit.

ISA 240 states that when the auditor is conducting an audit in accordance with ISAs they are responsible for obtaining reasonable assurance that the financial statements taken as a whole are free from material misstatement, whether caused by fraud or error. Owing to the inherent limitations of an audit, there is an unavoidable risk that some material misstatements of the financial statements may not be detected, even though the audit is properly planned and performed in accordance with the ISAs.

The auditor's responsibility for detection of fraud is therefore a secondary one to that of management and auditors face the same issues as management when it comes to detecting fraud through the concealment, controls override and often immaterial nature of fraud.

In addition to the challenges shared with management, the audit process is limited by the focus on material misstatements and by the nature of sampling whereby not every transaction will be examined. Auditors should, however, consider the risks of fraud when planning their audit and the control weaknesses which would increase the risk of fraud occurring. Auditors should conduct their audit with professional scepticism having awareness that override of controls may exist and that representations made to them may be false.

Overall, for both management and for auditors, fraud is hard to detect especially when collusion exists to enable override of controls and concealment of the fraud.

---

**Examiner's comments**

This question was set in the context of a non-audit assignment for a non-audit client. Candidates were asked to consider acceptance criteria for an investigative forensic appointment in response to a fraud at a manufacturing company. The scenario detailed a fraud where inventory was stolen, and the assignment was to quantify the fraud for an insurance claim. Most candidates demonstrated the ability to apply acceptance criteria with reference to the specific question. A minority of candidates discussed irrelevant considerations that appeared to have been learnt from a previous question set in a similar context. Whilst the criteria for assessment were similar, some of those points were not relevant in this case and candidates wasted time in the exam discussing issues that would only be relevant to an existing audit client.

Part (b)(i) of this question asked candidates to suggest the steps or procedures that could be used to quantify the fraud and answers here tended to be either very good or very poor. Good answers methodically went through the process of identifying the fictitious customer, extracting data on cancelled orders and matching that to missing inventory through an inventory count. Weaker candidates were those who approached this by listing pre-learned procedures or without taking in to account the assignment and scenario. Such candidates often suggested tests that were based on samples as would be relevant to an audit rather than trying to definitively quantify the loss. Other mistakes made here were focusing on sale price rather than cost or trying to trace the stolen inventory with reference to sales invoices despite the goods stolen not being invoiced. There was evidence of candidates listing procedures from a previous forensic investigation question that were not relevant to the scenario described and therefore could not be awarded credit.

Part (b)(ii) required candidates to identify and explain the deficiencies in controls that allowed the fraud to occur and recommend improvements. Candidates were often able to score maximum credit in this area by giving detailed explanations. Weaker candidates tended to identify the deficiency from the scenario but were unable to describe how it resulted in the fraud or made unspecific recommendations e.g. improve segregation of duties or someone should approve cancellations – to obtain full credit more detail was required such as who should approve a process or how duties should be segregated.

Part (c) required a discussion of factors making fraud hard to identify and was well answered by candidates that completed it.

| **ACCA marking guide** | | |
|---|---|---|
| | | *Marks* |
| **(a)** **Acceptance considerations** | | |
| Up to 2 marks for each issue explained. | | |
| • Scope of assignment | | |
| • Interaction with criminal investigation | | |
| • Form and contents of reports/audience | | |
| • Confidentiality (max 1 mark) | | |
| • Competence | | |
| • Resource availability (including ability to make deadlines) | | |
| • Customer due diligence requirements/reputational risks (award up to 1 additional mark for specific examples of information required as part of the customer due diligence) | | |
| **Maximum** | | **8** |
| **(b)** **(i)** **Procedures to quantify the loss** | | |
| 1 mark for each relevant procedure described. | | |
| • Meet with audit committee/management to understand and document what they know about the fraud and who might be involved | | |
| • Discuss with the company's legal team what is known about the fraud at present and the source of the information | | |
| • If possible, interview the whistle-blower to identify the potential staff involved and the timescales over which the fraud has been perpetrated | | |
| • Obtain the prior year report to management from the auditor and inspect auditor's reports to identify any deficiencies or discrepancies in inventories identified by the auditors | | |
| • Obtain/prepare a reconciliation of all orders placed including cancelled orders to all invoices raised to identify the total of all orders placed but not invoiced to establish the maximum potential value of the theft | | |
| • Arrange to conduct a full inventory count to identify discrepancies between the inventory records and physical inventory | | |
| • Investigate records of inventory written off to identify possible attempts to disguise the missing items | | |
| • Interview sales, warehouse, and accounting staff to identify the system in place for creating a sales order and for setting up customers within the sales and inventory systems | | |
| • Use data analytics to identify the total of cancelled orders within the inventory records system and any addresses which are associated with large volumes of cancellations | | |
| • Identify which cancelled orders are assigned to the sales representative identified by the whistle-blower | | |

|  | | |
|---|---|---|
| • Identify which customers those orders are assigned to and verify their existence within the invoicing system and, where possible, their registered business address to ensure they are genuine customers | | |
| • From this, identify fictitious customers and reconcile their cancelled orders to the inventory discrepancies identified | | |
| • Assess if the amounts ordered by the fictitious customers agree to the total discrepancies or if there is a further difference to be investigated | | |
| • Obtain inventory listing to identify the cost of the parts stolen and calculate the cost of the inventory identified as relating to the fictitious customer orders | | |
| • Using data analytics identify any other sales staff with unusual levels of cancelled sales dispatches to see if this is a wider issue | | |
| | **Maximum** | **6** |

**(ii)  Control deficiencies and contribution to fraud**

Up to 2 marks for each point explained with up to 1 mark per recommendation.

- Lack of segregation of duties and monitoring
    - lack of integration of systems
    - lack of monitoring of order cancellations
- Lack of segregation of duties in warehouse counts
- Additional implications
- Recommendations

|  | | |
|---|---|---|
| | **Maximum** | **6** |

**(c)  Difficulty in identifying fraud Generally, 1 mark per point explained.**

Generally, 1 mark per point explained.

- Management's responsibility
- Concealment
- Collusion
- Size of fraud relative to the business
- Auditor's responsibility
- Materiality
- Sampling risk
- Risk assessment and scepticism

|  | | |
|---|---|---|
| | **Maximum** | **5** |
| **Total** | | **25** |

**45   RETRIEVER**  *Walk in the footsteps of a top tutor*

**Top tutor tips**

*Part (a) requires evaluation of quality control, ethical and other professional matters arising. Typical issues to look out for in such a question are: whether the work has been assigned to the appropriate level of staff, whether sufficient time has been allocated for the audit, whether sufficient appropriate evidence has been obtained (e.g. have the ISAs been followed), whether any ethical threats are apparent (e.g. threats to objectivity or competence).*

*Part (b) deals with a forensic accounting service for a client who has been burgled and requested assistance determining the insurance claim. For planning matters, think about what happens at the planning stage for an audit and apply the principles to this engagement. For procedures, a common sense approach can be taken to quantify the extent of the loss.*

**(a)**   There are many concerns raised regarding quality control. Audits should be conducted with adherence to ISA 220 *Quality Control for an Audit of Financial Statements* and it seems that this has not happened in relation to the audit of the Retriever Group, which is especially concerning, given the Group obtained a stock exchange listing during the year. It would seem that the level of staffing on this assignment is insufficient, and that tasks have been delegated inappropriately to junior members of staff.

**Time pressure**

The junior's first comment is that the audit was time pressured. All audits should be planned to ensure that adequate time can be spent to obtain sufficient appropriate audit evidence to support the audit opinion.

It seems that the audit is being rushed and the juniors instructed not to perform work properly, and that review procedures are not being conducted appropriately. All of this increases the detection risk of the audit and, ultimately, could lead to an inappropriate opinion being given.

The juniors have been told not to carry out some planned procedures on allegedly low risk areas of the audit because of time pressure. It is not acceptable to cut corners by leaving out audit procedures. Even if the balances are considered to be low risk, they could still contain misstatements.

Directors' emoluments are related party transactions and are material by their nature and so should not be ignored. Any modifications to the planned audit procedures should be discussed with, and approved by, senior members of the audit team and should only occur for genuine reasons.

**Method of selecting sample**

ISA 530 *Audit Sampling* requires that the auditor shall select items for the sample in such a way that each sampling unit in the population has a chance of selection. The audit manager favours non-statistical sampling as a quick way to select a sample, instead of the firm's usual statistical sampling method. There is a risk that changing the way items are selected for testing will not provide sufficient, reliable audit evidence as the sample selected may no longer be representative of the population as a whole. Or that an insufficient number of items may be selected for testing.

The juniors may not understand how to pick a sample without the use of the audit firm's statistical selection method, and there is a risk that the sample may be biased towards items that appear 'easy to audit'. Again, this instruction from the audit manager is a departure from planned audit procedures, made worse by deviating from the audit firm's standard auditing methods, and likely to increase detection risk.

### Audit of going concern

Going concern can be a difficult area to audit, and given the Group's listed status and the fact that losses appear to have been made this year, it seems unwise to delegate such an important area of the audit to an audit junior. The audit of going concern involves many subjective areas, such as evaluating assumptions made by management, analysing profit and cash flow forecasts and forming an overall opinion on the viability of the business.

The going concern audit programme should be performed by a more senior and more experienced member of the audit team. This issue shows that the audit has not been well planned as appropriate delegation of work is a key part of direction and supervision, essential elements of good quality control.

### Review of work

The juniors have been asked to review each other's work which is unacceptable. ISA 220 requires that the engagement partner shall take responsibility for reviews being performed in accordance with the firm's review policies and procedures. Ideally, work should be reviewed by a person more senior and/or experienced than the person who conducted the work.

Audit juniors reviewing each other's work are unlikely to spot mistakes, errors of judgment and inappropriate conclusions on work performed. The audit manager should be reviewing all of the work of the juniors, with the audit partner taking overall responsibility that all work has been appropriately reviewed.

### Deferred tax

It is concerning that the client's financial controller is not able to calculate the deferred tax figure. This could indicate a lack of competence in the preparation of the financial statements, and the audit firm should consider if this impacts the overall assessment of audit risk.

The main issue is that the junior prepared the calculation for the client. Providing an audit client with accounting and bookkeeping services, such as preparing accounting records or financial statements, creates a self-review threat when the firm subsequently audits the financial statements. The significance of the threat depends on the materiality of the balance and its level of subjectivity.

Clients often request technical assistance from the external auditor, and such services do not, generally, create threats to independence provided the firm does not assume a management responsibility for the client. However, the audit junior has gone beyond providing assistance and has calculated a figure to be included in the financial statements.

The Group is listed and generally the provision of bookkeeping services is not allowed to listed clients. The Code states that in the case of an audit client that is a public interest entity, a firm shall not prepare tax calculations of current and deferred tax liabilities (or assets) for the purpose of preparing accounting entries that are material to the financial statements on which the firm will express an opinion.

The calculation of a deferred tax asset is not mechanical and involves judgments and assumptions in measuring the balance and evaluating its recoverability. The audit junior may be able to perform a calculation, but is unlikely to have sufficient detailed knowledge of the business and its projected future trading profits to be able to competently assess the deferred tax position. The calculation has not been reviewed and poses a high audit risk, as well as creating an ethical issue for the audit firm.

The deferred tax balance calculated by the junior should be assessed for materiality, carefully reviewed or re-performed, and discussed with management. It is unclear why the junior was discussing the Group's tax position with the financial controller, as this is not the type of task that should normally be given to an audit junior.

**Tax planning**

The audit junior should not be advising the client on tax planning matters. This is an example of a non-audit service, which can create self-review and advocacy threats to independence. As discussed above, the audit junior does not have the appropriate level of skill and knowledge to perform such work.

The junior's work on tax indicates that the audit has not been properly supervised, and that the junior does not seem to understand the ethical implications created. As part of a good quality control system, all members of the audit team should understand the objectives of the work they have been allocated and the limit to their responsibilities.

**(b)    (i)    Planning a forensic investigation**

Planning the investigation will involve consideration of similar matters to those involved in planning an audit.

The planning should commence with a meeting with the client at which the investigation is discussed. In particular, the investigation team should develop an understanding of the events surrounding the theft and the actions taken by the client since it occurred.

Matters that should be clarified with the client include:

- The objective of the investigation – to quantify the amount to be claimed under the insurance cover
- Whether the client has informed the police and the actions taken by the police so far
- Whether the thieves have been captured and any stolen goods recovered
- Whether the thieves are suspected to be employees of the Group
- Any planned deadline by which time the insurance claim needs to be submitted
- Whether the client has contacted the insurance company and discussed the events leading to the potential claim.

**Insurance policy**

The insurance policy should be scrutinised to clarify the exact terms of the insurance, to ensure that both the finished goods and stolen lorry will be included in the claim. The period of the insurance cover should be checked, to ensure that the date of the theft is covered, and the client should confirm that payments to the insurance company are up to date, to ensure the cover has not lapsed.

**Resources**

The audit firm should also consider the resources that will be needed to conduct the work. Kennel & Co has a forensic accounting department, so will have staff with relevant skills, but the firm should consider if staff with specific experience of insurance claims work are available.

**Access to information**

The client should confirm that the investigation team will have full access to information required, and are able to discuss the matter with the police and the insurance company without fear of breaching confidentiality.

**Output of the investigation**

The output of the investigation should be confirmed, which is likely to be a report addressed to the insurance company. It should be clarified that the report is not to be distributed to any other parties. Kennel & Co should also confirm whether they would be required to act as expert witness in the event of the thieves being caught and prosecuted.

---

*Tutorial note*

*Credit will also be awarded for explanations of acceptance issues such as the need for a separate engagement letter drawn up to cover the forensic investigation, outlining the responsibilities of the investigation team and of the client. Fees should also be discussed and agreed.*

---

**(ii)    Procedures**

- Watch the CCTV to form an impression of the quantity of goods stolen, for example, how many boxes were loaded onto the lorry.
- If possible, from the CCTV, determine if the boxes contain either mobile phones or laptop computers.
- Inspect the boxes of goods remaining in the warehouse to determine how many items of finished goods are in each box.
- Agree the cost of an individual mobile phone and laptop computer to accounting records, such as cost cards.
- Perform an inventory count on the boxes of goods remaining in the warehouse and reconcile to the latest inventory movement records.
- Discuss the case with the police to establish if any of the goods have been recovered and if, in the opinion of the police, this is likely to happen.
- Obtain details of the stolen lorry, for example the licence plate, and agree the lorry back to the non-current asset register where its carrying value should be shown.

**Examiner's comments**

This question contained two separate requirements in relation to the same client, the Retriever Group. The first requirement was largely based around quality control and ethics, the second to do with a forensic investigation. The scenario provided was not long, and candidates did not appear to be time pressured when attempting this question.

Requirement (a) described various matters that had arisen during the performance of the audit as described one of the audit juniors, including time pressure, deviations from the audit plan, and the type of work that had been performed by the audit juniors, some of which was inappropriate. The requirement asked candidates to evaluate the quality control, ethical and other professional issues arising in the planning and performance of the audit. Answers on the whole were satisfactory, and candidates seemed comfortable with applying their knowledge of quality control requirements and ethical threats to the scenario. Most answers were well structured, working through each piece of information and discussing the matters in a relevant way. There were a number of scripts where the maximum marks were awarded for this requirement.

The common strengths seen in many answers included:

- Identifying that the audit had not been planned well, as it was time pressured and the allocation of tasks to audit juniors was not commensurate with their knowledge and experience.

- Discussing the problems in the direction and supervision of the audit, including the significant issue of the audit manager instructing the juniors not to follow planned audit procedures.

- Appreciating that review procedures were not being performed in accordance with ISA requirements, and that audit juniors did not know the limit of their responsibilities.

- Explaining the ethical threats caused by the audit junior's inappropriate work on deferred tax and tax planning.

- Describing the lack of competence and integrity of the audit manager in allowing the audit to be performed to such poor quality.

- Recommending that the audit team members receive training on quality control and ethical issues, and that the audit files should be subject to a detailed quality control review with a view to some areas of the audit possibly being re-performed.

It was especially encouraging to see that most candidates were not just able to identify the problems but could also explain and evaluate them to some extent.

Requirement (b) contained a short scenario describing a burglary that had occurred at the Retriever Group. The Group's audit committee had asked the audit firm's forensic accounting department to provide a forensic accounting service to determine the amount to be claimed on the Group's insurance policy.

The requirement asked candidates to identify and explain the matters to be considered and steps to be taken in planning the forensic investigation, and for the procedures to be performed. Unfortunately answers to this requirement were overall unsatisfactory indicating that this is not a well understood part of the syllabus.

Some answers tended to include one or more of the following in relation to the first part of the requirement:

- A lengthy discussion of what a forensic investigation is, including long definitions, with no application to the scenario – this was not asked for. This tended to be based on rote learning and earned few, if any, marks.

- An assumption that management had already quantified the amount to be claimed, and that the forensic investigation would 'audit' that amount – leading to mostly irrelevant answer points.

- A discussion about fraud and the lack of integrity of management for 'allowing' the fraud to take place – this was often accompanied by lengthy speculation about the control deficiencies that failed to prevent the burglary from happening.

- A focus on whether adequate safeguards could be put in place to allow the audit firm's forensic accounting department to perform the investigation – this is a valid consideration to an extent, but the question did clearly state that there was no ethical threat.

- A discussion on the accounting treatment necessary for the stolen goods – again, not asked for.

In relation to the second part of the requirement, while some answers gave well described and relevant procedures to quantify the loss, many focused exclusively on determining the volume of goods stolen and said nothing about the value of them. Many suggested discussing the amount to be claimed with the insurance provider and comparing our figure with theirs, clearly not understanding the point of the forensic investigation being to provide the amount to be claimed in the first place. On the plus side, most answers included suggestions that reconciliation should be performed between the latest inventory count records and the amount of goods currently in the warehouse, though these were not often presented as procedures.

On the whole it was clear that many candidates were unprepared for a question requirement of this type, and that again it is apparent that a significant number of candidates rely on rote learnt knowledge and have difficulty to develop relevant answer points for a given scenario. Some candidates barely attempted this requirement, which for scripts achieving a mark that is a marginal fail is obviously a significant issue.

| Marking scheme | | |
|---|---|---|
| | | *Marks* |
| **(a)** | **Quality control, ethical and other professional matters**<br>Up to 2 marks for each matter evaluated (up to a maximum 3 marks for identification only)<br>– Time pressure<br>– Planned procedures ignored on potentially material item<br>– Sampling method changed – increases sampling risk<br>– Inappropriate review by juniors<br>– Inappropriate delegation of tasks<br>– Deferred tax – management not competent<br>– Deferred tax – self-review/management responsibility threat<br>– Tax planning – non-audit service with advocacy threat<br>– Junior lacks experience for this work regardless of ethical issues<br>– Junior not supervised/directed appropriately<br>– Overall conclusion | |
| | **Maximum** | 13 |
| **(b)** **(i)** | **Planning the forensic investigation**<br>Up to 1½ marks for each planning matter identified and explained (up to a maximum 2 marks for identification only)<br>– Develop understanding of the events surrounding the theft<br>– Meeting with client to discuss the investigation<br>– Confirm insurance policy details (period and level of cover)<br>– Consider resources for the investigation team<br>– Confirm access to necessary information<br>– Agree output of investigation<br>– Deadlines/fees<br>– Discuss confidentiality and ability to discuss with police/insurance company | |

| | | | |
|---|---|---|---|
| (ii) | **Procedures to be performed** | | |
| | 1 mark for each specific procedure recommended: | | |
| | – Watch the CCTV | | |
| | – If possible, from the CCTV, determine the type of goods stolen | | |
| | – Determine how many items of finished goods are in each box | | |
| | – Agree the cost of an individual item to accounting records | | |
| | – Perform an inventory count and reconcile to the latest inventory movement records | | |
| | – Discuss the case with the police to establish if any of the goods have been recovered | | |
| | – Obtain details of the stolen lorry and agree to the non-current asset register | | |
| | | Maximum | 12 |
| **Total** | | | 25 |

## 46 LARK & CO  *Walk in the footsteps of a top tutor*

### Top tutor tips

*Part (a)(i) covers the syllabus area of forensic accounting and asks for ethical and professional issues if your firm investigates the fraudulent activity. Think about the threats that can arise and how they could be safeguarded. Remember to explain and evaluate the significance of the threats. Part (a)(ii) requires the matters to be considered when planning the fraud investigation. For planning matters, think about what happens at the planning stage for an audit and apply the principles to this engagement.*

*Part (b) requires knowledge of the auditor's responsibilities when suspicious transactions are identified. Money laundering is a topic regularly examined and this requirement should be quite straightforward.*

*Part (c) covers professional scepticism and how to apply it. In this scenario the auditor has been given contradictory evidence from the client and the requirement asks for the further actions that should be taken by the auditor. You should think of ways in which to obtain further evidence to reach a conclusion as to which evidence can be relied on.*

**(a)** **(i)** An investigation into the alleged fraudulent activity is a forensic investigation. If Lark & Co were to conduct the forensic investigation, this would be a non-audit service performed for an audit client. Specifically, this investigation would be deemed a litigation support service.

### Tutorial note

*Litigation support services may include activities such as acting as an expert witness, calculating estimated damages or other amounts that might become receivable or payable as the result of litigation or other legal dispute, and assistance with document management and retrieval.*

Before a firm accepts an engagement to provide a non-audit service to an audit client, a determination should be made as to whether providing such a service would create a threat to independence. Self-review, self-interest and advocacy threats to independence may arise.

**Self-review threat**

The self-review threat exists because the forensic investigation will determine the monetary amount of the fraud, and the amount which Chestnut Co will attempt to recover from the fraudsters. Given the potential scale of the fraud, it could be that the amounts involved are material to the financial statements and therefore the audit team would be reviewing figures determined by members of the audit firm.

In addition, the forensic investigation team will, as part of their work, review systems and controls over expenses claimed by Chestnut Co's employees. This means that the forensic investigation team are also exposed to a self-review threat, as they will be reviewing systems and controls which have been considered during the audit of Chestnut Co's financial statements.

**Advocacy threat**

The advocacy threat arises because going to court and speaking as an expert witness in relation to the fraud would be seen as the audit firm promoting the interests of its client and supporting a position taken by management in an adversarial context.

**Self-interest threat**

A self-interest threat could also arise, as the forensic investigation may be a lucrative source of income for Lark & Co. This could create the perception that Lark & Co is reliant on Chestnut Co for income and impairs the objectivity of the firm.

The firm should evaluate the significance of these threats. In particular, the firm should consider the potential materiality of the amounts involved in the fraud, and the degree of subjectivity that may be involved in determining the amounts involved. If the matter is material, and would involve significant judgments, then no safeguards would reduce the threat to an acceptable level and the forensic investigation should not be conducted by the audit firm.

It is likely, however, that the investigation would not involve a significant degree of judgment and the investigation could be performed as long as safeguards were used, such as:

- Having a senior member of the audit firm, who was not involved in the forensic investigation review the results of the investigation and the impact on the financial statements.

- Performing an independent partner review on the audit of Chestnut Co.

- Ensuring that the forensic investigation is not performed by anyone involved in the audit engagement. Possibly the investigation could be performed by a different office of the firm.

The ethical situation must be discussed with those charged with governance of Chestnut Co. Depending on any relevant regulation in Chestnut Co's jurisdiction, it may not be possible for the audit firm to carry out this non-audit assignment, or it may be permitted with the approval of those charged with governance (or an audit committee, if one exists).

Furthermore, the fundamental ethical principles apply to all professional assignments, including a forensic investigation.

**Professional competence and due care**

Forensic investigations are specialist assignments and may require very specific skills, which will not be possessed by individuals unless they have undergone specific training. Lark & Co must consider whether there are any members of the firm who possess the necessary skills before accepting the assignment.

It is likely that relatively senior staff will need to be assigned to the investigation, which will bring necessary authority and experience to the investigation team. It should be considered whether Lark & Co is able to divert senior staff from other assignments at short notice. Resourcing the team could be a problem.

**Confidentiality**

In addition, confidentiality is a crucial issue in such investigations as members of the investigation team will have access to sensitive information which will be used as evidence in court. Any breach of confidentiality could jeopardise the integrity of the legal proceedings against the fraudsters. Anyone involved with the investigation must be made aware of these issues and confidentiality agreements should be signed.

(ii)   Discuss the purpose, nature and scope of the investigation. In particular, confirm whether evidence gathered will be used in criminal proceedings and in support of an insurance claim.

Confirm that Chestnut Co's objectives are to identify those involved with the fraud, and to quantify the amount of the fraud. This will help to clarify the terms of the engagement, which will be detailed in an engagement letter.

Determine the time-scale involved, whether Jack Privet needs the investigation to commence as soon as possible and the deadline for completing the investigation. This is necessary to determine the resources needed to perform the investigation, and whether resources need to be diverted from other assignments.

Enquire as to how many sales representatives have been suspended (i.e. are suspected of involvement in the fraud). This will help the firm to determine the potential scale of the investigation.

Gain an understanding as to how the fraud came to light (e.g. was it uncovered by internal audit or a member of the sales department) and who reported their suspicions to Jack Privet. This information will indicate how the investigation should commence (e.g. by interviewing the whistle-blower).

Determine whether Chestnut Co will provide resources to help with the investigation, e.g. members of the internal audit team could provide assistance in obtaining evidence.

Ask for Jack Privet's opinion as to why the fraud had not been prevented or detected by the company's internal controls. In particular, enquire if there has been a breakdown in controls over authorisation of expenses.

Determine whether recommendations to improve controls are required as an output of the investigative work.

Discuss the investigative techniques which may be used (e.g. interviewing the alleged fraudsters, detailed review of all expense claims made by sales representatives, analytical review of expenses) and ensure that investigators will have unrestricted access to individuals and documentation.

Enquire as to whether the police have been informed, and if so, the name and contact details of the person informed. It is likely that a criminal investigation by the police will take place as well as Lark & Co's own investigation.

Confirm that Chestnut Co grants permission to Lark & Co's investigation team to communicate with third parties such as the police and the company's lawyers regarding the investigation.

**(b) Implications**

The circumstances described by the audit senior indicate that Jack Heron may be using his company to carry out money laundering. Money laundering is defined as the process by which criminals attempt to conceal the origin and ownership of the proceeds of their criminal activity, allowing them to maintain control over the proceeds and, ultimately, providing a legitimate cover for the sources of their income. Money laundering activity may range from a single act, such as being in possession of the proceeds of one's own crime, to complex and sophisticated schemes involving multiple parties, and multiple methods of handling and transferring criminal property as well as concealing it and entering into arrangements to assist others to do so.

Heron's business is cash-based, making it an ideal environment for cash acquired through illegal activities to be legitimised by adding it to the cash paid genuinely by customers and posting it through the accounts. It appears that $2 million additional cash has been added to the genuine cash receipts from customers. This introduction of cash acquired through illegal activities into the business is known as 'placement'.

The fact that the owner himself posts transactions relating to revenue and cash is strange and therefore raises suspicions as to the legitimacy of the transactions he is posting through the accounts. Suspicions are heightened due to Jack Heron's refusal to explain the nature and reason for the journal entries he is making in the accounts.

The $2 million paid by electronic transfer is the same amount as the additional cash posted through the accounts. This indicates that the cash is being laundered and the transfer is known as the 'layering' stage, which is done to disguise the source and ownership of the funds by creating complex layers of transactions. Money launderers often move cash overseas as quickly as possible in order to distance the cash from its original source, and to make tracing the transaction more difficult. The 'integration' stage of money laundering occurs when upon successful completion of the layering process, the laundered cash is reintroduced into the financial system, for example, as payment for services rendered.

The secrecy over the reason for the cash transfer and lack of any supporting documentation is another indicator that this is a suspicious transaction. Jack Heron's reaction to being questioned over the source of the cash and the electronic transfer point to the fact that he has something to hide. His behaviour is certainly lacking in integrity, and even if there is a genuine reason for the journals and electronic transfer his unhelpful and aggressive attitude may cast doubts as to whether the audit firm wishes to continue to retain Heron Co as a client.

The audit senior was correct to be alarmed by the situation. However, by questioning Jack Heron about it, the senior may have alerted him to the fact that the audit team is suspicious that money laundering is taking place. There is a potential risk that the senior has tipped off the client, which may prejudice any investigation into the situation.

Tipping off is itself an offence, though this can be defended against if the person did not know or suspect that the disclosure was likely to prejudice any investigation that followed.

The amount involved is clearly highly material to the financial statements and will therefore have an implication for the audit. The whole engagement should be approached as high risk and with a high degree of professional scepticism.

The firm may wish to consider whether it is appropriate to withdraw from the engagement (if this is possible under applicable law and regulation). However, this could result in a tipping off offence being committed, as on withdrawal the reasons should be discussed with those charged with governance.

If Lark & Co continue to act as auditor, the audit opinion must be considered very carefully and the whole audit subject to second partner review, as the firm faces increased liability exposure. Legal advice should be sought.

**Nature of reporting**

The audit senior should report the situation in an internal report to Lark & Co's Money Laundering Reporting Officer (MLRO). The MLRO is a nominated officer who is responsible for receiving and evaluating reports of suspected money laundering from colleagues within the firm, and making a decision as to whether further enquiries are required and if necessary making reports to the appropriate external body.

Lark & Co will probably have a standard form that should be used to report suspicions of money laundering to the MLRO.

*Tutorial note*

*According to ACCA's Technical Factsheet 145 Anti-Money Laundering Guidance for the Accountancy Sector, there are no external requirements for the format of an internal report and the report can be made verbally or in writing.*

The typical content of an internal report on suspected money laundering may include the name of the suspect, the amounts potentially involved, and the reasons for the suspicions with supporting evidence if possible, and the whereabouts of the laundered cash.

The report must be done as soon as possible, as failure to report suspicions of money laundering to the MLRO as soon as practicable can itself be an offence under the money laundering regulations.

The audit senior may wish to discuss their concerns with the audit manager in more detail before making the report, especially if the senior is relatively inexperienced and wants to hear a more senior auditor's view on the matter. However, the senior is responsible for reporting the suspicious circumstances at Heron Co to the MLRO.

---

**Tutorial note**

*ACCA's Technical Factsheet 145 states that: 'An individual may discuss his suspicion with managers or other colleagues to assure himself of the reasonableness of his conclusions but, other than in group reporting circumstances, the responsibility for reporting to the MLRO remains with him. It cannot be transferred to anyone else, however junior or senior they are.'*

---

**(c)** **Discuss how professional scepticism should be applied to the audit of Coot Co's payroll and recommend any further actions that should be taken by the auditor**

The term professional scepticism is defined in ISA 200 *Overall Objectives of the Independent Auditor and the Conduct of an Audit in Accordance with ISAs* as follows: 'An attitude that includes a questioning mind, being alert to conditions which may indicate possible misstatement due to error or fraud, and a critical assessment of audit evidence'.

Professional scepticism means for example, being alert to contradictory or unreliable audit evidence, and conditions that may indicate the existence of fraud. If professional scepticism is not maintained, the auditor may overlook unusual circumstances, use unsuitable audit procedures, or reach inappropriate conclusions when evaluating the results of audit work. In summary, maintaining an attitude of professional scepticism is important in reducing audit risk.

In the case of the audit of Coot Co, the audit junior has not exercised a sufficient degree of professional scepticism when obtaining audit evidence. Firstly, the reliability of the payroll supervisor's response to the junior's enquiry should be questioned. Additional and corroborating evidence should be sought for the assertion that the new employees are indeed temporary.

The absence of authorisation should also be further investigated. Authorisation is a control that should be in place for any additions to payroll, so it seems unusual that the control would not be in place even for temporary members of staff.

If it is proved correct that no authorisation is required for temporary employees the audit junior should have identified this as a control deficiency to be included in the report to those charged with governance.

The contradictory evidence from comments made by management also should be explored further. ISA 500 *Audit Evidence* states that 'if audit evidence obtained from one source is inconsistent with that obtained from another... the auditor shall determine what modifications or additions to audit procedures are necessary to resolve the matter'.

Additional procedures should therefore be carried out to determine which source of evidence is reliable. Further discussions should be held with management to clarify whether any additional employees have been recruited during the year.

The amendment of payroll could indicate that a fraud ('ghost employee') is being carried out by the payroll supervisor. Additional procedures should be conducted to determine whether the supervisor has made any other amendments to payroll to determine the possible scope of any fraud. Verification should be sought as to the existence of the new employees. The bank accounts into which their salaries are being paid should also be examined, to see if the payments are being made into the same account.

Finally, the audit junior should be made aware that it is not acceptable to just put a note on the file when matters such as the lack of authorisation come to light during the course of the audit. The audit junior should have discussed their findings with the audit senior or manager to seek guidance and proper supervision on whether further testing should be carried out.

---

**Examiner's comments**

Requirement (a)(i) required an assessment of the ethical and professional issues raised by the request from the audit client to investigate the fraudulent activity. Most answers were satisfactory, identifying the main ethical threats (advocacy, self-review etc.) raised by the scenario and explaining them to an extent. Some answers also discussed whether the audit firm would have the necessary skills and resources to perform such a specialist piece of work. Some answers however tended to focus on why the audit firm had not discovered the fraud during the previous audit, and the possibility of the audit firm being sued for negligence or the need to 'discipline' the audit manager. Some answers also contained irrelevant discussions of the responsibilities of management and auditors in relation to fraud, and other answers used the fundamental principles as a framework for their answer, probably as this had been set on a previous exam paper, but with a completely different question requirement. Requirement (a)(ii) asked candidates to explain the matters that should be discussed in a meeting with the client, in terms of planning the forensic investigation. Some answers were very satisfactory, covering a wide range of matters including the timeframe, the required output of the investigation, and access to the client's accounting systems amongst others. Some answers however tended to simply list out the procedures that would be performed in conducting the investigation, or explain to the client's management the controls that should have been in place to stop the fraud in the first place.

Part (b)'s scenario described a cash-based business whose owner manager was acting suspiciously in relation to the accounting for cash sales. A large sum of cash had been transferred to an overseas bank account and the transaction had no supporting evidence. The requirement was to discuss the implications of these circumstances. This open requirement allowed for discussion of many different implications for the audit firm, included suspected fraud and/or money laundering, a poor control environment, the ethical implications of the owners intimidating behaviour, and problems for the audit firm in obtaining evidence. Most candidates covered a range of points and the majority correctly discussed fraud and/or money laundering. Weaker answers tended to focus on the materiality of the cash transferred to overseas, and seemed not to notice the client's suspicious behaviour. Candidates are reminded that they will often be expected to identify a key issue in a question scenario and that in a question of this type it is important to stop and think about what is happening in the scenario before rushing to start to write an answer. This question is a good example of one where a relatively short answer could generate a lot of

---

marks – if the scenario has been properly thought through before writing the answer. The requirement also asked for an explanation of any reporting that should take place by the audit senior. Candidates who had identified money laundering as an issue usually scored well here, describing the need to report to the audit firm's Money Laundering Reporting Officer, and what should be reported to them. Weaker answers discussed the auditor's report or that the fraud/money laundering should be reported to the client's management. This is not good advice given that the owner-manager was the person acting suspiciously and would have resulted in him being tipped off.

Part (c) described a client where unauthorised additions had been made to payroll, and contradictory audit evidence had been obtained. Candidates were asked to explain the term 'professional scepticism' and to recommend further actions to be taken by the auditor. Answers here were reasonably good, with most candidates able to attempt an explanation of the term, and most identifying poor controls leading to a possible fraud involving the payroll supervisor.

| | | | Marks |
|---|---|---|---|
| **Marking scheme** | | | |

| | | | Marks |
|---|---|---|---|
| **(a)** | **(i)** | **Ethical and professional issues**<br>Generally 1 mark per issue assessed:<br>– Non-audit service creates self-review threat<br>– Non-audit service creates advocacy threat<br>– Significance of threat to be evaluated<br>– Significance depends on materiality and subjectivity<br>– Examples of safeguards (1 mark each)<br>– Competence to provide service<br>– Resources to provide service<br>– Confidentiality agreements | |
| | | Maximum | 6 |
| | **(ii)** | **Matters to be discussed**<br>Generally 1 mark for each matter explained:<br>– Purpose, nature and scope of investigation<br>– Confirm objectives of investigation<br>– Time-scale and deadline<br>– Potential scale of the fraud<br>– How fraud reported to finance director<br>– Possible reasons for fraud not being detected by internal controls<br>– Resources to be made available to investigation team<br>– Whether matter reported to police | |
| | | Maximum | 6 |
| **(b)** | | **Money laundering**<br>**Implications of the audit senior's note**<br>1 mark for each matter discussed relevant to money laundering:<br>– Definition of money laundering<br>– Placement – cash-based business<br>– Owner posting transactions<br>– Layering – electronic transfer to overseas<br>– Secrecy and aggressive attitude<br>– Audit to be considered very high risk<br>– Senior may have tipped off the client<br>– Firm may consider withdrawal from audit<br>– But this may have tipping off consequences | |

**Reporting that should take place**

Generally 1 mark for each comment:

– Report suspicions immediately to MLRO
– Failure to report is itself an offence
– Examples of matters to be reported
– Audit senior may discuss matters with audit manager but senior responsible for the report

| | |
|---|---|
| Maximum | 8 |

**(c)** **Professional scepticism**

Generally 1 mark for each comment:

– Definition of professional scepticism
– Coot Co – evidence is unreliable and contradictory
– Absence of authorisation is fraud indicator
– Additional substantive procedures needed
– Management's comments should be corroborated
– Control deficiency to be reported to management/those charged with governance
– Audit junior needs better supervision/training on how to deal with deficiencies identified

| | |
|---|---|
| Maximum | 5 |
| **Total** | 25 |

**47 SQUIRE**  *Walk in the footsteps of a top tutor*

*Top tutor tips*

*Part (a) focuses on the review of interim financial information. This is a limited assurance engagement providing negative assurance. In part (i) you are asked for analytical procedures to perform during the review. Be careful to only give analytical procedures as other types of procedure are not relevant and will not score marks. Part (ii) requires matters to be considered in forming a conclusion on the interim financial statements. Even though this is not an audit engagement, the same approach can be taken as for audit completion questions which ask for matters to consider when reviewing the audit and forming a conclusion. Refer to the materiality of the warranty provision made in the previous year, discuss the appropriate accounting treatment and what should be done. In terms of the conclusion, remember that limited assurance will be given so the wording needs to reflect this.*

*Part (b) focuses on the governance and ethics areas of the syllabus. When dealing with ethical threats you must explain the threat. Take the discussion further by considering the significance of the threat. In this case, the situation involves the audit partner which makes the threat more significant. Finish off the discussion by stating any safeguards or actions the firm should implement.*

**(a)   (i)   Interim review analytical procedures**

Guidance on reviews of interim financial statements is provided in ISRE 2410 *Review of Interim Financial Information Performed by the Independent Auditor of the Entity*. The standard states that the auditor should plan their work to gather evidence using analytical procedures and enquiry.

The auditor should perform analytical procedures in order to discover unusual trends and relationships, or individual figures in the interim financial information, which may indicate a material misstatement.

Procedures should include the following:

- Comparing the interim financial information with anticipated results, budgets and targets as set by the management of the company.

- Comparing the interim financial information with:

    - comparable information for the immediately preceding interim period

    - the corresponding interim period in the previous year, and

    - the most recent audited financial statements.

- Comparing ratios and indicators for the current interim period with those of entities in the same industry.

- Considering relationships among financial and non-financial information. The auditor also may wish to consider information developed and used by the entity, for example, information in monthly financial reports provided to the senior management or press releases issued by the company relevant to the interim financial information.

- Comparing recorded amounts or ratios developed from recorded amounts, to expectations developed by the auditor. The auditor develops such expectations by identifying and using plausible relationships that are reasonably expected to exist based on the accountant's understanding of the entity and the industry in which the entity operates.

- Comparing disaggregated data, for example, comparing revenue reported by month and by product line or operating segment during the current interim period with that of comparable prior periods.

- Calculate the warranty provision as a percentage of new car sales up to 1 July 20X7 and compare with the year-end ratio to ensure the level of provision is consistent.

- Compare the warranty costs in the 6 month period with the warranty provision and assess whether the warranty provision appears reasonable given the current level of warranty claims.

As with analytical procedures performed in an audit, any unusual relationships, trends or individual amounts discovered which may indicate a material misstatement should be discussed with management. However, unlike an audit, further corroboration using substantive procedures is not necessary in a review engagement.

(ii)    **Review of interim financial statements**

Reviews of interim financial statements are governed by ISRE 2410 *Review of Interim Financial Information Performed by the Independent Auditor of the Entity.* Reviews are based on enquiries and analytical procedures, and having determined that Squire Co has changed its accounting treatment regarding the warranty provision, management must be asked to explain the reason for the change.

Interim financial statements should be prepared under the same financial reporting framework as annual financial statements. Therefore IAS *37 Provisions, Contingent Liabilities and Contingent Assets* should be applied.

It would appear correct that a warranty provision is not recognised for cars sold since 1 July 20X7, as Squire Co has no obligation relating to those sales. However, cars sold previous to that date are subject to a three-year warranty, so a warranty provision should continue to be recognised for the obligation arising in respect of those sales. Therefore Squire's interim financial statements understate liabilities and overstate profits.

The warranty provision as at 30 April represented 5.5% of total assets, therefore material to the financial statements. If the same warranty provision still needs to be recognised at 31 October, it would represent 5% of total assets, therefore material to the interim financial statements.

ISRE 2410 requires that when a matter comes to the auditor's attention that leads the auditor to question whether a material adjustment should be made to the interim financial information, additional inquiries should be made, or other procedures performed. In this case, the auditor may wish to inspect sales documentation to ensure that warranties are no longer offered on sales after 1 July. The auditor should also review customer correspondence to ensure that warranties on sales prior to 1 July are still in place.

If as a result of performing the necessary procedures, the auditor believes that a material adjustment is needed in the interim financial information, the matter must be communicated to the appropriate level of management, and if management fail to respond appropriately within a reasonable period of time, to those charged with governance. In order to avoid a modification of the report, it is likely that adjustment would be made by management to the interim financial statements.

If the amount remains unadjusted, meaning that the interim financial statements contain a material departure from the applicable financial reporting framework, the report on the review of interim financial information should contain a qualified or adverse conclusion. This is a modification of the conclusion, and the auditor must describe the reason for the modification, which is provided in a paragraph entitled 'Basis for Qualified Conclusion'.

The qualified conclusion would be worded as follows: 'Based on our review, with the exception of the matter described in the preceding paragraph, nothing has come to our attention that causes us to believe that the accompanying interim financial information does not give a true and fair view...'

Finally, the audit firm should consider whether it is possible to withdraw from the review engagement and resigning from the audit appointment.

**(b)** **(i)** **Ethical and professional matters**

**Temporary recruitment of audit partner**

Seconding a member of staff to an audit client may create a self-review threat. This would arise if the member of staff returns to the audit firm and considers matters or documentation which is the result of work which they performed while on assignment to the client.

In this situation, it is likely that the individual would be involved in preparing the financial systems of Gull Co for the flotation. If this is the case, it would create a significant threat to objectivity. This would be reduced if the role was focused on non-financial matters.

Additionally, the member of staff would work alongside employees of the client on a daily basis. This would overstep the normal professional boundary between auditor and client and may compromise the objectivity of the member of staff due to their familiarity with employees of the client.

In order to reduce this threat, the member of staff seconded to Gull Co should not be a current or future member of the audit team.

An additional risk would be if the seconded member of staff assumed managerial responsibilities of the client. This is not permitted. Given that Gull Co has specifically requested a partner, it appears as though they require someone senior, indicating that they may need someone to either make or significantly influence decision making.

In order to reduce this risk, the use of a less senior member of staff with relevant experience of the flotation process could be proposed and make it clear in the contract that they are not able to make decisions for Gull Co and that decision making will always remain their responsibility.

Alternatively, it could be recommended that Gull Co recruit the assistance of either the management or transaction advisory services team to assist them with the flotation as a separate engagement, thus circumventing the ethical threats identified.

**UK syllabus:** FRC Ethical Standard section 2 *Financial, business, employment and personal relationships,* states that an audit firm shall not enter into an agreement with an audited entity to provide a partner or employee to work for a temporary period as if that individual were an employee of the audited entity (a 'loan staff assignment') unless:

- the agreement is for a short period of time and does not involve staff or partners performing non-audit services which would not be permitted under FRC Ethical Standard section 5 *Non-audit/Additional services,* and

- the audited entity agrees that the individual concerned will not hold a management position, and acknowledges its responsibility for directing and supervising the work to be performed, which will not include such matters as making management decisions or exercising discretionary authority to commit the audited entity to a particular position or accounting treatment.

**Recruitment services**

In relation to the request to provide assistance in recruiting new members of the board, this could give rise to self-interest, familiarity or intimidation threats as the firm would essentially be advising on the recruitment of staff who will ultimately be in senior management positions and responsible for the running of and oversight of a listed company. These new members of staff may also go on to be included in any audit committee which the company sets up and will be responsible for assessing the independence of the external auditors. Being involved in any decision on who should be appointed to such a senior position is also likely to involve the firm taking on a management responsibility which is not appropriate. Given that Gull Co is potentially going to be a listed company, the audit firm should not be involved in any activity which involves searching for suitable candidates or undertaking any reference checks of prospective candidates. This request should be turned down due to the potential management responsibility involved.

*Tutorial note*

*Credit will be awarded for relevant comments relating to the professional benefits of accepting the assignment.*

(ii)     **Implications of governance and board structure on audit process**

**Structure of the board**

As a private company with the majority of shares held by the Brenner family, the auditor's report addressed to the shareholders as a body would have been aimed predominantly at the Brenner family. However, the predominance of the Brenner family may undermine the independence of the board. The board may be accustomed to operating in the interests of the family as the majority shareholders. However, once the company is listed, the board will be required to consider the interests of the new shareholders as a group. The executive members of the board are either Brenner family members or long-term employees of the company and potentially loyal to the existing ownership.

With only one non-executive director, the board currently lacks independent oversight and the opinions and decisions of the executive board may not be subject to appropriate levels of challenge and scrutiny.

In addition, non-executive board members are specifically required to scrutinise the performance of management, consider the integrity of the financial statements, determine director remuneration and participate in the appointment and removal of directors. With limited experience outside IT consultancy and limited time, the current non-executive is unlikely to be able to fulfil these roles effectively on their own.

There is no indication that management lacks integrity but the audit firm must remain sceptical of the motivations of the family, particularly leading up to a listing. There will be an incentive to overstate performance and position to inflate the value of the company.

With little effective oversight of the executive board, the audit firm must remain alert for this possibility, particularly when auditing matters involving management judgment in subsequent financial periods.

**UK syllabus:** As a company listed on the UK stock exchange, the company will be expected to comply with the UK Corporate Governance Code (the Code) or explain any departure from the Code in the annual report. The Code states that the board should include an appropriate combination of executive and non-executive directors (and, in particular, independent non-executive directors) such that no individual or small group of individuals can dominate the board's decision taking. The auditor, in line with Bulletin 2009/4 *Developments in corporate governance affecting the responsibilities of auditors in UK companies*, will be required to review the corporate governance statement produced by Gull plc for any inconsistencies and to report in line with the Bulletin.

**Audit committee**

The lack of any form of audit committee is a significant departure from corporate governance best practice. The audit committee fulfils a number of significant roles, including monitoring the integrity of the financial statements, reviewing internal financial controls, monitoring the independence of the external auditor and communicating with the external auditor on matters relating to the external audit. The audit committee should have a member with relevant financial expertise and this will become of even more importance once the company is listed.

In the absence of an audit committee, the auditor will have to communicate directly with the board including the requirement to communicate how the auditor has maintained their independence in line with ISA 260 *Communication with Those Charged with Governance*. This may affect the independence of the audit firm, or at least the perception of their independence. It may also reduce the effectiveness of communications between the auditor and the company. The audit committee is responsible for communicating relevant matters, such as deficiencies in internal control, up to the executive board for their consideration. Without an audit committee, matters of significance to the audit may not be given sufficient prominence by the board. Further, the audit committee is responsible for reviewing the integrity of the financial statements and internal controls and currently there is no-one at Gull Co capable of carrying out this role. Overall this may make it harder for the auditor to discuss and communicate key findings from the audit including the auditor's qualitative assessment of the company's accounting practices. Also with the lack of an objective audit committee, it may be harder for the auditor to fulfil their responsibilities to communicate any significant difficulties which are encountered during the audit.

**Listed status**

Further as a listed company, Gull Co will be subject to increased scrutiny and pressure to achieve performance levels, which may motivate the board to manipulate the financial statements to present an improved picture of performance. This increases the level of audit risk and is likely to have a significant impact on the firm's assessment of the risk of fraud and management override.

This is likely to have a significant impact on the firm's approach to auditing areas of the financial statements subject to judgment, such as management estimates and revenue recognition.

As a listed company, Gull Co may be required to produce more detailed financial statements probably in a shorter time frame and as mentioned above, the lack of financial expertise and lack of objective scrutiny by an audit committee may result in errors or omissions. This again increases the level of audit risk and more detailed testing may need to be performed to ensure compliance with appropriate accounting standards and listing rules.

Further, once listed, the auditor's report issued for Gull Co will be available to a much wider audience and will require additional disclosures in line with ISA 701 *Communicating Key Audit Matters in the Independent Auditor's Report*. This will add another level of work and complexity to the audit of Gull Co.

---

**Examiner's comments**

Requirement (a)(i) was unsatisfactorily answered by almost all candidates. This asked for the principal analytical procedures that should be used to gather evidence in a review of interim financial information. Candidates are repeatedly reminded that non-audit engagements are part of the syllabus, and likely to feature regularly in the examination. However, few candidates seemed to know the purpose of a review of interim financial information, which meant that their answers lacked clarity. Most answers could only suggest a comparison with the prior period, and hardly any answers mentioned the disaggregation of data, or comparison with budget. Only a handful of candidates seemed aware of the existence of ISRE 2410, *Review of Interim Financial Information Performed by the Independent Auditor of the entity,* on which the requirement is based. Some candidates confused a 'review of interim financial information' with an 'interim audit', despite the short scenario describing a review of interim financial information for the avoidance of any such confusion.

Requirement (a)(ii) was based on a scenario which described a review engagement that was taking place on the interim financial statements of a listed company. An accounting policy in relation to warranty provisions had been changed in the interim financial statements, and based on the information provided, candidates should have appreciated that the accounting treatment was incorrect. Figures were provided to enable materiality to be calculated. The requirement was to assess the matters that should be considered in forming an opinion on the interim financial statements, and the implications for the review report. Most answers were good at discussing the accounting treatment for the warranty provision, that the non-recognition was not appropriate, and the majority correctly assessed the materiality of the issue. Answers were inadequate in discussing the impact of this on the review report, being mostly unable to say much more than the auditor would need to mention it in the review report. There seemed to be a lack of knowledge on anything other than the standard wording for a review report, with many answers stating that the wording should be 'nothing has come to our attention' followed by a discussion that there actually was something to bring to shareholders' attention but with no recommendation as to how this should be done.

Part (b) had two elements, an ethics part regarding other services which were generally well answered and a second element which required the implications the governance structure and a potential listing may have on the audit process. Many candidates appeared to interpret this as a requirement to comment on how the governance structure of the client fell below best practice and how to improve that structure and did not address the audit implications at all. This is particularly disappointing given the recent examiner's article on the topic and again candidates are reminded to make sure that they read the requirements carefully.

---

| | | Marking scheme | | Marks |
|---|---|---|---|---|
| | | | | *Marks* |
| (a) | (i) | **Interim review analytical procedures**<br>Generally 1 mark per procedure:<br>– Comparisons to anticipated results<br>– Comparison to corresponding interim last year<br>– Comparison to last audited accounts<br>– Comparisons to similar entities<br>– Comparisons to non-financial data/ratios<br>– Develop auditor expectation using understanding of entity<br>– Disaggregation of data<br>– Calculate warranty as a percentage of sales<br>– Compare warranty costs with warranty provision | | |
| | | | Maximum | 7 |
| | (ii) | **Interim financial statement review**<br>Up to 1½ marks for each matter to be considered in forming conclusion/implication for report:<br>– Interim financial information should use applicable financial reporting framework<br>– Identify and explain unrecognised provision<br>– Correct calculation of materiality (1 mark)<br>– Communicate adjustment to management/TCWG<br>– If amount unadjusted, the conclusion will be qualified<br>– Reason for qualified conclusion to be explained in the report<br>– Consider withdrawing from engagement/resign from audit | | |
| | | | Maximum | 6 |
| (b) | (i) | **Ethical and professional matters**<br>In general up to 1 mark for each well explained point:<br>**Temporary recruitment of audit partner**<br>– Potential self-review threat<br>– Potential familiarity threat<br>– Potential management decision making threat<br>– Recommendations to reduce the potential threats described (1 mark each to a maximum of 2)<br>**Recruitment services**<br>– Potential self-interest, intimidation and familiarity threat<br>– Management responsibility in appointing senior management<br>– As listed entity, service cannot be provided<br>– Decline engagement | | |
| | (ii) | **Implications for audit process**<br>In general up to 1 mark for each well explained point:<br>– Lack of independence and oversight of board<br>– Ineffective non-executive board<br>– Need for increased auditor scepticism particularly in light of potential listing<br>– Increased fraud/manipulation risk which will need to be reflected in audit approach<br>– No effective audit committee<br>– Communication in line with ISA 260 harder with no objective audit committee<br>– Listed company with increased audit risk<br>– Extended auditor's report requirements | | |
| | | | Maximum | 12 |
| **Total** | | | | 25 |

# PROFESSIONAL AND ETHICAL CONSIDERATIONS

**48    THOMASSON & CO**  *Walk in the footsteps of a top tutor*

*Top tutor tips*

*Part (a) covers money laundering. Part (i) requires knowledge of money laundering requirements and the policies and procedures an accountancy firm should have in place to comply with the regulations. This is rote-learned knowledge from the text book and should be straightforward. Part (ii) requires application of knowledge to the scenario to evaluate whether there are any indicators of money laundering. Unusual transfers of cash, overly complex arrangements and uncertainty over the source of cash are all indicators of money laundering. You need to justify why you think the issues indicate money laundering. Very limited marks will be awarded for only listing the indicators.*

*Part (b) covers ethical and professional issues. Identify the type of threat, explain how the threat could influence the audit, discuss whether the threat is significant and finish off by explaining the safeguards the firm should take to reduce the threat to an acceptable level.*

**(a)    Money laundering**

**(i)    Policies and procedures for anti-money laundering programme**

Thomasson & Co should have established an anti-money laundering programme within the firm. As part of this programme, the firm should have appointed a money laundering reporting officer (MLRO) with an appropriate level of experience and seniority.

The audit firm should also have established internal reporting lines which should be followed to report any suspicions. Thomasson & Co will probably have a standard form which should be used to report suspicions of money laundering to the MLRO.

The typical content of an internal report on suspected money laundering may include the name of the suspect, the amounts potentially involved, and the reasons for the suspicions with supporting evidence if possible, and the whereabouts of the laundered cash. The firm's internal policies should have been set up to ensure that all pertinent information is captured in this standardised report.

Any individual in the audit firm who has suspicions of money laundering activities is then required to disclose these suspicions to the MLRO. The report must be done as soon as possible as any non-disclosure or failure to report such suspicions will constitute an offence under the money laundering regulations.

On receipt of the internal report, the MLRO must consider all of the circumstances surrounding the suspicions of money laundering activities, document this process and decide whether to report the suspicions to the appropriate external authorities. The audit firm has a legal duty to report even though this may conflict with the auditor's duty of confidentiality.

**Tutorial note**

*Credit will be awarded for other relevant answer points in relation to a firm's anti-money laundering programme.*

(ii)    **Evaluation of possible indicators of money laundering activities**

Money laundering is the process by which criminals attempt to conceal the true origin and ownership of the proceeds of criminal activity, allowing them to maintain control over the proceeds, and ultimately providing a legitimate cover for their sources of income.

In the case of Clean Co, the circumstances which may be indicative of money laundering activities include the following:

**Cash-intensive business**

Clean Co has a high level of cash-based sales (75%) and a high volume of individual sales reports. The nature of its business therefore creates a significant risk that illicit cash funds are being passed off as legitimate sales.

More specifically Mr Blackers' sale to a business associate for $33,000 may be an example of the placement of illegal funds in order to legitimise them as genuine sales. The size of the transaction in a business selling cleaning products and the round sum amount may be additional grounds for suspicion in relation to this transaction.

**International property transactions**

The performance of Mr Blackers' personal taxation computation has identified a significant number of transactions involving the purchase and sale of properties in international locations. These transactions may be examples of real estate laundering by Mr Blackers in his personal affairs. It is possible that he may be purchasing these properties with illegal funds ('placement') and then selling them in order to make funds appear legitimate ('integration').

A high volume of such transactions may also be indicative of the 'layering' of transactions in an attempt to make the original source of the funds more difficult to trace.

(b)    **Ethical and professional issues**

**Taxation services**

**Company tax computation**

The performance of the company tax computation creates a self-review threat. A self-review threat arises when an auditor reviews work which they themselves have previously performed – for example, if the external auditor is involved in the process of preparing the financial statements and then audits them. As a result, there is a risk that the auditor will not be sufficiently objective in performing the audit and may fail to identify any shortcomings in their own work. In this case therefore, a self-review threat to auditor independence arises because the tax calculation forms the basis of the tax payable and the tax charge in the financial statements and as such the audit team may be more likely to accept the tax calculations without adequate testing.

There is also a potential advocacy threat. An advocacy threat arises when the auditor is asked to promote or represent their client in some way. In this situation, there is a risk of the auditor being seen to promote the interests of Clean Co with a third party such as the tax authorities and therefore that the auditor will be biased in favour of the client and cannot be fully objective.

Completing tax returns does not generally create a threat of management involvement by the auditor, as completing the tax return may not involve the auditor making any judgements. Provided management takes responsibility for the returns, including any judgements which have been made, the threat to objectivity is not likely to be significant.

Where tax calculations have been prepared by the auditor for the purpose of preparing accounting entries, the IESBA International Code of Ethics for Professional Accountants (the Code) and the FRC Ethical Standard state that this may be acceptable for an unlisted audit client and that the firm should consider implementing safeguards in order to reduce the self-review threat to an acceptable level. In this case, these safeguards might have included, for example, using professionals who are not members of the audit team to prepare the tax computations. The tax services should be reviewed by an independent tax partner, or other senior tax employee.

Therefore, given that Clean Co is an unlisted client, Thomasson & Co should ascertain which members of staff performed the taxation services and should review whether the threat to independence has been adequately assessed before the taxation services were performed and whether adequate safeguards have been applied.

**Mr Blackers' personal tax computation**

From an ethical perspective, there is no prohibition in the Code or the FRC Ethical Standard on the preparation of personal tax returns for the directors of an audit client such as Clean Co. However, in this case the auditor should consider whether the preparation of Mr Blackers' personal tax return may result in the auditor being associated with criminal activities if the suspicions of money laundering activities noted above prove to be well founded.

The auditor should also consider the appropriateness of personal taxation services being billed to the company. Indeed, the preparation of Mr Blackers' personal tax return may be a taxable benefit which should be included in his tax return and the fee for this service may need to be reflected in his director's loan account with the company.

**Website and online sales system**

According to the Code and the FRC Ethical Standard, providing services to an audit client involving the design or implementation of IT systems which form a significant part of the internal control over financial reporting or generate information which is significant to the accounting records or financial statements on which the firm will express an opinion constitutes a self-review threat.

A self-review threat arises when an auditor reviews work which they themselves have previously performed – for example, if the external auditor is involved in the process of preparing the financial statements and then audits them. As a result, there is a risk that the auditor will not be sufficiently objective in performing the audit and may fail to identify any shortcomings in their own work.

In this case, the self-review threat arises as the new systems will produce data which will be used directly in the preparation of the financial statements. The audit process will therefore include reviewing and testing of financial data and systems which Thomasson & Co has helped to design and implement. As a result, there is a clear risk that the audit team may too readily place reliance on these systems.

With reference to Clean Co therefore, it is clear that providing assistance with the design and implementation of the website and online sales system will constitute a self-review threat as the auditor will audit sales figures which are generated by the system.

There is also a risk that the firm may assume a management responsibility if they become involved in making management decisions. In the case of revenue, this self-review threat may be heightened further by the auditor's reliance on controls testing and on analytical review of the data summaries generated by the new system.

---

*Tutorial note*

*UK syllabus: According to the FRC Ethical Standard, providing information technology services can create a management threat to independence. The management threat arises because the design and implementation of information systems is the responsibility of management. If the auditor becomes involved in making management decisions with regard to the website and online sales system, the perception that the auditor is independent of management would be impaired.*

---

It also seems clear that the new online sales system will be significant to the client's financial statements and records. Such a self-review threat may be too significant even for an unlisted client such as Clean Co unless appropriate safeguards are put in place.

Examples of possible safeguards which might assist in managing the self-review threat include the following:

- The client should acknowledge its responsibility for establishing and monitoring the system of internal controls and for the operating system and data it generates

- The respective responsibilities of the audit firm and the client should be clearly defined in a separate engagement letter in order to ensure that the client makes all management decisions in relation to the design and implementation process

- Thomasson & Co should use a separate team made up of non-audit staff to perform the systems design and implementation assignment and the work performed by this team should be subject to independent professional review.

If the self-review threat cannot be reduced to an acceptable level, or the engagement will result in the firm assuming a management responsibility, the service should not be provided.

**Office party**

The *Code* states that client hospitality (in this case the attendance at the office party by the audit team) may create a familiarity threat. A familiarity threat occurs when the auditor is too sympathetic or trusting of the client because of a close relationship with them. There is a risk therefore that as a result of attending the client office party, the audit staff may be getting too close to the client staff especially given that according to the audit senior, this practice has occurred every year. This close relationship may result in the audit team becoming less objective and less able to challenge explanations provided by the client.

The *Code* also states that gifts from a client to a member of the audit team may create a self-interest threat. A self-interest threat arises when the auditor derives a potential personal benefit from an audit client which may motivate them to behave in a manner which aims to protect that benefit. With reference to the office party therefore, the audit staff are receiving a direct financial benefit from the client (in this case in the form of vouchers).

Unless the value of such gifts is trivial and inconsequential, the self-interest threat would be too significant to mitigate with safeguards and the gifts should not be accepted.

The audit firm should consider introducing internal authorisation procedures in order to ensure transparency and to establish whether the value is trivial and inconsequential.

In this case, the value of $30 per head does appear to be trivial but the auditor might still consider declining the gifts in order to maintain a visible professional distance from a client which may be involved in criminal activities.

*Tutorial note*

*UK syllabus: There may be implications from the Bribery Act (2010). Under the Bribery Act, it is an offence to bribe another person or to be bribed yourself. This offence is widely defined and covers all bribes which are given or received to 'improperly perform' a function which is expected to be carried out in good faith, impartially, and where the person involved is in a position of trust. To ensure that there is no actual or perceived breach of the Bribery Act, the auditor might consider it prudent to decline the gifts and hospitality which has been offered by the client, even if it is trivial in monetary value.*

**Examiner's comments**

Requirement (a)(i) for four marks asked for a discussion of policies and procedures a firm should have in place in relation to an anti-money laundering programme. Most candidates were able to score full marks here. Candidates who did not score well either simply listed points with no discussion or confused the audit firm with the client and discussed controls over cash sales or places where the client could implement policies.

The second requirement (a)(ii), was for six marks and asked candidates to evaluate whether there were indicators of money laundering by the client or its staff. The majority of answers to this requirement were disappointing. Most candidates were able to correctly identify the indicators at the client which might suggest money laundering activities but made no attempt at explaining or evaluating those indicators. Simply stating sales are cash based or there is an off-shore bank account does not demonstrate an understanding of why these things are an indicator. Candidates would do well to add the word because at the end of such sentences to force them to explain why something is a red flag. For example "the company sales are 75% cash based. This is a potential indicator of money laundering because cash based sales are harder to trace." An even stronger answer would then relate this back to the stages of money laundering, giving a "So What?" to their answer. "This means that additional cash can be introduced alongside genuine sales. This would represent the placement stage of money laundering". Another mistake candidates often made in this part of the question was to discuss the risk of employee fraud/theft of the cash which was not required.

Part (c) was a 15-mark requirement to discuss the ethical and professional issues arising at the client. Candidates tended to perform poorly in this requirement. This was partly down to candidates not leaving enough time to properly address the requirement and partly because candidates are still not demonstrating the understanding of ethical issues or how to describe them sufficiently to attain marks. Candidates here also often showed a lack of detailed knowledge of the ethical guidance that would help them to properly analyse the issues in the question. In addition to the points on describing ethics made above in relation to question one, common mistakes made by candidates were to assume that invoicing the company for the tax work done on behalf of the directors was disallowed (rather than identifying that if the company was paying for his tax work, this should be considered director's remuneration and not part of the audit fee for disclosure and possible personal tax reasons) or stating that a trivial benefit provided to the auditors was not permitted which again is not the case, trivial hospitality benefits are permitted but should be approved by the firm. One of the most concerning points that was made in many answers was to correctly tie in the risk of money laundering at the client and the need to report this to the firm's money laundering reporting officer while avoiding tipping off but then to follow that with the suggestion that the firm resign from the client immediately and inform TCWG of the money laundering – so effectively then tipping off the client.

| | | Marking scheme | | Marks |
|---|---|---|---|---|

**(a)** **Money laundering**

**(i)** **Reporting duties and procedures**

Generally 1 mark per point

- Suspicions should be reported to nominated person within audit firm (MLRO); MLRO should possess suitable level of experience/seniority
- Audit firm should have established internal reporting lines which should be followed to report any suspicions
- Any individual in audit firm who has suspicions of money laundering activities must disclose them to MLRO; non-disclosure/failure to report constitutes an offence
- MLRO must consider all circumstances, document the process and decide whether to report to appropriate authorities; legal duty to report even though this may conflict with auditor's duty of confidentiality

Maximum **4**

**(ii)** **Indicators of money laundering**

Generally up to 2 marks for each well-explained point of explanation, for example:

**Cash intensive business**

- High level of cash sales and high volume of individual sales reports; risk illicit cash funds are being passed off as legitimate sales
- Mr Blackers' sale to business associate for $33,000 may be example of placement of illegal funds in order to legitimise them as genuine sales.

**International property transactions**

- May be example of real estate laundering by Mr Blackers in his personal affairs; may be purchasing international property with illegal funds (placement) and then selling them in order to make funds appear legitimate (integration)
- High volume of transactions and off-shore bank accounts in Mr Blackers' name may be indicative of layering of transactions in attempt to make original source of funds difficult to trace

Maximum **6**

**(b)** **Ethical and professional issues**

Generally 1 mark for each point identified and explained

**Taxation services**

- Company tax computation is self-review threat as tax calculation forms basis of tax payable and tax charge in financial statements
- Advocacy threat re acting on client's behalf with tax authorities
- Per IESBA *Code*, completing tax returns does not generally create threat to independence if management takes responsibility for returns including any judgments made
- Tax calculations for purpose of preparing accounting entries – may be acceptable for unlisted audit client; firm should consider safeguards, e.g. using professionals not members of audit team or independent senior/partner review
- Preparation of Mr Blackers' personal tax return may be taxable benefit which should be included in tax return and fee should be reflected in his director's loan account with the company
- Preparation of personal tax return may result in auditor being associated with criminal activities (i.e. money laundering as above)

AAA: ADVANCED AUDIT AND ASSURANCE (INT & UK)

**Website and online sales system**

- Self-review threat as auditor will audit sales figures generated by system
- New system appears to be significant to client's financial statements and records
- Risk assume management responsibility relating to design of system and controls
- Threat may be too significant even for unlisted client unless appropriate safeguards put in place
- Examples of possible safeguards include: client acknowledges responsibility for establishing and monitoring system of internal controls; client makes all management decisions re design and implementation process; client is responsible for operating system and data it generates; separate team made up of non-audit staff performs work with independent professional review (max 2 marks for safeguards)

**Office party**

- Client hospitality (attendance at party) may create familiarity risks as audit staff may be getting too close to client especially given that this happens every year
- Gifts may create self-interest risk as audit staff receiving direct financial benefit from client
- Unless value is trivial and inconsequential, threats would be too significant to mitigate with safeguards and should not be accepted
- Auditor should have internal authorisation procedures to establish whether value is trivial and inconsequential
- In this case, value appears trivial but auditor should consider declining given possible criminal activities by client staff

|  |  |
|---|---|
| Maximum | 15 |
| Total | 25 |

## 49 WESTON & CO  *Walk in the footsteps of a top tutor*

*Top tutor tips*

*Part (a) deals with tendering. For the tender document you need to identify ways in which you can sell your firm to the client. Try and match the firm with the prospective client from the information in the scenario. Don't just give rote learnt knowledge without applying it to the scenario.*

*Part (b) focuses on long association of senior personnel with an audit client. Identify the name of the threat and explain why long association creates an ethical issue. The requirement also asks for discussion of whether the engagement partner can become quality control reviewer of the same client in the future. Don't forget to include this in your answer.*

*Part (c) looks at the issue of providing a valuation service to an audit client. Identify and explain the threat but also discuss the significance of the threat. Finish off by suggesting the safeguards that can be applied to manage the threat, if applicable.*

**(a)    (i)    Matters to be included in the audit proposal**

**Outline of Weston & Co**

A brief outline of the audit firm, including a description of different services offered, and an outline of the firm's international locations. This will be important to Jones Co given that it wishes to expand into overseas markets and will be looking for an audit firm with experience in different countries. The document should also outline the range of services which Weston & Co can provide, and any specialism which the firm has in auditing recruitment companies.

**Identify the audit requirements of Jones Co**

There should be an outline of the statutory audit requirement in the country in which Jones Co is incorporated, to confirm that the company is now at the size which necessitates a full audit of the financial statements. As this is the first time an audit is required, it will be important to outline the regulatory framework and the duties of auditors and of management in relation to the audit requirement.

**Audit approach**

A description of the proposed audit approach, outlining the stages of the audit process and the audit methodology used by the firm should be given. The description should state that the audit will be conducted in accordance with ISA requirements. Weston & Co should emphasise the need for thorough testing of opening balances and comparatives given that this is the first year that the financial statements will be audited. The risk-based nature of the audit methodology should be explained, and that it will involve an assessment of accounting systems and internal controls. Controls may not be good given the limited resources of the accounting function, so the audit approach is likely to be substantive in nature.

The audit firm may at this stage wish to explain that while the audit should not be 'disruptive', the audit team will require some input from Jones Co's employees, especially the accountant, and other personnel including Bentley may need to make themselves available to respond to the audit firm's requests for information and to discuss matters relating to the audit.

**Communication**

The proposal should outline the various communications which will be made with those charged with governance during the audit process, and highlight the value added from such communications, for example, recommendations on any control deficiencies.

**Deadlines**

The audit firm should clarify the timescale to be used for the audit. Bentley has requested that the audit is completed within four months of the year end. This seems to be reasonable and it should be possible for the audit of a relatively small company with simple transactions and a full-time accountant to be completed within that timeframe.

### Quality control and ethics

Weston & Co should clarify its adherence to the ACCA *Code of Ethics*, and to International Standards on Quality Control. This should provide assurance that the audit firm will provide an unbiased and credible auditor's report. This may be important for the venture capitalists who will wish to gain assurance on the financial information which they are provided with in relation to their investment.

### Additional non-audit and assurance services

The audit proposal should describe the various non-audit and assurance related services which Weston & Co would be able to offer Jones Co. These may include, for example, business consultancy and corporate finance advice on overseas expansion and obtaining any necessary additional funding to help the planned overseas expansion.

This discussion should clearly state and emphasise that the provision of such services is subject to meeting ethical requirements and will be completely separate from the audit service.

### Tutorial note

*Credit will be awarded for discussion of other matters which may be included in the audit proposal, where the matters are relevant to the audit of Jones Co.*

**(ii)** **Matters to be considered in determining the audit fee**

Weston & Co needs to consider a number of matters in determining the audit fee. The commercial need for the firm to make a profit from providing the audit service needs to be considered alongside the client's expectations about the fee level and how it has been arrived at.

### Cost of providing the service

First, the audit firm should consider the costs of providing the audit service. This will include primarily the costs of the audit team, so the firm will need to assess the number and seniority of audit team members who will be involved, and the amount of time that they will spend on the audit. There may be the need for auditor's experts to be engaged, and the costs of this should be included if necessary.

Weston & Co will have standard charge out rates which are used when determining an audit fee and these should be used to estimate the total fee. Other costs such as travel costs should also be considered.

### Client expectations

Bentley Jones has made some comments in relation to the audit fee which have ethical and other implications. First, he wants the audit fee to be low, and says that he is willing to pay more for other services. One of the problems of a low audit fee is that it can affect audit quality, as the audit firm could be tempted to cut corners and save time in order to minimise the costs of the audit.

Offering an unrealistically low audit fee which is below market rate in order to win or retain an audit client is known as lowballing, and while this practice is not prohibited, the client must not be misled about the amount of work which will be performed and the outputs of the audit. The issue for the client is that an unrealistically low audit fee is unlikely to be sustainable in the long run, leading to unwelcome fee increases in subsequent years.

---

**Tutorial note**

*UK syllabus: FRC Ethical Standard section 4 states that the audit engagement partner must be satisfied and able to demonstrate that the audit engagement has assigned to it sufficient partners and staff with appropriate time and skill to perform the audit in accordance with all applicable auditing and ethical standards, irrespective of the audit fee to be charged. This means that the audit fee should be high enough to allow the use of appropriate resources and that a low fee cannot be tolerated if it would impact on audit quality.*

---

**Contingent fee**

The second issue is that Bentley Jones has suggested that the audit fee should be linked to the success of the company in expanding overseas, on which he wants the audit firm to provide advice. This would mean that the audit fee is being determined on a contingent fee basis. Contingent fees are fees calculated on a predetermined basis relating to the outcome of a transaction or the result of the services performed by the firm.

A contingent fee charged by a firm in respect of an audit engagement creates a self-interest threat which is so significant that no safeguards could reduce the threat to an acceptable level. Accordingly, a firm shall not enter into any such fee arrangement.

Weston & Co should explain to Bentley Jones that the audit fee will be determined by the level of audit work which needs to be performed, and cannot be in any way linked to the success of Jones Co or advice which may be given to the firm by its auditors. The fee will be determined by the grade of staff that make up the audit team and the time spent by each of them on the audit.

---

**Tutorial note**

*Credit will be awarded for discussion of other relevant current issues in relation to the setting of audit fees.*

---

**(b)** **Ethical threats created by long association of senior audit personnel and relevant safeguards**

When a senior auditor acts for an audit client for a long period, several ethical problems can arise. First, the professional scepticism of the auditor can be diminished. This happens because the auditor becomes too accepting of the client's methods and explanations, so stops approaching the audit with a questioning mind.

Familiarity and self-interest threats are created by using the same senior personnel on an audit engagement over a long period of time. The familiarity threat is linked to the issues relating to the loss of professional scepticism discussed above, and is due to the senior auditor forming a close relationship with the client's personnel over a long period of time.

As with any ethical threat, the significance of the threat should be evaluated and safeguards which reduce the threat to an acceptable level put in place. Matters which should be considered in evaluating the significance of the ethical threat could include the seniority of the auditor involved, the length of time they have acted for the client, the nature, frequency and extent of the individual's interactions with the client's management or those charged with governance and whether the client's management team has changed.

Examples of safeguards which can be used include:

- Rotating the senior personnel off the audit team

- Having a professional accountant who was not a member of the audit team review the work of the senior personnel

- Regular independent internal or external quality control reviews of the engagement.

*Tutorial note*

*INT syllabus:*

*In the case of a public interest company such as Ordway Co, the IESBA International Code of Ethics for Professional Accountants contains a specific requirement that an individual shall not be a key audit partner for more than seven years. After seven years the individual shall not be a member of the engagement team or be a key audit partner for the client for five years. This is known as the cooling off period, and during that period, the auditor shall not participate in the audit of the entity, provide quality control for the engagement, consult with the engagement team or the client regarding technical or industry-specific issues, transactions or events or otherwise directly influence the outcome of the engagement.*

*UK syllabus:*

*FRC Ethical Standard section 3 states that in the case of listed entities no one shall act as audit engagement partner for more than five years and that anyone who has acted as the audit engagement partner for a particular audited entity for a period of five years shall not subsequently participate in the audit engagement until a further period of five years has elapsed.*

Because Ordway Co is a listed company, the audit firm must remove Bobby from the audit team and not allow further contact with the client or the audit process. Bobby may not have any involvement with the audit of Ordway plc for the next five years.

Performing quality control work forms part of participating in the audit engagement. Therefore Bobby cannot act as engagement quality control reviewer for the audit of Ordway plc, having stepped down as audit engagement partner.

(c)     **Banbury Co**

Providing an actuarial valuation service is an example of providing a non-assurance service. The provision of such services can create threats to objectivity of self-review and self-interest.

The self-review threat arises because the defined benefit pension plan on which Weston & Co has been asked to provide a valuation service is included in the statement of financial position, and the audit firm would need to audit the figure which has been generated by a member of the firm. The self-interest threat arises from the fee which would be paid to the firm.

Weston & Co needs to evaluate the significance of the threats and whether safeguards could be used to reduce the threats to an acceptable level. In assessing the self-review threat the following factors should be considered:

*   Whether the valuation will have a material effect on the financial statements.

*   The extent of the client's involvement in determining and approving the valuation methodology and other significant matters of judgment.

*   The availability of established methodologies and professional guidelines.

*   For valuations involving standard or established methodologies, the degree of subjectivity inherent in the item.

*   The reliability and extent of the underlying data.

*   The degree of dependence on future events of a nature that could create significant volatility inherent in the amounts involved.

*   The extent and clarity of the disclosures in the financial statements.

A key matter to be considered is the materiality of the pension plan to Banbury Co's financial statements. Banbury Co is a listed company, and therefore a public interest entity. The Code and the FRC Ethical Standard state that an audit firm shall not provide valuation services to an audit client which is a public interest entity if the valuations would have a material effect, separately or in the aggregate, on the financial statements on which the firm will express an opinion.

Based on the 20X4 financial statements, the pension liability at the year-end represented only 0.3% of total assets and was immaterial. Weston & Co should consider whether there are any indications that the pension deficit may have become more significant during the year, which may have caused the balance to become material. In which case the audit firm should not provide the valuation service to Banbury Co.

An actuarial valuation involves significant subjectivity, for example, in determining the appropriate discount rate, and in estimating key variables to be used in the calculations. It is also unlikely that Banbury Co's management will possess sufficient knowledge and experience to have much involvement, if any, in the valuation. However, it may be possible to use safeguards to reduce the threats to an acceptable level.

Examples of such safeguards include:

*   Having a professional who was not involved in providing the valuation service review the audit or valuation work performed.

*   Making arrangements so that personnel providing such services do not participate in the audit engagement.

**Examiner's comments**

The first part of the question focused on practice management and client acceptance issues. The scenario described a potential new audit client, Jones Co, a small but rapidly growing company with ambitions to expand internationally. The audit firm had been approached to tender for the audit of Jones Co, and this would be the first year that the company required an audit. The company had previously had limited assurance reviews performed on its financial statements, and had one accountant using an off-the shelf accounting package. Requirement (a)(i) asked candidates to explain the specific matters to be included in the audit proposal document, other than those relating to the audit fee. This was quite well attempted by many, with almost all candidates understanding the main components of an audit proposal document such as a background of the audit firm, discussion of audit methodology, an outline of the firm's resources and timings and deadlines. Where candidates did not score well on this requirement was where the answer provided was very generic and was not made specific to the requirements of Jones Co. For example, some candidates ignored the fact that Jones Co had never previously been audited which would mean that management may have little appreciation of the audit process and as such the audit proposal should explain in some detail the responsibilities of management and the audit firm, and provide a detailed explanation of the audit process including key outputs. Requirement (a)(ii) went on to ask candidates to discuss the issues relating to determining the audit fee to be considered by the audit firm, assuming its appointment as auditor of Jones Co. Unfortunately many answers to this requirement did not identify the relevant matters in the question scenario, including the issue of contingent fees, intimidation on fees and lowballing that were implied by the comments made by the owner-manager of Jones Co. Better candidates were able to make the very valid point that the potential client needed a better understanding of the purpose of an audit and why it needs to be seen to be independent and tied this back to the content of the proposal document. Where these matters were not discussed, answers tended to be generic, and simply focused on the fact that audit fees should be determined by time, resources and charge-out rates. Many of the weaker answers did not focus on the specific nature of the question requirement, and instead discussed matters that had little to do with the audit fee, such as self-review threats and other irrelevant acceptance procedures such as customer due diligence.

Requirement (b) focused on a different audit client – Ordway Co, a listed company. The scenario briefly described that the current audit partner, having acted in that capacity for seven years was to be replaced by another partner, but wanted to stay in contact with the client and act as engagement quality control reviewer. Candidates were asked to explain the ethical threats raised by the long association of senior audit personnel with an audit client and the relevant safeguards to be applied. Candidates were also asked to determine whether the partner could in fact act as engagement quality control reviewer. This section was well attempted and most candidates correctly identified the familiarity threat and loss of professional scepticism that arises on a long association with an audit client, especially when dealing with senior audit personnel. Most candidates could also explain the relevant safeguards and demonstrated knowledge of the relevant requirements for listed entities. It was pleasing to see this syllabus area well understood by most candidates given its topical nature. The issue of whether the audit partner could remain in contact with the client by acting as engagement quality control reviewer was less well understood. While many candidates correctly suggested that this could not happen for ethical reasons, many others thought that it would be appropriate as long as further quality control reviews took place. Other candidates misinterpreted the question and thought that the partner was leaving the audit firm to work at the client.

Requirement (c) described the situation in which a listed client company had asked the audit firm to perform an actuarial valuation of its pension plan. The audit firm had an appropriately qualified person to perform the work, and as with the other requirements of this question, on the whole this was well attempted. Some answers failed to correctly calculate the materiality of the pension plan to the financial statements, and in some answers the fact that the client was a listed entity was not considered. However most candidates suggested an appropriate course of action in response to the ethical matters identified.

| Marking scheme | | | | Marks |
|---|---|---|---|---|
| (a) | (i) | **Matters to be included in the audit proposal** | | |
| | | Generally up to 1½ marks for each matter explained: | | |
| | | – | Outline of the audit firm | |
| | | – | Audit requirement of Jones Co | |
| | | – | Audit approach (allow up to 3 marks for well explained points made relevant to scenario) | |
| | | – | Deadlines | |
| | | – | Quality control and ethics | |
| | | – | Additional non-audit and assurance services | |
| | | | **Maximum** | 8 |
| | (ii) | **Matters to be considered in determining audit fee** | | |
| | | Generally up to 2 marks for each point discussed: | | |
| | | – | Fee to be based on staffing levels and chargeable hours | |
| | | – | Low fees can result in poor quality audit work and increase audit risk | |
| | | – | Lowballing and client expectation issues | |
| | | – | Contingent fees not allowed for audit services | |
| | | | **Maximum** | 6 |
| (b) | | **Long association of senior audit personnel** | | |
| | | Generally up to 1½ marks for each point discussed: | | |
| | | – | Loss of professional scepticism | |
| | | – | Familiarity and self-interest threats to objectivity | |
| | | – | Assessing the significance of the threat | |
| | | – | Appropriate safeguards (1 mark each where well explained to max of 3 marks) | |
| | | – | Specific rule applicable to public interest entities | |
| | | – | Conclusion on whether partner can perform EQCR role | |
| | | | **Maximum** | 6 |
| (c) | | **Banbury Co** | | |
| | | – | Valuation service creates self-review and self-interest threats | |
| | | – | Service cannot be provided if the pension deficit is material | |
| | | – | Calculate and comment on materiality | |
| | | – | Other matters to consider including level of subjectivity, lack of informed management (1 mark each) | |
| | | – | Safeguards may be used to reduce threat to acceptable level (1 mark each) | |
| | | | **Maximum** | 5 |
| **Total** | | | | **25** |

**50 DRAGON GROUP**  *Walk in the footsteps of a top tutor*

*Top tutor tips*

*Part (a) requires little more than common sense regarding why auditors may not wish to continue auditing a particular client.*

*Part (b) requires a basic knowledge of the contents of a tender document. You then need to develop this by applying your knowledge to the specific information given.*

*Part (c) asks you to consider the professional issues you need to consider before accepting a new client. This could include any aspect of audit quality control, ethics or general practice management.*

*Part (d) requires some basic knowledge and then some common sense suggestions about the difficulty of cross-border audit.*

**(a)     Reasons why a firm of auditors may decide not to seek re-election**

**Disagreement with the client**

The audit firm may have disagreed with the client for a number of reasons, for example, over accounting treatments used in the financial statements. A disagreement over a significant matter is likely to cause a breakdown in the professional relationship between auditor and client, meaning that the audit firm could lose faith in the competence of management. The auditor would be reluctant to seek re-election if the disagreement was not resolved.

**Lack of integrity of client**

The audit firm may feel that management is not acting with integrity, for example, the financial statements may be subject to creative accounting, or dubious business ethical decisions could be made by management, such as the exploitation of child labour. The auditor would be likely not to seek re-election (or to resign) in this case to avoid being associated with the client's poor decisions.

**Fee level**

The audit firm could be unable to demand a high enough audit fee from the client to cover the costs of the audit. In this situation the audit firm may choose not to offer itself for re-election, to avoid continuing with a loss making audit engagement, and consequently to use resources in a more commercially advantageous way.

**Fee payments**

The audit firm could have outstanding fees which may not be fully recovered due to a client's poor cash flow position. Or, the client could be slow paying, causing the audit firm to chase for payment and possibly affecting the relationship between the two businesses. In such cases the audit firm may make the commercial decision not to act for the client any longer.

**Resources**

The audit firm may find that it lacks the resources to continue to provide the audit service to a client. This could happen if the client company grows rapidly, financially or operationally, meaning that a larger audit team is necessary. The audit firm may simply lack the necessary skilled staff to expand the audit team.

**Competence**

The audit firm could feel that it is no longer competent to perform an audit service. This could happen for example if a client company diversified into a new and specialised business operation of which the audit firm had little or no experience. The audit firm would not be able to provide a high quality audit without building up or buying in the necessary knowledge and skills, and so may decide not to be considered for re-election.

**Overseas expansion**

A client could acquire one or several material overseas subsidiaries. If the audit firm does not have an associate office in the overseas location, the firm may feel that the risk and resources involved in relying on the work of other auditors is too great, and so decide not to act for the client any longer.

**Independence**

There are many ethical guidelines in relation to independence which must be adhered to by auditors, and in the event of a potential breach of the guidelines, the audit firm may decide not to seek re-election. For example, an audit firm may need to increase the audit fee if a client company grows in size. This could have the effect of increasing the fee received from the client above the allowed thresholds. As there would be no ethical safeguard strong enough to preserve the perception of independence, in this case the audit firm would not be able to continue to provide the audit service.

*Tutorial note*

*Other examples may be used to explain why the issue of independence could cause an audit firm not to seek re-election, e.g. audit firm takes on a financial interest in the client, close personal relationships develop between the firm and the client.*

**Conflicts of interest**

An audit firm may become involved in a situation where a conflict of interest arises between an existing audit client and another client of the firm. For example, an audit firm could take on a new audit client which is a competitor of an existing audit client. Although with the use of appropriate safeguards this situation could be successfully managed, the audit firm may decide that stepping down as auditor of the existing firm is the best course of action.

(b) **Matters to be included in tender document**

**Brief outline of Unicorn & Co**

This should include a short history of the firm, a description of its organisational structure, the different services offered by the firm (such as audit, tax, corporate finance, etc.), and the locations in which the firm operates.

The document should also state whether it is a member of any international audit firm network. The geographical locations in which Unicorn operates will be important given the multi-national structure of the Dragon Group.

### Specialisms of the firm

Unicorn & Co should describe the areas in which the firm has particular experience of relevance to the Dragon Group. It would be advantageous to stress that the firm has an audit department dedicated to the audit of clients in the retail industry, as this emphasises the experience that the firm has relevant to the specific operations of the group.

### Identification of the needs of the Dragon Group

The tender document should outline the requirements of the client, in this case, that each subsidiary is required to have an individual audit on its financial statements, and that the consolidated financial statements also need to be audited. Unicorn & Co may choose to include here a brief clarification of the purpose and legal requirements of an audit. The potential provision of non-audit services should be discussed, either here, or in a separate section of the tender document (see below).

### Outline of the proposed audit approach

This is likely to be the most detailed part of the tender document. Here the firm will describe how the audit would be conducted, ensuring that the needs of the Dragon Group (as discussed above) have been met. Typically contained in this section would be a description of the audit methodology used by the firm, and an outline of the audit cycle including the key deliverables at each phase of work. For example:

- How the firm would intend to gain business understanding at group and subsidiary level.

- Methods used to assess risk and to plan the audits.

- Procedures used to assess the control environment and accounting systems.

- Techniques used to gather evidence, e.g. the use of audit software.

How the firm would structure the audit of the consolidation of the group financial statements and how they would liaise with subsidiary audit teams.

The firm should clarify its adherence to International Standards on Auditing, ethical guidelines and any other relevant laws and regulations operating in the various jurisdictions relevant to the Dragon Group. The various financial reporting frameworks used within the group should be clarified.

### Quality control

Unicorn & Co should emphasise the importance of quality control and therefore should explain the procedures that are used within the firm to monitor the quality of the audit services provided. This should include a description of firm-wide quality control policies, and the procedures applied to individual audits. The firm may wish to clarify its adherence to International Standards on Quality Control.

### Communication with management

The firm should outline the various reports and other communication that will be made to management as part of the audit process. The purpose and main content of the reports, and the timing of them, should be outlined. Unicorn & Co may provide some 'added value' bi-products of the audit process. For example, the business risks identified as part of the audit planning may be fed back to management in a written report.

### Timing

Unicorn & Co should outline the timeframe that would be used. For example, the audits of the subsidiaries' financial statements should be conducted before the audit of the consolidated financial statements. The firm may wish to include an approximate date by which the group audit opinion would be completed, which should fit in, if possible, with the requirements of the group. If Unicorn & Co feel that the deadline requested by the client is unrealistic, a more appropriate deadline should be suggested, with the reasons for this clearly explained.

### Key staff and resources

The document should name the key members of staff to be assigned to the audit, in particular the proposed engagement partner. In addition, the firm should clarify the approximate number of staff to be used in the audit team and the relevant experience of the key members of the audit team. If the firm considers that external specialists could be needed, then this should be explained in this section of the document.

### Fees

The proposed fee for the audit of the group should be stated, and the calculation of the fee should be explained, i.e. broken down by grade of staff and hourly/daily rates per grade. In addition, invoicing and payment terms should be described, e.g. if the audit fee is payable in instalments, the stages when each instalment will fall due.

### Extra services

Unicorn & Co should ensure that any non-audit services that it may be able to offer to the Dragon Group are described. For example, subject to ethical safeguards, the firm may be able to offer corporate finance services in relation to the stock exchange listing that the group is seeking, although the provision of this non-audit service would need to be carefully considered in relation to independence issues.

(c) **Evaluation of matters to be considered**

### Size and location of the group companies

The Dragon Group is a large multi-national group of companies. It is extremely important that Unicorn & Co assesses the availability of resources that can be allocated to the audit team. The assignment would comprise the audit of the financial statements of all 20 current subsidiaries, the audit of the parent company's and the group's financial statements. This is a significant engagement which will demand a great deal of time.

The location of half of the group's subsidiaries in other countries means that the overseas offices of Unicorn & Co would be called upon to perform some or all of the audit of those subsidiaries. In this case the resource base of the relevant overseas offices should be considered to ensure there is enough staff with appropriate skills and experience available to perform the necessary audit work.

Unicorn & Co must consider if they have offices in all of the countries in which the Dragon Group has a subsidiary.

Depending on the materiality of the overseas subsidiaries to the group financial statements, it is likely that some overseas visits would be required to evaluate the work of the overseas audit teams. Unicorn & Co should consider who will conduct the visits (presumably a senior member of the audit team), and whether that person has the necessary skills and experience in evaluating the work of overseas audit teams.

### Planned expansion of the group

In light of the comments above, Unicorn & Co should consider that the planned further significant expansion of the group will mean more audit staff will be needed in future years, and if any subsidiaries are acquired in other countries, the audit is likely to be performed by overseas offices. The firm should therefore consider not only its current resource base in the local and overseas offices, but whether additional staff will be available in the future if the group's expansion goes ahead as planned.

### Relevant skills and experience

Unicorn & Co has an audit department specialising in the audit of retail companies, so it should not be a problem to find audit staff with relevant experience in this country.

On consolidation, the financial statements of the subsidiaries will be restated in line with group accounting policies and financial reporting framework, and will also be retranslated into local presentational currency. All of this work will be performed by the management of the Dragon Group. Unicorn & Co must evaluate the availability of staff experienced in the audit of a consolidation including foreign subsidiaries.

### Timing

It is important to consider the timeframe when conducting a group audit. The audit of each subsidiary's financial statements should be carried out prior to the audit of the consolidated financial statements. Unicorn & Co should consider the expectation of the Dragon Group in relation to the reporting deadline, and ensure that enough time is allowed for the completion of all audits. The deadline proposed by management of 31 December is only three months after the year end, which may be unrealistic given the size of the group and the multi-national location of the subsidiaries. The first year auditing a new client is likely to take longer, as the audit team will need to familiarise themselves with the business, the accounting systems and controls, etc.

### Mermaid Co – prior year modification

If Unicorn & Co accepts the engagement, the firm will take on the audit of Mermaid Co, whose financial statements in the prior year were in breach of financial reporting standards. This adds an element of risk to the engagement. Unicorn & Co should gather as much information as possible about the contingent liability, and the reason why the management of Mermaid Co did not amend the financial statements last year end. This could hint at a lack of integrity on the part of the management of the company.

The firm should also consider whether this matter could be significant to the consolidated financial statements, by assessing the materiality of the contingent liability at group level.

Further discussions should be held with the management of the Dragon Group in order to understand their thoughts on the contingency and whether it should be disclosed in the individual financial statements of Mermaid Co, and at group level. Contacting the incumbent auditors (after seeking relevant permission from the Dragon Group) would also be an important procedure to gather information about the modification.

**Minotaur Co – different business activity**

The acquisition of Minotaur Co represents a new business activity for the group. The retail business audit department may not currently have much, if any, experience of auditing a distribution company. This should be easily overcome, either by bringing in staff from a different department more experienced in clients with distribution operations, or by ensuring adequate training for staff in the retail business audit department.

**Highly regulated/reliance on financial statements and auditor's report**

The Group is listed on several stock exchanges, and is therefore subject to a high degree of regulation. This adds an element of risk to the engagement, as the management will be under pressure to publish favourable results. This risk is increased by the fact that a new listing is being sought, meaning that the financial statements and auditor's report of the group will be subject to close scrutiny by the stock exchange regulators.

There may be extra work required by the auditors due to the listings, for example, the group may have to prepare reconciliations of financial data, or additional narrative reports on which the auditors have to express an opinion under the rulings of the stock exchange. The firm must consider the availability of staff skilled in regulatory and reporting listing rules to perform such work.

**Previous auditors of Dragon Group**

Unicorn & Co should consider the reason why the previous audit firm is not seeking re-appointment, and whether the reason would impact on their acceptance decision. After seeking permission from the Dragon Group, contact should be made with the previous auditors to obtain confirmation of the reason for them vacating office (amongst other matters).

In conclusion, this is a large scale, multi-national group, which carries a fairly high level of risk. Unicorn & Co must be extremely careful to only commit to the group audit if it has the necessary resources, can manage the client's expectation in relation to the reporting deadline, is convinced of the integrity of management, and is confident to take on a potentially high profile client.

*Tutorial note*

*Credit will be awarded in this requirement for discussion of ethical matters which would be considered prior to accepting the appointment as auditor of the Dragon Group. However, as the scenario does not contain any reference to specific ethical matters, marks will be limited to a maximum of 2 for a general discussion of ethical matters on acceptance.*

**(d)** **Discuss how transnational audits may differ from other audits of historical information and how this may contribute to a higher level of audit risk in relation to the audit of Dragon Group.**

A transnational audit means an audit of financial statements which are or may be relied upon outside the audited entity's home jurisdiction for the purpose of significant lending, investment or regulatory decisions.

The Dragon Group is listed on the stock exchange of several countries, and is planning to raise more finance by a further listing, which means that the group is subject to the regulations of all stock exchanges on which it is listed, and so is bound by listing rules outside of its home jurisdiction. The group also contains many foreign subsidiaries, meaning that it operates in a global business and financial environment.

### Transnational audit and audit risk

### Application of auditing standards

Although many countries of the world have adopted International Standards on Auditing (ISAs), not all have done so, choosing instead to use locally developed auditing regulations. In addition, some countries use modified versions of ISAs. This means that in a transnational audit, some components of the group financial statements will have been audited using a different auditing framework, resulting in inconsistent audit processes within the group, potentially reducing the quality of the audit.

### Regulation and oversight of auditors

Similar to the previous comments on the use of ISAs, across the world there are many different ways in which the activities of auditors are regulated and monitored. In some countries the audit profession is self-regulatory, whereas in other countries a more legislative approach is used. This also can impact on the quality of audit work in a transnational situation.

### Financial reporting framework

Some countries use International Financial Reporting Standards, whereas some use locally developed accounting standards. Within a transnational group it is likely that adjustments, reconciliations or restatements may be required in order to comply with the requirements of the jurisdictions relevant to the group financial statements (i.e. the jurisdiction of the parent company in most cases). Such reconciliations can be complex and require a high level of technical expertise of the preparer and the auditor.

### Corporate governance requirements and consequent control risk

In some countries there are very prescriptive corporate governance requirements, which the auditor must consider as part of the audit process. In this case the auditor may need to carry out extra work over and above local requirements in order to ensure group wide compliance with the requirements of the jurisdictions relevant to the financial statements. However, in some countries there is very little corporate governance regulation at all and controls are likely to be weaker than in other components of the group. Control risk is therefore likely to differ between the various subsidiaries making up the group.

---

**Examiner's comments**

Requirement (a) was a short factual requirement, not related to the detail of the question scenario, which asked candidates to explain reasons why a firm of auditors may decide not to seek re-election as auditor. There were two main problems with answers to this requirement. Firstly, too few candidates actually provided an explanation of the reasons they gave. For example, an answer stated that the auditor had a disagreement with the client over something in the financial statements. While this is indeed a reason why the auditor may chose not to seek re-election, it is not an explanation, which would entail going on to say that the disagreement had caused a breakdown in the working relationship between the auditor and client, and that the auditor had lost faith in the competence and/or integrity of management.

---

The second requirement focused on the audit tendering process, and asked for matters to be included in a tender document to be presented to the Dragon Group. This requirement seemed to polarise candidates. Those candidates who tailored their answer to the question scenario tended to do well, with a significant proportion achieving close to the maximum marks available. However, candidates who provided a list of points to be included in ANY tender, regardless of the information provided about the prospective client, and about your audit firm, scored inadequately. In other words, it is important to apply knowledge to score well, as is true for any scenario-based question. Sound answers to (b) appreciated that the point of the tender document is to sell your audit firm's services to the client, and recommended points to include such as the global positioning of both audit firm and prospective client, the specialism of the audit firm in retail, and the firm's ability to potentially provide services relating to the expansion plans of the group, such as due diligence. Weak answers simply stated vague comments: 'we should discuss fees', 'we should set a deadline,' etc. Some answers confused a tender document with an engagement letter, and included points more suited to that document, such as a statement of responsibilities or a legal disclaimer. Inadequate answers to (b) were those that seemed to confuse the requirements with those of (c). Candidates are reminded that it is important to read ALL of the requirements of a question before beginning their answer, to avoid such confusion. Examples of statements commonly seen in answers to (b) which are more relevant to (c) are:

- 'are we competent to audit the group'

- 'can we audit the goodwill and foreign exchange transactions which are complex'

- 'will any of our audit staff want to go abroad to work'

- 'do any of our partners hold shares in Dragon Group'.

These comments definitely do not belong in a tender document, which should highlight the audit firm's capabilities to service the prospective client, rather than question the firm's competence or ability to take on the assignment. Such comments indicate a failure to read and understand the question requirement, as well as a lack of commercial awareness.

Requirement (c) asked candidates to evaluate the matters that should be considered before accepting the audit engagement. Answers here were weak, despite this being a regularly examined syllabus area. Most answers were not tailored to the question, and just provided a list of questions or actions, such as 'get permission to contact previous auditor', or 'check the integrity of management', and 'do we have the skill to audit foreign currencies'.

Providing a list of such comments will not generate enough marks to pass the question requirement. Better answers discussed, amongst other points:

- the risk posed by the numerous stock exchange listings of the potential client, and whether the audit fee would be enough to compensate for that risk

- the practical difficulties entailed in co-ordinating an audit of more than 20 companies across many different countries

- the tight deadline imposed by the potential client, especially in light of this being a first year audit, and the learning curve that the audit firm would need to go through.

Some candidates appeared to think that the audit would be too much trouble – a sizeable number of scripts contained comments such as 'auditing a company far from our main office would be tedious and inconvenient'. I would suggest that most audit firms, on being successful in a tender for an audit as significant as this, would consider the inconvenience worthwhile.

Requirement (d) was the worst answered on the paper. Clearly, very few candidates had studied the issue of transnational audits, and answers displayed a lack of knowledge. Answers appeared to be based mainly on guesswork, with common suggestions being 'language difficulties' and 'communication barriers'. However, some candidates could identify variations in auditing standards and financial reporting frameworks as issues contributing to high risk, but these points were rarely developed to their full potential.

| | Marking scheme | | |
|---|---|---|---|
| | | | *Marks* |
| **(a)** | **Identify and explain using examples why an audit firm may not seek re-election** | | |
| | Generally 1 mark per example | | |
| | – Disagreement | | |
| | – Lack of integrity | | |
| | – Fee level | | |
| | – Late payment of fees | | |
| | – Resources | | |
| | – Overseas expansion | | |
| | – Competence | | |
| | – Independence | | |
| | – Conflict of interest | | ─── |
| | | Maximum | **4** |
| | | | ─── |
| **(b)** | **Contents of tender document** | | |
| | Up to 1½ marks per matter described: | | |
| | – Outline of firm | | |
| | – Specialisms | | |
| | – Audit requirement of Dragon Group | | |
| | – Outline audit approach (max 3 marks if detailed) | | |
| | – QC | | |
| | – Communication with management | | |
| | – Timing | | |
| | – Key staff/resources | | |
| | – Fees | | |
| | – Extra services | | ─── |
| | | Maximum | **8** |
| | | | ─── |
| **(c)** | **Matters to consider re. acceptance** | | |
| | Generally ½ mark for identification, 1 further mark for explanation, from ideas list: | | |
| | – Large and expanding group – availability of staff now and in the future | | |
| | – Use of overseas offices | | |
| | – Visits to overseas audit teams | | |
| | – Skills/experience in retail/foreign subsidiaries consolidation | | |
| | – Timing – tight deadline | | |
| | – Mermaid Co – implication of prior year modification | | |
| | – Minotaur Co – implication of different business activity | | |
| | – Highly regulated – risk/additional reporting requirements | | |
| | – Reason for previous auditors leaving office | | ─── |
| | | Maximum | **6** |
| | | | ─── |
| **(d)** | **Transnational audits** | | |
| | Up to 2 marks per point explained | | |
| | – Definition of transnational audit and application to Dragon Group | | |
| | – Auditing standards | | |
| | – Regulation of auditors | | |
| | – Financial reporting standards | | |
| | – Corporate governance/control risk | | |
| | | | ─── |
| | | | **7** |
| | | | ─── |
| | **Total** | | **25** |
| | | | ─── |

**51    TONY GROUP**  *Walk in the footsteps of a top tutor*

***Top tutor tips***

*Part (a) deals with professional scepticism. This question followed the publication of a relevant technical article prior to the exam. Students are reminded to pay attention to technical articles published by the examining team in the run up to the exam.*

*Part (b) looks at how to apply professional scepticism to a situation. Think about whether there is any incentive for management to mislead the auditor and whether they appear to be trying to influence the audit by withholding information.*

*Part (c) is a straightforward requirement dealing with forensic procedures.*

**(a)**    Professional scepticism is defined in ISA 200 *Overall Objectives of the Independent Auditor and the Conduct of an Audit in Accordance with International Standards on Auditing* as an attitude that includes a questioning mind, being alert to conditions which may indicate possible misstatement due to error or fraud and a critical assessment of audit evidence.

ISA 200 requires the auditor to plan and perform an audit with professional scepticism, recognising that circumstances may exist which cause the financial statements to be materially misstated. It is important to use professional scepticism at all stages of the audit. Professional scepticism can reduce the risk of material misstatements caused by fraud going undetected.

Professional scepticism includes being alert to the existence of contradictory audit evidence and being able to assess assumptions and judgments critically and without bias, and being ready to challenge management where necessary. It is also important that the auditor considers the reliability of information provided by management during the audit.

Recently, regulatory bodies such as the IAASB have stressed the importance of the auditor's use of professional scepticism. The increased use of principles-based financial reporting frameworks such as IFRS Standards, and the prevalence of fair value accounting which introduces subjectivity and judgment into financial reporting are examples of the reasons why the use of professional scepticism by auditors is increasingly important. It is imperative that professional scepticism is applied to areas of financial reporting which are complex or highly judgmental.

Going concern assessments and related party transactions are also examples of areas where management must exercise judgment in determining the appropriate accounting treatment, and where the potential for management bias is high. Therefore these areas need to be approached with professional scepticism.

The application of professional scepticism is closely aligned with maintaining objectivity, and it is difficult to remain sufficiently sceptical when certain threats to objectivity are present. Ultimately, the exercise of professional scepticism should work to reduce audit risk by ensuring that the auditor has sufficient and appropriate evidence to support the audit opinion, and that all evidence obtained, especially in relation to areas of high risk of material misstatement, has been critically evaluated and is based on reliable information.

**(b)**  **(i)**  The finance director seems to be dictating the audit work to be performed. The audit manager should decide the extent of audit procedures in response to the risk of material misstatement identified. The manager should consider why the finance director seems so insistent that his file is used as the main source of audit evidence. He may be hiding something relevant to the impairment which would be revealed if the auditor looked at other sources of evidence.

The Group's profit before tax has fallen by 33.3%, indicating that a significant impairment loss amounting to more than the $50,000 calculated by the finance director may need to be recognised. There is a risk of material misstatement in that the impairment loss is understated, and there is a risk that management bias has resulted in an inappropriate determination of the loss.

The auditor therefore needs to be sceptical and alert for factors indicating that the loss is greater than that calculated by the finance director. Impairment testing is a complex and subjective area, and could be easily manipulated by management wishing to reduce the size of the loss recognised.

The audit manager should obtain corroborative evidence regarding the assumptions used and not just confirm that the assumptions are in line with management's risk assessment or the prior year audit file. The reliability of this source of evidence is not strong as it is prepared by management. An important part of professional scepticism is challenging management's assumptions, especially in an area of high judgment such as impairment testing.

The internal auditor checking the figures is also not a reliable source of evidence, as it is client-generated. The internal auditor may have been pressured to confirm the finance director's calculations.

Professional scepticism should also be applied to the comment that the assumptions are the same as in previous years. New factors impacting on impairment may have arisen during this year, affecting the determination of the impairment loss and up-to-date evidence on the assumptions used in this year's calculation should be sought.

The audit team should also remain alert when auditing balances and transactions other than goodwill in case there are other areas where Silvio does not appear to be providing all evidence required or where he is suggesting the audit approach to be taken.

While his comment does not seem to be intimidating in nature, the audit team should recognise that if Silvio does have something to hide in relation to the goodwill impairment, he may become more aggressive, in which case the matter should be brought to the attention of the firm's ethics partner and discussed with those charged with governance of the Group.

**(ii)**  **Audit procedures – impairment of goodwill**

- The assumptions used in the impairment test should be confirmed as agreeing with the auditor's understanding of the business based on the current year's risk assessment procedures, e.g. assess the reasonableness of assumptions on cash flow projections.

- Confirm that the impairment review includes the goodwill relating to all business combinations.

- Consider the impact of the auditor's assessment of going concern on the impairment review, e.g. the impact on the assumption relating to growth rates which have been used as part of the impairment calculations.

- Obtain an understanding of the controls over the management's process of performing the impairment test including tests of the operating effectiveness of any controls in place, for example, over the review and approval of assumptions or inputs by appropriate levels of management and, where appropriate, those charged with governance.

- Confirm whether management has performed the impairment test or has used an expert.

- The methodology applied to the impairment review should be checked by the auditor, with inputs to calculations, e.g. discount rates, agreed to auditor-obtained information.

- Develop an independent estimate of the impairment loss and compare it to that prepared by management.

- Confirm that the impairment calculations exclude cash flows relating to tax and finance items.

- Perform sensitivity analysis to consider whether, and if so how, management has considered alternative assumptions and the impact of any alternative assumptions on the impairment calculations.

- Check the arithmetic accuracy of the calculations used in the impairment calculations.

**Tutorial note**

*Credit will be awarded for other relevant audit procedures recommended.*

**(c)    Forensic investigation**

- Interview the two suspects and question them regarding the nature of the cash payments made to the customers prior to the signing of the contracts.

- Use computer-assisted audit techniques to identify all new customers in the year and any payments made to these customers, and total the amounts.

- Review the terms of the contracts with customers for any details of payments included in the contract, and understand the business rationale for any such payments.

**Tutorial note**

*It would be unusual for the Group to be making any payments to customers, so these terms would need to be viewed with professional scepticism.*

- Review the email and other correspondence entered into by the two suspects for any further information about the cash payments, e.g. specifically who the payments were discussed with.

- Perform tests of control on the authorisation of cash payments to find out if these payments were known to anyone operating in a supervisory capacity.

**Examiner's comments**

This question focused on professional scepticism, the audit of goodwill impairment, and a forensic investigation into alleged bribery payments made by several of the audit client's employees.

Requirement (a) was a discussion, asking candidates to explain the meaning of the term professional scepticism and to discuss its importance in planning and performing an audit. It was clear that many candidates had read and understood the contents of a recent article on the topic of professional scepticism. Most answers provided an appropriate definition of professional scepticism and went on to discuss how it links to audit quality. Stronger candidates also discussed how the auditor should apply professional scepticism when considering the risk of material misstatement associated with fraud and areas of the financial statements that rely on the application of judgment. Few candidates however, discussed the recent activities of the regulatory bodies in respect of professional scepticism.

The second part of the question involved a scenario which described how the finance director of the Tony Group was insisting that the audit firm should rely on a file prepared by him in their audit of goodwill impairment. The file contained workings and assumptions and had been checked by the Group's head of internal audit. The requirement asked candidates to discuss how professional scepticism should be applied to the scenario, and to explain the principal audit procedures to be performed on the impairment of goodwill. Many candidates were able to explain that the Group finance director was intimidating the audit firm, that his workings were not sufficient as a source of evidence, and that he may have something to hide. It was disappointing that few candidates appreciated that the Group's profit before tax had fallen significantly, and therefore the small impairment to goodwill suggested by the finance director was unlikely to be sufficient in the circumstances, and probably influenced by management bias. Most candidates did however realise that the audit firm should perform their own workings and not place complete reliance on the procedures that had been performed by the head of internal audit.

The requirement relating to procedures on goodwill impairment was poorly attempted. The evidence points provided by candidates for this requirement tended to revolve around recalculation or a discussion with management. Very few suggested specific procedures that would allow the auditor to develop their own expectation in terms of the impairment necessary, which could then be compared with the finance director's workings. This was disappointing, as impairment has featured in several exams as an audit issue and is a topic that candidates should be better prepared to tackle. Many candidates did not answer the question, and simply described the accounting treatment for goodwill, or suggested procedures that were relevant to the calculation of goodwill at acquisition but not relevant to a review of its impairment.

Requirement (c) asked candidates to recommend the procedures to be used in performing a forensic investigation. This was in relation to alleged bribery, whereby members of the Group's sales team were suspected of making payments to customers in order to secure contracts. Answers to this requirement were weak. Many candidates gave no procedures at all, therefore not answering the question set, and instead described agreeing the scope of the work or whether the investigation could be performed for ethical reasons.

Other candidates gave broad statements instead of procedures, such as "quantify the loss" without explaining how this could be done, or "interview the suspects" without saying what the purpose of this interview would be.

| | | **Marking scheme** | |
|---|---|---|---|
| | | | *Marks* |

**(a)**      **Professional scepticism discussion**

Generally up to 1½ marks for each point discussed, including:

- Definition of professional scepticism (1 mark for definition)
- Explaining professional scepticism
- Link between professional scepticism and ethics/objectivity
- Importance in relation to complex and subjective areas of the audit
- Importance in relation to the audit of going concern
- Discussion of regulatory bodies actions in relation to professional scepticism

                                                **Maximum**    **6**

**(b)**    **(i)**      **Applying professional scepticism**

Generally up to 1½ marks for each point discussed, and 1 mark for calculation of materiality.

- Risk that impairment loss understated due to Group's fall in profit
- The determination of the impairment loss is judgmental and subject to management bias
- Auditor should question the reasons for finance director's insistence that no other audit work is needed
- Evidence provided by the finance director is not reliable (client-generated)
- Assumptions are unlikely to have stayed the same since last year
- Audit team should remain alert for other instances where professional scepticism is needed
- Possible threat of intimidation by the finance director

                                                **Maximum**    **7**

      **(ii)**      **Procedures on impairment**

Generally 1 mark for each procedure explained:

- Review all assumptions used in preparing projected cash flows
- Confirm that the impairment review includes the goodwill relating to all business combinations
- Consider impact of auditor's assessment of the Group's going concern status
- Consider operating effectiveness of any controls in place
- Confirm whether management has performed the impairment test or used an expert
- Recalculate amounts based on auditor-generated inputs
- Develop an independent estimate of the impairment loss and compare to that prepared by management
- Confirm that the impairment calculations exclude cash flows relating to tax and finance items
- Perform sensitivity analysis
- Check the arithmetic accuracy of the calculations

                                                **Maximum**    **7**

**(c)**      **Procedures on alleged bribery payments**

Generally 1 mark for each procedure explained:

- Interview the two suspects
- Identify all new customers in the year and any payments made to these customers
- Review the terms of contracts with customers
- Review the email and other correspondence entered into by the two suspects
- Perform tests of control on the authorisation of cash payments

                                                **Maximum**    **5**

**Total**                                                           **25**

**52    SPANIEL**  *Walk in the footsteps of a top tutor*

*Top tutor tips*

*Part (a) requires a discussion of the risks of fraud in revenue recognition. In this situation, fraud involves manipulating the revenue figure in the financial statements to show a different picture. Therefore your answer should consider the ways in which management can achieve this.*

*Part (b) addresses the issue of auditor liability and whether the audit firm has been negligent due to failure to detect a fraud. Knowledge of the conditions for a negligence claim to succeed and discussion of each of these conditions in turn should help to score the marks available.*

*Part (c) is a discussion question regarding the difficulties auditing financial instruments and the matters to be considered when planning the audit of forward exchange contracts. For the first part, think about the risks associated with financial instruments. For the planning aspects, think about what the auditor does at the planning stage of an audit and why, and apply this to the specific area of financial instruments.*

**(a)**    There are a number of reasons why there should be a presumption that there are risks of fraud in revenue recognition.

### Management under pressure to achieve certain results

One reason is that managers of companies are often under pressure, particularly in listed companies, to achieve certain performance targets. The achievement of those targets often impacts their job security and their compensation. These performance targets often include measures of revenue growth, providing an incentive for management to use earnings management techniques.

In other companies there may be incentives to understate revenues, for example, to reduce reported profits and, therefore, company taxation charges. This may be more relevant to private limited companies where management may not be under such pressure to achieve revenue based targets.

### Volume of transactions

There is also usually a high volume of revenue transactions during a financial period. As the volume of transactions increases, the risk of failing to detect fraud and error using traditional, sample based auditing techniques also increases. This means that it is potentially easier for management to successfully manipulate these balances than other balances which are subject to a lower volume of transactions.

Material misstatement through the manipulation of revenue recognition can be readily achieved by recording revenue in an earlier or later accounting period than is proper or by creating fictitious revenues.

**Judgmental area**

Revenue recognition can also be a judgmental area. Examples include the recognition of revenues on long-term contracts, such as the construction of buildings, and from the provision of services. These require the estimation of the percentage of completion at the period end, increasing the scope for management to manipulate reported results.

**Complexity**

As well as requiring judgment, revenue recognition can also be a complex issue. For example, some sales have multiple elements, such as the sale of goods and the separate sale of related maintenance contracts and warranties. This added complexity increases the risk of manipulation.

**Cash sales**

In some companies, for example, those in the retail industry, a high proportion of revenue may be earned through cash sales. This increases the risk of the theft of cash and the consequent manipulation of recorded revenues to conceal this crime.

**Accounting fraud**

Methods of revenue manipulation have also featured prominently in cases of accounting fraud, such as Enron and Worldcom. The prevalence of these methods in modern accounting frauds and the failure of auditors to detect this in these cases suggests that it is one of the more common methods of earnings management and one which auditors should rightly consider as high risk.

**Not always high risk**

While revenue recognition in general may be considered a high risk area, it is not always the case. Companies with simple revenue streams or a low volume of transactions may be considered at low risk of fraud through revenue manipulations. Accordingly ISA 240 *The Auditor's Responsibility Relating to Fraud in an Audit of Financial Statements* permits the rebuttable of the fraud risk presumption for revenue recognition. One example of simple revenue streams would be where a company leases properties for fixed annual amounts over a fixed period of time. If this is the case, the reasons for not treating revenue as a high fraud risk area must be fully documented by the auditor.

**(b)** It is not the auditor's primary responsibility to detect fraud. According to ISA 240 *The Auditor's Responsibilities Relating to Fraud in an Audit of Financial Statements*, management is primarily responsible for preventing and detecting fraud. The auditor is required to obtain reasonable assurance that the financial statements are free from material misstatement whether caused by fraud or error.

The total amount estimated to have been stolen in the payroll fraud represents 5.6% of Spaniel's assets. If the amount has been stolen consistently over a 12-month period, then $3 million (8/12 × 4.5 million) had been stolen prior to the year end of 31 December 2012. $3 million is material, representing 3.8% of total assets at the year end. Therefore the fraud was material and it could be reasonably expected that it should have been discovered.

However, material misstatements arising due to fraud can be difficult for the auditor to detect. This is because fraud is deliberately hidden by the perpetrators using sophisticated accounting techniques established to conceal the fraudulent activity. False statements may be made to the auditors and documents may have been forged. This means that material frauds could go undetected, even if appropriate procedures have been carried out.

ISA 240 requires that an audit is performed with an attitude of professional scepticism. This may not have been the case. Spaniel Co is a long-standing client, and the audit team may have lost their sceptical attitude. Necessary tests of control on payroll were not carried out because in previous years it had been possible to rely on the client's controls.

It seems that ISAs may not have been adhered to during the audit of Spaniel Co. ISA 330 *The Auditor's Responses to Assessed Risks* requires that the auditor shall design and perform tests of controls to obtain sufficient appropriate audit evidence as to the operating effectiveness of relevant controls if the auditor's assessment of risks of material misstatement at the assertion level includes an expectation that the controls are operating effectively.

It can be acceptable for the auditor to use audit evidence from a previous audit about the operating effectiveness of specific controls but only if the auditor confirms that no changes have taken place. The audit partner should explain whether this was the case.

Substantive procedures have not been performed on payroll either. This effectively means that payroll has not been audited.

This leads to a conclusion that the audit firm may have been negligent in conducting the audit. Negligence is a common law concept in which an injured party must prove three things in order to prove that negligence has occurred:

- That the auditor owes a duty of care

- That the duty of care has been breached

- That financial loss has been caused by the negligence.

Looking at these points in turn, Groom & Co owes a duty of care to Spaniel Co, because a contract exists between the two parties. The company represents all the shareholders as a body, and there is an automatic duty of care owed to the shareholders as a body by the auditor.

A breach of duty of care must be proved for a negligence claim against the audit firm to be successful. Duty of care generally means that the audit firm must perform the audit work to a good standard and that relevant legal and professional requirements and principles have been followed. For an audit firm, it is important to be able to demonstrate that ISAs have been adhered to. Unfortunately, it seems that ISAs have been breached and so the audit firm is likely to have been negligent in the audit of payroll.

### Tutorial note

*Credit will be awarded for references to legal cases as examples of situations where audit firms have been found to have been negligent in performing an audit, such as Re Kingston Cotton Mill.*

Finally, a financial loss has been suffered by the audit client, being the amount stolen while the fraud was operating.

In conclusion, Spaniel Co is likely to be able to successfully prove that the audit firm has been negligent in the audit of payroll, and that Groom & Co is liable for some or all of the financial loss suffered.

**(c)** **The audit of financial instruments**

**Complex and difficult to understand**

There are many reasons why financial instruments are challenging to audit. The instruments themselves, the transactions to which they relate, and the associated risk exposures can be difficult for both management and auditors to understand.

If the auditor does not fully understand the financial instrument and its impact on the financial statements, it will be difficult to assess the risk of material misstatement and to detect errors in the accounting treatment and associated disclosures. Even relatively simple financial instruments can be complex to account for.

**Reliance on experts**

The specialist nature of many financial instruments means that the auditor may need to rely on an auditor's expert as a source of evidence. In using an expert, the auditor must ensure the objectivity and competence of that expert, and then must evaluate the adequacy of the expert's work, which can be very difficult to do where the focus of the work is so specialist and difficult to understand.

**Lack of evidence**

The auditor may also find that there is a lack of evidence in relation to financial instruments, or that evidence tends to come from management. For example, many of the financial reporting requirements in relation to the valuation of financial instruments are based on fair values. Fair values are often based on models which depend on management judgment. Valuations are therefore often subjective and derived from management assumptions which increase the risk of material misstatement.

**Professional scepticism**

It is imperative that the auditor retains professional scepticism in the audit of financial instruments, but this may be difficult to do when faced with a complex and subjective transaction or balance for which there is little evidence other than management's judgment.

### Internal controls

There may also be control issues relating to financial instruments. Often financial instruments are dealt with by a specialist department and it may be a few individuals who exert significant influence over the financial instruments that are entered into. This specialist department may not be fully integrated into the finance function, leading to the accounting treatment being dealt with outside the normal accounting system. Internal controls may be deficient and there may not be the opportunity for much segregation of duty. However, some companies will have established strong internal controls around financial instruments, leading to a lower risk of material misstatement.

### Planning implications

### Obtain an understanding of the accounting requirements

In planning the audit of Bulldog's financial instruments, the auditor must first gain an understanding of the relevant accounting and disclosure requirements. For example, the applicable financial reporting standards should be clarified, which are likely to be IFRS 9 *Financial Instruments* and IFRS 7 *Financial Instruments: Disclosures*. These standards can be complex to apply, and the auditor should develop a thorough understanding of how they relate to Bulldog's financial instruments.

### Obtain an understanding of the financial instruments

The auditor must also obtain an understanding of the instruments in which Bulldog Co has invested or to which it is exposed, including the characteristics of the instruments, and gain an understanding of Bulldog's reasons for entering into the financial instruments and its policy towards them.

### Resources

It is important that the resources needed to audit the financial instruments are carefully considered. The competence of members of the audit firm to audit these transactions should be assessed, and it may be that an auditor's expert needs to be engaged. If so, this should be explained to the client. Instructions will have to be drawn up and given to the expert to ensure that the work performed is in line with audit objectives and follows the relevant financial reporting requirements, for example, in relation to valuing the financial instruments.

### Consider internal controls

The audit planning should include obtaining an understanding of the internal control relevant to Bulldog's financial instruments, including the involvement, if any, of internal audit. An understanding of how financial instruments are monitored and controlled assists the auditor in determining the nature, timing and extent of audit procedures, for example, whether to perform tests on controls.

### Understand management's valuation method

Specific consideration should be given to understanding management's method for valuing financial instruments for recognition in the year-end financial statements. The valuation is likely to involve some form of estimate, and ISA 540 *Auditing Accounting Estimates, Including Fair Value Accounting Estimates and Related Disclosures* requires the auditor to obtain an understanding of how management makes accounting estimates and the data on which accounting estimates are based.

### Determine materiality

Finally, the materiality of the financial instruments should be determined and the significance of the risk exposure associated with them should be assessed.

**Examiner's comments**

The first part required candidates to discuss why auditors should presume that there is a risk of fraud in revenue recognition and this requirement was poorly answered with most candidates setting out lengthy explanations of the respective duties of the auditor and management for the identification and prevention of fraud and thereby not answering the question. Strong answers considered management bias and targets, judgments in complex business and cut-off errors.

Requirement (b) provided a scenario which described that an audit firm had given an unmodified audit opinion on Spaniel's financial statements, and that subsequent to the auditor's report being issued a fraud had been discovered that had been operating during the period covered by the auditor's report. The scenario also pointed out that the audit firm had not performed audit procedures in relation to the area in which the fraud was occurring, namely payroll. The requirement asked candidates to explain the matters to be considered in determining the audit firm's liability to Spaniel Co in respect of the fraud. There were some excellent answers to this requirement.

The best ones clearly outlined the factors that have to be proven to determine negligence, and applied them methodically to the scenario. The materiality of the fraud was considered, the duty of care owed to the audit client, and the fact that the auditor may not have been exercising professional scepticism during the audit due to the long-standing nature of the audit appointment. It was also appropriate to discuss the responsibilities of management and auditors in relation to fraud, and whether it is appropriate for auditors to rely on the conclusions reached in previous year's audit. Some answers tended to only provide a rote-learnt description of responsibilities in relation to fraud, and usually failed to reach an appropriate conclusion. With little application to the scenario there is limited scope for marks to be awarded.

Requirement (c) described a different audit client, Bulldog Co, which had expanded overseas and set up a treasury management function dealing with forward exchange contracts. The requirement was to discuss why the audit of financial statements is challenging and explain the matters to be considered in planning the audit of the forward exchange contracts. Answers here were extremely mixed in quality. Satisfactory answers focused on why financial instruments generally are difficult to audit, discussing their complex nature, the changing landscape of financial reporting requirements, the potential for both client and auditor to lack appropriate knowledge and skills, and the frequent need to rely on an expert. In terms of planning the audit, adequate answers focused on simple matters such as managing resources, obtaining an understanding of the nature of the contracts and the controls in relation to them, and assessing how management value the financial instruments. Inadequate answers did not include much reference to audit at all, and simply listed out financial reporting rules, with no consideration of audit implications other than saying that financial instruments are complex and subjective. There were very few references to relevant ISA requirements, and little evidence that the audit of complex matters such as financial instruments had been studied at all, even though it is a topical current issue.

| | | Marks |
|---|---|---|
| **Marking scheme** | | |

| | | *Marks* |
|---|---|---|
| **(a)** | **Fraud and revenue recognition** | |
| | Generally 1 mark for each point of discussion: | |
| | – Management targets/incentives | |
| | – High volume of transactions | |
| | – Use of judgment | |
| | – Complexity of accounting | |
| | – Cash sales | |
| | – Common in recent accounting frauds | |
| | – Not always complex/rebuttable permitted | |
| | **Maximum** | **7** |
| **(b)** | **Fraud and auditor's liability** | |
| | Generally up to 2 marks for each point explained: | |
| | – Auditor's responsibility in relation to fraud | |
| | – Materiality calculation of the fraud | |
| | – Reasons why fraud is hard to detect | |
| | – Audit firm may not have been sufficiently sceptical | |
| | – Non-adherence to ISAs on controls assessment and evidence obtained | |
| | – Discuss whether duty of care owed to client | |
| | – Discuss breach of duty of care | |
| | – Identify financial loss suffered and firm likely to have been negligent | |
| | **Maximum** | **12** |
| **(c)** | **Audit of financial instruments** | |
| | Generally up to 1½ marks for each point explained: | |
| | **Why is audit of financial instruments challenging?** | |
| | – Financial reporting requirements complex | |
| | – Transactions themselves difficult to understand | |
| | – Auditor may need to rely on expert | |
| | – Lack of evidence and need to rely on management judgment | |
| | – May be hard to maintain attitude of scepticism | |
| | – Internal controls may be deficient | |
| | **Planning implications** | |
| | – Obtain understanding of accounting and disclosure requirements | |
| | – Obtain understanding of client's financial instruments | |
| | – Determine resources, i.e. skills needed and need for an auditor's expert | |
| | – Consider internal controls including internal audit | |
| | – Understand management's method for valuing financial instruments | |
| | – Determine materiality of financial instruments | |
| | **Maximum** | **6** |
| **Total** | | **25** |

# UK SYLLABUS ONLY

**53   KRUPT**  *Walk in the footsteps of a top tutor*

*Top tutor tips*

*Part (a) asks for the penalties for fraudulent and wrongful trading. This is rote-learned knowledge from the text book and should be easy marks.*

*Part (b) requires application of knowledge of fraudulent and wrongful trading to the scenario to evaluate whether the client is guilty of either offence. Use the information in the scenario and take a logical approach to justify whether there is evidence of fraudulent or wrongful trading.*

**(i)   Potential liability and penalties as a result of actions for fraudulent and wrongful trading**

**Fraudulent trading**

Fraudulent trading is defined by the Insolvency Act 1986 (IA 1986) as carrying on the business of an insolvent company with the intent to defraud the company's creditors. Actions for fraudulent trading can be brought against any person who is knowingly a party to the fraudulent trading.

Fraudulent trading is a criminal offence and, as such, the burden of proof in a court action requires the prosecution's evidence to have established its case beyond reasonable doubt. In this regard, it is key to a successful action that the prosecution has established that intent was present in the defendant's actions.

The penalties and liability which may result from a successful action for fraudulent trading are imprisonment for up to 10 years, personal (civil) liability for the debts of company and disqualification from being a company director for up to 15 years.

**Wrongful trading**

Wrongful trading is defined as carrying on the business of an insolvent company when it ought to have been concluded that there was no reasonable prospect of the company avoiding insolvent liquidation and that the creditors of the company would therefore suffer losses. In contrast to fraudulent trading, it is not necessary to establish intent and wrongful trading is a civil wrong rather than a criminal offence. It is also significant that an action for wrongful trading can only be brought against company directors (including shadow directors).

As a civil wrong, the burden of proof for wrongful trading is the weaker test of the balance of probabilities. The penalties and liability which may result from a successful action for wrongful trading are personal (civil) liability of the directors for the debts of the company and disqualification from being a company director for up to 15 years.

(ii)    **Implications for Krupt Ltd**

Mr and Mrs Krupt appear to have bought a substantial quantity of goods on credit in order to ensure that the bank will have sufficient secured assets to cover its debt without having to call in the personal guarantee on the directors' house. The amounts involved in this transaction may be grounds for additional suspicion that the directors' actions were intended to defraud creditors – the inventory balance is now £1,250,000 (£750,000 + £500,000) which is just enough to cover the bank's secured loan.

The transaction will thereby effectively transfer the losses which the directors would otherwise suffer under their personal guarantees to the bank onto the company's unsecured creditors. If the transaction has been intentionally designed to achieve this outcome, the actions of Mr and Mrs Krupt would constitute fraudulent trading. The key issue in proving this would therefore be whether the evidence establishes this intent beyond reasonable doubt.

If a court were to conclude beyond reasonable doubt that it was intentional, imprisonment for up to 10 years, personal liability for the debts of the company and disqualification from being a company director for up to 15 years will all be possible penalties which the court may impose on Mr and Mrs Krupt.

Alternatively, if there is insufficient evidence of fraudulent trading, it may still be possible for creditors to bring a successful action for wrongful trading as a result of the weaker evidence test of the balance of probabilities and the fact that there is no need to establish intent. Moreover, it seems likely that an action for wrongful trading would succeed against Mr and Mrs Krupt. They are both directors of the company and there appears to be clear evidence based on the audit supervisor's findings that they ought to have realised that the creditors of the company would suffer losses.

As a result of a successful action for wrongful trading, it follows that the liquidator will be able to seize Mr and Mrs Krupt's domestic residence and other assets in order to swell the pool of assets available to distribute to all of the creditors of the company (including the unsecured creditors).

---

**Examiner's comments**

For the UK and IRL exams, this requirement was an insolvency question, the first part of which asked for the definitions and implications of fraudulent and wrongful / reckless trading. This section was disappointingly answered with the majority of candidates discussing either the concept of fraud or money laundering.

The second part of the question was the application of those definitions to a client that was clearly wrongful/reckless trading and potentially fraudulent trading. A very small minority appeared to have any knowledge of this part of the syllabus.

---

| | **Marking scheme** | |
|---|---|---|
| | | *Marks* |
| **(i)** | **Krupt Ltd** | |
| | Generally up to 1 mark for each point explained | |
| | **Fraudulent trading:** | |
| | – Definition: carrying on business of insolvent company with intent to defraud creditors | |
| | – Can apply to any person knowingly a party to fraudulent trading | |
| | – Burden of proof: beyond reasonable doubt (criminal offence) | |
| | – Penalties and liability (½ mark each): | |
| |    • Imprisonment up to 10 years | |
| |    • Personal (civil) liability for debts of company | |
| |    • Disqualification as company director for up to 15 years | |
| | **Wrongful trading:** | |
| | – Definition: carrying on business of insolvent company when ought to have concluded/realised that no reasonable prospect of avoiding insolvent liquidation (and that creditors would therefore suffer losses) | |
| | – Only applies to company directors (including shadow directors) | |
| | – Burden of proof: balance of probabilities (civil wrong) | |
| | – Penalties and liability (½ mark each): | |
| |    • Personal (civil) liability for debts of company | |
| |    • Disqualification as company director for up to 15 years | |
| **(ii)** | **Implications for Krupt Ltd:** | |
| | – Mr and Mrs Krupt appear to have bought substantial quantity of goods on credit in order to ensure that bank will have sufficient secured assets to cover its debt without having to call in the personal guarantee on the directors' house; transaction will effectively transfer losses on to unsecured creditors | |
| | – Amounts look suspicious in that there is now sufficient inventory to cover the secured loan from the bank, i.e. £750,000 + £500,000 = £1,250,000 compared to a loan of £1,200,000 | |
| | – If court concludes beyond reasonable doubt that this was intentional, imprisonment/personal liability/disqualification will all be possible penalties | |
| | – If court concludes insufficient evidence of fraudulent trading, it seems likely that wrongful trading will apply: Mr and Mrs Krupt are directors of company, clear evidence based on audit supervisor's findings that ought to have realised creditors would suffer losses | |
| | – liquidator will be able to seize Mr and Mrs Krupt's house (and other assets) to swell pool of assets available to distribute to all creditors of company (including unsecured) | |
| **Total** | | **10** |

## 54 KANDINSKY  *Walk in the footsteps of a top tutor*

### Top tutor tips

*Part (a) is a straightforward going concern question asking for indicators of problems and audit procedures to be performed. Here you should focus on the company's ability to pay its debts as they fall due.*

*Part (b) asks for alternatives to a creditor's voluntary liquidation and the implications of these. Make sure you address all parts of the requirement.*

**(a)** **Going concern matters**

**Revenue and profitability**

The extract financial statements show that revenue has fallen by 38.2%. Based on the information provided, operating profit was £1,150,000 in 20X4 but is only £340,000 in 20X5. Operating margins have fallen from 29.1% to 13.9% during the year and the fall in revenue and margin has caused the company to become loss-making this year.

These changes are highly significant and most likely due to the economic recession which will impact particularly on the sale of luxury, non-essential products such as those sold by Kandinsky Ltd. The loss-making position does not in itself mean that the company is not a going concern, however, the trend is extremely worrying and if the company does not return to profit in the 20X6 financial year, then this would be a major concern. Few companies can sustain many consecutive loss-making periods.

**Bank loan**

The bank loan is significant, amounting to 33.7% of total assets this year end, and it has increased by £500,000 during the year. The company appears to be supporting operations using long-term finance, which may be strategically unsound. The loan is secured on the company's properties, so if the company defaults on the payment due in June 20X6, the bank has the right to seize the assets in order to recoup their funds. If this were to happen, Kandinsky Ltd would be left without operational facilities and it is difficult to see how the company could survive. There is also a risk that there is insufficient cash to meet interest payments due on the loan.

**Trade payables**

The trade payables balance has increased by 38.5%, probably due in part to the change in terms of trade with its major supplier of raw materials. An extension to the payable payment period indicates that the company is struggling to manage its operating cycle, with the cash being generated from sales being insufficient to meet working capital requirements. Relations with suppliers could be damaged if Kandinsky Ltd cannot make payments to them within agreed credit terms, with the result that suppliers could stop supplying the company or withdraw credit which would severely damage the company's operations. There is also a risk that suppliers could bring legal action against the company in an attempt to recover the amounts owed.

**Borrowing facility**

Kandinsky Ltd has £500,000 available in an undrawn borrowing facility, which does provide a buffer as there is a source of cash which is available, somewhat easing the going concern pressures which the company is facing. However, the availability of the borrowing facility depends on certain covenants being maintained. The calculations below show that the covenants have now been breached, so the bank is within its right to withdraw the facility, leaving Kandinsky Ltd exposed to cash shortages and possibly unable to make payments as they fall due.

|  | Covenant | 20X5 | 20X4 |
|---|---|---|---|
| Interest cover | 2 | 340/520 = 0.65 | 1,150/500 = 2.3 |
| Borrowings to operating profit | 4:1 | 3,500/340 = 10.3:1 | 3,000/1,150 = 2.6:1 |

**Contingent liability**

The letter of support offered to a supplier of raw materials exposes Kandinsky Ltd to a possible cash outflow of £120,000, the timing of which cannot be predicted. Given the company's precarious trading position and lack of cash, satisfying the terms of the letter would result in the company utilising 80% of their current cash reserve – providing such support seems unwise, though it may have been done for a strategic reason, i.e. to secure the supply of a particular ingredient. If the financial support is called upon, it is not certain that Kandinsky Ltd would have the means to make the cash available to its supplier, which may create going concern issues for that company and would affect the supply of cane sugar to Kandinsky Ltd. There may also be legal implications for Kandinsky Ltd if the cash could not be made available if or when requested by the supplier.

**Audit procedures in relation to going concern matters identified**

- Obtain and review management accounts for the period after the reporting date and any interim financial accounts which have been prepared. Perform analytical review to ascertain the trends in profitability and cash flows since the year end.

- Read the minutes of the meetings of shareholders, those charged with governance and relevant committees for reference to trading and financing difficulties.

- Discuss with management the strategy which is being developed to halt the trend in declining sales and evaluate the reasonableness of the strategy in light of the economic recession and auditor's knowledge of the business.

- Review the company's current order book and assess the level of future turnover required to break-even/make a profit.

- Analyse and discuss the cash flow, profit and other relevant forecasts with management and review assumptions to ensure they are in line with management's strategy and auditor's knowledge of the business.

- Perform sensitivity analysis on the forecast financial information to evaluate the impact of changes in key variables such as interest rates, predictions of sales patterns and the timing of cash receipts from customers.

- Calculate the average payment period for trade payables and consider whether any increase is due to lack of cash or changes in the terms of trade.

- Obtain the contract in relation to the borrowing facility to confirm the covenant measures and to see if any further covenants are included in the agreement.

- Review correspondence with the bank in relation to the loan and the borrowing facility to gauge the bank's level of support for Kandinsky Ltd and for evidence of deteriorating relationships between the bank and the company's management.

- Obtain the bank loan agreement to confirm the amount of the loan, the interest rate and repayment dates and whether the charge over assets is specific or general in nature.

- Review the bank loan agreement for any clauses or covenants to determine whether there are any breaches.

- Obtain the letter of support in relation to the supplier to confirm the conditions under which Kandinsky Ltd would become liable for payment of the £120,000.

- Discuss with management the reason for the letter of support being given to the supplier to understand the business rationale and its implications, including why the supplier approached Kandinsky Ltd for the letter of support.

- Inspect minutes of management meetings where those charged with governance discussed the letter of support and authorised its issuance.

- Obtain any further documentation available in relation to the letter of support, for example, legal documentation and correspondence with the supplier, to confirm the extent of Kandinsky Ltd's involvement with the supplier and that no further amounts could become payable.

**(b)** The net liabilities position indicates that Viola Ltd is insolvent, meaning that if the company were to dispose of all of its assets, there would not be sufficient funds to pay off the company's liabilities. In a situation of insolvency coupled with operational difficulties like those being faced by Viola Ltd, if the company wishes to avoid liquidation the best option would be to place the company in administration.

### Administration

The aim of administration is to save the company if possible. The directors seek the assistance of experts and the company continues to operate. An insolvency practitioner is appointed to act as administrator, and will effectively take control of the company in an attempt to rescue it as a going concern.

Administration protects the company from the actions of creditors while a restructuring plan is prepared. This is important for Viola Ltd, which is struggling to manage its working capital, meaning that some creditor's balances may be long overdue and the creditors may already be considering actions to recover the amounts owed.

### Administration without a court order

Administration can commence without a court order. The directors themselves may be able to appoint an administrator, though this depends on the company's articles of association. Alternatively, the company (a majority of shareholders) or qualifying floating charge holders can apply for administration without going through the court. Given that Viola Ltd's bank loan is secured by a floating charge over the company's assets, the bank could have the right to appoint an administrator, depending on the terms of the floating charge. If the directors or the company commence appointing an administrator, notice must be given to any qualifying floating charge holders who are entitled to appoint an administrator.

### Administration with a court order

Alternatively, administration proceedings can involve a court order. The company (a majority of shareholders), the directors, one or more creditors or in rare cases the Justice and Chief Executive of the Magistrates' Court can apply to court for an administration order. The court will consider the application and will grant the administration order if it appears that the company is unable to pay its debts.

### Moratorium

Whichever method of appointment of an administrator is employed, the advantage for the company is that a moratorium over the company's debts commences. This means that no creditor can enforce their debt against the company during the period of administration and no security over the company's assets can be enforced. For Viola Ltd this would allow much needed breathing space and time to resolve the working capital problems and lack of cash.

### Statement of affairs

The administrator is likely to request that the directors prepare a statement of affairs detailing all of the company's assets and liabilities, information on the company's creditors and any security over assets.

Using the statement of affairs and other information, the administrator will prepare a proposal regarding the future of the company, in which the administrator recommends either a rescue plan to save the company, or states that the company cannot be saved. The proposal must be sent to all shareholders and creditors, and the proposal will be accepted or rejected. Decisions made by the creditors during the insolvency proceedings will be made using the 'deemed consent' process which means that provided the insolvency practitioner does not receive objections from 10% or more of the creditors by value, the proposed decision will be deemed to have been taken. Alternatively, a virtual meeting or electronic communication can be used to obtain creditor consent.

For Viola Ltd, the proposal is likely to focus on the probability of obtaining the new contracts which have been tendered for, and the availability of bank finance which depends on the contracts being secured. If the contracts are secured, then it may be possible to save the company. However, in the event that the contracts are not secured and there is limited demand from other customers, the administrator may well recommend liquidation of the company.

Administration can last for up to 12 months, but the administration period will end sooner if the administration has been successful, or where there is application to court by one or more creditors or by the administrator.

### Impact on directors

The impact on the directors is that they will lose control of the company and all operational decisions will be made by the administrator. The administrator has the power to remove or appoint directors.

### Impact on employees

The employees will remain employed unless the administrator decides that redundancies are an appropriate measure, and this could be a feature of any proposal to save the company. It must be noted that if the administrator recommends the winding up of Viola Ltd, then the loss of jobs will be inevitable.

### Voluntary liquidation

An alternative to administration is a voluntary liquidation, which can be initiated by creditors or by members. Liquidation means that the company will be wound up – the assets will be sold, proceeds used to pay the company's debts in a prescribed order, and any remaining funds would be distributed to the shareholders.

For a member's voluntary liquidation to take place, the shareholders must pass a resolution, which can be an ordinary or a special resolution depending on the articles of association. However, a member's voluntary liquidation can only take place if the directors make a declaration of solvency. This is a statutory declaration that the directors have made full enquiry into the affairs of the company, and their opinion is that it will be able to pay its debts. The declaration must also include a statement of the company's assets and liabilities. According to the information supplied, Viola Ltd is in a position of net liabilities and therefore it does not seem likely that the directors will be able to make this statement. Therefore a member's voluntary liquidation does not appear feasible.

### Conclusion

The recommendation therefore is for the company to be placed into administration, as this will protect the company from the actions of creditors and allow the administrator to consider all relevant facts before making a proposal on the future of the company.

---

**Examiner's comments**

This question presented information relating to two different clients. Initially candidates were required to identify indicators in the scenario which gave rise to going concern issues and then to state procedures to audit the going concern status of the company. In general, this was well attempted and candidates scored high marks, however those using a columnar approach tended to lack depth in their explanation of the factors identified in the question and overlooked some of the more encompassing audit procedures that did not arise from a specific scenario point.

The second part of the question was set around alternatives to insolvency for a company in financial distress. Answers to this requirement were mixed. Many candidates provided good answers, showing that they understood this syllabus area and could apply their knowledge to the scenario. Weaker answers were too vague, and some clearly did know this syllabus area well enough to provide any reasonable advice.

---

| | Marking scheme | Marks |
|---|---|---|

**(a)** **Identify and explain going concern matters**

Up to 2½ marks for matter identified and explained, to include 1 mark for relevant calculations:

- Revenue, operating margins and profitability
- Bank loan
- Trade payables
- Borrowing facility
- Contingent liability

**Audit procedures in respect of going concern matters**

Up to 1 mark for each well explained procedure:

- Review management accounts, perform analytical review
- Read the minutes of the meetings with shareholders
- Discuss with management the strategy which is being developed to halt the trend in declining sales
- Review the company's current order book
- Analyse and discuss the cash flow, profit and other relevant forecasts with management, review assumptions
- Perform sensitivity analysis on forecast
- Calculate the average payment period for trade payables
- Obtain the contract in relation to the borrowing facility to confirm the covenant measures
- Review correspondence with the bank in relation to the loan and the borrowing facility
- Obtain the bank loan agreement to confirm the amount of the loan, the interest rate, repayment dates and charge over assets
- Review the bank loan agreement for any clauses or covenants
- Obtain any further documentation available in relation to the letter of support
- Discuss the reason for the letter of support being given to the supplier
- Inspect minutes of meetings where TCWG discussed the letter of support
- Obtain legal documentation and correspondence with the supplier to determine level of involvement with the supplier

**Maximum** | **13**

**(b)** **Response to finance director's instructions**

Generally 1½ marks for each point explained

- Identify Viola Ltd as insolvent
- Purpose of administration
- Procedure – commencing administration without court order
- Procedure – commencing administration with a court order
- Moratorium over debts – advantage to the company
- Statement of affairs to be produced
- Administrator proposes rescue plan or liquidation
- Proposals agreed by members and creditors
- Period of administration and cessation of administration
- Impact on directors – lose control of the company
- Impact on employees – depends on recommendation of administrator
- Members' voluntary liquidation is a possibility but depends on declaration of solvency being made
- Conclusion/recommendation

**Maximum** | **12**

**Total** | **25**

**55   HUNT & CO**  *Walk in the footsteps of a top tutor*

*Top tutor tips*

*Part (a) requires knowledge of the difference between fraudulent and wrongful trading. You need to apply your knowledge to the scenario to assess whether the directors are guilty of either offence. The question also asks you to describe the impact of the compulsory liquidation for the employees and creditors. Make sure you identify all aspects of the requirement to avoid missing out on vital marks.*

*Part (b) (i) asks you to examine the information to determine whether the company is insolvent. This should be relatively straightforward. Consider whether the company has more liabilities than assets.*

*Part (b) (ii) asks you to set out the options available to the directors for the future of the company. This requires rote learned knowledge from the text book about the key aspects of liquidation and administration. The requirement specifically asks you to provide a recommendation so you must reach a conclusion as to the best way forward for the company.*

**(a)   Personal liability of company directors**

Normally, the directors of a company which is placed in liquidation do not have a personal liability for the debts of the company. However, the liquidator who is appointed to wind up the company will investigate the reasons for the insolvency, which includes an assessment of whether fraudulent or wrongful trading has taken place, in which case the directors may become liable to repay all or some of the company's debts.

Wrongful trading is defined under s.214 Insolvency Act 1986, and is the less serious of the two offences. Wrongful trading applies when:

- the company has gone into insolvent liquidation

- at some time before the commencement of the winding up of the company, the directors knew, or ought to have known, that there was no reasonable prospect that the company would avoid going into insolvent liquidation

- the directors did not take sufficient steps to minimise the potential loss to creditors.

In deciding whether or not a director of a company ought to have known or ascertained the company was insolvent, the liquidator will consider the general knowledge, skill and experience which may reasonably be expected of a reasonable diligent person carrying out the same functions as are carried out by that director. If a director has greater than usual skill, they would be judged by reference to their own capacity.

The liquidator needs to apply to the court to proceed with an action against a director for wrongful trading. If found guilty, the director faces a civil liability and can be ordered to make a contribution to the company's assets. A director is not likely to be found guilty if they can demonstrate that they took every step with a view to minimising the potential loss to the company's creditors which they ought to have taken.

Fraudulent trading is the more serious offence. Here, a director faces a criminal charge as well as a civil charge under the Insolvency Act. The definition of fraudulent trading is if in the course of the winding up of a company, it appears that any business of the company has been carried on with intent to defraud creditors of the company, or for any fraudulent purpose. Carrying on a business can include a single transaction.

It is harder to prove fraudulent trading than wrongful trading. Only those directors who took the decision to carry on the business, or played an active role are liable. If found guilty, directors may have to make personal contributions to the company's assets and the court can also impose fines or imprisonment on guilty directors.

In the case of Coxon Ltd's directors, it seems that there was a decision to continue to trade even when there were clear signs of the company's financial distress. The company continued to purchase goods even though the directors were aware of severe cash shortages and difficult trading conditions. Therefore the liquidator is likely to conclude that there is evidence of at least wrongful trading, especially on the part of the finance director, who should have known that the company was insolvent, and did not take all steps necessary to protect creditors.

### Impact of compulsory liquidation for employees and creditors

In a compulsory liquidation the employees are automatically dismissed. The liquidator effectively takes over control of the company, assuming management responsibility. The liquidator can require directors and other staff to assist with matters such as preparing and submitting the statement of affairs.

With regard to creditors, they have no involvement with the actual liquidation process, other than having the right to hold a meeting at which they appoint their choice of insolvency practitioner to act as liquidator.

The main impact of liquidation for both employees and creditors is the allocation of company assets at the end of the winding up. There is a prescribed order of priority for allocating company assets. Employees' salaries in arrears (subject to a maximum amount), pension contributions and holiday pay are all preferential creditors. This means that these amounts will be paid after liquidator's costs and fixed charge holders but before all other creditors.

Unsecured creditors and floating charge holders are paid next, followed by preference shareholders and finally members (equity shareholders). Trade creditors are likely to be unsecured creditors, so rank after employees for payment. They are protected to an extent by the 'prescribed part' which is a proportion of assets which is set aside for unsecured creditors. This means that they may not receive the full amount owed to them, but should receive a percentage of what is owed.

**(b)  (i)  Financial position of Jay Ltd**

The company is clearly suffering from a shortage of cash and is reliant on a bank overdraft to manage its working capital. It is unlikely that this situation can be sustained in the long run. However, there is a difference between a company suffering from a cash shortage and a company which is insolvent. Insolvency exists when a company is unable to pay its payables even if it sold all of its assets, in other words the company is in a position of net liabilities.

In order to determine whether Jay Ltd is insolvent it is necessary to look at its net asset or net liability position, using figures from the latest management accounts:

|  | £000 |
|---|---|
| Property, plant and equipment | 12,800 |
| Inventory | 500 |
| Trade receivables | 400 |
| Cash | 0 |
| Long-term borrowings | (12,000) |
| Trade payables | (1,250) |
| Bank overdraft | (1,400) |
| Net liabilities | (950) |

Jay Ltd appears to be insolvent, as it is in a position of net liabilities at 31 May 20X4.

**Tutorial note**

*Credit will be awarded where candidates discuss further issues to do with the company being in a position of net liabilities, such as the directors needing to take care to avoid conducting wrongful trading, and the implications of it.*

The management accounts show the very different results of 'Jay Sport' (JS) and 'Jay Plus' (JP). JS has clearly been badly affected by the revelation regarding one of its ingredients, with only a small amount of sales being made in the current financial year, and this business segment is loss-making overall. However, there seems to be continued demand for JP, which remains profitable. This indicates that the JP business segment may still be able to make a return for shareholders and creditors.

(ii)  **The future of the company – option 1: liquidation**

It may be decided that liquidation or 'winding up' is the best course of action. In this case the company's assets will be sold and a distribution made to its creditors with the proceeds. There is an order of priority for allocating the proceeds raised. Using the information available for Jay Ltd, and ignoring liquidator's costs, the long-term borrowings are secured by a fixed charge over property and rank high in the order of priority and would be paid before the other payables. The employees' wages of £300,000 rank as a preferential creditor and are paid next. Any proceeds remaining would be paid to unsecured creditors, then any residual amount to the shareholders. It is unlikely that the shareholders would receive anything in this case.

The directors cannot themselves begin liquidation proceedings. If they decide that this would be the best course of action for Jay Ltd, they can recommend that a creditor's voluntary winding up should be instigated. In this case a liquidator is appointed by the company's creditors, and a liquidation committee comprising both shareholders and creditors is established, so that the creditors have input to the conduct of the liquidation. A member's voluntary liquidation is not an option, as this form of liquidation can only be used for a solvent company.

If the directors take no action, then a creditor may end up applying to the court for a compulsory winding up order. Any creditor who is owed more than £750 can apply for this action to take place. The directors may wish to avoid the company being placed into compulsory liquidation as this means that employees are automatically dismissed.

In any liquidation the directors will have to stand down to be replaced by the liquidator, unless the liquidator decides to retain them.

### The future of the company – option 2: administration

Administration is a very different course of action. It aims to save the company, and an insolvency practitioner is appointed to take control of the company and to attempt to rescue it as a going concern. Administration protects the company from the actions of creditors while a restructuring plan is prepared.

Administration can commence without a court order. The directors themselves may be able to appoint an administrator where a company is unable to pay its debts, though this depends on the company's articles of association.

Alternatively, a majority of shareholders, the directors or one or more creditors can apply for administration through the court. It is likely to be more expensive and time consuming to apply to the court.

The administrator takes on the role of the directors, and within eight weeks of appointment must send a document to the company's shareholders and creditors in which they state their proposals for rescuing the company, or states that the company cannot be saved. In Jay Ltd's case, it is likely that the JS business segment would be discontinued, and further finance may need to be raised to support the JP segment.

### Conclusions and recommendation

From the information available, it seems that the JP range is still profitable, and could represent a way for the company to remain a going concern. The damage to the JS range does not seem to have tarnished the JP products, and therefore a rescue plan for the company may be feasible.

However, further information is needed before a definite decision is made. In particular, there may be costs that the company would be committed to continue to pay in relation to JS even if that part of the business were to cease to operate, for example, non-cancellable leases. From the information provided, and assuming that no large commitments are included in the overheads of JS, I would recommend that the directors consider an administration order for the company, which will give some breathing space for an appropriate strategy to be devised.

Administration may also benefit Jay Ltd's shareholders, who will continue to own their shares in what may become a more profitable and solvent business. It may also be preferential for the creditors for the company to continue to trade, as they may be more likely to receive the amounts owed to them through the continued operation of the company compared to a forced sale of its assets.

## Marking scheme

| | | | Marks |
|---|---|---|---|
| **(a)** | | **Wrongful and fraudulent trading** | |
| | | Up to 1½ marks for each matter explained: | |
| | | – Liquidator assesses reason for insolvency including director's actions | |
| | | – Definition of wrongful trading | |
| | | – Elements which must be proven for wrongful trading (up to 2 marks) | |
| | | – Matters looked at by court to determine liability – skill and experience | |
| | | – Implication of being found guilty of wrongful trading | |
| | | – Definition of fraudulent trading | |
| | | – Comment on or application of the above to Coxon Ltd's situation | |
| | | – Employees automatically dismissed but may assist liquidator if required | |
| | | – Creditors have limited role in liquidation other than ability to appoint liquidator | |
| | | – Employees rank as preferential creditors | |
| | | – Creditors can be secured, or unsecured and paid from prescribed part | |
| | | – Details of any impairment review conducted by management | |
| | | **Maximum** | **12** |
| **(b)** | **(i)** | **Examine financial position and determine whether the company is insolvent** | |
| | | Generally 1 mark per comment: | |
| | | – Calculation of net liabilities position of Jay Ltd | |
| | | – Determination that Jay Ltd is insolvent | |
| | | – Explanation of meaning of insolvency | |
| | | – Discussion of different results of JS and JP business segments | |
| | | **Maximum** | **4** |
| | **(ii)** | **Evaluate the option available to the directors** | |
| | | Up to 1½ marks per comment: | |
| | | – Explanation of meaning of liquidation | |
| | | – Application of order of priority in allocating proceeds of liquidation | |
| | | – Discussion of means of appointing an administrator | |
| | | – Benefits of administration over liquidation | |
| | | – Identify that a definite decision depends on further information | |
| | | – Overall recommendation | |
| | | **Maximum** | **9** |
| **Total** | | | **25** |

**56    BUTLER (A)**  *Walk in the footsteps of a top tutor*

---

*Top tutor tips*

*Part (a) (i) requires analytical procedures to be performed to help identify going concern issues. Be careful not to spend too much time on the calculations to the detriment of talking about the issues.*

*Part (a) (ii) asks for audit procedures to be performed on the cash flow forecast. Procedures should focus on obtaining evidence to support the assumptions which provide the basis for the forecast. It is important to remember that these events and transactions have not yet happened and therefore cannot be agreed to supporting documentation in the same way as historical figures.*

*Part (b) requires the procedures involved with placing a company into compulsory liquidation and the consequences to the key stakeholder groups of doing this. This requires rote learned knowledge from the text book.*

---

**(a)    (i)    Assessment of draft statement of financial position.**

**Overdraft**

The most obvious issue is that Butler Ltd currently does not have a positive cash balance. The statement of financial position includes an overdraft of £25 million. This lack of cash will make it difficult for the company to manage its operating cycle and make necessary interest payments, unless further cash becomes available.

**Net liabilities**

Butler Ltd is in a position of net liabilities, as indicated by the negative shareholders' funds figure. The company's retained earnings figure is now negative. Net liabilities and significant losses are both examples of financial conditions listed in ISA (UK) 570 *Going concern,* which may cast doubt about the going concern assumption.

**Loss-making**

Note 3 indicates that Butler Ltd has been loss-making for several years. Recurring losses are a further indication of going concern problems. Few companies can sustain many consecutive loss-making periods.

**Overstatement of assets**

There are several items recognised in the statement of financial position, which, if adjusted, would make the net liabilities position worse. For example, a deferred tax asset is recognised at £235 million. This asset should only be recognised if Butler Ltd can demonstrate that future profits will be sufficient to enable the recoverability of the asset. As Butler Ltd has been loss-making for several years, it is arguable that this asset should not be recognised at all.

---

Additionally, an intangible asset relating to development costs of £120 million is recognised. One of the criteria for the capitalisation of such costs is that adequate resources exist for completion of the development. Given Butler Ltd's lack of cash, this criteria may no longer be applicable. If adjustments were made to write off these assets, the net liabilities would become £580 million.

**Fixed charge**

Note 2 indicates that fixed charges exist over assets valued at £25 million. If Butler Ltd fails to make repayments to the creditor holding the charge over assets, the assets could be seized, disrupting the operations of Butler Ltd.

**Liabilities due for repayment**

There are significant short-term borrowings due for repayment – notably a bank loan of £715 million due for repayment in September 20X1. It is hard to see how Butler Ltd will be able to repay this loan given its current lack of cash. The cash flow forecast does not indicate that sufficient cash is likely to be generated post year end to enable this loan to be repaid.

**Provisions**

Provisions have been classified as non-current liabilities. Given that the provisions relate to customer warranties, it is likely that some of the provisions balance should be classified as a current liability. This potential incorrect presentation impacts on assessment of liquidity, as incorrect classification will impact on the cash flow required to meet the warranties obligation.

Butler Ltd's poor financial position means it is unlikely to be able to raise finance from a third party.

**Assessment of cash flow forecast**

From an overall point of view, the cash flow forecast indicates that by the end of August, Butler Ltd will still be in a negative cash position. As discussed above, this is particularly concerning given that a loan of £715 million is due to be repaid in September.

**Cash receipts from customers**

The assumption relating to cash receipts from customers seems optimistic. It is too simplistic to assume that anticipated economic recovery will lead to a sudden improvement in cash collection from customers, even if additional resources are being used for credit control.

**Inflows currently being negotiated**

£200 million of the cash receipts for this three-month period relate to loans and subsidies which are currently being negotiated and applied for. These cash inflows are not guaranteed, and if not received, the overall cash position at the end of the period will be much worse than currently projected.

**Financial assets**

The cash inflow for June 20X1 includes the proceeds of a sale of financial assets of £50 million. It is questionable whether this amount of cash will be generated, given the financial assets are recognised on the statement of financial position at £25 million. The assumed sales value of £50 million may be overly optimistic.

**Conclusion**

In conclusion, the cash flow forecast may not be reliable, in that assumptions are optimistic, and the additional funding is not guaranteed. This means that three months into the next financial year, the company's cash position is likely to have worsened, and loans and trade payables which are due for payment are likely to remain unpaid. This casts significant doubt as to the ability of Butler Ltd to continue operating as a going concern.

*Tutorial note*

*Credit will be awarded for calculation and explanation of appropriate ratios relevant to Butler Ltd's going concern status.*

(ii)    **Recommended audit procedures:**

- Discuss with management the reasons for assuming that cash collection from customers will improve due to 'anticipated improvement in economic conditions'. Consider the validity of the reasons in light of business understanding.

- Enquire as to the nature of the additional resources to be devoted to the credit control function, e.g. details of extra staff recruited.

- For the loan receipt, inspect written documentation relating to the request for finance from Rubery Ltd. Request written confirmation from Rubery Ltd regarding the amount of finance and the date it will be received, as well as any terms and conditions.

- Obtain and review the financial statements of Rubery Ltd, to consider if it has sufficient resources to provide the amount of loan requested.

- For the subsidy, inspect the application made to the subsidy awarding body and confirm the amount of the subsidy.

- Read any correspondence between Butler Ltd and the subsidy awarding body, specifically looking for confirmation that the subsidy will be granted.

- Regarding operating expenses, verify using previous months' management accounts, that operating cash outflows are approximately £200 million per month.

- Enquire as to the reason for the increase in operating cash outflows in August 20X1.

- Verify, using previous months' management accounts, that interest payments of £40 million per month appear reasonable.

- Confirm, using the loan agreement, the amount of the loan being repaid in August 20X1.

- Enquire whether any tax payments are due in the three month period, such as VAT.

- Agree the opening cash position to cash book and bank statement/bank reconciliation, and cast the cash flow forecast.

- Ensure that a cash flow forecast for the full financial year is received as three months' forecast is inadequate for the purposes of the audit.

- Enquire if those charged with governance have assessed the going concern assumption for a period of 12 months from the date of approval of the financial statements.

*Tutorial note*

*Marks would also be awarded for the more general procedures required under ISA 570 in relation to audit procedures on a cash flow forecast, such as evaluation of the reliability of underlying data, and requesting a written representation regarding the feasibility of plans for future action.*

**Conclusion**

The review of the draft statement of financial position and cash flow forecast shows that there are many factors indicating that Butler Ltd is experiencing going concern problems. In particular, the lack of cash, and the significant amounts due to be paid within a few months of the year end cast significant doubt over the use of the going concern assumption in the financial statements. The company has requested finance from its parent company, but even if this is forthcoming, cash flow remains a significant problem.

**(b) (i)** A company is usually placed into compulsory liquidation by a payable (creditor), who uses compulsory liquidation as a means to recover monies owed by the company. The payable (creditor) must petition the court and the petition is advertised in the *London Gazette. There* are various grounds for a petition to be made for compulsory liquidation. The most common ground is that the company is unable to pay its debts. In this case the payable (creditor) must show that he or she is owed more than £750 by the company and has served on the company at its registered office a written demand for payment. This is called a statutory demand. If the company fails to pay the statutory demand in 21 days and does not dispute the debt, then the payable (creditor) may present a winding up petition at court.

The application for a winding up order will be granted at a court hearing where it can be proven to the court's satisfaction that the debt is undisputed, attempts to recover have been undertaken and the company has neglected to pay the amount owed.

On a compulsory winding up the court will appoint an Official Receiver, who is an officer of the court. Within a few days of the winding up order being granted by the court, the Official Receiver must inform the company directors of the situation. The court order is also advertised in the *London Gazette.*

The Official Receiver takes over the control of the company and usually begins to close it down. The company's directors are asked to prepare a statement of affairs. The Official Receiver must also investigate the causes of the failure of the company.

The liquidation is deemed to have started at the date of the presentation of the winding up petition.

At the end of the winding up of the company, a final return is filed with the court and the Registrar. At this point the company is dissolved.

---

**Tutorial note**

*Credit will be awarded to candidates who explain other, less common, means by which a company may face a compulsory liquidation:*

*A shareholder may serve a petition for compulsory liquidation. The grounds for doing so would normally be based on the fact that that the shareholder is dissatisfied with the management of the company, and that it is therefore just and equitable to wind up the company. This action by the shareholder is only allowed if the company is solvent and if the shareholder has been a shareholder for at least six months prior to the petition.*

*Very occasionally, if the Crown believes that a company is contravening legislation such as the Trading Standards legislation or is acting against the public or government interest, it is possible for the company to be liquidated compulsorily. This is very serious action to take and is not used very regularly.*

---

   **(ii)**   Payables (creditors) – The role of the Official Receiver (or Insolvency Practitioner, if appointed), is to realise the company's assets, and to distribute the proceeds in a prescribed order. Depending on the amount of cash available for distribution, and whether the debt is secured or unsecured, payables (creditors) may receive some, all, or none of the amount owed to them.

Employees – All employees of the company are automatically dismissed. A prescribed amount of unpaid employee's wages, accrued holiday pay, and contributions to an occupational pension fund rank as preferential debts, and will be paid before payables (creditors) of the company.

Shareholders – Any surplus that remains after the payment of all other amounts owed by the company is distributed to the shareholders. In most liquidations the shareholders receive nothing.

| | | | Marking scheme | Marks |
|---|---|---|---|---|
| **(a)** | **(i)** | | **Going concern matters** | |

**(a)** **(i)** **Going concern matters**
Up to 1½ marks per matter identified and explained (maximum 3 marks for identification):
– Negative cash position
– Net liabilities position
– Recurring losses
– Possible adjustment to deferred tax and development intangible asset exacerbate net liabilities position (allow 3 marks max)
– Fixed charge over assets
– Significant short term liabilities
– Potential misclassified provisions
– Forecast to remain in negative cash position
– Assumptions re sales optimistic
– Receipt of loan and subsidy not guaranteed
– Assumption of sale value of financial assets could be optimistic

**Maximum**    **10**

**(ii)** **Procedures on cash flow forecast**
1 mark per specific procedure:
– Enquire regarding and consider validity of assumption re cash sales
– Inspect any supporting documentation re additional resources for credit control
– Seek written confirmation from Rubery Ltd re loan
– Review financial statements of Rubery Ltd re adequacy of resources
– Inspect subsidy application
– Seek third party confirmation that subsidy will be awarded
– Confirm cash outflows for operating expenses and interest appear reasonable
– Enquire about potentially missing cash outflows
– Agree date and amount of short term loan repayment to loan documentation
– Agree opening cash to cash book and bank statements

**Maximum**    **8**

**(b)** **(i)** **Procedures for compulsory liquidation**
1 mark each point explained:
– Creditors petition court for winding-up order
– Grounds for the petition must be demonstrated – usually an unpaid statutory demand
– Court appoints an Official Receiver
– Official Receiver informs company directors and takes control of company
– Shareholders can apply for compulsory liquidation (rare)
– The Crown can apply for compulsory liquidation (very rare)

**Maximum**    **4**

**(ii)** **Consequences for stakeholders**
1 mark each consequence explained:
– Payables (creditors)
– Employees
– Shareholders

**Maximum**    **3**

**Total**      **25**

# INT SYLLABUS ONLY

**57    KANDINSKY**  *Walk in the footsteps of a top tutor*

*Top tutor tips*

*Part (a) is a straightforward going concern question asking for indicators of problems and audit procedures to be performed. Here you should focus on the company's ability to pay its debts as they fall due.*

*Part (b) asks for a discussion of the relevance and measurability of the reported performance information. You need to think about whether the various stakeholder groups would be interested in such information or whether there is other information they would prefer to see (relevance). For measurability, think about whether the information would be readily available to report. Organisations may wish to report on performance matters but if that information is not reliably captured by the information systems the credibility of such information will be called into question.*

**(a)    (i)    Going concern matters**

**Revenue and profitability**

The extract financial statements show that revenue has fallen by 38.2%. Based on the information provided, operating profit was $1,150,000 in 20X4 but is only $340,000 in 20X5. Operating margins have fallen from 29.1% to 13.9% during the year and the fall in revenue and margin has caused the company to become loss-making this year.

These changes are highly significant and most likely due to the economic recession which will impact particularly on the sale of luxury, non-essential products such as those sold by Kandinsky Co. The loss-making position does not in itself mean that the company is not a going concern, however, the trend is extremely worrying and if the company does not return to profit in the 20X6 financial year, then this would be a major concern. Few companies can sustain many consecutive loss-making periods.

**Bank loan**

The bank loan is significant, amounting to 33.7% of total assets this year end, and it has increased by $500,000 during the year. The company appears to be supporting operations using long-term finance, which may be strategically unsound. The loan is secured on the company's properties, so if the company defaults on the payment due in June 20X6, the bank has the right to seize the assets in order to recoup their funds. If this were to happen, Kandinsky Co would be left without operational facilities and it is difficult to see how the company could survive. There is also a risk that there is insufficient cash to meet interest payments due on the loan.

**Trade payables**

The trade payables balance has increased by 38.5%, probably due in part to the change in terms of trade with its major supplier of raw materials. An extension to the payable payment period indicates that the company is struggling to manage its operating cycle, with the cash being generated from sales being insufficient to meet working capital requirements. Relations with suppliers could be damaged if Kandinsky Co cannot make payments to them within agreed credit terms, with the result that suppliers could stop supplying the company or withdraw credit which would severely damage the company's operations. There is also a risk that suppliers could bring legal action against the company in an attempt to recover the amounts owed.

**Borrowing facility**

Kandinsky Co has $500,000 available in an undrawn borrowing facility, which does provide a buffer as there is a source of cash which is available, somewhat easing the going concern pressures which the company is facing. However, the availability of the borrowing facility depends on certain covenants being maintained. The calculations below show that the covenants have now been breached, so the bank is within its right to withdraw the facility, leaving Kandinsky Co exposed to cash shortages and possibly unable to make payments as they fall due.

|  | Covenant | 20X5 | 20X4 |
|---|---|---|---|
| Interest cover | 2 | 340/520 = 0.65 | 1150/500 = 2.3 |
| Borrowings to operating profit | 4:1 | 3,500/340 = 10.3:1 | 3,000/1,150 = 2.6:1 |

**Contingent liability**

The letter of support offered to a supplier of raw materials exposes Kandinsky Co to a possible cash outflow of $120,000, the timing of which cannot be predicted. Given the company's precarious trading position and lack of cash, satisfying the terms of the letter would result in the company utilising 80% of their current cash reserve. Providing such support seems unwise, though it may have been done for a strategic reason, i.e. to secure the supply of a particular ingredient. If the financial support is called upon, it is not certain that Kandinsky Co would have the means to make the cash available to its supplier, which may create going concern issues for that company and would affect the supply of cane sugar to Kandinsky Co. There may also be legal implications for Kandinsky Co if the cash could not be made available if or when requested by the supplier.

(ii) **Audit procedures in relation to going concern matters identified**

- Obtain and review management accounts for the period after the reporting date and any interim financial accounts which have been prepared. Perform analytical review to ascertain the trends in profitability and cash flows since the year end.

- Read the minutes of the meetings of shareholders, those charged with governance and relevant committees for reference to trading and financing difficulties.

- Discuss with management the strategy which is being developed to halt the trend in declining sales and evaluate the reasonableness of the strategy in light of the economic recession and auditor's knowledge of the business.

- Review the company's current order book and assess the level of future turnover required to breakeven/make a profit.

- Analyse and discuss the cash flow, profit and other relevant forecasts with management and review assumptions to ensure they are in line with management's strategy and auditor's knowledge of the business.

- Perform sensitivity analysis on the forecast financial information to evaluate the impact of changes in key variables such as interest rates, predictions of sales patterns and the timing of cash receipts from customers.

- Calculate the average payment period for trade payables and consider whether any increase is due to lack of cash or changes in the terms of trade.

- Obtain the contract in relation to the borrowing facility to confirm the covenant measures and to see if any further covenants are included in the agreement.

- Review correspondence with the bank in relation to the loan and the borrowing facility to gauge the bank's level of support for Kandinsky Co and for evidence of deteriorating relationships between the bank and the company's management.

- Obtain the bank loan agreement to confirm the amount of the loan, the interest rate and repayment dates and whether the charge over assets is specific or general in nature.

- Review the bank loan agreement for any clauses or covenants to determine whether there are any breaches.

- Obtain the letter of support in relation to the supplier to confirm the conditions under which Kandinsky Co would become liable for payment of the $120,000.

- Discuss with management the reason for the letter of support being given to the supplier to understand the business rationale and its implications, including why the supplier approached Kandinsky Co for the letter of support.

- Inspect minutes of management meetings where those charged with governance discussed the letter of support and authorised its issuance.

- Obtain any further documentation available in relation to the letter of support, for example, legal documentation and correspondence with the supplier, to confirm the extent of Kandinsky Co's involvement with the supplier and that no further amounts could become payable.

**(b)    (i)    The relevance and measurability of the reported performance information**

**Relevance**

Performance information should be relevant to the users of that information. In the case of Rothko University, there is likely to be a wide range of interested parties including current and potential students who will be interested in the quality of the teaching provided and the likelihood of securing employment on completion of the university course. Other interested parties will include the government body which provides funding to the University, regulatory bodies which oversee higher education and any organisations which support the University's work, for example, graduate employers.

For current and potential students, performance measures such as the graduation rate and employability rate will be relevant as this will provide information on the success of students in completing their degree programmes and subsequently obtaining a job. This is important because students pay tuition fees to attend Rothko University and they will want to know if the investment in education is likely to result in employment. However, some students may be more interested in further study after graduation, so employability measures would be less relevant to them.

Students will be interested in the proportion of graduates who achieve a distinction as this may lead to better job prospects and a better return on the investment (of time and money) in their education.

Finally, students will find the performance measure on course satisfaction relevant because it indicates that the majority of students rated the quality of the course as high, an important factor in deciding whether to enrol onto a degree programme.

Stakeholders other than current and potential students may find other performance information more relevant to them, for example, potential graduate employers may be interested in the amount of work experience which is provided on the University's degree programme.

The performance measures are most relevant where they can be compared to the measures of other universities. Currently, the University has not provided comparative information and this is likely to make it difficult to assess the performance of the University over time and also makes the current year measures harder to gauge.

**Measurability**

In terms of measurability, as with many key performance indicators, it is sometimes difficult to precisely define or measure the performance information. Some of the measures are quite subjective, for example, the rating which a student gives to a course is down to personal opinion and it is difficult to substantiate, for example, the difference between a course rating of excellent and very good. Similarly, defining 'graduate level employment' could be subjective. Some measures will be easier to quantify, for example, the degree completion percentage, which will be based on fact rather than opinion.

There may also be problems in how the information is gathered, affecting the validity of the information. For example, only a sample of students may have completed a course evaluation, and possibly the most satisfied students were selected which will improve the measure.

**(ii)** **Examination procedures**

- Obtain a list detailing all of the University's performance objectives and the basis of measurement for each objective.

- Enquire of the University whether comparative information is available and if this information needs to be verified as part of the disclosure in the current year.

- For the graduation rate, obtain a list of students awarded degrees in 20X5, and a list of all students who registered on the degree programme and use this information to recalculate the %.

- For academic performance, review minutes of meetings where degree results were discussed and approval given for the award of distinction to a number of students.

- For a sample of students awarded a distinction, confirm each student's exam results to supporting documentation, e.g. information in their student files, notices of exam results sent to the student and confirm that the grades achieved qualify for a distinction being awarded.

- Inspect any documentation issued at events such as degree award ceremonies to confirm the number of students being awarded a distinction.

- Obtain supporting documentation from the University for the employability rate and discuss with appropriate personnel, for example, the careers centre, the basis of the determination of the rate.

- For the employability rate, a confirmation could be sent to a sample of students asking for the details of their post-graduation employment.

- If the University supplies references for students seeking employment, inspect the references issued in 20X5 and contact the relevant company to see if the student was offered employment.

- For course satisfaction, inspect the questionnaires or surveys completed by students from which the % was derived, and recalculate.

- Enquire if there is any other supporting documentation on course satisfaction, for example, minutes of student and lecturer meetings about the quality of courses.

---

**Examiner's comments**

This question presented information relating to two different clients. Initially candidates were required to identify indicators in the scenario which gave rise to going concern issues and then to state procedures to audit the going concern status of the company. In general, this was well attempted and candidates scored high marks, however those using a columnar approach tended to lack depth in their explanation of the factors identified in the question and overlooked some of the more encompassing audit procedures that did not arise from a specific scenario point.

---

The second part of the question focused on the audit of performance information and required candidates to discuss the relevance and measurability of key performance indicators (KPIs) in respect of a University and to describe how they might be audited. Well prepared candidates were able to discuss the issues surrounding measuring and determining relevant performance information and were able to draw on the information included in the recent examiner's article on this topic to the scenario. Some candidates did not focus on the question requirement and attempted to describe the theory of public sector KPIs. Many candidates were unprepared and left this requirement out altogether.

| Marking scheme | | | | Marks |
|---|---|---|---|---|
| **(a)** | **(i)** | **Identify and explain going concern matters** | | |
| | | Up to 2½ marks for matter identified and explained, to include 1 mark for relevant calculations: | | |
| | | – | Revenue, operating margins and profitability | |
| | | – | Bank loan | |
| | | – | Trade payables | |
| | | – | Borrowing facility | |
| | | – | Contingent liability | |
| | | | **Maximum** | 9 |
| | **(ii)** | **Audit procedures in respect of going concern matters** | | |
| | | Up to 1 mark for each well explained procedure: | | |
| | | – | Review management accounts, perform analytical review | |
| | | – | Read the minutes of the meetings with shareholders | |
| | | – | Discuss with management the strategy which is being developed to halt the trend in declining sales | |
| | | – | Review the company's current order book | |
| | | – | Analyse and discuss the cash flow, profit and other relevant forecasts with management, review assumptions | |
| | | – | Perform sensitivity analysis on forecast | |
| | | – | Calculate the average payment period for trade payables | |
| | | – | Obtain the contract in relation to the borrowing facility to confirm the covenant measures | |
| | | – | Review correspondence with the bank in relation to the loan and the borrowing facility | |
| | | – | Obtain the bank loan agreement to confirm the amount of the loan, the interest rate, repayment dates and charge over assets | |
| | | – | Review the bank loan agreement for any clauses or covenants | |
| | | – | Obtain any further documentation available in relation to the letter of support | |
| | | – | Discuss the reason for the letter of support being given to the supplier | |
| | | – | Inspect minutes of meetings where TCWG discussed the letter of support | |
| | | – | Obtain legal documentation and correspondence with the supplier to determine level of involvement with the supplier | |
| | | | **Maximum** | 6 |

**(b)** **(i)** **The relevance and measurability of the reported performance information**

Generally up to 1 mark for each point explained:

–   1 mark for explaining why each measure would be relevant to an existing or potential student (4 measures in total, so maximum 4 marks)
–   Problems in defining the measures
–   Problems in quantifying the measures – some are subjective
–   Issues in validity of the reported information
–   Lack of comparative information

**(ii)** **Examination procedures**

Up to 1 mark for well described procedures:

–   Obtain a list detailing all of the University's performance objectives and the basis of measurement for each objective
–   Discuss with University the availability of comparative information and requirement to include in current year report
–   For the graduation rate, obtain a list of students awarded degrees in 20X5, and a list of all students who registered on the degree programme and use this information to recalculate the %
–   For academic performance, review minutes of meetings where degree results were discussed and approval given for the award of distinction to a number of students
–   Agree a sample of students' exam results to supporting documentation, e.g. information in their student files, notices of exam results sent to the students
–   Inspect any documentation issued at events such as degree award ceremonies to confirm the number of students being awarded a distinction
–   Obtain supporting documentation from the University for the employability rate and discuss with appropriate personnel, for example, the careers centre, the basis of the determination of the rate
–   For the employability rate, a confirmation could be sent to a sample of students asking for the details of their post-graduation employment
–   If the University supplies references for students seeking employment, inspect the references issued in 20X5 and contact the relevant company to see if the student was offered employment
–   For course satisfaction, inspect the questionnaires or surveys completed by students from which the % was derived, and recalculate
–   Enquire if there is any other supporting documentation on course satisfaction, for example, minutes of student and lecturer meetings about the quality of courses

|                                    |    |
|------------------------------------|----|
| **Maximum**                        | 10 |
| **Total**                          | 25 |

**58    PUBLIC SECTOR ORGANISATIONS**  *Walk in the footsteps of a top tutor*

*Top tutor tips*

*This question is not taken from a previous exam, but has been added to the exam kit to give you the opportunity to practise requirements relating to the INT syllabus area of public sector performance information.*

(a)    **Performance audits** aim to provide management with assurance and advice regarding the effective functioning of its operational activities.

**Performance information** is information published by public sector bodies regarding their objectives and the achievement of those objectives.

(b)    **Performance targets**

    (i)    **Local police department**

- Reduce the number of crimes by x%

- Reduce the number of offenders re-offending by x%

- Reduce the number of deaths caused by dangerous driving x%

- Increase public satisfaction to x%

    (ii)    **Local hospital**

- Reduce emergency department waiting times to a maximum of x hours

- Reduce the maximum waiting time for an operation to x weeks

- Reduce the number of infections contracted in the hospital by x%

- Reduce the number of re-admissions to hospital by x%

    (iii)    **Local council**

- Increase public satisfaction to x%

- To build x number of council houses in the next 5 years

- To spend $x on road maintenance and improvements each year

- To increase council tax by a maximum of the rate of inflation

*Tutorial note*

*Credit will be awarded for any other relevant examples.*

*A target does not have to be SMART. Targets are typically more generalised than an objective.*

**(c)** **Stakeholder groups**

**(i)** **Police department**

| Stakeholder | Use |
|---|---|
| Government e.g. Home Office | To ensure that police departments are achieving the targets set by the government. |
| | To report to taxpayers on how government money in this area is being used to achieve the stated objectives. |
| Local residents | Residents may wish to know the level of crime in their area to assess the performance of their local police department. |
| Prospective residents | Prospective residents may use such information to decide whether to move to a particular town/city. If the crime rate is high they may decide not to move there. |

**(ii)** **Local hospital**

| | |
|---|---|
| Local residents | To assess the performance of their local hospital as this will be of importance if they were ever to be admitted to hospital. |
| Patients awaiting treatment | Patients awaiting treatment may have a choice of hospital from which to receive treatment. In this case, patients are likely to choose the option with the lowest infection rates, highest success rates for a particular operation/procedure, or the quickest treatment time. |
| Government e.g. Department for Health | To ensure that hospitals are achieving the targets set by the government. |
| | To report to taxpayers on how government money in this area is being used to achieve the stated objectives. |

**(iii)** **Local council**

| | |
|---|---|
| Local residents | To assess the performance of their local council and how their taxes are being used. |
| Suppliers/contractors | Suppliers/contractors will be interested to see the plans for the future to assess if there will be additional work being tendered. For example if the council has set a target to build an additional 1000 houses in the coming year, local building firms may be able to bid for the work. |
| Government e.g. Department for Communities and Local Government | To ensure that councils are achieving the targets set by the government. |
| | To report to taxpayers on how government money in this area is being used to achieve the stated objectives. |

*Tutorial note*

*Credit will be awarded for any other relevant examples e.g. employees to assess whether there is the possibility of redundancies if the target is to reduce costs significantly.*

**(d)    Difficulties**

All relevant information may not be reported (e.g. number of crimes or number of hospital infections) therefore it may appear as though there has been improvement when problems may not have been recorded completely.

Where information is completely recorded, accuracy of the information may be an issue. The public sector organisation needs to have good internal controls in place in respect of this information in the same way as internal controls would be expected to be in place in respect of financial information.

Definitions of certain targets and measures may be ambiguous resulting in matters going un-recorded due to public sector employees recording the information in a different way. Information may be classified differently by different members of staff unless specific training is given.

Even so, information may not be comparable between different police departments/ hospitals/councils if each interpret the definitions in a different way.

There is also the risk that public sector departments will falsify the figures that have been reported if they are failing to meet the targets set by the government. This may be difficult for the auditor to detect as it is unlikely there will be alternative forms of corroborative evidence to highlight discrepancies.

| | | | Marks |
|---|---|---|---|
| **Marking scheme** | | | |
| (a) | **Definitions** Up to 1 for each definition<br>– Performance audit<br>– Performance information | | |
| | | Maximum | 2 |
| (b) | **Performance targets** 1 mark per performance target. Max of 3 per public sector body. | | |
| | | Maximum | 9 |
| (c) | **Stakeholder groups** ½ mark per stakeholder group and 1 mark per reason for using the performance information. | | |
| | | Maximum | 9 |
| (d) | **Difficulties** Up to 1 ½ per point made.<br>– Completeness<br>– Accuracy<br>– Ambiguity of targets<br>– Comparability<br>– Risk of falsification | | |
| | | Maximum | 5 |
| **Total** | | | 25 |

# Section 5

# SPECIMEN EXAM QUESTIONS

**ALL THREE questions are compulsory and MUST be attempted**

1    ADAMS GROUP  *Walk in the footsteps of a top tutor*

It is 1 July 20X5. You are a manager in Dando & Co, a firm of Chartered Certified Accountants responsible for the audit of the Adams Group, a listed entity for the year ended 31 May 20X5. The Group operates in the textile industry, buying cotton, silk and other raw materials to manufacture a range of goods including clothing, linen and soft furnishings. Goods are sold under the Adams brand name, which was acquired by the Group many years ago. Your firm was appointed as auditor in January 20X5.

You have been provided with the following exhibits:

1    An email which you have received from Joss Dylan, the audit engagement partner.

2    Information about the Adams Group's general background and activities.

3    Extracts from the draft Group financial statements for the year ending 31 May 20X5.

4    Notes from a meeting held between Joss Dylan and the Group's finance director and representatives from its audit committee.

**Required:**

**Respond to the instructions in the email from the audit engagement partner.    (46 marks)**

**Note: The split of the mark allocation is shown in the partner's email (Exhibit 1).**

**Professional marks will be awarded for the presentation and logical flow of the briefing notes and the clarity of the explanations provided.    (4 marks)**

**(Total: 50 marks)**

**Exhibit 1: Email from audit engagement partner**

| To: | Audit manager |
| --- | --- |
| From: | Joss Dylan |
| Subject: | Adams Group audit planning |
| Date: | 1 July 20X5 |

Hello

I need you to begin planning the audit of the Adams Group (the Group) for the year ended 31 May 20X5. As you know, we have been appointed to audit the Group financial statements, and we have also been appointed to audit the financial statements of the parent company and of all subsidiaries of the Group except for a foreign subsidiary, Lynott Co, which is audited by a local firm, Clapton & Co. All components of the Group have the same year end of 31 May, report under IFRS Standards and in the same currency.

Using the information provided, I require you to prepare briefing notes for my use, in which you:

(a)     Evaluate the audit risks to be considered in planning the audit of the Group. Your evaluation should utilise analytical procedures for identifying relevant audit risks.

**(20 marks)**

(b)     Explain the matters to be considered, and the procedures to be performed, in respect of planning to use the work of Clapton & Co.     **(8 marks)**

(c)     Design the principal audit procedures to be performed in respect of the following balances recognised as non-current assets in the Group statement of financial position:

(i)     $12 million recognised as investment in associate, and     **(5 marks)**

(ii)     $8 million recognised as a brand name.     **(5 marks)**

(d)     Using the information provided in Exhibit 4, identify and evaluate any ethical threats and other professional issues which arise from the requests made by the Group audit committee.     **(8 marks)**

**Thank you.**

**Exhibit 2 – Background and structure of the Adams Group**

The Group structure and information about each of the components of the Group is shown below:

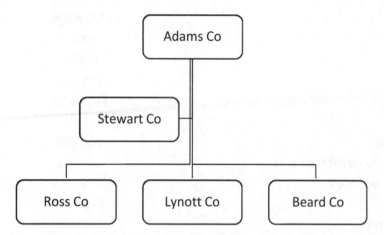

Ross Co, Lynott Co and Beard Co are all wholly owned, acquired subsidiaries which manufacture different textiles. Adams Co also owns 25% of Stewart Co, a company which is classified as an associate in the Group statement of financial position at a value of $12 million at 31 May 20X5. The shares in Stewart Co were acquired in January 20X5 for consideration of $11.5 million. Other than this recent investment in Stewart Co, the Group structure has remained unchanged for many years.

**Information relevant to each of the subsidiaries**

Adams Co is the parent company in the group and its main activities relate to holding the investments in its subsidiaries and also the brand name which was purchased many years ago. Adams Co imposes an annual management charge of $800,000 on each of its subsidiaries, with the charge for each financial year payable in the subsequent August.

Ross Co manufactures luxury silk clothing, with almost all of its output sold through approximately 200 department stores. Ross Co's draft statement of financial position recognises assets of $21.5 million at 31 May 20X5. Any silk clothing which has not been sold within 12 months is transferred to Lynott Co, where the silk material is recycled in its manufacturing process.

Lynott Co is located in Farland, where it can benefit from low cost labour in its factories. It produces low price fashion clothing for the mass market. A new inventory system was introduced in March 20X5 in order to introduce stronger controls over the movement of inventory between factories and stores. Lynott Co is audited by Clapton & Co, and its auditor's reports in all previous years have been unmodified. Clapton & Co is a small accounting and audit firm, but is a member of an international network of firms. Lynott Co's draft statement of financial position recognises assets of $24 million at 31 May 20X5.

Beard Co manufactures soft furnishings which it sells through an extensive network of retailers. The company is cash-rich, and surplus cash is invested in a large portfolio of investment properties, which generate rental income. The Group's accounting policy is to measure investment properties at fair value. Beard Co's draft statement of financial position recognises assets of $28 million at 31 May 20X5, of which investment properties represent $10 million.

### Exhibit 3 – Extracts from draft Group consolidated financial statements

### Draft consolidated statement of profit or loss and other comprehensive income

|  | Year ended 31 May 20X5 | Year ended 31 May 20X4 |
|---|---|---|
|  | $000 | $000 |
|  | Draft | Actual |
| Revenue | 725,000 | 650,000 |
| Cost of sales | (463,000) | (417,500) |
| Gross profit | 262,000 | 232,500 |
| Other income – rental income | 200 | 150 |
| Operating expenses | (250,000) | (225,000) |
| Operating profit | 12,200 | 7,650 |
| Net finance cost | (1,000) | (1,000) |
| Profit before tax | 11,200 | 6,650 |
| Income tax expense | (1,500) | (1,000) |
| Profit for the year | 9,700 | 5,650 |
| Other comprehensive income: |  |  |
| Gain on investment property revaluation | 1,000 | 3,000 |
| Total comprehensive income | 10,700 | 8,650 |

**Draft consolidated statement of financial position**

| | 31 May 20X5 | 31 May 20X4 |
|---|---|---|
| | $000 | $000 |
| | **Draft** | **Actual** |
| **Non-current assets** | | |
| Property, plant and equipment | 45,000 | 45,000 |
| Investment property (recognised at fair value) | 10,000 | 7,500 |
| Intangible asset – brand name (recognised at cost) | 8,000 | 8,000 |
| Investment in associate | 12,000 | – |
| | 75,000 | 60,500 |
| **Current assets** | | |
| Inventory | 12,000 | 6,000 |
| Receivables | 10,500 | 6,600 |
| Cash | 10,000 | 22,000 |
| | 32,500 | 34,600 |
| **Total assets** | 107,500 | 95,100 |
| **Equity and liabilities** | | |
| Share capital | 35,000 | 35,000 |
| Retained earnings | 34,000 | 24,600 |
| | 69,000 | 59,600 |
| **Non-current liabilities** | | |
| Bank loan | 20,000 | 20,000 |
| **Current liabilities** | | |
| Trade payables | 16,000 | 13,500 |
| Tax payable | 2,500 | 2,000 |
| | 18,500 | 15,500 |
| **Total equity and liabilities** | 107,500 | 95,100 |

Exhibit 4 – Notes from discussion with Group audit committee and finance director

**Recent publicity**

During the year, the Group attracted negative publicity when an investigation by a well-known journalist alleged that child-labour was being used by several suppliers of raw materials to Lynott Co. The Group refuted the allegations, claiming that the suppliers in question had no contract to supply Lynott Co, and that the Group always uses raw materials from ethically responsible suppliers. The media coverage of the issue has now ended. The Group finance director is confident that the negative publicity has not affected sales of the Group's products, saying that in fact sales are buoyant, as indicated by the increase in Group revenue in the year.

**Systems and accounting policies**

The Group has a policy of non-amortisation of the Adams brand name. The brand name was acquired many years ago and is recognised at its original cost. The previous audit firm accepted the policy due to the strength of the brand name and the fact that the Group spends a significant amount each year on product development and marketing aimed at supporting the brand. The Group has maintained a good market share in the last few years and management is confident that this will continue to be the case.

As part of management's strategy to increase market share, a bonus scheme has been put in place across the Group under which senior managers will receive a bonus based on an increase in revenue.

The Group's accounting and management information systems are out of date, and the Group would like to develop and implement new systems next year. The audit committee would like to obtain advice from Dando & Co on the new systems as they have little specialist in-house knowledge in this area.

**Financing**

In addition, the audit committee requests that the Group audit engagement partner attends a meeting with the Group's bank, which is planned to be held the week after the auditor's report is issued. The purpose of the meeting is for the Group to renegotiate its existing lending facility and to extend its loan, and will be attended by the Group finance director, a representative of the audit committee, as well as the bank manager. The Group is hoping that the audit partner will be able to confirm the Group's strong financial position at the meeting, and also confirm that the audit included procedures on going concern, specifically the audit of the Group's cash flow forecast for the next two years, which the bank has requested as part of their lending decision.

**2** **BRADLEY**  *Walk in the footsteps of a top tutor*

It is 1 July 20X5. The audit of Bradley Co's financial statements for the year ended 30 April 20X5 is nearly complete, and the auditor's report is due to be issued next week. Bradley Co operates steel processing plants at 20 locations and sells its output to manufacturers and engineering companies. You are performing an engagement quality control review on the audit of Bradley Co, as it is a significant new client of your firm.

**(a)** One of the audit assistants who has been working on the audit of Bradley Co made the following comments when discussing the completion of the audit with you:

'I was assigned to the audit of provisions. One of the provisions, amounting to $10,000, relates to a legal claim made against the company after an employee was injured in an accident at one of the steel processing plants. I read all of the correspondence relating to this, and tried to speak to Bradley Co's legal advisers, but was told by the finance director that I must not approach them and should only speak to him about the matter. He said that he is confident that only $10,000 needs to be recognised and that the legal advisers had confirmed this amount to him in a discussion of the matter. I noted in the audit working papers that I could not perform all of the planned audit procedures because I could not speak to the legal advisers. The audit manager told me to conclude that provisions are correctly recognised in the financial statements based on the evidence obtained, and to move on to my next piece of work. He said it didn't matter that I hadn't spoken to the legal advisers because the matter is immaterial to the financial statements.

'We received the final version of the financial statements and the chair's statement to be published with the financial statements yesterday. I have quickly looked at the financial statements but the audit manager said we need not perform a detailed analytical review on the financial statements as the audit was relatively low risk. The manager also said that he had discussed the chair's statement with the finance director so no further work on it is needed. The audit has been quite time-pressured and I know that the client wants the auditor's report to be issued as soon as possible.'

**Required:**

**Explain the quality control and other professional issues raised by the audit assistant's comments, discussing any implications for the completion of the audit.**

**(10 marks)**

**(b)** The schedule of uncorrected misstatement included in Bradley Co's audit working papers is shown below, including notes to explain each matter included in the schedule. The financial statements recognise revenue of $2.5 million, and total assets of $35 million. The audit engagement partner is holding a meeting with management tomorrow, at which the uncorrected misstatements will be discussed.

| | | Statement of profit or loss | | Statement of financial position | |
|---|---|---|---|---|---|
| | | Debit | Credit | Debit | Credit |
| | | $ | $ | $ | $ |
| 1 | Share-based payment scheme | 300,000 | | | 300,000 |
| 2 | Restructuring provision | | 50,000 | 50,000 | |
| 3 | Estimate of additional allowance required for slow-moving inventory | 10,000 | | | 10,000 |
| **Totals** | | 310,000 | 50,000 | 50,000 | 310,000 |

1 A share-based payment scheme was established in September 20X4. Management has not recognised any amount in the financial statements in relation to the scheme, arguing that due to the decline in Bradley Co's share price, the share options granted are unlikely to be exercised. The audit conclusion is that an expense and related equity figure should be included in the financial statements.

2 A provision has been recognised in respect of a restructuring involving the closure of one of the steel processing plants. Management approved the closure at a board meeting in April 20X5, but only announced the closure to employees in May 20X5. The audit conclusion is that the provision should not be recognised.

3 The allowance relates to slow-moving inventory in respect of a particular type of steel alloy for which demand has fallen. Management has already recognised an allowance of $35,000, which is considered insufficient by the audit team.

**Required:**

**(i)  Explain the matters which should be discussed with management in relation to each of the uncorrected misstatements; and**

**(ii)  Assuming that management does not adjust the misstatements, justify an appropriate audit opinion and explain the impact on the auditor's report.**

The following mark allocation is provided as guidance for this requirement:

**(i)  10 marks**

**(ii)  5 marks**

**(15 marks)**

**(Total: 25 marks)**

**3  WATERS**  *Walk in the footsteps of a top tutor*

**(a)** Following recent changes to its *International Code of Ethics for Professional Accountants* (the *Code*), in relation to audit firms providing non-assurance services to audit clients, the IESBA commented that:

'The performance of non-assurance services may create threats to independence of the firm or members of the audit team. Such threats include self-review, self-interest and advocacy threats. Further, if a firm were to assume a management responsibility for an audit client, the threats created would be so significant that no safeguards could reduce the threats to an acceptable level. However, there are varying views on what constitutes a management responsibility and as such it is in the public interest to enhance the clarity and guidance on this topic in the *Code*.'

**Required:**

**Discuss the changes made to the *Code* in relation to non-assurance services and evaluate the arguments for and against auditors providing non-assurance services to audit clients.** **(8 marks)**

**(b)** It is 1 July 20X5. You are a manager in Hunt & Co, a firm which offers a range of services to audit and non-audit clients. You have been asked to consider a potential engagement to review and provide a report on the prospective financial information of Waters Co, a company which has been an audit client of Hunt & Co for six years. The audit of the financial statements for the year ended 31 May 20X5 has just commenced.

Waters Co operates a chain of cinemas across the country. Currently its cinemas are out of date and use projectors which cannot show films made using new technology, which are becoming more popular. Management is planning to invest in all of its cinemas in order to attract more customers. The company has sufficient cash to fund half of the necessary capital expenditure, but has approached its bank with a loan application of $8 million for the remainder of the funds required. Most of the cash will be used to invest in equipment and fittings, such as new projectors and larger screens, enabling new technology films to be shown in all cinemas. The remaining cash will be used for refurbishment of the cinemas. Prior to finalising the application for the funding from the bank, the finance director has also asked if the audit engagement partner will assist him in presenting the final version of the strategic plan, in relation to the refurbishment, to the board as he knows that Hunt & Co has several clients in the industry and the partner will be able to confirm that the plan is consistent with what others in the industry are doing.

The draft forecast statements of profit or loss for the years ending 31 May 20X6 and 20X7 are shown below, along with the key assumptions which have been used in their preparation. The unaudited statement of profit or loss for the year ended 31 May 20X5 is also shown below. The forecast has been prepared for use by the bank in making its lending decision, and will be accompanied by other prospective financial information including a forecast statement of cash flows.

### Forecast statement of profit or loss

| | Year ended 31 May 20X5 Unaudited $000 | Note to forecast information | Year ending 31 May 20X6 Forecast $000 | Year ending 31 May 20X7 Forecast $000 |
|---|---|---|---|---|
| Revenue | 35,000 | 1 | 43,000 | 46,000 |
| Operating expenses | (28,250) | 2 | (31,500) | (32,100) |
| | | | | |
| Operating profit | 6,750 | | 11,500 | 13,900 |
| Finance costs | (1,700) | | (2,000) | (1,900) |
| | | | | |
| Profit before tax | 5,050 | | 9,500 | 12,000 |

**Note 1:** The forecast increase in revenue is based on the following assumptions:

(i) All cinemas will be fitted with new projectors and larger screens to show new technology films by September 20X5.

(ii) Ticket prices will increase from $7.50 to $10 from 1 September 20X5.

**Note 2:** Operating expenses include mainly staff costs, depreciation of property and equipment, and repairs and maintenance to the cinemas.

**Required:**

(i) Explain the matters to be considered by Hunt & Co before accepting the engagement to review and report on Waters Co's prospective financial information.

(7 marks)

(ii) Assuming the engagement is accepted, describe the examination procedures to be used in respect of the forecast statement of profit or loss. (6 marks)

(iii) Discuss the content of the report which would be issued on the prospective financial information, explaining the level of assurance which is provided. (4 marks)

(Total: 25 marks)

# Section 6

# ANSWERS TO SPECIMEN EXAM

1    ADAMS GROUP  *Walk in the footsteps of a top tutor*

### Top tutor tips

*The first requirement asks for audit risks, i.e. the risks of material misstatement and any detection risks. Knowledge of the examinable accounting standards is essential to answer this question. For the areas of the financial statements, explain how the client might have incorrectly accounted for the balances. Detection risk is the risk the auditor does not detect the misstatements in the financial statements. Look out for information in the scenario that indicates it is a new audit client or a client which operates from multiple locations which may make it difficult for the auditor to visit the locations required to obtain sufficient appropriate evidence.*

*Part (b) asks for matters to be considered before using the work of a component auditor. This should be straightforward rote learned knowledge applied to the scenario.*

*Part (c) asks for procedures in respect of the investment in associate and brand name. Procedures are very regularly examined as a follow on from audit risks. Make sure the procedures are adequately described so that the person performing the procedure will know what to do.*

*Part (d) asks for ethical threats and other professional issues arising. When discussing ethical threats try to evaluate the significance of the threat as this will affect how the auditor should manage the threat.*

*Don't forget to present your answer in a briefing note format and include an introduction and a conclusion as well as subheadings to get the professional marks.*

**Briefing notes**

To:          **Joss Dylan, Audit engagement partner**

From:        **Audit manager**

Subject:     **Audit planning for the Adams Group**

Date:        **1 July 20X5**

**Introduction**

These briefing notes are prepared for use by the audit engagement partner of the Adams Group, and relate to the planning of the audit of the Group for the year ended 31 May 20X5. The notes contain an evaluation of audit risk, and the matters to be considered in respect of using the work of Clapton & Co, and the relevant procedures to be performed. The notes also detail the procedures to be conducted in relation to the investment in Stewart Co, an associate of the group and the Adams brand name. Finally, the notes discuss the ethical and professional issues which need to be addressed as a result of the requests made by the audit committee of the Adams Group.

**(a)      Evaluation of audit risk**

**New audit client**

The Group is a new client of our firm which may create detection risk as we have no previous experience with the client. However, thorough planning procedures which focus on obtaining a detailed knowledge and understanding of the Group and its activities will minimise this risk. We need to obtain a thorough understanding of each of the subsidiaries as they are all significant components of the Group, with Ross Co, Lynott Co and Beard Co's assets representing respectively 20%, 22.3% and 26% of Group assets. There is also a significant risk that comparative information and opening balances are not correct.

**Analytical review**

Relevant trends and ratio calculations:

–      Revenue increased by 11.5%

–      Gross profit increased by 12.7%

–      Operating profit increased by 59.5%

–      Cash fallen by 54.5%

–      Inventories increased by 100%

–      Receivables increased by 59.1%

|                    | 20X5  | 20X4  |
| ------------------ | ----- | ----- |
| Gross margin       | 36.1% | 35.8% |
| Operating margin   | 1.7%  | 1.2%  |
| Interest cover     | 12.2  | 7.7   |
| Current ratio      | 1.8   | 2.2   |
| Gearing            | 22.5% | 25.1% |

### Revenue

The analytical review indicates that the Group's revenue generation and profitability has improved during the year. There could be valid business reasons to explain the trends, however, the audit team should be alert for possible overstatement of revenue and understatement of expenses.

The risk is increased due to the bonus scheme which gives rise to a risk of material misstatement at the financial statement level. Management will be biased towards accounting treatments which lead to overstatement of revenue, for example, the early recognition of revenue.

There is also a risk of management manipulation of the financial statements due to the renegotiation of the Group's lending facilities, for example, it would be favourable to present a good interest cover to the bank as an analysis of interest cover is likely to feature in their lending decision.

### Current assets

The current ratio has fallen, largely due to the significant reduction in cash of 54.5%. Other changes within current assets could indicate audit risk, as both inventories and trade receivables have increased significantly, by 100% and 59.1% respectively. Given that revenue has increased by only 11.5% in the year, these increases appear very large and could indicate potential overstatement.

### Property, plant and equipment

The analytical review also reveals that the amount recognised in respect of property, plant and equipment has not changed over the year. This seems unlikely to be reasonable, as the Group would presumably have incurred some capital expenditure in the year, disposed of some assets and charged depreciation. There are implications for operating profit, which, for example, is overstated if any necessary depreciation has not been charged.

### Brand name – lack of amortisation

The brand is material at 7.4% of Group assets. It is recognised in the statement of financial position as an intangible asset which is appropriate given that the brand is a purchased intangible asset. However, the asset is recognised at its original cost and there is risk attached to the policy of non-amortisation of the brand.

IAS 38 *Intangible Assets* states that an intangible asset with a finite useful life is amortised, and an intangible asset with an indefinite useful life is not. The risk is that the assumption that the brand has an indefinite life is not correct, and that the asset is overstated and operating expenses understated through the lack of an annual amortisation charge against the asset.

### Brand name – potential impairment

There is also a risk that the brand could be impaired given the bad publicity and allegations made by the journalist against the Group. IAS 36 *Impairment of Assets* requires an impairment review to be carried out when indicators of potential impairment exist.

The allegations may have damaged the Group's reputation, with consequential impact on revenue and cash flows, though the increase of 11.5% in the Group's revenue could indicate that this is not the case, as claimed by the Group finance director. However, sales of certain products could be in decline, and the fact that inventories have doubled in value could indicate problems in selling some of the Group's products.

The risk is that if any necessary impairment has not been recognised, the asset is overstated and operating expenses understated by the amount of the impairment loss.

### Associate – lack of Group knowledge of accounting treatment

A new associate has been acquired during the year, which gives rise to several risks. It is material at 11.2% of Group assets.

Because this is the first addition to the Group for many years, there is an inherent risk that the Group lacks accounting knowledge on the appropriate accounting treatment. Associates are accounted for under IAS 28 *Investments in Associates and Joint Ventures*, which states that an entity with joint control of, or significant influence over, an investee shall account for its investment in an associate or a joint venture using the equity method.

There is a risk that the equity method has not been properly applied. The investment in the associate recognised in the statement of financial position has increased in value since acquisition by $0.5 million, presumably due to the inclusion of the Group's share of profit arising since investment. There is a risk that this has not been calculated correctly, for example, it is not based on the correct share of profit, and the investment may therefore be over- or understated.

### Associate – possible impairment

Risk also arises in relation to any possible impairment of the investment, which may cause it to be overstated in both the individual financial statements of Adams Co, and the Group financial statements.

### Associate – disclosure of income

There is a disclosure issue, as the Group's share of post-investment profit of Stewart Co should be recognised in profit or loss, and IAS 1 *Presentation of Financial Statements* requires that the profit or loss section of the statement of profit or loss shall include as a line item the share of the profit or loss of associates accounted for using the equity method.

The draft statement of profit or loss and other comprehensive income does not show income from the associate as a separate line item. It may have been omitted or netted against operating expenses, and the risk is inappropriate presentation of the income from investment.

### Associate – classification

There is a risk that the investment should not have been classified as an associate. According to IAS 28, if an entity holds, directly or indirectly, 20% or more of the voting power of the investee, it is presumed that the entity has significant influence, unless it can be clearly demonstrated that this is not the case.

If the 25% holding does not give rise to significant influence, for example, if the shares do not convey voting rights, it should be classified as an investment rather than an associate. There is a risk of inappropriate classification, recognition and measurement of the investment in Stewart Co.

### Ross Co's inventory in multiple locations

A risk arises in relation to inventory, which is held in each of the department stores. There is a risk that controls are not sufficiently strong in respect of the movement of inventory and counting procedures at the year-end, as it will be hard for Ross Co to ensure that all locations are subject to robust inventory counting procedures. This control risk leads to potential over or understatement of inventory and cost of sales.

### Systems and controls

The audit committee states that the Group's systems are out of date. This may give rise to control risk across the Group as a whole. In addition, Lynott Co has implemented a new inventory control system. A new system introduced during the year can create control risk.

With any new system, there are risks that controls may take time to develop or be properly understood, and the risk of error in relation to inventories is relatively high.

### Beard Co's investment properties

The investment properties are material to both Beard Co's individual financial statements, representing 35.7% of its total assets, and also to the Group's financial statements, representing 9.3% of Group assets.

According to IAS 40 *Investment Property*, an entity can use either the fair value model or the cost model to measure investment property. When the fair value model is used the gain is recognised in profit or loss. The draft consolidated statement of profit or loss and other comprehensive income includes the investment property revaluation gain as other comprehensive income rather than as profit or loss, and therefore the gain is not presented in accordance with IAS 40.

An accounting error may have been made in the adjustment made to increase the value of the investment property. The statement of financial position shows an increase in value of investment properties of $2.5 million, however, the gain in the statement of profit or loss and other comprehensive income is stated at $1 million. There is a risk that the gain is understated and part of the gain may have been classified elsewhere in profit or loss. The gain as stated in the statement of profit or loss and other comprehensive income is material at 9.3% of total comprehensive income.

It would be important to obtain information on the type of properties which have been invested in, and whether there have been any additions to the portfolio during the year, as part of the movement in the investment property balance during the year could be explained by acquisitions and disposals. Information should also be obtained on any disposals of investment properties during the year, and whether a profit or loss was made on such disposals.

The possible error discussed above in relation to the presentation of the investment property gain is also relevant to the comparative information, which may also be materially misstated. This increases the risk that other balances and transactions in prior years have been incorrectly accounted for. The use of professional scepticism should be stressed during the audit, and further procedures planned on opening balances and comparative information.

Further information should be sought from the previous auditor of the Group in relation to the accounting treatment for the investment properties, and whether it had been identified as an error, in which case the auditor's reports of both Beard Co and the Group should have been modified. A review of prior year auditor's reports is necessary, as well as a review of the previous audit firm's working papers, assuming permission is given for this to take place.

### Bonus scheme

It is noticeable from the draft statement of financial position that there is no accrual recognised in respect of the bonus scheme, unless it has been included inappropriately in trade or tax payables. This indicates a potential understatement of liabilities and overstatement of profit if any necessary accrual has not been made for any bonus which is payable.

### Management charges

The management charges imposed by the parent company on the subsidiaries represent inter-company transactions. In the individual financial statements of each subsidiary, there should be an accrual of $800,000 for the management charge payable in August 20X5, and Adams Co's individual financial statements should include $2.4 million as a receivable. There is a risk that these payables and the corresponding receivable have not been accrued in the individual financial statements.

At Group level, the inter-company balances should be eliminated on consolidation. If this has not happened, the liabilities and receivables in the Group financial statements will be overstated, though there would be no net effect on Group profit if the balances were not eliminated.

*Tutorial note*

*Credit will also be awarded for comments on relevant issues to do with transfer pricing and relevant tax implications which have not been considered and recognised appropriately in the financial statements.*

### Inventory

The draft consolidated statement of financial position shows that inventory has doubled in the year. Given that the Group is involved in retail, there could be issues to do with obsolescence of inventory, leading to potentially overstated inventory and overstatement of profit if any necessary write down is not recognised. This may be especially the case for the mass market fashion clothing made by Lynott Co. Inventory is material to the Group, representing 11.2% of Group assets.

### Inter-company transfers

Ross Co transfers goods to Lynott Co for recycling when its goods are considered obsolete. There is a risk that at Group level the inter-company trading is not eliminated on consolidation, which would lead to overstated receivables and payables. In addition, if the inventory is transferred at a profit or loss, which is then not realised by the Group at the year-end, the Group inventory figure and operating profit could be over- or understated if any necessary provision for unrealised profit or loss is not recognised.

**Goodwill**

The draft consolidated statement of financial position does not recognise goodwill, which is unusual for a Group with three subsidiaries. It may be that no goodwill arose on the acquisitions, or that the goodwill has been fully written off by impairment. However, there is a risk of understatement of intangible assets at the Group level.

**Component auditor**

Lynott Co is audited by an overseas firm of auditors. This may introduce audit risk in that Dando & Co will be relying to some extent on their work. Careful planning will be needed to reduce this risk to a minimum, and this is discussed in the next section of the briefing notes.

---

*Tutorial note*

*Credit will be awarded for relevant calculations which form part of relevant analytical review performed, such as calculations relating to profit margins, liquidity and gearing, and for discussion which is relevant to the evaluation of audit risk. Credit will also be awarded for discussion of other relevant audit risks, for example, risks associated with the lack of a deferred tax figure in the statement of financial position, and the change in effective tax rate.*

---

**(b)** **Matters to be considered and procedures to be performed in respect of using the work of Clapton & Co**

The requirements in respect of using the work of component auditors are given in ISA 600 *Special Considerations – Audits of Group Financial Statements (Including the Work of Component Auditors)*. ISA 600 requires that if the Group engagement team plans to request a component auditor to perform work on the financial information of a component, the Group engagement team shall obtain an understanding of four matters.

– The Group engagement team should ascertain whether the component auditor understands and will comply with the ethical requirements which are relevant to the group audit and, in particular, is independent. When performing work on the financial information of a component for a group audit, the component auditor is subject to ethical requirements which are relevant to the group audit. Given that Clapton & Co is based in Farland, the ethical requirements in that location may be different, possibly less stringent, to those followed by the Group.

– The component auditor's professional competence should also be assessed, including whether the component auditor has the relevant industry specific skills and technical knowledge to adequately obtain evidence on the component. As Lynott Co reports under IFRS Standards, there is less likelihood of Clapton & Co having a knowledge gap in terms of the Group's applicable financial reporting framework than if the company used local accounting rules. The fact that Clapton & Co is a member of an international network means it is likely to have access to regular training programmes and technical updates which adds to the credibility of their audit work.

---

- The Group audit team should also gain an understanding of Clapton & Co's resource base to ensure it can cope with the work required by the Group. There should also be evaluation of whether the Group engagement team will be able to be involved in the work of the component auditor to the extent it is necessary to obtain sufficient appropriate audit evidence.

- Whether the component auditor operates in a regulatory environment which actively oversees auditors should be understood. The Group audit team should ascertain whether independent oversight bodies have been established in the jurisdiction in which Clapton & Co-operates, to oversee the auditing profession and monitor the quality of audit. This allows greater reliance to be placed on their work.

In addition to the matters required to be considered in accordance with ISA 600 discussed above, the risk of material misstatement in the subsidiary being audited by the component auditor must be fully assessed, as areas of high risk may require input from the Group audit team, and not be subject to audit solely by the component auditors. For areas of high risk, such as Lynott Co's inventories, the Group audit team may consider providing instructions to the component auditor on the audit procedures to be performed.

**Procedures:**

- Review the local ethical code (if any) followed by Clapton & Co, and compare with the IESBA *International Code of Ethics for Professional Accountants* for any significant difference in requirements and principles.

- Obtain confirmation from Clapton & Co of adherence to any local ethical code and the IESBA *Code*. Establish through discussion or questionnaire whether Clapton & Co is a member of an auditing regulatory body, and the professional qualifications issued by that body.

- Obtain confirmations of membership from the professional body to which Clapton & Co belongs, or the authorities by which it is licensed.

- Discuss the audit methodology used by Clapton & Co in the audit of Lynott Co, and compare it to those used under ISAs (e.g. how the risk of material misstatement is assessed, how materiality is calculated, the type of sampling procedures used).

- A questionnaire or checklist could be used to provide a summary of audit procedures used.

- Ascertain the quality control policies and procedures used by Clapton & Co, both firm-wide and those applied to individual audit engagements.

- Request any results of monitoring or inspection visits conducted by the regulatory authority under which Clapton & Co operates.

(c) **Audit procedures to be performed**

(i) **Investment in associate**

- Obtain the legal documents relating to the share acquisition, and review to confirm the terms and conditions including the number of shares purchased and the voting rights attached to each share.

- Agree the cost of investment of $11.5 million to the legal documentation and to Adams Co's bank statement and cash book.

–   Review the minutes of Group management meetings to understand the business rationale for the investment, and to confirm that the Group intends to exercise significant influence over Stewart Co, for example, through appointment of board members.

–   Obtain management's calculation to determine the $12 million recognised in the Group financial statements, review the method of the calculation for compliance with IAS 28.

–   Obtain the financial statements of Stewart Co to confirm the amount of profit made in the year and confirm that the Group's share of that profit is included in the Group financial statements.

–   Enquire with management as to whether any impairment review of the investment in Stewart Co has taken place, and if so, obtain management's workings and review the assumptions used and the method of calculation.

**(ii)  Adams brand name**

–   Obtain the Group's marketing budget and plans, and review to confirm that there is adequate support of the brand name through advertising.

–   Obtain the results of any market research which has been recently carried out by the Group and review its conclusions, for example, on the market share of the Group's product lines.

–   Given the materiality of the brand name, consider using an expert in brand valuation to provide a fair value for the brand, which can then be compared to the amount recognised in the financial statements.

–   Discuss with management whether in their opinion there are any indicators that the brand name is impaired, in particular discussing the impact of the bad publicity on sales.

–   Obtain written representation from management that in their opinion the brand is not impaired at the year-end.

**(d)  Ethical matters**

**Advice on accounting and management information systems**

The first threat relates to the audit committee's request for our firm to provide advice on the new accounting and management information systems to be implemented next year. If the advice were given, it would constitute the provision of a non-assurance service to an audit client. The IESBA's *International Code of Ethics for Professional Accountants* has detailed guidance in this area and specific requirements in the case of a public interest entity such as the Group which is a listed entity.

The *Code* states that services related to IT systems including the design or implementation of hardware or software systems may create a self-review threat. This is because when auditing the financial statements the auditor would assess the systems which they had recommended, and an objective assessment would be difficult to achieve as the auditor would be reluctant to find errors or shortcomings in the recommendations and work performed by their firm. There is also a risk of assuming the responsibility of management, especially as the Group apparently has little experience in this area, so would rely on the auditor's suggestions and be less inclined to make their own decision.

In the case of an audit client which is a public interest entity, the Code states that an audit firm shall not provide services involving the design or implementation of IT systems which form a significant part of the internal control over financial reporting or which generate information which is significant to the client's accounting records or financial statements on which the firm will express an opinion.

Therefore the audit firm should not provide a service to give advice on the accounting systems. With further clarification on the nature of the management information systems and the update required to them, it may be possible for the audit firm to provide a service to the Group, as long as those systems are outside the financial reporting system. However, it may be prudent for the audit firm to decline offering any advice on systems to the client especially as Adams Group is a listed entity.

### Meeting with the bank

Second, the audit committee has asked the audit engagement partner to attend a meeting with the bank, the objective of the meeting being the renegotiation of the Group's lending facilities. This is an advocacy threat to objectivity, as the audit partner will be supporting the client in its renegotiation and may be perceived as supporting or confirming the Group's financial position.

If the partner were to attend the meeting and confirm the strength of the Group's financial position, or confirm any work performed on the cash flow forecast, there could be legal implications. These actions would potentially expose Dando & Co to liability, it could be perceived that the audit firm is in some way guaranteeing the loan or guaranteeing that the Group is in a position to service the debt. The partner should not attend the meeting or be seen to be supporting the Group in its attempt to raise further finance.

These ethical issues should be discussed with those charged with governance of the Group, with an explanation provided as to why the audit firm cannot attend the meeting with the bank.

### Conclusion

These briefing notes have shown that the audit risk of this engagement is relatively high, largely due to the existence of potential management bias, a change to the group structure in the year and a requirement to place reliance on the work of another audit firm, and the risks associated with the brand. As this is our firm's first audit of the Adams Group, an audit strategy needs to be developed to focus on these areas, as well as dealing with the additional planning issues associated with relying on the component auditor.

---

**Examiner comments**

This question was based on planning the audit of a new client – the Adams Group. The Group comprised a parent company, three subsidiaries, one of which was located overseas, and an associate which had been acquired during the year. Information relevant to each of the components of the Group was detailed in the form of narrative notes and draft consolidated financial statements were also provided. The notes contained information on the Group's activities, details of inter-company transactions, a portfolio of investment properties held by one of the subsidiaries, a new system introduced in relation to inventory, and a bonus for management based on revenue. Details were also provided in respect of the auditors of the overseas subsidiary, which had retained the services of a small local firm.

---

The first requirement asked candidates to evaluate the audit risks to be considered in planning the audit of the Group. This is a very typical requirement for the first question in the paper, and while it was encouraging to see that many candidates had clearly revised this part of the syllabus, there were many whose answers were extremely disappointing. The best answers worked through the information provided in the question to identify the various audit risks, and evaluated them by, including an assessment of materiality and a discussion of the significance of the risks identified. Most candidates proved able to include a discussion of the most obvious of the risks in their briefing notes, including the management bonus, the classification of the associate, the valuation of investment properties and the potential control risk caused by implementing a new system during the year. Only the better candidates identified the risks arising from the opening balances and comparative information (due to this being a new audit client for the firm), the lack of presentation of income from the associate in the Group statement of profit or loss, the incorrect treatment of the investment property revaluation gains (which should be recognised as part of profit for the year) and the change in the effective tax rate. The best answers included in their evaluation of each audit risk an identification of the risk factor from the scenario (e.g. the measurement of the investment properties), a determination of materiality where possible given the information in the question, a clear comment on the appropriateness of the accounting treatment where relevant, and the impact on the financial statements (e.g. not cancelling inter-company transactions would lead to overstated revenue, cost of sales, receivables and payables). The key weakness present in many answers was the poor quality of explanations. Most candidates could identify a reasonable range of risks but could not develop their answer to demonstrate a clear evaluation of that risk, in a suitable structure, like the one discussed above. For example, having identified that the portfolio of investment properties would give rise to some kind of audit risk, many candidates would then attempt to expand their answer with vague comments such as 'there is risk this is not accounted for properly', 'there is risk in the accounting treatment' or 'there is risk that IAS 40 will not be followed'. This type of comment does not represent a detailed evaluation of audit risk and does not earn credit.

Other weaknesses seen in many answers included:

- Incorrect materiality calculations or stating that a balance is material without justification

- Incorrect analysis of the financial statements provided or incorrect trend calculations, the most common of which was stating that inventory had increased by 50% when it had doubled

- Too much emphasis on business risk with no development or discussion of the audit implications

- Not using the draft financial statements at all to identify audit risks

- Not identifying from the scenario that all Group members use the same financial reporting framework and report in the same currency, leading to sometimes lengthy discussion of irrelevant matters

- Long introductions including definitions of audit risk, showing a lack of appreciation of the fact that the notes are for an audit partner, and general discussions about audit planning

- Lack of understanding of certain accounting treatments such as equity accounting for associates and the correct treatment of investment properties

- Focusing on goodwill – despite the fact that no goodwill was recognised in the Group financial statements many answers discussed at length that it must be tested for impairment annually

- Suggesting that the bonus scheme would lead to manipulation of expenses, when the bonus was based on revenue.

Requirement (b) asked candidates to explain the matters to be considered, and the procedures to be performed, in respect of planning to use the work of the component auditor. This requirement was relatively well attempted, with the majority of answers covering a range of relevant matters and associated procedures. It was clear that many candidates had studied this part of the syllabus, and could apply their knowledge to the question scenario. Most candidates identified that the component audit firm was a small firm, so resourcing the audit could be an issue, and that due to its overseas location there may be differences in the ethical code and auditing standards used by the firm. Weaker answers incorrectly discussed the problem of the overseas subsidiary not reporting under IFRS Standards (the question clearly stated that it did) and tended to focus on accounting issues rather than answering the question requirement. Some answers were also very brief for the marks available, amounting to little more than a few sentences or a short list of bullet points.

The UK and Ireland (IRL) adapted papers had a slightly different style in that the question requirements were not separated out. The candidates attempting these adapted papers dealt well with the style of question requirements, and on the whole devoted an appropriate amount of time to the discussion of each of the requirements.

There were four professional marks available, and most candidates secured at least two of these marks by providing an introduction and using headings to create an appropriate structure for their answer. Too few answers contained a conclusion, and a significant minority of answers included a heading for a conclusion, but with nothing written underneath that heading, so the conclusion mark could not be awarded. Candidates are reminded that practising past exam questions with a careful review of model answers is essential in order to build up a good technique for audit planning requirements such as seen in this question.

| Marking scheme | Marks |
|---|---|
| **(a)** **Audit risk evaluation**<br>In relation to the matters listed below:<br>Up to 3 marks for each audit risk evaluated unless otherwise indicated.<br>In addition, 1 mark for relevant ratios and ½ mark for relevant trends to a maximum of 3 marks.<br>Relevant materiality calculations will be awarded to a maximum of 3 marks.<br>  – New audit client (max 2 marks)<br>  – Analytical review:<br>    • Increased revenue and profitability, risk of overstatement<br>    • Increased current ratio, risk of overstatement of current assets<br>    • Unusual trend in PPE, risk of over- or understatement<br>  – Brand name – indefinite useful life and lack of amortisation<br>  – Brand name – potential impairment and overstatement if not recognised<br>  – Equity accounting – measurement of associate and possible impairment<br>  – Disclosure of income from associate<br>  – Classification as an associate | |

|  |  |
|---|---|
| - Ross Co's inventory – control issues relating to multi-location of inventory | |
| - Lynott Co's new inventory control system | |
| - Beard Co's investment property – measurement of the gain | |
| - Beard Co's investment property – incorrect classification of gain | |
| - Possible error in comparative information and need for scepticism | |
| - Bonus scheme – inherent risk of overstating revenue (max 2 marks) | |
| - Elimination of management charges | |
| - Inventories – movement in the year and potential overstatement (max 2 marks) | |
| - Inter-company trading (inventories) | |
| - Goodwill – none recognised (max 2 marks) | |
| - Reliance on component auditor (max 2 marks) | |

**Maximum**      20

**(b)** **Using the work of a component auditor**

Up to 2 marks for each matter explained:
- Compliance with ethical requirements
- Professional competence
- Sufficient involvement in component auditor's work/resources
- Existence of a regulated environment
- Assess level of risk in the subsidiary audited by the component auditor

1 mark for each relevant procedure:
- Review the local ethical code (if any) and compare with the IESBA *Code*
- Obtain confirmation from Clapton & Co of adherence to any local ethical code and the IESBA *Code*
- Establish whether Clapton & Co is a member of an auditing regulatory body, and the professional qualifications
- Obtain confirmations from the professional body to which Clapton & Co belong, or the authorities by which it is licensed
- Discuss the audit methodology used by Clapton & Co in the audit of Lynott Co, and compare it to those used under ISAs
- A questionnaire or checklist could be used to provide a summary of audit procedures used
- Ascertain the quality control policies and procedures used by Clapton & Co, both firm-wide and those applied to individual audit engagements
- Request any results of monitoring or inspection visits conducted by the regulatory authority under which Clapton & Co operates

**Maximum**      8

**(c)** **Procedures to be performed**

Generally 1 mark for each well explained audit procedure:

**(i)** **Investment in associate**
- Obtain and review the legal documents for key information
- Agree the cost of investment of $11.5 million to the legal documentation and bank statement and cash book
- Review the minutes of Group management meetings for understanding of the rationale behind the investment and means of exercising significant influence
- Obtain and review management's calculation to determine the $12 million
- Obtain the financial statements of Stewart Co to confirm the amount of profit made in the year and confirm that the Group's share of that profit is included in the Group financial statements

|  |  |
|---|---|
| – Enquire with management as to whether any impairment review of the investment in Stewart Co has taken place, and if so, obtain management's workings and review the assumptions used and the method of calculation | |
| **Maximum** | 5 |

**(ii)** **Adams brand name**
 – Obtain the Group's marketing budget and plans, and review to confirm that there is adequate support of the brand name through advertising
 – Obtain and review the results of any market research which has been recently carried out
 – Consider using an expert in brand valuation to provide a fair value for the brand, which can then be compared to the amount recognised in the financial statements
 – Discuss with management whether in their opinion there are any indicators that the brand name is impaired, in particular discussing the impact of the bad publicity on sales
 – Obtain written representation from management that in their opinion the brand is not impaired at the year-end

|  |  |
|---|---|
| **Maximum** | 5 |

**(d)** **Ethical issues**
Generally up to 1 mark for each relevant point of discussion/explanation:
 – Advice on new systems is a non-assurance service to an audit client
 – Gives rise to a self-review threat and risk of taking on management responsibility (1 mark for each threat explained)
 – Advice on new systems should not be given where systems form significant part of internal control over financial reporting
 – Risk increased because Group is listed entity, service should not be provided
 – Attending meeting with bank is an advocacy threat
 – Legal implication for the firm if partner 'confirms' work performed
 – Partner should not attend meeting with bank
 – Matters and reasons for declining services should be discussed with Group audit committee

|  |  |
|---|---|
| **Maximum** | 8 |

**Professional marks**
Overall presentation, structure and logical flow of the briefing notes, and for the clarity of the evaluation and explanations provided.

|  |  |
|---|---|
| **Maximum** | 4 |
| **Total** | 50 |

**2    BRADLEY**  *Walk in the footsteps of a top tutor*

*Top tutor tips*

*Part (a) asks for quality control and other professional issues raised in relation to the completion of the audit. Quality control issues are increasingly common in the exam. Consider whether the audit has been performed in accordance with professional standards and whether the auditor has conducted the work with professional scepticism and due professional care.*

*Part (b) (i) asks for matters to be discussed with management in relation to three uncorrected misstatements. You can take the same approach as a 'matters' question i.e. state whether the issue is material, the accounting treatment required and the risk to the financial statements.*

*For part (b) (ii) you need to state the impact to the auditor's report if the client does not amend the financial statements. Consider the aggregate effect of the misstatements to assess whether there is a material misstatement. State the impact to both the report and opinion as a result of the issues. Don't waste time stating the reporting implications if the issues are corrected as this is not part of the requirement.*

**(a)    Quality control, ethical and other issues**

**Provision**

The first comment made by the audit assistant shows that the audit of the provision in relation to the legal claim has not been properly carried out, and it would seem that there is not sufficient, appropriate audit evidence to conclude that provisions are fairly stated.

First, the finance director telling the audit assistant not to approach the company's legal advisers would appear to be placing a limitation on the evidence which can be obtained. Also, the finance director could have used his seniority to intimidate the audit assistant.

The situation indicates that the finance director may be trying to hide something, and professional scepticism should be exercised. Possibly the finance director knows that the amount which should be provided is much larger than the $10,000, and he is reluctant to recognise a larger liability in the financial statements or that the legal advisers are aware of other provisions which should be included in the financial statements which are currently not being recognised.

As the key risk for provisions is understatement, the audit team should not so readily accept the finance director's assessment that the amount included is complete. The audit team should challenge his statement regarding the adequacy of the provision and ask for written evidence, for example, confirmation from the legal advisers.

It is also concerning that the audit manager told the audit assistant to conclude on the audit work when the planned procedures had not been performed. This does not provide good direction to the audit team and increases audit risk. There could be a material misstatement if the provision is significantly understated, and there is not sufficient evidence on the audit file to currently support the conclusions drawn.

### Overall review

It is a requirement of ISA 520 *Analytical Procedures* that analytical procedures are performed at the overall review stage of the audit. An objective of ISA 520 is that the auditor should design and perform analytical procedures near the end of the audit which assist the auditor when forming their opinion as to whether the financial statements are consistent with the auditor's understanding of the entity.

It is unlikely that the audit senior's 'quick look' at Bradley Co's financial statements is adequate to meet the requirements of ISA 520 and audit documentation would seem to be inadequate. Therefore if the audit manager, or another auditor, does not perform a detailed analytical review on Bradley Co's financial statements as part of the completion of the audit, there is a breach of ISA 520. Failing to perform the final analytical review could mean that further errors are not found.

The auditor will not be able to check that the presentation of the financial statements conforms to the requirements of the applicable financial reporting framework. It is also doubtful whether a full check on the presentation and disclosure in the financial statements has been made. The firm should evidence this through the use of a disclosure checklist.

The lack of final analytical review increases audit risk. Because Bradley Co is a new audit client, it is particularly important that the analytical review is performed as detection risk is higher than for longer-standing audit engagements where the auditor has developed a cumulative knowledge of the audit client.

The fact that the audit manager suggested that a detailed review was not necessary shows a lack of knowledge and understanding of ISA requirements. An audit client being assessed as low risk does not negate the need for analytical review to be performed, which the audit manager should know. Alternatively, the audit manager may have known that analytical review should have been performed, but regardless of this still instructed the audit senior not to perform the review, maybe due to time pressure. The audit manager should be asked about the reason for his instruction and given further training if necessary.

The manager is not providing proper direction and supervision of the audit assistant, which goes against the principles of ISA 220 *Quality Control for an Audit of Financial Statements*, and ISQC1 *Quality Control for Firms that Perform Audits and Reviews of Financial Statements and other Assurance and Related Services Engagements*. Both of these discuss the importance of the audit team having proper direction and supervision as part of ensuring a good quality of audit engagement performance.

### Chair's statement

The final issue relates to the chair's statement. ISA 720 *The Auditor's Responsibilities Relating to Other Information* requires that the auditor shall read the other information to identify material inconsistencies, if any, with the audited financial statements.

The audit manager has discussed the chair's statement but this does not necessarily mean that the manager had read it for the purpose of identifying potential misstatements, and it might not have been read at all.

Even if the manager has read the chair's statement, there may not be any audit documentation to show that this has been done or the conclusion of the work. The manager needs to be asked exactly what work has been done, and what documentation exists. As the work performed does not comply with the ISA 720 requirements, then the necessary procedures must be performed before the auditor's report is issued. This is especially important as the necessary paragraphs will need to be included within the auditor's report setting out that the other information has been obtained, the responsibility that the auditor has for the other information explained and whether anything needs to be reported in relation to any inconsistencies.

Again, the situation could indicate the audit manager's lack of knowledge of ISA requirements, or that a short-cut is being taken, probably as a result of time pressure. In either case the quality of the audit is in jeopardy.

**(b) (i) Evaluation of uncorrected misstatements**

During the completion stage of the audit, the effect of uncorrected misstatements must be evaluated by the auditor, as required by ISA 450 *Evaluation of Misstatements Identified during the Audit*. In the event that management refuses to correct some or all of the misstatements communicated by the auditor, ISA 450 requires that the auditor shall obtain an understanding of management's reasons for not making the corrections and shall take that understanding into account when evaluating whether the financial statements as a whole are free from material misstatement. Therefore a discussion with management is essential in helping the auditor to form an audit opinion.

ISA 450 also requires that the auditor shall communicate with those charged with governance about uncorrected misstatements and the effect that they, individually or in aggregate, may have on the opinion in the auditor's report.

Each of the matters included in the schedule of uncorrected misstatements will be discussed below and the impact on the auditor's report considered individually and in aggregate.

**Share-based payment scheme**

The adjustment in relation to the share-based payment scheme is material individually to profit, representing 12% of revenue. It represents less than 1% of total assets and is not material to the statement of financial position.

IFRS 2 *Share-based Payment* requires an expense and a corresponding entry to equity to be recognised over the vesting period of a share-based payment scheme, with the amount recognised based on the fair value of equity instruments granted. Management's argument that no expense should be recognised because the options are unlikely to be exercised is not correct.

IFRS 2 would classify the fall in Bradley Co's share price as a market condition, and these are not relevant to determining whether an expense is recognised or the amount of it.

Therefore management should be requested to make the necessary adjustment to recognise the expense and entry to equity of $300,000. If this is not recognised, the financial statements will contain a material misstatement, with consequences for the auditor's opinion.

**Restructuring provision**

The adjustment in relation to the provision is material to profit, representing 2% of revenue. It represents less than 1% of total assets so is not material to the statement of financial position.

The provision appears to have been recognised too early. IAS 37 *Provisions, Contingent Liabilities and Contingent Assets* requires that for a restructuring provision to be recognised, there must be a present obligation as a result of a past event, and that is only when a detailed formal plan is in place and the entity has started to implement the plan, or announced its main features to those affected.

A board decision is insufficient to create a present obligation as a result of a past event. The provision should be recognised in May 20X5 when the announcement to employees was made.

Management should be asked to explain why they have included the provision in the financial statements, for example, there may have been an earlier announcement before 30 April 20X5 of which the auditor is unaware.

In the absence of any such further information, management should be informed that the accounting treatment of the provision is a material misstatement, which if it remains unadjusted will have implications for the auditor's opinion.

**Inventory allowance**

The additional slow-moving inventory allowance which the auditor considers necessary is not material on an individual basis to either the statement of profit or loss or the statement of financial position, as it represents only 0.4% of revenue and less than 1% of total assets.

Despite the amount being immaterial, it should not be disregarded, as the auditor should consider the aggregate effect of misstatements on the financial statements. ISA 450 does state that the auditor need not accumulate balances which are 'clearly trivial', by which it means that the accumulation of such amounts clearly would not have a material effect on the financial statements. However, at 0.4% of revenue the additional allowance is not trivial, so should be discussed with management.

This misstatement is a judgmental misstatement as it arises from the judgments of management concerning an accounting estimate over which the auditor has reached a different conclusion. This is not a breach of financial reporting standards, but a difference in how management and the auditor have estimated an uncertain amount.

Management should be asked to confirm the basis on which their estimate was made, and whether they have any reason why the allowance should not be increased by the amount recommended by the auditor.

If this amount remains unadjusted by management, it will not on an individual basis impact the auditor's report.

(ii)     **Impact on auditor's report**

When considering their opinion, the auditor must conclude whether the financial statements as a whole are free from material misstatement. In order to do this, they must consider whether any remaining uncorrected misstatements are material, either on an individual basis or in aggregate.

**Aggregate materiality position**

In aggregate, the misstatements have a net effect of $260,000 ($310,000 − $50,000), meaning that if left unadjusted, profit will be overstated by $260,000 and the statement of financial position overstated by the same amount. This is material to profit, at 10.4% of revenue, but is not material to the statement of financial position at less than 1% of total assets.

**Impact on auditor's report**

The misstatements in relation to the share-based payment scheme and restructuring provision are individually material to the statement of profit or loss and therefore management should be requested to make this adjustment as the statement of profit or loss is materially misstated if the adjustments are not made by management. According to ISA 705 *Modifications to the Opinion in the Independent Auditor's Report*, the auditor shall modify the opinion in the auditor's report when the auditor concludes that, based on the audit evidence obtained, the financial statements as a whole are not free from material misstatement.

The type of modification depends on the significance of the material misstatement. In this case, these misstatements in aggregate are material to the financial statements, but are unlikely to be considered pervasive even though they relate to a number of balances in the financial statements as they do not represent a substantial proportion of the financial statements. This is supported by the fact that the adjustment is not material to the statement of financial position and it is therefore unlikely that the auditor will conclude that the financial statements as a whole are misleading.

Therefore a qualified opinion should be expressed, with the auditor stating in the opinion that except for the effects of the matters described in the basis for qualified opinion paragraph, the financial statements show a true and fair view.

The basis for qualified opinion paragraph should be placed immediately after the opinion paragraph, and should contain a description of the matters giving rise to the qualification This should include a description and quantification of the financial effects of the misstatement.

The remaining uncorrected misstatement in relation to the inventory allowance is, individually, immaterial to the financial statements and although management should be encouraged to amend all misstatements, failure to amend the inventory allowance will have no impact on the auditor's report. It should be emphasised to management that failure to correct the allowance will have an impact on future periods. If management intends to leave uncorrected misstatements, written confirmation of their immaterial nature should be obtained via a written representation.

**Examiner's comments**

This question scenario was set at the completion stage of the audit of Bradley Co, a significant new audit client, with the auditor's report due to be issued in the next week.

Requirement (a) provided some information in the form of a comment made by the audit senior, who indicated that there may have been some problems with the performance of the audit. The concerns raised included the lack of a detailed review of the final version of the financial statements and the chairman's statement had been discussed with the finance director but no further work had been conducted. The justification for not carrying out these tasks was the conclusion by the audit manager that the audit was relatively low risk. The requirement asked candidates to explain the quality control and other professional issues raised by the audit senior's comments. Candidates did not perform well on this requirement, which was somewhat surprising as in the past questions on quality control issues have been well attempted. Only a minority of candidates were able to identify that the audit of a significant new client could not be classified as low risk, and that a final review would be needed on the financial statements at the completion stage of the audit. Very few candidates however mentioned that final analytical review is a requirement of ISA 520 *Analytical Procedures* and even fewer could explain why the final review is so important prior to the issuance of the auditor's report. In respect of the work performed on the chairman's statement, few candidates identified that there was a lack of documentation of the work performed, but most at least understood the auditor's responsibilities in relation to the chairman's statement. Generally the answers to this requirement were not made relevant to the information given in the scenario and instead mentioned general features of quality control such as the need for supervision and review. This will earn minimal credit, as marks are severely limited when answer points are not related to the scenario. Many answers discussed at length the reporting implications of uncorrected inconsistencies in the chairman's statement, but discussing this in a lot of detail was not answering the question requirement.

Requirements (b)(i) and (b)(ii) dealt with the evaluation of misstatements and their potential implications for the auditor's opinion and report. The information was presented as a schedule of proposed adjustments to uncorrected misstatements in relation to three issues – a share-based payment scheme, a restructuring provision, and slow-moving inventory. In each case the auditor's proposed correcting journal was presented, along with an explanation of the audit findings and audit conclusion on the matter. Requirement (b)(i) asked for an explanation of the matters to be discussed with management in relation to each of the uncorrected misstatements, for nine marks, and requirement (b)(ii) asked candidates to justify an appropriate audit opinion assuming that management does not make the proposed adjustments. Both requirement (b)(i) and (b)(ii) were not well attempted. Answers were much too brief for the marks available and unfortunately many candidates could not competently demonstrate that they understand the topic of auditors' reports. Firstly in relation to the share-based payment, the required financial reporting requirements were not well understood, with most candidates suggesting that a provision should be created rather than an adjustment made to equity, which was disappointing as this detail was actually given in the question. In relation to the restructuring provision, many candidates did not consider the specific requirements of IAS 37 *Provisions, Contingent Liabilities and Contingent Assets* in relation to restructuring provisions, and instead applied the general recognition criteria for provisions to the scenario. The slow-moving inventory was better dealt with, as most candidates could explain that inventory should be measured at lower of cost and net realisable value. On the whole, the only marks that many candidates were awarded in this requirement were for materiality calculations.

There seems to be very little knowledge or understanding of ISA 450 *Evaluation of Misstatements Identified during the Audit* with almost no candidates differentiating between judgmental misstatements and misstatements caused by a breach of International Financial Reporting Standards requirements.

The answers in relation to the impact on the auditor's report were also disappointing. Only the very best candidates considered the aggregate effect of the misstatements in discussing the audit opinion. Many attempted to aggregate the misstatements themselves, coming to the wrong total, even though this had been given in the question. Weaker candidates simply stated that each of the material misstatements would result in a qualified 'except for' opinion. Some candidates suggested that the inventory adjustment should be discussed in an Emphasis of Matter or Other Matter paragraph because it was immaterial, clearly demonstrating a complete misunderstanding of when it is appropriate to use these paragraphs. Candidates must learn when an Emphasis of Matter paragraph should be used; it is not a substitute to be used when the candidate cannot decide between a modified and an unmodified audit opinion.

Candidates must appreciate that the process of justifying an audit opinion and explaining the implication for the auditor's report is a core area of the syllabus. It is regularly examined and it should not come as a surprise to see this topic in the exam. The presentation of information in this question was in a new style, but this should not have made the question more difficult, in fact having information presented in the form of journals with totals given should make understanding the question easier. Further the structure of the requirement into two distinct sections should have helped candidates understand that they were being asked to consider the issues first and then to aggregate the effect of the misstatements before assessing the impact on the auditor's report.

| | Marking scheme | |
|---|---|---|
| **(a)** | **Explanation of quality control and other professional issues** | *Marks* |
| | Generally up to 1 mark for each point explained: | |
| | – Insufficient audit evidence obtained in relation to legal provision | |
| | – Possible limitation of scope imposed by management and intimidation threat | |
| | – Matter is immaterial but the issue is potential understatement of provisions | |
| | – Further procedures should be performed, necessary to exercise professional scepticism | |
| | – Audit manager's instructions are not appropriate and increase detection risk | |
| | – Analytical review mandatory at the final review stage | |
| | – Objective to ensure that financial statements consistent with auditor's understanding | |
| | – A quick look unlikely to be sufficient | |
| | – The fact that it is deemed low-risk does not negate the need for analytical review | |
| | – Lack of analytical review increases audit risk | |
| | – Other information must be read with objective of identifying material inconsistencies | |
| | – Manager to be questioned to see what work has been done and what documentation exists | |
| | – Likely that chair's statement needs to be properly read and audit conclusion documented | |
| | – Audit manager lacks understanding of ISA requirements | |
| | – Audit manager may need further training | |
| | – Time pressure increases detection risk and impacts on the quality of the audit performed | |
| | **Maximum** | **10** |

|  |  |  |  |
|---|---|---|---|

**(b)**    **(i)**    **Explain matters to be considered in forming audit opinion**

Generally 1 mark for each point explained:

- ISAs require auditor to understand management's reason for not adjusting misstatements
- ISAs require auditor to communicate impact of unadjusted misstatement on opinion

**Share-based payment:**

- Materiality assessment including appropriate calculation
- Fall in share price not valid reason for not recognising expense and credit to equity
- Material misstatement due to breach of financial reporting standards, encourage management to make necessary adjustment

**Provision:**

- Materiality assessment including appropriate calculation
- Provision recognised too early, obligating event when closure announced
- Material misstatement due to breach of financial reporting standards
- Consider if any additional information to explain recognition of provision e.g. announcement before year end which auditor unaware of
- Encourage management to make necessary adjustment

**Inventory allowance:**

- Materiality assessment including appropriate calculation
- Discussion of difference between clearly trivial, immaterial and material items
- Misstatement is a matter of judgment rather than fact
- Management should still be encouraged to make adjustment but no impact on audit opinion if not done

                                                             **Maximum**      **10**

**(ii)**    **Impact on auditor's report:**

Generally up to 1 mark per point explained:

- Determination of aggregate impact of adjustments and combined materiality
- Material misstatement and modified opinion necessary
- Discussion and conclusion as to whether opinion should be qualified or adverse
- Basis for qualified opinion paragraph to include a description and quantification of the financial effects of the misstatement

                                                             **Maximum**      **5**

**Total**      **25**

**3**   **WATERS**  *Walk in the footsteps of a top tutor*

*Top tutor tips*

*Part (a) requires a discussion of the arguments for and against providing non-assurance services to audit clients. A good discussion should look at both sides of the argument.*

*Matters to consider before accepting an engagement should be straightforward as this question has been asked on many previous exam papers. Think about what might cause the accountancy firm to decline the work e.g. level of risk, insufficient resources.*

*Examination procedures need to focus on assessing the reasonableness of the assumptions used to prepare the forecast. Remember that these transactions have not happened as of yet so you will not be able to inspect invoices, etc. Instead, think about how the client determined the forecast figures and assess whether that is reasonable. Analytical procedures and inquiries will be the main procedures to use. There may be some documents you can inspect such as quotations for new equipment.*

*In the final part of the question apply your knowledge of auditor's reports to the assurance report on the forecast to identify the contents of the report. Make sure you address the second element of the requirement which asks for an explanation of the level of assurance provided by the report.*

**(a)**   **Non-assurance services**

The issue of auditors providing non-assurance services to audit clients has been topical for many years, and there are many arguments for and against their outright prohibition. IESBA conducted a review of the *International Code of Ethics for Professional Accountants* (the *Code*) and made a number of changes to the guidance, tightening the services which can be provided, with a particular focus on public interest entities.

The amendments mean that the *Code* no longer permits the provision of normally prohibited non-assurance services in emergency situations to public interest clients, such as certain bookkeeping and taxation services. The provisions in the *Code* relating to management responsibility were strengthened to ensure better understanding of what constitutes a management responsibility. It continues to be emphasised in the *Code* that auditors must not assume management responsibility when providing non-assurance services to audit clients.

The *Code*, while not providing an exhaustive list, sets out a number of examples of activities which may result in management responsibility. A number of new activities have been explicitly added, including being involved in the strategic direction of the company, hiring of personnel and reporting to those charged with governance on behalf of management, and thus effectively making these activities prohibited in line with the *Code*.

There are varying views on whether it is appropriate for auditors to provide non-assurance services to their clients. For example, governance regulations in some jurisdictions can be relatively lenient. For example, the UK Corporate Governance Code requires the audit committee to review and monitor the external auditor's independence and objectivity. This includes the audit committee evaluating and approving the provision of non-audit services by the audit firm. This assessment would include consideration of whether the audit firm was complying with the relevant ethical guidance. In contrast, the US Sarbanes-Oxley Act takes a stricter approach and prohibits audit firms from providing other services to audit clients.

Those arguing in favour of outright prohibition suggest that this would be a simple way to eliminate the threats to objectivity, which the provision of non-assurance services to audit clients creates. The IESBA quote states that several threats to objectivity are created when performing such services. A self-review threat arises when the auditor, in performing additional services for the client, performs work which impacts on the financial statements, meaning that the auditor is reviewing their own figures, or matters over which they have provided guidance or advice. An example could be where the audit firm performs a valuation service on a matter which is material to the financial statements.

Depending on the nature of the additional service, an advocacy threat may arise, where the audit firm is perceived to be supporting the interests of their client. This could happen, for example, if the audit firm advises their client in relation to a legal dispute or tax tribunal.

In particular, non-audit services can be very lucrative, leading potentially to a self-interest threat. The greater the volume and financial significance of the non-assurance services provided, the greater the risk that the auditor will have relationship and economic reasons not to challenge management's views and positions with the necessary degree of professional scepticism.

It has also been argued that outright prohibition would benefit the market and competition within the audit market, allowing smaller audit firms to provide the services which larger firms would no longer be able to offer to their audit clients or conversely allow smaller firms to ascertain a larger proportion of the external audit market.

However, there are also many arguments which support auditors providing these additional services. By having the same firm provide the audit and the non-assurance service, the client benefits in two ways. The audit firm will already possess a good knowledge and understanding of the client and its operating environment, resulting in deeper insight and a better quality service being provided. This will then lead to cost benefits, as the non-assurance service will be provided in a more efficient way.

Audit firms would also argue that participation in services such as due diligence reviews and forensic investigations allows the audit firm to understand their clients' business and risks better and to obtain insights into management's objectives and capabilities which are useful in an audit context. This may reduce audit risk.

Many non-assurance services can be safely provided as long as steps are taken to assess potential threats to objectivity, and to adequately address those risks, for example, by the use of separate teams to provide audit and non-assurance services.

However, in the case of public interest entities, such as listed companies, the IESBA has taken the view that no safeguards are available to reduce the risks to an acceptable level in the case of some non-assurance services and it continues to emphasise that the auditor shall not become involved in activities which result in them assuming any form of management responsibility.

**(b)** **(i)** Before accepting the engagement to examine Waters Co's prospective financial information, there are several matters to be considered.

**Ethical matters**

A significant matter is whether it is ethically acceptable to perform the engagement. The engagement would constitute a non-assurance service provided to an audited entity which may create self-interest, self-review and advocacy threats to independence.

**Advocacy threat**

In this case, the advocacy threat may be deemed particularly significant as Hunt & Co could be perceived as promoting the client's position to the bank. The engagement should only be provided if safeguards can be used to reduce the threat to an acceptable level, which may include:

- Having a professional accountant who was not involved with the non-assurance service review the non-assurance work performed or otherwise advise as necessary.

- Discussing ethical issues with those charged with governance of the client.

- Using separate teams to work on the audit and on the PFI engagement.

**Assuming management responsibilities**

The request by the finance director to assist him in presenting the final version of the strategic plan to the board also needs to be considered. The request to be involved in confirming that the plan is consistent with competitors suggests that if the board is not satisfied the company may not move forward with the plan or apply for the bank funding. If the engagement partner is involved, this would likely result in the firm taking on a management responsibility as they are essentially supporting the strategic direction suggested by management.

Further, by attending the presentation the partner could be seen to be communicating with the board on behalf of management. Both of these activities are now referenced as management activities in the *Code* and therefore the firm should advise the finance director that Hunt & Co may be able to perform the review for the purposes of the bank but the firm will not be able to take part in the presentation.

**Requirements of ISAE 3400 *The Examination of Prospective Information***

As well as ethical matters, ISAE 3400 *The Examination of Prospective Information* requires that certain matters are considered before the engagement is accepted.

**Scope of the work**

Hunt & Co must also consider the specific terms of the engagement. For example, the firm will need to clarify whether the bank has requested an assurance report to be issued, and what exact information will be included in the application to the bank. It is likely that more than just a forecast statement of profit or loss is required, for example, a forecast statement of cash flows and accompanying narrative, including key assumptions is likely to be required for a lending decision to be made.

### Intended use of the information

ISAE 3400 also requires that consideration should be given to the intended use of the information, and whether it is for general or limited distribution. It seems in this case the assurance engagement and its report will be used solely in connection with raising bank finance, but this should be confirmed before accepting the engagement.

### Period covered by the PFI

The period covered by the prospective financial information and the key assumptions should also be considered. ISAE 3400 states that the auditor should not accept an engagement when the assumptions used are clearly unrealistic or when the auditor believes that the prospective financial information will be inappropriate for its intended use. For example, the assumption that the necessary capital expenditure can take place by September 20X5 may be overly optimistic.

### Resources and skills

The firm should also consider whether there are staff available with appropriate skills and experience to perform the PFI engagement, and the deadline by which the work needs to be completed. If the work on the cinemas is scheduled to be completed by September 20X5, presumably the cash will have to be provided very soon, meaning a tight deadline for the engagement to be performed.

(ii)  **Examination procedures**

- Agreement that the accounting policies used in preparing the forecast statement of profit or loss are consistent with those used in historical financial information and comply with IFRS Standards.

- The forecast should be cast to confirm accuracy.

- The time frame of the work to be carried out needs to be discussed with management, with enquiry being made to ascertain how the work can be carried out in such a short period of time, for example, will all cinemas be closed for the period of refurbishment? This will help to confirm the accuracy of the revenue and expenses recognised.

- Review of market research documents and review of prices charged by competitors showing new technology films to support the assumption regarding increase in price and consumer appetite for the films.

- Analytical review followed by discussion with management on the trend in revenue, which is forecast to increase by 22.9% and 7% in the years to 31 May 20X6 and 20X7 respectively.

- Consider the capacity of the cinemas and the number of screenings which can take place to assess the reasonableness of projected revenue.

- Analytical review of the composition of operating expenses to ensure that all expenses are included at a reasonable amount. In 20X5, operating expenses are 80.7% of revenue, but this is forecast to reduce to 73.4% in 20X6 and to 69.8% in 20X7, indicating understatement of forecast expenses.

- Review the list of operating expenses to ensure that any loss to be recognised on the disposal of old equipment has been included, or that profit on disposal has been netted off.

- Quotations received from potential suppliers of the new technology should be reviewed to verify the amount of the capital expenditure and therefore that depreciation included in the forecast statement of profit or loss appears reasonable.

- Recalculation of depreciation expense and confirmation that depreciation on the new technology has been included and correctly calculated and agrees to the forecast statement of financial position.

- Recalculation of finance cost to ensure that interest payable on the new bank loan has been included, with confirmation of the rate of interest to bank documentation.

- Review of capital expenditure budgets, cash flow forecasts and any other information to accompany the forecast statement of profit or loss for consistency, and confirmation that the amount planned to be spent on the cinemas can be met with the amount of finance applied for as well Waters Co's own cash balance.

(iii) **Report on prospective financial information**

ISAE 3400 contains requirements on the content of a report on prospective financial information, stating that it should contain, in addition to a title, addressee and being appropriately signed and dated:

- Identification of the prospective financial information.

- A reference to the ISAE or relevant national standards or practices applicable to the examination of prospective financial information.

- A statement that management is responsible for the prospective financial information including the assumptions on which it is based.

- When applicable, a reference to the purpose and/or restricted distribution of the prospective financial information.

- An opinion as to whether the prospective financial information is properly prepared on the basis of the assumptions and is presented in accordance with the relevant financial reporting framework.

- Appropriate caveats concerning the achievability of the results indicated by the prospective financial information.

**Level of assurance**

In terms of the assurance level, the report will include a statement of negative assurance as to whether the assumptions provide a reasonable basis for the prospective financial information. This is a lower level of assurance than that given in an audit of historical financial information. The assurance provided is limited due to the future orientation of the information subject to review, and because the nature of the investigative procedures performed are less detailed and substantive in nature.

**Examiner's comments**

The scenario centred on Waters Co, an audit client, that had approached your firm to provide a report on prospective financial information which would be used by the company's bank in making a significant lending decision. The amount advanced would be used to upgrade the cinemas operated by Waters Co and a forecast statement of profit or loss was provided in the scenario, along with some of the assumptions used in its preparation by management.

Requirement (b)(i) asked candidates to explain the matters to be considered by the audit firm before accepting the engagement to report on the prospective financial information. The quality of answers here was quite good, with almost all candidates making a reasonable attempt to discuss relevant matters including ethical issues, resource availability, the scope of the engagement and the nature of the assumptions used in the forecast. Where candidates scored less well on this requirement it was often due to lack of application to the scenario. A minority of answers amounted to little more than a bullet point list, often posed as questions (e.g. 'are there any ethical matters to consider', 'who is the report for', 'why is the report needed'), and while these are matters to consider the lack of any application to the scenario limits the amount of credit that can be awarded.

Requirement (b)(ii) asked for examination procedures to be used in respect of the forecast statement of profit or loss, assuming the engagement is accepted. This was also quite well attempted by many candidates, who used the information provided to generate specific and relevant enquiries and other procedures. Weaker answers tended to write very vague comments which were not tailored to the scenario or explained, or were just incorrect, such as. 'obtain representations', 'agree forecast to audited financial statements', 'check whether assumptions are realistic', 'perform analytical procedures'.

| Marking scheme | | |
|---|---|---|
| | | *Marks* |

**(a)**    **Discussion on non-assurance services**

Generally 1 mark for each point of discussion:

- IESBA *Code* has been amended to restrict the provision of non-assurance services especially to public interest entities in emergency situations
- Examples – bookkeeping and tax no longer allowed services
- *Code* contains enhanced guidance on management responsibilities
- Examples – involvement in recruitment and strategic direction of the company
- Different approaches used in different jurisdictions, e.g. UK comply or explain approach, US legislative approach
- Arguments against provision are based on threats to objectivity, e.g. self-review threat, advocacy threat, self-interest threat (1 mark each explained with relevant example)
- Arguments in favour of provision focus on audit firms' enhanced understanding of client, and the firms being in the best position to offer the services to their clients
- Safeguards may be used to reduce threats to an acceptable level in some situations

                                               **Maximum**    **8**

**(b)**    **(i)**    **Matters to consider before accepting the engagement**

Up to 1 mark for each matter explained:

- Independence – types of threats raised
- Appropriate safeguards (max 2 marks)
- Request for assistance with presenting the strategic plan is a management responsibility
- No safeguards can reduce threat to an acceptable level and the assistance should not be provided
- Competence and time frame
- Elements to be included in the application and intended use
- Key assumptions and time period covered

                                               **Maximum**    **7**

         **(ii)**    **Examination procedures**

1 mark for each described procedure.

- Agreement that the accounting policies used in preparing the forecast information are consistent with those used in historical financial information and comply with IFRS Standards
- The forecast should be cast to confirm accuracy
- Review of capital expenditure forecasts
- Quotations received from potential suppliers of the new technology should be reviewed
- The time frame of the work to be carried out needs to be discussed with management
- Review of market research documents and review of prices charged by competitors
- Analytical review followed by discussion with management on the trend in revenue
- Revenue is forecast to increase by 22.9% and 7% in the years to 31 May 20X6 and 20X7 respectively
- Analytical review of the composition of operating expenses
- In 20X5, operating expenses are 80.7% of revenue, but this is forecast to reduce to 73.4% in 20X6 and to 69.8% in 20X7
- Recalculation of depreciation expense and agreement to forecast statement of financial position
- Recalculation of finance cost to ensure that interest payable with confirmation of the rate of interest to bank documentation

                                               **Maximum**    **6**

| | | | | |
|---|---|---|---|---|
| **(iii)** | **Content of the report** | | | |

**(iii)** **Content of the report**

½ mark for each relevant content element identified (up to 2 marks) and up to 2 marks for discussion of the level of assurance provided.

- Content elements:
  - reference to relevant ISAE or national standards
  - statement of management responsibility
  - reference to purpose and distribution of report
  - opinion on basis of assumptions and application of relevant financial reporting framework
  - caveats on achievability of results
- Assurance is based on negative assurance
- Assurance limited by future orientation of the subject matter and nature of procedures used

| | |
|---|---|
| **Maximum** | 4 |
| **Total** | 25 |

# Section 7

# REFERENCES

The Board (2019) *IFRS 15 Revenue From Contracts with Customers*. London: IFRS Foundation.

The Board (2019) *IFRS 16 Leases*. London: IFRS Foundation.